ENCOUNTERS: READINGS AND THE WORLD

*E*ncounters
Readings and the World

Pat C. Hoy II
New York University

Robert DiYanni
Pace University

The McGraw-Hill Companies, Inc.

New York   St. Louis   San Francisco   Auckland   Bogotá
Caracas   Lisbon   London   Madrid   Mexico City
Milan   Montreal   New Delhi   San Juan
Singapore   Sydney   Tokyo   Toronto

McGraw-Hill

A Division of The *McGraw·Hill* Companies

Encounters: Readings and the World

Copyright © 1997 by The McGraw-Hill Companies, Inc. All rights reserved. Printed in the United States of America. Except as permitted under the United States Copyright Act of 1976, no part of this publication may be reproduced or distributed in any form or by any means, or stored in a data base or retrieval system, without the prior written permission of the publisher.

Acknowledgments appear on pages 773 to 777, and on this page by reference.

This book is printed on acid-free paper.

1 2 3 4 5 6 7 8 9 0 DOC DOC 9 0 9 8 7 6

ISBN 0-07-030639-7

This book was set in ITC Berkeley Book by The Clarinda Company.
The editors were Tim Julet and David A. Damstra;
the production supervisor was Richard A. Ausburn;
the designer was Lisa Delgado.
R. R. Donnelley & Sons Company was printer and binder.

Cover photograph: Keith Carter, *Mojo*

Hoy, Pat C.
     Encounters : readings and the world / Pat C. Hoy II, Robert DiYanni.
       p.   cm.
     Includes index.
     ISBN 0–07–030639–7
     1. College readers. 2. English language—Rhetoric.   I. DiYanni, Robert. II. Title.
PE1417.H69 1997
808'.0427—dc20   96–3470

About the Authors

Pat C. Hoy II, director of the Expository Writing Program and Professor of English at New York University, has also held appointments as Professor of English, U.S. Military Academy, and as senior preceptor in the Expository Writing Program and director of the Summer Writing Program, Harvard University. He received his B.A. from the U.S. Military Academy and his Ph.D. from the University of Pennsylvania.

Professor Hoy is the author of *Reading and Writing Essays: The Imaginative Tasks* (McGraw-Hill) and *Instinct for Survival: Essays by Pat C. Hoy II* (U. of Georgia Press). He is coeditor of *Prose Pieces: Essays and Stories* and *Women's Voices: Visions and Perspectives*. He is coauthor with Robert DiYanni of *The Scribner Handbook for Writers*.

His essays on pedagogy appear in *Literary Nonfiction: Theory, Criticism, Pedagogy* (Southern Illinois University Press), *How Writers Teach Writing* (Prentice-Hall), and *What Do I Know?: Reading, Writing, and Teaching the Essay* (Boynton). He has also published essays in *Sewanee Review, Virginia Quarterly Review, Agni, Twentieth Century Literature,* and *South Atlantic Review.* Five of his essays have been selected as "Notables" in *Best American Essays.*

Professor Hoy regularly teaches freshman composition.

Robert DiYanni is Professor of English at Pace University, Pleasantville, New York, where he teaches courses in literature, writing, and humanities. He has also taught at Queens College of the City University of New York, at New York University in the Graduate Rhetoric Program, and most recently in the Expository Writing Program at Harvard University. He received his B.A. from Rutgers University (1968) and his Ph.D. from the City University of New York (1976).

Professor DiYanni has written articles and reviews on various aspects of literature, composition, and pedagogy. His books include *The McGraw-Hill Book of Poetry; Women's Voices; Reading Poetry; Like Season'd Timber: New Essays on George Herbert;* and *Modern American Poets: Their Voices and Visions* (a text to accompany the Public Broadcasting Television series that aired in 1988). With Pat C. Hoy II he wrote *The Scribner Handbook for Writers.* He is currently at work on *An Introduction to the Humanities.*

Table of Contents with List of Artworks

A SPECTRUM OF STUDENT WRITING 79

A SPECTRUM OF PROFESSIONAL WRITING 125

ARTWORKS[*]

Artist	Painting	Writer
Mary Cassatt	*The Family*	MARY GORDON
Lisa Fifield	*Running Elk*	BARRY LOPEZ, LESLIE MARMON SILKO, LOREN EISELEY
Edward Hopper	*Nighthawks*	MARK STRAND
Jean A. Ingres	*La Grande Odalisque*	ELIZABETH MACDONALD
Piet Mondrian	*Composition in Yellow and Blue*	JAMES RHEE

[*]Except for the DeChirico and Trutat paintings, all the works listed are in the color insert.

Annotated Table of Contents

C

C

one drives the other back with the suddenness of two dogs who have
been conversing in tones too low for an onlooker to hear.

Our stories do freeze the frames of our experience, but those stories
also carry meaning as old as life itself. Embedded in each is a nugget
of truth. The truth varies, of course, according to the way we tell the
stories. But without them, we are lost, cut adrift.

I was saved from sin when I was going on thirteen. But not really
saved. It happened like this.

I am not tragically colored. There is no great sorrow dammed up in
my soul, nor lurking behind my eyes. I do not mind at all. I do not
belong to the sobbing school of Negrohood who hold that nature
somehow has given them a lowdown dirty deal and whose feelings
are all hurt about it.

When my mother killed herself I was looking for a job. That was fifteen years ago. I had no money and no food. On the pleasure side I
was down to my last pack of Pall Malls plus half a bottle of J & B. I
needed to find work because I needed to be able fully to support
myself and my eight-year-old son, very fast.

I wished every sentence, everything I knew, that began with England
would end with "and then it all died; we don't know how, it just all
died." At that moment, I was thinking, who are these people who
forced me to think of them all the time, who forced me to think that
the world I knew was incomplete, or without substance, or did not
measure up because it was not England; that I was incomplete, or
without substance, and did not measure up because I was not English.

Oppressed people cannot remain oppressed forever. The yearning for
freedom eventually manifests itself, and that is what has happened to
the American Negro. Something within has reminded him of his
birthright of freedom, and something without has reminded him that
it can be gained.

Falling into life wasn't easy, and I suspect that is why I hunger for
such awkward symmetry today. Having lost the use of my legs dur-

ing the polio epidemic that swept across the eastern United States during the summer of 1944, I was soon immersed in a process of rehabilitation that was, at least when looked at in retrospect, as much spiritual as physical.

can society—flaws rooted in historic inequalities and longstanding cultural stereotypes. How we set up the terms for discussing racial issues shapes our perception and response to these issues.

the dark and dirty old training rings and in the makeshift cages, whatever light is generated, whatever excitement, whatever beauty, must come from original sources—from internal fires of professional hunger and delight, from the exuberance and gravity of youth. It is the difference between planetary light and the combustion of stars.

At first, I did not know the sex of my three goslings. But nothing on two legs grows any faster than a young goose, and by early fall it was obvious that I had drawn one male and two females. You tell the sex of a goose by its demeanor and its stance—the way it holds itself, its general approach to life. A gander carries his head high and affects a threatening attitude. Females go about with necks in a graceful arch and are less aggressive.

Kingston plays with this image of culturized feminine weakness throughout "On Discovery." The binding [of feet] can also be compared to other symbols of feminine vanity, such as the tight elastic of a brassiere, the metal wire inside corsets, or even the hot sticky nylon pantyhose, which bring no pleasure to any woman.

The fact remains that there is no such land, that never in the known history of the world has there been evidence that any such Land of Women ever existed. Why, then, does Kingston tack it onto the story in such an awkward yet prominent fashion? She does it to remind us, as my mother tried to remind me, that women can do anything, even turn the world upside down to show that a man can be anything—even a woman.

Many say that finding a significant other is one of the greatest things that can happen to a man. A man needs someone to care about, someone to listen to, someone to love. But everything comes at a price, and, oftentimes, the price is exorbitantly high.

White's essays are not the armor of an embittered man. His works stand as quietly defiant acts, as bursts of value in the face of technological progress. . . . Nostalgic, he nevertheless confronts chaos and decay. Natural decay is sad, but it is not to be struggled against. Artificial decay—the oppressive, mechanized deterioration induced by War and Industry—is too big finally to be vanquished, but can be held at bay, kept at a safer distance from life.

C

E. B. White's work, from his essays to his children's literature, is
replete with eggs—as objects of natural beauty and as sources of life.
. . . White's eggs are rich with meaning; they are links in a never-
ending cycle of life; they are sources of continuity in a world fragmented by passing time. And even in those essays that do not figure
literal eggs, the sanctity, the beauty, and the fragility of life that they
represent pervade White's work.

Thematic Table of Contents

Within the configurations described below, many essays are listed more than once. Such listing speaks of the richness of the essays themselves. They are not about just one issue, one topic. Placing essays in several categories allows us to see how they bear up under multiple readings, yielding insight and evoking new questions every time we look into them.

Family and Community

These essays explore and examine issues related to family and community—life at home as well as life in the larger community beyond the hearth: the extended family, the hometown, the nation, the world. Inherent in these explorations are inquiries into parenting and the power of home, ethnicity and language, identity and growth, race and racism, disease and trauma, shelter and conflict within the state.

Gender, Identity, and Sexuality

These essays, many of them listed under several configurations in this thematic table of contents, remind us how complex and interesting issues of gender, identity, and sexuality can be, how difficult they are to understand isolated from one another. Additionally, perhaps gender, identity, and sexuality can be understood only in the context of family and community. As you will discover, the first two configurations are not discrete. Reading these essays, we begin to see that searches for identity—an individual's move toward independence and wholeness—almost always take the searchers back to their beginnings, no matter how long the journey, how arduous the pilgrimage.

Writing and Language

Although these essays are about much more than writing and the use of language, they bring to our attention the very nature of composing—the act of using language to confirm ourselves, to construct a sense of what we think the world is like, to give voice to our vision of how things are, or were, or could be.

Race

These essays point toward diversity, tolerance, and complication, but they do not offer tidy solutions to the thorny issues associated with race and ethnicity. Instead they raise questions about the difficulty of resolution, the importance of sovereignty, and the wisdom of difference.

Courage

These essays suggest a variety of ways in which we might revalue the notion of courage—courage in the face of opposition, disease, the unknown, physical pain, torture, death, loss, the challenges of sport.

The Mysteries

These essays dare to reach out toward what we cannot always see, cannot quantify precisely, cannot easily pin down. Yet what these writers reach out for—what's there just beyond seeing—they manage, somehow, to make palpable, momentarily accessible to us: truth, connectedness, things of the spirit, animal secrets, beauty, creation, imagination, time's complexity, tribal wisdom, aging, the nature of dying. We are reminded, indirectly, of the power of language to recover what has been lost, what, over time, we have learned to leave out of our rational investigations and, perhaps, out of our lives as well.

Looking at Art

In these essays we get to see writers using art objects to help them develop their ideas, but we see as well how writers can become artists, creating art out of the ordinary, the commonplace—a car race, an island, a battlefield, a drawing in the earth, a wound to the eye, a death. We gain access to the writer's transfiguring imagination, and we get to see that imagination at work.

Rhetorical Table of Contents

Essays That Alternate Between Presenting Experience and Exploring an Idea

These essays introduce personal experience as the basis—or rather one of the bases—for exploring an idea or a series of related ideas. Some, like Dillard's "Living Like Weasels" and Gordon's "Mary Cassatt," explore an idea extensively at the end, following the story of the writer's experience. Others, like White's "The Ring of Time" and Davenport's "The Geography of the Imagination," work back and forth between description and exploration.

Essays That Sneak the Idea in Through Image or Metaphor

The essays in this group work largely by implication. The writers of these essays do not state their claims about an idea explicitly. Instead they work by suggestion, using details and images to convey their attitudes and perspectives. Some, like Ehrlich's "Looking for a Lost Dog," talk about one thing (the symbolic meaning) in terms of another (the literal action described in the essay). Others, like Kincaid's "On Seeing England for the First Time," let readers determine the author's implied point from the selection of detail.

Essays That Move Systematically Between Evidence and Idea

The essays in the following group typically present their ideas in a direct and straightforward manner. The writers of these essays state their claims and then support them with evidence. Some, like Bowman's "Gender Switching" and Son's "Men at the Mercy of Women," are analytical and thus use details of the texts analyzed as evidence to support the writer's interpretation. Others, like Dorris's "Fetal Alcohol Syndrome" and Tuchman's "History by the Ounce," argue their cases by bringing logic and analysis to bear on ideas and evidence not contained in a single text or place.

Essays That Use Humor and Irony

The following essays use humor to engage their readers and to convey the writers' attitudes toward their subjects. Some, like Pickering's "Trespassing" and Abbott's "The True Story of Why I Do What I Do," employ a humorous narrative voice that is fun to listen to. Others, like Fussell's "Indy" and Wolfe's "The Right Stuff," use techniques of irony to create a satiric tone. Still others, such as White's "The Geese" and Hughes's "Salvation," blend humor with sadness.

Essays That Celebrate

This group of essays celebrates their authors' subjects. The writers of these pieces convey a sense of excitement about their subjects, carrying readers along on a wave of energy and enthusiasm. The authors write from a desire to share their perspectives and to convey their admiration or love, as Hoagland does about his turtles; Gordon, about the paintings of Mary Cassatt; and Neffinger, about his uncle, a master builder of houses of cards.

Essays That Lament or Condemn

These essays express dismay, anger, disgust, as well as other critical perspectives. Some, like West's "Race Matters," Shilts's "Talking AIDS to Death," and Dorris's "Fetal Alcohol Syndrome," propose solutions for serious social problems. Others, including White's "The Geese" and Jordan's "Many Rivers to Cross," lament life's pain.

Essays That Describe Scenes and Situations

These essays contain sharply described scenes and clearly identified situations. The writers use the scenes and situations to establish what is important to them. Through carefully arranged, precise details, these writers bring their scenes and situations vividly before their readers, allowing descriptive detail and action to express attitude and convey meaning.

Essays That Speculate on the Unknown

These essays wonder and wander. The writers do not argue points or explain their ideas succinctly and clearly from the start. Instead, they choose to explore an idea's implications and ramifications. They invite readers to share their wondering and also their amazement at what they have discovered through their reading and their experience.

Essays That Persuade, Explain, Urge

The following essays are passionate in their convictions. They aim to convince readers of something that the writers hold dear. Their tone sometimes becomes urgent and insistent, in keeping with the intensity of the writers' feelings. Some of the essays, like Staples's "Just Walk on By," express indignation. Others, like Mairs's "On Being a Cripple," express dissatisfaction. Still others, like Selzer's "A Mask on the Face of Death," express a kind of quiet desperation.

Essays That Analyze Issues

This group of essays centers on issues of race, gender, class, and ethnicity. Morrison and Baldwin analyze what being black means in America today, while Gordimer analyzes the place of whites in South Africa. Other writers, including Anzaldúa and Rodriguez, address issues of cultural difference for Hispanic and Latin Americans, analyzing as well, issues of gender and sexual disposition. Still others in this group, including Dorris, Momaday, and Silko, consider issues faced by Native Americans.

Essays Linked with Works of Art

The following essays either refer directly to or can be linked indirectly with particular paintings or types of art. Some writers, including MacDonald, Davenport, Rhee, and Strand, analyze the work of artists such as Ingres, de Chirico, Wood, Mondrian, and Hopper, linking the artworks with ideas they develop in their essays. Other writers, including Hughes, Gordon, and Didion, describe works of art by painters such as Picasso, Cassatt, and O'Keeffe by telling stories. Additional ways of linking art with an essay's ideas appear in Danto's "Gettysburg," in which military battlefields are viewed as works of art, and Neffinger's "House of Cards," in which the writer connects an idea about the relationship between beauty and destruction with the art of building houses with playing cards.

Preface for the Instructor

If writing is thinking and discovery and selection and order and meaning, it is also awe and reverence and mystery and magic.

TONI MORRISON

Perception sees analogies—the relationship between things and ideas; it is observation plus comment, and as much the comment of the emotions as of the mind.

HOLBROOK JACKSON

Different kinds of essays affect readers in different ways. Some readers respond enthusiastically to informal, familiar essays that explore, searching as they go along for the elusive answer to a nagging question; other readers respond more readily to essays that get right to the main idea, arguing or defending in some reasonable way a point of view. The first kind of essay lets readers in on the writer's thinking, so they can participate in the exploration or inquiry; the second type concerns itself more with presenting the fruits of thinking, making a claim and justifying it.

Good essays, however, are rarely so tidy, and they often defy easy classification. Truly satisfying essays often manage to do both these things at once—to give us a sense of writers' thinking even as they manage to make their claims, working in an exploratory way, while moving forward, methodically, to persuade us.

Looking into these various forms of the essay—the exploratory, the argumentative, the combined—seeing how they work, what they have to say, student writers can gain a clearer sense of what they might be able to do in their own essays. Reading and studying these essays, they can learn something about possibilities; they learn about writing as well as about the ideas in the essays.

We have selected the essays in this book with care and with the help of astute readers so that students can begin to glimpse new possibilities as writers, new opportunities in life. Opening up such possibilities is the overarching aim of this collection.

The Tables of Contents

We have arranged the essays alphabetically by author so that we do not limit the way students can see them. The essays sit there in the collection and in the first table of contents, waiting for the sampling; in the annotated table of contents, each listing is accompanied by an inviting quotation that points toward the essay's richness. The thematic table of contents suggests ways to group the essays according to many of our culture's most compelling preoccupations: family and community; gender, identity, and sexuality; writing and language; race; courage; the mysteries; and art. Moreover, for each of the thematic configurations, we have provided a brief explanation that highlights social and thematic implications. These thematic headings, however, are suggestive rather than definitive. Within the collection, there are many more ways to group the essays.

We have provided still another way of looking at these essays. The rhetorical table of contents suggests *how* the essays make meaning, rather than *what* they might mean. That table points toward writerly concerns rather than cultural or personal ones. Our rhetorical categories are not entirely traditional; they seek to move beyond established boundaries, suggesting unique ways for students to think about the way writers write. The categories highlight techniques and call attention to the various ways writers create meaning.

Headnotes and Questions

We have kept the author headnotes brief so as not to distract readers from the essays themselves and to avoid preempting students' responses to them. Our concluding comment in each headnote points to a single feature of the essay, hinting at an idea or pointing toward an interesting element of the essay's style—nothing more.

Our suggestions for thinking, connecting, and writing that follow each essay point across the collection and outside it to related ideas, corresponding essays, complementary poems, and interesting writing techniques. These suggestions help students discover things to write about; they provide clues about how to write, how to develop their ideas. Taken together, the suggestions reflect our strong sense of the many ways that reading, thinking, and writing intertwine to enrich our classrooms and our lives.

The Spectrum of Student Writing

Perhaps the most compelling aspect of this collection is the spectrum of student writing that complements the spectrum of essays by the professionals. The student essays point the way for other students, giving them a chance to see just how some of these essays were developed, what the writing leading up to the final essays looked like. The student essays, like the ones written by professionals, represent the spectrum of essays we mentioned at the outset.

At one end of the spectrum are exploratory essays based largely on writers' lived experiences; at the other end are essays more traditionally academic, argumentative. Essays of the first type, exemplified by Tom Ceraulo's "The Burden of Pride," Michael Cohen's "You Can Shave the Beast, but the Fur Will Grow Back," and Gian Neffinger's "House of Cards," charm as they amble from story to story, their implicit complexity masked by narrative seduction and a playful intimacy. Beneath the surface of these experience-based essays, and in and around the stories included within them, the writers explore in ways that point to the more assertive mode of the analytical and argumentative essay. But they persuade in a more casual, some might say more hospitable, way.

The more argumentative essays usually make a more explicit claim to complexity, but they are intellectually playful as well. Ruth Chung's analysis of Virginia Woolf's "Old Mrs. Grey," David Reich's argument about Amy Tan's "Mother Tongue," and James Rhee's interpretation of a Mondrian painting exemplify this more analytical and objective mode. The idea in each of these essays emerges quickly, and the essays are all efficiently organized. Yet you will find in each the twists and turns of the essayist's mind playing over rich material, entertaining doubt, making concessions while also making a point.

All the student essays, wherever they fall on the spectrum, have much in common—a basic three-part structure (beginning, middle, and ending), an interest in ideas, a concern for clarity, an inherent coherence. But each is different in its own right, in the way it moves from the beginning through the middle to the end, in the particular writer's way of thinking about a chosen subject, in the many ways each writer tells stories or amasses evidence gleaned from reading, in the way each causes us to see ourselves or the world in which we live. The collection of student essays overall invites us to see their obvious differences while encouraging us to search for their more intriguing similarities: the rigor, complexity, and subtle analysis that underlie the more apparent surface differences.

Instead of focusing primarily on the ends of the spectrum, we have included some student essays that combine the best features of the exploratory and the argumentative—the ambling, personal nature of the one with the more distanced, analytical rigor of the other. Student essays that accomplish this combining feat in compelling ways are Kristen E. Hughes's "I Will Be My Own Hero," which begins with the writer's encounter with Picasso's *Guernica* and leads to an exploration of an idea about heroism and gender; Elizabeth MacDonald's "Odalisque," which combines her interest in beauty and suffering with her interest in paintings by Ingres and de Chirico; and Han N. Pham's essay "Down the Unwritten Path," which focuses on cultural continuities and discontinuities and draws on the experience of her Vietnam-born parents and grandparents while reflecting on the evidence gleaned from her reading of Frances Fitzgerald's *Fire in the Lake*.

To some extent, all the student essays, even those we have identified as closer to one end of the spectrum than the other, resist easy classification. They do not want to be pigeonholed. These three student pieces—"I Will Be My Own Hero," "Odalisque," "Down the Unwritten Path"—along with the two essays explored in detail in the student introduction, provide elegant yet varied examples of how student writers can effectively negotiate the spectrum.

Two Student Writers at Work

For the two student essays in the introduction, we have provided a detailed explanation of how they came to be written. We give the assignments that led to the essays and show you how the students responded to those assignments—their preliminary exercises and their initial drafts. For Maile Meloy's "The Voice of the Looking Glass," we supply the two brief exercises that she developed into the first full draft of her essay. We present her preliminary writing clean, without a reader's comments; we then show the first draft with the instructor's marginal comments and intertextual annotations. Following this draft, we include a portion (about half) of Maile's second draft, along with comments about changes and additions she made. Then we print the final version of her essay without annotations or comments to allow students to see for themselves what additional revisions Maile made. This snapshot of her work allows students to see as well how Maile's reading and thinking, along with instructor conferences and collaboration with classmates, helped her revise and develop her essay.

In addition to Maile Meloy's exploratory essay, which weaves in analysis and interpretation of texts as she pursues an idea, we have provided a second student essay, Robynn Stacy Maines's analysis of Gretel Ehrlich's "Looking for a Lost Dog." For Robynn's essay, too, we present exercises and drafts as well as her finished piece. As with Maile's essay, we give students the assignments that led Robynn to her essay. For her exercises and drafts, we have included student responses to her work in progress, their questions and comments, along with her instructor's annotations. For Robynn's second draft, which we present in excerpt, we include her own editing and revising without further annotations and comments.

We have presented these two different types of student essays in detail, with the assignments and excerpted drafts, to show students how to build up a strong and fully developed piece of writing that evolves over time from a number of smaller pieces. We show the writing process in all its messy complexity and recursiveness. We want students to see that regardless of the type of essay being written, they can build toward strong essays over time when they rethink what they are doing and attend to others' comments about their writing.

The Spectrum of Professional Writing

Those compelling student essays give *Encounters: Readings and the World* its distinctiveness. But the student essays develop out of a broad spectrum of professional writing in the rest of the collection. The professional essays also touch both ends of the exploratory-argumentative spectrum, but most of them rest comfortably in between. A highly personal piece such as Zora Neale Hurston's "How It Feels to Be Colored Me" is complemented by Cornel West's "Race Matters," a more rigorously analytical piece. While some essays situate themselves at the ends of the spectrum (Scott Russell Sanders's "Wayland" and Lee K. Abbott's "The True Story of Why I Do What I Do," for example, on the personal side and Mark Strand's "Crossing the Tracks to Hopper's World" and Susan Sontag's "AIDS and Its Metaphors" on the analytical side), the vast majority of essays in the book move across the middle of the spectrum.

An essay such as Barry Lopez's "The Stone Horse," for example, yokes Lopez's love of animals with his fascination about historical, archeological detail. Arthur Danto's "Gettysburg" combines Danto's firsthand knowledge of the historic battlefield with his propensity to cross the boundary lines of traditional academic disciplines (in this case, art and philosophy and military history). Both writers give us pleasurable insight into just how malleable the form of the essay can be. Neither of their essays loses any of its academic force or credibility as a result of the two writers' deep personal attachments to their subjects.

Indeed, these essays are more persuasive and, we can guess, more rigorous, because of Lopez's and Danto's personal attachments. Reading the essays, we have the distinct feeling that we are reading about important subjects that have to do with their lives and with the lives we ourselves are trying to live. Lopez is deeply curious about animals and has spent long periods of time in the wilderness studying them. His published study of wolves—*Of Wolves and Men*—is as thorough as the work of the most detached scientist, but his concern about the wolf is anything but detached. He nudges us always in the direction of mystery rather than the direction of certainty, and when, in his essay, he brings us upon the stone horse, it is to cause us, finally, to contemplate the horse's heritage, and ours.

Danto peers into the history of warfare, but he looks at history through the particular details of the Gettysburg battlefield, especially the statue of an infantry soldier—his uniform, his weapon, his vulnerability at a moment in history when technology was drastically changing the nature and consequence of organized fighting. Danto's interest in art and his background as a philosopher enable him to see there on that battlefield what others could not see—about the soldier, about the battlefield itself, about war, about us. Lopez and Danto take us close to their subjects, but their investigations are rigorous and, at the same time, personal, sometimes moving; these essayists seem to be inviting us, personally, into conversations about the broader implications of their ideas about destruction and preservation.

Two Writers in Depth along with Student Essays About the Writers' Work

In addition to supplying a range of professional writing for students to read, study, learn from, and work with, we have included two writers whose work is represented with multiple selections. We reprint three selections by Maxine Hong Kingston and three by E. B. White, and include extensive headnotes that provide biographical information while offering rhetorical perspectives on their work.

Along with the multiple selections by Kingston and White, we have included student essays based on those writers' works. Kingston's brief "On Discovery" is complemented by three student essays that analyze and interpret it. Two of these essays are by women, one young and of Asian descent, the other an older student of European descent. The third piece was written by a third-year male, who was pursuing a degree in engineering. You will not be surprised that the three essayists read Kingston's piece in very different ways.

The student writing based on the work of E. B. White does something different. Instead of analyzing a single essay by White, Christian D'Andrea, in "The Human Atlas: Locating E. B. White," refers to half a dozen of White's essays as he attempts to define the mind of the writer as reflected in the essays. Although not a formal research essay, D'Andrea's piece includes parenthetical citations for each of his references to White's essays.

Radhika A. Jones's research essay on White represents the more familiar and traditional type of researched piece. Like D'Andrea's essay on White, Jones's contains an idea, a thesis she presents early and develops throughout her argument. Unlike D'Andrea's essay, Jones's looks beyond White's essays, and includes references to his letters and his famous children's books, especially *Charlotte's Web*. As a research essay, it also includes references to secondary sources, a list of works cited, and parenthetical in-text citations, which follow MLA formatting guidelines.

The Artwork

Because we have seen how well students respond to visual stimuli, especially to art, we have included ten reproductions of paintings in *Encounters: Readings and the World*. These works are not merely decorative. Nor are they included simply as stimuli for writing exercises and assignments. Rather, each painting is closely linked with one or more professional or student essays. Although the table of contents identifies each of these links, it does not indicate how the essayists associate the art with their ideas.

In her essay, "Odalisque," Elizabeth MacDonald discusses paintings by de Chirico and Ingres and comments along the way on a photograph of Rita Hayworth (not reprinted). Mark Strand and James Rhee analyze and contemplate the Hopper and Mondrian paintings as they work out their own ideas. Guy Davenport in his "Geography of the Imagination" takes inspiration from Grant Wood's *American Gothic* just as Kristen E. Hughes does from Picasso's *Guernica,* in her essay "I Will Be My Own Hero." Henri Trutat's *Reclining Bacchante,* though not specifically mentioned by John Berger in "Ways of Seeing: Men Looking at Women," is

powerfully exemplified by his argument and by the student essay that
cites Berger—Maile Meloy's "The Voice of the Looking Glass." Joan Didion
refers to Georgia O'Keeffe's paintings. And Mary Gordon refers equally
favorably to the work of Mary Cassatt. Finally, Lisa Fifield's *Running Elk*
can be linked with issues of gender and culture in the essays by Leslie
Marmon Silko, Loren Eiseley, and Barry Lopez—among others—but these
links must be made in the reader's imagination; they are not suggested or
worked out in the essays. Image and imagination working together create
the links.

The fact that visual images stimulate students' imaginations is apparent not only in the student essays reprinted in *Encounters: Readings and the
World* but also in the many ways other visual texts, especially personal
and family photographs, stimulate thought and evoke feeling—in the
reader and in the classroom. Two other outstanding examples of what
happens when students confront these images and begin to make use of
them in their writing can be found in Maile Meloy's "The Voice of the
Looking Glass" and Han N. Pham's "Down the Unwritten Path."

Final Note

We believe that the student and professional essays in *Encounters: Readings
and the World* will give you and your students a basis for exciting writing
courses. We have suggested some ways for using these essays, but we are
less concerned with proposing a particular methodology than with
emphasizing the richness of the essays in this collection. The essays can
tell you much that you need to know about developing classes suited to
your own visions and to your students' needs. Implicit in this collection,
of course, is our own sense of what we think of as good writing.

We would like to thank the following reviewers for their helpful com-
ments and suggestions: Victoria Boynton, SUNY College at Cortland;
Hilda Carey, Boston College; Donald Hammar, Ricks College; Robert
Lorenzi, Camden County College; Robert Noreen, California State Uni-
versity/Northridge; Donnalee Rubin, Salem State University; and Peter
Valenti, Fayetteville State University.

We welcome your questions and comments about our selections and
about our suggestions for teaching. We can be reached through McGraw-
Hill or through our respective institutions. Please call us.

Pat C. Hoy II
Robert DiYanni

ENCOUNTERS: READINGS AND THE WORLD

*I*ntroduction for the Student

Indeed much of the attraction of writing is that it opens life.

SAM PICKERING

The book cover for this collection of stunning essays invites you to begin thinking about yourself and your writing in new, reflective ways. Sitting wherever you are, looking out onto a part of the world—your room, the scene outside your window, the open space around the park bench—sitting there in that very space, you can also look into your self. Within such a convoluted context, looking out and looking in, writers write; they begin the intriguing, and sometimes frustrating, process of rubbing themselves up against the world, trying to make sense simultaneously of their lives (or themselves) and the world around them. From that vantage point, where you can look out and look within, you can find the beginnings for your writing.

But, of course, there is more; you are not alone. Besides yourself and the scene outside your window, besides your experience and whatever else you eventually come to learn about that world outside, there is also the work of other writers, other thinkers—others who have come before you and have begun to make sense of experience. Those others have left for you the work they have already done.

Once upon a time, those other writers were starting just where you are—at the beginning, at that place where you look within and look without, learning to make sense of what you see. A critical part of that process of turning experience and insight into words involves looking and then looking again, and then thinking about what you have seen.

Read an essay once, look at a painting once, and it may not seem to say much to you; it may not stir your imagination. But take the time to look again, and you may very well find something that did not seem to be there

1

at first glance. We come to know whatever we know piecemeal, by accumulation, by reflection. Rarely does clarity come to us all at once. Looking, relooking, noting the differences and reflecting about them—that is what it takes. Inevitably, if you include *writing* in that process—looking, jotting down notes and impressions, waiting a day if you can, looking again, noting differences, writing out your thoughts—you will almost certainly discover that your writing enabled you to see better, yielded something you could not have predicted. Writing has discovery in it.

The essays in this collection, written both by students and by professional writers, invite you to make discoveries as you read, write, think, and reflect about them. At the beginning of the book, we give you examples of student writing that is grounded in some of the essays and paintings in this collection. These student essays are there so that you can see how others have responded to the essays and paintings from this collection. The student essays are there, too, to give you insight into how essays actually evolve. In some cases, you will observe the entire process followed by the student writers as they respond to assignments, develop draft essays, collaborate with other writers (classmates and teachers), and revise their work. Looking at the way these other student writers work, you can begin to discover ways of working that are suited to your individual needs as a reader and as a writer. There is not one right way; there are many ways. This book should help you discover your own ways of reading and writing.

Let us imagine that you are picking up this book for the first time, that you have not been introduced to it by your teacher or by others who have looked into it. No one else has given you a map for your reading. If you look at the first table of contents, you will note that the book has three parts: (1) A Spectrum of Student Writing, (2) A Spectrum of Professional Writing, and (3) Two Professional Writers: Related Student Essays. Although that table of contents may seem forbidding to you because, for the most part, you see nothing but a long list of authors and titles with only a few clear distinctions, it permits you to see at a glance how the book is organized and what is in it. Other tables will help you see the collection in other ways.

The second table, an annotated table of contents, offers teasing invitations into the essays themselves—brief quotations, hints about what awaits you. The third table, a thematic table of contents, does some *connecting* work for you, highlighting and configuring a number of topics: family and community; gender, identity, and sexuality; writing and language; race; courage; the mysteries; and looking at art. Although there are, of course, many other ways for you to group the essays in the collection, these initial configurations give you a sense of how various essays might be related to one another. The fourth table, a rhetorical table of contents, highlights writing techniques. Instead of suggesting *what* the essays mean, it suggests *how* the essays mean. This table groups essays according to some of the ways writers create meaning.

Mark your place in this introduction, and turn to the annotated table of contents (p. xiii), the one with the inviting quotations. Begin to read, skipping around as you see fit, until you land on an idea or an essay that grabs your attention. Turn to that essay, start reading, and stay with the essay until the writer causes you to lose interest. Then turn back again to the annotated table of contents and repeat the process two or three times, sampling other essays in the collection. During that recursive process, take the time, at least once, to look at the reproductions of art. When you have finished your sampling, prepare for reflection.

Open your reading journal (any notebook that you will be able to use again and again to record your thoughts), and list the essays that you sampled. Write down the authors' names and the titles. Ask yourself these questions, and jot down notes about each of them: What do the essays I sampled have in common? Why did I choose those essays so readily? What do my selections say about my personal interests? What ideas interested me in those essays? What caused me to stop reading and turn back to the table of contents? What, if anything, did the art reproductions have to do with the essays I sampled?

As you sampled the essays, questioned them, wrote about them, and reflected about what you had done, you were, at the same time, inadvertently configuring a group of essays; you were grouping them according to something that interested you, something that may have been hidden from you at the outset. Now, try that process one more time as you look back at the essays you sampled before. Repeat the reading and reflecting, but slow down a bit. Then reflect, in writing, about what happened during your reexamination: What did you learn? Did your own writing reveal anything to you?

The reading, writing, and reflecting that you have just completed previews and encapsulates a process that you will repeat over and over during your college years. What may seem strange and unfamiliar about it now will more than likely become second nature. This process is fundamental to learning, and it resembles a more formal research process. You begin with an inclination or a hunch and set out to investigate it by reading, questioning what you read, taking notes, reflecting, doing more reading and more reflecting until you have an idea worth writing about. Getting the idea occupies you at first, and then you turn to evaluating the idea and building up, through reading and writing, your confidence in that idea. That investigative and evaluative process leads finally to your research essay, in which you present and justify your findings. But without the initial curiosity, without the preliminary reading and questioning, without the reflecting, there will more than likely be no idea, nothing to write about. Reading, writing, and reflecting carry you along.

Drafting and Revising Essays

et us look now at the work of two students as they move through the reading, writing, and reflecting process in writing essays. We'll catch glimpses of them doing a lot of preliminary work on the way to completing their essays, work that involves reading, questioning, writing, and reflecting. In the beginning, these students are set in motion by writing exercises given them by their instructors, but there comes a point in the process where they are on their own to make sense of what they're learning. We cannot show you what it looked like inside their heads as they sorted things out, but we can help you see how these students got to a place where they began to have something to say and were learning how to say it effectively.

What these students are doing, you can do as well. Observing how they did much of their preliminary work should help you do yours. But, remember, these examples are not prescriptive. No two students will ever work in exactly the same way. You will have to figure out what works best for you. These examples simply suggest possibilities and allow you to look in on other students doing their work.

Let us look first at the work of Maile Meloy, who was learning to make use of her own experience. In her freshman writing course, she and the other students had already learned to tell stories about their experiences and to make use of the stories in *exploratory* essays, such as those written by Tom Ceraulo, Michael Cohen, and Gian Neffinger (pp. 81–93). These informal essays explore ideas; they are written so that you as a reader actually have the pleasure of observing the writers as they think about their ideas, developing them as they go along in their essays. Writers of exploratory essays are always looking for elusive answers to nagging questions. Exploratory essays are grounded in the familiar, everyday world in which we all live. These essays depend on stories of experience,

5

but they need not confine themselves exclusively to such stories. On many occasions, exploratory essayists make use of paintings, other essays, movies—anything that helps the writers develop their ideas.

Maile Meloy's instructor wanted students to start thinking about art as well as about their own experiences. To help students get started, the instructor asked them to respond to two different writing exercises. For the first, they were asked to describe a picture or photograph that meant something to them. They were asked both to describe the picture and to explain its importance, all in about 200 to 400 words. Students in the class chose many different kinds of pictures. Some selected masterpieces hanging in prominent museums. Others chose posters from their bedrooms at home or from their college dorm rooms. Still others selected pictures from newspaper and magazine advertisements. Maile, along with several other classmates, chose to write about a photograph.

I have a photograph of myself at graduation, with my hair down and fuchsia and plumeria leis piled around my neck. I am laughing, with my mouth open, head tilted, and eyes cast to the side, at something the photographer has said. It is not posed; I am caught in a spontaneous, joyful moment by the gaze of the camera. I have looked at that picture a lot. It is the way I want to be seen in everyday, spontaneous moments, when soft studio lights are not at my rescue and I am vulnerable. I am pleased with the image.

When asked for the photograph, my instinctive response was, "But it's the only copy I have," which I blurted out before I realized how narcissistic I sounded. We are not to let on that we monitor ourselves so closely. We are to be head-tossing and laughing-eyed with out being conscious of our beauty. Loveliness is to ooze naively from our pores. Why would I need pictures of myself? Because I like them. They are interesting to me.

I like to see myself in relation to other people, see myself how other people see me. I study photographs of myself intently, critically--always appraising, always analyzing, carefully recording the information I see there.

I take other opportunities to survey and record--most women do. I have mastered a swift glance over my right shoulder at mirrors and windows as I walk by, careful not to linger and let voyeurs hidden behind reflective glass see my interest in my own image. The left profile is less reassuring, and with scarcely a conscious thought I place people to my right, when it can be subtly maneuvered, so that their view is optimal. This self-observation is not vanity. It is a play for approval, and a request to be treated well, with respect and admiration.

For the second exercise, students were asked to tell a story or to present a situation that had some *connection* with what they had written about in the first exercise—their picture and its importance. Maile chose to write about her mother and her thoughts about appearance, particularly the appearance of women. Notice how Maile's thoughts about appearance conflict to some extent with her mother's. Notice, too, how Maile linked her second exercise with her first.

My mother despises our appearance-oriented environment and lives in fear that I have bought into it. She has sometimes lamented that I was not born unattractive; she is afraid I will have everything given to me, that I'll never know what it is to really earn rewards. She too has bought into the system, however, and perhaps it is that which she laments. Five foot two, beautiful and blonde, a southern-Californian ex-Homecoming Queen, she has been handed a lot on that tarnished silver platter of prettiness. And while carefully maintaining that prettiness, she has despised it. My petite mother always wanted to be tall, dark-haired and magnificent so that people would take her seriously. Unable to transform her appearance, she instead majored in microbiology, which she hated, in an attempt to earn the respect that she craved.

She has since abandoned microbiology and her model-loveliness is beginning to abandon her. It makes me nervous. Old slides of her from college and early marriage are stunning but disconcerting, serving as my own personal *memento mori.* They are my reminder of the death and disappearance of youth and of what is culturally defined as desirable. I wish I could look forward to such changes, to rejoice in the richness that replaces outward worth. But I shudder with the vanity of youth and dread the wrinkles and sagging flesh of age.

Because of my dread of becoming what she is, and what other older women are, I expect intimidation and jealousy. And because I watch other women to compare them to myself and judge myself accordingly, I experience intimidation and jealousy.

Maile's two exercises were read in class by members of her work group. They were also read and commented on by the instructor. Her readers asked Maile questions about her experience and her ideas. Her instructor encouraged her to think about something she had read that had some bearing on the stories she was telling; her instructor also encouraged other students to tell Maile about what they knew or had read that might shed some light on the complicated questions raised by her stories, questions about appearance and image.

Maile's draft follows, along with annotations and interlinear comments by her instructor. Notice how Maile used a pair of epigraphs (brief quotations at the beginning of her draft) that she gleaned from her reading. (You can read the Berger piece on pp. 158–162.) Notice, too, how Maile introduced brief quotations from other writers into the text of her essay, without letting the voices of those other writers take over her draft. She maintained control, using their words and thoughts to stimulate and clarify her own thinking. Maile used those quotations to clarify her ideas for her readers as well.

Maile Meloy
Paper #3
Expos 17, DiYanni
4/11/91

The girl was ugly.   I was bored during
the whole journey.

Casanova
History of My Life

A woman must continually watch herself.
She is almost continually accompanied
by her own image of herself.   Men look
at women.   Women watch themselves
being looked at.

John Berger
Ways of Seeing

Reverse the order of your epigraphs.

From the moment I became conscious

of cause and effect I have been con-

scious of the importance of my own

appearance.   Little girls (and little

quickly? early? both?

boys) learn quickly that the way women

depends on?

are treated is relative to the way

they appear.   [Because, as John Berger

says in his book, *Ways of Seeing,* "how

she appears to others, and ultimately

how she appears to men, is of crucial

This second sentence is not quite right. Try alternatives?

Move this Berger "Because..." part to the end of the paragraph?

importance for what is normally thought of as the success of her life," [It is] *(handwritten: It / =)* a woman's ever-present task to monitor her image, not to survey a situation to determine the appropriate action *(handwritten: as)* a man does, but to survey herself and define the way she wishes others to act toward her.]

(handwritten margin note: Make this bracketed part a sentence in itself.)

I have a photograph of myself at graduation, with my hair down and fuchsia and plumeria leis piled around my neck. I am laughing, with my mouth open, head tilted, and eyes cast to the side, at something the photographer has said. It is not posed; I am caught in a spontaneous, joyful moment by the gaze of the camera. ¶ I have

(handwritten margin note: New paragraph needed here?)

looked at that picture a lot. It is the way I want to be seen in everyday, spontaneous moments, when soft studio

lights are not at my rescue and I am
vulnerable. I am pleased with the image.
And / *I am* ~~When~~ asked for the photograph, my   *No new paragraph here.*
instinctive response ~~was,~~ *is,* "But it's the
only copy I have," which I blurted out
before I realized how narcissistic I
sounded. We are not to let on that we
monitor ourselves so closely. We are
to be head-tossing and laughing-eyed
with out being conscious of our
beauty. ~~Loveliness is to ooze naively
from our pores.~~ ¶ Why ~~I would~~ *do* I need
pictures of myself? Because I like
them. They are interesting to me. I
like to see myself in relation to
other people *to* see myself how other
people see me. I study photographs of
myself intently, critically--always
appraising, always analyzing, carefully
recording ~~the information~~ *what* I see there.
regarding? evaluating? assessing?

I take other opportunities to survey and record. ~~most~~ **Most** women do. I have mastered a swift glance over my right shoulder at mirrors and windows as I walk by, careful not to linger and let voyeurs [hidden behind reflective glass] see my interest in my own image. The left profile is less reassuring, and with scarcely a conscious thought I place people to my right. ~~when it can be subtly maneuvered, so that their view is optimal.~~ ¶ ~~It~~ **This self-regard** is not vanity. ~~this self observation.~~ It is a play for approval, and a request to be treated well, with respect and admiration. It says, "I don't want to bore you during the entire journey."

My mother despises the appearance-oriented environment in which women live, and **she** fears that I have bought into

[margin note: Do you need this bracketed material?]

it. She has sometimes lamented that I

was not born unattractive; she is

afraid I will have everything given to

me, that I'll never know what ^it^ is to

really earn rewards. She too has

bought into the system, however, and

perhaps it is that which she laments.

Five foot two, beautiful and blonde, a

southern-Californian ex-Homecoming

Queen, she has been handed a lot on

the tarnished silver platter of pretti-

ness. And while carefully maintaining

that prettiness, she has despised it.

She has always wanted to be tall,

dark-haired and magnificent so that

people would take her seriously. [(It *Delete sentence in brackets?*

is interesting to note that her friend

Diane, who is tall, dark-haired, and

magnificent, has wanted since her first

bas mitzvah to be short, cute, and

blonde.)] (My mother ~~trapped~~ **Trapped** in her

surfer-girl image and unable to trans-

form her appearance, instead majored in

microbiology, which she hated, in an

attempt to earn the respect ~~that~~ she

craved.

She has since abandoned microbiol-

ogy and her model-loveliness is begin-

ning to abandon her. It makes me ner-

vous. Old slides of her from college

show how   she was.   Are the slides

and early marriage ~~are~~ gorgeous ~~but~~   **gorgeous?**

But these images are   to remind us? one? me?

disconcerting, serving <u>as a reminder</u> of

the death and disappearance of youth

and of what is culturally defined as

desirable. I wish I could look for-

ward to such changes, to rejoice in

the inner richness that replaces out-

ward worth, but I shudder with the

vanity of youth and dread the wrinkles

and sagging flesh of age.

Because of my dread of becoming

what she is, and what other older

women are, I expect intimidation and

jealousy. And because I watch other

women, ~~to~~ compar~~e~~ myself to them and measuring myself against?

judg~~e~~ myself accordingly, I experience

intimidation and jealousy. The dynam-

ics of this watching myself/watching

you watching me phenomenon create what

Margaret Atwood has dubbed "that pale-

mauve hostility that you so often find

between women." It is a shared

secret, that we watch ourselves so

carefully while feigning nonchalance.

We appraise other women as a man

would, appraise ourselves as a man

would, and weigh the results. It is

strangely comforting to find the other

wanting. I think most women hate this

trap, and hate the pale-mauve hostility.   But we learn it as we learn to

walk and to wear our hair in pigtails

the way daddy likes it.   It is our way

of surviv~~ed~~ **ing** in the world we are born

into: one in which, like it or not, we

must continually impress men.   As

Berger says, a woman's "own sense of

being in herself is supplanted by a

sense of being appreciated as herself

by another."

> This is a richly suggestive notion. It could be elaborated.

We are taught this meticulous self-

observation.   At the onset of puberty,

among the other ridiculously sexist

boy-catching hints we receive, girls

are often instructed to "learn how to

take a compliment."   In other words,

we are expected to accept another per-

son's sense of us as they have

expressed it, and to consider it a

reward.   By accepting it we add it to

our expectations of ~~ourself~~ **ourselves**--our checklist as we glance into the mirrors of
shop windows, listen to ourselves
speak, or choose our clothes, opinions
and other accessories.

Nice. I like this shift and mix of "things" and "more-than-things."

   When a girl "takes a compliment,"
she accepts the reward and accepts, as
well, the requirement ~~which~~ **that** earned her
the compliment. ~~They~~ **Both** ~~both~~ become
internalized. She now needs to be
able to earn that other person's sense
of her from herself. She practices
her "disarming smile" in mirrors, concentrates on "poise," and makes sure
she's being "a good listener." Not
all compliments are "taken," of course,
although they may be acknowledged with
a polite "thank you." Some are discarded because they do not fit her
image as the watcher in her sees it,

and these rejects can be disconcerting as they suggest a discrepancy between the internal surveyor and the external one. But true compliments, the ones that congratulate a girl's or woman's muta-ble, monitored perception of herself, are internalized and added to the checklist.

Begin a new sentence?

I do not want to be John Berger's pathetically trapped woman, to merely "appear," and to be a composite of other people's perceptions of me. I do not want to value appearance over action. But I cannot escape the habit of constantly having one eye on my own image. In windows, mirrors and in photographs, in other people's glances, and in by images of myself. I am my own mind I am haunted continually critiquing my appearance, my reactions, my gestures, my speech.

~~observes~~ of ***Of*** one of ~~of his~~ ***the*** women char-

acters, ***a Steven Sondheim song sings:*** "Look at her looking, forever

in that mirror. What does she see?"

¶She sees the self she must continually

present: the self the world perceives.

Maile—You've done it again: you've written what will soon become a truly wonderful essay. The insights here are sharp, rich, complex. The language is often brilliant and beautiful! But the paper needs one more draft — for stylistic scrutiny, refining, tightening, fine-tuning.

After receiving responses from both her classmates and her instructor, Maile prepared another draft of her essay. In this draft, she introduced an experience she had while walking on a city street—an encounter with a homeless person. When Maile saw the woman, it seemed like nothing more than an unexpected encounter, and she quickly put the experience aside. But later, as she read her draft, the experience came back to her; it clarified what she was thinking about. Maile decided, finally, to use that experience to begin her essay, placing it directly before her earlier introduction. You will notice other changes Maile made in her essay: changes in phrasing; the addition of details to heighten our awareness; ideas and quotations from a book of feminist literary criticism that she linked up with her experience and the story about her mother. (Notice, too, that Maile reversed the order of her epigraphs.)

What follows represents approximately half of Maile's second full draft of her essay. The portions described above are included, along with a few additional paragraphs. This draft is presented without marginal or interlinear comments.

A woman must continually watch herself. She
is almost continually accompanied by her own
image of herself. Men look at women. Women
watch themselves being looked at.

> John Berger
> Ways of Seeing

The girl was ugly. I was bored during the
whole journey.

> Casanova
> *History of My Life*

I have been haunted for several days by the
image of one of the homeless people in the city.
She sits huddled in a doorstep in a beige coat
with a scarf tied around her head, and she
clutches a large white plastic bag. The first
time I saw her I found myself staring, wondering
at her face, which was colored a deep pink. As I
neared her, I could make out the cakey texture of
makeup and I caught the sickeningly sweet chemical
smell of the pink powder that covered her entire
face: forehead, wrinkled cheeks, lips, eyes, eyebrows, and ears, and that was smeared across the
lapels of her coat and mixed with the pattern of
her headwrap. I fixed my eyes back on the side-

walk, which was covered with white face powder,
and braced for the inevitable request for money.
It didn't come. She didn't even notice me; her
eyes were riveted to a spot in the corner of the
the doorstep. I glanced back at that spot as I
passed, expecting to see a mirror into which she
was staring so intently. There was nothing there.
Only the concrete wall stared back at her.

Later in the day she was gone, and only a
white outline of her seated form remained in the
scattered face powder on the sidewalk, along with
a sandwich in a baggie that someone must have
given her, abandoned there with one bite taken.
Disconcerted, I sought my own reflection in a shop
window, to replace that of the trembling, staring,
caricature of misplaced female vanity I had seen
that morning. Even as I caught my own eye, I saw
the irony in my means of escape. This poor, ill
woman, to whom her own presented, made-up self is
more important than food, has been in my thoughts

as a final stage in the obsession with our appearance that women learn from early childhood. There but for the grace of something--perhaps our own awareness of our appearances trap--go all women.

Why do I need pictures of myself? Because I like them. They are interesting to me. I like to see myself in relation to other people, to see myself how other people see me. I study photographs of myself intently, critically--always appraising, always analyzing, carefully assessing what I see there.

I take other opportunities to survey and assess. Most women do. I have mastered a swift glance over my right shoulder at mirrors and windows as I walk by, careful not to linger and let voyeurs behind the glass see my interest in my own image. The left profile is less reassuring, and with scarcely a conscious thought I place people to my right. This self-observation is not vanity. It is a play for approval, and a request to be treated well, with respect and admiration.   It

says, "I don't want to bore you during the entire

journey."

Sandra M. Gilbert and Susan Gubar quote Laura

Riding as an epigraph to the first chapter of *The*

Madwoman in the Attic:

> And the lady of the house was seen only as she
> appeared in each room, according to the nature
> of the lord of the room.   None saw the whole
> of her, none but herself.   For the light which
> she was was both her mirror and her body.   None
> could tell the whole of her, none but herself.

The chapter, entitled "The Queen's Looking Glass,"

makes some important observations about "images of

women," especially as portrayed in the Grimm

brother's fairy tale, "Little Snow White." They

note that "female bonding is extraordinarily dif-

ficult in patriarchy: women almost inevitably turn

against women because the voice of the looking-

glass sets them against each other" (38).   Thus we

are set up as rivals for each other by the male

voice of the looking glass, and Gilbert and Gubar

see little hope for female solidarity. They share
Anne Sexton's view that Snow White must inevitably
become the wicked Queen. Having escaped from one
display case (the glass coffin), she has traded it
for another, the mirror in the Prince's home
(41-42). To escape her new prison she must become
the witch. She must become assertive and therefore monstrous and misogynistic to destroy the
"angel woman" Galatea in herself (42).

That the perfect Snow White should become the
evil Queen is horrifying to me, although Gilbert
and Gubar endorse the witch's actions and sympathize with her. It rings true, however, and it
turns me to look at my relationship with my own
mother. She despises the appearance-oriented
environment in which women live, and she fears
that I have bought into it. She has sometimes
lamented that I was not born unattractive; she is
afraid I will have everything given to me, that
I'll never know what it is to really earn rewards.

She too has bought into the system, however, and perhaps it is that which she laments. Five feet two, beautiful and blonde, a southern-Californian ex-Homecoming Queen, she has been handed a lot on the tarnished silver platter of prettiness. And while carefully maintaining that prettiness, she has despised it. She has always wanted to be tall, dark-haired and magnificent so that people would take her seriously. My mother, trapped in her surfer-girl image and unable to transform her appearance, instead majored in microbiology, which she hated, in an attempt to earn the respect she craved.

She has since abandoned microbiology and her model-loveliness is beginning to abandon her. It makes me nervous. Old pictures of her from college and early marriage are breathtaking, with her tousled hair, her smooth tan skin, her perfect cheekbones, and her brilliant Homecoming Queen smile. (Holly Near, singing of her own Queen experience, has observed, "That's what Homecoming

Queens do, is smile.") These images, however, are

disconcerting. They are reminders for me of the

death and disappearance of youth and of what is

culturally defined as desirable. I wish I could

look forward to such changes, to rejoice in the

inner richness that replaces outward worth, but I

shudder with the vanity of youth and dread the

wrinkles and sagging flesh of age. I delight with

Snow White that I am still "the fairest of them

all."

    As good as that second draft is, it benefited from further reflection and revision. Maile decided, for example, that she preferred her original introduction to the one based on the old woman in the street. So she moved the paragraphs about the woman back to a later section of her essay. Maile also elaborated on a reference to a Stephen Sondheim song, which she used to conclude her essay. And she made other adjustments of word choice and sentence style.

    Here is the final version of Maile's essay, one that she built up over a period of about four weeks. Remember that this fine essay did not emerge full-blown from Maile's mind all at once. She thought about it repeatedly over an extended period of time. She relied on her experiences, she read, she wrote, collaborated with other classmates, worked with her instructor, revised, and continued to refine and develop her idea until she had an essay that pleased her. Her idea about appearance, her sense of the way women monitor themselves, her conviction that both men and women have something to do with this monitoring—all these notions grew out of Maile's experiences, her living and her reading. She cared about these experiences, cared about making sense of them, and her concern shows in her essay. That concern carried her through the writing and motivated her; it carries the reader along as well in Maile's final essay.

The Voice of the Looking Glass

Maile Meloy

> A woman must continually watch herself. She is almost
> continually accompanied by her own image of herself. Men look
> at women. Women watch themselves being looked at.
>
> JOHN BERGER
> *Ways of Seeing*

> The girl was ugly. I was bored during the whole journey.
>
> CASANOVA
> *History of My Life*

From the moment I became conscious of cause and effect I have been conscious of the importance of my own appearance. Little girls (and little boys) learn early that the way women are treated is determined by the way they appear. John Berger, in *Ways of Seeing*, has gotten it right. It is a woman's ever-present task to monitor her image, not to survey a situation to determine the appropriate action, as a man does, but to survey herself and define by her presentation the way she wishes others to act toward her.

I have a photograph of myself at graduation, with my hair down and fuschia and plumeria leis piled around my neck. I am laughing, with my mouth open, head tilted, and eyes cast to the side, at something the photographer has said. The picture is not posed; I am caught in a spontaneous, joyful moment by the gaze of the camera.

I have looked at that picture a lot. It is the way I want to be seen in everyday, spontaneous moments, when soft studio lights are not at my rescue and I am vulnerable: I am pleased with the image. When I am asked for the photograph, my instinctive response is, "But it's the only copy I have," which I blurt out before I realize how narcissistic I sound. We are not to let on that we monitor ourselves so closely. We are to be head-tossing and laughing-eyed without being conscious of our beauty.

Why do I need pictures of myself? Because I like them. They are interesting to me. I like to see myself in relation to other people, to see myself the way other people see me. I study photographs of myself intently, critically—always appraising, always analyzing, carefully assessing what I see there.

I take other opportunities to survey and assess. Most women do. I have mastered a swift glance over my right shoulder at mirrors and windows as I walk by, careful not to linger and let voyeurs behind the glass see my interest in my own image. The left profile is less reassuring, and with scarcely a conscious thought I place people to my right. This self-observation is not vanity. It is a play for approval, and a request to be treated well, with respect and admiration. It says, "I don't want to bore you during the entire journey."

The result of the demand for women to be beautiful, combined with a woman's need for approval, according to Berger, is that a woman's "own sense of being in herself is supplanted by a sense of being appreciated by another." Laura Riding's epigraph to the first chapter of Sandra M. Gilbert and Susan Gubar's *The Madwoman in the Attic* addresses this replacement of a woman's self-image with a male's-eye view:

> And the lady of the house was seen only as she appeared in each room, according to the nature of the lord of the room. None saw the whole of her, none but herself. For the light which she was was both her mirror and her body. None could tell the whole of her.

The chapter, entitled "The Queen's Looking Glass," makes some important observations about "images of women," especially as portrayed in the Grimm brothers' fairy tale "Little Snow White." They note that "female bonding is extraordinarily difficult in patriarchy: women almost inevitably turn against women because the voice of the looking glass sets them against each other" (38). Thus we are set up as rivals for each other by the male voice of the looking glass, and Gilbert and Gubar see little hope for female solidarity. They share Anne Sexton's view that Snow White must inevitably become the wicked Queen. Having escaped from one display case (the glass coffin), she has traded it for another, the mirror (41–42). The Prince's home itself is a prison, the same one her mother encountered, where she appears "according to the nature of the lord of the room." To escape her new prison she must become the witch. She must become assertive and therefore monstrous and misogynistic to destroy the "angel woman" Galatea in herself (42).

That the perfect Snow White should become the evil Queen is horrifying to me, although Gilbert and Gubar endorse the witch's actions and sympathize with her. It rings true, however, and it turns me to look at my relationship with my own mother. She despises the appearance-oriented environment in which women live, and she fears that I have bought into it. She has sometimes lamented that I was not born unattractive; she is afraid I will have everything given to me, that I'll never know what it is to really earn rewards. She too has bought into the system, however, and perhaps it is that which she laments. Five feet two, beautiful and blonde, a southern-Californian ex-Homecoming Queen, she has been handed a lot on the tarnished silver platter of prettiness. And while carefully maintaining that prettiness, she has despised it. She has always wanted to be tall, dark-haired and magnificent so that people would take her seriously. My mother, trapped in her surfer-girl image and unable to transform her appearance, instead majored in microbiology, which she hated, in an attempt to earn the respect she craved.

She has since abandoned microbiology, and her model-loveliness is beginning to abandon her. It makes me nervous. Old pictures of her from college and early marriage are breathtaking, with her tousled hair, her smooth tan skin, her perfect cheekbones, and her brilliant Homecoming Queen smile. (Holly Near, singing of her own Queen experience, has observed, "That's what Homecoming Queens do, is smile.") These images, however, are disconcerting. They are reminders for me of the death and disappearance of youth and of what is culturally defined as desirable. I wish I could look forward to such changes, to rejoice in the inner richness that replaces outward worth, but I shudder with the vanity of youth and dread the wrinkles and sagging flesh of age. I delight with Snow White that I am still "the fairest of them all."

Because of my dread of becoming what my mother is, and what other older women are, I expect intimidation and jealousy. And because I watch other women, measuring myself against them and judging myself accordingly, I experience intimidation and jealousy. The dynamics of this watching myself/watching you watching me phenomenon create what Margaret Atwood has dubbed "that pale-mauve hostility that you often find among women." It is a shared secret, that we watch ourselves so carefully while feigning nonchalance. We appraise other women as a man would, appraise ourselves as a man would, and weigh the results. It is strangely comforting to find the other wanting. I think most women hate this trap, and hate the pale-mauve hostility. But we learn it as we learn to walk and to wear our hair in pigtails the way daddy likes it. It is our way of surviving in the world we are born into: one in which, like it or not, we must continually impress men.

We are taught our meticulous self-observation; it is a learned activity. At the onset of puberty, among the other ridiculously sexist boy-catching hints we receive, girls are often instructed to "learn how to take a compliment." We are expected to accept another person's sense of us as they have expressed it, and to consider it a reward. By accepting it we add it to our expectations of ourself—our checklist as we glance into the mirrors of shop windows, listen to ourselves speak, or choose our clothes, opinions, and other accessories.

When a girl "takes a compliment," she accepts the reward and accepts, as well, the requirement that earned her the compliment. Both become internalized. She now needs to be able to earn that other person's sense of her from herself. She practices her "disarming smile" in mirrors, concentrates on "poise," and makes sure she's being "a good listener." Not all compliments are "taken," of course, although they may be acknowledged with a polite "thank you." Some are discarded because they do not fit her image as the watcher in her sees it, and these rejects can be disconcerting as they suggest discrepancy between the internal surveyor and the external one, but true compliments, the ones that congratulate a girl's or woman's mutable, monitored perception of herself, are internalized and added to the checklist.

Sometimes the internal surveyor goes out of control. I have been haunted for several days by the image of one of the homeless people in the city. She sits huddled in a doorstep in a beige coat with a scarf tied around her head, and she clutches a large white plastic bag. The first time I saw her I found myself staring, wondering at her face, which was colored a deep pink. As I neared her, I could make out the cakey texture of makeup and I caught the sweet chemical smell of the pink powder that covered her entire face: forehead, wrinkled cheeks, lips, eyes, eyebrows, and ears, and that was smeared across the lapels of her coat and mixed with the pattern of her headwrap. I fixed my eyes back on the sidewalk, which was covered with white face powder, and braced for the inevitable request for money. It didn't come. She didn't even notice me; her eyes were riveted to a spot in the corner of the doorstep. I glanced back at that spot as I passed, expecting to see a mirror into which she was staring so intently. There was nothing there. Only the concrete wall stared back at her.

Later in the day she was gone, and only a white outline of her seated form remained in the scattered face powder on the sidewalk, along with a sandwich in a baggie that someone must have given her, abandoned there with one bite taken. Disconcerted, I sought my own reflection in a shop window, to replace that of the trembling, staring caricature of female vanity I had seen that morning. Even as I caught my own eye, I saw the irony in my means of escape. This poor, ill woman, to whom her own made-up self is more important than food, exists at the outer edge of the obsession with appearance that women learn from childhood.

I do not want to be John Berger's pathetically trapped woman, to merely "appear," and to be a composite of other people's perceptions of me. I do not want to value appearance over action, but I cannot escape the habit of constantly having one eye on my own image. In mirrors and windows, in photographs, in other people's glances, and in my own mind I am haunted by images of myself. I am continually critiquing my appearance, my reactions, my gestures, and my speech. I am already caught in the queen's looking glass, already in conspiracy with the made-up old woman in the street.

A Stephen Sondheim character sings of his mistress, "Look at her looking, forever in that mirror. What does she see?" He need not ask, for she sees through his eyes. She sees herself as lover, as desirable object, and as rival before she sees herself as a woman. She sees herself in relation to him and in light of his expectations, and she sees her imperfections in that light. She sees Snow White fading and growing old and yet she clings to the façade. It is what she knows.

Let's look now at a different kind of essay, an *analytical/argumentative* one written by Robynn Stacy Maines, who became excited about Gretel Ehrlich's essay "Looking for a Lost Dog" (pp. 229–233). Once Robynn discovered that the essay was not really about the lost dog, she was able to pay attention to the way Ehrlich developed her ideas about thinking. What she found in that essay interested her so much that she wanted to write about it. She wanted to analyze Ehrlich's essay, break it down into its many parts, look at it, see how it worked, and then write an essay about her discoveries. But we're getting ahead of ourselves. Let's go back to the beginning—to the process of discovery. Students were asked to respond to the following writing exercise:

EXERCISE 1

Select an essay by one of the contemporary essayists in this collection and write a 500-word analysis focusing on the essay's images or metaphors, or both.

Here is Robynn's response to the exercise, along with marginal and interlinear annotations that show the comments of one of her student readers and her instructor.

In Gretel Ehrlich's "Looking for a

Lost Dog," the first significant

metaphor or image is the dog. [The *This implies a paradoxical dimension, doesn't it?*

essay begins by representing it simply

as itself: a lost dog. But as the

essay's theme begins to emerge, the

dog takes on a metaphorical essence:

of things lost.] Ehrlich's first

straight forward approach to the idea

at play is in her sentence in para-

graph eleven: "To find what's lost;

to lose what's found." It is at this

point that the dog becomes symbolic.

He represents the concept that the

things we go looking for are not nec-   *Well put.*

essarily the things we will find. [The

dog is not, at least in this episode, *Do you need this last sentence?*

found, ~~but~~ *though* many other and perhaps more

significant things are.

The underlying idea of the essay

emerges clearly in paragraph eleven, *Why skip ahead? Talk about 9 first and then develop into 11.*

but it is in paragraph nine that we

get our first real taste of what that

idea may resemble. Ehrlich uses the *Could you try to combine these sentences into one?*

image of the trees with lost blossoms

and her feeling of having "caught

strangers undressed" to jolt us into

feeling, if not fully comprehending

yet, the sensation of her unfolding

idea. We experience the reaction of

surprise that catching strangers

undressed would generate. And so we *What idea? Be more specific in your reference to the idea of Ehrlich's essay.*

are effectively prepared to understand

the idea that the essay begins to

bring out.

Ehrlich next introduces the greater

significance of losing and finding.
Here is where the waterfall image
comes into play in order to help
illustrate how even the most obvious
and present things--truths perhaps,
about ourselves, about what we truly
need from life--can be concealed, just
as the falls are hidden behind rose
thickets. In fact, these things
appear "lost"--for we can't see them--
precisely because we are too close to
them. And Ehrlich then takes the
metaphor further to include the mind,
and how it can feel at times that we
are "losing our minds" when in fact,
we are merely too close to them to see
them, understand them, clearly. And
so we feel overwhelmed, the way one
might feel about an impressionist
painting up close: it seems to have no

Lovely.

Good metaphor.

meaning until you distance yourself and take in the congruent whole.

[This being too close to what is lost to know how to find it, how to recognize it, is like one end of a cord which ties up a bundle.] The other end is in the form of the symbolism of walking, meandering and as in the Thoreau quote in paragraph twelve, water. Through these images Ehrlich demonstrates the other notion that completes the idea: that to find something, or to soothe loss or calm maddening desire, one must set out "with a purpose but no destination" (paragraph 17). Water seems random, and it is as a substance. But it has a nature, a method, as Thoreau said, always "seeking the shortest course to the sea" (paragraph 12).

Awkward sentence.

You must read Annie Dillard. (Let's talk about her work in conference).

to

Isn't this really three ideas?

And so Ehrlich's walk itself, which had a purpose: to find the dog, also *a walk* *was* without *a* destination. The discover-ies, however were enormous, *both* gentle and unexpected. Before her walk *Ehrlich* ~~she~~ was feeling discontented, longing for things either lost or not yet found: love, more from life. Her distress had created so much "noise" that it had become depressing. By taking a meandering, purposeful yet destination-less walk, she came to discover things that were different than what she thought she needed, but which removed the longing nonetheless.

Good use of "meandering".

Good analysis.

The cottonwood "lunatic with bird-song" is perhaps the most compelling image, appropriately, because the pic-ture and sound of it pulls together those two cord ends, drawing up the whole bundle that is the theme. The ← *Good metaphor.*

tree is full of birds, but to see only

the birds it to miss the grandeur of

the "symphony" of the whole tree. And *Good analysis in this paragraph.*

the use of lunacy is potent because it

recalls her earlier mention of losing

one's mind. The fullness of Ehrlich's

idea culminates with the image of this

tree which is so much more, heaving

upward, like her own raucous mind,

full of noise yet astonishing in its *quiet*

presence.

And so, by the end "it is enough

to make a shadow" because living

itself is enough, and full of discov- *I don't understand this phrase. Can you elaborate just a bit?*

ery enough, to outweigh whatever is lost.

The second writing exercise called for a second look, a reconsidera-
tion of the selected essay.

EXERCISE 2

Return to the essay you analyzed in Exercise 1 and provide an overview of it by
discussing its structure and organization. You can do this overview in different

ways, the simplest perhaps being to describe what the writer does in each paragraph or group of paragraphs, taken in order. Or you can decide for yourself what features of the essay's organization or structure to comment on.

Robynn wrote the following response:

The first major structural compo-

nent of "Looking For a Lost Dog" may

be the title itself, for it embodies   *Tighten*

~~at first glance,~~ a simple introduction   *a little.*

to the situation around which the

essay's theme will be woven. It tells

us that we are going to hear about the

process of looking for a dog, yet its

simplicity, its overly direct, almost

obvious nature, implies that the dog

and the process of looking will ~~come~~

~~to~~ take on greater meaning. Other-

wise, how much depth could simply try-

ing to find a dog possess? The first

two paragraphs hold more or less to

the first sense of the title: "I

started off this morning looking for

my lost dog." This first line is
blunt, to the point. Ehrlich gets the
obvious aspect of the story out of the
way immediately in paragraphs one and
two with snappy descriptions of the
dog and how he's been lost before.
We're almost compelled to skim right
through this part, for even within
their quickness, there is the faintest
impression that more is coming which
we become anxious to discover: ". . .
his right leg is crooked where it
froze to the ground," and "When we put
our ears to the ground, we could hear
the hole that had swallowed him."
What oddities, what different angles to
take ~~in~~ regarding otherwise normal
things. We don't know it yet, but
Ehrlich has planted the ~~subconscious~~
seed of her theme.

Paragraphs three and four then, are the tender sprout. Ehrlich's humorous description of herself "cupping my hands behind my ears--mule-like--and pricking them all the way forward or back to hear what's happened or what's ahead," (paragraph 3) and the quote from her friend about life being polyphonic and hearing having "to do with the great suspiration of life everywhere," (paragraph 4) bring the concept of seeing--or hearing--life in unexpected ways into sharp focus. In fact, she plays somewhat thing of a trick on us here, allowing us to believe we've got her figured out. We can gloat a little, thinking how cleverly we've uncovered her idea. But read on we must, for the satisfaction of having our cleverness confirmed.

"But back to the dog." (paragraph 5) What? There's more? Of course, we think, she must try to find the dog by looking and listening differently than she normally would. We still feel ourselves right along with her, ahead a little even, as she begins to meander into descriptions of the countryside. Lovely, we may think, but isn't it getting a bit off the point? And then, there's the bit on Navajo "hand tremblers." The quotation at the end: "Lots of noise, but noise that's hard to hear" is at first glance baffling. It has the very effect of what it says. We find ourselves suddenly confused by the "noise" of this and the last paragraph's illustrative qualities, and begin to wonder if in fact they did have a place. Perhaps we weren't so clever. Better read on.

Paragraph 7 and the image of the falls leads us into more description and more uncertainty, until the end of the paragraph: "The falls roar, but they're overgrown . . . and the closer I get, the harder it is to see the water. Perhaps that is how it will be in my search for the dog." Aha! There is more here. Not only must we look at things in different ways, but there is a reason why we don't see things clearly. Sometimes they are hidden! We are almost too excited at seeing this idea sprout a new stem to stop and wonder what it may be that keeps the things we look for hidden.

Ehrlich gives us a reprieve for a moment with paragraph eight, where she launches into a story about how the

dog was bitten by rattlesnakes and
nearly died. But she inserts a quiet
reminder here that the dog is a
metaphor. We should be on the lookout
for more of what he represents.

　　Paragraph nine carries us visually
on Ehrlich's walk with vibrant pictures
of the landscape and the sensations it
brings her. The images of glaring
mountains, "the black sky (hanging)
over like a frown," and the sensation
of being pulled downstream by the
"string of cottonwoods whose tender
leaves are the color of limes," are so
beautiful, they transfix us and make
us nearly forget that there is a theme
to discover fully here. And so in
this dazed state, Ehrlich pounces with
the image of the blossom-less trees
making her feel as if she "has caught

strangers undressed." Drawn into her
description as we are, we can't help
but feel the astonishment that such a
sight would provoke. We are effectively snapped into the mindset of
witnessing the unexpected. And so we
are sensationally prepared for the
first congruent taste of the essay's
theme which is carried to us much like
the birds in paragraph 10 on fierce
spring winds. It drops neatly and
concisely into place with the first
sentence of paragraph 11: "To find
what's lost; to lose what's found."
It's so simple, like the title, but by
this point, we have enough information
to know that "to find what's lost"
takes a new kind of vision and an eye
toward the unexpected. But the second
half of that sentence: "to lose what's

found" is what really compels us.
Ehrlich loses no time in drawing on
our curiosity by giving us an example
of something that can seem lost at
times: the mind. And immediately, she
rebukes the concept that the mind can
be lost by comparing it to the falls:
"We can lose sight of what is too
close." She is off and running now
with the theme at work. She keeps on
a steady course, ironically, by bringing in a Thoreau quote about a saunterer having the nature of water: it
appears random, yet "is all the while
sedulously seeking the shortest course
to the sea."

Paragraph 13 and its meanderings
into Ehrlich's "longings--for what I'm
not, for what is impossible, for people I love who can't be in my life

. . ." seem at first undirected, misplaced, as do the descriptions in
paragraphs 14 and 15 about Ehrlich's
seeming irrational expectations of herself. But then, if we allow ourselves
a reminder, we are struck by the earlier Thoreau quote: "The saunterer, in
the good sense, is no more vagrant
than the meandering river . . ." Paragraph 16 is a sort of preparation for
the unity to come in that it plays the
organized image of a Japanese garden
against the tumultuous one of the
"tortured junipers and tumbled boulders." She nearly stumbles, yet catches
the perfect sight of an unexpected
locust in a bird's nest. Everything
is out of place, but strangely perfected and wonderful to behold.

"Some days I think this one place

isn't enough," (paragraph 17) tells us what she believes she has lost, that she wants to find more from life perhaps. But then she comes across the "towering cottonwood . . . lunatic with birdsong" and the completion of the essay's idea is before us. "Today it is enough to make a shadow" (paragraph 18) because by allowing herself to meander, with vision for the unexpected, she has learned to let go of what she thought she needed and instead discover what she'd really lost: those elements of discovery in life itself that sustain us beyond any loss lesser than that of life itself.

Lovely.

A fine analysis of the essay's idea — and a good overview of it. When you write your essay draft, however, do not structure it according to a linear march through Ehrlich's paragraphs. Very nice insights throughout. Great work throughout this analysis, Robynn.

Notice how in this second exercise Robynn continued to analyze the images of Ehrlich's essay. This time, however, she was able to comment more extensively on how the images affect the reader—both herself as an individual reader and other readers as well.

Notice, too, how she found new ways to frame her understanding of Ehrlich's achievement in "Looking for a Lost Dog." And notice how often Robynn quoted specific phrases and passages from Ehrlich's writing to illustrate the observations she made about the essay.

Robynn looked very closely at individual paragraphs, paying attention to the language and images in those paragraphs. In the process of analyzing, she saw more in Ehrlich's essay than she did when she wrote her first exercise. Looking again paid off. She, like Ehrlich in her search, found more than she bargained for.

Once the exercises had been completed and Robynn had a chance to think about them and about Ehrlich's essay, she was ready to begin work on the first draft of her essay. She was ready to find a way to tell readers what she had discovered.

Robynn Stacy Maines
"The Essay"
Professor DiYanni
Essay #2, First Draft
July 14, 1993

GRETEL EHRLICH's "LOOKING FOR A LOST
DOG": AN ANALYSIS

Better, more catchy title?

In "Looking for a Lost Dog" Gretel

Ehrlich has accomplished a feat of

communication both subtle and powerful.

The remarkable thing is that the power

is the subtlety and the subtlety the

power, so that the essay itself, its

structure and the actual experience of

reading it, is an intricately devised

reflection of its ~~message.~~ *theme.* Wherever

Avoid "message". It's too telegraphic.

Ehrlich employs ~~an element, whether it~~

~~be~~ a metaphor, an image, or an anec-

dote ~~which illustrates the message she~~ *her idea,*

~~wishes~~ to convey she simultaneously

I'd suggest some re-writing here, some fine-tuning. I've provided one possibility.

adds a physical dimension to the essay

itself, like raising a mirror against

another, creating infinitely reflecting
mutually?

images of each into the other.   In
in an infinite regression?

other words, ~~her message is infinitely~~
Ehrlich conveys not just an idea,

~~present in both the words she uses and~~
but an experience — an experience, in

~~the experience of the reader as he or~~
fact, that both mirrors her idea and

~~she reads the essay.~~   ~~Her~~ accomplish-
dramatizes it.   Ehrlich's

ment of this is so subtle, the reader

is nearly unconscious of the impression

being made, which reinforces the idea

of "Looking for a Lost Dog."

      The title is the first and perhaps

the most subtle of ~~the~~ double mirror-
Ehrlich's   's.

~~like tools.~~   It embodies more than a

simple introduction to the situation

around which the essay's theme will

weave.   It tells us that we are going

to hear about the process of looking

for a dog, yet its simplicity, its

overly direct, almost obvious nature,

implies that the dog and the process

of looking will come to take on

greater meaning; [otherwise how much   Cut?

depth could simply trying to find a

dog possess?] Such an expectation is

immediately reinforced by the Thoreau

quote ~~inserted~~ as ~~a prelude~~. Its con-

Ehrlich uses an epigraph.

nection to the forthcoming story as

presumed by the title isn't entirely   *Titles don't*
                                             presume —
apparent--it doesn't need to be, so   *readers do.*

indicated? suggested?

early on--yet it entices us, with its

message that "the most valuable

suggestion?

thoughts which I entertain are anything

but what I thought. Nature abhors a

vacuum, and if I can only walk with

sufficient carelessness I am sure to

be filled." Our thought at this point

may be that the essay is surely going

to be highly philosophical. We may

even prepare ourselves for an intellec-

tual excursion. But then Ehrlich

throws us for a loop with the first
two paragraphs which hold more or less
to the first sense of the title: "I
started off this morning looking for
my lost dog." This first line is
blunt, to the point. Ehrlich gets the
obvious aspect of the story out of the
way immediately ~~in paragraphs one and two~~ with <u>snappy</u> descriptions of the
dog and how he's been lost before.

> I like this surprising adjective here.

We're almost compelled to skim right
through this part, for even within
their quickness, there is the faintest
impression that more is coming which
we become anxious to discover: ". . .
his right leg is crooked where it
froze to the ground," and "When we put
our ears to the ground, we could hear
the hole that had swallowed him."
What oddities, what different angles to

take in regard to otherwise normal
things. We don't know it yet *at this point in reading the essay,* but
Ehrlich has planted the ~~subconscious.~~
seed of her theme.

Paragraphs three and four then, are
the tender sprout. Ehrlich's humorous
description of herself "cupping my
hands behind my ears--mule-like--and
pricking them all the way forward or
back to hear what's happened or what's
ahead," (paragraph 3) and the quote
from her friend about life being polyphonic and hearing having "to do with
the great suspiration of life everywhere," (paragraph 4) bring the concept
of seeing--or hearing--life in unexpected ways into sharp focus. In
fact, she plays *something* ~~somewhat~~ of a trick on
us here, allowing us to believe *that* we've
got her figured out. We can gloat a

little, thinking how cleverly we've

uncovered her idea. But read on we

must, for the satisfaction of having

our cleverness confirmed.

"But back to the dog." (paragraph

5) What? There's more? Of course, *This shift in your tone is distracting. Delete?*

we think, she must try to find the dog

by looking and listening differently

than she normally would. We still

feel ourselves right along with her,

ahead a little even, as she begins to

meander into descriptions of the coun-

tryside. Lovely, we may think, but

isn't ~~it~~ *she* getting a bit off the point?

And then, there's the ~~bit on~~ *description of* Navajo

"hand tremblers." The quotation at the

end: "Lots of noise, but noise that's

hard to hear" is at first glance baf-

fling. It has the very effect of what

it is communicating. We find ourselves suddenly confused by the "noise"

of this and the last paragraph's

illustrative qualities, and begin to

wonder if in fact they ~~did~~ do have a

place. [Perhaps we weren't so clever.   Cut?(Not needed.)

Better read on.]

  Paragraph 7 and the image of the

falls leads us into more description   Rather than

and more uncertainty, until the end of   emphasizing the paragraph numbers, em-

the paragraph: "The falls roar, but   phasize instead the image.

they're overgrown . . . and the closer   Use as a transition the sound of

I get, the harder it is to see the   the noisy roaring falls.

water. Perhaps that is how it will be

in my search for the dog." Aha! we think,

/There is more here. Not only must we

look at things in different ways, but

there is a reason why we don't see

things clearly. Sometimes they are

hidden! We are almost too excited at

seeing this idea sprout a new stem to

stop and wonder what it may be that

keeps the things we look for hidden.

Ehrlich gives us a reprieve for a

moment ~~with paragraph eight~~, ~~where~~ **when** she

(handwritten note in right margin: Again, play down "hide", or omit the paragraph numbers.)

launches into a story about how the

dog was bitten by rattlesnakes and

nearly died, and how they've been wor-

ried about him (about losing him?).

It's subtle, but she inserts a quiet

reminder here that the dog is a

metaphor. ~~We should be on the lookout~~

~~for more of what he represents.~~

Then she shifts direction again and

~~Paragraph nine~~ **a** carries us visually

on ~~Ehrlich's~~ **a** walk **filled** with vibrant pictures

of the landscape and the sensations it

brings her. The images of glaring

mountains, "the black sky (hanging)

over like a frown," and the sensation

of being pulled downstream by the

"string of cottonwoods whose tender

leaves are the color of limes," are so

beautiful ~~that~~ they transfix us and make us
[*that* inserted above with caret]

nearly forget that there is a theme to

discover ~~fully~~ here.   And so <u>in this</u>

dazed state, Ehrlich <u>pounces</u> with the
[*better word?* written above *pounces*]

image of the blossom-less trees making

her feel as if she "has caught

strangers undressed."   Drawn into her

description as we are, we can't help

but feel the astonishment that such a

sight would provoke.   We are effec-

tively snapped into the mind set of

witnessing the unexpected.¶ And so we

are sensationally prepared for the

first congruent taste of the essay's

theme which is carried to us much like

the birds ~~in paragraph 10~~ on fierce

spring winds.¶ It drops neatly and

concisely into place with the first

sentence of paragraph 11: "To find

[Marginal annotations: "Is Ehrlich dazed?" / "New paragraph here?" / "or here?"]

what's lost; to lose what's found."
It's so simple~~—~~like the title. ~~but by~~ By however, this point, we have enough information to know that "to find what's lost" requires ~~takes~~ a new kind of vision and an eye toward the unexpected. As the essay's theme begins to emerge, the dog now takes on a metaphorical essence: of things lost. ~~It is at this point that~~ The ~~the~~ dog ~~becomes~~ (symbolic) ~~He~~ repre-sents the concept that the things we go looking for are not necessarily the things we will find. The dog is not, at least in this episode, found, though many other and perhaps more significant things are. ¶ Ehrlich's **Start a new paragraph?** straightforward placement of a major thematic concept here has a satiating quality, for it rewards our sense of comprehension, But ~~but~~ the second half of

the sentence: "to lose what's found"
compels us to venture beyond this initial understanding. This is a perfect
example of the mirroring quality present throughout the essay. The words
themselves "to lose what's found" mirror the preceding words "to find
what's lost." But that is only one
dimension of the strategy. The other
and even more powerful effect is that
the concept itself reflects the idea
we've already come to understand up to
this point in the essay. What's more,
the introduction of it is so confusing
yet obviously pertinent, that we fall
~~completely~~ prey to our own rambling
curiosity. ¶ Ehrlich loses no time in   *New paragraph?*
drawing on our curiosity by giving us
an example of something that can seem
lost; at times the mind. She then

immediately rebukes the concept that
the mind can be lost by comparing it
to the falls: "We can lose sight of
what is too close." We can feel overwhelmed, the way one might feel about
an impressionist painting up close: it
seems to have no meaning until you
distance yourself and take in the congruent whole.   Ehrlich is off and running now with the theme at work. She
keeps on a steady course, ironically,
by bringing in a Thoreau quote about a
saunterer having the nature of water:
it appears random, yet "is all the
while sedulously seeking the shortest
course to the sea." Being too close
to what is lost, to know how to find
                  and
it ⌃ how to recognize it is like one
end of a cord which ties up a bundle.
The other end is ~~in the form of the~~

symbolized by walking, meandering and,

as in the Thoreau quote in paragraph

twelve, water. Through these images

Ehrlich demonstrates the other notion

that completes the idea: that to find

something, or to soothe loss or calm

maddening desire, one must set out

"with a purpose but no destination"

(paragraph 17). Water seems random,

and it is as a substance. But it has

a nature, a method, which, as Thoreau says, is

always "seeking the shortest course to

the sea" (paragraph 12).

The meanderings

of Ehrlich's "longings--for what I'm

not, for what is impossible, for peo-

ple I love who can't be in my life

. . ." seem at first undirected, mis-

placed, as do the descriptions about Ehrlich's seem-

Explain the connection.

ing irrational expectations of herself.
But then, if we allow ourselves a
reminder, we are struck by the earlier
Thoreau quote: "The saunterer, in the
good sense, is no more vagrant than
the meandering river. . . ." ~~Paragraph~~
~~16~~ is a sort of preparation for the
unity to come in that it plays the
organized image of a Japanese garden
against the tumultuous one of the
"tortured junipers and tumbled boulders." She nearly stumbles, yet
catches the perfect sight of an unexpected locust in a bird's nest.
Everything is out of place, but
strangely perfect.

You'll need a transition to this next image.

And so Ehrlich's walk itself, which
started out with a purpose: to find
the dog, also is without destination.
The discoveries, however, are enormous,

A great ending.

gentle and unexpected. Before her walk she was feeling discontent**ed,** longing for things either lost or not yet found: love, more from life. Her distress had created so much "noise" that it had become depressing. By taking a meandering, purposeful yet destinationless walk, ~~she~~ **Ehrlich** came to discover things that were different than what she thought she needed, but which removed the longing nonetheless.

The cottonwood "lunatic with birdsong" is perhaps the most compelling image, appropriately, because the picture and sound of it pulls together those two cord ends, drawing up the whole bundle that is the theme. The tree is full of birds, but to see only the birds is to miss the grandeur of the "symphony" of the whole tree. And the use of lunacy is potent because it

recalls her earlier mention of losing

one's mind. The fullness of Ehrlich's

idea culminates with the image of this

tree which is so much more, heaving

upward, like her own raucous mind,

full of noise yet astonishing in its

presence.

And so, by the end "it is enough

to make a shadow" because living

itself is enough, and full of discov-

ery enough, to outweigh whatever is

lost.

Robynn— This is a beautiful analysis. Do as good a job as you can with your next draft. Then consider perhaps doing some further fine-tuning a couple of weeks later, after you've had a chance to get away from the piece.

Robynn's first draft contained many excellent features. It was based on a clear idea about Ehrlich's essay; that idea was Robynn's thesis. Look back to the last half of her first paragraph. The draft presented aptly chosen passages from Ehrlich's essay to illustrate that thesis. And in the draft,

Robynn made important connections between Ehrlich's images, quoting Ehrlich's language to illustrate and demonstrate the idea and movement of mind so central to "Looking for a Lost Dog."

In her second draft, Robynn worked hard to improve many of her sentences and to retain her emphasis on Ehrlich's imagery. Her analysis of imagery was the key to her own thesis. Writing this second draft, Robynn wanted to eliminate the sense that she was plodding through Ehrlich's essay paragraph by paragraph, listing in order the things she noticed. She focused primarily on Ehrlich's images rather than on where they appeared in the essay.

Here are a few paragraphs from Robynn's second draft:

```
    This meandering of thought contin-

ues into Ehrlich's friend's observation

that life is polyphonic and that hear-

ing "has to do with the great suspira-

tion of life everywhere." The concept

of seeing--or hearing--life in unex-

pected ways, all at once comes into

sharp focus, like turning a random

corner during a walk through a city

and coming suddenly upon a cathedral.

In fact, Ehrlich plays something of a

trick on us here, allowing us to

believe we've got her figured out.

The use of this rather grand concept
```

and especially the ominous sounding "suspiration" just feels like revelation. ~~We can gloat a little, thinking how cleverly we've uncovered her idea.~~ We're drawn forward ~~though~~ by our desire to have that ~~cleverness~~ revelation affirmed.

Prepared as we are for ~~a philosophical~~ verification of our conclusion, we are jolted by the next sentence: "But back to the dog." This ~~sharp~~ unexpected return to the ordinary, to the bluntness of the beginning is surprising. ~~Ehrlich has returned us to a simple story about a lost dog and we are thrown off balance with this unexpected turn. But then we think, of course, she must try to find the dog by looking and listening differently than she normally would. We still feel ourselves right along~~

~~with her, ahead a little even~~ **As** she

begins to meander once again, into **lovely**

descriptions of the countryside**,**
we begin to feel lost.
~~Lovely, we may think, but isn't she~~

~~getting a bit off the point?~~ By the

time she brings us to the description

of Navajo "hand tremblers" and the

quotation at the end**:** "Lots of noise,

but noise that's hard to hear**,**" we may

feel thoroughly baffled. But all of

this has the very effect of what ~~it~~ **Ehrlich** is

communicating: we ~~find ourselves~~ **are** ~~sud-~~

~~denly~~ confused by the "noise" of this

and the last paragraph's illustrative

qualities **.** ~~and begin to wonder if in~~

~~fact they do have a place.~~

The image of the falls with its own

noise leads us into more description

and more uncertainty, until the end of

the paragraph: "The falls roar, but

they're overgrown . . . and the closer

I get, the harder it is to see the

water. *Perhaps that is how it will be* **(my italics). In one sentence,**

in my search for the dog. ~~Aha! we~~ **confusion culminates in meaning.**

~~think, there is more here.~~ Not only

must we look at things in different

ways, but there is a reason why we

don't see things clearly: sometimes

they are hidden. We are **ready to** ~~almost too~~

explore this new idea with

~~excited at seeing this idea sprout a~~

Ehrlich, ready for its pertinence

~~now stem to stop and wonder what it~~

to finding the dog.

~~may be that keeps the things we look~~

~~for hidden.~~ **But**

~~And~~ then, again, with our curiosity **Is this a real verb?**

Instead of taking us on

peaked, Ehrlich diverges. ~~back to the~~

the expected route of applying philosophy to the search,

~~dog, this time into a story about how~~

she wanders into an ordinary story about how

he was bitten by rattlesnakes and

nearly died. ~~and how they've been wor-~~

~~ried about him (about losing him?).~~

prosaic images of the

By continuing to return us to the dog

just when we feel ready to explore her

underlying ideas, Ehrlich inserts a

quiet reminder that the dog is a

He represents the things we look for consciously, which lead us to other, less obvious discoveries.

metaphor. He also ~~plays the role of~~ *acts as a pivot point* ~~fulcrum~~ for the twists and turns of

twists and turns don't have a fulcrum.

the essay, so that within the mirror-

ing effect, the dog is the anchor for

the wandering from confusion to under-

standing which takes place throughout.

The crossouts and the interlinear rewriting, as well as the marginal revisions, are exclusively Robynn's. In looking carefully at her revisions, you will notice how much clearer they make her essay. Even so, Robynn continued to work on revising her essay, partly because she saw how far it had already come from those early exercises. But the more she worked, the more she looked back into Ehrlich's essay and into her own, the more she kept seeing, and she wanted to comment on those observations and improve her analysis.

Here, then, is the final version of Robynn's analytical essay on Gretel Ehrlich's "Looking for a Lost Dog."

Finding a Dog Not Lost in "Looking for a Lost Dog"

Robynn Stacy Maines

In "Looking for a Lost Dog" Gretel Ehrlich employs an effective strategy in making the essay itself, its structure and the actual experience of reading it, an intricate reflection of its theme. Wherever Ehrlich delivers elements of her idea through metaphor, imagery or anecdote, she simultaneously adds a physical dimension to the essay itself, like raising a mirror against another, creating mutual reflections of the central idea both in the essay and in the experience of reading it.

The essay begins with a sort of drifting into reverie, the prose itself resembling the wanderings of the mind. Physical descriptions of the dog lead to a story of how he fell into a hole once, and how they could hear him whining. This image spills over into musings about the positioning of our ears making us narcissistic, so that "we can only hear what's right next to us or else the internal monologue inside." It has such a rambling effect that we almost miss the significance of "the internal monologue inside." In fact, Ehrlich carries us right by it on the meandering stream of her own "internal monologue" into a humorous description of herself "cupping my hands behind my ears—mule-like—and pricking them all the way forward or back to hear what's happened or what's ahead." It's as if she herself, in her own inner conversation, doesn't notice that she's foreshadowed her own thoughts.

Her approach almost compels us to skim right through this part, so that we come close to overlooking a few of the other gems throughout this opening segment. Without being obvious though, they radiate the faintest impression that more is coming, and despite the lightheartedness, we become eager to discover the meaning behind these things: "his right leg is crooked where it froze to the ground," and "when we put our ears to the ground, we could hear the hole that had swallowed him." What oddities, what different angles to take in regard to otherwise normal things. We are not aware of it at this point in reading the essay, but Ehrlich has introduced us to a portion of her idea, that things are not always as they appear. She has also employed the subtle mirroring, for the very rambling nature of her prose introduces us to another key component of her theme: the importance of meandering as a means of discovery.

This meandering of thought continues into Ehrlich's friend's observation that life is polyphonic and that hearing "has to do with the great suspiration of life everywhere." The concept of seeing—or hearing—life in unexpected ways, all at once comes into sharp focus. The use of this rather grand concept and especially the ominous-sounding "suspiration" just feels like revelation, and we are drawn forward by a desire to have that revelation affirmed.

Prepared as we are for verification of our conclusion, we are jolted by the next sentence: "But back to the dog." This unexpected turn into the ordinary throws us off balance, the more so because she doesn't return to the dog at all, but instead begins to meander once again, this time into lovely descriptions of the countryside. We begin to feel lost. By the time she brings us to the description of Navajo "hand tremblers" and the quotation at the end, "Lots of noise, but noise that's hard to hear," we may feel thoroughly baffled. But all of this embodies the very effect of what Ehrlich is communicating: we are confused by the "noise" of this and the last paragraph's illustrative qualities, and begin to wonder if they signify something not yet discovered.

The image of the falls with its own noise leads us into more description and more uncertainty, until the end of the paragraph: "The falls roar, but they're overgrown . . . and the closer I get, the harder it is to see the water. *Perhaps that is how it will be in my search for the dog*" (my italics). In one sentence, confusion culminates in meaning. Not only must we look at things in different ways, but there is a reason why we don't see things clearly: sometimes they are hidden. We are ready to explore this new idea, ready for its pertinence to finding the dog when, again with our curiosity piqued, Ehrlich diverges once more.

Instead of taking us on the expected route of applying philosophy to the search, Ehrlich wanders into an ordinary story about how the dog was bitten by rattlesnakes and nearly died. By continuing to return us to prosaic images of the dog just when we feel ready to explore her underlying ideas, Ehrlich inserts a quiet reminder that the dog is a metaphor. He represents the things we look for consciously, but which lead us instead to other, less obvious discoveries. He also acts as a pivot point for the twists and turns of the essay, so that within the mirroring effect, the dog is the anchor for the wandering from confusion to understanding which takes place throughout our reading.

Ehrlich moves us forward with this sense of random thinking and into random walking with vibrant pictures of the landscape and the sensations it brings her. The images of glaring mountains, "the black sky (hanging) over like a frown," and the sensation of being pulled downstream by the "string of cottonwoods whose tender leaves are the color of limes," are so beautiful that they transfix us and make us nearly forget that there is a theme to discover. And so having effectively lulled us into something of a mesmerized state, Ehrlich surprises us with the image of the blossomless trees making her feel as if she "has caught strangers undressed." Drawn into her description as we are, we can't help but feel the astonishment that such a sight would provoke. We are effectively snapped into the mind-set of witnessing the unexpected and sensationally prepared for the first congruent taste of the essay's theme, which is carried to us much like the birds flying north on fierce spring winds.

It drops neatly and concisely into place with the first sentence of paragraph 11: "To find what's lost; to lose what's found." It's so simple, like the title. By this point, however, we have enough information to know that "to find what's lost" takes a new kind of vision and an eye toward the unexpected.

Ehrlich's straightforward placement of a major thematic concept here has a satiating quality, for it rewards our sense of comprehension. But the second half of that sentence —"to lose what's found"—compels us to venture beyond this initial understanding. This is a perfect example of the mirroring quality present throughout the essay. The words themselves "to lose what's found" mirror the preceding words "to find what's lost." But that is only one dimension of the strategy. The other and even more profound effect is that the concept itself is a reflection of the message we've already come to understand up to this point in the essay. What's more, the introduction of it is so confusing, yet obviously pertinent, that we fall prey to our own rambling curiosity.

Ehrlich loses no time in drawing on our curiosity by giving us an example of something that can seem lost at times: the mind. She then immediately rebukes the concept that the mind can be lost by comparing it to the falls: "We can lose sight of what is too close." We can feel overwhelmed, the way one might feel about an impressionist painting up close: it seems to have no meaning until you distance yourself and take in the congruent whole. Ehrlich is off and running now with the theme at work. She keeps on a steady course, ironically, by bringing in a Thoreau quotation about a saunterer having the nature of water: it appears random, yet "is all the while sedulously seeking the shortest course to the sea."

Being so close to what is lost that you can't find or recognize it, is like one end of a cord which ties up a bundle. The other end is in the symbolism of walking, meandering, and the nature of water. Through these images Ehrlich demonstrates the other notion that completes the idea: that to find something, or to soothe loss or calm maddening desire, one must set out "with a purpose but no destination." Water appears random, yet it has a nature, a method, as Thoreau said, always "seeking the shortest course to the sea."

The meandering of the essay into Ehrlich's "longings—for what I'm not, for what is impossible, for people I love who can't be in my life" seems at first undirected, misplaced, as do the descriptions of Ehrlich's seemingly irrational expectations of herself. But then, if we allow ourselves a reminder, we are struck by the Thoreau quotations: "The saunterer, in the good sense, is no more vagrant than the meandering river" and "if I can only walk with sufficient carelessness I am sure to be filled." Ehrlich's walk, as well as her "internal monologue," has carried her to this place of inner speculation. Her "hybrid anguish spends itself as recklessly and purposefully as water" so that whatever it is that is empty, or lost, inside her can be filled, or found. This intrusion of emotion is no intrusion at all, but the destination of her meandering. Its misplaced, sudden sensation is appropriate, for its effect on the reader mirrors the idea that the most obvious and present things are often those which are most difficult to recognize.

The momentum of the essay toward the end reflects that of Ehrlich's thoughts as one begins to play rapidly into the next. Ehrlich's strange notion that she could "sniff out a scent" causes her to question herself and then to relate this to a similar situation in Japan when she thought she would "break into fluent Japanese." It is as if we are witnessing her mind's connections, for the image of the Japanese garden seems to grow out of her thoughts of Japan. This apparently discursive run of images recalls the beginning of the essay and its similar ramblings. The difference is that now nothing is ignored or breezed by. The organized image of a Japanese garden plays directly against the tumultuous one of the "tortured junipers and tumbled boulders." She nearly stumbles, yet catches the perfect sight of an unexpected locust in a bird's nest. Everything is out of place, but strangely perfect.

This perfect sensation allows us to not worry about the dog, even if we do wonder about him. We've come to understand that his purpose was not to provide a destination, but to create impetus for the meandering. And so Erlich's walk itself, which started out with the purpose of finding the dog, also is without destination. The discoveries, however, are enormous, gentle and unexpected. Before her walk she was discontented and longing for things either lost or not yet found: love, more from life. Her distress had created so much "noise" that it had become depressing. By taking a meandering, purposeful yet destinationless walk, she came to discover things that were different than what she thought she needed, but which removed the longing nonetheless.

The cottonwood "lunatic with birdsong" is perhaps the most compelling image, appropriately, because the picture and sound of it pull together those two cord ends, drawing up the whole bundle that is the theme. The tree is full of birds, but to see only the birds is to miss the grandeur of the "symphony" of the whole tree. And the use of lunacy is potent because it recalls her earlier mention of losing one's mind. The fullness of Erlich's idea culminates with the image of this tree which is so much more, heaving upward, like her own raucous mind, full of noise yet astonishing in its presence.

And so, by the end "it is enough to make a shadow," because living itself is enough, and full of discovery enough, to outweigh whatever is lost.

Watching these two student writers at work, you can see how their interests developed, how they began by reading, writing, and reflecting. Again and again, they revised their work. Often after initial drafting, they did more reading, listened to their classmates and their instructors, and then wrote again, all in an effort to say what they had discovered and to say it clearly and effectively. Maile wrote an essay that depended very much on stories about her own experiences, but she enriched those stories and her essay with ideas and quotations from other written sources. Robynn focused on a close, analytical reading of Gretel Ehrlich's essay; her evidence came from that essay. She created an essay out of a close reading of another essay. In each case, these students' excitement and enthusiasm came from their discoveries and their desire to tell others what they were learning. Remember, they started with nothing more than an inclination and a little reading. Everything else followed.

The essays and the accompanying reproductions in this book call you, each of you, into reflection—asking you to think about that world outside your window, the fascinating world within, and the many representations of those worlds that appear in the essays and paintings. Therein you find your sources, the beginnings for your writing.

A Spectrum of Student Writing

The nine essays in this section of the anthology were all written by students for their first-year college writing courses. The final version of each essay (the version printed here) was preceded by a series of exercises and drafts and by comments from classmates and from the writing teacher.

Pedagogical notes are provided for each of the subsections that follow, notes that will help you identify the kind of essay you are reading.

Familiar/Exploratory Essays

I n this group of essays, students tell stories about their own experiences, and they use these stories to develop and illustrate ideas. These essays, grounded in the familiar and commonplace, explore as they go along; the writers are looking for the elusive answers to nagging questions. You get to see them thinking, working out their ideas. Tom Ceraulo wonders about masculinity; Michael Cohen, about the burden of living in New York City; Gian Neffinger, about the fragility of beauty. Their conclusions are tentative; their ideas are fluid, capable of further analysis. The exploration of a good idea can go on and on; as experience and evidence change, so do the ideas, over time, ever so slightly.

T om Ceraulo

The Burden of Pride

A month ago, I looked at this stark image of Michael Stipe and was immediately stricken by it. His face was marked by a tall diamond of emotion and concern. His wide eyes seemed to reach out to a troubled soul. He did not seem like a man; I was certain, on that first occasion that I studied the black-and-white photograph, that he was one of the angels dreamed up by the wondrous mind of filmmaker Wim Wenders. Like Damiel and Cassiel, the silent observers Wenders chronicles in "Wings of Desire" and "Faraway, So Close," his face was simple, and it seemed at once quite human and not human at all. The being that I saw in the first examination of the photograph was a being that I had a desire both to emulate and to be comforted by. I liked being in its presence. But each successive time that I viewed the photograph, something darker emerged from it. Stipe gradually began to look like an abandoned soul. Where once he seemed egoless, he then began to seem like a man whose ego had been shattered. I began to see a reluctance in the waves of skin that rose up between his eyes. Then I detected unbearable apprehension in him. His shaven scalp, marked by stubble, began to give him the aura of a man dying of cancer or AIDS, looking back on his life in sadness as it is being stripped away from him. The eyes that I initially envisioned reaching out to comfort someone then could have just as easily been staring in despair at a blank wall. I no longer desired to emulate the being in the photograph; its presence would now make me feel uncomfortable.

I was bothered by the regression that the photograph had undergone before my mind's eye. I do admit that Wenders' angels come to mind whenever I am moved by something, so it was nice, in a way, that I was able to shake them from their hold on me as I more carefully studied the picture. Still, what I was left with did not move me; it left me cold. So how, I wondered, could something that warmed my heart so much at first now seem so empty?

The answer to that question struck me, and I'm still not comfortable with it. As I looked deeper and deeper into that emotional photograph, what I began to uncover was *myself*. In the end it did not seem to matter that I was looking at an image of Michael Stipe; I could have just as well been staring at a mirror. I had no desire to emulate him or be in his presence. All of the demons that I do all I can to hide were flooding my consciousness: my desire to be the compassionate onlooker that the angels are, my tendency to look back in sadness as the world around me changes, my reluctance to try new things (many of which later turn out to be the treasures of my life), and my constantly waning self-confidence. These demons are safely tucked away in the recesses of my mind when I'm out in the world. They are allowed to come out very infrequently— usually late at night, in relative seclusion, through a song I am writing or the restless thoughts that are coming to me as I try to sleep. And when they come out, I see that they are larger than I am and—probably due to the fact that they spend a lot of time locked up deep inside of me—far more potent than any of my more common thoughts and concerns. What interests me most about them is the reason I keep them tucked away. It is very likely due to a masculine preoccupation. As a male, I'm not *supposed* to have fears or crazy aspirations, so I hide them from the world; I suspect that all men do this to some extent.

It seems odd to me that I hide many of my feelings of inadequacy to the extent that I do, since I have always seen myself as lacking the masculine bravado displayed by many of my male friends. I've never taken to the locker-room boasting that I see firsthand when I am in a room with men only. Whenever I am subject to this, I usually just politely smile or nod at whatever guy is talking, expressing my disgust with his statements to myself. It seems that I identify more with my female friends. Perhaps this has something to do with the fact that I am a creative person, and creativity is a more feminine quality; I'm not quite sure. But I am sure that, like all men, I feel an innate need to stow away what is bothering me about myself. I still harbor this very masculine reflex to hide behind a strong-looking façade.

Perhaps I don't hide behind a façade of superiority or boastfulness, but I still hide. There's never anything wrong in my life, as far as others can see—because I don't *let* them see on a regular basis. The great John Lennon, who late in his life was a househusband with a very assertive, working wife, spent much of his early life as an insecure man who hid behind a sardonic wit and tough exterior. On top of this unhealthy habit, he was falsely projected around the world as a god, a man who could do no wrong, as the Beatles became an unprecedented phenomenon. Perhaps in an attempt to undertake the impossible task of living up to the majestic image his fans had of him, Lennon let his poor self-confidence be viewed by the world in only a few of the songs he wrote as a Beatle. And even in the songs he did put some of his troubled inner self into, a catchy pop melody and a fast tempo took the listener's attention away from the insecurity conveyed in the lyrics. "Help!" has lyrics that clearly convey despair, for example, but is performed as a rock'n'roll number. Lennon, as so many men in our society do, was hinting at his emotional distress with the song and hoping that someone would take notice. But his hints were far too subtle for others to catch on to, as are the hints of many men.

It's little wonder why Lennon took refuge in drugs and alcohol during the periods in his life when he was simultaneously trying to live up to his superhuman image and to suppress the self-doubt that was buried inside of him. While the rest of the world was worshiping the Beatle, he secretly felt that he was, in his own words, "a loser." Perhaps a man can portray himself as a tough, problem-free individual without his true feelings getting to him too often, but if he also is burdened with the task of living up to hero worship as well, he is bound to lose his mind; any additional burden, for that matter, might cause him to lose his mind. Lennon turned to drugs, which made him numb to both his personal problems and his audience's lofty expectations.

The concept of men hiding their feelings of inadequacy brings to mind "Perfect Blue Buildings," a Counting Crows song written by singer-songwriter Adam Duritz. "Beneath the dust and love and sweat that hangs on everybody," Duritz sings, "there's a dead man trying to get out." That "dead man" is the one inside of me that I try to hide: the one who strives to be that compassionate observer, the one who can't help but dwell on faded glory when it is time to move on, the one who hesitates to try something different, and the one who is painfully unsure of himself. Like the narrator of "Perfect Blue Buildings," I "try to keep myself away from me" because of society's expectations, or what I perceive them to be.

I find it both interesting and appropriate that Duritz specifically says that it is a "dead *man* trying to get out," though he may not have considered this while writing the song. Men do seem to leave an integral part of themselves to die "beneath the dust and love and sweat" far more frequently than women, due to the inherent aversion that men have to showing weakness. We desire to be in control of ourselves and everything that surrounds us. When we see that this control is impossible to attain, we build up an exterior that conveys to the world the false notion that we have it. I, for example, try so hard to be a perceptive, compassionate observer. I realize time and again that this is impossible, so as a sort of compensation (or perhaps as a way of saving my masculine ego), I *act* as if I am that observer.

"You got an attitude of everything I ever wanted," Adam Duritz sings later in that same song, "I got an attitude of need." The character he portrays in the song is, at that point, a man who is facing his demons in a private setting. He's letting the "dead man" out by confessing his true feelings to a mirror in a lonely room at 4:30 A.M. He has to let it out sometime; all humans do. But because society expects men to be strong and unaffected by inner turmoil, he is forced to let it out in private. Talking to another person might be the best thing for him, but he disregards this; the burden of pride that has been placed upon his shoulders denies him the healthy expression of his problems to another. This notion brings me to a thought involving my obsession with Wenders' angel films: am I so attracted to the concept of unseen spiritual beings having the ability to listen to my thoughts because I cannot express many of my thoughts to another person?

It strikes me as strange that males do not seem to hold back displaying their emotions when they are angry. Perhaps this is acceptable to the masculine psyche because the display of anger or hate—frequently in the form of violence—is a more masculine act. It has crossed my mind that when we vent our anger through violent acts, we are trying show those around us that we are fighting against what is bothering us—that we are involved in an active struggle with our demons to attain that elusive control. In truth, we're just frustrated; we know the demons are bigger than we are, yet we can't bring ourselves to accept that fact. So if we're not playing the role of angry beasts lashing out against what bothers us, we keep what bothers us inside. Either way, we satisfy our pride while losing more and more of what makes us human.

And it doesn't help that many of our heroes and leaders are, like Lennon, expected to be superhuman. In our culture, we expect our men to be definitive in their convictions, and this is most clearly seen in America's Presidents. Ronald Reagan seemingly put together solutions to our nation's problems without even thinking. He believed in simple remedies. He was "decisive." And his approval ratings were consistently high during his presidency. Bill Clinton, on the other hand, is not so certain of what should be done to solve many problems. He has to read up on the issues at hand. He "waffles" in his stances on the issues. He comes across as a man who is more open about his feelings than the stone-faced Reagan was. And his approval ratings remain low. Clinton is not being the tough, masculine leader that Americans desire. Unlike Reagan, Clinton does not satisfy the public's expectations of a masculine leader—he seems more *human*, more like the men we all (at least subconsciously) know lie beneath our abrasive exteriors. It seems logical to me, as I consider all of this, that we have yet to have a female President. We will not have a female chief executive until we, as a culture, discard our expectation that men should act any less human than women.

This notion brings me back to that stark, black-and-white image of Michael Stipe. I'm beginning to realize that I didn't see myself—and men in general—in the photograph only when Stipe seemed to be in desperation. I also saw myself in Stipe when he had the aura of one of Wenders' angels—or, perhaps more accurately, when he seemed to me to be participating in the masculine act of trying to appear less human. As I kept studying his image and, in effect, stripping away his mask, I was also studying my self-image and stripping away my own mask—and the mask of males in my culture. The burden of pride causes us all to tuck away important parts of ourselves. The demons we tuck away eat away at us, and our "dead men" fight to get out. But in our foolish attempt to be what we inherently feel men are supposed to be, we constantly disregard these warning signs—and our true identities continue to slip away.

M ichael Cohen

You Can Shave the Beast, but the Fur Will Grow Back

I live in Brooklyn, New York City. I was born and bred there. I am one of eight million New Yorkers. New York City is sometimes described as a "melting pot," meaning we are like different Kool-Aid powders that dissolve into a uniform color and flavor. My view differs, though. I think we are eight million different insoluble liquids layered one on top of the other, appearing like oil floating on water. When stirred, these liquids are rustled from their respective positions, almost coming together, only to revert to their original separated composition a second later. I'm sorry, Dr. King, we haven't all "sat at the same table" yet. This polarization and social indifference, I believe, stems from the ruthless, heart-hardening, cutthroat environment of our city. But underneath this coarseness, I wonder if there isn't a sliver of pillow-soft care and empathy for those wishing to escape the city's coldness?

New Yorkers are stereotypically known as a crass and rude group, devoid of compassion. Having visited other places in the world, I can frankly attest that I have never experienced apathy so widely spread throughout a populace as I have felt living in New York. The "New York attitude" isn't unique to lower-class individuals who are down on their luck; it transcends class, wealth, stature, and race. It's evident in the Wall Street white collar, the ghetto rogue, the chubby mother of three—and me. It's a compelling force. I've been trained, conditioned like one of Dr. Pavlov's dogs, to behave this way; to bark on demand, to push as I'm being shoved, to hate when hated.

I was sucked into the vacuum of hate at an early age. When I was twelve years old, I got a taste of the caustic malice that would grow, like a cancer, steady and imperceptible, eventually decomposing my soul as I got older. I was riding my bicycle in my relatively safe neighborhood (keep in mind, safe, compared to places like Harlem and Bed-Stuy, might not be considered so safe in terms of average America; you still had to be smart and keep your head up on the street), minding my own business, and rode by two kids who were walking. As I passed them, one of them spat at me and said, "fuckin' Jew." I continued riding, my ear drenched in this person's gooey, bacteria-laden saliva, and my innocence told me this was normal because when I reached the next intersection a man making a left turn drove by me and yelled out a similar epithet from his car. The exact words don't matter. It's the faces, the sneers of hatred, the furrowed brows of enmity that have caused me to become another jaded member of this regressing social zoo. The very hate I was taught to loathe, for my race has been scapegoated and hated since the dawn of mankind, was now slowly becoming part of me. Being swept away by the malevolent New York attitude caused me to ignore this paradox that was taken captive by my anger, shackled to the back wall of my conscience, pleading me to listen, to stop hating. This overpowering ethic was bestial, fit for animals, not humans. I'm not talking about any lovable bunny rabbits or timid deer, mind you. I'm talking about vicious animals, like New York, cat-sized, hairy, filthy, germ-carrying rats that don't scurry when something bigger comes their way, that line their holes with a dead one's crumbs, that gnaw their way into basements so they can pillage someone's food supply.

I was surrounded by these animals; therefore, I could only expect to become a fuming, smileless, growling animal—like them.

I got older and learned to drive. Now I was the one yelling "you fuckin' guido!" or "muthafuckin' nigga'!" or "bastard spic!" It was natural animal instinct. Anyway, who'd you expect me to love!? The nightly eleven o'clock newscasts I saw on my TV weren't filled with ivory-clean, safe, suburban "nothing doing" stories. I saw murdered priests, burnt synagogues, shootings, arsons, gang rapes, babies disposed of in trash dumpsters, death, and more death. I saw Rashid Baz and Lemrick Nelson. Baz, an Arab livery driver, sprayed bullets with reckless abandon into a van transporting a group of Hasidic young men on the Brooklyn Bridge. He killed one. Why'd he do it? No excuse could explain it, not the Koran, not the Muslim fundamentalist doctrine, not anything. Nelson, today a free man, was found with a bloody knife on his person the night Yankel Rosenbaum was murdered in Crown Heights, Brooklyn. The blood was positively identified as Rosenbaum's. Nelson was part of the angry mob that surrounded Rosenbaum and chanted, like something out of *Lord of the Flies,* "Kill the Jew! Kill the Jew!" But this hunt wasn't fictional; it happened on an everyday Brooklyn street. For such atrocities I can only accept one reason: we are New Yorkers; we are animals, predators; we grew up angry and wanted to see the bloodshed of others we didn't like. A consistent diet of spoon-fed images of hate-drenched violence penetrated our consciences. Now, we are immune, desensitized. It's okay to hate, for there's no one to love. Having pondered this, I've told myself that this attitude can't possibly evolve into a formula for happiness, but being too busy clawing and biting my way around in the real world, I was not keen enough to contemplate change yet.

I wonder if I acquired an education, would I become human or merely a smarter, craftier animal? Every morning I take the subway to Manhattan so I can acquire this education. On an elevated platform I wait for the F-train. Off in the distance, to my left, I see the old parachute ride apparatus in Coney Island that looks like the Space Needle in Seattle. It serves no function nowadays, except to remind us how we've degenerated. When that apparatus was working, Coney Island was in its heyday. On hot days, hundreds of thousands would flock there to enjoy the beach, the rides, the carnival-like atmosphere, and Nathan's franks. It was a happy New York. Today, Coney Island is dilapidated and scary. High crime, drug traffic, and poverty have ravaged the area, not unlike dozens of other neighborhoods throughout the city. To my right, I see the Twin Towers, formally known as the World Trade Center, standing tall, very tall. I take for granted, sometimes, that it is one of the tallest skyscrapers in the world. To me, it's just another big building. But now, from so far away, it shines like a polished jewel, surveying the mind-blowing industrious pace of its city below. Looking up close from the plaza between One and Two World Trade Center, one can understand and can't deny that these structures probably can withstand the impact of a 747 jumbo jet, as its structural engineers proudly contend. It thrives nonstop, lit throughout the night. When six Muslims bombed it two years ago it merely coughed black smoke for a couple of days and resumed its frantic pace soon afterwards. It is an icon of the unrelenting, dog-eat-dog capitalism and greed that embodies New York and has driven many to ledge-jumping. I stand between these two polar edifices, wondering if I am another gear in this machine of a city, if I will ever escape New York's contagious, mass-produced animal destiny.

Travis Bickle, the title character in the Martin Scorsese film *Taxi Driver*, drove and saw "filth and scum" daily. Disgusted, he felt they should be "washed away, just the way rain washes away the dirt on the street." Bickle built up an arsenal of guns and hate. He consummated his frustration by killing a pimp and a gangster and was lauded as a New York hero because he helped return a twelve-year-old prostitute to her white American family. Through violence, he transformed his discontent. My ideology differs from Bickle's, but I wonder if it's possible for me to affect my environment, to enact a change from its current bleak decline. Can I be like Bickle and separate myself from the vacuum suck of this powerful city?

Or can I be like the Flatiron Building on the lower Fifth Avenue corner, where a fork splits Broadway and Fifth from their brief intersection? The Flatiron has a unique teardrop shape. From the long sides of the building it appears as any other normal building. The way the windows are situated on its face gives the illusion that the Flatiron has the equivalent sides and depth of a normal square or rectangular building, like the Empire State Building, would have. But as you walk around its base and turn the corner, the building curves smoothly, appearing thin and sleek, defying the expectation of another square side. It was built early in this century. It is a timeless, classic work of architectural art. It bucks the trend of New York buildings that appear gaudy and modern to grab attention, only to fall out of vogue when their trendy quality is dated. I wish to elude my carnivorous counterparts' bloodthirsty jaws in this pan-competitive city, but will I stand modest and proud in the end, like the Flatiron, having survived my inner battle for compassion in a soul-less environment?

The F-train takes me home at the end of my day. It is packed as I get on. I'm one amongst Black, Hindu, Asian, White, Jewish, Hispanic, and so on. With each stop, weary bodies depart and file themselves away in their respective neighborhoods. After forty minutes I grab my backpack and prepare to get off, too. Through the window I see a majestic sun setting in pretty tones of orange and red. As I get off the train I see the Coney Island parachute apparatus straight ahead. Its days in the sun are long gone. It looks at me, its construct antiquated, as if it's weeping, warning me, "You're next. Your fate . . . like mine." I turn around, shunning its somber expression, trying to find a glimmer of hope in something, only to face the daunting World Trade Center. Straight-faced, like a banker letting you know your loan request has been denied, it tells me, with a confident clean-shaven-and-starched-collar-executive coolness, "Don't even think about it. You can't change a thing. Not a chance." I want to defy this unfair proclamation. I want to break out and become human, with my own mind, my own will to care. I want to rise above and break the mold of the carbon copy, mean beast this city wants me to become. I refuse to regress.

As I descend the stairs, from the platform to the street below, I accidentally bump hard into somebody. I offer an apology to this fellow and stick my hand out in goodwill. He responds with a vile grunt and an ice-cold stare and mumbles, "Fuck off," before hurriedly scurrying away. Predictable, like a hackneyed cliché from the tobacco-chewing mouth of a vociferous Texas football coach in a half-time motivational talk with his players, is the behavior of this rough-hewn New Yorker.

I tried leading this horse to water. He refused to drink. This new-found compassion to lead, to rectify, has lifted my soul halfway out of the hostile, rancorous dark New York mire. The remaining half of my soul is being held back by the stubborn horses whose reins I'm holding onto. They refuse to join me, to whinny and trot along the green meadows of tolerance. They keep bucking. But letting go will only pull me back in.

G ian Neffinger

House of Cards

My uncle is an artist, a master craftsman. He does not paint or sculpt or write or draw, at least not particularly well; these things are not his specialty. My Uncle Pete is a master builder of the House of Cards. He says he built his first such house when he was four, and although grandmother tends to doubt this claim, it is certain that he has worked at his skill for some time.

At family gatherings he would build the most magnificent structures imaginable, anything from a cottage complete with windows to a modern skyscraper eight stories tall. No high-rise was ever more of a feat to construct than one of Uncle Pete's masterpieces. At the crucial moment, when all of the family cringed and looked away, his hand was steady, his movements effortlessly precise. And when the occasional indoor breeze did drift through and fell his fragile giant, he simply sighed and sipped his coffee.

When at last he had finished, resisting the inexorable temptation to add just one more wing, he stood back to witness the sum of all the whims that went into its creation. Having duly admired it, he then turned his attention to another matter, that of choosing The Card. After careful analysis he rendered his decision; "That's the one." At this cue my cousin Andy and I began to salivate with anticipation. Who would get to pull out *the* card?

The Pulling of the Card was always saved as an after-dinner treat, but well before the appointed hour, Andy and I would examine the card in question and envision the fateful event like a child adoring a package under the tree on Christmas Eve. Surely it was great fun, watching Uncle Pete enlist each card into his conspiracy to defy the universal law of gravitation, but what made all of his efforts worthwhile to us was not the spectacle of completion but the spectacle of destruction. For upon the pulling of that one card, all of the delicate relationships that held the structure

91

aloft dissolved, and that brilliant conspiracy was reduced to a scattered pile of playing cards, each as ordinary as the next. It was amazing how little disturbance it took; just to bump it would suffice. The only good way to get a sense of the delicate precision involved in creating it was to touch it gently, to try to alter it ever so slightly, and have it crumple to nothing. Andy and I used to promise each other the most outrageous things we could think of in exchange for the other's turn to tinker with The Card.

It was a unique phenomenon, the fall of a house of cards. Having not actually witnessed it, you might guess it would be fun to watch, but for all the wrong reasons. Mother never understood at all; she thought we were just being beastly, destroying the card house just as we destroyed our Lego airplanes and our matchbox cars and our new Sunday slacks. It was not anything malicious at all. "Malicious" is laughing at the blood dribbling from Tyler Evans' nose after my friend Pete clocked him. But Andy and I never had anything against Uncle Pete's houses; in fact we liked them. Malice had nothing to do with it.

Part of the appeal of getting to pull The Card was the sense of power—that's the part Andy and I fought over. Of course, we fought over everything that even vaguely resembled a privilege. But I remember, when no one was around, I used to go into the china cabinet, carefully bring out the beautiful, rose-colored heirloom teapot and hold it out at arm's length over the hard wood floor. The first time I tried this I was nervous—after all, what if I slipped? That would require some wild explaining—even if I did tell the truth, no one would believe me, and they would suspect something far more treacherous instead. That first time I got scared; I clutched the teapot against me and proceeded to carefully return it to its proper place. But something drew me back, until, after several visits, I would grandly swing my arm out to its full extension, as if presenting a trophy of war, and I would admire the finely crafted treasure, pausing only to glance at the unforgiving oak surface below. And I would think to myself, "I could, of course. I could just drop it, and no amount of surgery and no amount of prayer could ever bring it back." And oh, how I smiled!

When the house fell, when the invisible hand of physics let go and the cards fell in chaos, something powerful happened. Having that power between thumb and forefinger was a grand feeling. After all of the care that had gone into its assembly, it seemed ironic that it must all end with the tiniest of movements. Perhaps it was irony that made the moment magic. It would certainly seem equal to the task; it was irony that made the *Titanic* legend great. Had it not been billed as the Unsinkable Ship, its sinking would not have been so remarkable, and the world would never have had cause to learn that eight-ninths of an iceberg's mass lie concealed below the water's surface.

Whatever the meaning hidden in that final moment of splendor, one thing is sure: a sudden demise grants a certain timelessness. A. E. Housman, in his poem "To an Athlete Dying Young," tells of a champion who died in his prime, before his renown faded. He took his championship crown to his grave, where he could never be dethroned. Thus went the *Titanic*. It met its end as the pinnacle of naval technology, and now, whenever anyone thinks of the mightiest ship ever to cruise the open sea, none think of Old Ironsides, bobbing in its secure harbor with its heavy cargo of tourists; none think of the newest, most massive cruise liners or battleships, for the *Titanic* owns the title of mightiest—has owned it since that fateful night, and will own it forever.

So goes the house of cards—quickly, gloriously. No such house ever lasted long enough to suffer the indignities of time and fortune. Most great monuments are not nearly as lucky. Their features are worn away by time, or tourists; their renown is drowned in the wake of Progress. Their beauty is never apprehended; it just slowly fades away.

When I first came across the tragic hero in literature, I felt as if I had met him somewhere before. Here was a man, arguably a great man, who reached the pinnacle of his greatness in his own destruction. In his ruin, he proves himself, revealing, to the swift, the moral: "What a piece of work is a man!" and leaving even the stupid with a sense of wonder at the spectacle they have witnessed. The exceptional character placed in an unnatural circumstance makes for an extraordinary event, stretching the boundaries of our comprehension.

My Uncle Pete builds tragic heroes as a hobby; my cousin and I stage the plays: we circle, examine, touch gently, then grasp The Card, pause for a moment, and pull.

To this day I've never met anyone who could build a house of cards as well as Uncle Pete. To this day Andy and I take turns performing the after-dinner ritual; we have long since retired our Legos and our matchbox cars, but I don't know if we'll ever surrender our childhood rights to The Card. After all, better us than the breeze. What does a breeze know about beauty?

Analytical/Argumentative Essays

These essays focus on the close analysis of texts—two essays and one painting. These three writers did a great deal of exploring before they began writing their essays; as they wrote their preliminary drafts, they were not only trying to figure out what the essays and the painting meant to them but also looking into just how that meaning was conveyed. Analyzing, they were taking the texts apart and putting them back together in their minds, all as a way of understanding what they were reading.

In their essays, they tell us the results: what the texts mean to them and how they convey that meaning. These essays are more direct, more certain about their conclusions than those exploratory essays in the first group. But you still get to see these writers thinking as they make their claims about the texts and use the evidence they have selected from the essays and the painting to help us understand those claims. Ruth Chung argues about the importance of details in "Old Mrs. Grey," showing us how those details help us understand Woolf's idea. David Reich adds a new twist to the meaning of standard English, taking a stand against one of Amy Tan's claims in "Mother Tongue," and James Rhee makes a case about Mondrian's brutality in *Composition in Yellow and Blue*.

R uth Chung

On Virginia Woolf's "Old Mrs. Grey"

In her essay "Old Mrs. Grey," Virginia Woolf paints a picture of a ninety-two-year-old woman whose supreme desire is to die. There is no action or movement in this portrait; Mrs. Grey merely sits alone in a corner of her house. Woolf's short, page-long description depicts the sufferings not only of a single individual but also of the old and the gray in general. And yet it is clear that the purpose of this piece is more than the extraction of sympathy. Woolf expresses her view that a life of such suffering is not worth living. She asserts that the physical and mental agonies of old age should not be prolonged on humanitarian grounds.

Throughout the essay, Woolf uses Mrs. Grey's house and the landscape outside to describe the old woman's mental state. Woolf's description of the house and the rolling fields and hills seems to be just another picturesque view of England's countryside. From the context of Mrs. Grey's pain and her desire to die, however, the house, with its door wide open may represent her body on the verge of death. The comparison may run still deeper. Woolf describes Mrs. Grey's mind as open and ready to be enveloped and swallowed by death's rays. It also follows that the image of the fields and hills, described as places of "stainless and boundless rest; space unlimited; untrodden grass; wild birds flying," comes to represent the pure, unblemished paradise, the haven from pain for which Mrs. Grey yearns. It could also simply be a representation of death, a state of being (or not being) that everyone must eventually face, a time when "even the busiest, most contented suddenly let fall what they hold."

Woolf further describes Mrs. Grey's longing for death, using light as a symbol to enhance our understanding of that longing. Through the seven foot by four opening of Mrs. Grey's front door, sunshine pours in from the outside, putting "embarrassing pressure" on the fire burning in the grate

which appears "only as a small spot of dusty light feebly trying to escape."
Here, the fire burning in the grate may represent the appeals and delights
of life, which have become dreary to Mrs. Grey when compared to the
lure of the after-life, the sweet respite of death, as represented by the
streaming sunshine from outside. Mrs. Grey is so enamored by the
prospect of going to such a paradise of rest and relief, that living for the
present becomes pointless; it seems silly to do the week's wash "when out
there over the fields over the hills, there is no washing; no pinning of
clotheslines; mangling and ironing; no work at all."

The idea of a new life dawning is also represented by "morning
spreading seven foot by four green and sunny," which tries to infiltrate the
house and beckons to Mrs. Grey through the front door. Mrs. Grey welcomes this light as much as she welcomes death, but the light has not yet
been able to permeate the whole house. She has put so much hope into
this state of rest, that "when the colour went out of the doorway, she
could not see the other page which is then lit up." This "other page" represents Mrs. Grey's present chapter of life, which has potential, even in her
pain, to be enjoyable and fulfilling. But Mrs. Grey can only see this life as
she sees the fire burning in the grate, which becomes dim in the light of
her suffering and pain. She is so weary of her life that "her eyes had
ceased to focus themselves. . . . they could see but without looking." It
isn't that she is physically blind, but that her pain is so great that it is all
she can see. It could also be that nothing in her present life seems to be
worth looking at because she cannot appreciate the little pleasures of life:
"She had never used her eyes on anything minute and difficult; merely
upon faces, and dishes and fields."

However, it is not fair to take Mrs. Grey's suffering lightly either, for
she suffers excruciating pain. Woolf compares her pain to a sadistic snake:
"a zigzag of pain, wriggling across the door, pain that twisted her legs as
it wriggled; jerked her body to and fro like a marionette." Woolf also
speaks of a sharp, cutting pain by describing Mrs. Grey's body as being
"wrapped around the pain as a damp sheet is folded over a wire . . .
spasmodically jerked by a cruel invisible hand." The startling image of
Mrs. Grey that these comparisons create, of her body writhing, twisting
like a live wire shows the sufferings the elderly must endure and explains
Mrs. Grey's state of mind, her abnormal eagerness for death.

Woolf gives readers further insight into Mrs. Grey's mental anguish by
taking us into her mind as well as allowing us to hear what she has to say.
Mrs. Grey looks back to her active childhood, her entrance into the adult
world, and the time spent with her eleven brothers and sisters. But these
memories can only bring her sorrow and loneliness when she compares

those times to the present. She is literally jerked back to reality by a convulsion: "The line jerked. She was thrown forward in her chair." Her old body is sick and deteriorating and all of her siblings have died; she has even survived her husband and her children.

The tone of Mrs. Grey's voice as she mumbles is not bitter, for she has no energy to complain. Woolf's fragmented sentences reflect Mrs. Grey's tiredness as though she doesn't have even enough energy to speak: "'All dead. All dead. . . . My brothers and sisters. And my husband gone. My daughter too. But I go on.'" Her words also have an almost Mother Goose–rhyme quality to them: "'I'm an ignorant old woman. I can't read or write and every morning I crawls downstairs, I say I wish it were day.'" This suggests a regression into a childish state, into senility, but the words are coherent, expressing her feelings of debilitation and inadequacy. While her words have no stint of bitterness in them, they evoke pity. Her daily supplications to God—"O let me pass"—show how desperately she yearns to be relieved of her suffering. The thought of Mrs. Grey crawling downstairs and falling into bed by herself every day is especially poignant and helps readers understand Mrs. Grey's fatigue and loneliness.

In the last paragraph of her essay, Woolf concludes by laying blame for Mrs. Grey's suffering on humanity. Again, she makes her point using comparisons. She asserts that it is the hand of humanity that jerks so cruelly on the wire of pain, that "puts out the eyes and the ears," that "pinions" the bodies of the elderly on those wires by trying to keep them alive. The elderly are like tortured birds, pinned to a barn door, like "a rook that still lives, even with a nail through it." Woolf suggests that we, humanity, are responsible for prolonging their sufferings by caring for them and by trying to ameliorate their lives "with a bottle of medicine, a cup of tea, a dying fire." Our efforts to alleviate suffering inflict and prolong pain.

Perhaps Woolf is not really blaming humanity for the sufferings of the elderly but merely reprimanding all of us for being unaware of what we might be doing to cause such suffering. Perhaps she is merely voicing her own ambivalence about euthanasia. And yet her strong language in the last paragraph and her suggestive details throughout the essay suggest that Mrs. Grey is suffering unmercifully and that she longs to walk out that door of her house into those expansive fields to a new and deserved freedom. She longs to take flight, not to stay "pinioned" to a barn door. Woolf wants us to think about Mrs. Grey's pain and her desire, and she wants as well to have us realize that our kindnesses toward the elderly may be misdirected. Woolf wants us to know that helping Mrs. Grey may very well mean helping her die.

David Reich

"Mother Tongue" and Standard English: Amy Tan's Literary Fusion and Ours

In her essay "Mother Tongue," Amy Tan writes about the language she grew up with, the "broken English" that her immigrant Chinese mother spoke at home (198). This language shaped the way she "saw things, expressed things, made sense of the world" (198), but it also caused her a great deal of suffering. For one thing, it actually made her feel ashamed of her mother; though her mother was a mature woman, many Americans treated her as if she were a child because of her poor English (198). In addition, Ms. Tan herself was discouraged from becoming a writer because of a general perception that Asians have difficulty with language (201).

At first, Ms. Tan's way of dealing with language discrimination was to prove that she could speak standard English as well as anyone; she always took pains to use perfect grammar and complex structure in order to impress people with her "mastery over the language" (201). Thus, for Ms. Tan, standard English represented an escape from the stigma of home's "broken" English—in other words, an escape from home. Because it represented an escape from home, her standard English also represented an escape from all she associated with home—all of her early childhood memories, all of her relationships with people, and all of the important things in her life—so that in the end her standard English was a language that was in many ways "bland" (200), in many ways barren of the thought and emotion that was inside her since it focused on rejecting one part of her life instead of affirming another part. When Ms. Tan realized that in writing standard English she was escaping the world that mattered to her and was deliberately writing to nobody at all, she resolved to switch instead to a language she knew much better—her "mother tongue." Once she switched, she made sure to write with a reader in mind—her mother—so that the things she wrote were always personal efforts at communication and sense, and the language she used was always loaded with the imagery of very real human interactions (201–202).

When Ms. Tan began to write using her mother tongue—the language of her soul—the things she wrote became expressions of her soul. Surprisingly, though, Ms. Tan's switch to a more authentic language did not involve a rejection of standard English in the same way that her earlier switch from one language to another had involved a rejection of her mother tongue. In fact, her writing is rendered in grammatical English, which Ms. Tan had initially perceived as "standard"—that is, as foreign and sterile. The important part of Ms. Tan's mother tongue is its imagery and the way in which it is true to life, not its brokenness, so that the reader (and the writer, too) loses little and gains much when she translates her mother's many "Englishes" into comprehensible and "perfect" form (201–202).

There is something very unusual and exciting about standard English that allows Ms. Tan to incorporate her mother tongue into it. Standard English, after all, can be as much a mother tongue as any other subspecies of the language. It is in fact my own mother tongue, the language of my upbringing, and is for me as "vivid, direct," and "full of observation and imagery" (198) as Ms. Tan's mother tongue. But standard English is also different from other mother tongues, and in some sense isn't a mother tongue at all, because it is larger than any particular ethnicity; it's not even "white" English. Because it is spoken in several countries and by people of many different backgrounds, it cannot be associated with a particular world view in the way that Ms. Tan's mother tongue can be associated with the world view of Chinese immigrants or the relationship between a particular mother and daughter. Standard English is larger than other "Englishes" (196)—it is a framework for living rather than a program for living—so that a person like me, who is in quest of his mother tongue, must realize that he cannot so simply say that "my mother tongue is standard English." Instead, he must look more deeply into the English he speaks in order to identify the essential part of his internal language, and only then can he try to understand its relationship to the standard English with which he publicly expresses himself in speech and writing.

I learned my real mother tongue at home, as did Ms. Tan. Through it I learned to value and articulate certain ideas and to think in particular ways, so that ever since, those issues and ways of thinking and forms of articulation have been among the most important influences in my life. In her essay "And We Walk Through," Christella Wong provides a clear way of thinking about the functions of standard English and mother tongue. Language, she writes, is a "door between worlds," serving both as "entrance and barrier" (1). Ms. Tan's mother tongue was initially a barrier or a "closed door" because the difference between her mother's broken English and society's standard English caused her to abandon, for a time, that deeply understood mother tongue in favor of a more sterile language. On the other hand, standard English was for me an "open door," a powerful link between my private world and the public world around me, because the shared vocabulary of the two worlds allowed me to move between them with ease. Moreover, as a writer, I feel comfortable living in the world of standard English—it is not a means to an end but rather an end in itself—so that when I write about something, I am often interested and even struck by what I write. At this point, the language of my writing becomes more than an external thing, more than an assay into the outside world—it becomes the language of my soul. It is also at this point—when living in a world of language becomes an end in itself rather than a means to an end—that Ms. Tan's writing becomes the language of her soul. Once she begins to live in the world of her writing, it does not matter whether she is writing in broken English or English that is grammatically correct; all that matters is that she is writing and that she understands what she writes. Thus, when Ms. Tan chooses to incorporate her mother tongue into standard English, to fuse her two worlds, standard English becomes her open door.

Language, after all, is transcendent, allowing individuals to communicate and take communion with the world around them. The fusion of standard English and mother tongue, of the outer voice with the inner, is the point of transcendence for all writers, their transition from struggling with language to living it. For Amy Tan, justification as a writer lies in the process of living her text, not in the process of changing it. As long as she lives her text, and integrates her mother tongue with standard English so that language is a medium and not an impediment, and so that the world around her is exciting and can be understood in an intimate but also slightly distanced way, she is being honest and true to herself. And if honest and true, she will then be interested in what she herself has to say, and in some sense, though she speaks a mother tongue with a particular reader in mind, she is really speaking to herself, to her own excitement, and she herself—not her mother—has become the primary reader for her own work.

Once Ms. Tan becomes her own reader, she transcends the limitations of both mother tongue and standard English, and everything she writes becomes both absolutely public and intensely personal. In this sense, as a writer who has achieved a measure of transcendence, Amy Tan inhabits that rare space where a writer's private domain becomes the domain of all her readers, so that what she creates in some sense concerns everybody as well as nobody, and is, in another sense, the estate of each individual reader. Ms. Tan's readers therefore sympathize with her story even if it isn't written in their own mother tongue. They are responding to what is distilled from that mother tongue, which is less a particular ethnicity than a literary province where the speakers of a language may use its familiar textures to communicate thoughts and emotions that are universal and real. Even more, they sympathize with her because of her lucid writing, her undogmatic conviction, and her ability to draw her readers into her text—into her life. She makes them feel at home there, in the mesh of her life and text, so that they are forced to concede, even before they are intellectually convinced, and whether or not her words make any sense in a large way, that what she says has validity, and that the language she speaks is not only her "mother tongue," but all of ours.

Works Cited

Tan, Amy. "Mother Tongue." *The Best American Essays 1991*. Ed. Joyce Carol Oates and Robert Atwan. New York: Ticknor, 1991. 196–202.

Wong, Christella. "And We Walk Through," in Pat C. Hoy II, *Expository Writing 16, Fall Term 1992–1993*. Harvard University, 1992. 1.

J ames Rhee

Contending with Mondrian's "Composition in Yellow and Blue"

This painting, simple enough, is brutally complex.

Two heavy, black lines cut through the canvas. They form right angles with each other, but, more important, form right angles with the edges of the painting. Four rectangles are produced, the largest in the upper right-hand corner, the smallest opposite it in the lower left-hand corner, and two of equal size in the remaining corners. Simple, but with a twist.

Look at the painting carefully, and notice that dividing a rectangle using two lines perpendicular to it and to each other always creates at least two congruent rectangles. That may seem like an irrelevant point, but the artist took it into thoughtful consideration. For in his painting, there are no shapes of equal area or perimeter or appearance, but only disturbing little quirks.

He took the rectangles in the upper left and lower right corners of the canvas, which were, as you recall, equal, and he quite terribly perverted them. He colored the upper left one a bright yellow, a yellow that eclipses its pure, unadulterated white neighbors. But he did worse things to its diagonal partner, irrevocably disrupting the harmony that once existed in the painting.

He took this hapless rectangle in the lower right corner and caged it in with a black border. But not an ordinary black border, for that would have been too merciful. It was a black border indented several inches in on the right and elevated ever so slightly off the bottom of the canvas. The once proud and haughty rectangle, suddenly considerably diminished in size, was now the smallest of the four originals.

But did the artist finish his slicing and dicing here? No. He had to increase the painting's complexity, add further incongruities to give his work that final abstract dimension. He took what had been severed from the lower right rectangle, and with this excess created two more small rectangles with another bold stroke of black. And yet he was not finished. For to complement the bright yellow, he colored the top of these two small miniature offspring a bright blue.

And now the work was complete. A total of six rectangles: three whites of varying sizes, a yellow, a blue, and another white surrounded on all four sides by black. The ominous borders remain staunch in their position, too heavy to yield and too black to challenge.

To a casual passerby, the painting is only this—six rectangles with a couple of odd colors. To me, it is a canvas replete with hostile division and deliberate contention.

Combination Essays

These essays manage to combine exploration and analysis, bringing together stories of experience as well as textual evidence from essays, novels, and paintings. We are able to see the writers exploring their ideas while also being rigorously analytical and persuasive. Kristen E. Hughes, contemplating Picasso's *Guernica,* hits upon an idea about masculinity and then tells us what it means to be a female hero. Elizabeth MacDonald, working under the influence of the images of Ingres, de Chirico, and Hayworth, gives us a sense of what it means to suffer in the service of beauty. Han N. Pham takes us "Down the Unwritten Path," leading us into cultural continuities and discontinuities as she draws on the experience of her Vietnam-born parents and grandparents and the evidence gleaned from Frances Fitzgerald's *Fire in the Lake.*

K̲risten E. Hughes

I Will Be My Own Hero

> I'll walk, but not in old heroic traces,
> And not in paths of high morality,
> And not among the half-distinguished faces,
> The clouded forms of long-past history.
>
> —CHARLOTTE BRONTË

In Picasso's *Guernica,* a bull stands implacably over a screaming woman with a dead child in her arms. Above and aloof from her and the other broken humans below, the bull may represent the German Luftwaffe, which bombed the small town of Guernica in 1937, or the ruthless *caudillo* Franco, or even the masculine pursuit of war itself. The bull's eyes remain expressionless despite the chaos and destruction around him, his ears and horns are simple and sharp. As I looked up at the bull a few years ago in Madrid, I found I hated and feared his strength, his virile indifference to the pain in the faces of the other figures in *Guernica;* yet I also felt awe and admiration. In a perverse way I love his pride and his independence. Sometimes I wonder if there is any of him in me. I wonder too if I want him there.

I used to have a secret hope that inside me there was a Hero who would take over my life and who only suffered from a lack of confidence. I always hoped that my Hero would take charge and make the decision to go adventuring, like Ulysses, across the world. I wanted to be able to say what Tennyson's Ulysses said: "I am become a name;/ For always roaming with a hungry heart/ Much have I seen and known." I yearned also to have "drunk delight of battle with my peers,/Far on the ringing plains of windy Troy" (10–12). What I lacked, I told myself, was opportunity. If the place and time were right, I could be brave and adventuresome, I imagined. I consoled myself for a long time, believing that somewhere within me was a "hungry heart" that would earn me power and glory: I would be Ulysses or Elizabeth the First, a monarch like the best of them. But only a few years ago I began to question what it was exactly that I was worshiping and what it was that I wanted to be.

I always wanted to be a boy when I was younger because I thought that only men (or very unusual women) could become heroic adventurers, and become "honour'd" in the world: they were the ones the inspirational poems were written about. Once on a Saturday morning when my father was home from work, the desire nagged bitterly. We sat in the kitchen, and it was dark enough that the lights were still on, yet the rays of the morning sun were slanting into my eyes through the trees and the French windows, and they glinted on Craig's curly blond hair. My mother and my father sat debating my brother's prospects around the breakfast dishes and the strewn remains of the morning paper. As Daddy planned his boy's future, his voice swelled with male pride I wanted so much to ridicule. Eventually I scooted my chair back from the table and walked away. When I was only halfway up the stairs my eyes were full of tears. Reaching my room I lay on my bed and sobbed and sobbed, pressing my pillow into my face, wishing that my father would show the personal interest in me Craig never seemed to appreciate.

I waited a long time for that recognition, and the waiting tempered my needs. As I gained my own footing, paying attention to what was going on around me, I began to question much of what I considered masculine. One day at school there was the usual argument in the common room during lunch hour. That day Tammy took on the five of us, and eventually, exasperated or defeated, she stormed off pouting. Later, after I had forgotten the whole scene, she walked back into the room after our group had broken up—Tammy tells me now that it was after classes. Her face was damp, and her hair a tangled mess. She begged me to come into the hall with her, and because she looked so worried, so pale, I followed her and listened.

"Kristen, there's something I need to tell you, if you'll listen. And you have to promise never to tell anyone else, not ever; it's been worrying me all day. Will you promise me?" She was pleading with an unusual intensity, and I couldn't imagine what she wanted to say.

"I'm not sure," I stammered, "that's a very difficult promise to . . ."

"Please, will you promise me?" she repeated. I swore I would never tell. She went on: "I need someone to understand, I can't go on like this. My mother has two broken ribs—Dad did it a couple of nights ago. He came home very late, after eating dinner with friends from work, and found an empty wine bottle on the living room floor. He accused Mummy of being an alcoholic. I was upstairs but came down when I heard the noise. But it was only after I left that he hit her. I don't know what to do, and this isn't the first time."

I don't remember the rest of what Tammy said; it has blended in my memory with other stories she has told me since. Shocked and confused, I tried to find out what she wanted to do. Nothing, was the answer. I remember the blinking T.V. screen behind her head announcing the week's events in school, the black wires dangling from the ceiling to the box on the wall.

Tammy says now that her father has the mental age of a five-year-old and that he doesn't know what he is doing, and that is why he breaks her mother's ribs. The violence in men, she would say, is the violence of the boy who rips the wings off flies, and burns ants by concentrating sunlight through a magnifying glass, just as my golden-haired brother used to do not so long ago. On lazy summer afternoons, as if practicing an obscure sacrificial rite, my brother would construct a pyre of grass and dry leaves on our stone patio and lure insects to them with crumbs of food; then, as he angled his glass just so, the pyre and the bodies would go up in flames. The composed and aloof expression on his face suggested that the whole experience was nothing but an experiment for him. He went on calmly to teach the art to our younger brother. Like Tammy's father, he seemed unaware of the pain he might be causing, or the memories he was leaving behind.

These days I no longer adore Ulysses. Though I occasionally desire his "hungry heart," when I think that he had to drink "delight in battle" to satisfy his hunger, I feel betrayed. I am horrified by the thought of my hero fighting, killing, standing proud on the "ringing plains of Troy" bloody sword in hand. Tammy's father and my brother played havoc with that illusion of mine, and I have found too that my own hungry heart can lead me astray.

I too have destroyed life. The six little bodies were those of baby gerbils. All together they had fit snugly into the palm of my hand and wriggled under the water less and less until their movements had stopped, and they were dead. My gerbils had been reproducing every month— every month there was a new litter of ugly, blind, pink babies—and eventually I decided that I could stand the mess and the visitors' oohs and aahs no longer. So I came up with a master plan: I sentenced the babies to a watery death. My father offered to help, but I refused to allow him the honor. It was my operation, and I was going to carry it out with the skill, nerve, and command of a general under fire. But I found that I didn't have the heart for it. I have no respect for what I did.

I wanted, and still want, the admiration of my father. I want the attention of independent boys. I want to be a hero myself. But I no longer stand in awe of the male hero's virile power. I have resented my own father's indifference and have seen the aftermath of violence, and have had boyfriends leave me without a trace of regret. Their tough indifference has wounded me. Alice Walker says, "I saw in [Martin Luther King, Jr.] . . . the hero for whom I had waited so long." She saw in him a model of non-violence. I am sure, though, that it was not just her adoration for Dr. King that made Walker what she is now; it was her own determination, her own inner resolve. It is not by aspiring to be a great man, or even by fol-lowing one that I can find my answers. So now I am involved in a new search for a hero within me, but this time the hero will not be a bull, or a Ulysses, or even a Tudor queen.

There is a man, a solitary, adventurous, and heroic man, in Gabriel García Márquez's *One Hundred Years of Solitude,* whose grand illusion of war is shattered, and he can no longer act the soldier. Colonel Aureliano Buendía lives out the remainder of his life in the solitude of his workshop, making, melting, and remaking little gold fishes. "He had had to start thirty-two wars and had had to violate all of his pacts with death and wal-low like a hog in the dungheap of glory in order to discover the privileges of simplicity almost forty years later" (163). But Buendía's are not the priv-ileges of old age that I want for myself. He never makes anything that lasts. He melts down the fishes he crafts. He only makes to destroy and to remake. Soldiering was all that he knew. Years after Buendía's death his great-great-nephew—his namesake—looks for the history of his parent-age. All the local priest remembers of the old colonel is that a street in town had once borne his name.

After Aureliano Buendía gave up his warring, he could never find the man within himself who could live a quiet life well; he did not have the inner resources he needed to turn his energies to life and the community where he lived. He left nothing of lasting value.

Perhaps it was Nathan, more than any of those other men, who opened my eyes. With Nathan I tried to claim something I had no right to. I didn't know it at the time. Nathan was proud, and inevitably I loved him. I saw in him the boy I wanted to be. He was a dark knight with a beautiful cold smile, a would-be rower, and a chain-smoker at the age of

sixteen. I never knew exactly who he was. He was a stranger to me as
Colonel Aureliano Buendía had been a stranger to his own mother.
Nathan had a faraway look in his eyes, as if he was always dreaming of
some other place. I longed to tame him, make him interested in me. But
he never even asked me how I felt, and he never praised me. I would
dress up for him and suffer for days waiting for him to call.

When Nathan finally got around to coming, he would say, "Kris, I'm
going out to a film with the guys tonight and then we're going to get
trashed at Kim's house since his parents are in Majorca."

"What about tomorrow?" I would ask.

"Sorry, out rowing tomorrow. Do you want to hear a great song we
invented yesterday? It goes like this.

I woke up this morning, tanananana,

And wha'du you know, tanananana, . . ."

And I would listen just to hear him talk.

One night he left me for another girl, no explanations, nothing. I
hated him and his righteous arrogance, but I think I still love the wild
spirit in him. I still yearn to live a life that seems an answer to my own
desires. But I can't be indifferent to those around me, can't quite see how
my heart can close itself to all the others.

The soldier, the bull, the boy have reasons for killing and inflicting
pain, I think, and I cannot understand them. On the one hand they want
to gain glory and exalt themselves. A natural part of the glory-making is
defeating others, triumphing in battle, controlling other lives. On the
other hand, the childish delight in torture, in violence, only exists in some
of them. I have seen it in Tammy's father, in my brother, in Pinkie, and in
me. Pinkie, the seventeen-year-old gangster and Catholic boy in Graham
Greene's *Brighton Rock,* believed the only life after death was in Hell:

> Pinkie stood looking down on the greying hair; he felt no pity at all; he
> wasn't old enough for pity. . . . A leather-jacket buzzed up the pane
> and the Boy caught it in his hand. It vibrated like a tiny watch spring in
> his palm. He began to pull off the legs and wings one by one. "She loves
> me," he said, "she loves me not. I've been out with my girl, Spicer."
> (134)

The girl, Rose, he threatened with vitriol, and subsequently married so
that she wouldn't implicate him in a murder. She was willing; she idolized
him and thought she shared something with him, that they were the
same: Catholic and quiet. Violent, Pinkie was frigid and a virgin. He

derived his pleasure not from sex, not from Rose, but from cutting people up with his razor blade, from torture. I see some of the dispassionate glee that Pinkie feels when he is thinking about vitriol, or a razor, in the eyes of the toro as he stands over Guernica's destruction. I also see that delight in the eyes of some men, and I turn away. I want to follow a new hero who will also turn away.

Tammy's revelation to me about her father changed the way I thought about heroism and the seductive power of virility. I recognize that the fear I felt looking up at the bull on the huge canvas of *Guernica* two years ago in Spain came from my knowledge of the pain and terror Tammy's father inflicts on her and her mother. What I learned from Nathan was more important than he was to me: what I had been seeking was not to be found where I had been looking. I realized that Nathan worked very hard for his "hard" cool image; and though he never told me what joy it brought him, I know now that it would never satisfy me.

I am finding a new Hero in myself to follow. She can be violent at times, because she can be everything, but she will always be sorry. No matter how hungry her heart, indifference will not suit her. She has an indomitable will but is never proud for long.

Works Cited

Brontë, Charlotte. "Stanzas." In *The New Oxford Book of Victorian Verse.* Ed. Christopher Ricks. New York: Oxford University Press, 1990.

Greene, Graham. *Brighton Rock.* New York: Viking, 1953.

Márquez, Gabriel García. *One Hundred Years of Solitude.* Trans. Gregory Rabassa. New York: Avon, 1971.

Tennyson, Lord Alfred. "Ulysses." In *The New Oxford Book of Victorian Verse.* Ed. Christopher Ricks. New York: Oxford University Press, 1990.

Walker, Alice. "The Civil Rights Movement: What Good Was It?" *In Search of Our Mothers' Gardens.* New York: Harcourt Brace, 1984. 119-29.

Elizabeth MacDonald

Odalisque

I am in eighth grade—perhaps two weeks, or even a week before all the trouble started—and walking one evening with a friend on the east side of Manhattan. I catch sight of my reflection in a plateglass window and, in these formative years, observe what I am becoming. My hair is short and less feminine at this time, my face rounder, my body plumper. I was happy with what I saw.

I am in ninth grade and my waist is the thickness of a bottleneck. Lying on my bed I hear my parents talking about me as they walk along the hall.

"This diet has gone on too long," my mother is saying, "she's gotten very weak."

"She is very thin," says my father.

I am in tenth grade and fatter than I have ever been. In a book written during the Twiggy-influenced sixties I read that every day that you fast you lose two pounds of fat. This seems easier than recovering the discipline that I had once in such abundance and have now lost. I begin a regimen in which I eat enormous amounts for a few days and fast on the others. I want very much to regain the beauty that was once mine, to rediscover the indestructible, perfect creature of angles and spare planes that lies hidden under this amorphous mass of lumps. I want more than anything to be thin again. This seems to be a way. For a desperate girl who has no assurance that she will ever be desirable almost no price is too high.

I do not remember the first time that I made myself throw up. It may have been in eleventh grade, but the circumstances have faded under the shame and horror. As I understand it, many people try self-induced vom-

111

iting. Few are successful on the first attempt and most give up. Some of us persist: some of us even become quite talented.

In that talent I originally found salvation. Self-indulgence and beauty seemed, for the first time, compatible. I could give myself everything I wanted and retain the figure of the ascetic. I could have my cake, and I could eat it too. Nothing, however, is that easy. Maintaining the façade becomes indispensable. Every compliment is a knife in the gut and an impulse to retain what I have, though I pay, and pay dearly. There is a line in Yeats' "Adam's Curse" that cries bitterness—

> To be born woman is to know—
> Although they do not talk of it at school—
> That we must labor to be beautiful

I have only just discovered that I have been misquoting these lines for years. In my mind the last line, though essentially the same, has always had a slightly different nuance.

> . . . We must suffer to be beautiful.

The most famous photograph of Rita Hayworth, as Gilda, immortalizes her as an extraordinary beauty. In black satin she stands, mysterious and gorgeous—a stunning beauty, with allure and come-hither confidence. Her skin glows alabaster against a black background and on her beautiful face, slightly turned to the side, is a look of encouragement and, conversely, knowing distance. She tilts her chin up in the arrogance of her beauty: she knows very well that she stops traffic and hearts. Her hair is long, her waist is small, and her strapless dress clings to her perfect figure. Her self-presentation is more than feminine; it is the essence of female. Rita Hayworth played a woman all men wanted and all women wanted to be. She sets the standard of what it is to be an ideal woman— a flesh Goddess.

I have heard that she could not reconcile her beauty and herself, that she felt herself to be an illusion created by lights and other people's vision of what she should be. You could never tell that from this photograph. This woman revels in nothing more than her sexuality and beauty. And for all that, all the power and joy in her physical presence that she presents to the world in this still, Rita Hayworth never believed in the image she presented. She felt that the façade was fraudulent and that she was two people inhabiting a beautiful shell whose two sides were irreconcilable. Her most famous quotation is a cry of pain. "Every man I ever knew went to bed with Gilda and woke up with me." They saw in her the realization of all their dreams and found that she was just a woman. Men looked in her for Gilda and a goddess. Inside she knew that she was as mortal as Mary Sixpack and she could not bear the split between her image and what she felt to be her real self. She suffered in her beauty.

In the margins of most of my notebooks is the sketch of a woman's head in a three-quarter view. Her hair is long and her cheekbones are far more pronounced than mine will ever be, no matter how thin I get. Her jaw is very defined. I gave her a name once, a name that has much to do with ethereality and fragility and a name as imaginary as is Gilda. I only christen the sketches that turn out well with that name. I only want to draw a Gilda, and I only want to be a Gilda, even knowing what Gilda did to Rita Hayworth.

I would never presume to compare my looks with those of Rita Hayworth, but I am a woman, and I know about laboring. I too have learned that there is a price to be paid for beauty. I live the same deception as she did. I am not what I seem, and the deception battles my soul.

"Yes, I am attracted," I overheard him say once, "but I don't think she's my type." He did not know me at that point. I was a shell and a body, long hair and green eyes and long legs and a small waist, nice curves for one so thin. I know that he wants the flesh envelope that I walk in. I and others have seen him looking at me, my hair, my face, my legs. He has twisted around in chairs to watch me as I go by, and I know that he is aware of me whenever I am around him. My physicality is a magnet. He wants and he wants, but he just wants a body. He does not want me. He himself is easy in his corporeality: he has the athlete's presence and the athlete's ability to live within his skin and take pleasure in the way his body works. I think I felt that if he—so easy in his skin—believed in my entirety then I too would believe. Only my body sold. Uninterested in the interior, he cannot divorce himself of his attraction for the façade, and I am caught. The façade always sells first, and therefore the façade must always be maintained, no matter what.

I met him for breakfast one morning this winter when the snow was falling softly. I walked alone in the quiet of early morning. I could feel the snow collecting on the gauze of my hair. Alone with him in a near-empty dining hall, I felt cold, and my food had no taste. I ate very little. After breakfast I disappeared.

Sometimes, when I have disappeared and I am unrecognizable, invisible, I run my hands over the planes of my face, telling myself that I am, I am, I am. I exist, I am alive, I tell myself, running my fingertips over the sockets of bone in which those green eyes lie, and I discover the line of my jaw beneath my skin. My eyelashes tickle my hands, and my hands worship my flesh and my bones. I am reassuring myself that somewhere under my rib cage my heart beats, that though invisible I am not gone.

I remember the first time I threw up blood.

The modern artist Giorgio de Chirico painted in a classical manner. His subjects seem to be informed by Italian Renaissance models but the classical vision has been tortured and twisted and made strange. His paintings recede into depth in skewed perspective, and nature has been warped into something that is both recognizable and alien. In his lonely, dark settings the shadows are like none ever seen in reality but are still frighteningly real. "There are more enigmas in the shadow of a man who walks in the sun," he said, "than in all the religions of past, present and future." In the medium he devoted his life to he could find no answers: mysteries were easier than a simple darkness, the shadow of a man in the sun. The lines of his paintings are invariably ruler straight, but there is no peace or ease to be found in his art. His paintings are disorienting: they are the representation of a human imbalance and uncertainty in the world.

I am uneasy in my shell.

The neoclassical artist Ingres painted figures of dubious anatomical construction but used the questions to glorify the beauty of the human shape rather than to disorient the viewer. It is the male body that is said to represent best the human form for its shape follows the lines of the core and is undisguised by curves and softness. Ingres painted women. In "The Turkish Bath" many women lie in splendor, impossibly twisted into sensuous shapes. He celebrates the disguising curves and softness, emphasizing them, asserting roundness as beautiful. In another celebration of Woman, "La Grande Odalisque," a beautiful woman reclines alone [see color insert]. I first saw this painting in grisaille, a technique that simulates statuary, molding the human shape in shades of gray.
The body of this Turkish harem slave is everything that I wish I could permit mine to be. It is voluptuous and smooth; it is classically feminine.

In the line of breast and hip, of round arm and thigh, globes and arcs connect and flow, defining grace and beauty. Hers is a celebration of existence, of the flesh and the senses. Nude she reclines, luxuriating in herself as a living being and a body. Her setting reflects and enhances the luxury of her being: royal blue, oriental cushions, self-indulgence and self-love. She cares for her own pleasure. Her skin is pale, and the feminine aspects of her figure have been emphasized to the point of distortion. Her shoulders are narrow; her waist is small, and her lower back is far too long. The elongation highlights the flesh at the hip and leads into her legs. They appear shorter than they would were she thin. Her feet and hands are fragile, her visible eye luminous, and the bones of her face have a delicate beauty. She is direct and beautiful. She is sensuous and sensual. She is enigmatic and she is feminine. Her glance over her round shoulder beckons and arrogantly asserts her power. Nude, she revels in herself as a sexual being. She does not hide.

In my dreams, though, I take on the attributes not of the Odalisque, but of my impossibly idealized sketch. The world celebrates my fragility and stunning physical presence. I define gorgeous. The earth congratulates itself that I pass time on its surface. I am delicate and so breathtakingly beautiful that I put Gilda to shame.

Ingres chose not to make his Odalisque's body anatomically correct. By the standards of reality it is warped and strangely twisted, wrong like de Chirico's perspective. Her arm and her lower back are far too long, her leg twists around her other leg. Her body is more than imperfect, it is impossible, but in its impossibility the necessities of bone and blood have been sacrificed to the beauty of line and form. Where de Chirico skews perspective to disorient, Ingres twists a body and liberates it. Without the bones that constrain the normal human figure, she is freer in her flesh. She is more conscious of her own power and presence. She inhabits her body in joy, accepting it, loving her curves and sensuality, hedonism inherent in the hookah and crumpled sheets. She flows feminine.

In Ingres' world—though not in mine—she need not suffer to be easy in her skin.

GIORGIO DE CHIRICO, MELANCHOLY AND MYSTERY OF A STREET, 1914. OIL ON CANVAS, 34¼ × 28½ IN. PRIVATE COLLECTION. © SIAE/VAGA, NY.

H_an N. Pham

Down the Unwritten Path

> To the Traditional Vietnamese, the nation consisted of a
> landscape and the past of the family. . . . the family was the
> essence, the cell as it were, that contained the design for the
> whole society.
>
> FRANCES FITZGERALD
FIRE IN THE LAKE

My family has never posed for a family portrait, as most families
do. Perhaps this is because we've never had the time or the
patience to drag ourselves down to the local photographer and
smile with clenched sincerity, eyes checking watch, fingernails tapping
impatiently on the corner table. Or perhaps it is because we've never
placed much value in "normal" family traditions: the family vacations
untaken, the sweet babybooks never bought, the dinner table never used
except for the solitary click clicking of a pair of chopsticks. Sometimes.
And always alone. In any case, our family history is inscribed in each of
us; its struggles mark us, but most notably it marks the women in my
family—my grandmother, my mother, me. We, the life-givers and unspoken historians of our family legacy, carry with us, in our faces, in our
actions, the unwritten history of our family—past, present, and perhaps,
future.

I

Imagine now, just a picture of a woman laughing. That's all. A woman
so small in her stature that she could fade into the gray carpet, the gray

wall. Only she doesn't. Somehow her vitality has leaked out into her clothing, from the magenta pumps with elfin toes, to the white blouse peeking out from under the suit so blue it seems the tailor took a portion of the deep blue sky stretched somewhere between dawn and twilight, added a dash of the Caribbean Sea, and filled the entire length with white sunlight until it was bursting, bursting with blue. This suit, left alone, could have danced waltzes with more passion than most people. Yet it was the woman within who brought the final touch.

My mother is the woman laughing in the picture.

She is the kind of mother that carries with her a sweet scent of motherhood wherever she goes: her arms are soft, her eyes kind, her full pink lips are always trembling to kiss you. Lips that never thought that they would have to utter to her children, "Your father is leaving me." Not us. Not my brother and me. Just her alone. She never expected it to happen to her, this fragmentation of the family, this abrupt dismissal by her husband. But she accepted it with the quiet obedience so characteristic of any woman raised in Old Vietnam. Looking at her, within her, listening to the words that fall from lips that might have well been my grandmother's, or her mother's before her, I hear the essence of all the Vietnamese cultural values that her mother instilled in her and she sought to instill in me: Obey your parents. Obey your husband. Be ladylike. You are a girl; not a boy. Then I realize that she is, for me, for my children, the last rickety bridge that sways somewhere between Old Vietnam and my new America.

II

I am sitting cross-legged on the floor, the soles of my pink feet staring at me with a chubby softness. I watch my grandmother, who is leaning heavily against the back of the broken recliner, her rough-skinned hands lying awkwardly in her lap, palms upward, slightly tilted toward one another as if one hand is asking the other, "What are we to do now?"

I am interviewing her for a required English project, a report entitled "Words of the Wise and Experienced." I am asking her about her childhood, the way she was raised. She tells me, in a throaty voice that dips now and then into bitterness, that she was raised to work every day, in the fields, in the kitchen, at home, at school. She was not spoiled like *American* children, her small black eyes focusing quickly on me before they slip back out of focus. She could cook, clean, sew, raise chickens, a garden, children—every accomplishment needed of a wife ticked off on wrinkled fingers swollen with arthritis.

Looking at her weary face, I try to ask a simpler question, a happier one. "And your husband?" I ask.

She mouths a few sentences in trailing Vietnamese whispers. "He was chosen for me. He not pretty-boy. But my parents chose him, and you must always listen to your parents. So we married, and he was my husband." She stops, as if that was all there was to her marriage. He was her husband. Perhaps she believed her parents when they told her that if she listened to them, then she would always have happiness.

My grandfather stayed behind with his mistress, their former chambermaid, when my grandmother left Vietnam with her daughter and son-in-law and their children, all staking their futures on a leaking boat, filled with peasants and squawking poultry that rained colored feathers, which rocked out onto the black, rolling sea under the cover of night. She would not see my grandfather again for ten years, when she was reunited with him in America. With him came my half-uncle, child of the other woman. To save face, she allows him to call her "Mother."

III

In Vietnam, perhaps in any Asian culture, a woman's life is taking care of her family, in pleasing her husband. A woman without a family is poor, and pitied. A woman whose husband speaks poorly of her, who abuses and mocks her, is a shame to the community. A woman who speaks up against this is an embarrassment. But, perhaps the worst, is a woman whose husband has left her. She then becomes the forgotten spirit of the community, someone to look down upon, to sidle by with a snicker and whispered remarks, a woman to be shunned.

Two generations of my family's women have experienced unhappiness in their married life. Two women wove small deceptions to hide their shame. My grandmother accepted into her life, without a murmur, a strange fifteen-year-old boy who called her "Mother." My mother, when my father moved into his own house many miles away, taught me to say that my father was at work and would return home late every time someone called him. She begged me to learn to tell happy family stories when I visited my other grandmother, my father's mother, in Los Angeles.

Through her, I learned how to smile in the face of misery at home, at school, anywhere.

IV

It has been about two years since my father left.

It may be a little shorter, or a little longer; I have accepted it so well I have forgotten. There was never an event that caused my father to storm out of the house, no outburst, no slamming of the door. Sometimes, in my sleep, with eyes shut tight, I can hear past echoes of my father yelling at my mother, of my brother yelling at my father, of my mother crying and yelling at the world for an outlet from the pain. I know now that my father did not leave because of a mistress, as so many are quick to ask me when they find out. It is as FitzGerald related in one section of her book, *"a [Vietnamese] man is not an independent character . . . but a social role—he must always act in the correct manner, no matter what it costs him."* My father left because he could no longer play the role of the strong Vietnamese husband, who had complete control of his household, whose wife was always pretty and delicate, whose children were quiet and obedient. He could not play his Vietnamese role to perfection in America.

He, too, had his secret shame.

V

So many generations have flowed between the rice paddy fields and the hedges of cane, so that "the sense of limitation and enclosure was as much a part of traditional life as of the life of the nation." In the end, the lives of the Vietnamese people concentrated solely on the land and the family. The land was the constant element that sheltered the family from outside influences and helped the family to perpetuate its sacred values and traditional roles of the family: husband and wife, father and son, mother and daughter. However, every tradition, every value, stemmed from the land and was tied intricately to it—"as long as Vietnamese Society remained a closed system, intellectual foundations remained flawless and immobile . . . without their land, they were without a social identity"—*Fire in the Lake.*

So, by passing from Vietnam into America, my family forsook its identity, and began anew.

VI

The arguments have faded long ago. My father no longer tries to run away; he comes every Friday to pick up my mother so they can pass the weekend together. He always smiles quietly at me, and laughs, eyes glistening with a suspicious moistness every time I hug him and pat his balding head, forgiving him. My mother still does everything to please him. Even when he left, she helped him buy furniture and decorations for his home. She proudly proclaims that his garden is the prettiest on the block; she spent many hours crouched on the soft, green grass, happily weeding and making a nest for the seeds she had bought, carefully pouring her love into the earthen beds so that on the day the flowers peeked above their rims of soil to surround that lonely house far away, my father, too, would drink the love that fell from their perfumed petals, poured from the hands of my mother, given freely from the hearts of his family.

The shame has passed.

VII

The suffocating Vietnamese culture that taught my mother, and her mother, and many mothers before to always obey, and tread softly, and speak quietly, is giving way to mine: an American culture where the women stand tall beside the men, where one opinion is weighed against the other on the basis of intelligence, not sex. The women need never flinch, or bow their heads. I can stamp my feet, yell as loud as I want, and never hide here. No one will ever be able to tell me that I must obey my husband, and bear the burdens of the struggles of my family alone, as if I am afraid to be shunned by the community when I let on that I am not perfect, that my family is not the perfect Vietnamese family.

VIII

On the face of my grandmother is the story of Old Vietnam, complete with cultural, social, and family values, etched in the lines of her cheeks, her mouth, her eyes. Then, encountering the picture of my mother, described in the beginning of her laughing at work, taken during our own family crises, you would never realize that the woman so vibrant with laughter had not laughed for many months. But, if you look carefully, you might be able to see the threads of my family's future in the picture, in my mother's stance, and the way her head falls back as she laughs.

Imagine now, only a woman, young or old, in a picture laughing. Laughing with her feet planted firmly on the ground, toes spread out wide to claim her space. Laughing with her body tall and straight, shoulders thrown back with confidence. Laughing with a bob of black hair bouncing back from a head bent backwards, as if leaning back from the weight of the huge smile, open to show two rows of glistening white teeth and a curled pink tongue, that tickles the face open with happiness. Laughing, with twinkling black Asian eyes squeezed tight above a snub nose that rises above the round cheeks like a little hill about to topple over.

This image of the woman, my mother, is the final piece to the fragmented picture described in the beginning, where initially you could only see a woman, in vibrant clothes, laughing. Here you see the entire being: my mother, whole, happy, and strong. And, just as easily, perhaps you can picture me, in the same stance, with the same confidence, laughing, or my daughter after me, or the daughter after that. For the picture could be any of us, now, in the future, laughing with the strength that generations of women before us have passed on to us.

Together, we are the women of our family, holding in our actions, our tears, and our laughter the living etches of our family history—from the Old Vietnam that is my grandmother sitting wearily against the back of the broken recliner, across the rickety bridge that is my mother struggling to find laughter, continuing on to me—the daughter who carries our family's fresh, unwritten pages on into America.

Han N. Pham's essay—one version of it at least—ends here, with the beautiful images of her mother as a rickety bridge uniting her mother's and her old world of Vietnam with her and her daughter's new world of America, the pages of their lives here remaining to be written.

As readers and writers ourselves, we love the essay as it stands. As teachers, however, we wondered whether there wasn't something more that Han could include, something more about her mother and her father. So we asked her the following questions:

• What is there from your grandmother's tradition that has been transported to America and that allows your mother to laugh in the picture of her you describe?

• Can you explain a bit further the connection between what remains from your grandmother's tradition in making your mother the woman she became and you the woman you are becoming?
• How does your father figure into the equation with you and your mother? Can you tell us more about the image of your father living by himself and yet your mother feeling a need to help him?

After thinking about these questions, Han wrote an additional section, which follows. She prefaced her new concluding extension with a note to us that reads in part: "The clue—the image of my father living by himself and my mother giving in to him . . . In the investment of herself for his benefit there is love . . . He is forgiven no matter what he has done . . . You were right in assuming that the clue lay with my father. Read on."

IX

Reflections on "Down the Unwritten Path"

I remember the period of time surrounding my father's leaving and the careful shattering of our family structure so well, as if it was an old movie reel creaking slow images past the eyes of my mind. I remember yelling at my mother, my voice catching as it reeled toward the heights of our vaulted ceiling in desperate, demanding tones: Why don't you stand up to him? Why do you let him treat you that way? Why are you so obedient? I remember her staring at me in a strange way as I screamed out that last word, "obedient."

She knew that I didn't understand. But now I do.

"Down the Unwritten Path" forced me to give voice to the feelings that had struggled unheard; the same concepts that had caused me to emblazon an angry "weak" against my family have now led to the word that is the foundation for these pages—"strong": the sacred concepts of family, its roles, and its honor. It is no exaggeration to say that these concepts were as essential to my family as they were to Vietnam, one viewing itself as a miniature model of the larger, who, in turn, viewed herself as a nation merely perpetuating an enlarged role of the family—an endless cycle of complete roundness, a healthy circle pouring joy and prosperity from past generations into the new.

When my grandmother traveled to America, leaving behind her a nation still smoking in the ruins of the Vietnam War, she brought with her a strange commodity that she had already instilled in her daughter, who had just begun her married life in America—stability. I remember scoffing at the thought of the typical Asian man-and-woman relationship, so barbaric in its command that husband speak, wife obey. When my grandmother accepted my half-uncle into her life, when my mother never yelled back when she should have, could have, when she helped nurture my father's garden and pick out his furniture, I called it "obedience."

I was wrong.

Although this essay is clearly a tribute to the women in my family, the key truly does lie in their relationship with their men: their husbands, fathers, and sons. It is not obedience that keeps harsh words from spilling out in reply to the same, nor is it obedience that causes a woman to "give" so unselfishly to her husband. It is, rather, a deep, ancient understanding that the family is total—that determination, perseverance, and a strong love are needed to do these little tasks that the "civilized" world, with former citizens like me, scoff at. They are not taught to remain silent in the time of crises; their actions alone state that they understand the situation, and are willing to wait silently as they "ride out the storm" very much like the mother who learns to purse her lips while waiting for her obstinate child to learn by doing what she has told him he should not do. These actions do not depict a weak flower, swayed by the winds of struggle; they depict, instead, the silent dignity and honor that surround women who stand, face into the wind, weathering it by planting seeds to await the spring rains and whispering strength into the ears of "Americanized" children asking questions for a school report.

Love, honor, roles, relationships, strength, determination, family— these are the words that form an endless chain into the past, connecting my grandmother, my mother, and me with the other side of the sacred circle—our brothers, husbands, and fathers. They are all boats that help us weather the storm as they carry us to the New World and toward other lands.

A Spectrum of Professional Writing

L ee K. Abbott
(b.1947)

L ee K. Abbott was raised in southern New Mexico in the small town of Las Cruces. He received a B.A. (1970), an M.A. (1973) from New Mexico State University, and an M.F.A. from the University of Arkansas in 1977. In 1989 he became a professor of English at Ohio State University. His stories, collected in five volumes, have appeared in a variety of magazines and literary journals, including *Harper's* and *The Kenyon Review*. Abbott has been awarded numerous prizes, and his stories have been included in *Best American Short Stories* (1985 and 1987), *The Pushcart Prize* volumes (1987 and 1989), and the *O. Henry Prize Stories* (1984). His work has also been twice nominated for a Pulitzer Prize.

In "The True Story of Why I Do What I Do," Abbott explains not only his reasons for writing but also his sense of "truth." The essay is interesting for the questions it raises about how writers reveal their various truths and why some of them rely on fiction to convey those truths. It is also noteworthy for its highly individual and engaging voice.

The True Story of Why I Do What I Do

All stories are true stories, especially the artful lies we invent to satisfy the wishful thinker in us, for they present to us, in disguise often and at great distance, the way we are or would want to be. Told to us in a lingo as unique as a fingerprint, they address our up-and-down, our here-and-now. They come, I think, from a desire, as irresistable as love itself, to fix on the page a moment, suffered or made up, when something—one puny thing or idea or person—revealed itself and so turned off the Boom-Boom-Boom which usually deafens us to ourselves. Happily-ended or not, stories are the truth we leave behind, like crumbs, to say how we've come and what was there to see.

To be inspirational, as high-minded and upward-looking as the foolish half of me mostly aims to be, I have to tell you about my father—as crazed, driven and cross-hearted a hero as I have ever known. His analogues have appeared in dozens of my stories: he's the gentleman, in golf togs or business suit, throwing the epic tantrum, careening hither and thither in a men's locker or banker's office; he's the one, in the fiction I invent, with the outraged moral intelligence, the one who hectors and harangues, the one telling another (usually me, you can guess) how to behave and when to beware and what is likely to be the dry end of things we love.

In fiction, he is imperious, forbidding as a Puritan God, sharp-minded as an out-of-town lawyer, stiff as pig bristle, wiry and unforgiving; in fiction, the made-up landscape I am a sometime citizen in, he suffers and is redeemed (or he is not), does the wrong thing and is shamed (or is not), comes to insight and is crushed (or is not). In fiction, given its unities and shape and its epiphanies, I comprehend my father. I know exactly what he meant when he told me that you could tell a gentleman by his hand shake and his shoe shine. I know, and can articulate, what significance there is in the properly mowed lawn, what wisdom there is in the order of dried dishes. In fiction, I know—maybe as Flannery O'Connor did—why the heathen rage.

In life, however—which, messy and improbable and ephemeral, is not good fiction—I had no idea what made his world spin round and round. The facts were clear to me, not the flesh. He went to Dartmouth, I knew. He pole-vaulted cross-handed. One brother died on the Bataan Death March; his sister in a boating accident on Lake Sasebo in Maine. His father went blind in the last years of his life; his mother squandered an inheritance of at least one million dollars. He was a roué, I heard, a slick-haired rake who hung out on the pier at Old Orchard Beach and went down to Miami in the winter. He married my mother, the over-pampered daughter of a Canadian insurance executive, in Harligen, Texas while he was at gunnery school in WWII. They lived in Panama, where I was born. He ran the National Guard in Illinois, where my brother was born. He played one year of professional golf. He became a career military man, went to England, Korea, Germany, resigned his commission twice because somebody, or something, infuriated him.

If it is true, as Willa Cather says, that the "basic material a writer works with is acquired before the age of fifteen," then by the time I was a sopho-more in high school in Las Cruces, New Mexico, already telling my teach-ers and myself that I was going to be a writer, the material I had acquired I'd got from him: a duke's mixture of soirées, of country clubs and officers' clubs, of colorful compadres named Red and Goonch and Uncle Inches—the whole of it tragic and tearful to the aggressively poetic kid I was then. My mother was a drunk, institutionalized when I was twelve; my father was a drinker. He had psoriasis on his knobby knees and knobby elbows, he smoked like the dickens, he threw a wedge at the TV, he dressed in pink polkadots for the Club Championship, he banished me to my room forever, he expected my brother and me to know the truth and speak it invari-ably—this was my material, a hodge-podge of goo and muck and human blah-blah-blah the responsibility for which I was absolutely unaware of until the inspirational summer afternoon I am partly here to yap about.

Once upon a time (Isn't this the rhetoric, in truth, that opens every fairytale we survive and want to write about?), my father and I found our-selves alone at home. I want to say it was a Sunday, for in my memory the day, if not the events themselves, have a liturgical, quasi-holy "feel." In my memory, that attic atop the shoulders where everything truly felt is found, there is that Sunday light, crooked and mote-filled and lazy, and that Sun-day time, heavy and ever in danger of wobbling to a halt. My father, in his bermuda shorts and golf shirt, is in the TV room, drinking the rum thing he preferred; he had the habit, annoying I think now, of dumping his half-used ice cubes back in the freezer, a habit the girl who became my wife told me was disgusting every time I made her a Coke and it tasted like hooch. I am in the living room, I think, listening to records; more likely, I am reading—*Sports Illustrated,* the *National Geographic, Life* magazine.

My taste in those days ran to the quick, the immediate—prose of the slash-and-burn kind. *Mila 18* by Leon Uris, *The Naked and the Dead* (still an excellent book, by the way), Alistair MacClean's high seas adventures. I saw myself writing a book like those one day—a book, conceived out of testosterone and *Nugget*-style macho, a book as pithy and direct as a dust jacket blurb: "Mr. Abbott," the endorsement would run, "writes like an assassin. He's the 'Aaarrgghh' the yellow yammer when they spy the vast What-Not opening to greet them." I had, I thought then, no experience (this was long before I realized that Henry James was correct when he said that "experience was an atmosphere of the mind"). I was just a kid, after all. Skinny, with a flat-top and fifteen pimples, half my mind tilted toward girls, the other half tilted toward glory (which would, in the reasoning I was the victim of, get me girls).

The hours passed that Sunday afternoon as they always do when I cast myself back into the dangerous tides that are my past: the clock above the antique writing desk chiming on the quarter-hour, the father wandering between the refrigerator and liquor cabinet, Pee Wee Reese or Dizzy Dean saying in the TV room what the Dodgers were doing; the son in another room cobbling together in his fertile but screwy imagination a tale of swashbuckling and hair-raising, a narrative of guns and grateful bimbos and nick-of-time derring-do. We were in our elements, him and me: one, the older, tuned to the stupid clatter of the exterior world; the other, the younger flesh of him, tuned to the twilight interior world of fetch-and-keep, of fantasy. Then he burst into the living room, eyed me as if wondering for the last time whether I was up to the burden he was about to pitch my way, and said, a little drunkenly, "Come with me."

He had been thinking about himself, it is clear now. An inventory, check mark after check mark after check mark, had been taken: three heart attacks, a fist-sized hunk of his lung removed at William Beaumont General Hospital in Ft. Bliss, the yips on the putting green, Homeric-like anger, frustration at a life twisted which-away, hopes high as heaven he believed in, bitterness at being less than the hero he'd promised himself he'd be. I didn't know this at the time I followed him outdoors and into the utility rooms at the end of the car port. I knew only that he was semi-sloshed. I knew only that he was fifty-six years old, gray-headed and tough. I knew he hated going to work at the post office, his job in those days, where he supervised and inspected and, unhappiest of all for him, had to tattle on those who stole money or stamps or swiped somebody's *Playboy* magazine.

"See this, Kit?" he said. He was standing in the center of the utility room, lawn mower here, gas can there, the walls hung with tools I never got the sense of. Golf clubs were in there, a bucket of practice balls, cans of oil, greasy rags, a hoe, a rake, a cheap hardware store of goodies that smelled old and used and too sweet. "You want to be a writer, huh?" he said, sweeping his arms, then pulling me after him. He snarled the word; it was sound which scorned ignorance and innocence. Against the wall, high as the ceiling, were stacked his footlockers and steamer trunks, from the Army of the United States and from the regiments that were the families of his own father, innkeeper Lyman Kittredge Abbott of Portland, Maine. I like to think now that I knew we were coming to something, my father and I, that he was going to say words to me and I, perhaps for the first time, was going to understand him precisely. I like to think now that I was smart enough to know that I was in the presence of a truth grander than the two of us, a truth the price of which we go paying forever, a truth more dire than the knowing that we die and do not rise. This is the moment, I like to think of myself thinking then, when you discover how hard the world is, when what you've cleaved to is cleaved from you with a broadaxe.

Then he assaulted those lockers and trunks. In a fury, huffing and puffing, he snatched them down, one by one, hollering "Timber!" when the uppermost went tumbling. They crashed and banged, and I tried backing up a little, as he flung one behind him and scrambled over another to reach a third. He was hollering, you have to know, all the New England notes of his voice echoing in that now cramped room, and maybe I was some scared. This was the temper I'd witnessed elsewhere— on the golf course, behind the wheel of his Ford, in the living room when someone in the big world made a ding-a-ling out of himself. But there was more than anger here: there was pain, the particular kind of which was personal and buried deep in his bones, pain for which there is no Latin name or medicine or machine, other than fiction, to account for.

"Write it all down!" he was shouting. "Write it all goddam down!"

And it was here, from a certain X-spot in the world, 1855 Cruse, that my father, teetering from booze and the awful weight of his own life, was taking seriously, in a manner I couldn't yet, what purpose writing ought to have. Here it is, he was in effect saying. Crated and stored, catalogued and preserved, year by used-up year, place by rotten place. Here it is: the come and go of it, the building and collapse of it, the joy and weep of it. Here it is, he was saying. All the tissues and nerves and human jingle-jangle, that want and excess of it, the rigamarole and whirling, damaged creatures we are. And all you have to do, son and boy, is write it down. Write it all goddam down.

This, I submit, is the inspirational part. If we write for any larger purpose than a simple good time—and, believe me, there is nothing at all
wrong with a good time—it is, I think, because we all feel, less and more,
the obligation we have to our fathers, to our mothers, to all the folks,
linked by biology or not, who have raised us; an obligation, as essential to
our moral natures as our hearts are to long life, to the places we were
raised in and in the knowledge we learned there. We want, I hope,
because there is no other way to do it, to write it down, to transform it,
to set it straight. At our best, we do not write for the money alone, though
money is nice; nor do we write for fame, though fame is likewise nice. We
write, beginner and professional alike, because, though half-frightened,
we want to know what is in the trunks and lockers we lug forward
through time, what vital secrets they can be sprung to reveal.

CONSIDERATIONS

Thinking

Explain the paradox at the beginning of Abbott's opening sentence: "All stories are true stories, especially the artful lies we invent to satisfy the wishful
thinker in us."

What, according to Abbott, is the primary function of stories? What do stories enable writers to do?

Is this essay about Abbott's father? About the writer's relationship with his
father? About the father's response to the son's ambition? Explain.

Connecting

To what extent can you relate to Abbott's comment that he "had no idea what
made his [father's] world spin round and round"? To what extent do you understand your parents' goals and dreams, their hopes and fears and feelings?

Lee K. Abbott was a young man, still in school, during the scene he describes
with his father telling him to "Write it all down! Write it all goddam down!" What
is the relationship between Abbott's writerly vocation and his father's demand?

Compare Abbott's assessment of the value of stories with Tim O'Brien's in
"How to Tell a True War Story."

Writing

Write a piece explaining why you do what you do or why you want to do
whatever it is that you envision yourself doing with your life. Try to account for
what has motivated you, what may have pushed, prodded, propelled you in the
direction you are heading.

Compare Abbott's notions about the truths of fiction with Scott Russell
Sanders's notion of the falseness of fact in "Wayland."

Gloria Anzaldúa
(b.1942)

Gloria Anzaldúa was raised in southwest Texas. She describes
herself as "a border woman," living between the Mexican and
Anglo cultures. Her books include two edited volumes: *This Bridge
Called My Back: Writing by Radical Women of Color* (1983) and *Haciendo
Caras: Making Face/Making Soul* (1990). The following selection, from
Borderlands/La Frontera (1987), crosses language borders by mixing
Spanish and English while combining various essay genres, such as
autobiography, critical theory, and argument.

How to Tame a Wild Tongue

"We're going to have to control your tongue," the dentist says, pulling out all the metal from my mouth. Silver bits plop and tinkle into the basin. My mouth is a motherlode.

The dentist is cleaning out my roots. I get a whiff of the stench when I gasp. "I can't cap that tooth yet, you're still draining," he says.

"We're going to have to do something about your tongue," I hear the anger rising in his voice. My tongue keeps pushing out the wads of cotton, pushing back the drills, the long thin needles. "I've never seen anything as strong or as stubborn," he says. And I think, how do you tame a wild tongue, train it to be quiet, how do you bridle and saddle it? How do you make it lie down?

Who is to say that robbing a people of its language is less violent than war?

RAY GWYN SMITH

I remember being caught speaking Spanish at recess—that was good for three licks on the knuckles with a sharp ruler. I remember being sent to the corner of the classroom for "talking back" to the Anglo teacher when all I was trying to do was tell her how to pronounce my name. "If you want to be American, speak 'American.' If you don't like it, go back to Mexico where you belong."

"I want you to speak English. *Pa' hallar buen trabajo tienes que saber hablar el inglés bien. Qué vale toda tu educación si todavía hablas inglés con un 'accent',*" my mother would say, mortified that I spoke English like a Mexican. At Pan American University, I and all Chicano students were required to take two speech classes. Their purpose: to get rid of our accents.

Attacks on one's form of expression with the intent to censor are a violation of the First Amendment. *El Anglo con cara de inocente nos arrancó la lengua.* Wild tongues can't be tamed, they can only be cut out.

OVERCOMING THE TRADITION OF SILENCE

> *Ahogadas, escupimos el oscuro.*
> *Peleando con nuestra propia sombra*
> *el silencio nos sepulta.*

En boca cerrada no entran moscas. "Flies don't enter a closed mouth" is a saying I kept hearing when I was a child. *Ser habladora* was to be a gossip and a liar, to talk too much. *Muchachitas bien criadas,* well-bred girls don't answer back. *Es una falta de respeto* to talk back to one's mother or father. I remember one of the sins I'd recite to the priest in the confession box the few times I went to confession: talking back to my mother, *hablar pa' 'tras, repelar. Hocicona, repelona, chismosa,* having a big mouth, questioning, carrying tales are all signs of being *mal criada.* In my culture they are all words that are derogatory if applied to women—I've never heard them applied to men.

The first time I heard two women, a Puerto Rican and a Cuban, say the word *"nosotras,"* I was shocked. I had not known the word existed. Chicanas use *nosotros* whether we're male or female. We are robbed of our female being by the masculine plural. Language is a male discourse.

> And our tongues have become
> dry   the wilderness has
> dried out our tongues   and
> we have forgotten speech.
>
> IRENA KLEPFISZ

Even our own people, other Spanish speakers *nos quieren poner candados en la boca.* They would hold us back with their bag of *reglas de academia.*

> *Oyé como ladra:*
> *el lenguaje de la frontera*
>
> *Quien tiene boca se equivoca.*
>
> MEXICAN SAYING

"*Pocho,* cultural traitor, you're speaking the oppressor's language by speaking English, you're ruining the Spanish language," I have been accused by various Latinos and Latinas. Chicano Spanish is considered by the purist and by most Latinos deficient, a mutilation of Spanish.

But Chicano Spanish is a border tongue which developed naturally. Change, *evolución, enriquecimiento de palabras nuevas por invención o adopción* have created variants of Chicano Spanish, *un nuevo lenguaje. Un lenguaje que corresponde a un modo de vivir.* Chicano Spanish is not incorrect, it is a living language.

For a people who are neither Spanish nor live in a country in which Spanish is the first language; for a people who live in a country in which English is the reigning tongue but who are not Anglo; for a people who cannot entirely identify with either standard (formal, Castilian) Spanish nor standard English, what recourse is left to them but to create their own language? A language which they can connect their identity to, one capable of communicating the realities and values true to themselves—a language with terms that are neither *español ni inglés,* but both. We speak a patois, a forked tongue, a variation of two languages.

Chicano Spanish sprang out of the Chicanos' need to identify ourselves as a distinct people. We needed a language with which we could communicate with ourselves, a secret language. For some of us, language is a homeland closer than the Southwest—for many Chicanos today live in the Midwest and the East. And because we are a complex, heterogeneous people, we speak many languages. Some of the languages we speak are

1. Standard English
2. Working class and slang English
3. Standard Spanish
4. Standard Mexican Spanish
5. North Mexican Spanish dialect
6. Chicano Spanish (Texas, New Mexico, Arizona, and California have regional variations)
7. Tex-Mex
8. *Pachuco* (called *caló*)

My "home" tongues are the languages I speak with my sister and brothers, with my friends. They are the last five listed, with 6 and 7 being closest to my heart. From school, the media, and job situations, I've picked up standard and working class English. From Mamagrande Locha and from reading Spanish and Mexican literature, I've picked up Standard Spanish and Standard Mexican Spanish. From *los recién llegados,* Mexican immigrants, and *braceros,* I learned the North Mexican dialect. With Mexicans I'll try to speak either Standard Mexican Spanish or the North Mexican dialect. From my parents and Chicanos living in the Valley, I picked up Chicano Texas Spanish, and I speak it with my mom, younger brother (who married a Mexican and who rarely mixes Spanish with English), aunts, and older relatives.

With Chicanas from *Nuevo México* or *Arizona* I will speak Chicano Spanish a little, but often they don't understand what I'm saying. With most California Chicanas I speak entirely in English (unless I forget). When I first moved to San Francisco, I'd rattle off something in Spanish, unintentionally embarrassing them. Often it is only with another Chicana *tejano* that I can talk freely.

Words distorted by English are known as anglicisms or *pochismos.* The *pocho* is an anglicized Mexican or American of Mexican origin who speaks Spanish with an accent characteristic of North Americans and who distorts and reconstructs the language according to the influence of English. Tex-Mex, or Spanglish, comes most naturally to me. I may switch back and forth from English to Spanish in the same sentence or in the same word. With my sister and my brother Nune and with Chicano *tejano* contemporaries I speak in Tex-Mex.

From kids and people my own age I picked up *Pachuco. Pachuco* (the language of the zoot suiters) is a language of rebellion, both against Standard Spanish and Standard English. It is a secret language. Adults of the culture and outsiders cannot understand it. It is made up of slang words from both English and Spanish. *Ruca* means girl or woman, *vato* means guy or dude, *chale* means no, *simón* means yes, *churro* is sure, talk is *periquiar, pigionear* means petting, *que gacho* means how nerdy, *ponte águila* means watch out, death is called *la pelona.* Through lack of practice and not having others who can speak it, I've lost most of the *Pachuco* tongue.

CHICANO SPANISH

Chicanos, after 250 years of Spanish/Anglo colonization, have developed significant differences in the Spanish we speak. We collapse two adjacent vowels into a single syllable and sometimes shift the stress in certain words such as *maíz/maiz, cohete/cuete.* We leave out certain consonants when they appear between vowels: *lado/lao, mojado/mojao.* Chicanos from South Texas pronounce *f* as *j* as in *jue (fue).* Chicanos use "archaisms," words that are no longer in the Spanish language, words that have been evolved out. We say *semos, truje, haiga, ansina,* and *naiden.* We retain the "archaic" *j,* as in *jalar,* that derives from an earlier *h* (the French *halar* or the Germanic *halon* which was lost to standard Spanish in the sixteenth century), but which is still found in several regional dialects such as the one spoken in South Texas. (Due to geography, Chicanos from the Valley of South Texas were cut off linguistically from other Spanish speakers. We tend to use words that the Spaniards brought over from Medieval Spain. The majority of the Spanish colonizers in Mexico and the Southwest came from Extremadura—Hernán Cortés was one of them—and Andalucía. Andalucians pronounce *ll* like a *y,* and their *d's* tend to be absorbed by adjacent vowels: *tirado* becomes *tirao.* They brought *el lenguaje popular, dialectos y regionalismos.*)

Chicanos and other Spanish speakers also shift *ll* to *y* and *z* to *s.* We leave out initial syllables, saying *tar* for *estar, toy* for *estoy, hora* for *ahora* (*cubanos* and *puertorriqueños* also leave out initial letters of some words). We also leave out the final syllable such as *pa* for *para.* The intervocalic *y,* the *ll* as in *tortilla, ella, botella,* gets replaced by *tortia* or *tortiya, ea, botea.* We add an additional syllable at the beginning of certain words: *atocar* for *tocar, agastar* for *gastar.* Sometimes we'll say *lavaste las vacijas,* other times *lavates* (substituting the *ates* verb endings for the *aste*).

We used anglicisms, words borrowed from English: *bola* from ball, *carpeta* from carpet, *máchina de lavar* (instead of *lavadora*) from washing machine. Tex-Mex argot, created by adding a Spanish sound at the beginning or end of an English word such as *cookiar* for cook, *watchar* for watch, *parkiar* for park, and *rapiar* for rape, is the result of the pressures on Spanish speakers to adapt to English.

We don't use the word *vosotros/as* or its accompanying verb form. We don't say *claro* (to mean yes), *imagínate,* or *me emociona,* unless we picked up Spanish from Latinas, out of a book, or in a classroom. Other Spanish-speaking groups are going through the same, or similar, development in their Spanish.

LINGUISTIC TERRORISM

> *Deslenguadas. Somos los del español deficiente.* We are your linguistic nightmare, your linguistic aberration, your linguistic *mestisaje,* the subject of your *burla.* Because we speak with tongues of fire we are culturally crucified. Racially, culturally, and linguistically *somos huérfanos*—we speak an orphan tongue.

Chicanas who grew up speaking Chicano Spanish have internalized the belief that we speak poor Spanish. It is illegitimate, a bastard language. And because we internalize how our language has been used against us by the dominant culture, we use our language differences against each other.

Chicana feminists often skirt around each other with suspicion and hesitation. For the longest time I couldn't figure it out. Then it dawned on me. To be close to another Chicana is like looking into the mirror. We are afraid of what we'll see there. *Pena.* Shame. Low estimation of self. In childhood we are told that our language is wrong. Repeated attacks on our native tongue diminish our sense of self. The attacks continue throughout our lives.

Chicanas feel uncomfortable talking in Spanish to Latinas, afraid of their censure. Their language was not outlawed in their countries. They had a whole lifetime of being immersed in their native tongue; generations, centuries in which Spanish was a first language, taught in school, heard on radio and TV, and read in the newspaper.

If a person, Chicana or Latina, has a low estimation of my native tongue, she also has a low estimation of me. Often with *mexicanas y latinas* we'll speak English as a neutral language. Even among Chicanas we tend to speak English at parties or conferences. Yet, at the same time, we're afraid the other will think we're *agringadas* because we don't speak Chicano Spanish. We oppress each other trying to out-Chicano each other, vying to be the "real" Chicanas, to speak like Chicanos. There is no one Chicano language just as there is no one Chicano experience. A monolingual Chicana whose first language is English or Spanish is just as much a Chicana as one who speaks several variants of Spanish. A Chicana from Michigan or Chicago or Detroit is just as much a Chicana as one from the Southwest. Chicano Spanish is as diverse linguistically as it is regionally.

By the end of this century, Spanish speakers will comprise the biggest minority group in the United States, a country where students in high schools and colleges are encouraged to take French classes because French is considered more "cultured." But for a language to remain alive it must be used. By the end of this century English, and not Spanish, will be the mother tongue of most Chicanos and Latinos.

So, if you want to really hurt me, talk badly about my language. Ethnic identity is twin skin to linguistic identity—I am my language. Until I can take pride in my language, I cannot take pride in myself. Until I can accept as legitimate Chicano Texas Spanish, Tex-Mex, and all the other languages I speak, I cannot accept the legitimacy of myself. Until I am free to write bilingually and to switch codes without having always to translate, while I still have to speak English or Spanish when I would rather speak Spanglish, and as long as I have to accommodate the English speakers rather than having them accommodate me, my tongue will be illegitimate.

I will no longer be made to feel ashamed of existing. I will have my voice: Indian, Spanish, white. I will have my serpent's tongue—my woman's voice, my sexual voice, my poet's voice. I will overcome the tradition of silence.

> My fingers
> move sly against your palm
> Like women everywhere, we speak in code.
> MELANIE KAYE/KANTROWITZ

"Vistas," corridos, y comida:

MY NATIVE TONGUE

In the 1960s, I read my first Chicano novel. It was *City of Night* by John Rechy, a gay Texan, son of a Scottish father and a Mexican mother. For days I walked around in stunned amazement that a Chicano could write and could get published. When I read *I Am Joaquín* I was surprised to see a bilingual book by a Chicano in print. When I saw poetry written in Tex-Mex for the first time, a feeling of pure joy flashed through me. I felt like we really existed as a people. In 1971, when I started teaching High School English to Chicano students, I tried to supplement the required texts with works by Chicanos, only to be reprimanded and forbidden to do so by the principal. He claimed that I was supposed to teach "American" and English literature. At the risk of being fired, I swore my students to secrecy and slipped in Chicano short stories, poems, a play. In graduate school, while working toward a Ph.D., I had to "argue" with one adviser after the other, semester after semester, before I was allowed to make Chicano literature an area of focus.

Even before I read books by Chicanos or Mexicans, it was the Mexican movies I saw at the drive-in—the Thursday night special of $1.00 a carload—that gave me a sense of belonging. *"Vámonos a las vistas,"* my mother would call out and we'd all—grandmother, brothers, sister, and cousins—squeeze into the car. We'd wolf down cheese and bologna white bread sandwiches while watching Pedro Infante in melodramatic tearjerkers like *Nosotros los pobres,* the first "real" Mexican movie (that was not an imitation of European movies). I remember seeing *Cuando los hijos se van* and surmising that all Mexican movies played up the love a mother has for her children and what ungrateful sons and daughters suffer when they are not devoted to their mothers. I remember the singing-type "westerns" of Jorge Negrete and Miquel Aceves Mejía. When watching Mexican movies, I felt a sense of homecoming as well as alienation. People who were to amount to something didn't go to Mexican movies, or *bailes,* or tune their radios to *bolero, rancherita,* and *corrido* music.

The whole time I was growing up, there was *norteño* music sometimes called North Mexican border music, or Tex-Mex music, or Chicano music, or *cantina* (bar) music. I grew up listening to *conjuntos,* three- or four-piece bands made up of folk musicians playing guitar, *bajo sexto,* drums, and button accordion, which Chicanos had borrowed from the German immigrants who had come to Central Texas and Mexico to farm and build breweries. In the Rio Grande Valley, Steve Jordan and Little Joe Hernández were popular, and Flaco Jiménez was the accordion king. The rhythms of Tex-Mex music are those of the polka, also adapted from the Germans, who in turn had borrowed the polka from the Czechs and Bohemians.

I remember the hot, sultry evenings when *corridos*—songs of love and death on the Texas-Mexican borderlands—reverberated out of cheap amplifiers from the local *cantinas* and wafted in through my bedroom window.

Corridos first became widely used along the South Texas/Mexican border during the early conflict between Chicanos and Anglos. The *corridos* are usually about Mexican heroes who do valiant deeds against the Anglo oppressors. Pancho Villa's song, *"La cucaracha,"* is the most famous one. *Corridos* of John F. Kennedy and his death are still very popular in the Valley. Older Chicanos remember Lydia Mendoza, one of the great border *corrido* singers who was called *la Gloria de Tejas.* Her *"El tango negro,"* sung during the Great Depression, made her a singer of the people. The ever-present *corridos* narrated one hundred years of border history, bringing news of events as well as entertaining. These folk musicians and folk songs are our chief cultural mythmakers, and they made our hard lives seem bearable.

I grew up feeling ambivalent about our music. Country-western and rock-and-roll had more status. In the fifties and sixties, for the slightly educated and *agringado* Chicanos, there existed a sense of shame at being caught listening to our music. Yet I couldn't stop my feet from thumping to the music, could not stop humming the words, nor hide from myself the exhilaration I felt when I heard it.

There are more subtle ways that we internalize identification, especially in the forms of images and emotions. For me food and certain smells are tied to my identity, to my homeland. Woodsmoke curling up to an immense blue sky; woodsmoke perfuming my grandmother's clothes, her skin. The stench of cow manure and the yellow patches on the ground; the crack of a .22 rifle and the reek of cordite. Homemade white cheese sizzling in a pan, melting inside a folded *tortilla*. My sister Hilda's hot, spicy *menudo, chile colorado* making it deep red, pieces of *panza* and hominy floating on top. My brother Carito barbequing *fajitas* in the backyard. Even now and 3,000 miles away, I can see my mother spicing the ground beef, pork, and venison with *chile*. My mouth salivates at the thought of the hot steaming *tamales* I would be eating if I were home.

Si le preguntas a mi mamá, "¿Qué eres?"

> Identity is the essential core of who we are as individuals, the conscious experience of the self inside.
>
> GERSHEN KAUFMAN

Nosotros los Chicanos straddle the borderlands. On one side of us, we are constantly exposed to the Spanish of the Mexicans, on the other side we hear the Anglos' incessant clamoring so that we forget our language. Among ourselves we don't say *nosotros los americanos, o nosotros los españoles, o nosotros los hispanos.* We say *nosotros los mexicanos* (by *mexicanos* we do not mean citizens of Mexico; we do not mean a national identity, but a racial one). We distinguish between *mexicanos del otro lado* and *mexicanos de este lado.* Deep in our hearts we believe that being Mexican has nothing to do with which country one lives in. Being Mexican is a state of soul—not one of mind, not one of citizenship. Neither eagle nor serpent, but both. And like the ocean, neither animal respects borders.

Dime con quien and as y te diré quien eres.
(Tell me who your friends are and I'll tell you who you are.)

MEXICAN SAYING

Si le preguntas a mi mamá, "¿Qué eres?" te dirá, "Soy mexicana." My brothers and sister say the same. I sometimes will answer *"soy mexicana"* and at others will say *"soy Chicana" o "soy tejana."* But I identified as *"Raza"* before I ever identified as *"mexicana"* or "Chicana."

As a culture, we call ourselves Spanish when referring to ourselves as a linguistic group and when copping out. It is then that we forget our predominant Indian genes. We are 70–80 percent Indian. We call ourselves Hispanic or Spanish-American or Latin American or Latin when linking ourselves to other Spanish-speaking peoples of the Western hemisphere and when copping out. We call ourselves Mexican-American to signify we are neither Mexican nor American, but more the noun "American" than the adjective "Mexican" (and when copping out).

Chicanos and other people of color suffer economically for not acculturating. This voluntary (yet forced) alienation makes for psychological conflict, a kind of dual identity—we don't identify with the Anglo-American cultural values and we don't totally identify with the Mexican cultural values. We are a synergy of two cultures with various degrees of Mexicanness or Angloness. I have so internalized the borderland conflict that sometimes I feel like one cancels out the other and we are zero, nothing, no one. *A veces no soy nada ni nadie. Pero hasta cuando no lo soy, lo soy.*

When not copping out, when we know we are more than nothing, we call ourselves Mexican, referring to race and ancestry; *mestizo* when affirming both our Indian and Spanish (but we hardly ever own our Black) ancestry; *Chicano* when referring to a politically aware people born and/or raised in the United States; *Raza* when referring to Chicanos; *tejanos* when we are Chicanos from Texas.

Chicanos did not know we were a people until 1965 when Cesar Chavez and the farmworkers united and *I Am Joaquín* was published and *la Raza Unida* party was formed in Texas. With that recognition, we became a distinct people. Something momentous happened to the Chicano soul—we became aware of our reality and acquired a name and a language (Chicano Spanish) that reflected that reality. Now that we had a name, some of the fragmented pieces began to fall together—who we were, what we were, how we had evolved. We began to get glimpses of what we might eventually become.

Yet the struggle of identities continues, the struggle of borders is our reality still. One day the inner struggle will cease and a true integration take place. In the meantime, *tenémos que hacer la lucha. ¿Quién está protegiendo los ranchos de mi gente? ¿Quién está tratando de cerrar la fisura entre la india y el blanco en nuestra sangre? El Chicano, si, el Chicano que anda como un ladrón en su propia casa.*

Los Chicanos, how patient we seem, how very patient. There is the quiet of the Indian about us. We know how to survive. When other races have given up their tongue we've kept ours. We know what it is to live under the hammer blow of the dominant *norteamericano* culture. But more than we count the blows, we count the days the weeks the years the centuries the aeons until the white laws and commerce and customs will rot in the deserts they've created, lie bleached. *Humildes* yet proud, *quietos* yet wild, *nosotros los mexicanos-Chicanos* will walk by the crumbling ashes as we go about our business. Stubborn, persevering, impenetrable as stone, yet possessing a malleability that renders us unbreakable, we, the *mestizas* and *mestizos,* will remain.

CONSIDERATIONS

Thinking

What argument does Anzaldúa make for the need for a Chicano Spanish? Why does she characterize it as "a forked tongue"? And why does she say that "often it is only with another Chicana *tejano* that [she] can talk freely"?

What cultural values are associated with the different languages and dialects Anzaldúa describes? Which are most important to her and why?

Connecting

To what extent does Anzaldúa's discussion of her languages reflect your own linguistic experience? Did you find yourself connected to or disconnected from her discourse? Where, especially, and why?

Relate what Anzaldúa says about language to what Amy Tan says about her "Englishes" in "Mother Tongue."

Writing

Write an essay describing, illustrating, and exploring the different languages or dialects you use. Explain where and when you use them, with whom you use them, and why.

*J*ames Baldwin
(1924–1987)

James Baldwin was born in Harlem and became, at fourteen, a preacher. At seventeen, he abandoned the ministry and devoted himself to the craft of writing. Baldwin received institutional support in the form of fellowships to help sustain him while he wrote his first two novels: *Go Tell It on the Mountain* (1953) and *Giovanni's Room* (1956). Sandwiched between these two works was a collection of essays, *Notes of a Native Son* (1955), which many readers consider his finest work.

In his essays, Baldwin struggled to define himself as an American, as a writer, and as a black man, all of which, for Baldwin, were inextricably intertwined. In coming to terms with what was the most difficult thing in his life (his blackness), Baldwin revealed himself to be a passionate and eloquent writer, whose most frequent subject has been the relations between the races.

Notes of a Native Son provides a perspective on a series of personal experiences and public events that led Baldwin to understand the destructive power of hatred and its threat to destroy his own life. The essays are remarkable for their descriptive power and rhetorical eloquence.

In "Stranger in the Village," Baldwin describes a period of time he spent in a Swiss mountain village—the only black man the villagers had ever encountered. He conveys a sense of his differentness and in the process raises questions about the extent to which a black man can ever be fully a part of European culture.

Stranger in the Village

From all available evidence no black man had ever set foot in this tiny Swiss village before I came. I was told before arriving that I would probably be a "sight" for the village; I took this to mean that people of my complexion were rarely seen in Switzerland, and also that city people are always something of a "sight" outside of the city. It did not occur to me—possibly because I am an American—that there could be people anywhere who had never seen a Negro.

It is a fact that cannot be explained on the basis of the inaccessibility of the village. The village is very high, but it is only four hours from Milan and three hours from Lausanne. It is true that it is virtually unknown. Few people making plans for a holiday would elect to come here. On the other hand, the villagers are able, presumably, to come and go as they please—which they do: to another town at the foot of the mountain, with a population of approximately five thousand, the nearest place to see a movie or go to the bank. In the village there is no movie house, no bank, no library, no theater; very few radios, one jeep, one station wagon; and, at the moment, one typewriter, mine, an invention which the woman next door to me here had never seen. There are about six hundred people living here, all Catholic—I conclude this from the fact that the Catholic church is open all year round, whereas the Protestant chapel, set off on a hill a little removed from the village, is open only in the summertime when the tourists arrive. There are four or five hotels, all closed now, and four or five bistros, of which, however, only two do any business during the winter. These two do not do a great deal, for life in the village seems to end around nine or ten o'clock. There are a few stores, butcher, baker, *épicerie*, a hardware store, and a money-changer—who cannot change travelers' checks, but must send them down to the bank, an operation which takes two or three days. There is something called the *Ballet Haus,* closed in the winter and used for God knows what, certainly not ballet, during the summer. There seems to be only one schoolhouse in the village, and this for the quite young children; I suppose this to mean that their older brothers and sisters at some point descend from these mountains in order to complete their education—possibly, again, to the town just below. The landscape

146

is absolutely forbidding, mountains towering on all four sides, ice and snow as far as the eye can reach. In this white wilderness, men and women and children move all day, carrying washing, wood, buckets of milk or water, sometimes skiing on Sunday afternoons. All week long boys and young men are to be seen shoveling snow off the rooftops, or dragging wood down from the forest in sleds.

The village's only real attraction, which explains the tourist season, is the hot spring water. A disquietingly high proportion of these tourists are cripples, or semi-cripples, who come year after year—from other parts of Switzerland, usually—to take the waters. This lends the village, at the height of the season, a rather terrifying air of sanctity, as though it were a lesser Lourdes. There is often something beautiful, there is always something awful, in the spectacle of a person who has lost one of his faculties, a faculty he never questioned until it was gone, and who struggles to recover it. Yet people remain people, on crutches or indeed on deathbeds; and wherever I passed, the first summer I was here, among the native villagers or among the lame, a wind passed with me—of astonishment, curiosity, amusement, and outrage. That first summer I stayed two weeks and never intended to return. But I did return in the winter, to work; the village offers, obviously, no distractions whatever and has the further advantage of being extremely cheap. Now it is winter again, a year later, and I am here again. Everyone in the village knows my name, though they scarcely ever use it, knows that I come from America—though, this, apparently, they will never really believe: black men come from Africa—and everyone knows that I am the friend of the son of a woman who was born here, and that I am staying in their chalet. But I remain as much a stranger today as I was the first day I arrived, and the children shout *Neger! Neger!* as I walk along the streets.

It must be admitted that in the beginning I was far too shocked to have any real reaction. In so far as I reacted at all, I reacted by trying to be pleasant—it being a great part of the American Negro's education (long before he goes to school) that he must make people "like" him. This smile-and-the-world-smiles-with-you routine worked about as well in this situation as it had in the situation for which it was designed, which is to say that it did not work at all. No one, after all, can be liked whose human weight and complexity cannot be, or has not been, admitted. My smile was simply another unheard-of phenomenon which allowed them to see my teeth—they did not, really, see my smile and I began to think that, should I take to snarling, no one would notice any difference. All of the physical characteristics of the Negro which had caused me, in America, a very different and almost forgotten pain were nothing less than miraculous—or infernal—in the eyes of the village people. Some thought my hair was the color of tar, that it had the texture of wire, or the texture of cotton. It was jocularly suggested that I might let it all grow long and make myself a winter coat. If I sat in the sun for more than five minutes some daring creature was certain to come along and gingerly put his fingers on my hair, as though he were afraid of an electric shock, or put his hand on my hand, astonished that the color did not rub off. In all of this, in which it must be conceded there was the charm of genuine wonder and in which there was certainly no element of intentional unkindness, there was yet no suggestion that I was human: I was simply a living wonder.

I knew that they did not mean to be unkind, and I know it now; it is necessary, nevertheless, for me to repeat this to myself each time I walk out of the chalet. The children who shout *Neger!* have no way of knowing the echoes this sound raises in me. They are brimming with good humor and the more daring swell with pride when I stop to speak with them. Just the same, there are days when I cannot pause and smile, when I have no heart to play with them; when, indeed, I mutter sourly to myself, exactly as I muttered on the streets of a city these children have never seen, when I was no bigger than these children are now: *Your* mother *was a nigger.* Joyce is right about history being a nightmare—but it may be the nightmare from which no one *can* awaken. People are trapped in history and history is trapped in them.

There is a custom in the village—I am told it is repeated in many villages—of "buying" African natives for the purpose of converting them to Christianity. There stands in the church all year round a small box with a slot for money, decorated with a black figurine, and into this box the villagers drop their francs. During the *carnaval* which precedes Lent, two village children have their faces blackened—out of which bloodless darkness their blue eyes shine like ice—and fantastic horsehair wigs are placed on their blond heads; thus disguised, they solicit among the villagers for money for the missionaries in Africa. Between the box in the church and the blackened children, the village "bought" last year six or eight African natives. This was reported to me with pride by the wife of one of the bistro owners and I was careful to express astonishment and pleasure at the solicitude shown by the village for the souls of black folk. The bistro owner's wife beamed with a pleasure far more genuine than my own and seemed to feel that I might now breathe more easily concerning the souls of at least six of my kinsmen.

I tried not to think of these so lately baptized kinsmen, of the price paid for them, or the peculiar price they themselves would pay, and said nothing about my father, who having taken his own conversion too literally never, at bottom, forgave the white world (which he described as heathen) for having saddled him with a Christ in whom, to judge at least from their treatment of him, they themselves no longer believed. I thought of white men arriving for the first time in an African village, strangers there, as I am a stranger here, and tried to imagine the astounded populace touching their hair and marveling at the color of their skin. But there is a great difference between being the first white man to be seen by Africans and being the first black man to be seen by whites. The white man takes the astonishment as tribute, for he arrives to conquer and to convert the natives, whose inferiority in relation to himself is not even to be questioned; whereas I, without a thought of conquest, find myself among a people whose culture controls me, has even, in a sense, created me, people who have cost me more in anguish and rage than they will ever know, who yet do not even know of my existence. The astonishment with which I might have greeted them, should they have stumbled into my African village a few hundred years ago, might have rejoiced their hearts. But the astonishment with which they greet me today can only poison mine.

And this is so despite everything I may do to feel differently, despite my friendly conversations with the bistro owner's wife, despite their three-year-old son who has at last become my friend, despite the *saluts* and *bonsoirs* which I exchange with people as I walk, despite the fact that I know that no individual can be taken to task for what history is doing, or has done. I say that the culture of these people controls me—but they can scarcely be held responsible for European culture. America comes out of Europe, but these people have never seen America, nor have most of them seen more of Europe than the hamlet at the foot of their mountain. Yet they move with an authority which I shall never have; and they regard me, quite rightly, not only as a stranger in their village but as a suspect latecomer, bearing no credentials, to everything they have—however unconsciously—inherited.

For this village, even were it incomparably more remote and incredibly more primitive, is the West, the West onto which I have been so strangely grafted. These people cannot be, from the point of view of power, strangers anywhere in the world; they have made the modern world, in effect, even if they do not know it. The most illiterate among them is related, in a way that I am not, to Dante, Shakespeare, Michelangelo, Aeschylus, Da Vinci, Rembrandt, and Racine; the cathedral at Chartres says something to them which it cannot say to me, as indeed would New York's Empire State Building, should anyone here ever see it. Out of their hymns and dances come Beethoven and Bach. Go back a few centuries and they are in their full glory—but I am in Africa, watching the conquerors arrive.

The rage of the disesteemed is personally fruitless, but it is also absolutely inevitable; this rage, so generally discounted, so little understood even among the people whose daily bread it is, is one of the things that makes history. Rage can only with difficulty, and never entirely, be brought under the domination of the intelligence and is therefore not susceptible to any arguments whatever. This is a fact which ordinary representatives of the *Herrenvolk,* having never felt this rage and being unable to imagine it, quite fail to understand. Also, rage cannot be hidden, it can only be dissembled. This dissembling deludes the thoughtless, and strengthens rage, and adds, to rage, contempt. There are, no doubt, as many ways of coping with the resulting complex of tensions as there are black men in the world, but no black man can hope ever to be entirely liberated from this internal warfare—rage, dissembling, and contempt having inevitably accompanied his first realization of the power of white men. What is crucial here is that, since white men represent in the black man's world so heavy a weight, white men have for black men a reality which is far from being reciprocal; and hence all black men have toward all white men an attitude which is designed, really, either to rob the white man of the jewel of his naïveté, or else to make it cost him dear.

The black man insists, by whatever means he finds at his disposal, that the white man cease to regard him as an exotic rarity and recognize him as a human being. This is a very charged and difficult moment, for there is a great deal of will power involved in the white man's naïveté. Most people are not naturally reflective any more than they are naturally malicious, and the white man prefers to keep the black man at a certain human remove because it is easier for him thus to preserve his simplicity and avoid being called to account for crimes committed by his forefathers, or his neighbors. He is inescapably aware, nevertheless, that he is in a better position in the world than black men are, nor can he quite put to death the suspicion that he is hated by black men therefore. He does not wish to be hated, neither does he wish to change places, and at this point in his uneasiness he can scarcely avoid having recourse to those legends which white men have created about black men, the most usual effect of which is that the white man finds himself enmeshed, so to speak, in his own language which describes hell, as well as the attributes which lead one to hell, as being as black as night.

Every legend, moreover, contains its residuum of truth, and the root function of language is to control the universe by describing it. It is of quite considerable significance that black men remain, in the imagination, and in overwhelming numbers in fact, beyond the disciplines of salvation; and this despite the fact that the West has been "buying" African natives for centuries. There is, I should hazard, an instantaneous necessity to be divorced from this so visibly unsaved stranger, in whose heart, moreover, one cannot guess what dreams of vengeance are being nourished; and, at the same time, there are few things on earth more attractive than the idea of the unspeakable liberty which is allowed the unredeemed. When, beneath the black mask, a human being begins to make himself felt one cannot escape a certain awful wonder as to what kind of human being it is. What one's imagination makes of other people is dictated, of course, by the laws of one's own personality and it is one of the ironies of black-white relations that, by means of what the white man imagines the black man to be, the black man is enabled to know who the white man is.

I have said, for example, that I am as much a stranger in this village today as I was the first summer I arrived, but this is not quite true. The villagers wonder less about the texture of my hair than they did then, and wonder rather more about me. And the fact that their wonder now exists on another level is reflected in their attitudes and in their eyes. There are the children who make those delightful, hilarious, sometimes astonishing grave overtures of friendship in the unpredictable fashion of children; other children, having been taught that the devil is a black man, scream in genuine anguish as I approach. Some of the older women never pass without a friendly greeting, never pass, indeed, if it seems that they will be able to engage me in conversation; other women look down or look away or rather contemptuously smirk. Some of the men drink with me and suggest that I learn how to ski—partly, I gather, because they cannot imagine what I would look like on skis—and want to know if I am married, and ask questions about my métier. But some of the men have accused *le sale nègre*—behind my back—of stealing wood and there is already in the eyes of some of them that peculiar intent, paranoiac malevolence which one sometimes surprises in the eyes of American white men when, out walking with their Sunday girl, they see a Negro male approach.

There is a dreadful abyss between the streets of this village and the streets of the city in which I was born, between the children who shout

Neger! today and those who shouted *Nigger!* yesterday—the abyss is experience, the American experience. The syllable hurled behind me today expresses, above all, wonder: I am a stranger here. But I am not a stranger in America and the same syllable riding on the American air expresses the war my presence has occasioned in the American soul.

For this village brings home to me this fact: that there was a day, and not really a very distant day, when Americans were scarcely Americans at all but discontented Europeans, facing a great unconquered continent and strolling, say, into a marketplace and seeing black men for the first time. The shock this spectacle afforded is suggested, surely, by the promptness with which they decided that these black men were not really men but cattle. It is true that the necessity on the part of the settlers of the New World of reconciling their moral assumptions with the fact—and the necessity—of slavery enhanced immensely the charm of this idea, and it is also true that this idea expresses, with a truly American bluntness, the attitude which to varying extents all masters have had toward all slaves.

But between all former slaves and slave-owners and the drama which begins for Americans over three hundred years ago at Jamestown, there are at least two differences to be observed. The American Negro slave could not suppose, for one thing, as slaves in past epochs had supposed and often done, that he would ever be able to wrest the power from his master's hands. This was a supposition which the modern era, which was to bring about such vast changes in the aims and dimensions of power, put to death; it only begins, in unprecedented fashion, and with dreadful implications, to be resurrected today. But even had this supposition persisted with undiminished force, the American Negro slave could not have used it to lend his condition dignity, for the reason that this supposition rests on another: that the slave in exile yet remains related to his past, has some means—if only in memory—of revering and sustaining the forms of his former life, is able, in short, to maintain his identity.

This was not the case with the American Negro slave. His is unique among the black men of the world in that his past was taken from him, almost literally, at one blow. One wonders what on earth the first slave found to say to the first dark child he bore. I am told that there are Haitians able to trace their ancestry back to African kings, but any American Negro wishing to go back so far will find his journey through time abruptly arrested by the signature on the bill of sale which served as the entrance paper for his ancestor. At the time—to say nothing of the circumstances—of the enslavement of the captive black man who was to become the American Negro, there was not the remotest possibility that he would ever take power from his master's hands. There was no reason to suppose that his situation would ever change, nor was there, shortly, anything to indicate that his situation had ever been different. It was his necessity, in the words of E. Franklin Frazier, to find a "motive for living under American culture or die." The identity of the American Negro comes out of this extreme situation, and the evolution of this identity was a source of the most intolerable anxiety in the minds and the lives of his masters.

For the history of the American Negro is unique also in this: that the question of his humanity, and of his rights therefore as a human being, became a burning one for several generations of Americans, so burning a question that it ultimately became one of those used to divide the nation. It is out of this argument that the venom of the epithet *Nigger!* is derived. It is an argument which Europe has never had, and hence Europe quite sincerely fails to understand how or why the argument arose in the first place, why its effects are so frequently disastrous and always so unpredictable, why it refuses until today to be entirely settled. Europe's black possessions remained—and do remain—in Europe's colonies, at which remove they represented no threat to European identity. If they posed any problem at all for the European conscience, it was a problem which remained comfortingly abstract: in effect, the black man, *as a man*, did not exist for Europe. But in America, even as a slave, he was an inescapable part of the general social fabric and no American could escape having an attitude toward him. Americans attempt until today to make an abstraction of the Negro, but the very nature of these abstractions reveals the tremendous effects the presence of the Negro has had on the American character.

When one considers the history of the Negro in America it is of the greatest importance to recognize that the moral beliefs of a person, or a people, are never really as tenuous as life—which is not moral—very often causes them to appear; these create for them a frame of reference and a necessary hope, the hope being that when life has done its worst they will be enabled to rise above themselves and to triumph over life. Life would scarcely be bearable if this hope did not exist. Again, even when the worst has been said, to betray a belief is not by any means to have put oneself beyond its power; the betrayal of a belief is not the same thing as ceasing to believe. If this were not so there would be no moral standards in the world at all. Yet one must also recognize that morality is based on ideas and that all ideas are dangerous—dangerous because ideas can only lead to action and where the action leads no man can say. And dangerous in this respect: that confronted with the impossibility of remaining faithful to one's beliefs, and the equal impossibility of becoming free of them, one can be driven to the most inhuman excesses. The ideas on which American beliefs are based are not, though Americans often seem to think so, ideas which originated in America. They came out of Europe. And the establishment of democracy on the American continent was scarcely as radical a break with the past as was the necessity, which Americans faced, of broadening this concept to include black men.

This was, literally, a hard necessity. It was impossible, for one thing, for Americans to abandon their beliefs, not only because these beliefs alone seemed able to justify the sacrifices they had endured and the blood that they had spilled, but also because these beliefs afforded them their only bulwark against a moral chaos as absolute as the physical chaos of the continent it was their destiny to conquer. But in the situation in which Americans found themselves, these beliefs threatened an idea which, whether or not one likes to think so, is the very warp and woof of the heritage of the West, the idea of white supremacy.

Americans have made themselves notorious by the shrillness and the brutality with which they have insisted on this idea, but they did not invent it; and it has escaped the world's notice that those very excesses of which Americans have been guilty imply a certain, unprecedented uneasiness over the idea's life and power, if not, indeed, the idea's validity. The idea of white supremacy rests simply on the fact that white men are the creators of civilization (the present civilization, which is the only one that matters; all previous civilizations are simply "contributions" to our own) and are therefore civilization's guardians and defenders. Thus it was impossible for Americans to accept the black man as one of themselves, for to do so was to jeopardize their status as white men. But not so to accept him was to deny his human reality, his human weight and complexity, and the strain of denying the overwhelmingly undeniable forced Americans into rationalizations so fantastic that they approached the pathological.

At the root of the American Negro problem is the necessity of the American white man to find a way of living with the Negro in order to be able to live with himself. And the history of this problem can be reduced to the means used by Americans—lynch law and law, segregation and legal acceptance, terrorization and concession—either to come to terms with this necessity, or to find a way around it, or (most usually) to find a way of doing both these things at once. The resulting spectacle, at once foolish and dreadful, led someone to make the quite accurate observation that "the Negro-in-America is a form of insanity which overtakes white men."

In this long battle, a battle by no means finished, the unforeseeable effects of which will be felt by many future generations, the white man's motive was the protection of his identity; the black man was motivated by the need to establish an identity. And despite the terrorization which the Negro in America endured and endures sporadically until today, despite the cruel and totally inescapable ambivalence of his status in his country, the battle for his identity has long ago been won. He is not a visitor to the West, but a citizen there, an American, as American as the Americans who despise him, the Americans who fear him, the Americans who love him— the Americans who became less than themselves, or rose to be greater than themselves by virtue of the fact that the challenge he represented was inescapable. He is perhaps the only black man in the world whose relationship to white men is more terrible, more subtle, and more meaningful than the relationship of bitter possessed to uncertain possessor. His survival depended, and his development depends, on his ability to turn his peculiar status in the Western world to his own advantage and, it may be, to the very great advantage of that world. It remains for him to fashion out of his experience that which will give him sustenance, and a voice.

The cathedral of Chartres, I have said, says something to the people of this village which it cannot say to me; but it is important to understand that this cathedral says something to me which it cannot say to them. Perhaps they are struck by the power of the spires, the glory of the windows; but they have known God, after all, longer than I have known him, and in a different way, and I am terrified by the slippery bottomless well to be found in the crypt, down which heretics were hurled to death, and by the obscene, inescapable gargoyles jutting out of the stone and seeming to say that God and the devil can never be divorced. I doubt that the villagers think of the devil when they face a cathedral because they have never been identified with the devil. But I must accept the status which myth, if nothing else, gives me in the West before I can hope to change the myth.

Yet, if the American Negro has arrived at his identity by virtue of the absoluteness of his estrangement from his past, American white men still nourish the illusion that there is some means of recovering the European innocence, of returning to a state in which black men do not exist. This is one of the greatest errors Americans can make. The identity they fought so hard to protect has, by virtue of that battle, undergone a change: Americans are as unlike any other white people in the world as it is possible to be. I do not think, for example, that it is too much to suggest that the American vision of the world—which allows so little reality, generally speaking, for any of the darker forces in human life, which tends until today to paint moral issues in glaring black and white—owes a great deal to the battle waged by Americans to maintain between themselves and black men a human separation which could not be bridged. It is only now beginning to be borne in on us—very faintly, it must be admitted, very slowly, and very much against our will—that this vision of the world is dangerously inaccurate, and perfectly useless. For it protects our moral high-mindedness at the terrible expense of weakening our grasp of reality. People who shut their eyes to reality simply invite their own destruction, and anyone who insists on remaining in a state of innocence long after that innocence is dead turns himself into a monster.

The time has come to realize that the interracial drama acted out on the American continent has not only created a new black man, it has created a new white man, too. No road whatever will lead Americans back to the simplicity of this European village where white men still have the luxury of looking on me as a stranger. I am not, really, a stranger any longer for any American alive. One of the things that distinguishes Americans from other people is that no other people has ever been so deeply involved in the lives of black men, and vice versa. This fact faced, with all its implications, it can be seen that the history of the American Negro problem is not merely shameful, it is also something of an achievement. For even when the worst has been said, it must also be added that the perpetual challenge posed by this problem was always, somehow, perpetually met. It is precisely this black-white experience which may prove of indispensable value to us in the world we face today. This world is white no longer, and it will never be white again.

CONSIDERATIONS

Thinking

In what ways was Baldwin a "stranger" in the Swiss village? What does his experience in Europe contribute to his understanding of race relations in America?

How important are the historical references Baldwin includes? What is their purpose?

Connecting

Relate what Baldwin says about race in this essay with what he says in *Notes of a Native Son*.

Compare Baldwin's feeling of displacement with that described by Brent Staples in "Just Walk on By."

Writing

Write an essay describing an experience in which you felt yourself to be something of a stranger or an outsider. Try to account for the sense of difference you experienced.

Write an essay about a place you lived in or visited for a short time. Try to account for what the place and its people were like.

J ohn Berger (b.1926)

J ohn Berger is a writer and a critic of international repute. His books
include the novels *G* and *A Fortunate Man,* and the critical works
About Looking and *Ways of Seeing*—among a number of others. His art
criticism is animated by a social and cultural critical impulse. He aims to
see works of art in context, considering the societal values they embody,
and encouraging his readers to see such works in relation to other images
from contemporary life, especially those in film, advertising, and
photography.

The following selection, "Ways of Seeing: Men Looking at Women,"
is excerpted from Berger's brief but insightful book about the cultural
values revealed and concealed in western art. Berger focuses here on
ways women see themselves in the regard of men, and how men's looking at women influences the ways they look at themselves.

FELIX TRUTAT, *RECLINING BACCHANTE,* 1845. MUSÉE DES BEAUX-ARTS, DIJON.

Ways of Seeing:
Men Looking at Women

According to usage and conventions which are at last being questioned but have by no means been overcome, the social presence of a woman is different in kind from that of a man. A man's presence is dependent upon the promise of power which he embodies. If the promise is large and credible his presence is striking. If it is small or incredible, he is found to have little presence. The promised power may be moral, physical, temperamental, economic, social, sexual—but its object is always exterior to the man. A man's presence suggests what he is capable of doing to you or for you. His presence may be fabricated, in the sense that he pretends to be capable of what he is not. But the pretense is always towards a power which he exercises on others.

By contrast, a woman's presence expresses her own attitude to herself, and defines what can and cannot be done to her. Her presence is manifest in her gestures, voice, opinions, expressions, clothes, chosen surroundings, taste—indeed there is nothing she can do which does not contribute to her presence. Presence for a woman is so intrinsic to her person that men tend to think of it as an almost physical emanation, a kind of heat or smell or aura.

To be born a woman has been to be born, within an allotted and confined space, into the keeping of men. The social presence of women has developed as a result of their ingenuity in living under such tutelage within such a limited space. But this has been at the cost of a woman's self being split into two. A woman must continually watch herself. She is almost continually accompanied by her own image of herself. Whilst she is walking across a room or whilst she is weeping at the death of her father, she can scarcely avoid envisaging herself walking or weeping. From earliest childhood she has been taught and persuaded to survey herself continually.

And so she comes to consider the *surveyor* and the *surveyed* within her as the two constituent yet always distinct elements of her identity as a woman.

She has to survey everything she is and everything she does because how she appears to others, and ultimately how she appears to men, is of crucial importance for what is normally thought of as the success of her life. Her own sense of being in herself is supplanted by a sense of being appreciated as herself by another.

Men survey women before treating them. Consequently how a woman appears to a man can determine how she will be treated. To acquire some control over this process, women must contain it and interiorize it. That part of a woman's self which is the surveyor treats the part which is the surveyed so as to demonstrate to others how her whole self would like to be treated. And this exemplary treatment of herself by herself constitutes her presence. Every woman's presence regulates what is and is not 'permissible' within her presence. Every one of her actions— whatever its direct purpose or motivation—is also read as an indication of how she would like to be treated. If a woman throws a glass on the floor, this is an example of how she treats her own emotion of anger and so of how she would wish it to be treated by others. If a man does the same, his action is only read as an expression of his anger. If a woman makes a good joke this is an example of how she treats the joker in herself and accordingly of how she as a joker woman would like to be treated by others. Only a man can make a good joke for its own sake.

One might simplify this by saying: *men act* and *women appear.* Men look at women. Women watch themselves being looked at. This determines not only most relations between men and women but also the relation of women to themselves. The surveyor of woman in herself is male: the surveyed female. Thus she turns herself into an object—and most particularly an object of vision: a sight.

CONSIDERATIONS

Thinking

What distinction does Berger make with regard to a man's and a woman's "presence"? With regard to a man's and a woman's power? With regard to the relationship between power and presence for men and women?

How important, according to Berger, is a woman's image of herself? To what extent is her self-image influenced by the male gaze?

To what extent do you share Berger's belief that "*men act* and *women appear*"? Why?

Do women, as Berger suggests, turn themselves into objects? If so, to what extent are men complicit in that transformation? Why?

Connecting

To what extent can you, as a man or a woman, relate to what Berger says about men and women in this piece? Why?

After reading Maile Meloy's "The Voice of the Looking Glass," account for the ways in which Meloy uses Berger. Consider how you might use Meloy's techniques in your own writing.

Examine various images of women in the media, in public life, in business, and at home. To what extent do the images of women found in one or more of those places support, illustrate, or qualify Berger's ideas about women?

After reading Elizabeth MacDonald's "Odalisque" and Berger's ideas about women, what do you think Berger would have to say about "Odalisque"? Why?

Writing

Write an essay in which you examine images of women in advertising or in western painting in light of Berger's claims. You can begin with Trutat's *Reclining Bacchante* and Ingres's *La Grande Odalisque* (see the essay by Elizabeth MacDonald). You may wish to include consideration of Cassatt's *The Family* and Wood's *American Gothic* (color insert).

Write an essay in which you examine the depiction of women by one or more writers in this book, again, in light of Berger's argument. You may wish to read one essay or more than one. You may also wish to go beyond those included in the book. But for a start, look at these: Joan Didion's "Georgia O'Keeffe," Nancy Mairs's "On Being a Cripple," Alice Walker's "Beauty: When the Other Dancer Is the Self."

J udith Ortiz Cofer (b.1952)

J udith Ortiz Cofer is a novelist, poet, and essayist whose work has appeared in magazines and literary reviews such as *Glamour, The Georgia Review,* and *The Kenyon Review.* Her work includes *The Line of the Sun,* a novel; *Terms of Survival* and *Reaching for the Mainland,* poetry collections; *Peregrina,* a chapbook; and *Silent Dancing,* essays and poems. She has won fellowships from the National Endowment for the Arts, the Florida and Georgia Councils for the Arts, and the Bread Loaf Writers' Conference.

"Silent Dancing" focuses on the way imported cultural values affected the lives of Puerto Ricans who moved in the 1950s into a newly formed ethnic enclave in Paterson, New Jersey, just across the Hudson River from New York City. Cofer is especially interested in the way the new culture affects those who move into it. In "Silent Dancing" she gives us glimpses of that turmoil through a retrospective look at a home movie filmed during her childhood in her new home.

Silent Dancing

We have a home movie of this party. Several times my mother and I have watched it together, and I have asked questions about the silent revelers coming in and out of focus. It is grainy and of short duration, but it's a great visual aid to my memory of life at that time. And it is in color— the only complete scene in color I can recall from those years.

We lived in Puerto Rico until my brother was born in 1954. Soon after, because of economic pressures on our growing family, my father joined the United States Navy. He was assigned to duty on a ship in Brooklyn Yard—a place of cement and steel that was to be his home base in the States until his retirement more than twenty years later. He left the Island first, alone, going to New York City and tracking down his uncle who lived with his family across the Hudson River in Paterson, New Jersey. There my father found a tiny apartment in a huge tenement that had once housed Jewish families but was just being taken over and transformed by Puerto Ricans, overflowing from New York City. In 1955 he sent for us. My mother was only twenty years old, I was not quite three, and my brother was a toddler when we arrived at *El Building,* as the place had been christened by its newest residents.

My memories of life in Paterson during those first few years are all in shades of gray. Maybe I was too young to absorb vivid colors and details, or to discriminate between the slate blue of the winter sky and the darker hues of the snow-bearing clouds, but that single color washes over the whole period. The building we lived in was gray, as were the streets, filled with slush the first few months of my life there. The coat my father had bought for me was similar in color and too big; it sat heavily on my thin frame.

I do remember the way the heater pipes banged and rattled, startling all of us out of sleep until we got so used to the sound that we automatically shut it out or raised our voices above the racket. The hiss from the valve punctuated my sleep (which has always been fitful) like a nonhuman presence in the room—a dragon sleeping at the entrance of my childhood. But the pipes were also a connection to all the other lives being lived around us. Having come from a house designed for a single family back in Puerto Rico—my mother's extended-family home—it was curious to know that strangers lived under our floor and above our heads, and that the heater pipe went through everyone's apartments. (My first spanking in Paterson came as a result of playing tunes on the pipes in my room to see if there would be an answer.) My mother was as new to this concept of beehive life as I was, but she had been given strict orders by my father to keep the doors locked, the noise down, ourselves to ourselves.

It seems that Father had learned some painful lessons about prejudice while searching for an apartment in Paterson. Not until years later did I hear how much resistance he had encountered with landlords who were panicking at the influx of Latinos into a neighborhood that had been Jewish for a couple of generations. It made no difference that it was the American phenomenon of ethnic turnover which was changing the urban core of Paterson, and that the human flood could not be held back with an accusing finger.

"You Cuban?" one man had asked my father, pointing at his name tag on the Navy uniform—even though my father had the fair skin and light-brown hair of his northern Spanish background, and the name Ortiz is as common in Puerto Rico as Johnson is in the United States.

"No," my father had answered, looking past the finger into his adversary's angry eyes. "I'm Puerto Rican."

"Same shit." And the door closed.

My father could have passed as European, but we couldn't. My brother and I both have our mother's black hair and olive skin, and so we lived in El Building and visited our great-uncle and his fair children on the next block. It was their private joke that they were the German branch of the family. Not many years later that area too would be mainly Puerto Rican. It was as if the heart of the city map were being gradually colored brown—*café con leche*[1] brown. Our color.

The movie opens with a sweep of the living room. It is "typical" immi-grant Puerto Rican decor for the time: The sofa and chairs are square and hard-looking, upholstered in bright colors (blue and yellow in this instance), and cov-ered with the transparent plastic that furniture salesmen then were so adept at convincing women to buy. The linoleum on the floor is light blue; if it had been subjected to spike heels (as it was in most places), there were dime-sized indenta-

---

[1]*café con leche:* Coffee with cream. In Puerto Rico it is sometimes prepared with boiled milk. [All footnotes in this essay are author notes.—EDS.]

tions all over it that cannot be seen in this movie. The room is full of people dressed up: dark suits for the men, red dresses for the women. When I have asked my mother why most of the women are in red that night, she has shrugged, "I don't remember. Just a coincidence." She doesn't have my obsession for assigning symbolism to everything.

The three women in red sitting on the couch are my mother, my eighteen-year-old cousin, and her brother's girlfriend. The novia *is just up from the Island, which is apparent in her body language. She sits up formally, her dress pulled over her knees. She is a pretty girl, but her posture makes her look insecure, lost in her full-skirted dress, which she has carefully tucked around her to make room for my gorgeous cousin, her future sister-in-law. My cousin has grown up in Paterson and is in her last year of high school. She doesn't have a trace of what Puerto Ricans call* la mancha *(literally, the stain: the mark of the new immigrant—something about the posture, the voice, or the humble demeanor that makes it obvious to everyone the person has just arrived on the mainland). My cousin is wearing a tight, sequined, cocktail dress. Her brown hair has been lightened with peroxide around the bangs, and she is holding a cigarette expertly between her fingers, bringing it up to her mouth in a sensuous arc of her arm as she talks animatedly. My mother, who has come up to sit between the two women, both only a few years younger than herself, is somewhere between the poles they represent in our culture.*

It became my father's obsession to get out of the barrio, and thus we were never permitted to form bonds with the place or with the people who lived there. Yet El Building was a comfort to my mother, who never got over yearning for *la isla*. She felt surrounded by her language: The walls were thin, and voices speaking and arguing in Spanish could be heard all day. *Salsas* blasted out of radios, turned on early in the morning and left on for company. Women seemed to cook rice and beans perpetually—the strong aroma of boiling red kidney beans permeated the hallways.

Though Father preferred that we do our grocery shopping at the supermarket when he came home on weekend leaves, my mother insisted that she could cook only with products whose labels she could read. Consequently, during the week I accompanied her and my little brother to *La Bodega*—a hole-in-the-wall grocery store across the street from El Building. There we squeezed down three narrow aisles jammed with various products. Goya's and Libby's—those were the trademarks that were trusted by *her mamá*, so my mother bought many cans of Goya beans, soups, and condiments, as well as little cans of Libby's fruit juices for us.

And she also bought Colgate toothpaste and Palmolive soap. (The final *e* is pronounced in both these products in Spanish, so for many years I believed that they were manufactured on the Island. I remember my surprise at first hearing a commercial on television in which Colgate rhymed with "ate.") We always lingered at La Bodega, for it was there that Mother breathed best, taking in the familiar aromas of the foods she knew from Mamá's kitchen. It was also there that she got to speak to the other women of El Building without violating outright Father's dictates against fraternizing with our neighbors.

Yet Father did his best to make our "assimilation" painless. I can still see him carrying a real Christmas tree up several flights of stairs to our apartment, leaving a trail of aromatic pine. He carried it formally, as if it were a flag in a parade. We were the only ones in El Building that I knew of who got presents on both Christmas day AND *dia de Reyes*, the day when the Three Kings brought gifts to Christ and to Hispanic children.

Our supreme luxury in El Building was having our own television set. It must have been a result of Father's guilt feelings over the isolation he had imposed on us, but we were among the first in the barrio to have one. My brother quickly became an avid watcher of Captain Kangaroo and Jungle Jim, while I loved all the series showing families. By the time I started first grade, I could have drawn a map of Middle America as exemplified by the lives of characters in "Father Knows Best," "The Donna Reed Show," "Leave It to Beaver," "My Three Sons," and (my favorite) "Bachelor Father," where John Forsythe treated his adopted teenage daughter like a princess because he was rich and had a Chinese houseboy to do everything for him. In truth, compared to our neighbors in El Building, *we* were rich. My father's Navy check provided us with financial security and a standard of life that the factory workers envied. The only thing his money could not buy us was a place to live away from the barrio—his greatest wish, Mother's greatest fear.

In the home movie the men are shown next, sitting around a card table set up in one corner of the living room, playing dominoes. The clack of the ivory pieces was a familiar sound. I heard it in many houses on the Island and in many apartments in Paterson. In "Leave It to Beaver," the Cleavers played bridge in every other episode; in my childhood, the men started every social occasion with a hotly debated round of dominoes. The women would sit around and watch, but they never participated in the games.

Here and there you can see a small child. Children were always brought to parties and, whenever they got sleepy, were put to bed in the host's bedroom.

Babysitting was a concept unrecognized by the Puerto Rican women I knew: A responsible mother did not leave her children with any stranger. And in a culture where children are not considered intrusive, there was no need to leave the children at home. We went where our mother went.

Of my preschool years I have only impressions: the sharp bite of the wind in December as we walked with our parents toward the brightly lit stores downtown; how I felt like a stuffed doll in my heavy coat, boots, and mittens; how good it was to walk into the five-and-dime and sit at the counter drinking hot chocolate. On Saturdays our whole family would walk downtown to shop at the big department stores on Broadway. Mother bought all our clothes at Penney's and Sears, and she liked to buy her dresses at the women's specialty shops like Lerner's and Diana's. At some point we'd go into Woolworth's and sit at the soda fountain to eat.

We never ran into other Latinos at these stores or when eating out, and it became clear to me only years later that the women from El Building shopped mainly in other places—stores owned by other Puerto Ricans or by Jewish merchants who had philosophically accepted our presence in the city and decided to make us their good customers, if not real neighbors and friends. These establishments were located not downtown but in the blocks around our street, and they were referred to generically as *La Tienda, El Bazar, La Bodega, La Botánica*. Everyone knew what was meant. These were the stores where your face did not turn a clerk to stone, where your money was as green as anyone else's.

One New Year's Eve we were dressed up like child models in the Sears catalogue: my brother in a miniature man's suit and bow tie, and I in black patent-leather shoes and a frilly dress with several layers of crinoline underneath. My mother wore a bright red dress that night, I remember, and spike heels; her long black hair hung to her waist. Father, who usually wore his Navy uniform during his short visits home, had put on a dark civilian suit for the occasion: We had been invited to his uncle's house for a big celebration. Everyone was excited because my mother's brother Hernan—a bachelor who could indulge himself with luxuries—had bought a home movie camera, which he would be trying out that night.

Even the home movie cannot fill in the sensory details such a gathering left imprinted in a child's brain. The thick sweetness of women's perfumes mixing with the ever-present smells of food cooking in the kitchen: meat and plantain *pasteles*, as well as the ubiquitous rice dish made special with pigeon peas—*gandules*—and seasoned with precious *sofrito*[2] sent up from the Island by somebody's mother or smuggled in by a recent traveler. *Sofrito* was one of the items that women hoarded, since it was hardly ever in stock at La Bodega. It was the flavor of Puerto Rico.

The men drank Palo Viejo rum, and some of the younger ones got weepy. The first time I saw a grown man cry was at a New Year's Eve party: He had been reminded of his mother by the smells in the kitchen. But what I remember most were the boiled *pasteles*—plantain or yucca rectangles stuffed with corned beef or other meats, olives, and many other savory ingredients, all wrapped in banana leaves. Everybody had to fish one out with a fork. There was always a "trick" pastel—one without stuffing—and whoever got that one was the "New Year's Fool."

There was also the music. Long-playing albums were treated like precious china in these homes. Mexican recordings were popular, but the songs that brought tears to my mother's eyes were sung by the melancholy Daniel Santos, whose life as a drug addict was the stuff of legend. Felipe Rodríguez was a particular favorite of couples, since he sang about faithless women and brokenhearted men. There is a snatch of one lyric that has stuck in my mind like a needle on a worn groove: *De piedra ha de ser mi cama, de piedra la cabezera . . . la mujer que a mi me quiera . . . ha de quererme de veras. Ay, Ay, Ay, corazón, porque no amas.*[3] . . . I must have heard it a thousand times since the idea of a bed made of stone, and its connection to love, first troubled me with its disturbing images.

The five-minute home movie ends with people dancing in a circle—the creative filmmaker must have set it up, so that all of them could file past him. It is both comical and sad to watch silent dancing. Since there is no justification for the absurd movements that music provides for some of us, people appear frantic, their faces embarrassingly intense. It's as if you were watching sex. Yet for years I've had dreams in the form of this home movie. In a recurring scene, familiar faces push themselves forward into my mind's eyes, plastering their features into distorted close-ups. And

---

[2]*sofrito:* A cooked condiment. A sauce composed of a mixture of fatback, ham, tomatoes, and many island spices and herbs. It is added to many typical Puerto Rican dishes for a distinctive flavor.

[3]*De piedra ha de ser . . . amas:* Lyrics from a popular romantic ballad (called a *bolero* in Puerto Rico). Freely translated: "My bed will be made of stone, of stone also my headrest (or pillow), the woman who (dares to) loves me, will have to love me for real. Ay, Ay, Ay, my heart, why can't you (let me) love. . . ."

I'm asking them: "Who is *she*? Who is the old woman I don't recognize? Is she an aunt? Somebody's wife? Tell me who she is."

"See the beauty mark on her cheek as big as a hill on the lunar land-scape of her face—well, that runs in the family. The women on your father's side of the family wrinkle early; it's the price they pay for that fair skin. The young girl with the green stain on her wedding dress is *La Novia*—just up from the Island. See, she lowers her eyes when she approaches the camera, as she's supposed to. Decent girls never look at you directly in the face. *Humilde,* humble, a girl should express humil-ity in all her actions. She will make a good wife for your cousin. He should consider himself lucky to have met her only weeks after she arrived here. If he marries her quickly, she will make him a good Puerto Rican-style wife; but if he waits too long, she will be corrupted by the city—just like your cousin there."

"She means me. I do what I want. This is not some primitive island I live on. Do they expect me to wear a black mantilla on my head and go to mass every day? Not me. I'm an American woman, and I will do as I please. I can type faster than anyone in my senior class at Central High, and I'm going to be a secretary to a lawyer when I graduate. I can pass for an American girl anywhere—I've tried it. At least for Italian, any-way—I never speak Spanish in public. I hate these parties, but I wanted the dress. I look better than any of these *humildes* here. *My* life is going to be different. I have an American boyfriend. He is older and has a car. My parents don't know it, but I sneak out of the house late at night sometimes to be with him. If I marry him, even my name will be Amer-ican. I hate rice and beans—that's what makes these women fat."

Your *prima*[4] is pregnant by that man she's been sneaking around with. Would I lie to you? I'm your *Tía Política,*[5] your great-uncle's common-law wife—the one he abandoned on the Island to go marry your cousin's mother. *I* was not invited to this party, of course, but I came anyway. I came to tell you that story about your cousin that you've always wanted to hear. Do you remember the comment your mother made to a neigh-bor that has always haunted you? The only thing you heard was your cousin's name, and then you saw your mother pick up your doll from the couch and say: 'It was as big as this doll when they flushed it down the toilet.' This image has bothered you for years, hasn't it? You had nightmares about babies being flushed down the toilet, and you won-dered why anyone would do such a horrible thing. You didn't dare ask

---

[4]*prima:* Female cousin.
[5]*Tía Política:* Aunt by marriage.

your mother about it. She would only tell you that you had not heard her right, and yell at you for listening to adult conversations. But later, when you were old enough to know about abortions, you suspected.

"I am here to tell you that you were right. Your cousin was growing an *Americanito* in her belly when this movie was made. Soon after she put something long and pointy into her pretty self, thinking maybe she could get rid of the problem before breakfast and still make it to her first class at the high school. Well, *Niña,*[6] her screams could be heard downtown. Your aunt, her mamá, who had been a midwife on the Island, managed to pull the little thing out. Yes, they probably flushed it down the toilet. What else could they do with it—give it a Christian burial in a little white casket with blue bows and ribbons? Nobody wanted that baby—least of all the father, a teacher at her school with a house in West Paterson that he was filling with real children, and a wife who was a natural blonde.

"Girl, the scandal sent your uncle back to the bottle. And guess where your cousin ended up? Irony of ironies. She was sent to a village in Puerto Rico to live with a relative on her mother's side: a place so far away from civilization that you have to ride a mule to reach it. A real change in scenery. She found a man there—women like that cannot live without male company—but believe me, the men in Puerto Rico know how to put a saddle on a woman like her. *La Gringa,*[7] they call her. Ha, ha, ha. *La Gringa* is what she always wanted to be. . . ."

The old woman's mouth becomes a cavernous black hole I fall into. And as I fall, I can feel the reverberations of her laughter. I hear the echoes of her last mocking words: *La Gringa, La Gringa!* And the conga line keeps moving silently past me. There is no music in my dream for the dancers.

When Odysseus visits Hades to see the spirit of his mother, he makes an offering of sacrificial blood, but since all the souls crave an audience with the living, he has to listen to many of them before he can ask questions. I, too, have to hear the dead and the forgotten speak in my dream. Those who are still part of my life remain silent, going around and around in their dance. The others keep pressing their faces forward to say things about the past.

My father's uncle is last in line. He is dying of alcoholism, shrunken and shriveled like a monkey, his face a mass of wrinkles and broken arteries. As he comes closer I realize that in his features I can see my whole family. If you were to stretch that rubbery flesh, you could find my father's

---

[6]*Niña:* Girl.
[7]*La Gringa:* Derogatory epithet used here to ridicule a Puerto Rican girl who wants to look like a blonde North American.

face, and deep within *that* face—my own. I don't want to look into those eyes ringed in purple. In a few years he will retreat into silence, and take a long, long time to die. *Move back, Tio,* I tell him. *I don't want to hear what you have to say. Give the dancers room to move. Soon it will be midnight. Who is the New Year's Fool this time?*

CONSIDERATIONS

Thinking

How does Cofer use color to underscore her ideas in the first third of her essay?

How do you account for the different attitudes that Cofer's mother and father had about isolating the family within El Building? Can you detect Cofer's attitude about those differences? How does that family conflict over values manifest itself in other ways throughout the essay?

How would you characterize the differences in values within Cofer's extended family—expecially those between the men and the women and those between the newly arrived Puerto Ricans and those who have begun to adapt to the new culture?

Connecting

Cofer uses both television and the home movie to help her develop her ideas. Is one of these forms of visual evidence more effective than the other, or do the two kinds of evidence simply allow her to reveal different things? Explain.

Make a list of the various times when silence comes into play in the essay. What is the overall effect of silence on the final impression that Cofer creates? Do you want to remain silent in face of what you learn, or do you want to speak out? What might your decision have to do with your own ethnicity?

Read Sharman Apt Russell's "Homebirth." What connections can you make between the women in that essay and the women in "Silent Dancing"—and between the men in the two essays?

Writing

Select a moment from your own life when you chose to remain silent and you now realize you should have spoken up. Write an essay that gives readers a clear perspective on how you feel about that decision now.

Choose a family photograph or a home video that you were a part of. Write about your choice, telling us about what was going on outside the frame of the photograph or the video, what observers now cannot see or know about without your help. In light of what the photograph or video represents to you now, try to account for the significance of what remains unseen or unexamined.

Arthur C. Danto
(b.1924)

Arthur C. Danto is the Johnsonian Professor of Philosophy at Columbia University. His work is distinguished by the ease and elegance that accompany his moves across academic disciplines. He is the art critic for *The Nation* and the author of several books of philosophy, including *The Philosophical Disenfranchisement of Art, Narration and Knowledge,* and *Connection to the World.* He is the recipient of the Lionel Trilling Award and the George S. Polk Award for criticism, Guggenheim Fellowships, and two appointments as a Fulbright scholar.

In "Gettysburg," Danto examines Civil War memorial art in general and the Gettysburg battlefield in particular as a way of exploring the moral boundaries of war.

Gettysburg

Then the whole of things might be different
From what it was thought to be in the beginning,
before an angel bandaged the field glasses.

JOHN ASHBERY

Pity-and-terror, the classically prescribed emotional response to tragic representation, was narrowly restricted to drama by the ancient authorities. In my view, tragedy has a wider reference by far, and pity-and-terror is aroused in me by works of art immeasurably less grand than those which unfold the cosmic undoings of Oedipus and Agamemnon, Antigone, Medea, and the women of Troy. The standard Civil War memorial, for example, is artistically banal by almost any criterion, and yet I am subject to pity-and-terror whenever I reflect upon the dense ironies it embodies. I am touched that the same figures appear and reappear in much the same monument from village to village, from commons to green to public square, across the American landscape. The sameness only deepens the conveyed tragedy, for it is evidence that those who subscribed funds for memorials, who ordered their bronze or cast-iron cement effigies from catalogues or from traveling sales representatives, so that the same soldier, carrying the same musket, flanked by the same cannons and set off by the same floral or patriotic decorations, were blind to the tragedy that is, for me, the most palpable quality of these cenotaphs. That blindness is a component of the tragedy inherent in the terrible juxtaposition of the most deadly armaments and ordnance known up to that time, with what, under those conditions, was the most vulnerably clad soldiery in history.

The Civil War infantryman is portrayed in his smart tunic and foraging cap. Take away the musket, the bayonet and the cartridge case, and he would be some uniformed functionary—messenger, conductor, bellhop, doorman. This was the uniform he fought in, as we know from countless drawings and photographs that have come down to us from the Civil War. Armed, carrying a knapsack, he moved across the battlefield as though on dress parade. But the weapons he faced were closer in design and cold effectiveness to those standard in the First World War, fifty years in his future, than to those confronted by Napoleon's troops at the Battle of Waterloo, fifty years in his past. What moves me is the contradiction between the code of military conduct, symbolically present in his garments but absent from his gun. We see, instead of the chivalry and romanticism of war as a form of art, the chill implacable indifference to any consideration other than maiming and death, typical of the kind of total combat the Civil War became. That contradiction was invisible when the memorials were raised, and it is its invisibility today that moves me to pity-and-terror.

The rifled musket—one with a helically grooved bore giving a stabilizing spin to the bullet and making possible a flat trajectory—was known in the eighteenth century, but it was used then primarily for hunting. The smooth-bore musket was military issue. There is an affecting Yankee pragmatism in the fact that the citizen-soldiers of the American Revolution should have used their hunting weapons to such effect against the celebrated "Brown Bess"—a smooth-bore musket with its barrel shortened and browned—that the rifled musket had to be adopted by British and European armies. But the Brown Bess had been Wellington's weapon in Belgium, in the style of warfare conducted on the classical battlefield, with disciplined infantry firing in ranks at short distance: a row of blasts from these muskets, as from deadly popguns, could be pretty effective in stopping or driving back an opposed line. Even the rifled musket, at that time, used the round ball. The elongated, cylindroconoidal bullet was invented only afterward, by Captain John Norton, in 1823, and though it has been acclaimed as the greatest military invention since the flintlock, Wellington could not see how it improved on the Brown Bess, as indeed it did not if battle were conducted as Wellington understood it. The elongated bullet, with its lowered wind resistance making its charge much more powerful, was understood by Sir William Napier as profoundly altering the nature of infantry, turning the infantry soldier into a "long-range assassin." Napier intuited that a change in the conduct of battle at any point would entail a change at every point—like what Heidegger calls a *Zeugganzes*— a complex of instruments, men and arms forming a total system which functions *as* a totality. Napier's objection implies the very code that the Civil War uniform embodies, and defines a certain moral boundary, the other side of which is not war so much as slaughter. Rifling, the Norton bullet and the percussion cap, established as superior to the flintlock by 1839, certainly changed the face of warfare. There was no room in the new complex for the cavalry charge, as had to be learned in the Charge of the Light Brigade in 1854, and relearned in the Civil War. In any case, the standard Civil War issue was the 1861-model Springfield rifle: percussion lock, muzzle-loading, .58 caliber, shooting a 480-grain conical Minié bullet. It was effective at a thousand yards, deadly accurate at three hundred. The smooth-bore was of limited effectiveness at one hundred to one hundred twenty yards. Civil War soldiers faced the kind of fire that made obsolete the way they were used by generals who learned about battle at West Point and had studied the Napoleonic paradigms. The guns faithfully depicted in the Civil War memorial statue made the style and gallantry of the men who carried them obsolete. Even the brass button would be a point of vulnerability in battles to come.

The 1903 and 1917 Springfield models were used by American infantry in the First World War. Increased muzzle velocity flattened trajectory; the ammunition clip, easy to change, speeded charging the magazine. But those rifles were fired over the cusp of trenches and the steel helmets protected the riflemen's heads. Of course, helmets have existed since ancient times and, in fact, were worn by Prussian and Austrian observers at Gettysburg, though more for ostentation than protection. They were brightly polished. "The sword carries greater honor than the shield" could be repeated by a military historian in very recent years, giving a reason why Robert E. Lee should have achieved greater honor through losing glamorously than his opponent, George Meade, earned through winning stolidly, by fighting a defensive battle. Lee had been mocked as "The King of Spades" when he used entrenchments at Chancellorsville. The steel helmet reduced injuries in the First World War by about seventy-five percent. The casualties at Gettysburg, for the three days of the battle, totaled about 51,000, of which 7,058 were outright deaths. The Roman legions were better protected, and their sanitary conditions were better than those prevailing in the 1860s. A wound in the July heat festered and went gangrenous quickly. There were 33,264 wounded. The wagon train that carried the Confederate wounded away under driving rains on July 5 was seventeen miles long. Over 10,000 were unaccounted for, and I suppose their bones would still be turned up at Gettysburg had the battlefield not become a military park. In any case I am uncertain they would have worn helmets if they had had them, for they were men who lived and died by an exalted concept of honor. You went to your death like a soldier, head held high under your jaunty cap. "As he passed me he rode gracefully," Longstreet wrote, years after, of Pickett leading his stupendous charge, "with his jaunty cap raked well over on his right ear and his long auburn locks, nicely dressed, hanging almost to his shoulders.

He seemed rather a holiday soldier than the general at the head of a column which was about to make one of the grandest, most desperate assaults recorded in the annals of war." Longstreet thought the great charge a terrible mistake. He thought Lee wrong from the start at Gettysburg. Lee was deaf to Longstreet for the same reason that mourners and patriots across America were blind to the message of their memorials. Longstreet is my hero.

I recently trudged the battle lines at Gettysburg. The scene of that great collision had, according to the architectural historian Vincent Scully, been transformed by the National Park Service into a work of art, and I was curious to see, in the first instance, how the locus of agony and glory should have been preserved and transfigured under the glass bell of aesthetic distance into a memorial object. An interest in memorial art and in the moral boundaries of war would have sufficed to move me as a pilgrim to what, since the Gettysburg Address, we have thought of as consecrated ground. But I had also been enough unsettled by a recent remark of Gore Vidal's that had come up in the civil strife between *Commentary* and *The Nation,* in regard to Norman Podhoretz's patriotism, to want to think out for myself whether, as Vidal claimed, the American Civil War is our Trojan War. Podhoretz had pretended to a greater interest in the Wars of the Roses than in the Civil War, and this had greatly exercised Vidal, whose family had participated on both sides and thus had internalized the antagonisms that divided the nation. The Trojan War was not of course a civil conflict. A better paradigm might have been the epic wars between the Pandavas and Kauravas, as recounted in the *Mahabharata* and given moral urgency in the *Bhagavad Gita,* where the fact that it is a *civil* war was deemed by the great warrior Arjuna—until he was persuaded otherwise by the god Krishna a compelling reason not to fight. No one's remembered ancestors participated in the Trojan War when it in fact was their Trojan War in the sense Vidal must have intended, when the Homeric poems had emerged out of the mists to define the meaning of life, strife, love and honor for a whole civilization. The Civil War, if it were to be our Trojan War in that sense, would have to be so even for those whose families were elsewhere and indifferent when it took place. It has not received literary embodiment of the right sort to affect American consciousness as the *Iliad* affected Greek consciousness (Troy affected Roman consciousness through the *Aeneid*). And so a further question that directed me was whether the artistic embodiment of a battlefield into a military park might serve to make it our Trojan War in the required way, where one could not pretend an indifference to it because it was now the matrix of our minds and our beings.

Like Tewkesbury, where the climactic battle of the Wars of the Roses took place in 1471, the name Gettysburg has an irresistibly comic sound, good for a giggle in music hall or vaudeville. It could, like Podunk, serve as everyone's name for Nowheresville, the boondocks, the sticks. It was one of hundreds of "-burgs" and "-villes" named after forgotten worthies (James Gettys had been given the site by William Penn), indicating, before the place "became terrible"—Bruce Catton's phrase—simply where life went on. Gettysburg in 1863 was the seat of Adams County and a poky grove of Academe, with a college and a seminary. But Gettysburg was no Troy: the battle was *at* but not *for* Gettysburg. When Lee withdrew on July 5, its 2,400 inhabitants had ten times that number of dead and wounded to deal with, not to mention mounds of shattered horses: the miasma of putrefaction hung over the town until winter. Gettysburg became host to a cemetery large in proportion to its size, though there is a strikingly prophetic Romanesque gatehouse at Evergreen Cemetery, which gave its name to Cemetery Hill and Cemetery Ridge, and which seemed waiting to welcome the alien dead: you can see artillery emplacements in front of it in a surviving photograph. You can count the houses in Gettysburg in another photograph of the time, looking east from Seminary Ridge. That the battle was there, between Cemetery Ridge and Seminary Ridge, was an artifact of the war. Gettysburg was not somebody's prize. Longstreet called it "ground of no value." It was a good place for a battle, but though it is clear that there had to be a battle someplace soon, it could have happened in any number of other burgs or villes. Meade, knowing there was to be a battle, would have preferred Pipes Creek as its site. Lee was heading for Harrisburg, a serious city and the capital of the state, and decided to *accept* battle instead, knowing he would have to do so somewhere, and Gettysburg, by geological accident, was as good a place as any to fight.

In his novel *Lincoln,* Gore Vidal puts Mary Lincoln in the War Room with her husband. She is supposed to have had, according to the novel, a certain military intuition, and Vidal describes her looking at a map, pointing to the many roads leading in and out of Gettysburg, and saying, in effect, My goodness—whoever controls Gettysburg controls everything. Perhaps this in fact is intended to underscore Mary Lincoln's acute frivolity: if it meant, really, to show how the mind of a general got lodged in the pretty head of the President's wife, it simply shows the limits of Vidal's own military intuition. Gettysburg was not that kind of place. It was not, for example, like Monte Cassino, anchoring a line because it controlled roads up the Italian peninsula, so that when it fell, its defenders were obliged to fall back to the next line of defense. Gettysburg really *was* nowhere, of no importance and no consequence: like Waterloo it was illuminated by the sheer *Geworfenheit* of war. The essence of war is accident.

This is how it happened to happen there. It was known in Washington in late June that Lee was somewhere in Pennsylvania, but not known where he was exactly. Despite the telegraph and the *New York Times,* there is a sense in which men were as much in the dark in regard to one another's whereabouts as they might have been in England in the fifteenth century, fighting the Wars of the Roses. Lee had heard rumors that the Army of the Potomac was somewhere east of him, but he had no clear idea of where. This, too, was a matter of accident. In classical warfare, the cavalry served as the eyes of the army. But Lee's glamorous and vain cavalry leader, Jeb Stuart, was off on a toot of his own, seeking personal glory. He turned up only on the last day of the battle of Gettysburg, trailing some useless trophies. Buford, a Union cavalry general, sent out to look for the suspected Confederate troops, more or less bumped into General Pettigrew's brigade marching along the Chambersburg Pike into Gettysburg to requisition shoes. They collided, as it were, in the fog, and each sent word that the enemy was near. Buford perceived that it was good ground for a battle and sent for reinforcements. Lee perceived that it was a good *moment* for battle and began to concentrate his forces. It happened very fast: the next day was the first day of the engagement, July 1.

Here is Longstreet's description of the site:

> Gettysburg lies partly between Seminary Ridge on the West and Cemetery Ridge on the South-east, a distance of about fourteen hundred yards dividing the crests of the two ridges.

This is a soldier's description, not the imagined description of a novelist's personage: you can deduce the necessary orders to infantry and artillery from Longstreet's single sentence. The battle seethed and boiled between the two ridges, as if they were its containing walls. Gettysburg had the bad luck to lie partly between the ridges. It had the good luck to lie between them *partly.* There was only one accidental, civilian death: the battle took place, mainly, to the south of the village. The ridges formed two facing natural ramparts, as though two feudal lords had built their walls within catapult distance of each other.

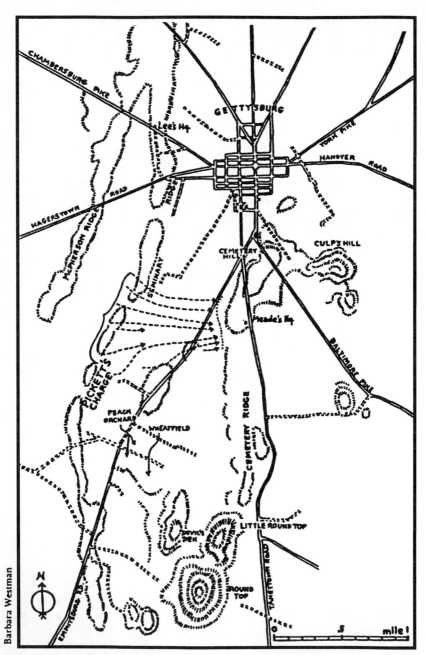

CHAMBERSBURG PIKE

GETTYSBURG

Lee's Hq

YORK PIKE

HANOVER ROAD

HAGERSTOWN ROAD

McPHERSON RIDGE

SEMINARY RIDGE

CULP'S HILL

CEMETERY HILL

Meade's Hq

BALTIMORE PIKE

PICKETT'S CHARGE

PEACH ORCHARD

WHEATFIELD

CEMETERY RIDGE

DEVIL'S DEN

LITTLE ROUND TOP

ROUND TOP

N

EMMITSBURG ROAD

TANEYTOWN ROAD

0   ½   mile 1

Barbara Westman

GETTYSBURG • JULY 3, 1863 • 2:30 P.M.

To visualize the terrain, draw a vertical line and label it Seminary Ridge. This is where the Confederate Army formed its line, along the crest. They seized it after a heated battle with Buford's forces, which, despite reinforcements, were driven fourteen hundred yards east to Cemetery Ridge. Now draw a line parallel and to the right of Seminary Ridge, only curve it to the right at the top, to form a sort of fishhook. This was the shape of the Union line, indeed called "The Fish-hook," on July 2 and 3. (Gettysburg is a dot between the lines, just about where the hook begins its curve.) Where the barb would be is Culp's Hill. Farther back along the shaft is Cemetery Hill. At the eye of the hook is Big Round Top, at a distance of about four miles from Cemetery Hill. About half its height, and upshaft, is Little Round Top. The four hills served as battle towers. The rampart itself slopes to the west to form what is designated a *glacis* in the vocabulary of fortification. It was a formidable defensive position, but Seminary Ridge too would have been a formidable defensive position. "If we could only take position here and have them attack us through this open ground!" Lee's chief of artillery, Porter Alexander, recalled having thought. "We were in no such luck—the boot, in fact, being upon the other foot." A defensive war was not what had brought Lee north and onto enemy territory. He had to attack if there was to be battle.

Longstreet did not think there needed to be battle. Standing beside Lee, he surveyed the Union position with his field glasses for a very long time, turned to Lee and said,

> If we could have chosen a point to meet our plans of operation, I do not think we could have found a better one than that upon which they are now concentrating. All we have to do is throw our army around by their left, and we shall interpose between the Federal Army and Washington. We can get a strong position and wait, and if they fail to attack us we shall have everything in condition to move back tomorrow night in the direction of Washington.

"No," said General Lee—the words are famous and fateful—"the enemy is there and I am going to attack him there."

Perhaps Longstreet was wrong: Meade was as cautious a man as he. Why need Meade have attacked them, even though between Washington and its army? Lee's supply line was long and vulnerable, and Meade might have ringed any position he would take and wait out a siege. Still, wars are fought not so much by generals as by governments, and Longstreet knew that Washington would pressure Meade to attack, needing a victory and in fear for Washington itself. And Lee was probably right: if he could crush Meade's army here, where it was, he would have free access to Washington or Baltimore or Philadelphia. He needed or thought he needed a *brilliant* victory. He had invaded the North not for conquest but to astonish. And he could sustain a defeat as Meade could not. If Meade were defeated, pressure to negotiate would be exerted on Lincoln by the Peace Party in the Union. There might be foreign recognition. And morale would have been disastrously lowered since the Union had just undergone a series of brutal defeats. He might, on the symbolic date of July Fourth, achieve independence for the South. Whereas if he lost at Gettysburg, well, he could have swaggered back to his own territory, as after a dashing raid, trailing glory. Besides, rounding the Federal left would have baffled his troops, who had driven the enemy back to that position. Morale is a precious factor, a form of power. Lee would have to *smash* the Union left. He would have to take Little Round Top, as he nearly succeeded in doing on the second day of battle.

A battlefield has something of the metaphysical complexity of a work of art: it stands to the terrain on which it is spread as a work of art stands to the physical object to which it belongs. Not every part of the physical object is really a part of the work of art—we do not take the weave of canvas into consideration in identifying the meaning of a picture, for example, since there is no coherent way in which we can read the roughness of his surfaces into, say, the iconographic program of Tintoretto's Scuola di San Rocco. We rarely consider the fact that a surface is dry when interpreting a painting. Richard Wollheim, in his recent Mellon Lectures, borrowed from phenomenology the useful term "thematization," and would use it to say that not every part or property of the physical object is "thematized" by the work. Doubtless the concept can be taken further—I am seeking to thematize the contradiction, which most would not even see as there, in Civil War memorial statuary. But what I want to say here is that battle thematizes certain features of the terrain, transforming them into what soldiers call "ground." At Gettysburg, the flanking hills of the Federal line were thematized in this sense on the second day of battle; Cemetery Hill and the sweep of field and meadow between the ridges were thematized on the third and last day. It is doubtful the two ridges would have been so thematized in an imagined encounter between Napoleon and Wellington: their artillery would not have reached far enough, and besides, the explosive shell had not been invented in 1815. (Its invention meant the end of the wooden battleship.) What would be the point of lobbing cannon balls across the fields? One follows the structure of battle by grasping successive thematizations. War is a deadly artist. A battlefield is already more than halfway to a work of art.

On July 2, Lee strove to take either or both Culp's Hill and Little Round Top. Meade's defensive line along Cemetery Ridge would have been untenable had Lee succeeded: he would have had to draw back to Pipes Creek, and it would have been a defeat. The fighting that afternoon was fierce but uncoordinated—each commander had difficulties with his generals—and the outcome of the engagement was sufficiently ambiguous that Lee could interpret it as a victory. Still, no thanks to General Daniel Sickles, the tempestuous Federal general who had left Little Round Top undefended, both the contested hills remained, it may have seemed precariously, in Union hands. Had Meade's engineering chief, Gouverneur Warren, not happened to see that no one was holding the crest at Little Round Top and on his own authority diverted troops to its defense in the very nick of time, the outcome of that day's fighting would have been different.

It is worth contemplating Little Round Top from the perspective of weaponry. Little Round Top was called "the Rocky Hill" by the Confederates—armies improvise a nomenclature with their thematizations. Its slopes are strewn with heavy boulders of the kind that, piled up, gave the name "Devil's Den" to an adjacent site. It is full of ad hoc shelters and one-man fortresses, and offers an object lesson in the military imagination. It cried out for a kind of weapon—the grenade—which was to be indispensable to infantry in the World Wars but which was considered extinct at the time of the Civil War because of the increase in range and accuracy of muzzled arms. Grenades had been intensely employed in seventeenth-century tactics (when a grenadier was a special physical type, like a shot-putter). It came into its own again in the Russo-Japanese war. The field mortar, with its high trajectory, would also have done wonders at Devil's Den, with its freestone breastworks and God-given sniper nests. Civil War battle seems to have been imagined as something that takes place on a field, between massed armies. The grenade and mortar, conceived of as suited to storming fortresses, were inscrutable in 1863, even though all the technology was in place for the manufacture of the lightweight grenades that re-entered the armory half a century later. The weaponry determined the order of thematization, and particularly the field between the ridges on which Pickett's charge was to take place on July 3 was something generals understood or thought they understood. Longstreet knew they did not.

On July 3, Lee had determined to attack Meade's center. This was his reasoning: Meade, he believed, would infer that Lee was seeking to turn his flanks and would renew the attack on the anchoring hills. So Meade would move reinforcements to right and left, leaving the center weak. Meade's reasoning was this: Lee would reason as he in fact reasoned, so the right thing was to reinforce the center. In classical warfare there is a kind of language—armies communicate through guns (as the United States and the Soviet Union today communicate through nuclear testing): a cannonade announces a charge. All that morning the Federal officers and men watched the enemy concentrate its artillery—150 guns focused on the Union center. "A magnificent sight," according to Henry Hunt, chief of artillery on the Union side: "Never before had such a sight been witnessed on this continent, and rarely, if ever, abroad." The Union employed about 200 pieces in that battle, and a duel opened up at about 1 P.M. that lasted nearly two hours: nothing on that scale had ever taken place before. But the state of explosive chemistry in the mid-nineteenth century raised severe cognitive problems for the Confederate force. What was used then was black gunpowder, which created dense smoke. The exploding shells cast a smoke screen over Cemetery Ridge, concealing from Confederate artillery chief Porter Alexander that he was shooting too high, and that his shells were falling behind the Union line. By accident, he hit a dozen caissons of ammunition to Meade's rear. Union Major General Hunt decided to conserve ammunition for the attack to come, and ordered fire to cease. Alexander took this as a sign that he had silenced the Federal guns, and signaled Pickett to move forward. Smoke still hung blackly over Cemetery Ridge, but at a certain moment of no return a breeze lifted it and Pickett's men saw, in Allan Nevins's words, "the full panoply of Union strength in its terrifying grandeur, a double line of infantry in front, guns frowning beside them, and reserves in thick platoons further back." Until that moment, none of Lee's officers had any real idea of what power had been building up behind the sullen ridge. Had his cavalry been operative, Lee would not have charged. He fought blind.

It was in Pickett's grand charge up the slopes of Cemetery Ridge that the tragic contradiction between arms and uniform became palpable. Pickett's superb veterans, fresh in this battle, marched according to a magnificent code into a wall of fire. It was the brutal end to an era of warfare, the last massed charge. The triumph of slaughter over chivalry gave rise to Sherman's horrifying march through Georgia and South Carolina, to total war, to the firebombing of Dresden, to Hiroshima and Nagasaki, to the rolled grenade in the full jetliner. "It was the most beautiful thing I ever saw," exclaimed Colonel Fremantle, a British observer at Longstreet's side. The sentiment was widely shared. Pickett's charge was what war was all about in that era; it had the kind of beauty that made Lee remark, at the Battle of Fredericksburg, "It is well that war is so terrible—we should grow too fond of it." Longstreet wrote: "That day at Gettysburg was one of the saddest in my life." I think he was more or less alone in this feeling. I do not think Gettysburg was perceived as the awful defeat it was by the South, at least not then, since news of Grant's victory at Vicksburg had not yet come, nor do I think it was received as a great victory, least of all in Washington, or by Lincoln, who cared only that Meade should press his advantage. What no one could see, just because the doors of the future always are closed, was that beauty on that occasion was only the beginning of terror.

The bodies were rolled into shallow trenches, and the armies moved off to other encounters. Some 3,500 Union dead are today neatly buried in concentric arcs alongside Evergreen Cemetery. Seventeen acres were set aside for this, weeks after the battle, and it was here, before the landscaping was altogether completed, that Lincoln delivered the address which is so enshrined in the national consciousness today that it requires an effort of severe deconstruction to perceive it as a cry of victory as gloating as anything that issued from the coarse throat of Ajax. The Gettysburg Battlefield Memorial Association was chartered in 1864 and began acquiring land which was absorbed into the National Military Park established, without debate so far as I can discover, by an act of Congress in 1895. In 1933 it came under the jurisdiction of the National Park Service, which transformed it in an unforgiving way. There is an historical preservation I applaud but a political overlay that distresses me.

It is always moving to visit a battlefield when the traces of war itself have been erased by nature or transfigured by art, and to stand amid memorial weapons, which grow inevitably quaint and ornamental with the evolution of armamentary technology, mellowing under patinas and used, now, to punctuate the fading thematizations of strife. The first cannon to be fired at the Battle of Gettysburg stands by the memorial to Buford near MacPherson's Farm, like a capital letter to mark the beginning of a ferocious sentence. Four cannons form Cushing's battery stand, like four exclamation points, to mark its end at the point where Pickett's men penetrated the Union line only to be surrounded. General Francis Walker uses a Homeric metaphor to describe Pickett's charge:

As the spear of Menelaus pierced the shield of his antagonist, cut
through the shining breastplate, but spared the life, so the division of
Pickett, launched from Seminary Ridge, broke through the Union
defense, and for the moment thrust its head of column within our lines,
threatening destruction to the Army of the Potomac.

When I was a soldier, I was often struck, as by a paradox, that at the very
moment that artillery was pounding somewhere, somewhere else men
and women in soft clothing were touching glasses and carrying on flirta-
tions; and that before and after this moment, but in this place, the peaceful pursuit of human purposes would go innocently forward, that families
would picnic where men were being killed. And I was overwhelmed after
the war by the thick peace that had settled back over places I had seen
sharded: Salerno, Velletri, Cassino, Anzio. There is that sense today at
Gettysburg, as tourists consult their maps and point across to not very
distant hills and ridges, or listen to patient guides rehearse the drama of
those three days in July 1863. The statue of General Lee, on his elegant
horse, Traveller, stands just where Lee himself stood, and faces, across the
open field traversed by Pickett's division, to where an appropriately less
flamboyant effigy of Meade looks west from Cemetery Ridge. The copse of
trees that Lee had singled out as the point to head for still stands not far
from Meade's statue, segregated by an iron fence, as if a sacred grove.
Ranks of cannons point across, from ridge to ridge, and the sites are
strewn with touching, simple monuments, placed by the units that were
there so that it would always be remembered that they were there. The
most florid monument celebrates the Pennsylvania presence (there are
537 Pennsylvanians buried in the National Cemetery, and 867 New Yorkers—the largest representation by state there). There is an art history of
Gettysburg to be written, but the meaning that comes through, even without it, is that a momentous collision occurred here, and that it was connected with the high and generous feelings that are appropriate, after a
battle, between those who fought it.

The Park Service's pamphlet of 1950 recommends an itinerary with
fourteen stops—it maps onto the Stations of the Cross if you have an
appetite for numerical correspondences. It is chronological. You begin
where the battle began, at MacPherson's Ridge at 8 A.M. on July 1. You
now follow a trail south along Seminary Ridge, and you may pause in
front of Lee's statue and recite the thought Faulkner insisted was in the
breast of every Southern boy: it is, there, eternally "still not yet two
o'clock on that July afternoon in 1863." Edging the Peach Orchard, where

Sickles formed a reckless salient and lost a leg, you mount Round Top and head north to The Copse of Trees and Meade's headquarters. You pause at the cemetery and end, not quite appropriately, at Culp's Hill. In 1950, as today, you would leave 1863 from time to time and enter the present, for the acreage of the Battle Park is intersected, here and there, with fragments of mere unthematized Pennsylvania, along whose roads tractors and trucks drive past restaurants and service stations on one or another civilian errand. The almost cubist interpenetration of past and present, war and peace, is semiotically moving in its own right.

The itinerary of 1950 was dropped from revised editions of the pamphlet, in 1954 and 1962, and today the visit has a different structure. Today you enter the park, amidst many monuments, along "High-Water Mark Trail." There are no Confederate markers among the celebratory monuments: instead, there is "High-Water Mark Monument," erected by "us" to show how far "they" reached. It was not really a high-water mark. There was no flood: this was not Genghis Khan, but one of the gentlest occupations the world has ever seen. It was, exactly as General Walker put it, a spear point which penetrated but did not slay—a Homeric poet would have supposed a god or goddess deflected the weapon. Lee was the spearman—Menelaus, if the analogy appeals (except Menelaus triumphed). If we construe the Military Park as a monumentary text, it now reads *not* as the history of a great battle between heroic adversaries, but as the victory of the Union. The text begins where the victory was won. As a text, the park is now a translation into historical landscape of the Gettysburg Address. Small wonder it "fell like a wet blanket," as Lincoln afterward said. Small wonder the *Harrisburg Patriot* editorialized the "silly remarks" this way: "For the credit of the Nation we are willing that the veil of oblivion shall be dropped and that they shall be no more repeated or thought of." Half the men who fell there did not fight for what Lincoln said was achieved there, and of those who might have, Lincoln's were not in every case the reasons they were there. It was an inappropriate political speech on an occasion that called for generosity, vaunting and confessional. The language is concealingly beautiful, evidence that Auden is after all right that time worships language "and forgives / Everyone by whom it lives."

I can understand, or might be able to understand, how a literary scholar, though patriotic, might find the Wars of the Roses of greater interest than the American Civil War, even if he should have no special concern with the ambitions of Lancaster and York. Henry VI, the subject of an early tragedy of Shakespeare, founded Kings College, Cambridge. But the main reason, I should think, for being interested in the civil wars of the fifteenth century in England is connected with one main reason for being interested in our Civil War. The Wars of the Roses were of an unparalleled brutality and were fought by mercenaries. It was total warfare, and the sickening experience of having one's land run over by one's countrymen but acting like brigands and in the royal pay lingered for centuries in British consciousness. Henry VI also founded Eton, on whose playing fields the British Empire is said to have been won by practices governed by the rules of fair combat and respect for the opponent. The unspeakable conduct of battle on the Continent—think of the Thirty Years War—until the eighteenth century, when Anglicization began to define the moral outlines of military conduct, must have confirmed the legacy of the Wars of the Roses in the English mind.

My sense is that the high-minded perception of the soldierly vocation is embodied in the uniform, the insignia, the flags and the vulnerability of the militia depicted in sculpture of the Civil War. The other form of war is embodied in the weapons. If there is a high-water mark in the history of modern war, it was in Pickett's gallant and foregone assault. It has been growing darker and darker ever since. I am not certain this is a basis for seeing the Civil War as "our" Trojan War. In a sense, something is not a Trojan War if it is *ours:* the Trojan War speaks to what is universal and human, regardless of political division and national culture. I am not certain that the idea of Union has any more meaning than or as much meaning as Helen of Troy, as justification for pitched combat. If the Civil War is to address humanity as the Trojan War does, it must itself be addressed at a different level than any that has so far been reached. Gettysburg is a good place to begin.

CONSIDERATIONS

Thinking

What do you think Danto means by "the triumph of slaughter over chivalry" in this sentence about Pickett's charge at Cemetery Ridge: "The triumph of slaughter over chivalry gave rise to Sherman's horrifying march through Georgia and South Carolina, to total war, to the firebombing of Dresden, to Hiroshima and Nagasaki, to the rolled grenade in the full jetliner"? What does that phrase about slaughter and chivalry have to do with those Civil War memorials that interest Danto so profoundly?

What is Danto's complaint about the "concealingly beautiful" language of Lincoln's Gettysburg Address, and what does that complaint have to do with what

Danto calls (borrowing Richard Wollheim's language from phenomenology) "thematization"?

Connecting

Throughout this essay, Danto refers to other wars, especially the Trojan War. How does he make use of those other wars, and why does he object so much to Gore Vidal's notion that Gettysburg was "our" Trojan War?

Consider these stanzas from Robert Lowell's poem "For the Union Dead":

> On a thousand small town New England greens,
> the old white church holds their air
> of sparse, sincere rebellion; frayed flags
> quilt the graveyards of the Grand Army of the Republic.

> The stone statues of the abstract Union Soldier
> grow slimmer and younger each year—
> wasp-waisted, they doze over muskets
> and muse through their sideburns . . .

What do you think Danto would say to Lowell about this image of the soldiers? What do you think Lowell would say to Danto about his essay?

Writing

After reading Lincoln's Gettysburg Address, write a letter to Danto about his assessment of the address, explaining why you agree or disagree with that assessment.

Go to a military battlefield or to a museum that contains the artifacts of war. Select one artifact, research it, and write an essay about an idea of yours that arises from your research and reflection.

Guy Davenport
(b.1927)

Guy Davenport, professor of English at the University of Kentucky, was educated at Duke University; Merton College, Oxford; and Harvard University. Davenport's books include volumes of essays and stories.

The following selection, "The Geography of the Imagination," comes from a book of the same title. In it, Davenport displays his wide-ranging erudition and his remarkable ability to make connections among the most disparate materials. His essay is noteworthy for its imaginative daring and for its careful attention to details of the works and objects he brings into his discussion.

The Geography of the Imagination

Thc difference between the Parthenon and the World Trade Center, between a French wine glass and a German beer mug, between Bach and John Philip Sousa, between Sophocles and Shakespeare, between a bicycle and a horse, though explicable by historical moment, necessity, and destiny, is before all a difference of imagination.

Man was first a hunter, and an artist: his earliest vestiges tell us that alone. But he must always have dreamed, and recognized and guessed and supposed, all skills of the imagination. Language itself is continuously an imaginative act. Rational discourse outside our familiar territory of Greek logic sounds to our ears like the wildest imagination. The Dogon, a people of West Africa, will tell you that a white fox named Ogo frequently weaves himself a hat of string bean hulls, puts it on his impudent head, and dances in the okra to insult and infuriate God Almighty, and that there's nothing we can do about it except abide him in faith and patience.

This is not folklore, or a quaint custom, but as serious a matter to the Dogon as a filling station to us Americans. The imagination; that is, the way we shape and use the world, indeed the way we *see* the world, has geographical boundaries like islands, continents, and countries. These boundaries can be crossed. That Dogon fox and his impudent dance came to live with us, but in a different body, and to serve a different mode of the imagination. We call him Brer Rabbit.

We in America are more sensitive than most to boundaries of the imagination. Our arrival was a second one; the misnamed first arrivers must still bear a name from the imagination of certain Renaissance men, who for almost a century could not break out of the notion that these two vast continents were the Indies, itself a name so vague as to include China, India, and even Turkey, for which they named our most delicious bird.

The imagination has a history, as yet unwritten, and it has a geography, as yet only dimly seen. History and geography are inextricable disciplines. They have different shelves in the library, and different offices at the university, but they cannot get along for a minute without consulting the other. Geography is the wife of history, as space is the wife of time.

191

When Heraclitus said that everything passes steadily along, he was not inciting us to make the best of the moment, an idea unseemly to his placid mind, but to pay attention to the pace of things. Each has its own rhythm: the nap of a dog, the precession of the equinoxes, the dances of Lydia, the majestically slow beat of the drums at Dodona, the swift runners at Olympia.

The imagination, like all things in time, is metamorphic. It is also rooted in a ground, a geography. The Latin word for the sacredness of a place is *cultus*, the dwelling of a god, the place where a rite is valid. *Cultus* becomes our word *culture*, not in the portentous sense it now has, but in a much humbler sense. For ancient people the sacred was the vernacular ordinariness of things: the hearth, primarily; the bed, the wall around the yard. The temple was too sacred to be entered. Washing the feet of a guest was as religious an act as sharing one's meals with the gods.

When Europeans came to the new world, they learned nothing on the way, as if they came through a dark tunnel. Plymouth, Lisbon, Amsterdam, then the rolling Atlantic for three months, then the rocks and pines, sand and palms of Cathay, the Indies, the wilderness. A German cartographer working in Paris decided to translate the first name of Amerigo Vespucci into Latin, for reasons best known to himself, and call the whole thing America. In geography you have maps, and maps must have the names of places on them.

We new-world settlers, then, brought the imagination of other countries to transplant it in a different geography. We have been here scarcely a quarter of the time that the pharaohs ruled Egypt. We brought many things across the Atlantic, and the Pacific; many things we left behind: a critical choice to live with forever.

The imagination is like the drunk man who lost his watch, and must get drunk again to find it. It is as intimate as speech and custom, and to trace its ways we need to reeducate our eyes. In 1840—when Cooper's *The Pathfinder* was a bestseller, and photography had just been made practical—an essay called "The Philosophy of Furniture" appeared in an American magazine. Dickens made fun of Americans for attending lectures on the philosophy of anything, the philosophy of crime on Monday, the philosophy of government on Wednesday, the philosophy of the soul on Thursday, as Martin Chuzzlewit learned from Mrs. Brick. The English, also, we know from Thomas Love Peacock's satirical novels, were addicted to the lecture. The great French encyclopedia, its imitators, and the periodical press had done their work, and audiences were eager to hear anybody on any subject. Crowds attended the lectures of Louis Agassiz on zoology and geology (in 1840 he was explaining the Ice Age and the nature of glaciers, which he had just discovered); of Emerson, of transcendentalists, utopians, home-grown scientists like John Cleve Symmes, of Cincinnati, who explained that the globe is open at the poles and another world and another humanity resident on the concavity of a hollow earth; and even Thoreau, who gave lectures in the basements of churches.

This "Philosophy of Furniture" was by an unlikely writer: Edgar Allan Poe. In it he explains how rooms should be decorated. "We have no aristocracy of the blood," says this author who was educated at a university founded by Thomas Jefferson, "and having therefore as a natural, and indeed as an inevitable thing, fashioned for ourselves an aristocracy of dollars, the *display of wealth* has here to take the place and perform the office of the heraldic display in monarchial countries."

We are familiar with Poe's anxiety about good taste, about the fidelity of the United States to European models. What we want to see in this essay is a clue to the structure of Poe's imagination, which Charles Baudelaire thought the greatest of the century, an imagination so fine that Paul Valéry said it was incapable of making a mistake.

Poe's sense of good taste in decoration was in harmony with the best English style of the early Victorian period; we recognize his ideal room as one in which we might find the young Carlyles, those strenuous aesthetes, or George Eliot and Elizabeth Gaskell—a glory of wallpaper, figured rugs, marble-top tables, tall narrow windows with dark red curtains, sofas, antimacassars, vases, unfading wax flowers under bell jars, a rosewood piano, and a cozy fireplace. The amazing thing is that Poe emphasizes lightness and grace, color and clarity; whereas we associate his imagination with the most claustrophobic, dark, Gothic interiors in all of literature.

On our walls, Poe says, we should have many paintings to relieve the expanse of wallpaper—"a glossy paper of silver-grey tint, spotted with small arabesque devices of a fainter hue." "These are," he dictates, "chiefly landscapes of an imaginative cast—such as the fairy grottoes of Stanfield, or the lake of the Dismal Swamp of Chapman. There are, nevertheless, three or four female heads, of an ethereal beauty—portraits in the manner of Sully."

In another evocation of an ideal room, in a sketch called "Landor's Cottage" he again describes a wall with pictures: ". . . three of Julien's exquisite lithographs *à trois crayons,* fastened to the wall without frames. One of these drawings was a scene of Oriental luxury, or rather voluptuousness; another was a 'carnival piece', spirited beyond compare; the third was a

Greek female head—a face so divinely beautiful, and yet of an expression so provokingly indeterminate, never before arrested my attention."

Poe titled the collection of his stories published that year *Tales of the Grotesque and Arabesque*. These two adjectives have given critics trouble for years. *Grotesque,* as Poe found it in the writings of Sir Walter Scott, means something close to *Gothic,* an adjective designating the Goths and their architecture, and what the neoclassical eighteenth century thought of mediæveal art in general, that it was ugly but grand. It was the fanciful decoration by the Italians of grottoes, or caves, with shells, and statues of ogres and giants from the realm of legend, that gave the word *grotesque* its meaning of *freakish, monstrous, misshapen.*

Arabesque clearly means the intricate, nonrepresentational, infinitely graceful decorative style of Islam, best known to us in their carpets, the geometric tile-work of their mosques, and their calligraphy.

Had Poe wanted to designate the components of his imagination more accurately, his title would have been, *Tales of the Grotesque, Arabesque, and Classical.* For Poe in all his writing divided all his imagery up into three distinct species.

Look back at the pictures on the wall in his ideal rooms. In one we have grottoes and a view of the Dismal Swamp: this is the grotesque mode. Then female heads in the manner of Sully: this is the classical mode. The wallpaper against which they hang is arabesque.

In the other room we had a scene of oriental luxury: the arabesque, a carnival piece spirited beyond compare (Poe means masked and costumed people, at Mardi Gras, as in "The Cask of Amontillado" and "The Masque of the Red Death"): the grotesque, and a Greek female head: the classical.

A thorough inspection of Poe's work will disclose that he performs variations and mutations of these three vocabularies of imagery. We can readily recognize those works in which a particular idiom is dominant. The great octosyllabic sonnet "To Helen," for instance, is classical, "The Fall of the House of Usher" is grotesque, and the poem "Israfel" is arabesque.

But no work is restricted to one mode; the other two are there also. We all know the beautiful "To Helen," written when he was still a boy:

> Helen, thy beauty is to me
> Like those Nicaean barks of yore,
> That gently, o'er a perfumed sea,
> The weary, way-worn wanderer bore
> To his own native shore.

On desperate seas long wont to roam,
Thy hyacinth hair, thy classic face,
Thy Naiad airs have brought me home
To the glory that was Greece
And the grandeur that was Rome.

Lo! in yon brilliant window niche
How statue-like I see thee stand,
The agate lamp within thy hand!
Ah, Psyche, from the regions which
Are Holy Land!

The words are as magic as Keats, but what is the sense? Sappho, whom Poe is imitating, had compared a woman's beauty to a fleet of ships. Byron had previously written lines that Poe outbyrons Byron with, in "the glory that was Greece/And the grandeur that was Rome." But how is Helen also Psyche; who is the wanderer coming home? Scholars are not sure. In fact, the poem is not easy to defend against the strictures of critics. We can point out that *Nicaean* is not, as has been charged, a pretty bit of gibberish, but the adjective for the city of Nice, where a major shipworks was: Marc Antony's fleet was built there. We can defend *perfumed sea*, which has been called silly, by noting that classical ships never left sight of land, and could smell orchards on shore, that perfumed oil was an extensive industry in classical times and that ships laden with it would smell better than your shipload of sheep. Poe is normally far more exact than he is given credit for.

That window-niche, however, slipped in from Northern Europe; it is Gothic, a slight tone of the grotto in this almost wholly classical poem. And the closing words, "Holy Land," belong to the Levant, to the arabesque.

In "The Raven" we have a dominant grotesque key, with a vision of an arabesque Eden, "perfumed from an unseen censer / Swung by Seraphim whose footfalls tinkled on the tufted floor," and a grotesque raven sits on a classical bust of Pallas Athene. That raven was the device on the flag of Alaric the Visigoth, whose torch at Eleusis was the beginning of the end of Pallas's reign over the mind of man. Lenore (a name Walter Scott brought from Germany for his horse) is a mutation of Eleanor, a French mutation of Helen.

Were we to follow the metamorphoses of these images through all of Poe—grotesque, or Gothic; arabesque, or Islamic; classical, or Graeco-Roman—we would discover an articulate grammar of symbols, a new, as yet unread Poe. What we shall need to understand is the meaning of the symbols, and why they are constantly being translated from one imagistic idiom to another.

The clues are not difficult, or particularly arcane. Israfel for instance is an arabesque, and Roderick Usher a grotesque Orpheus; Orpheus himself does not appear in Poe in his native Greek self. But once we see Orpheus in Usher, we can then see that this masterpiece is a retelling of his myth from a point of view informed by a modern understanding of neuroses, of the inexplicable perverseness of the human will. That lute, that speaking guitar, all those books on Usher's table about journeys underground and rites held in darkness—all fit into a translation by Poe of a classical text into a Gothic one. "The Gold Bug," as Northrop Frye has seen, is strangely like the marriage of Danaë; the old black who lowers the gold bug is named Jupiter. Danaë was shut up in a treasure house and a riddle put her there.

Where do these images come from? The Mediterranean in the time of Columbus was from its western end and along its northern shore Graeco-Roman, what historians call the Latin culture, and at its eastern end, and along its southern shore, Islamic. So two thirds of Poe's triple imagery sums up the Mediterranean, and fed his imagination with its most congenial and rich portion. The Gothic style has its home in northern Europe, "my Germany of the soul" as Poe put it. He was always ambiguous about the culture with which, ironically, he is identified. Death, corruption, and dreariness inhere in the Gothic. Poe relates it to melancholia, hypersensitivity, madness, obsession, awful whirlpools in the cold sea, ancient houses spent and crumbling. Is there some pattern here from his own life? There is a real House of Usher, still standing, not in a gloomy Transylvanian valley by a black tarn, but in Boston, Massachusetts, where Poe was born, and where his barely remembered mother played the first Ophelia on an American stage, a rôle definitively Gothic in Poe's scheme of modes.[1]

Poe's sense of Islam, which we can trace to Byron and Shelley, derived as well from the explorers Burckhardt, Volney, and John Lloyd Stephens. The angel Israfel is not, as Poe wants us to believe, in the Koran, but from George Sale's introduction to his translation of the *Koran* by way of Thomas Moore.

The classical was being restated before Poe's eyes in Charlottesville by an old man who said he loved a particular Greek temple as if it were his mistress. Jefferson had the undergraduates up to dinner at Monticello two at a time, in alphabetical order. *P* is deep in the alphabet; Poe was

---

[1] Fiske Kimball, *Domestic Architecture of the American Colonies and of the Early Republic* (New York: Dover, 1966), p. 275.

expelled and the old man dead before the two most astute readers of Alexander von Humboldt in the United States could face each other over a platter of Virginia ham.

Poe's imagination was perfectly at home in geographies he had no knowledge of except what his imagination appropriated from other writers. We might assume, in ignorance, that he knew Paris like a Parisian, that Italy and Spain were familiar to him, and even Antarctica and the face of the moon.

The brothers Goncourt wrote in their journal as early as 1856 that Poe was a new kind of man writing a new kind of literature. We have still to learn that his sensibility was radically intelligent rather than emotional.

When he compares the eyes of Ligeia to stars, they are the binary stars that Herschel discovered and explained in the year of Poe's birth (the spectroscopic double Beta Lyra and the double double Epsilon Lyra, to be exact), not the generalized stars of Petrarchan tradition. We have paid too little attention to this metaphysical Poe; and we scarcely understand Europeans when they speak of the passion they find in his poetry. What are we to think of the Russian translator of Poe, Vladimir Pyast, who, while reciting "Ulalume" in a St. Petersburg theater, went stark raving mad? Russians treasure the memory of that evening.

Night after night, from 1912 to 1917, a man who might have been the invention of Poe, sat in a long, almost empty room in a working-class district of Berlin, writing a book by candle light. *Might have been the invention of Poe*—he was basically a classicist, his doctoral thesis was on Heraclitus, his mind was shaped by Goethe, Nietzsche, von Humboldt, and Leo Frobenius, the anthropologist and cultural morphologist. Like Poe, he thought in symbols.

He was Oswald Spengler. His big book, *The Decline of the West,* was meant to parallel the military campaigns of the Wermacht in 1914–1918, which by pedantic adherence to tactics and heroic fervor was to impose German regularity and destiny upon Europe. Spengler's book, like the Wermacht, imposed only a tragic sense that history is independent of our will, ironically perverse, and, a nightmare.

The value of *The Decline of the West* is in its poetry of vision, its intuition of the rise, growth, and decline of cultures. By culture Spengler meant the formative energy of a people, lasting for thousands of years. A civilization is the maturity of a culture, and inevitably its decline. His feeling for the effeteness of a finished culture was precisely that of Poe in "The Fall of the House of Usher" and "The Murders in the Rue Morgue"—both stories about the vulnerability of order and civilized achievement.

Spengler's most useful intuition was to divide world cultures into three major styles: the Apollonian, or Graeco-Roman; the Faustian, or Western-Northern European; and the Magian, or Asian and Islamic. Historians instantly complained that the cultures of our world may not be divided into three but into seventy-six distinct groups.

What interests us, however, is that Spengler's categories are exactly those of Edgar Allan Poe.

And those of James Joyce. Look at the first three stories of Joyce's *Dubliners*. The first is concerned with a violation of rites that derive from deep in Latin culture by way of the Roman Mass, the second takes its symbols from chivalry, the moral codes of Northern knighthood, and the third is named "Araby." This triad of symbolic patterns is repeated four more times, to achieve fifteen stories. The first three chapters of *Ulysses* also follow this structure, even more complexly; and the simplest shape to which we can summarize *Ulysses* is to say that it is about a man, Leopold Bloom, in a northern European, a Faustian-technological context, who is by heritage a Jew of Spengler's Magian culture, who is made to act out the adventures of Ulysses, exemplar of classical man.

"We have museum catalogues but no artistic atlases," the great French historian and cultural geographer Fernand Braudel complains in his *The Mediterranean and the Mediterranean World in the Age of Philip II,* "We have histories of art and literature but none of civilization."

He suspects that such a map of the arts would disclose the same kind of historical structure that he has demonstrated for food, clothing, trade routes, industrial and banking centers; and that our understanding of our imaginative life would take on as yet unguessed coherence and hitherto uncomprehended behavior.

Such a map would presumably display such phenomena as the contours of the worship of Demeter and Persephone, coinciding with grain-producing terrain, and with the contours of Catholicism. This would not surprise us. It might also show how the structure of psychology and drama nourished by grain-producing cultures persists outside that terrain, continuing to act as if it were inside, because its imaginative authority refuses to abdicate.

How else can we explain a story like O. Henry's "The Church with the Overshot Wheel"? In this poignant little tale, set in the pinewoods of North Carolina, a miller's daughter named Aglaia (a name commensurate with the style of naming girls in the Fancy Names Belt) is kidnapped by shiftless rovers who take her to Atlanta. The miller in his grief moves away to the Northwest, becomes prosperous and a philanthropist, naming his best brand of flour for his lost daughter whom he supposes to be dead. In her memory he has his old mill rebuilt as a church, endowing it handsomely, but keeping its overshot wheel. The community becomes a summer resort for people of modest means; and of course O. Henry has the orphan daughter come to it as a grown woman, and in a typical denouement, her memory of a song she used to sing as a child, together with an accidental spill of flour over her father, who is visiting the old mill, reunites them. O. Henry, perhaps unconsciously, has retold the myth of Persephone, using a name, Aglaia, "the bright girl," which was one of the epithets of Persephone, deification of wheat, and all the elements of the myth, transposed to twentieth-century America: the rape that brought devastation, the return and reunion that brought healing and regeneration.

I find an explanation of this story according to the theory of Jungian archetypes—patterns imprinted in the mind—unsatisfactory. It is better to trace O. Henry's plot and symbols backward along geographical lines, through myths brought across the Atlantic from the Mediterranean, through books and schoolrooms, through libraries and traditions, and to assess his story as a detail in the structure of a culture of strong vitality which decided on the expressiveness of certain symbols five thousand years ago, and finds them undiminished and still full of human significance.

The appeal of popular literature must lie precisely in its faithfulness to ancient traditions. The charming little children's book by Carlo Collodi, *Le Avventuri di Pinocchio,* can scarcely claim to be included in a history of Italian literature, and yet to a geographer of the imagination it is a more elegant paradigm of the narrative art of the Mediterranean than any other book since Ovid's *Metamorphoses,* rehearses all the central myths, and adds its own to the rich stock of its traditions. It reaches back to a Gnostic theme known to both Shakespeare and Emily Dickinson: "Split the stick," said Jesus, "and I am there." It combines Pygmalion, Ovid, the book of Jonah, the Commedia dell'Arte, and Apuleius; and will continue to be a touchstone of the imagination.

The discovery of America, its settlement, and economic development, were activities of the Renaissance and the Reformation, Mediterranean tradition and northern acumen. The continuities of that double heritage have been longlasting. The *Pequod* set out from Joppa, the first Thoreau was named Diogenes, Whitman is a contemporary of Socrates, the *Spoon River Anthology* was first written in Alexandria; for thirty years now our greatest living writer, Eudora Welty, has been rewriting Ovid in Mississippi. "The Jumping Frog of Calaveras County" was a turn for a fifth-century Athenian mime.

A geography of the imagination would extend the shores of the Mediterranean all the way to Iowa.

Eldon, Iowa—where in 1929 Grant Wood sketched a farmhouse as the background for a double portrait of his sister Nan and his dentist, Dr. B. H. McKeeby, who donned overalls for the occasion and held a rake. Forces that arose three millennia ago in the Mediterranean changed the rake to a pitchfork, as we shall see.

Let us look at this painting to which we are blinded by familiarity and parody. In the remotest distance against this perfect blue of a fine harvest sky, there is the Gothic spire of a country church, as if to seal the Protestant sobriety and industry of the subjects. Next there are trees, seven of them, as along the porch of Solomon's temple, symbols of prudence and wisdom.

Next, still reading from background to foreground, is the house that gives the primary meaning of the title, *American Gothic*, a style of architecture. It is an example of a revolution in domestic building that made possible the rapid rise of American cities after the Civil War and dotted the prairies with decent, neat farmhouses. It is what was first called in derision a balloon-frame house, so easy to build that a father and his son could put it up. It is an elegant geometry of light timber posts and rafters requiring no deep foundation, and is nailed together. Technically, it is, like the clothes of the farmer and his wife, a mail-order house, as the design comes out of a pattern-book, this one from those of Alexander Davis and Andrew Downing, the architects who modified details of the Gothic Revival for American farmhouses. The balloon-frame house was invented in Chicago in 1833 by George Washington Snow, who was orchestrating in his invention a century of mechanization that provided the nails, wire-screen, sash-windows, tin roof, lathe-turned posts for the porch, door-knobs, locks, and hinges—all standard pieces from factories.

We can see a bamboo sunscreen—out of China by way of Sears Roebuck—that rolls up like a sail: nautical technology applied to the prairie. We can see that distinctly American feature, the screen door. The sash-windows are European in origin, their glass panes from Venetian technology as perfected by the English, a luxury that was a marvel of the eighteenth century, and now as common as the farmer's spectacles, another revolution in technology that would have seemed a miracle to previous ages. Spectacles begin in the thirteenth century, the invention of either Salvino degl'Armati or Alessandro della Spina; the first portrait of a person wearing specs is of Cardinal Ugone di Provenza, in a fresco of 1352 by Tommaso Barisino di Modena. We might note, as we are trying to see the geographical focus that this painting gathers together, that the center for lens grinding from which eyeglasses diffused to the rest of civilization was the same part of Holland from which the style of the painting itself derives.

Another thirteenth-century invention prominent in our painting is the buttonhole. Buttons themselves are prehistoric, but they were shoulder-fasteners that engaged with loops. Modern clothing begins with the buttonhole. The farmer's wife secures her Dutch Calvinist collar with a cameo brooch, an heirloom passed down the generations, an eighteenth-century or Victorian copy of a design that goes back to the sixth century B.C.

She is a product of the ages, this modest Iowa farm wife: she has the hair-do of a mediæval madonna, a Reformation collar, a Greek cameo, a nineteenth-century pinafore.

Martin Luther put her a step behind her husband; John Knox squared her shoulders; the stock-market crash of 1929 put that look in her eyes.

The train that brought her clothes—paper pattern, bolt cloth, needle, thread, scissors—also brought her husband's bib overalls, which were originally, in the 1870s, trainmen's workclothes designed in Europe, manufactured here by J. C. Penney, and disseminated across the United States as the railroads connected city with city. The cloth is denim, from Nîmes in France, introduced by Levi Strauss of blue-jean fame. The design can be traced to no less a person than Herbert Spencer, who thought he was creating a utilitarian one-piece suit for everybody to wear. His own example was of tweed, with buttons from crotch to neck, and his female relatives somehow survived the mortification of his sporting it one Sunday in St. James Park.

His jacket is the modification of that of a Scots shepherd which we all still wear.

Grant Wood's Iowans stand, as we might guess, in a pose dictated by the Brownie box camera, close together in front of their house, the farmer looking at the lens with solemn honesty, his wife with modestly averted eyes. But that will not account for the pitchfork held as assertively as a minuteman's rifle. The pose is rather that of the Egyptian prince Rahotep, holding the flail of Osiris, beside his wife Nufrit—strict with pious rectitude, poised in absolute dignity, mediators between heaven and earth, givers of grain, obedient to the gods.

This formal pose lasts out 3000 years of Egyptian history, passes to some of the classical cultures—Etruscan couples in terra cotta, for instance—but does not attract Greece and Rome. It recommences in northern Europe, where (to the dismay of the Romans) Gaulish wives rode beside their husbands in the war chariot. Kings and eventually the merchants of the North repeated the Egyptian double portrait of husband and wife: van Eyck's Meester and Frouw Arnolfini; Rubens and his wife Helena. It was this Netherlandish tradition of painting middle-class folk with honor and precision that turned Grant Wood from Montparnasse, where he spent two years in the 1920s trying to be an American post-Impressionist, back to Iowa, to be our Hans Memling.

If Van Gogh could ask, "Where is my Japan?" and be told by Toulouse-Lautrec that it was Provence, Wood asked himself the where-abouts of his Holland, and found it in Iowa.

Just thirty years before Wood's painting, Edwin Markham's poem, "The Man with the Hoe" had pictured the farmer as a peasant with a life scarcely different from that of an ox, and called on the working men of the world to unite, as they had nothing to lose but their chains. The painting that inspired Markham was one of a series of agricultural subjects by Jean Françcois Millet, whose work also inspired Van Gogh. A digging fork appears in five of Van Gogh's pictures, three of them variations on themes by Millet, and all of them are studies of grinding labor and poverty.

And yet the Independent Farmer had edged out the idle aristocrat for the hand of the girl in Royal Tyler's "The Contrast," the first native Amer-ican comedy for the stage, and in Emerson's "Concord Hymn" it is a battle-line of farmers who fire the shot heard around the world. George III, indeed, referred to his American colonies as "the farms," and the two Georges of the Revolution, Hanover and Washington, were proudly farm-ers by etymology and in reality.

The window curtains and apron in this painting are both calico printed in a reticular design, the curtains of rhombuses, the apron of cir-cles and dots, the configuration Sir Thomas Browne traced through nature and art in his *Garden of Cyrus,* the quincunxial arrangement of trees in orchards, perhaps the first human imitation of phyllotaxis, acknowledging the symmetry, justice, and divine organization of nature.

Curtains and aprons are as old as civilization itself, but their presence here in Iowa implies a cotton mill, a dye works, a roller press that prints calico, and a wholesale-retail distribution system involving a post office, a train, its tracks, and, in short, the Industrial Revolution.

That revolution came to America in the astounding memory of one man, Samuel Slater, who arrived in Philadelphia in 1789 with the plans of all Arkwright's, Crompton's, and Hargreaves's machinery in his head, put himself at the service of the rich Quaker Moses Brown, and built the first American factory at Pawtucket, Rhode Island.

The apron is trimmed with rickrack ribbon, a machine-made substitute for lace. The curtains are bordered in a variant of the egg-and-dart design that comes from Nabataea, the Biblical Edom, in Syria, a design which the architect Hiram incorporated into the entablatures of Solomon's temple—"and the chapiters upon the two pillars had pomegranates also above, over against the belly which was by the network: and the pomegranates were two hundred in rows round about" (1 Kings 7:20) and which formed the border of the high priest's dress, a frieze of "pomegranates of blue, and of purple, and of scarlet, around about the hem thereof; and bells of gold between them round about" (Exodus 28:33).

The brass button that secures the farmer's collar is an unassertive, puritanical understatement of Matthew Boulton's eighteenth-century cut-steel button made in the factory of James Watt. His shirt button is mother-of-pearl, made by James Boepple from Mississippi fresh-water mussel shell, and his jacket button is of South American vegetable ivory passing for horn.

The farmer and his wife are attended by symbols, she by two plants on the porch, a potted geranium and sanseveria, both tropical and alien to Iowa; he by the three-tined American pitchfork whose triune shape is repeated throughout the painting, in the bib of the overalls, the windows, the faces, the siding of the house, to give it a formal organization of impeccable harmony.

If this painting is primarily a statement about Protestant diligence on the American frontier, carrying in its style and subject a wealth of information about imported technology, psychology, and aesthetics, it still does not turn away from a pervasive cultural theme of Mediterranean origin— a tension between the growing and the ungrowing, between vegetable and mineral, organic and inorganic, wheat and iron.

Transposed back into its native geography, this icon of the lord of metals with his iron sceptre, head wreathed with glass and silver, buckled in tin and brass, and a chaste bride who has already taken on the metallic thraldom of her plight in the gold ovals of her hair and brooch, are Dis and Persephone posed in a royal portrait among the attributes of the first Mediterranean trinity, Zeus in the blue sky and lightning rod, Poseidon in the trident of the pitchfork, Hades in the metals. It is a picture of a sheaf of golden grain, female and cyclical, perennial and the mother of civilization; and of metal shaped into scythe and hoe: nature and technology, earth and farmer, man and world, and their achievement together.

CONSIDERATIONS

Thinking

What does Davenport mean by "the imagination"? What are its abilities and functions? In what sense does imagination reflect geographical boundaries? To what extent can those boundaries be crossed? Why is crossing boundaries important?

Davenport's erudition is vast and his imagination boundless. Select one example of Davenport's erudition and explain how it contributes to the imaginative power of his essay.

Connecting

Davenport's essay revels in making connections, the more far-fetched the better. Summarize the connections he makes between any three examples he cites.

Choose a painting or a photograph with which you are familiar and try to look at it the way Davenport looks at Grant Wood's *American Gothic* (p. 200), which Davenport describes in detail through his essay.

Writing

Write an essay in which you explore connections between three different things. They can be things you've seen, heard, read about, heard about, wondered about. Try to discover some connections that are not immediately obvious.

Write a letter to Guy Davenport asking him questions, offering him suggestions, or otherwise discussing with him observations you have about his essay.

MARY CASSATT, *THE FAMILY,*
1924.

OIL ON CANVAS, 32 1/4 ×
26 1/8 IN.

THE CHRYSLER MUSEUM,
NORFOLK, VIRGINIA. GIFT OF
WALTER P. CHRYSLER, JR.,
71.498.

LISA FIFIELD, *RUNNING ELK,*
1993.

WALTERCOLOR, GOUACHE, AND
ACRYLIC ON PAPER, 22 × 30 IN.

COLLECTION OF PAT HOY.
© 1993 LISA FIFIELD.

EDWARD HOPPER, *NIGHTHAWKS*, 1942.
OIL ON CANVAS, 84.1 × 152.4 CM, FRIENDS OF AMERICAN ART COLLECTION, 1942.51.
PHOTOGRAPH © 1995, THE ART INSTITUTE OF CHICAGO. ALL RIGHTS RESERVED.

JEAN AUGUSTE DOMINIQUE INGRES, *LA GRANDE ODALISQUE*, 1814.
OIL ON CANVAS, 2 FT 11 1/4 IN × 5 FT 3 3/4 IN.
LOUVRE, PARIS. ERICH LESSING/ART RESOURCE, NY.

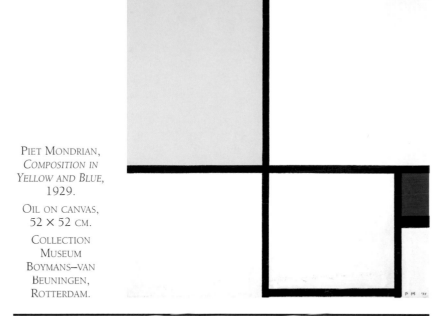

PIET MONDRIAN,
*COMPOSITION IN
YELLOW AND BLUE,*
1929.

OIL ON CANVAS,
52 × 52 CM.

COLLECTION
MUSEUM
BOYMANS–VAN
BEUNINGEN,
ROTTERDAM.

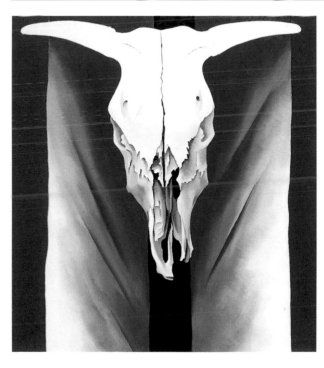

GEORGIA O'KEEFFE,
*COW'S SKULL: RED,
WHITE AND BLUE,*
1931.

OIL ON CANVAS,
39 7/8 × 35 7/8 IN.

THE METROPOLITAN
MUSEUM OF ART,
ALFRED STIEGLITZ
COLLECTION, 1952
(52.203).

PABLO PICASSO, *GUERNICA*, 1937.
OIL ON CANVAS, 11 FT 5 1/2 IN. × 25 FT 5 3/4 IN.
© COPYRIGHT ARS, NY. CENTRO DE ARTE REINA SOFIA, MADRID. GIRAUDON/ART
RESOURCE, NY.

GRANT WOOD,
AMERICAN GOTHIC,
1930.

OIL ON BEAVER
BOARD, 74. 3 ×
62.4 CM, FRIENDS
OF AMERICAN ART
COLLECTION,
1930.934.

PHOTOGRAPH ©
1995, THE ART
INSTITUTE OF
CHICAGO. ALL
RIGHTS RESERVED.

J oan Didion
(b.1934)

J oan Didion is a writer of great diversity. She has published five nonfiction works: *Slouching Toward Bethlehem, The White Album, Salvador, Miami,* and *After Henry;* four novels: *Run River, Play It As It Lays, The Book of Common Prayer,* and *Democracy;* and sketches, reviews, and screenplays. In all of Didion's work, there is a subtle, understated longing for a less complex, more stable world than the one we live in, but there is no whining, no refusal to go forward. Neither is hers a solipsistic vision. Facing the personal, facing the self, is to face the world on the barest of terms: alone.

We catch glimpses of Didion's toughness by the way she writes about and admires Georgia O'Keeffe's "hardness." She turns that hardness into something far more intriguing than fluttering eyelashes and submissiveness.

Georgia O'Keeffe

"**W**here I was born and where and how I have lived is unimportant," Georgia O'Keeffe told us in the book of paintings and words published in her ninetieth year on earth. She seemed to be advising us to forget the beautiful face in the Stieglitz photographs. She appeared to be dismissing the rather condescending romance that had attached to her by then, the romance of extreme good looks and advanced age and deliberate isolation. "It is what I have done with where I have been that should be of interest." I recall an August afternoon in Chicago in 1973 when I took my daughter, then seven, to see what Georgia O'Keeffe had done with where she had been. One of the vast O'Keeffe "Sky Above Clouds" canvases floated over the back stairs in the Chicago Art Institute that day, dominating what seemed to be several stories of empty light, and my daughter looked at it once, ran to the landing, and kept on looking. "Who drew it," she whispered after a while. I told her. "I need to talk to her," she said finally.

My daughter was making, that day in Chicago, an entirely unconscious but quite basic assumption about people and the work they do. She was assuming that the glory she saw in the work reflected a glory in its maker, that the painting was the painter as the poem is the poet, that every choice one made alone—every word chosen or rejected, every brush stroke laid or not laid down—betrayed one's character. *Style is character.* It seemed to me that afternoon that I had rarely seen so instinctive an application of this familiar principle, and I recall being pleased not only that my daughter responded to style as character but that it was Georgia O'Keeffe's particular style to which she responded: this was a hard woman who had imposed her 192 square feet of clouds on Chicago.

"Hardness" has not been in our century a quality much admired in women, nor in the past twenty years has it even been in official favor for men. When hardness surfaces in the very old we tend to transform it into "crustiness" or eccentricity, some tonic pepperiness to be indulged at a distance. On the evidence of her work and what she has said about it, Georgia O'Keeffe is neither "crusty" nor eccentric. She is simply hard, a straight shooter, a woman clean of received wisdom and open to what she sees. This is a woman who could early on dismiss most of her contemporaries as "dreamy," and would later single out one she liked as "a very poor painter." (And then add, apparently by way of softening the judgment: "I guess he wasn't a painter at all. He had no courage and I believe that to create one's own world in any of the arts takes courage.") This is a woman who in 1939 could advise her admirers that they were missing her point, that their appreciation of her famous flowers was merely sentimental. "When I paint a red hill," she observed coolly in the catalogue for an exhibition that year, "you say it is too bad that I don't always paint flowers. A flower touches almost everyone's heart. A red hill doesn't touch everyone's heart." This is a woman who could describe the genesis of one of her most well-known paintings—the "Cow's Skull: Red, White and Blue" owned by the Metropolitan—as an act of quite deliberate and derisive orneriness. "I thought of the city men I had been seeing in the East," she wrote. "They talked so often of writing the Great American Novel— the Great American Play—the Great American Poetry. . . . So as I was painting my cow's head on blue I thought to myself, 'I'll make it an American painting. They will not think it great with the red stripes down the sides—Red, White and Blue—but they will notice it.'"

The city men. The men. They. The words crop up again and again as this astonishingly aggressive woman tells us what was on her mind when she was making her astonishingly aggressive paintings. It was those city men who stood accused of sentimentalizing her flowers: "I made you take time to look at what I saw and when you took time to really notice my flower you hung all your associations with flowers on my flower and you write about my flower as if I think and see what you think and see—and I don't." *And I don't.* Imagine those words spoken, and the sound you hear is *don't tread on me.* "The men" believed it impossible to paint New York, so Georgia O'Keeffe painted New York. "The men" didn't think much of her bright color, so she made it brighter. The men yearned toward Europe so she went to Texas, and then New Mexico. The men talked about Cézanne, "long involved remarks about the 'plastic quality' of his form and color," and took one another's long involved remarks, in the view of this angelic rattlesnake in their midst, altogether too seriously. "I can paint one of those dismal-colored paintings like the men," the woman who regarded herself always as an outsider remembers thinking one day in 1922, and she did: a painting of a shed "all low-toned and dreary with the tree beside the door." She called this act of rancor "The Shanty" and hung it in her next show. "The men seemed to approve of it," she reported fifty-four years later, her contempt undimmed. "They seemed to think that maybe I was beginning to paint. That was my only low-toned dismal-colored painting."

Some women fight and others do not. Like so many successful guerrillas in the war between the sexes, Georgia O'Keeffe seems to have been equipped early with an immutable sense of who she was and a fairly clear understanding that she would be required to prove it. On the surface her upbringing was conventional. She was a child on the Wisconsin prairie who played with china dolls and painted watercolors with cloudy skies because sunlight was too hard to paint and, with her brother and sisters, listened every night to her mother read stories of the Wild West, of Texas, of Kit Carson and Billy the Kid. She told adults that she wanted to be an artist and was embarrassed when they asked what kind of artist she wanted to be: she had no idea "what kind." She had no idea what artists did. She had never seen a picture that interested her, other than a pen-and-ink Maid of Athens in one of her mother's books, some Mother Goose illustrations printed on cloth, a tablet cover that showed a little girl with pink roses, and the painting of Arabs on horseback that hung in her grandmother's parlor. At thirteen, in a Dominican convent, she was mortified when the sister corrected her drawing. At Chatham Episcopal Institute in Virginia she painted lilacs and sneaked time alone to walk out to where she could see the line of the Blue Ridge Mountains on the horizon. At the Art Institute in Chicago she was shocked by the presence of live models and wanted to abandon anatomy lessons. At the Art Students League in New York one of her fellow students advised her that, since he would be a great painter and she would end up teaching painting in a girls' school, any work of hers was less important than modeling for him. Another painted over her work to show her how the Impressionists did trees. She had not before heard how the Impressionists did trees and she did not much care.

At twenty-four she left all those opinions behind and went for the first time to live in Texas, where there were no trees to paint and no one to tell her how not to paint them. In Texas there was only the horizon she craved. In Texas she had her sister Claudia with her for a while, and in the late afternoons they would walk away from town and toward the horizon and watch the evening star come out. "That evening star fascinated me," she wrote. "It was in some way very exciting to me. My sister had a gun, and as we walked she would throw bottles into the air and shoot as many as she could before they hit the ground. I had nothing but to walk into nowhere and the wide sunset space with the star. Ten watercolors were made from that star." In a way one's interest is compelled as much by the sister Claudia with the gun as by the painter Georgia with the star, but only the painter left us this shining record. Ten watercolors were made from that star.

CONSIDERATIONS

Thinking

What do you think about hardness—"a straight shooter, a woman clean of received wisdom and open to what she sees"—in a woman? In a man?

To what extent does Didion's celebration of O'Keeffe's aggressiveness turn on itself, raising the possibility that O'Keeffe may have needed the men to set her work in motion?

Referring to the men, O'Keeffe makes this judgment: "I made you take time to look at what I saw and when you took time to really notice my flower you hung all your associations with flowers on my flower and you write about my flower as if I think and see what you think and see—and I don't." Aren't we bound inevitably to hang all our associations on whatever we are looking at? To what extent can we ever see what is there before us—seeing the object as it really is?

Connecting

In his famous preface to *The Renaissance,* a collection of essays about painters, Walter Pater says that the critic's primary aim is not—as Matthew Arnold had claimed—to see the object (whether painting, book, poem, personality) as it really is, but to "know one's impression of the object as it really is." Which of these men seems closer to describing the way Didion gives us O'Keeffe's work?

What is the connection between Texas and New Mexico and what *you* see in O'Keeffe's paintings? Do those flowers actually have anything to do with the American southwest? Speculate.

Just how much of Didion do you find in her analysis of O'Keeffe?

Writing

Go to your college library and look at a collection of O'Keeffe's paintings. Imagine why Didion's seven-year-old daughter, after looking at "Sky Above Clouds," exclaimed to her mother about O'Keeffe, "I need to talk to her." Didion offers an explanation of why she thinks her daughter wanted to see O'Keeffe. Assume that you are Didion's daughter; consider your mother's conjecture, and write your own reasons for wanting to talk to O'Keeffe.

In his essay "On Not Looking at Pictures," E. M. Forster says that paintings send him off on "alien visions." He has a hard time holding his imagination to the painting. Select one of O'Keeffe's paintings, focus on just what you can see there in the painting, and write about it. Then set your mind free and write about your associations. Which reaction do you prefer? Explain.

A nnie Dillard
(b.1945)

A nnie Dillard has taught creative writing at Wesleyan University in
Connecticut. She lived for a time in Roanoke, Virginia, a setting
she used to wonderful effect in her first book, *Pilgrim at Tinker
Creek*, which won a Pulitzer Prize. Since then, Dillard has spent quite a lot
of time living on Puget Sound, as well as writing a number of books,
including *Living by Fiction,* a critical study; *Teaching a Stone to Talk,* a
collection of essays; and *An American Childhood,* a portion of her
autobiography. Dillard's essays can be demanding both intellectually and
emotionally.

Her essay "Living Like Weasels" is both surprising and intellectually
provocative. One of its most notable features is its images suggesting the
weasel's tenacity—images that Dillard introduces in the opening
paragraphs of her essay.

Living Like Weasels

A weasel is wild. Who knows what he thinks? He sleeps in his underground den, his tail draped over his nose. Sometimes he lives in his den for two days without leaving. Outside, he stalks rabbits, mice, muskrats, and birds, killing more bodies than he can eat warm, and often dragging the carcasses home. Obedient to instinct, he bites his prey at the neck, either splitting the jugular vein at the throat or crunching the brain at the base of the skull, and he does not let go. One naturalist refused to kill a weasel who was socketed into his hand deeply as a rattlesnake. The man could in no way pry the tiny weasel off, and he had to walk half a mile to water, the weasel dangling from his palm, and soak him off like a stubborn label.

And once, says Ernest Thompson Seton—once, a man shot an eagle out of the sky. He examined the eagle and found the dry skull of a weasel fixed by the jaws to his throat. The supposition is that the eagle had pounced on the weasel and the weasel swiveled and bit as instinct taught him, tooth to neck, and nearly won. I would like to have seen that eagle from the air a few weeks or months before he was shot: was the whole weasel still attached to his feathered throat, a fur pendant? Or did the eagle eat what he could reach, gutting the living weasel with his talons before his breast, bending his beak, cleaning the beautiful airborne bones?

I have been reading about weasels because I saw one last week. I startled a weasel who startled me, and we exchanged a long glance.

Twenty minutes from my house, through the woods by the quarry and across the highway, is Hollins Pond, a remarkable piece of shallowness, where I like to go at sunset and sit on a tree trunk. Hollins Pond is also called Murray's Pond; it covers two acres of bottomland near Tinker Creek with six inches of water and six thousand lily pads. In winter, brown-and-white steers stand in the middle of it, merely dampening their hooves; from the distant shore they look like miracle itself, complete with miracle's nonchalance. Now, in summer, the steers are gone. The water lilies have blossomed and spread to a green horizontal plane that is terra firma to plodding blackbirds, and tremulous ceiling to black leeches, crayfish, and carp.

211

This is, mind you, suburbia. It is a five-minute walk in three directions to rows of houses, though none is visible here. There's a 55 mph highway at one end of the pond, and a nesting pair of wood ducks at the other. Under every bush is a muskrat hole or a beer can. The far end is an alternating series of fields and woods, fields and woods, threaded everywhere with motorcycle tracks—in whose bare clay wild turtles lay eggs.

So. I had crossed the highway, stepped over two low barbed-wire fences, and traced the motorcycle path in all gratitude through the wild rose and poison ivy of the pond's shoreline up into high grassy fields. Then I cut down through the woods to the mossy fallen tree where I sit. This tree is excellent. It makes a dry, upholstered bench at the upper, marshy end of the pond, a plush jetty raised from the thorny shore between a shallow blue body of water and a deep blue body of sky.

The sun had just set. I was relaxed on the tree trunk, ensconced in the lap of lichen, watching the lily pads at my feet tremble and part dreamily over the thrusting path of a carp. A yellow bird appeared to my right and flew behind me. It caught my eye; I swiveled around—and the next instant, inexplicably, I was looking down at a weasel, who was looking up at me.

Weasel! I'd never seen one wild before. He was ten inches long, thin as a curve, a muscled ribbon, brown as fruitwood, soft-furred, alert. His face was fierce, small and pointed as a lizard's; he would have made a good arrowhead. There was just a dot of chin, maybe two brown hairs' worth, and then the pure white fur began that spread down his underside. He had two black eyes I didn't see, any more than you see a window.

The weasel was stunned into stillness as he was emerging from beneath an enormous shaggy wild rose bush four feet away. I was stunned into stillness twisted backward on the tree trunk. Our eyes locked, and someone threw away the key.

Our look was as if two lovers, or deadly enemies, met unexpectedly on an overgrown path when each had been thinking of something else: a clearing blow to the gut. It was also a bright blow to the brain, or a sudden beating of brains, with all the charge and intimate grate of rubbed balloons. It emptied our lungs. It felled the forest, moved the fields, and drained the pond; the world dismantled and tumbled into that black hole of eyes. If you and I looked at each other that way, our skulls would split and drop to our shoulders. But we don't. We keep our skulls. So.

He disappeared. This was only last week, and already I don't remember what shattered the enchantment. I think I blinked, I think I retrieved my brain from the weasel's brain, and tried to memorize what I was seeing, and the weasel felt the yank of separation, the careening splashdown into real life and the urgent current of instinct. He vanished under the wild rose. I waited motionless, my mind suddenly full of data and my spirit with pleadings, but he didn't return.

Please do not tell me about "approach-avoidance conflicts." I tell you I've been in that weasel's brain for sixty seconds, and he was in mine. Brains are private places, muttering through unique and secret tapes—but the weasel and I both plugged into another tape simultaneously, for a sweet and shocking time. Can I help it if it was a blank?

What goes on in his brain the rest of the time? What does a weasel think about? He won't say. His journal is tracks in clay, a spray of feathers, mouse blood and bone: uncollected, unconnected, loose-leaf, and blown.

I would like to learn, or remember, how to live. I come to Hollins Pond not so much to learn how to live as, frankly, to forget about it. That is, I don't think I can learn from a wild animal how to live in particular—shall I suck warm blood, hold my tail high, walk with my footprints precisely over the prints of my hands?—but I might learn something of mindlessness, something of the purity of living in the physical senses and the dignity of living without bias or motive. The weasel lives in necessity and we live in choice, hating necessity and dying at the last ignobly in its talons. I would like to live as I should, as the weasel lives as he should. And I suspect that for me the way is like the weasel's: open to time and death painlessly, noticing everything, remembering nothing, choosing the given with a fierce and pointed will.

I missed my chance. I should have gone for the throat. I should have lunged for that streak of white under the weasel's chin and held on, held on through mud and into the wild rose, held on for a dearer life. We could live under the wild rose wild as weasels, mute and uncomprehending. I could very calmly go wild. I could live two days in the den, curled, leaning on mouse fur, sniffing bird bones, blinking, licking, breathing musk, my hair tangled in the roots of grasses. Down is a good place to go, where the mind is single. Down is out, out of your ever-loving mind and back to your careless senses. I remember muteness as a prolonged and giddy fast, where every moment is a feast of utterance received. Time and events are merely poured, unremarked, and ingested directly, like blood pulsed into my gut through a jugular vein. Could two live that way? Could two live under the wild rose, and explore by the pond, so that the smooth mind of each is as everywhere present to the other, and as received and as unchallenged, as falling snow?

We could, you know. We can live any way we want. People take vows of poverty, chastity, and obedience—even of silence—by choice. The thing is to stalk your calling in a certain skilled and supple way, to locate the most tender and live spot and plug into that pulse. This is yielding, not fighting. A weasel doesn't "attack" anything; a weasel lives as he's meant to, yielding at every moment to the perfect freedom of single necessity.

I think it would be well, and proper, and obedient, and pure, to grasp your one necessity and not let it go, to dangle from it limp wherever it takes you. Then even death, where you're going no matter how you live, cannot you part. Seize it and let it seize you up aloft even, till your eyes burn out and drop; let your musky flesh fall off in shreds, and let your very bones unhinge and scatter, loosened over fields, over fields and woods, lightly, thoughtless, from any height at all, from as high as eagles.

CONSIDERATIONS

Thinking

What does Dillard mean by suggesting that we can live like the weasel? To what extent are weasel life and human life analogous? In what ways do they differ, and how are those differences suggested in Dillard's essay?

What do you think is Dillard's purpose in "Living Like Weasels"? Where do you find her argument most clearly articulated?

Connecting

What is the relationship between the story Dillard tells in the first paragraph and the story she recounts in the second paragraph?

Explain how Dillard connects her experience with weasels with her reading about them.

Compare Dillard's presentation of her experience with the weasel with Edward Hoagland's description of his experiences with turtles in "The Courage of Turtles."

Writing

Write an essay in which you explore your relationship to the natural world. You may wish to base your essay on one or more experiences you have had in nature. Or you may wish to center your essay on a literary work that reflects a concern with nature.

Write an essay describing some of your own encounters with animals and what you have learned from those experiences.

M ichael Dorris (b.1945)

Michael Dorris, a member of the Modoc tribe, has published widely on Native American life. His work includes a collection of short stories, *Working Men;* a novel, *A Yellow Raft in Blue Water;* and a fictional collaboration with his wife, the writer Louise Erdrich, *The Crown of Columbus.*

Dorris has also written a powerful book about fetal alcohol syndrome, *The Broken Cord,* which won a National Book Critics Circle Award. The following essay on fetal alcohol syndrome is collected with many other of Dorris's pieces of nonfiction in *Paper Trail.* The essay is notable for its directness and honesty in portraying the severity of the problem and for a deeply passionate urgency that animates Dorris's powers of persuasion.

Fetal Alcohol Syndrome: A Parent's Perspective

nlike so many good people—scientists and social workers and politicians—who have chosen out of the kindness of their hearts and the dictates of their social consciences to become knowledgeable about fetal alcohol syndrome and fetal alcohol effect, to work with their victims, to demand prevention, I was dragged to the subject blindfolded, kicking and screaming. I'm the worst kind of expert, a grudging, reluctant witness, an embittered amateur, and, above all else: a failure. A parent.

I'm a living, breathing encyclopedia of what hasn't worked in curing or reversing the damage to one child prenatally exposed to too much alcohol. Certain drugs temporarily curbed my son's seizures and hyperactivity but almost certainly had dampening effects on his learning ability and personality development. Fifteen years of special education—isolation in a classroom, repetitive instruction, hands-on learning—maximized his potential but didn't give him a normal IQ. Psychological counseling—introspective techniques, group therapy—had no positive results, and may even have encouraged his ongoing confusion between what is real and what's imagined.

Brain surgery hasn't worked.

Anger hasn't worked.

Patience hasn't worked.

Love hasn't worked.

When you're the parent of an FAS or FAE child, your goals change with the passing years. You start with seeking solutions: ideas and regimens to penetrate the fog that blocks your son's or daughter's ability to comprehend rules, retain information, or even be curious. You firmly believe—because it has to be true—that the answers are "out there." It's just a matter of locating them. You go through teachers and their various learning theories like so many Christmas catalogues received in the mail, determined to find the perfect gift, the right combination of toughness and compassion, optimism and realism, training and intuition. Once you find a likely prospect, you badger her (in my experience, most teachers of

216

"learning disabled" [LD] children seem to be women), demand results, attempt to coerce with praise or threat. You become first an ally, then increasingly a pain in the neck, a judgmental critic, an ever-persistent, occasionally hysterical, nuisance. When the teacher, worn out and frustrated, eventually gives up on your child, decides he's beyond her ability or resources to help, she's as glad to see *you* go as she's relieved that your son won't be back to remind her of her limitations. "With a crazy, irrational parent like that," you imagine her saying to her colleagues, "no wonder the kid has problems."

Do I sound paranoid, cynical? I wasn't always this way, but I'm the product of a combined total of fifty years of dealing with alcohol-damaged children—for not only does the son I wrote about in *The Broken Cord* suffer from fetal alcohol syndrome, but his adopted brother and sister are, to a lesser and greater extent, victims of fetal alcohol effect.

For years, my wife and I and our extended families had no choice but to become a kind of full-time social service agency specializing in referrals, the admissions policies of various expensive institutions, the penalties meted out under the juvenile justice system, the nightmares of dealing with uninformed, often smug, bureaucrats given by default responsibility for people who can't make it on their own in contemporary America. We were forced to progress from attending increasingly sour PTA meetings to learning the intricacies of intelligence testing—hoping that the score will come in below 70 and thus qualify a child for legal disability. We've had to become acquainted with the admissions policies and maximum length of stays at institutions like Covenant House, Boystown, and the Salvation Army. We've paid out well over $150,000, not counting what our insurance has covered, for our children's primary and secondary special school tuitions, counseling, doctors of every sort, experimental medical procedures, Outward Bound for Troubled Youth, and private camps for the learning disabled. We have managed to try every single avenue that's been suggested to us by well-meaning people who should know what might benefit our sons and daughter, and nothing—*nothing*—has consistently worked for more than a few months.

Our older children, now all adults or nearly so, often cannot function independently, cannot hold jobs, tell the truth, manage money, plan a future. They have all at one time or another been arrested or otherwise detained for shoplifting, inappropriate sexual conduct, and violent behavior. Despite all our efforts to protect them, they have periodically come under the influence of people who, for instance, worship Satan or take advantage of them physically, mentally, and/or financially. They maintain no enduring friendships, set for themselves no realistic goals, can call upon no bedrock inner voice to distinguish moral from amoral, safe from dangerous.

Okay: maybe it's us. Maybe we're incredibly dysfunctional parents. We've spent years feeling guilty and inadequate, holding on to the belief that if only we could become better, more resourceful, more sympathetic, more enlightened in our expectations and requirements, we could alter the bleak future that seems to lie in store or have already arrived for our adopted children. Like every self-reflective father and mother, we can recall our failures, our lapses, our losses of temper, and time after time we have added up these shortcomings to see if they balance the devastating total of our sons' and daughter's current situations. *The Broken Cord* was written, at least in part, to further this process, to assign guilt—if not wholly to us, then to somebody, something—to make not just sense of a senseless waste, but a difference. If every avenue of investigation were explored, maybe something would be discovered that could reverse the fate of not just any anonymous afflicted fetus, child, or adult, but of *our* children.

But what the book yielded was worse than the least I had expected. Not only was there no magic trick, no scientific breakthrough that could produce a "cure," but from the outpouring of letters that have come from around the country it is clear that our family's private sorrow is far from unusual. In the year and a half since *The Broken Cord* was published, we have heard from more than two thousand parents of FAS and FAE victims. All love their children, and almost none have given up hope. But none of them knows what the hell to do next.

The hardest group to answer are the parents of very young children, children who seem from the symptoms described to be clearly fetal alcohol affected. I recognize these parents: in the early stages of denial, full of the surety that answers exist. They want practical advice, experts to consult, books to read, innovative doctors to visit. They want to head off the unpleasant disappointments chronicled in my book, to save their child— and themselves—from such a miserable chain of events. If *The Broken Cord* had been written by somebody else, I would have mailed just such a letter to its author. I would have been skeptical of his pessimism, sure that I could do better, last longer, be smarter, succeed where he had failed. So when I answer the letters I receive, I root for those parents, applaud their confidence, ask them to write back and tell me when things improve. So far, there has been no good news.

Almost equally difficult to absorb is the mail I receive from parents whose FAS and FAE children are older than ours. They write with the weary echo of experience, the products of many cycles of raised expectations followed by dejection. They tell of their "fifty-two-year-old child," or their FAE adult daughter who's just given birth to her third FAS baby and is pregnant again and still drinking. They tell of children serving twenty-year prison terms or, in one case, of a "sweet" son sentenced to the death penalty for an impulsive murder for which he has never shown the slightest remorse. They tell of children raised in privilege who are now lost among the homeless on a distant city's streets, of children once so loving and gentle who have been maimed from drug use or knife fights, or, as is so often the case, who have been raped. They tell of innocents become prostitutes, of suicide attempts, and always, always, of chemical dependency. They tell of children whose whereabouts are unknown, or who are dead at twenty-five. This is not the way it was supposed to happen, these parents cry. It's not fair. It's not right.

We read these letters and wonder: is *this in store?*

I've even heard from adults diagnosed with fetal alcohol effect—one of them with a Ph.D. from Harvard and several others with master's degrees. These are highly intelligent people, the Jackie Robinsons of FAE, who have had to become specialists on themselves. Through years of observing their own trials and errors, of watching how "normal" people behave in a given context and analyzing how that contrasts with their own uncertain reactions, some of them have worked out complicated formulas to simulate a greater connection to the world than they in fact possess. One woman carries in her purse a card on which is typed a series of questions she explicitly asks herself in an attempt to gauge the consequences of her possible responses to an unprecedented situation: What would so-and-so do in this instance? What will people probably think if I do *x, y,* or *z?* She's compensating for life in a universe that's slightly, almost imperceptibly alien, and trying to speak a language whose idiom and nuance are forever just beyond her automatic reach.

The correspondence we've received from around this country, and lately from around the world, has magnified exponentially our particular family experience, but hasn't contradicted it. The letter I've waited for but which has yet to arrive is the one that begins, "I've read your book and you're dead wrong," or "My child was diagnosed as having FAS but we fixed it by doing the following things and now, five years later, he's perfectly fine."

To what extent does this preventable scourge affect American Indian people? The answer, like so much about FAS, is ambiguous. On the one hand, prenatal exposure to ethanol impairs a fetus in exactly the same ways whether its mother is a member of a country club in Greenwich, Connecticut, or an ADC mom on the White Earth reservation. Every human being during development is vulnerable, fragile, easy to poison; ethnicity acts as neither a shield nor a magnet. Yes, "drinking age" matters, diet counts, smoking and other drug use will exacerbate the damage done by alcohol, but all things considered, no woman is physically destined to give birth to an FAS baby.

The factors that really make a difference have to do with ephemeral things: strong family and community support for abstinence, access to good prenatal care and chemical dependency treatment, clear and widespread information on the dangers of drinking during pregnancy. And it's here that Native American women are at a severe disadvantage. Health programs on reservations have been among the first things cut when the federal budget gets tight; clinics are shut down, counselors laid off, preventive educational campaigns scrapped. Access to organizations like Planned Parenthood is, in many tribal communities, impossible. Poverty, unemployment, despair—familiar elements in the daily lives of too many Indian people—lead to alcohol and other drug abuse. The causes of the problem, and the solutions, are so much bigger and more complex than just saying no.

When you factor in to the statistics on FAS and FAE those having to do with prenatal exposure to crack cocaine—which seems to produce in children many of the same learning disabilities as too much alcohol—we are looking at hundreds of thousands of impaired babies born in this country annually. In ten years that's three million people. By the time the first generation counted is twenty years old, it's six million, and that's assuming a stable rate—not the current geometrically accelerating one. How does our society handle this onslaught, on either a local or a national level? How do we make laws that apply equally to those of us who can understand the rules and to a significant minority who, through no fault of their own, can't? How do we preserve individual liberty, free choice, safe streets, mutual trust, when some members of society have only a glancing grasp of moral responsibility? How do we cope with the growing crime rate among young people, with "wilding," with trying to teach the unteachable?

The thorny ethical issue that has troubled me most in thinking about the social impact of FAS and other such lifelong but preventable afflictions concerns responsibility. When, if ever, are we, one-on-one or collectively, obliged to intervene? It's becoming increasingly clear that FAS victims beget more FAS victims: a pregnant woman who can't calculate the long-term consequences of her decisions is a hard case for prenatal counseling. It is difficult if not impossible to convince her to defer an immediate gratification because nine months or nine years later her hypothetical child might suffer from a night of partying. That child is an abstraction, a hazy shadow at best, and the argument is a great deal less compelling than the draw of another drink or fix.

Some studies have suggested that compared with the "average" woman, female FAS and FAE victims start having children younger, continue for a longer period of years to produce them, and ultimately conceive and bring to term more offspring. They are less likely to seek prenatal care, to abstain from dangerous activities during their pregnancies, and to keep custody of their babies. Statistically a woman who's given birth to an FAS baby has almost an eight out of ten chance to do so again, if she continues drinking, and subsequent siblings are likely to be even more impaired than the first.

These often abandoned or removed children, whether adopted or institutionalized, are ultimately our culture's victims and therefore are its responsibility. How to cope? At the absolute minimum, how do we—especially in a tight economy—pay the medical bills, build the prisons, construct the homeless shelters? How do we train special education teachers to function indefinitely with no hope of success, or ordinary citizens how to forgive behaviors that are irritating at best, threatening or dangerous at worst? How do we teach compassion for a growing class of people who are likely to exhibit neither pity nor gratitude, who take everything society has to offer and have almost nothing constructive to give back? How do we maintain the universal franchise to vote, the cornerstone of our political system? How do we redefine "guilty or not guilty" to apply to heartless acts committed by people who are fundamentally incapable of comprehending the spirit of the law?

To me these questions can be understood if not answered by a simple analogy: Imagine we saw a blind woman holding a child by the hand attempt to cross a busy street. The traffic was fast, she guessed wrong, and before our eyes her child was struck by a truck and killed. A tragedy we would never forget. Then a year later we come by the same intersection again, and again there's the woman, but with a new child. The light is against her but she doesn't see and tries to cross to the other side. The child is hit, terribly injured, as we stand by helplessly and watch. The next year it happens again, and the next, and the next. How many times must it happen before we become involved? Before we take the woman's arm or hold up our hand to stop the cars or carry her child or at least tell her when the signal is green? How many children are too many? When do their rights to safe passage assert themselves? And how long before the mother herself is killed?—for remember, she's a victim and at grave risk, too. It does no good to blame her, to punish her for the result of her blindness. Once the street is crossed the child is dead. The mother needs help and we need to find a decent way to provide it. If we turn our backs, we stop being innocent bystanders and become complicit in the inevitable accident, accessories after the fact.

Despite all his recent fame since *The Broken Cord*'s publication, Abel continues to be fired from menial jobs, to lose places to live. He hasn't made a single lasting friend, hasn't received a friendly personal phone call, hasn't read a book unless you count *Garfield*. He's twenty-three and lonely, without being able to think of the name to describe that emotion or figure out and persevere in any action to alleviate it.

My wife and I had to go out of town on business last week. When we returned we called Abel's new residence and were greeted by the chilling report that he had apparently "forgotten" to eat from Thursday through Sunday and had lost a considerable amount of weight.

Abel isn't considered to be sufficiently impaired to qualify for a state-run facility for the disabled, so his only option is to board in a private home close enough to walk to the truck stop where he works part-time. As it happened, the perfectly nice husband and wife who maintain this home had a family emergency that necessitated that they be gone the same weekend that Louise and I were away. They left Abel's food, clearly marked for each day, on a special shelf in the refrigerator, but in their absence—that is, without the cue of their direct, repeated instructions at meal time—it had not occurred to our adult son that the hunger he had to have felt could be sated simply by feeding himself.

And Abel is the easy one, the most fortunate of our three adopted children, because he is at least unambiguously diagnosable. The state of New Hampshire, financially strapped as it is, has no choice but to examine him and conclude "LD." Minimal services are provided: a social worker takes him to the dentist and checks on his living situation a couple of times a month. He's finally eligible for social security and Medicaid benefits, providing he doesn't earn more than $500 a month. Strangers and friends who interact with him think, "Ah, retarded," instead of "stupid," "rude," or "dangerous." They make allowances.

Our two other older children, however, are another story. Their respective birth mothers drank in sprees while pregnant—not heavily enough to produce full FAS symptoms in their offspring, but . . . heavily enough. Almost certainly fetal alcohol affected, our son and daughter are now nineteen and almost sixteen, respectively, and they have fallen apart, right on the FAE schedule. My son has been on the street since, at seventeen, he chose to quit the last of the many special schools and treatment centers we found for him, starting at age fourteen. That final place was the only one that didn't kick *him* out. He's intellectually capable of a normal life, but he often lacks judgment, empathy, perspective, the patience to set long-term goals and then work to accomplish them.

Our daughter, at Boystown for the last two years after having been expelled from three "regular" schools for shoplifting or for failing to pass any courses since the sixth grade, has recently discovered satanism. She has carved an upside-down cross into her arm with a ballpoint pen, twice. After seeing *Dances with Wolves* she's become convinced that the reservation where she was born (and where her birth mother is currently in jail again for drunk and disorderly conduct) is like the happy community in the movie, and so has refused to cooperate with her house parents in any way because she hopes to be sent to South Dakota. Helpful people from the Omaha Indian Center, as well as Louise and I and a dozen others, have tried to explain to her the huge gap between fantasy and fact, between antiseptic fiction and the ragged poverty of Rosebud reservation, but it doesn't penetrate.

Every parent is helpless, that's a given, virtually a cliché. The children of hippies become CPAs or join the army, rural kids move to the city as soon as they can buy a ticket, passing on their way the teenage urban cowboys en route to the wide open spaces. But the utter helplessness of an FAS or FAE parent is of another magnitude. We stand by, throwing one temporary impediment after another into the path of boys and girls seemingly bent upon engineering their own destruction. Many of us hear at one time or another the standard advice of the stumped psychological counselor: let your kids sink to the bottom, then they'll start to work their way back up. Well, we come to discover that in the case of our "special" children, the bottom is very deep indeed. At each plateau, a new descent is immediately sought, and if the levels of Dante's *Inferno* spring to mind, it's not inappropriate. For an FAS or FAE child who doesn't understand rules or morality, honesty or loyalty (except as applying to the exigencies of the moment), the drop is that of an elevator once the cable has been severed.

Louise and I are not the persons to consult for a benign or inspirational message. Hope has become our enemy—a trickster who lies in wait, who reappears in dreams and then pulls the rug from under us time after time. Our afflicted children are beyond placebos, beyond the reach of platitude. Our sons and oldest daughter were brainwashed by alcohol before they were born, casualties in this battle. We have fought the aftereffects of their prenatal exposure to ethanol for twenty years—tried every tactic we could think of or that was suggested to us by specialists—and we barely made a dent in their fates.

When one son calls me from a reservation phone booth and speculates about how he might steal a car and drive to Seattle, it's not much consolation to think that the sum of all our efforts may have merely forestalled this moment in his life by a year or so. We know that buried within the brooding adult Abel resides a sweet little boy, capable of responding with affection if the right buttons are pushed—but try to convince his co-workers when he forgets to punch in on time.

Let us make no mistake about one point: we're not *facing* a crisis, we're *in* one, though official statistics can be deceiving. A couple of years ago South Dakota, a state with at that time no resident dysmorphologist (the only doctor, except for a geneticist, fully trained to diagnose FAS or FAE), reported a grand total of two FAS births—during the same period in which my friend Jeaneen Grey Eagle, director of Project Recovery in Pine Ridge, estimated that somewhere between one-third and one-half of the infants born in certain communities of her reservation were at high risk due to heavy maternal drinking. Underdiagnosis, unfortunately, does not equal small numbers.

But what can we do about it? Each person must provide his or her own answers. Some of us—the scientists—can study the biochemistry involved in fetal damage from drugs, learn to predict which women are most at risk and when, figure out how much ethanol, if any, is tolerable. Others—advocates and politicians—can address the issue of prevention: get out the word, make pests of ourselves, speak up even when it makes our friends uncomfortable, fight for the future of a child not yet even conceived. Still others—social workers, psychologists, and educators—can tackle the needs of the here and now, of the tens of thousands of FAS and FAE men, women, and children who exist on the margins of society. We can devise effective curricula, learning regimens, humane models for dependent care.

If we, today, put our minds to it, if only we did our part, we might not obliterate fetal alcohol syndrome on a global level, but, in all candor, we could save many lives, many mothers, many babies. All it takes is nine months of abstinence, a bit longer if a mother breast feeds. Three hundred thousand separate and discrete solutions, three hundred thousand miracles, and it's a clean year.

And finally some of us, the parents into whose care these children have been given, whether by birth or adoption, can try to get through another day, to survive the next unexpected catastrophe, to preserve a sense of humor. We laugh at things that really aren't funny—quite the contrary—but we laugh, without malice, for relief. When Abel went with me last fall to his annual case management meeting, he was asked to list all the accomplishments in the past twelve months about which he felt especially proud. He drew a blank.

"Then, tell us what you've been doing since we met here last year," the man directed—and Abel complied.

"Well, I went down the stairs and I opened the door," he began. "Then I got into the car and my father took me home. For supper we had . . ." Abel tried to remember that anonymous meal he polished off some 365 days before, stalled, and looked to me for help.

"Next question," I suggested, and the social worker consulted his list. "Tell me what things you really *don't* like to do," he invited.

Abel's eyes lit. This was an easy one. "I don't like to dig up burdocks," he stated.

I blinked in surprise. Abel hadn't dug up burdocks in three years. He was simply using a response that had worked in the past.

"Wait a minute," I said. "Abel, thousands of people all over the country have read your chapter at the end of the book about how you dug up those burdocks to help us. People liked that part so much I think that's why they gave our book that prize you have sitting on your dresser. People are very proud of you for what you did. I know it wasn't fun to dig up those plants, but you should feel good that you did it."

Abel was having an especially polite day. He smiled at me, cocked his head, and asked: "What book would that be?"

The grind doesn't get easier and it doesn't go away. FAS victims do not learn from experience, do not get well. Louise keeps a diary and a while ago she glanced back over the past four years. That can be dangerous, because there are some things you don't notice until you take the long view. It turned out that as a family we hadn't had a single period longer than three consecutive days in all that time when one of our alcohol-impaired children was not in a crisis—health, home, school—that

demanded our undivided attention. It often seems to us that their problems define our existence as well as their own, and in that respect perhaps
we are in a small way the forecast of things to come for this country. How
many children of chemically dependent parents have perished in house
fires, from malnutrition, from lack of medical care, from exposure? Are
these, also, options protected under the rubric of an adult's right to
choose to drink or take drugs beyond the point of responsible self-
control? Who are these lost babies but the victims of "victimless" crime?
Certainly if they survive, the penalties they suffer are ongoing. The prisons to which they are confined exist without the possibility of parole.

FAS is not a problem whose impact is restricted to its victims. It's not
just a woman's issue, not just a man's. No one is exempted. These are
everybody's children.

I am descended from the Modoc tribe on my father's side, and I can't
help but think of a historic parallel to my present circumstances. In the
late nineteenth century the Modocs were engaged in what history calls
"the Last Indian War." It consisted of about fifty hungry men, women, and
children leaving the Oregon reservation to which they had been
assigned—a reservation owned and operated by their traditional enemies,
the Klamath—and returning to the Northern California lands they had
previously occupied. As was the custom in those days, they were pursued
by the cavalry and a full military force—who had a terribly hard time
locating them, since the Modocs were hiding in a moonscape of lava beds.
But find them they eventually did.

A few of the captured leaders were executed without trial, but what to
do with the rest? A group of about twenty adult Modocs were given a
choice: either be shipped to a cholera-ridden prison camp in Indian Territory (now Oklahoma) or work the vaudeville circuit with A. B. Meacham,
the former Indian agent who had been the source of many of the tribe's
troubles. Meacham, you see, had a dynamite idea: America had read in
newspapers about the savage Modocs, now the public must be allowed to
see them in person.

For more than a year, in cities and towns throughout this country,
between a troop of jugglers and a knife-throwing act, the final agonized
moments of the "war" were restaged. The Modoc POWs were assigned
new, more "Indian-sounding" names, costumed in the kind of fringe-and-
feather outfits the audience expected Indians to wear, and commanded to
re-create, twice a day, six nights a week, plus two additional matinee performances, the moment of their final defeat.

I know how they must have felt.

People have asked me whether it was "cathartic" to write *The Broken Cord* and then see it have some impact on national awareness. The answer is no. There's no catharsis when you're the parent of an FAS or FAE child or adult.

On my book tour, I one day found myself on a Seattle TV talk show. During the commercial break the hostess chided me for not revealing enough of my *feelings* about the plight of my oldest son. "You want feelings, get Barry Manilow," I told her, but it did no good. The next time I looked at the monitor, there was my face, and lest anyone miss the point, it had a caption: *Tragic Dad.*

That's hardly the identity I expected when I became a father. I speak out publicly today as a living anecdote, a walking warning label, a Chatty Cathy doll who spews forth a version of the same cautionary tale whenever the string is pulled. Our unhappy personal chronicle, the struggle of many well-intentioned and initially optimistic people to alter for the better the life of one damaged little boy, has to the great surprise of my wife and myself become a kind of flagship sound bite for prenatal sobriety, and yet mostly my role is not to warn but to mourn—and that's easier done in private. To be best known for one's saddest story is not the road to notoriety anyone would willingly choose.

CONSIDERATIONS

Thinking

What is Dorris's central point? How convincingly does he present it? What kinds of evidence does he introduce in its support?

What, if anything, do you think should be done about women who drink during pregnancy? Should there be some way to protect their unborn children—perhaps even at the expense of the women's individual freedom?

Connecting

Dorris introduces a number of analogies into his argument. Consider the effectiveness of Dorris's analogy of women who have given birth to children suffering from fetal alcohol syndrome to the blind woman crossing a busy street. Consider also his comparison of public response to FAS and those who suffer from it with the experience and treatment accorded the Modoc Indians.

Compare Dorris's discussion in this essay with Richard Selzer's description of AIDS in "A Mask on the Face of Death." Consider the way each essayist presents information about the disease he describes and consider the extent to which each makes judgments about the behavior that contributes to the suffering caused by each disease.

Writing

Do some research on fetal alcohol syndrome. Write an essay in which you incorporate what you learn from your research and connect that information with Dorris's argument and the evidence he presents in its support.

Read the foreword to *The Broken Cord*—an essay by Dorris's wife, Louise Erdrich, about their son Abel. Compare Erdrich's essay with Dorris's.

Gretel Ehrlich
(b.1946)

E ducated at Bennington, the UCLA Film School, and the New School for Social Research, Gretel Ehrlich now lives in California, where she grew up. *The Solace of Open Spaces,* her first book of essays about her life in Wyoming, won the Harold B. Vurcell Memorial Award. She has also written a novel *(Heart Mountain)* about Japanese internment during World War II, a second collection of essays *(Islands, Universe, and Home)*, and, most recently, a long narrative *(A Match to the Heart)* detailing her physical and spiritual recovery after being struck by lightning. Her other awards include a Whiting Foundation grant for "Spring," and a Guggenheim Fellowship.

"Looking for a Lost Dog" turns from the dog to a pursuit of the "peregrine saunterings of the mind." As Ehrlich follows her own deep longings, her interest shifts to the struggle that takes place in our lives between "impulse and reason, logic and passion."

Looking for a Lost Dog

The most valuable thoughts which I entertain are anything but what *I* thought. Nature abhors a vacuum, and if I can only walk with sufficient carelessness I am sure to be filled.

HENRY DAVID THOREAU

I started off this morning looking for my lost dog. He's a red heeler, blotched brown and white, and I tell people he looks like a big saddle shoe. Born at Christmas on a thirty-below-zero night, he's tough, though his right front leg is crooked where it froze to the ground.

2   It's the old needle-in-the-haystack routine: small dog, huge landscape, and rugged terrain. While moving cows once, he fell in a hole and disappeared. We heard him whining but couldn't see him. When we put our ears to the ground, we could hear the hole that had swallowed him.

3   It's no wonder human beings are so narcissistic. The way our ears are constructed, we can only hear what's right next to us or else the internal monologue inside. I've taken to cupping my hands behind my ears— mule-like—and pricking them all the way forward or back to hear what's happened or what's ahead.

4   "Life is polyphonic," a Hungarian friend in her eighties said. She was a child prodigy from Budapest who had soloed on the violin in Paris and Berlin by the time she was twelve. "Childishly, I once thought hearing had mostly to do with music," she said. "Now that I'm too old to play the fiddle, I know it has to do with the great suspiration of life everywhere."

5   But back to the dog. I'm walking and looking and listening for him, though there is no trail, no clue, no direction to the search. Whimsically, I head north toward the falls. They're set in a deep gorge where Precambrian rock piles up to ten thousand feet on either side. A raven creaks overhead, flies into the cleft, glides toward a panel of white water splashing over a ledge, and comes out cawing.

6   To find what is lost is an art in some cultures. The Navajos employ "hand tremblers," usually women, who go into a trance and "see" where the lost article or person is located. When I asked one such diviner what

230

it was like when she was in trance, she said, "Lots of noise, but noise that's hard to hear."

7 Near the falls the ground flattens into a high-altitude valley before the mountains rise vertically. The falls roar, but they're overgrown with spruce, pine, willow, and wild rose, and the closer I get, the harder it is to see the water. Perhaps that is how it will be in my search for the dog.

8 We're worried about Frenchy because last summer he was bitten three times by rattlesnakes. After the first bite he walked toward me, reeled dramatically, and collapsed. I could see the two holes in his nose where the fangs went in, and I felt sure he was dying. I drove him twenty miles to the vet; by the time we arrived, Frenchy resembled a monster. His nose and neck had swollen as though a football had been sewn under the skin.

9 I walk and walk. Past the falls, through a pass, toward a larger, rowdier creek. The sky goes black. In the distance snow on the Owl Creek Mountains glares. A blue ocean seems to stretch between, and the black sky hangs over like a frown. A string of cottonwoods whose new, tender leaves are the color of limes pulls me downstream. I come into the meadow with the abandoned apple orchard. The trees have leaves but have lost most of their blossoms. I feel as if I had caught strangers undressed.

10 The sun comes back, and the wind. It brings no dog, but ducks slide overhead. An Eskimo from Barrow, Alaska, told me the reason spring has such fierce winds is so birds coming north will have something to fly on.

11 To find what's lost; to lose what's found. Several times I've thought I might be "losing my mind." Of course, minds aren't literally misplaced—on the contrary, we live too much under them. As with viewing the falls, we can lose sight of what is too close. It is between the distant and close-up views that the struggle between impulse and reason, logic and passion takes place.

12 The feet move; the mind wanders. In his journals Thoreau wrote: "The saunterer, in the good sense, is no more vagrant than the meandering river, which is all the while sedulously seeking the shortest course to the sea."

13 Today I'm filled with longings—for what I'm not, for what is impossible, for people I love who can't be in my life. Passions of all sorts struggle soundlessly, or else, like the falls, they are all noise but can't be seen. My hybrid anguish spends itself as recklessly and purposefully as water.

14 Now I'm following a game trail up a sidehill. It's a mosaic of tracks—elk, deer, rabbit, and bird. If city dwellers could leave imprints in cement,

it would look this way: tracks would overlap, go backward and forward like the peregrine saunterings of the mind.

15   I see a dog's track, or is it a coyote's? I get down on my hands and knees to sniff out a scent. What am I doing? I entertain expectations of myself as preposterous as when I landed in Tokyo—I felt so at home there that I thought I would break into fluent Japanese. Now I sniff the ground and smell only dirt. If I spent ten years sniffing, would I learn scents?

16   The tracks veer off the trail and disappear. Descending into a dry wash whose elegant, tortured junipers and tumbled boulders resemble a Japanese garden, I trip on a sagebrush root. I look. Deep in the center of the plant there is a bird's nest, but instead of eggs, a locust stares up at me.

17   Some days I think this one place isn't enough. That's when nothing is enough, when I want to live multiple lives and be allowed to love without limits. Those days, like today, I walk with a purpose but no destination. Only then do I see, at least momentarily, that everything is here. To my left a towering cottonwood is lunatic with birdsong. Under it I'm a listening post while its great gray trunk—like a baton or the source of something—heaves its green symphony into the air.

18   I walk and walk: from the falls, over Grouse Hill, to the dry wash. Today it is enough to make a shadow.

CONSIDERATIONS

Thinking

About halfway through this essay, references to the dog get more and more scarce. Where do you last sense the dog's presence? What do you think his disappearance suggests about the essay's meaning?

What do you suppose Ehrlich means by this revelation: "My hybrid anguish spends itself as recklessly and purposefully as water"? Cite evidence from the essay to back up your interpretation.

Look carefully at the last two paragraphs. What signs do you find of solace? Of compromise?

Connecting

How does Ehrlich help you understand Thoreau's idea that "the most valuable thoughts which I entertain are anything but what *I* thought"?

What do you suppose Ehrlich's Hungarian friend meant about hearing "the great suspiration of life everywhere"? Why do you think Ehrlich quotes her?

Make five columns on a blank sheet of paper and list one of the senses at the top of each. Read through the essay again and keep track of the references to each of the five senses. How does that exercise alter your sense of the essay's meaning?

Now read Robynn Stacy Maines's essay "Finding a Dog Not Lost in 'Looking for a Lost Dog.'" How does Maines's essay help you understand Ehrlich's? Explain.

Writing

Select a sentence from Ehrlich's essay—as she did from Thoreau's—to use as the epigraph for your own essay. Develop that essay to deepen the understanding of the sentence you chose.

Jot down a list of the people and the quotations Ehrlich introduces in her essay. Then make a list of her most compelling images. Write a paragraph about each list, explaining how the list helps you understand the essay.

L oren Eiseley
(1907–1977)

A lthough Loren Eiseley was an anthropologist by profession—a professor and once the provost of the University of Pennsylvania—he considered himself a writer. Other labels, some self-generated (social philosopher, scientist, naturalist, fugitive, drifter), satisfied him less. What he wrote most and liked best were the pieces he called "concealed" essays, essays in which "personal anecdote [is] allowed gently to bring under observation thoughts of a more purely scientific nature." His works include *The Immense Journey, Darwin's Century, The Firmament of Time, The Unexpected Universe, The Invisible Pyramid, The Night Country, All the Strange Hours, The Star Thrower,* three volumes of poetry, and *The Lost Notebooks of Loren Eiseley.* His many awards include the Joseph Wood Krutch Medal, in 1976, for significant contribution toward the improvement of life and the environment.

"The Dance of the Frogs" takes us into that territory between the scientific world of rationality and the more ineffable world of the spirit.

The Dance of the Frogs

I

He was a member of the Explorers Club, and he had never been outside the state of Pennsylvania. Some of us who were world travelers used to smile a little about that, even though we knew his scientific reputation had been, at one time, great. It is always the way of youth to smile. I used to think of myself as something of an adventurer, but the time came when I realized that old Albert Dreyer, huddling with his drink in the shadows close to the fire, had journeyed farther into the Country of Terror than any of us would ever go, God willing, and emerge alive.

He was a morose and aging man, without family and without intimates. His membership in the club dated back into the decades when he was a zoologist famous for his remarkable experiments upon amphibians—he had recovered and actually produced the adult stage of the Mexican axolotl, as well as achieving remarkable tissue transplants in salamanders. The club had been flattered to have him then, travel or no travel, but the end was not fortunate. The brilliant scientist had become the misanthrope; the achievement lay all in the past, and Albert Dreyer kept to his solitary room, his solitary drink, and his accustomed spot by the fire.

The reason I came to hear his story was an odd one. I had been north that year, and the club had asked me to give a little talk on the religious beliefs of the Indians of the northern forest, the Naskapi of Labrador. I had long been a student of the strange mélange of superstition and woodland wisdom that makes up the religious life of the nature peoples. Moreover, I had come to know something of the strange similarities of the "shaking tent rite" to the phenomena of the modern medium's cabinet.

"The special tent with its entranced occupant is no different from the cabinet," I contended. "The only difference is the type of voices that emerge. Many of the physical phenomena are identical—the movement of powerful forces shaking the conical hut, objects thrown, all this is familiar to Western physical science. What is different are the voices projected.

235

Here they are the cries of animals, the voices from the swamp and the mountain—the solitary elementals before whom the primitive man stands in awe, and from whom he begs sustenance. Here the game lords reign supreme; man himself is voiceless."

A low, halting query reached me from the back of the room. I was startled, even in the midst of my discussion, to note that it was Dreyer.

"And the game lords, what are they?"

"Each species of animal is supposed to have gigantic leaders of more than normal size," I explained. "These beings are the immaterial controllers of that particular type of animal. Legend about them is confused. Sometimes they partake of human qualities, will and intelligence, but they are of animal shape. They control the movements of game, and thus their favor may mean life or death to man."

"Are they visible?" Again Dreyer's low, troubled voice came from the back of the room.

"Native belief has it that they can be seen on rare occasions," I answered. "In a sense they remind one of the concept of the archetypes, the originals behind the petty show of our small, transitory existence. They are the immortal renewers of substance—the force behind and above animate nature."

"Do they dance?" persisted Dreyer.

At this I grew nettled. Old Dreyer in a heckling mood was something new. "I cannot answer that question," I said acidly. "My informants failed to elaborate upon it. But they believe implicitly in these monstrous beings, talk to and propitiate them. It is their voices that emerge from the shaking tent."

"The Indians believe it," pursued old Dreyer relentlessly, "but do *you* believe it?"

"My dear fellow"—I shrugged and glanced at the smiling audience— "I have seen many strange things, many puzzling things, but I am a scientist." Dreyer made a contemptuous sound in his throat and went back to the shadow out of which he had crept in his interest. The talk was over. I headed for the bar.

II

The evening passed. Men drifted homeward or went to their rooms. I had been a year in the woods and hungered for voices and companionship. Finally, however, I sat alone with my glass, a little mellow, perhaps, enjoying the warmth of the fire and remembering the blue snowfields of the North as they should be remembered—in the comfort of warm rooms.

I think an hour must have passed. The club was silent except for the ticking of an antiquated clock on the mantel and small night noises from the street. I must have drowsed. At all events it was some time before I grew aware that a chair had been drawn up opposite me. I started.

"A damp night," I said.

"Foggy," said the man in the shadow musingly. "But not too foggy. They like it that way."

"Eh?" I said. I knew immediately it was Dreyer speaking. Maybe I had missed something; on second thought, maybe not.

"And spring," he said. "Spring. That's part of it. God knows why, of course, but we feel it, why shouldn't they? And more intensely."

"Look—" I said. "I guess—" The old man was more human than I thought. He reached out and touched my knee with the hand that he always kept a glove over—burn, we used to speculate—and smiled softly.

"You don't know what I'm talking about," he finished for me. "And, besides, I ruffled your feelings earlier in the evening. You must forgive me. You touched on an interest of mine, and I was perhaps overeager. I did not intend to give the appearance of heckling. It was only that . . ."

"Of course," I said. "Of course." Such a confession from Dreyer was astounding. The man might be ill. I rang for a drink and decided to shift the conversation to a safer topic, more appropriate to a scholar.

"Frogs," I said desperately, like any young ass in a china shop. "Always admired your experiments. Frogs. Yes."

I give the old man credit. He took the drink and held it up and looked at me across the rim. There was a faint stir of sardonic humor in his eyes.

"Frogs, no," he said, "or maybe yes. I've never been quite sure. Maybe yes. But there was no time to decide properly." The humor faded out of his eyes. "Maybe I should have let go," he said. "It was what they wanted. There's no doubting that at all, but it came too quick for me. What would you have done?"

"I don't know," I said honestly enough and pinched myself.

"You had better know," said Albert Dreyer severely, "if you're planning to become an investigator of primitive religions. Or even not. I wasn't, you know, and the things came to me just when I least suspected—But I forget, you don't believe in them."

He shrugged and half rose, and for the first time, really, I saw the black-gloved hand and the haunted face of Albert Dreyer and knew in my heart the things he had stood for in science. I got up then, as a young man in the presence of his betters should get up, and I said, and I meant it, every word: "Please, Dr. Dreyer, sit down and tell me. I'm too young to be saying what I believe or don't believe in at all. I'd be obliged if you'd tell me."

Just at that moment a strange, wonderful dignity shone out of the countenance of Albert Dreyer, and I knew the man he was. He bowed and sat down, and there were no longer the barriers of age and youthful ego between us. There were just two men under a lamp, and around them a great waiting silence. Out to the ends of the universe, I thought fleetingly, that's the way with man and his lamps. One has to huddle in, there's so little light and so much space. One—

III

"It could happen to anyone," said Albert Dreyer. "And especially in the spring. Remember that. And all I did was to skip. Just a few feet, mark you, but I skipped. Remember that, too.

"You wouldn't remember the place at all. At least not as it was then." He paused and shook the ice in his glass and spoke more easily.

"It was a road that came out finally in a marsh along the Schuylkill River. Probably all industrial now. But I had a little house out there with a laboratory thrown in. It was convenient to the marsh, and that helped me with my studies of amphibia. Moreover, it was a wild, lonely road, and I wanted solitude. It is always the demand of the naturalist. You understand that?"

"Of course," I said. I knew he had gone there, after the death of his young wife, in grief and loneliness and despair. He was not a man to mention such things. "It is best for the naturalist," I agreed.

"Exactly. My best work was done there." He held up his black-gloved hand and glanced at it meditatively. "The work on the axolotl, newt neoteny. I worked hard. I had—" he hesitated—"things to forget. There were times when I worked all night. Or diverted myself, while waiting the result of an experiment, by midnight walks. It was a strange road. Wild all right, but paved and close enough to the city that there were occasional street lamps. All uphill and downhill, with bits of forest leaning in over it, till you walked in a tunnel of trees. Then suddenly you were in the marsh, and the road ended at an old, unused wharf.

"A place to be alone. A place to walk and think. A place for shadows to stretch ahead of you from one dim lamp to another and spring back as you reached the next. I have seen them get tall, tall, but never like that night. It was like a road into space."

"Cold?" I asked.

"No. I shouldn't have said 'space.' It gives the wrong effect. Not cold. Spring. Frog time. The first warmth, and the leaves coming. A little fog in the hollows. The way they like it then in the wet leaves and bogs. No moon, though; secretive and dark, with just those street lamps wandered out from the town. I often wondered what graft had brought them there. They shone on nothing—except my walks at midnight and the journeys of toads, but still . . ."

"Yes?" I prompted, as he paused.

"I was just thinking. The web of things. A politician in town gets a rake-off for selling useless lights on a useless road. If it hadn't been for that, I might not have seen them. I might not even have skipped. Or, if I had, the effect—How can you tell about such things afterwards? Was the effect heightened? Did it magnify their power? Who is to say?"

"The skip?" I said, trying to keep things casual. "I don't understand. You mean, just skipping? Jumping?"

Something like a twinkle came into his eyes for a moment. "Just that," he said. "No more. You are a young man. Impulsive? You should understand."

"I'm afraid—" I began to counter.

"But of course," he cried pleasantly. "I forget. You were not there. So how could I expect you to feel or know about this skipping. Look, look at me now. A sober man, eh?"

I nodded. "Dignified," I said cautiously.

"Very well. But, young man, there is a time to skip. On country roads in the spring. It is not necessary that there be girls. You will skip without them. You will skip because something within you knows the time—frog time. Then you will skip."

"Then I will skip," I repeated, hypnotized. Mad or not, there was a force in Albert Dreyer. Even there under the club lights, the night damp of an unused road began to gather.

IV

"It was a late spring," he said. "Fog and mist in those hollows in a way I had never seen before. And frogs, of course. Thousands of them, and twenty species, trilling, gurgling, and grunting in as many keys. The beautiful keen silver piping of spring peepers arousing as the last ice leaves the ponds—if you have heard that after a long winter alone, you will never forget it." He paused and leaned forward, listening with such an intent inner ear that one could almost hear that far-off silver piping from the wet meadows of the man's forgotten years.

I rattled my glass uneasily, and his eyes came back to me.

"They come out then," he said more calmly. "All amphibia have to return to the water for mating and egg laying. Even toads will hop miles across country to streams and waterways. You don't see them unless you go out at night in the right places as I did, but that night—

"Well, it was unusual, put it that way, as an understatement. It was late, and the creatures seemed to know it. You could feel the forces of mighty and archaic life welling up from the very ground. The water was pulling them—not water as we know it, but the mother, the ancient life force, the thing that made us in the days of creation, and that lurks around us still, unnoticed in our sterile cities.

"I was no different from any other young fool coming home on a spring night, except that as a student of life, and of amphibia in particular, I was, shall we say, more aware of the creatures. I had performed experiments"—the black glove gestured before my eyes. "I was, as it proved, susceptible.

"It began on that lost stretch of roadway leading to the river, and it began simply enough. All around, under the street lamps, I saw little frogs and big frogs hopping steadily toward the river. They were going in my direction.

"At that time I had my whimsies, and I was spry enough to feel the tug of that great movement. I joined them. There was no mystery about it. I simply began to skip, to skip gaily, and enjoy the great bobbing shadow I created as I passed onward with that leaping host all headed for the river.

"Now skipping along a wet pavement in spring is infectious, particularly going downhill, as we were. The impulse to take mightier leaps, to soar farther, increases progressively. The madness worked into me. I bounded till my lungs labored, and my shadow, at first my own shadow, bounded and labored with me.

"It was only midway in my flight that I began to grow conscious that I was not alone. The feeling was not strong at first. Normally a sober pedestrian, I was ecstatically preoccupied with the discovery of latent stores of energy and agility which I had not suspected in my subdued existence.

"It was only as we passed under a street lamp that I noticed, beside my own bobbing shadow, another great, leaping grotesquerie that had an uncanny suggestion of the frog world about it. The shocking aspect of the thing lay in its size, and the fact that, judging from the shadow, it was soaring higher and more gaily than myself.

"'Very well,' you will say"—and here Dreyer paused and looked at me tolerantly—"'Why didn't you turn around? That would be the scientific thing to do.'

"It would be the scientific thing to do, young man, but let me tell you it is not done—not on an empty road at midnight—not when the shadow is already beside your shadow and is joined by another, and then another.

"No, you do not pause. You look neither to left nor right, for fear of what you might see there. Instead, you dance on madly, hopelessly. Plunging higher, higher, in the hope the shadows will be left behind, or prove to be only leaves dancing, when you reach the next street light. Or that whatever had joined you in this midnight bacchanal will take some other pathway and depart.

"You do not look—you cannot look—because to do so is to destroy the universe in which we move and exist and have our transient being. You dare not look, because, beside the shadows, there now comes to your ears the loose-limbed slap of giant batrachian feet, not loud, not loud at all, but there, definitely there, behind you at your shoulder, plunging with the utter madness of spring, their rhythm entering your bones until you too are hurtling upward in some gigantic ecstasy that it is not given to mere flesh and blood to long endure.

"I was part of it, part of some mad dance of the elementals behind the show of things. Perhaps in that night of archaic and elemental passion, that festival of the wetlands, my careless hopping passage under the street lights had called them, attracted their attention, brought them leaping down some fourth-dimensional roadway into the world of time.

"Do not suppose for a single moment I thought so coherently then. My lungs were bursting, my physical self exhausted, but I sprang, I hurtled, I flung myself onward in a company I could not see, that never outpaced me, but that swept me with the mighty ecstasies of a thousand springs, and that bore me onward exultantly past my own doorstep, toward the river, toward some pathway long forgotten, toward some unforgettable destination in the wetlands and the spring.

"Even as I leaped, I was changing. It was this, I think, that stirred the last remnants of human fear and human caution that I still possessed. My will was in abeyance; I could not stop. Furthermore, certain sensations, hypnotic or otherwise, suggested to me that my own physical shape was modifying, or about to change. I was leaping with a growing ease. I was—

"It was just then that the wharf lights began to show. We were approaching the end of the road, and the road, as I have said, ended in the river. It was this, I suppose, that startled me back into some semblance of human terror. Man is a land animal. He does not willingly plunge off wharfs at midnight in the monstrous company of amphibious shadows.

"Nevertheless their power held me. We pounded madly toward the wharf, and under the light that hung above it, and the beam that made a cross. Part of me struggled to stop, and part of me hurtled on. But in that final frenzy of terror before the water below engulfed me I shrieked, 'Help! In the name of God, help me! In the name of Jesus, stop!'"

Dreyer paused and drew in his chair a little closer under the light. Then he went on steadily.

"I was not, I suppose, a particularly religious man, and the cries merely revealed the extremity of my terror. Nevertheless this is a strange thing, and whether it involves the crossed beam, or the appeal to a Christian deity, I will not attempt to answer.

"In one electric instant, however, I was free. It was like the release from demoniac possession. One moment I was leaping in an inhuman company of elder things, and the next moment I was a badly shaken human being on a wharf. Strangest of all, perhaps, was the sudden silence of that midnight hour. I looked down in the circle of the arc light, and there by my feet hopped feebly some tiny froglets of the great migration. There was nothing impressive about them, but you will understand that I drew back in revulsion. I have never been able to handle them for research since. My work is in the past."

He paused and drank, and then, seeing perhaps some lingering doubt and confusion in my eyes, held up his black-gloved hand and deliberately pinched off the glove.

A man should not do that to another man without warning, but I suppose he felt I demanded some proof. I turned my eyes away. One does not like a webbed batrachian hand on a human being.

As I rose embarrassedly, his voice came up to me from the depths of the chair.

"It is not the hand," Dreyer said. "It is the question of choice. Perhaps I was a coward, and ill prepared. Perhaps"—his voice searched uneasily among his memories—"perhaps I should have taken them and that springtime without question. Perhaps I should have trusted them and hopped onward. Who knows? They were gay enough, at least."

He sighed and set down his glass and stared so intently into empty space that, seeing I was forgotten, I tiptoed quietly away.

CONSIDERATIONS

Thinking

There seem to be two Eiseleys in this essay—the young scientist and the older man looking back, reflecting. What does this sentence, uttered by the younger man, tell you about their differences: "I have seen many strange things, many puzzling things, but I am a scientist"?

Recounting his dance with the frogs, Dreyer tries to account for the force that moved him so close to the water. How effectively does his language serve him? Explain.

Connecting

Do you believe in the "mad dance of the elementals behind the show of things"?

Was Dreyer, as he claimed, "free," released from "demoniac possession," when he turned away at the wharf, or was he more free when he skipped with the frogs? How do you know?

How does Eiseley actually entice you to believe in the dance? What are his techniques?

Writing

Decide whether you think "The Dance of the Frogs" is a tale or an essay, and make that decision the point of an essay. Support your conclusion by citing evidence from specimen pieces (other tales, other essays) or from any other general sources about those two forms of literature. You might also consider other Eiseley essays.

Write a short essay about how Eiseley uses light and shadow to convey meaning.

E. M. Forster
(1879–1970)

E.M. Forster is known to us primarily through his novels and the movies that have been based on them, especially *A Room with a View* and *Howards End*. Forster was also a fine essayist, deft, with a wry sense of humor and a quiet, understated contempt for pomposity. His two most important collections of essays—*Abinger Harvest* and *Two Cheers for Democracy*—although personal and familiar, offer a far-reaching sense of history.

"What I Believe" offers a quiet warning about wars and the men who get us into them; it offers as well a defense of "the sensitive, the considerate and the plucky."

What I Believe

I do not believe in Belief. But this is an age of faith, and there are so many militant creeds that, in self-defence, one has to formulate a creed of one's own. Tolerance, good temper and sympathy are no longer enough in a world which is rent by religious and racial persecution, in a world where ignorance rules, and science, who ought to have ruled, plays the subservient pimp. Tolerance, good temper and sympathy—they are what matter really, and if the human race is not to collapse they must come to the front before long. But for the moment they are not enough, their action is no stronger than a flower, battered beneath a military jack-boot. They want stiffening, even if the process coarsens them. Faith, to my mind, is a stiffening process, a sort of mental starch, which ought to be applied as sparingly as possible. I dislike the stuff. I do not believe in it, for its own sake, at all. Herein I probably differ from most people, who believe in Belief, and are only sorry they cannot swallow even more than they do. My law-givers are Erasmus and Montaigne, not Moses and St. Paul. My temple stands not upon Mount Moriah but in that Elysian Field where even the immortal are admitted. My motto is "Lord, I disbelieve—help thou my unbelief."

I have, however, to live in an Age of Faith—the sort of epoch I used to hear praised when I was a boy. It is extremely unpleasant really. It is bloody in every sense of the word. And I have to keep my end up in it. Where do I start?

With personal relationships. Here is something comparatively solid in a world full of violence and cruelty. Not absolutely solid, for psychology has split and shattered the idea of a "Person," and has shown that there is something incalculable in each of us, which may at any moment rise to the surface and destroy our normal balance. We don't know what we are like. We can't know what other people are like. How, then, can we put any trust in personal relationships, or cling to them in the gathering political storm? In theory we cannot. But in practice we can and do. Though A is not unchangeably A or B unchangeably B, there can still be love and loyalty between the two. For the purpose of living one has to assume that the personality is solid, and the "self" is an entity, and to ignore all contrary evidence. And since to ignore evidence is one of the characteristics of faith, I certainly can proclaim that I believe in personal relationships.

Starting from them, I get a little order into the contemporary chaos. One must be fond of people and trust them if one is not to make a mess of life, and it is therefore essential that they should not let one down. They often do. The moral of which is that I must, myself, be as reliable as possible, and this I try to be. But reliability is not a matter of contract— that is the main difference between the world of personal relationships and the world of business relationships. It is a matter for the heart, which signs no documents. In other words, reliability is impossible unless there is a natural warmth. Most men possess this warmth, though they often have bad luck and get chilled. Most of them, even when they are politicians, *want* to keep faith. And one can, at all events, show one's own little light here, one's own poor little trembling flame, with the knowledge that it is not the only light that is shining in the darkness, and not the only one which the darkness does not comprehend. Personal relations are despised today. They are regarded as bourgeois luxuries, as products of a time of fair weather which is now past, and we are urged to get rid of them, and to dedicate ourselves to some movement or cause instead. I hate the idea of causes, and if I had to choose between betraying my country and betraying my friend, I hope I should have the guts to betray my country. Such a choice may scandalize the modern reader, and he may stretch out his patriotic hand to the telephone at once and ring up the police. It would not have shocked Dante, though. Dante places Brutus and Cassius in the lowest circle of Hell because they had chosen to betray their friend Julius Caesar rather than their country Rome. Probably one will not be asked to make such an agonising choice. Still, there lies at the back of every creed something terrible and hard for which the worshipper may one day be required to suffer, and there is even a terror and a hardness in this creed of personal relationships, urbane and mild though it sounds. Love and loyalty to an individual can run counter to the claims of the State. When they do—down with the State, say I, which means that the State would down me.

This brings me along to Democracy, "even Love, the Beloved Republic, which feeds upon Freedom and lives." Democracy is not a Beloved Republic really, and never will be. But it is less hateful than other contemporary forms of government, and to that extent it deserves our support. It does start from the assumption that the individual is important, and that all types are needed to make a civilisation. It does not divide its citizens into the bossers and the bossed—as an efficiency-regime tends to do. The people I admire most are those who are sensitive and want to create something or discover something, and do not see life in terms of power, and such people get more of a chance under a democracy than elsewhere. They found religions, great or small, or they produce literature and art, or they do disinterested scientific research, or they may be what is called "ordinary people," who are creative in their private lives, bring up their children decently, for instance, or help their neighbours. All these people need to express themselves; they cannot do so unless society allows them to do so, and the society which allows them most liberty is a democracy.

Democracy has another merit. It allows criticism, and if there is not public criticism there are bound to be hushed-up scandals. That is why I believe in the Press, despite all its lies and vulgarity, and why I believe in Parliament. Parliament is often sneered at because it is a Talking Shop. I believe in it *because* it is a talking shop. I believe in the Private Member who makes himself a nuisance. He gets snubbed and is told that he is cranky or ill-informed, but he does expose abuses which would otherwise never have been mentioned, and very often an abuse gets put right just by being mentioned. Occasionally, too, a well-meaning public official starts losing his head in the cause of efficiency, and thinks himself God Almighty. Such officials are particularly frequent in the Home Office. Well, there will be questions about them in Parliament sooner or later, and then they will have to mind their steps. Whether Parliament is either a representative body or an efficient one is questionable, but I value it because it criticises and talks, and because its chatter gets widely reported.

So Two Cheers for Democracy: one because it admits variety and two because it permits criticism. Two cheers are quite enough: there is no occasion to give three. Only Love the Beloved Republic deserves that.

What about Force, though? While we are trying to be sensitive and advanced and affectionate and tolerant, an unpleasant question pops up: does not all society rest upon force? If a government cannot count upon the police and the army, how can it hope to rule? And if an individual gets knocked on the head or sent to a labour camp, of what significance are his opinions?

This dilemma does not worry me as much as it does some. I realise that all society rests upon force. But all the great creative actions, all the decent human relations, occur during the intervals when force has not managed to come to the front. These intervals are what matter. I want them to be as frequent and as lengthy as possible, and I call them "civilisation." Some people idealise force and pull it into the foreground and worship it, instead of keeping it in the background as long as possible. I think they make a mistake, and I think that their opposites, the mystics, err even more when they declare that force does not exist. I believe that it exists, and that one of our jobs is to prevent it from getting out of its box. It gets out sooner or later, and then it destroys us and all the lovely things which we have made. But it is not out all the time, for the fortunate reason that the strong are so stupid. Consider their conduct for a moment in the Niebelung's Ring. The giants there have the guns, or in other words the gold; but they do nothing with it, they do not realise that they are all-powerful with the result that the catastrophe is delayed and the castle of Walhalla, insecure but glorious, fronts the storms. Fafnir, coiled round his hoard, grumbles and grunts; we can hear him under Europe today; the leaves of the wood already tremble, and the Bird calls its warnings uselessly. Fafnir will destroy us, but by a blessed dispensation he is stupid and slow, and creation goes on just outside the poisonous blast of his breath. The Nietzschean would hurry the monster up, the mystic would say he did not exist, but Wotan, wiser than either, hastens to create warriors before doom declares itself. The Valkyries are symbols not only of courage but of intelligence; they represent the human spirit snatching its opportunity while the going is good, and one of them even finds time to love. Brünnhilde's last song hymns the recurrence of love, and since it is the privilege of art to exaggerate, she goes even further, and proclaims the love which is eternally triumphant and feeds upon freedom, and lives.

So that is what I feel about force and violence. It is, alas! the ultimate reality on this earth, but it does not always get to the front. Some people call its absences "decadence"; I call them "civilisation" and find in such interludes the chief justification for the human experiment. I look the other way until fate strikes me. Whether this is due to courage or to cowardice in my own case I cannot be sure. But I know that if men had not looked the other way in the past, nothing of any value would survive. The people I respect most behave as if they were immortal and as if society was eternal. Both assumptions are false: both of them must be accepted as true if we are to go on eating and working and loving, and are to keep open a few breathing holes for the human spirit. No millennium seems likely to descend upon humanity; no better and stronger League of Nations will be instituted; no form of Christianity and no alternative to Christianity will bring peace to the world or integrity to the individual; no "change of heart" will occur. And yet we need not despair, indeed, we cannot despair; the evidence of history shows us that men have always insisted on behaving creatively under the shadow of the sword; that they have done their artistic and scientific and domestic stuff for the sake of doing it, and that we had better follow their example under the shadow of the aeroplanes. Others, with more vision or courage than myself, see the salvation of humanity ahead, and will dismiss my conception of civilisation as paltry, a sort of tip-and-run game. Certainly it is presumptuous to say that we *cannot* improve, and that Man, who has only been in power for a few thousand years, will never learn to make use of his power. All I mean is that, if people continue to kill one another as they do, the world cannot get better than it is, and that since there are more people than formerly, and their means for destroying one another superior, the world may well get worse. What is good in people—and consequently in the world—is their insistence on creation, their belief in friendship and loyalty for their own sakes; and though Violence remains and is, indeed, the major partner in this muddled establishment, I believe that creativeness remains too, and will always assume direction when violence sleeps. So, though I am not an optimist, I cannot agree with Sophocles that it were better never to have been born. And although, like Horace, I see no evidence that each batch of births is superior to the last, I leave the field open for the more complacent view. This is such a difficult moment to live in, one cannot help getting gloomy and also a bit rattled, and perhaps short-sighted.

In search of a refuge, we may perhaps turn to hero-worship. But here we shall get no help, in my opinion. Hero-worship is a dangerous vice, and one of the minor merits of a democracy is that it does not encourage it, or produce that unmanageable type of citizen known as the Great Man. It produces instead different kinds of small men—a much finer achievement. But people who cannot get interested in the variety of life, and cannot make up their own minds, get discontented over this, and they long for a hero to bow down before and to follow blindly. It is significant that a hero is an integral part of the authoritarian stock-in-trade today. An efficiency-regime cannot be run without a few heroes stuck about it to carry off the dullness—much as plums have to be put into a bad pudding to make it palatable. One hero at the top and a smaller one each side of him is a favourite arrangement, and the timid and the bored are comforted by the trinity, and, bowing down, feel exalted and strengthened.

No, I distrust Great Men. They produce a desert of uniformity around them and often a pool of blood too, and I always feel a little man's pleasure when they come a cropper. Every now and then one reads in the newspapers some such statement as: "The coup d'etat appears to have failed, and Admiral Toma's whereabouts is at present unknown." Admiral Toma had probably every qualification for being a Great Man—an iron will, personal magnetism, dash, flair, sexlessness—but fate was against him, so he retires to unknown whereabouts instead of parading history with his peers. He fails with a completeness which no artist and no lover can experience, because with them the process of creation is itself an achievement, whereas with him the only possible achievement is success.

I believe in aristocracy, though—if that is the right word, and if a democrat may use it. Not an aristocracy of power, based upon rank and influence, but an aristocracy of the sensitive, the considerate and the plucky. Its members are to be found in all nations and classes, and all through the ages, and there is a secret understanding between them when they meet. They represent the true human tradition, the one permanent victory of our queer race over cruelty and chaos. Thousands of them perish in obscurity, a few are great names. They are sensitive for others as well as for themselves, they are considerate without being fussy, their pluck is not swankiness but the power to endure, and they can take a joke. I give no examples—it is risky to do that—but the reader may as well consider whether this is the type of person he would like to meet and to be, and whether (going farther with me) he would prefer that this type should *not* be an ascetic one. I am against asceticism myself. I am with the old Scotsman who wanted less chastity and more delicacy. I do not feel that my aristocrats are a real aristocracy if they thwart their bodies, since bodies are the instruments through which we register and enjoy the world. Still, I do not insist. This is not a major point. It is clearly possible to be sensitive, considerate and plucky and yet be an ascetic too; if anyone possesses the first three qualities, I will let him in! On they go—an invincible army, yet not a victorious one. The aristocrats, the elect, the chosen, the Best People—all the words that describe them are false, and all attempts to organise them fail. Again and again Authority, seeing their value, has tried to net them and to utilise them as the Egyptian Priesthood or the Christian Church or the Chinese Civil Service or the Group movement, or some other worthy stunt. But they slip through the net and are gone; when the door is shut, they are no longer in the room; their temple, as one of them remarked, is the Holiness of the Heart's Affection, and their kingdom, though they never possess it, is the wide-open world.

With this type of person knocking about, and constantly crossing one's path if one has eyes to see or hands to feel, the experiment of earthly life cannot be dismissed as a failure. But it may well be hailed as a tragedy, the tragedy being that no device has been found by which these private decencies can be transmitted to public affairs. As soon as the people have power they go crooked and sometimes dotty as well, because the possession of power lifts them into a region where normal honesty never pays. For instance, the man who is selling newspapers outside the Houses of Parliament can safely leave his papers to go for a drink and his cap beside them: anyone who takes a paper is sure to drop a copper into the cap. But the men who are inside the Houses of Parliament—they cannot trust one another like that, still less can the Government they compose trust other governments. No caps upon the pavement here, but suspicion, treachery and armaments. The more highly public life is organised the lower does its morality sink; the nations of today behave to each other worse than they ever did in the past, they cheat, rob, bully and bluff, make war without notice, and kill as many women and children as possible; whereas primitive tribes were at all events restrained by taboos. It is a humiliating outlook—though the greater the darkness, the brighter shine the little lights, reassuring one another, signaling: "Well, at all events, I'm still here. I don't like it very much, but how are you?" Unquenchable lights of my aristocracy! Signals of the invincible army! "Come along—anyway, let's have a good time while we can." I think they signal that too.

The Saviour of the future—if ever he comes—will not preach a new Gospel. He will merely utilise my aristocracy, he will make effective the good will and the good temper which are already existing. In other words, he will introduce a new technique. In economics, we are told that if there was a new technique of distribution, there need be no poverty, and people would not starve in one place while crops were being ploughed under in another. A similar change is needed in the sphere of morals and politics. The desire for it is by no means new; it was expressed, for example, in theological terms by Jacopone da Todi over six hundred years ago. "*Ordina questo amore, O tu che m'ami,*" he said; "O thou who lovest me—set this love in order." His prayer was not granted, and I do not myself believe that it ever will be, but here, and not through a change of heart, is our probable route. Not by becoming better, but by ordering and distributing his native goodness, will Man shut up Force into its box, and so gain time to explore the universe and to set his mark upon it worthily. At present he only explores it at odd moments, when Force is looking the other way, and his divine creativeness appears as a trivial by-product, to be scrapped as soon as the drums beat and the bombers hum.

Such a change, claim the orthodox, can only be made by Christianity, and will be made by it in God's good time: man always has failed and always will fail to organise his own goodness, and it is presumptuous of him to try. This claim—solemn as it is—leaves me cold. I cannot believe that Christianity will ever cope with the present worldwide mess, and I think that such influence as it retains in modern society is due to the money behind it, rather than to its spiritual appeal. It was a spiritual force once, but the indwelling spirit will have to be restated if it is to calm the waters again, and probably restated in a non-Christian form. Naturally a lot of people, and people who are not only good but able and intelligent, will disagree here; they will vehemently deny that Christianity has failed, or they will argue that its failure proceeds from the wickedness of men, and really proves its ultimate success. They have Faith, with a large F. My faith has a very small one, and I only intrude it because these are strenuous and serious days, and one likes to say what one thinks while speech is comparatively free: it may not be free much longer.

The above are the reflections of an individualist and a liberal who has found liberalism crumbling beneath him and at first felt ashamed. Then, looking around, he decided there was no special reason for shame, since other people, whatever they felt, were equally insecure. And as for individualism—there seems no way of getting off this, even if one wanted to. The dictator-hero can grind down his citizens till they are all alike, but he cannot melt them into a single man. That is beyond his power. He can order them to merge, he can incite them to mass-antics, but they are obliged to be born separately, and to die separately, and, owing to these unavoidable termini, will always be running off the totalitarian rails. The memory of birth and the expectation of death always lurk within the human being, making him separate from his fellows and consequently capable of intercourse with them. Naked I came into the world, naked I shall go out of it! And a very good thing too, for it reminds me that I am naked under my shirt, whatever its colour.

CONSIDERATIONS

Thinking

This essay was written in 1938, on the brink of a second major war in Europe. Why do you suppose Forster capitalizes "Belief," "Age of Faith," "Democracy," and "Great Men"?

Why does Forster give only two cheers for democracy instead of three?

Why does Forster distrust "Great Men"?

Connecting

What does Forster accomplish by looking first at personal relationships, friendship, and Democracy before he turns to Force, hero worship, and his special aristocracy?

What is the effect of the figurative language Forster uses throughout the essay: "science" playing the "subservient pimp"; "Tolerance, good temper and sympathy," whose action in 1938 is "no stronger than a flower, battered beneath a military jack-boot"; "breathing holes for the human spirit" and "under the shadow of the aeroplanes"; and "efficiency-regime"?

Writing

In a well-developed paragraph, explain what Forster means by "creativeness." In a second paragraph, explain why the notion is so important to him in light of his argument against Force.

Write your own essay titled "What I Believe." Make it more than a mere listing of your beliefs. Instead, like Forster, develop a thoughtful exploration of two or three of your central convictions.

Paul Fussell
(b.1924)

Paul Fussell, the Donald T. Regan Professor of English at the University of Pennsylvania, is the author of *The Great War and Modern Memory,* which won the National Book Award in 1976 along with the National Book Critics Circle Award and the Ralph Waldo Emerson Award from Phi Beta Kappa. Fussell's other works include *The Boy Scout Handbook and Other Observations, Thank God for the Atom Bomb,* and *Wartime: Understanding and Behavior in the Second World War.* His essays on war, class, and culture seek to expose our excesses; they reveal as well Fussell's penetrating wit and acerbic sensibility. Occasionally, as in "Indy," they also reveal a touch of sentimentality about American rituals, albeit couched in irony.

"Indy" is Fussell's attempt to put the Indy 500 into national perspective, thereby revealing the ritual that informs the race. In what Fussell sees as a taming of the machine, he sees as well an alternative to war.

Indy

Nineteen eighty-two was a bad year for motor racing. Making a practice run at the Indianapolis Motor Speedway, driver Gordon Smiley was killed, just a week after driver Gilles Villeneuve was killed in Belgium. These two horrors let loose a cascade of objections to motor racing, most of them based on the assumption that human beings are rational creatures, despite the evidence to the contrary that was pouring in from the South Atlantic, where in the Falkland Islands Argentinians and British were shooting and shelling each other to death over matters of national pride and publicity. While that mass murder was in progress, some journalists chose to find auto racing a scandal. In *Time* magazine, Tom Callahan deplored the whole enterprise of the Indianapolis 500: "Some 450,000 people," he wrote, "will perch or picnic at the Speedway on Sunday. Nobody knows how many of them are ghouls spreading their blankets beside a bad intersection." This reprehension of ghoulishness was attended by four gruesome color photographs of Smiley's bloody accident designed to gratify the ghoul in all readers. At the same time, Frank Deford was setting off his anti-Indy blast in *Sports Illustrated,* finding the race not a sport but a mere hustling of automotive products ("The drivers at Indy look much less like athletes than like a lot of congested billboards"). He concluded that among the spectators lurk a significant number of "barbarians." George Vecsey, in the sports pages of *The New York Times,* suggested that the Indy race is becoming too dangerous to be regarded as a sport. "I can see accidents," he said, "on the Long Island Expressway."

Were these people right? Is the Indy 500 a sporting event, or is it something else? And if something else, is it evil or benign? I went there to find out.

Although the automotive industry moved to Detroit early in this century, Indianapolis is still a motor city, swarming with car washes and auto-parts stores, and the sign on the road into town from the airport, WELCOME TO INDIANAPOLIS: CROSSROADS OF AMERICA, seems to imply that you're entering a place best reached by car. Here, nobody walks. One day I walked two and a half miles along Sixteenth Street to the Speedway, and in that one

hour found myself literally the only person not in an automobile. Returning a few hours later, I was still the only walker, with the exception of a
man who accosted me and tried to borrow sixty-two cents.

To a Northeasterner, Indianapolis seems at first a strangely retrograde
repository of piety and patriotism. When I arrived, an editorial in the only
paper in town was raising a populist voice in a call for school prayer, and
a front-page box offered "Today's Prayer" just above "Today's Chuckle."
After a short sojourn in Indianapolis one is no longer surprised at the
imperious sign in the store window, GO TO CHURCH SUNDAY. Catholics
wishing to arrive at the 500-mile race very early Sunday morning, like
everyone else, have their needs cared for by the Archdiocese of Indianapolis, which has ruled that the race-going faithful may fulfill their holy
Sunday obligation "by attending Mass the evening before." Indianapolis
seems the sort of place where the President expects no one to guffaw or
shout, "Oh, come off it!" when he asserts that someone or something is
"in my prayers." In fact, the President would love Indianapolis. Driving to
the Speedway, the motorist passes a billboard advertising (of course) cars,
but bellowing also GOD BLESS AMERICA. At the Speedway, even at qualifying
trials weeks before the race, the national anthem is played at every opportunity, and the official program carries odd vainglorious ads like one
inserted by the International Association of Machinists and Aerospace
Workers: "PRIDE—Pride helped build America into the greatest nation on
earth."

"Naptown" is what many locals call Indianapolis, and it does seem a
somnolent place. Although it's a city and not a town, it's hard not to think
of the Hoosier Booth Tarkington and those long, warm, sleepy afternoons
when Penrod and Sam found nothing whatever to do. As I experienced
the slowness of the Indianapolis pace—every transaction seems to drag on
interminably, every delay is welcomed with friendly patience—I began to
wonder whether speed and danger were not celebrated there one day a
year just for the sheer relief and novelty of it, life being, on all other days,
so safe, slow, and predictable. But friendly as well, it must be said. An
elderly man flushing the urinal next to mine at the Speedway Motel,
astonished at the noisy vigor of the flush, turned to me and although we'd
not been introduced, kindly made me the audience for his observation,
"Gawd, the *suction* on that son of a bitch! If you dropped it *in* there, you'd
really lose it!" Ron Dorson, an authority on the anthropology of Indy,
observes that although "in most public social settings . . . it is considered
socially deviant for strangers to approach one another," at the Speedway
things are different. There, "it becomes perfectly acceptable to engage total

strangers in conversation about lap times, automotive technology, Speedway management, or race-driver intrigue." Something of pioneer individualism seems to linger in this friendliness, and on race Sunday, when you
behold the infield crowded with campers, tents, trailers, and R.V.s, their
occupants cooking and drawing water and cosseting children and making
love in the friendliest fashion, you realize what the Indy setting really is.
It's an early-nineteenth-century American pioneer campsite surrounded,
as if fortuitously, by an early-twentieth-century two-and-a-half-mile track.
And you almost begin to wonder if it's not the camping out, that primeval
American ceremony of innocence, rather than the race and its excite-
ments and hazards, that has drawn these multitudes here.

I'd say the people can be divided into three social classes: the middles,
who on race day, in homage to the checkered flag, tend to dress all in
black and white and who sit in reserved seats; the high proles, who watch
standing or lolling in the infield, especially at the turns, "where the action
is"; and the uglies, the overadvertised, black-leathered, beer-sodden, pot
headed occupiers of that muddy stretch of ground in the infield at the
first turn known as the Snake Pit. These are the ones who, when girls
approach, spiritlessly hold up signs reading SHOW US YOUR TITS. These
uglies are sometimes taken to be the essence of Indy, and they are those
Frank Deford probably has in mind when he speaks of "barbarians." But
they are not the significant Indy audience. The middle class is—all those
nice unstrenuous types arriving at the Speedway in cars bearing Purdue
and Indiana State stickers.

The middles are privileged to participate in an exclusive social event,
the classy pit promenade. Beginning three hours before the start, anyone
who can wangle a pit pass strolls slowly up and down in the space
between the pits and the track proper, all dressed up and watched envi-
ously—that is the hope, at least—by the tens of thousands of social infe-
riors confined to the stands. On race morning in Indianapolis this is the
stylish place to be, a place where one wouldn't dare show oneself
unshaven or in dirty clothes. Many spandy-clean black-and-white getups
are to be seen there, including trousers with two-inch black-and-white
squares. Even though the social tone is compromised a bit by the presence of journalistic onlookers (that's how I got there), the thing struck me
as comparable with some of the great snob social operations of the world,
like appearing in or near the royal box at Ascot or visibly sipping champagne while watching the cricket at Lord's or even nodding slightly to
well-dressed friends while ambling slowly down the Champs Élysées. But

this Indy promenade is distinctly for middle-class people. The upper-middle class is not to be found at Indy. If you're the sort of person drawn to the U.S. Open or the America's Cup races at Newport, you're not likely to be seen at the Speedway.

From the outset, devotees of motor racing have felt anxieties about its place on the class-status ladder. Is motor racing on a par with cockfighting and female mud wrestling, or is it up there with pro football and even, perhaps, tennis? The surprise registered by an Indianapolis paper after the race in 1912 speaks volumes, socially: "There has been no better-mannered gathering in Indianapolis. . . . There was no pushing, no crowding, no profanity, no discourtesies." When the Chief Steward issues his portentous injunction, "Gentlemen, start your engines," we may feel that the first word insists a bit too much. Presumably, if women drivers were to become a regular feature at Indy, the formula would have to include "Ladies and . . . ," which some might think a further advance toward gentility. Janet Guthrie, who has so far been the only woman to participate (three times), says: "I think that racing's image needs all the help it can get. It has traditionally been a lowbrow image." Before being killed in the Austrian Grand Prix in 1975, Mark Donohue, who had graduated not just from college but from Brown, raced at Indy and sensed what an anomaly he was there. "I was considered different from the other Indy drivers," he said. "I had gone to college, I was articulate, and I didn't swear a lot."

The sense that racing will naturally sink proleward unless rigorously disciplined is what one takes away from a reading of the rule book promulgated by the United States Auto Club, the official supervisor of Indy racing. Cars are not to bear "undignified names," "improper language or conduct" is forbidden, and everything must be neat and clean at all times, just as a gentleman would wish: "*Appearance:* cars, crews, and all pit personnel whose appearance detracts from the character of the program may be excluded." (What's that aimed at, long hair? Terrible acne? Effeminate gestures?)

A similar aspiration to respectability seems partially responsible for the euphemisms that abound at Indy. Just as the self-conscious middle class may remark that someone has passed away (sometimes *over*), the Indy public-address announcer will inform the spectators that "We have a fatality." Instead of saying that there's been a terrible smash-up on the third turn, he'll say, "We have a yellow light." A car never hits the wall, it "gets into" it, or even "kisses" it. When a hurtling car comes into contact with the concrete wall, the driver may be said to have "visited cement city." Driver Danny Ongais, badly injured in a crash in 1981, spoke of it later not as the crash or even the accident but as "the incident." Everywhere there is the gentleman's feeling that if you pretend something has not happened, it has not. Thus the rule prohibiting cars from adding oil during the race. Adding oil would publicly acknowledge, as racing journalist Terry Reed points out, "that a car is blowing (or leaking) its original supply on the track, making the course even more hazardous." Almost immediately after Gordon Smiley's car and body nauseatingly stained the wall, it was repainted, white and pure. After that his tire marks on the third turn ran oddly into an immaculate expanse of white.

As Danny Ongais's indirection suggests, there are psychological as well as social reasons for all this euphemism. Racing is now deadly dangerous, with speeds over 200 miles an hour the rule. That makes more true than ever Jackie Stewart's point: "Motor racing will always be dangerous because you are always going too fast for things around you." Johnny Rutherford adds: "Very few drivers—maybe only a handful—are capable of running two hundred miles an hour." An example of one guy who wasn't, some say in Indianapolis, was the late Gordon Smiley. At least that's the way they rationalize in order to admit to no defect in the conditions, only in the weaker aspirants, thus making racing seem a wholesome and natural illustration of Darwinian selection. A pervasive atmosphere of risk shrouds a top driver's professional life. In June 1970, Jackie Stewart had occasion to realize that in the past months he'd "seen more of life and death than most people see in two lifetimes. Four weeks after Jimmy died, it was Mike Spence at Indianapolis; four weeks later, another friend, Ludovico Scarfiotti; four weeks more, to the day, it was Jo Schlesser in Rouen; and two weeks ago, Bruce McLaren at Goodwood. Now it's Piers. It just keeps on." The U.S.A.C. rule book says explicitly that "Automobile racing is a hazardous undertaking," and it implies it all the way through as when it notes that all drivers are required to remove dentures before starting or when it lays down precise specifications for easily detached steering wheels, "to aid in removing injured drivers from cars."

I have been really scared quite a bit, most notably in the infantry in the Second World War, when shells whined closer and closer and I waited for the final one to tear me to pieces. But I had another moment of sheer terror on May 22, 1982, at eleven in the morning, on the third day of qualifying at Indy, when I entered the Speedway through an underpass running beneath the track itself and for the first time heard those cars screaming by just overhead. They give off not just an almost unbearable sudden noise, but shocking heat and concussion as well. In their appalling *whoosh* is the quintessential menace of the Machine. Not even an observer feels entirely safe at the Speedway, and indeed the spectators are in actual danger all the time—from hurtling machines, tires, and fragments, and from the deadly methanol fuel, which burns with a scarcely visible flame, consuming ears and noses and fingers before onlookers are even aware that the victim is on fire. No wonder "13" is, by U.S.A.C. edict, never used in car numbering.

No wonder, either, that the rituals of the Indy world are so strenuously male, macho as all get-out. Women, even wives and girlfriends, weren't allowed in the pits until 1970. In 1976 Janet Guthrie, intent on breaking the male barrier for the first time, couldn't get her car to go fast enough to qualify for a starting position, but on her way to her car to try, as the journalist Dan Gerber remembers,

> she is stopped by two slightly beer-crazed twenty-year-olds.
> "Hey, Janet," one of them calls, "You gonna qualify?"
> "I hope so," she replies, smiling, perhaps a little nervously.
> "Well, we don't," the other boy calls back to her. "We hope you crash and burn where we can see you."

Actually, to understand just how male Indy is, you have only to scrutinize the famous Borg-Warner trophy, awarded annually to the winner after he has drunk from the traditional quart bottle of milk—not carton, bottle, for this is Indy which, except for speed, has made very few concessions to the modern world. On top of the Borg-Warner trophy is a silver male figure ten inches tall, signaling the finish of a race by vigorously deploying a checkered flag, despite the curious fact that he's quite naked and exhibiting a complete set of realistic male genitals, instead of what we might expect of Indiana, a cache-sexe, consisting maybe of a windblown bit of fabric. There he stands, quite immodestly undraped—unlike, say, the modest figure in front of Rockefeller Center—proclaiming for all to see the ideal maleness toward which Indy aspires.

The ideal whiteness too. Indy, as Ron Dorson says, is "a show staged by white people for a white audience." Blacks are so rare among the spectators that you notice them specifically, and of course there are no black drivers, nor threat of any. (There was once a Jewish driver, Mauri Rose, but that's another story.) At a local cocktail party I broached the black topic as politely as I could and was told by one woman that blacks abjured the race because you had to sit for hours in the hot sun and, as is well known, blacks can't bear to sit in the sun. Phoned for his views, the local NAACP spokesman fulminated, asserting that the situation is a scandal but that all black representations had been ineffective. Once Indy is over and the Speedway emptied for another year, you see a lot of blacks there working for a week to sweep up the six million pounds of litter the crowd leaves (together with odd left-behinds like sets of teeth, and each time, two or three quite decent cars inexplicably abandoned forever in the infield).

The combined weight of the litter suggests the size of the crowd, estimated (the Speedway declines to issue a precise count) at around 400,000. That's half the total population of the state of Montana. And the size of the crowd suggests another thing that's being celebrated beside speed. A name for it would be gigantism. Indy is the biggest of everything, "the largest single-day sporting event in the world," as local publicity says, and as Roger Penske adds, for the drivers it's "the biggest race in the world to win"; both the purse and the publicity are the largest. There is more press coverage—over 4,000 media people are there—than of any similar event. So gigantic is the track that a spectator sees only a tiny segment of it. Thus the public-address announcer is indispensable, performing over (naturally) "the world's largest public-address system" to tell you what you are missing. This means that every event is mediated through language: "We have a yellow light." The Indy public-address and radio announcers have always become public personages, even stars, and young Paul Page, who recently succeeded Sid Collins as the radio "Voice of the Indianapolis Five Hundred," is as famous there as, say, Alistair Cooke is elsewhere.

It's not just the announcing that makes Indy so curiously a language event. It's the advertising, the sight of grown men proud to be walking around in caps that say VALVOLINE or GOODYEAR. The cars themselves, plastered with decals (CHAMPION, DIEHARD, STP), have been called "the world's fastest billboards." So precise are the contracts between advertisers and drivers that drivers are allowed to appear bareheaded only for the brief moment between removing the helmet and clapping on the required prole-cap, reading DOMINO'S PIZZA or QUAKER STATE. Officially, Indy is a celebration of "progress" in the motor-car and rubber-tire industries (the tires are supplied gratis by Goodyear). It's supposed to be a testing ground for improvements destined to make their way into your passenger car. But unofficially, it's a celebration of the charm of brand names, a recognition of their totemic power to confer distinction on those who wear, utter, or display them—and secondary distinction on those in the stands who recognize and respond to them. You achieve vicarious power by wearing the right T-shirt or cap and thus allying yourself with successful enterprises like BUDWEISER or GATORADE. By this display of "legible clothing," as Alison Lurie calls it, you fuse your private identity with external commercial success, redeeming your insignificance and becoming, for the moment, somebody. (A cruel and ironic end for Whitman's highly American awareness of the Self and the Other.) Even the lucky wearers of the coveted pit passes are vouchsafed this feeling of power, for the badges, not content to be merely what they are, are also little ads—for CHEVROLET CAMARO, the year I was there. A person unable to read (a real "barbarian," maybe) would get very little out of Indy.

Obviously there's much more going on here than is commonly imagined by what Naptowners are likely to refer to as "the eastern press," and there's certainly more going on than an overpowering desire to see someone killed. There is a powerful and in my view benign element of ritual purgation about Indy, and the things purged are precisely such impurities as greed, vulgarity, snobbery, and sadism.

The events just before the race, presented always in the same order and with the same deliberate, ample timing, are enough to hint at this ritual element. It is a Sunday morning, a time once appropriate for other rituals of purgation. When I inquired why the race was held on Sunday despite protests from the local Baptists about profaning the Sabbath and the inconvenience of closed liquor stores, I was told that Monday, the holiday, was always available as a rain date. But the race seems to gravitate to a Sunday for deeper reasons.

We've entered the Speedway very early, at 7:00 or 8:00 in the morning, although the crazies will have poured in, already blotto on beer and clad in T-shirts proclaiming the wearer TOO DRUNK TO FUCK, when the gates open at 5:00. We're all anticipating the hour of start, 11:00, the hour when church services traditionally begin. By 9:30 virtually everyone involved in the unvarying pre-start ceremonies is in place. At 9:45, as—I'm quoting the official program—"the Purdue University Band plays 'On the Banks of the Wabash,'" the race cars, still inert, silent, dead things, a threat to no one, are pushed by hand from the pits to their starting positions on the too narrow track, where they are formed up into the eleven rows of a viciously hazardous but thoroughly traditional three-abreast arrangement. At 10:34 the Chief Steward makes a stately ritual circuit in the pace car, officially inspecting the track for impurities one last time. At 10:44, all rise: "The Star-Spangled Banner." At 10:47, heads bowed for the invocation, delivered by a local divine, who prays for a safe race and reminds us of the dead of all our wars—and all past Indys. One minute later, "Taps." It is Memorial Day, you suddenly remember. Two minutes after "Taps," the band plays, very slowly, "Back Home in Indiana." By this time I find that I am crying, for me always an empirical indication, experienced at scores of weddings and commencements, that I am taking part in a ritual. By the time the portentous voice issued its command to the gentlemen, I was ready to be borne out on a litter. And the race hadn't even started yet.

If, while witnessing these things, you come to understand that Indy has something more to do with Memorial Day than coincidence, you also realize that there's some ritual meaning in the event's occurring at the moment recognized as the division between spring and summer. For Dan Gerber, listening as a boy annually to the Voice of the Indianapolis Five Hundred meant—release. "It meant school was getting out and I could get sunburned and go fishing and spend three months on Lake Michigan." It has meant something similar to me: the university year has ended, grades have been turned in, no more pressure, no more anxiety, from that quarter at least, until fall. Indy, says the man who for years has commanded the corps of six hundred ushers, "is spring tonic to me." I know what he means.

As with a great many contemporary experiences, the meaning of Indy is elusive because it won't fit familiar schemes of classification. Rationalists, trying to make sense of its competitive dimension, will conclude that news about it belongs on the sports page. But then Warner Wolf, the TV sports commentator, appalled by the destruction of Villeneuve and Smiley, argues that racing is not a sport at all and indignantly defames it as merely a thing about machines. Although there probably is a legitimate sport called "motor sport," indulged in largely by amateurs, Wolf is right in perceiving that what takes place at Indy is not really a sport. The essence of Indy is in its resemblance to other rituals in which wild, menacing, nonhuman things are tamed.

I am thinking of the rodeo and the bullfight. Subduing beasts that, unsubdued, would threaten man—that's the ritual enacted by rodeo, and, with some additional deepening of the irrational element, of the bullfight as well. Just as at Indy, you can get hurt trying to subdue wild horses, killed trying to dominate bulls. Virility, *cojones,* figure in each of these, as the little silver man indicates they do at Indy. Warner Wolf is also right when he notes that Indy is a thing about machines, but it's about machines only the way rodeos would be about broncos if no men were there to break them and bullfights about *toros* if no *toreros* were there to command them. Indy enacts the ritual taming and dominating of machines, emphasizing the crucial distinction between man and machine, the one soft and vulnerable but quick with courage and resource, the other hard and threatening but witless and unimaginative, stupid, indeed. The cars are at Indy so that men can be shown able to dominate them, and the wonder and glory of the dominators is the point. Indy is thus like a great Sunday-morning proclamation of the dignity of man, and no number of discarded chicken bones or trampled beer cans can change that. Like former Sunday morning rituals, Indy insists that people are worth being saved. If the machine should win, onlookers—sadists excepted—do not feel pleasure. The reasons the extinction of the space shuttle *Challenger* was so distressing are many, but one was certainly the spectacle of the machine, in that case, winning. Those aboard lost their lives not to something like a hurricane or an earthquake, but to a machine. The servant had suddenly turned master, and a vicious, violent master at that.

Do some people, regardless, come to see drivers killed? Probably, but as irrelevant a tiny number of the sick as those who enjoy seeing a bullfight ruined by a goring. If you see someone die at Indy, you are seeing that the machine has won, and that's opposed to everything the ritual is saying. No one enjoyed the moment in the 1987 race when a tire flew off one of the cars and killed a spectator. That was a victory for the machine, and like all such victories, it was messy and inartistic. A longtime student of the race, Sam Posey, seems to get the point when he considers the pleasure spectators take in identifying themselves with the driver-tamer of the machine. When things go wrong and the crowd sees a driver killed, he says, "They are terribly shocked and extremely depressed. They wish they had not been there." What the spectator wants to see is the machine crashing, disintegrating, wheels flying off, and in the end the man springing out and waving, "I'm okay." "Because that's the moment of the greatest thrill," says Posey. "That's when man has conquered the machine. The machine has bitten back, but the man jumps out laughing and therefore the spectator's dream of immortality is confirmed." Immortality: hence, value, and value much longer lasting than that conferred on the congeries of steel, aluminum, and rubber by the mere age of the machine.

I was at Indy during a week when every day brought worse news and more terrible images of people's limbs blown off in the South Atlantic, and perhaps the contrast between that spectacle and the Greatest Spectacle in Racing made Indy seem especially therapeutic. No one was hurt all the time I was there, the only injuries being sunburns and hangovers. I went looking for something mean, but what I found was not that at all. If Indy is in one sense about beer, in a deeper sense it's about milk, as the winning driver's victory refreshment suggests. A full-page ad in the official program, inserted by "Your Local Indiana Dairy Farmer," designated milk "the Drink of Champions" and noted that "over the past six years milk has powered the 'Fastest Rookie.'" Indy, the program also said, is "an American Tradition." It would be hard to find one ministering more comprehensively to the national spirit.

CONSIDERATIONS

Thinking

Why do you suppose Fussell likens the Indy 500 to "an early-nineteenth-century American pioneer campsite" and calls it a "primeval American ceremony of innocence"? Does he make similar comparisons elsewhere in the essay?

Why do you suppose Fussell includes the information about blacks in his essay? Why not Asians, Chicanos, other nonwhites?

What exactly does Fussell mean by that "powerful" and "benign element of ritual purgation" that takes place at Indy? How does Fussell's crying relate to that purgation? Is his crying consistent with what you can discern about his attitude toward the race and the crowd? Explain.

Connecting

Select a spectator event that you are familiar with and recall the crowds. Can you figure out a class structure in that crowd comparable to the "social classes" Fussell discerned at the racetrack?

Compare the way Fussell peoples his essay with local characters and uses their dialogue with the way Gretel Ehrlich uses her characters in "Looking for a Lost Dog." What does that comparison reveal about writing techniques?

What is the relationship between Fussell and all those sports writers he quotes? How does he use them in his essay?

Writing

Write an essay in which you consider what Fussell calls "the spectator's dream of immortality." Extend your inquiry to another sport or activity that you know a great deal about.

If Fussell went to the Indy 500 "looking for something mean," what do you think he found? Write your response to someone else in your class, exchange responses, and compare them.

A nne Ellen Geller (b.1967)

A nne Ellen Geller is studying for her Ph.D. at New York University, where she teaches in the expository writing program. Since graduating from Mount Holyoke, she has served as assistant to the chairman of the board for the Citizens Committee for New York, supporting neighborhood, block, tenant, and youth organizations in the city. She has also had fellowships at NYU and with the New York City Writing Project. She recently received the Naomi Kitay Fellowship, a Mount Holyoke alumni award in creative and critical writing.

In "The Truth, Teased Out, and Told," Geller questions whether their rituals of intimacy actually keep women who claim to be friends from ever really knowing one another.

The Truth, Teased Out, and Told

We drank a lot at the after party at the bridegroom's grandmother's house in Manchester by the Sea. We had all already drunk our way through the wedding, so perhaps I should say that at the after party we drank a lot more. That's the kind of night it was. The kind of night when being sober is being in the same place, at a different party.

There were four of us who hadn't all been together since college, five if you count the bride, but she was busy hostessing and hugging, and she appears in the first few scenes of the evening only as a walk-on and, even later, only as a sort of apparition, who breezes in and assures us that anything we end up doing is okay. I wonder now if she meant anything she could think of, or anything we could.

It was early in the day when I was dared to kiss the best man, the brother of the groom, arrogant, ruddy cheeked, curly haired Douglas, who later lorded over the after party in his tuxedo and bare feet. Tongue they told me, and proof. But, in the end, no one demanded any proof and all that was important was that I missed the start of everything happening because I was down on the rocks by the ocean with the best man. But it is still good to joke about the evening using that story when we don't want to talk about what else happened.

The waitress slipped serving the first course of the reception lunch, and my dressed salad slid down my sleeve. A soft red pepper hung off my shoulder, lettuce caught at the inside bend of my elbow. "I'm sorry, I'm so sorry, please forgive me," the waitress said over and over again. I slipped out of the oil soaked silk jacket, and we thought the disaster had been a slight one, but when I got up to rub away at the stains in the ladies room, everyone at the table gasped. The dressing had pooled on my chair. A dark egg-shaped stain adorned the back of my skirt.

"If anyone can pull it off, you can," someone said.

"You know how to work something like this," someone else added.

I'm not sure I have ever concentrated so hard to form a smile. But I had a reputation to uphold, so when I began my pursuit of the best man as the guests started dancing, I found myself turning and exhibiting the stain for him with a flourish that would have made Vanna White green with envy.

Just teasing. Just joking. Just playing around. My grandmother never liked it when my sister and I teased each other as adults. "You look so homely," my grandmother would say to me and then to my sister. "Doesn't she look homely," she would ask, giving each of us a chance to evaluate the other. We were all dressed up at those times, makeup carefully applied for a holiday dinner. That was teasing to her. Saying something that could not be true, even when my sister and I felt it could be.

My grandmother did not like it when I mocked and made fun of my sister's dumpy and disheveled East Village look. "Now, now," she would say to me. And she would take my sister aside. But she would not say never mind. She would not say my joke wasn't so. She would ask my sister about her newest paintings, and she would carefully examine her five earrings, exclaiming with delight as she fingered each set of dangling beads.

Now, when I listen to women around me measure themselves against other women, saying, "Such traditionalists," "What cut-throat professionals," I like to interrupt the patter by asking questions. My grandmother taught me that the details of a woman's life are what sharpen her edges, give her dimension, bring her alive, and set that one woman apart from all other women. "I teased her, that was the only way I could talk to her," I, and most other women, have said at one time or another. Our teasing is informed by what we think we know, what we think we have figured out, about the other woman. What we still want to know.

At the after party the alcohol blurred the laughing crowd of people. Two labradors ran about, licking, knocking over drinks that had been set down on the stone terrace, barking insistently for us to share our hors d'oeuvres. It became darker, and cool, an early September evening on the North Shore. When the best man and I wandered off we came upon two of my friends sitting side by side just below the grass line, and I gave them my shoes. I slipped along on the rocks, down, down, closer to the waves. A painting teacher once told a friend of mine that the lightest light in the dark of a painting should be darker than the darkest dark in the light, and I remember thinking that there's something about the dark by the ocean at night that always seems so bright. I had a plastic cup in one hand and the weight of that drink was just enough to throw me off balance. Douglas held my forearm to steady me and called me, "Girl," with a slurred g.

I'm sure my memory works only one way, and I feel now as Alice did speaking with the White Queen, "I can't remember things before they happen." What my female friends did to one another that night, each of us had already done many times before. Let everyone into your experiences or be alone, share or suffer. Secrets, crushes, notes, a glimpse at a first bra, lessons learned while we were still girls.

At Camp Mohawk, my day camp, we played truth or dare at a sleepover when I was a Mohican. It was the summer I was twelve. Tired with anxiety, I called my mother the following morning, told her I had a sore throat, and asked her to pick me up. For weeks afterward I dreamed of the small dark bunk room where by day we changed in and out of our bathing suits and ate our lunch when it was raining. I dreamt of the circle of those of us who had been awake, sitting Indian-style, knees knocking against those of the girl on either side. I chose truth and I said, no, I had never kissed a boy. My friend Tracy chose dare. What did she know, what had she already experienced at that young age that she did not want to risk sharing? She was willing, it seemed, to do whatever the other girls could conceive. I still remember what she looked like standing on the roof, alone, the lights of the camp paths illuminating her thin summer nightgown so her legs showed through. We all crowded around the window, looking out at her, stifling laughs into quiet giggles so that our counselors would not storm into the room.

Now I feel like Tracy, and my truths are not so willingly shared, but even the mature Mohicans still huddle. After work they sit around steaming cappuccinos or tall glasses of white wine, and they demand from me tastier tidbits than those I had at twelve.

Truth or dare. As open as women are, I think that we hardly ever say to one another exactly what it is we're thinking. So the line that separates a truth from a dare is a blurry one. So blurry in fact, that telling the truth sometimes becomes the posing of a dare. And, a dare, however silent or loud it may be, can become an acknowledgement of the truth.

I know it is this way, even with my mother. We have reached a point where I tell her most everything, save my birth control method, the balance on my Mastercard bill, the last time I spoke to an ex-boyfriend she thought was long gone. Yet, every now and again, I am indiscreet. I savor disclosure. So, in conversations with her, I sometimes slip in a reference to something that I know will be too much for her.

Daughters of feminists. That's what one author calls my generation of women. She says we have not accepted our mothers' dreams, expectations, and formulations, "wholesale." She suggests that the readers of her book look at what the daughters my age "reject, what they accept, how they juggle the elements." True enough, I want some of what my mother had. All of what she suffered, I refuse. This rejecting and accepting has been easy. Sometimes I like to share with my mother something she will find too brazen, too filled with sexual insinuation, too sassy, too impolite. Even over the phone I can hear her recoil, and I hang up pleased.

But the juggling is difficult. How can I keep who I am up in the air, I often wonder. My mother knows all and admits to knowing nothing. I told my mother that the best man was handsome. I'm saving the rest of the story for another time.

Send old and silly pictures of you and Allison, said the little note from Allison's sister that was inside the invitation for Allison's bridal shower. We're putting together a collage of all her friends. Months later, I would meet many of these women in person at the wedding, and I would watch them interact. They were previewed in stills that did them little justice.

All I could find in my album and my drawer of photo envelopes were pictures of Allison and her ex-boyfriends. I knew a little something about Allison that I could send along, and I knew enough not to share it. I finally found two photographs that I wanted to contribute. In one Allison and I are both guests at a wedding. We stand with arms around one another, each of us holding up our skirts. "Show us a little thigh," is what I believe we were asked to do. I'm in a giddy dress, short with a blue and white polka dotted skirt, and there is a huge blue bow fastened just above my behind.

I wonder how many of those pictures scared Allison when she looked at them. I wonder if she saw herself in those old and silly pictures, or if she saw someone else. Someone she didn't recognize. Someone she didn't know. They were pictures of moments, the lengths of camera flashes. They were sent in by women who came to a luncheon bearing gifts and then pointed to themselves up there on that posterboard. Those women said to one another, that's the time Allison and I went to, that's one when Allison and I were ———.

The second picture I sent shows Allison at my graduation from college. Her skin is already tanner than it should have been that early in the spring, but always the marine biologist, she had just returned from diving somewhere where it was warm. Oh, Allison, those pictures and those women don't say a thing about you, and at the same time they say everything there is to say. You did become the bride who dove into the country club pool in her wedding gown.

When Edith Wharton describes two aged female friends sitting side by side on a parapet in Rome she speaks of how "they visualized each other, each through the wrong end of her little telescope." Sometimes I have thought a friend was more fragile than she was. Sometimes I have imagined her to be more daring, more experienced, more prepared. And always I have been convinced that I had evidence, reasons, examples for what she had been or become. Trust in a relationship between women means that two women are constantly interpreting each other. And sometimes interpretation can be wrong.

Once, when my friend Kate came to visit me, I told her I would take her to a party in Harlem. She seemed wary, but I assured her it would be an adventure.

At the party, my friend Kevin stayed in the candlelit living room with the dancers and the filmmakers and the basketball players, while Kate and I stood in the bedroom and talked to a lone lawyer and his friend, the banker.

I wanted to move inside. I wanted to stretch out on the floor by Kevin and lounge on the pillows, lean my head back and look at the ceiling through my cat glasses while everyone talked. I wanted to run my hand back and forth across the back of the friend's Doberman. She was sleek and warm and sweet. She wandered around the party, but she kept returning to me to lean against the side of my leg.

"I guess you need a Doberman if you're going to live here," Kate whispered to me as the dog brushed by her.

Kate told the lawyer about how she dropped out of law school. The banker told me about golf. Kate announced that what she really wanted to do was teach. Someday she would quit her job and teach. We had spent the morning walking around Central Park talking about how she might make this change, its implications, the excitement of it. The lawyer said why haven't you already quit, why haven't you already started teaching. Kate smiled. I wanted to tell him that it was obvious that she wasn't ready yet, but that was something I would have said about her, and not in front of her. She hadn't said she wasn't ready.

In fact she had talked all morning about being ready and then she followed the description of her readiness with a litany of everything she had to do to prepare.

Women have been encouraged to support one another, to train themselves to see things that another woman can't see in herself. Is it any wonder that we no longer know how to step outside of our interlocked views of one another? We have learned to look through microscopic lenses to determine the expectations of men. For men were the ones feminism defined over and over again as the other. Our mothers told us that we were women of a new generation. We could have anything we wanted. But women have still not learned to set expectations for themselves. Each of us seems to be kept from knowing ourselves by our need to know each other.

The entire time the lawyer was cross-examining her, Kate stood with her arms folded in front of her. Every now and then she looked at her watch.

One of the women in the living room had bought Kevin a set of tarot cards, which he brought into the bedroom.

"Ask a question," he said, "pick a card."

Kate said okay, and within minutes the wish spread was laid out across the table. Her entire future, love to come, fortune to find, danger to avoid, right there before our eyes. Would what she wanted most appear with the next card, or would what she most feared? She looked nervous, afraid of having her cards read, afraid of exposure, suddenly aware and fearful of what we might all be able to see.

We waited patiently through the shuffling and then we all watched the first few cards turned, but truth had already been exposed. Losing interest in what was obvious, the lawyer and the banker became all innuendo, and Kate began to giggle. Kevin handed over the cards and faded into the crowd of the hallway and all I could see was his goatee.

"Maybe we should go," Kate said to me quietly a little while later when the lawyer held the deck of cards to the ear of the banker and whispered something. "It's getting awfully late." I knew, and I think she did too, that the lawyer was about to ask how she was getting home, where she was staying.

Out on the street it had become busy. This was not a New York that Kate had ever seen. The red and blue and green lights of the corner bodega were flashing. Triangular flags across Broadway flapped and blew. A man was yelling on the pay phone. One woman screamed to another, "Mira, mira." We walked a block to the bus stop and stood. Kate said nothing, and looked north on Broadway.

"Let's wait for the bus. It should come soon," I said to Kate. A big group of teenagers walked by, loose jeans down around their hips, baseball caps on backwards. Kate watched them and pulled the collar of her coat around her neck and held it with her leather gloved hands.

The day after that party Kate and I went to breakfast at a greasy coffee shop right in my neighborhood. She admitted that she had been afraid at the apartment in Harlem, and I realized that I had liked knowing that the night before. My friends liked knowing that I would kiss the best man, and I did not surprise them. I have to wonder sometimes if I have any idea who I am without measuring myself against the woman someone else thinks I have become.

When the best man and I walked back up from the rocks at the after party, I couldn't find my shoes, and I couldn't find my friends. I asked the almost faceless figures crowded on the terrace where they were as I straightened my sweater and tried to untangle my salty, seasprayed hair. Someone said "Inside, upstairs." My friend Beth was sitting in the living room alone, at one end of a small sofa.

Beth was the one of the group I had not seen or spoken to over the years. The first thing I had noticed about her, seeing her that wedding weekend after so long, was that she looked thinner, more witchly pinched and artificially pristine than I remembered. I've never met Beth's mother, although I've heard of her again and again from the others. She is legendary, the ice-queen, who has to serve and clear moving around the dinner table in the proper direction, even if the only guests are Beth's college friends. Perhaps it was a certain composure Beth was taught by her mother that kept her from being the woman I think she wanted to be the night of the after party. I imagine that night, she acted, and reacted, just as the ice-queen would have. Or is it that she acted and reacted just as we would have expected her to?

We're so seldom reacting to the woman who's right before us, as she knows herself. We're thinking of her as the collage of everything we know about her, everything we imagine her to be. I hold a friend close, but by seeing her for who I think she is, I am always holding her away. A friend who sees herself only as I see her is hiding from who she could be, and from me.

Upstairs, Kate lay on a single bed, her face to the wall, in the room where we had changed out of the clothes we wore to the ceremony and the reception. Her knees were curled to her chin, her arms wrapped around them. She was sobbing, heaving, shaking. She was saying that she had done something terrible, something horrible, something any of us could have done—did she say that last part or did we just think it. We would never forgive her she said. I'm sorry, I'm sorry, please, please forgive me. The room was spinning, spinning, in different directions I think for each of us. I lay down and curled against her. I held her tight as she shook. Her body seemed slight, but maybe that was only because I had been holding the much larger best man, fifteen, twenty minutes, an hour earlier. She leaned over and threw up on the floor, and we all rushed to clean it up.

It turned out that sitting on the rocks Kate had been drunk enough to share something with Beth, and Beth was the one of us whose composite of Kate was least accurate. Kate shared her secret the first time, and then over and over, to each of us, wanting, I suppose, all of us to feel close to her. And the truth she shared was a truth like any other handed over in that way. It could have been a specific truth or any of the truths that women have grown accustomed to hearing from one another. I've had an affair. I've had an abortion. I was raped. My lover hits me. I have AIDS. You would have had an older brother had I not given him up for adoption. I'm a lesbian.

But truth stops us like a barrier and holds us back. We cannot feel close to the one who has shared because she is not the woman we knew, not the woman we had constructed out of all we thought we knew. Usually the woman who has said what we have been asked to hear is vastly different from the woman we thought we knew. She is unfamiliar, she is ugly, she is a stranger we must come to know.

Facing the truth. Once you find you've seen in a woman what you've never seen before, what's next? I suppose that even I am afraid of those times when I might catch a glimpse of myself and not realize that the woman I see is me.

Beth didn't ask Kate to help her construct a new image, a new understanding. The rest of us surrounded Kate, held her, rubbed her back. Investigators quoted in today's paper tell me that even in a resting state women's brains are involved in symbolic actions. This is no surprise to women. We are so good at these acts, we do them in our sleep. Much sympathy, a little advice, a great deal of storytelling.

A friend and I have an ongoing competition we call story-of-the-year. It's ritualistic. For her, and for me, story-of-the-year serves to measure the passing of time. Each New Year's we judge. Whose tale from the past twelve months is most outrageous, most surprising. Who has done something shockingly daring, who has survived having something done to her that has been most out of her control. There is something reassuring in the replaying of these tales. Adrienne Rich tells us that "the most important thing one woman can do for another is to illuminate and expand her sense of actual possibilities." When I'm reviewing my stories, I can see for myself the outer limits of the woman I am. And these stories take on a different dimension, still, set next to those of my friend. Perhaps some day I will be able to scrutinize my experiences on my own, without the need to compare.

I remember walking by Beth and Kate sitting on the rocks as I wandered off from that after party. I was smug and sure in the face of Kate's dare that I kiss the best man. I gave them my shoes, and barefoot I cut my foot on a rock. It began to hurt as I was holding Kate. It hurt weeks later, too. The cut was on the bottom of my foot, the soft part of my sole.

At parties when I was in elementary school we would play the statue dance. Music plays and the children dance, but when the music stops each child must stand in place, still as a statue, or she is out. As the game has worn on, as my group of female friends age and change, there are only two or three of us standing perfectly still, without laughing, without crying, without switching legs when the music stops, and catches us in the act.

Weeks after the wedding, my foot finally scabbed hard, hurt more in a different way, and then healed. But, Kate no longer talks to Beth. She says she just can't call her a friend. I heard that Beth called Kate once on New Year's. It was inevitable, I suppose, in the spirit of Auld Lang Syne. But Beth has never, ever, since the party at Allison's wedding talked with Kate about the disclosure, tried to make sense of it, explained how she felt or why she couldn't face what she heard.

Kate still wonders aloud sometimes about what Beth thinks of her. I wonder about both of them, and myself. I wonder daringly if it really is our need to know one another that makes it our destiny to never know ourselves. Or if it is just that women have accepted that paradox for so long that we know to do nothing but live our lives by the reading of the cards someone else offers us, a reading that can never be the truth.

CONSIDERATIONS

Thinking

Alice Fasano, a writing teacher, has spoken of an essay's main idea as its "central passion." What do you consider the central passion of Anne Ellen Geller's essay? Write out your answer in two or three sentences.

Do you think Geller's generalizations about women are sound? Does your experience contradict or call into question Geller's central idea? Explain.

Connecting

Consider Geller's title: "The Truth, Teased Out, and Told." Explain the "Teased Out" part of the title in relation to the rest of the essay. What does it mean?

What is there in the essay itself that causes you either to trust or to distrust Geller and her ideas?

Read Maxine Hong Kingston's essays in this anthology. What do you suppose Kingston would have to say about Geller's women?

Writing

In what ways does Geller make use of other women writers in her essay? Do their words simply decorate the essay, or do they help Geller make some important points about women? Explain.

Speculate about whether you think a man could have written Geller's essay, or at least could have raised for consideration her ideas about women.

Write an essay about men's relationships with other men, as you understand those relationships.

D iana Hume George
(b.1948)

D iana Hume George, a poet, essayist, and literary critic, is also a professor of English at Pennsylvania State University (Behrend College). *Blake and Freud,* a book of literary criticism, was nominated for a Pulitzer Prize. She is also the author of *Oedipus Anne: The Poetry of Anne Sexton* and a volume of her own poetry, *The Resurrection of the Body.* George's work has appeared in *The Missouri Review, The Georgia Review, The Ontario Review, Spoon River Quarterly,* and *Best American Essays 1990.*

"Wounded Chevy at Wounded Knee," written on the occasion of a visit to the site of the 1890 massacre at Wounded Knee, South Dakota, gives George an opportunity to write a searching inquiry into the modern plight of Native Americans, while coming to terms with her own long-standing confusion about her relationship to these "indigenous peoples of North America." She is the mother of a "half-Indian son."

Wounded Chevy at Wounded Knee

Pine Ridge Sioux Reservation, July 1989

"If you break down on that reservation, your car belongs to the Indians. They don't like white people out there." This was our amiable motel proprietor in Custer, South Dakota, who asked where we were headed and then propped a conspiratorial white elbow on the counter and said we'd better make sure our vehicle was in good shape. To get to Wounded Knee, site of the last cavalry massacre of the Lakota in 1890 and of more recent confrontations between the FBI and the American Indian Movement, you take a road out of Pine Ridge on the Lakota reservation and go about eight miles. If you weren't watching for it you could miss it, because nothing is there but a hill, a painted board explaining what happened, a tiny church, and a cemetery.

The motel man told us stories about his trucking times, when by day his gas stops were friendly, but by night groups of Indian men who'd been drinking used to circle his truck looking for something to steal—or so he assumed. He began carrying a .357 Magnum with him "just in case." Once he took his wife out to Pine Ridge. "She broke out in hives before we even got there." And when they were stopped on the roadside and a reservation policeman asked if they needed help, she was sure he was going to order her out of the car, steal it, and, I suppose, rape and scalp her while he was at it. As the motel man told us these contradictory stories, he seemed to be unaware of the irony of warning us that the Indians would steal our car if they got a chance and following with a story about an Indian who tried to help them just in case they might be having trouble.

He did make a distinction between the reservation toughs and the police. He wasn't a racist creep, but rather a basically decent fellow whose view of the world was narrowly white. I briefly entertained the notion of staying awhile, pouring another cup of coffee, and asking him a few questions that would make him address the assumptions behind his little sermon, but I really wanted to get on my way, and I knew he wasn't going to change his mind about Indians here in the middle of his life in the middle of the Black Hills.

Mac and I exchanged a few rueful remarks about it while we drove. But we both knew that the real resistance to dealing with Indian culture on these trips that have taken us through both Pueblo and Plains Indian territories hasn't come from outside of our car or our minds, but rather from within them. More specifically, from within me. For years Mac has read about the Plains Indians with real attentiveness and with an openness to learning what he can about the indigenous peoples of North America. He reads histories, biographies, novels, and essays, thinks carefully about the issues involved, remembers what he has read, informs himself with curiosity and respect about tribes that have occupied the areas we visit. For a couple of years he urged me toward these materials, many of which have been visible around our home for years: *Black Elk Speaks, In a Sacred Manner We Live, Bury My Heart at Wounded Knee,* studies of Indian spiritual and cultural life. While we were in Lakota country this time, he was reading Mari Sandoz's biography of Crazy Horse. But he has long since given up on getting me to pay sustained attention to these rich materials, because my resistance has been firm and long-standing. I am probably better informed about Indian life than most Americans ever thought of being, but not informed enough for a thoughtful reader and writer. My resistance has taken the form of a mixture of pride and contempt: pride that I already know more than these books can tell me, and contempt for the white liberal intellectual's romance with all things Indian. But my position has been very strange perhaps, given that I was married to an American Indian for five years, lived on a reservation, and am the mother of a half-Indian son.

I've been mostly wrong in my attitudes, but it's taken me years to understand that. Wounded Knee is where I came to terms with my confusion, rejection, and ambivalence, and it happened in a direct confrontation with past events that are now twenty years old. My resistance broke down because of an encounter with a young Lakota named Mark, who is just about my own son's age.

I grew up in the 1950s and 1960s in a small white community on the edge of the Cattaraugus Seneca Indian Reservation in western New York State. Relations between Indians and whites in my world were bitter, and in many respects replicated the dynamics between whites and blacks in the South, with many exceptions due to the very different functions and circumstances of these two groups of people of color in white America. The school system had recently been integrated after the closing of the Thomas Indian School on the reservation. The middle-class whites wanted nothing to do with the Indians, whom they saw as drunkards and degenerates, in many cases subhuman. When I rebelled against the

restraints of my white upbringing, the medium for asserting myself
against my parents and my world was ready-made, and I grabbed it.

I began hanging out on the reserve with young Indians and shifted
my social and sexual arena entirely to the Indian world. I fell in love with
an idea of noble darkness in the form of an Indian carnival worker, got
pregnant by him, married him, left the white world completely, and
moved into his. Despite the fact that this was the sixties, my actions
weren't politically motivated; or, rather, my politics were entirely personal
at that point. While my more aware counterparts might have done some
of the same things as conscious political and spiritual statements, I was
fifteen when I started my romance with Indians, and I only knew that I
was in love with life outside the constricting white mainstream, and with
all the energy that vibrates on the outer reaches of cultural stability. My
heart and what would later become my politics were definitely in the right
place, and I have never regretted where I went or what I came to know.
But for twenty years that knowledge spoiled me for another kind of
knowing.

Whatever my romantic notions were about the ideal forms of American Indian wisdom—closeness to the land, respect for other living creatures, a sense of harmony with natural cycles, a way of walking lightly in
the world, a manner of living that could make the ordinary and profane
into the sacred—I learned that on the reservation I was inhabiting a world
that was contrary to all these values. American Indian culture at the end
of the road has virtually none of these qualities. White America has
destroyed them. Any culture in its death throes is a grim spectacle, and
there can be no grimmer reality than that endured by people on their way
to annihilation.

I did not live among the scattered wise people or political activists of
the Seneca Nation. I did not marry a nominal American Indian from a
middle-class family. I married an illiterate man who dropped out of school
in the seventh grade and was in school only intermittently before that. He
traveled around the East with carnivals, running a Ferris wheel during the
summer months, and logged wood on the reservation during the winter—
when he could get work. Home base was an old trailer without plumbing
in the woods, where his mother lived. He drank sporadically but heavily,
and his weekends, often his weekdays, were full of pool tables, bar
brawls, the endlessness of hanging out with little to do. He didn't talk
much. How I built this dismal life into a romanticized myth about still
waters running deep gives me an enduring respect for the mythopoeic,
self-deluding power of desire, wish, will.

When I was married to him my world was a blur of old cars driven by drunk men in the middle of the night, of honky-tonk bars, country music, late night fights with furniture flying, food stamps and welfare lines, stories of injury and death. The smell of beer still sickens me slightly. I was sober as a saint through all of this, so I didn't have the insulation of liquor, only of love. I lived the contrary of every white myth about Indian life, both the myths of the small-town white racists and those of the smitten hippies. When I finally left that life behind, extricating myself and my child in the certain knowledge that to stay would mean something very like death for both of us, I removed myself in every respect. I knew how stupid white prejudice was, understood the real story about why Indians drank and wasted their lives, felt the complexities so keenly that I couldn't even try to explain them to anyone white. But similarly, I knew how birdbrained the lovechild generation's romance with Indian culture was.

My husband went on to a career of raping white women that had begun during—or maybe before—our marriage. When he was finally caught, convicted, and sent to Attica, I was long since done with that part of my life. My son pulled me back toward it with his own love for his father, and I still keep in touch with my husband's mother on the reservation, sometimes helping her to handle white bureaucracy, but that's all. I heard at a remove of miles, of cons, it seemed, about the early deaths of young men I'd known well—deaths due to diabetes, to lost limbs, or to car wrecks at high speed—and I felt something, but I didn't have to deal with it. When I tried to think about that past life in order to put it into some kind of perspective, no whole picture emerged. When I tried to write about it, no words would come. And when I tried to be open to learning something new about Indians in America on my trip, my heart closed up tight, and with it my mind. When I went to Wounded Knee, the wounds of these other Indians half a continent and half a lifetime away were a part of the landscape.

We pull off to the side of the road to read the billboard that tells what happened here. "Massacre of Wounded Knee" is the header, but upon close inspection you see that "Massacre" is a new addition, painted over something else. "Battle," perhaps? What did it used to say, I wonder, and hope I'll run into a local who can tell me. While I'm puzzling over this, an old Chevy sputters into the pull-off and shakes to a stop. It's loaded with dark faces, a young man and an older woman with many small children. The man gets out and walks slowly to the front of the car, rolling up his T-shirt over his stomach to get air on his skin. As he raises the hood, a Comanche truck pulls in beside him with one woman inside. It's very hot, and I weave a little in the glare of sun. Suddenly I see the past, superimposed on this hot moment. I've seen it before, again and again, cars full of little Indian kids in the heat of summer on the sides of roads. I glance again, see the woman in the front seat, know that she's their mother or their aunt. She looks weary and resigned, not really sad. She expects this.

And then in another blink it's not only that I have seen this woman; I have *been* this woman, my old car or someone else's packed with little kids who are almost preternaturally quiet, wide-eyed and dark-skinned and already knowing that this is a big part of what life is about, sitting in boiling back seats, their arms jammed against the arms of their brother, their sister, their cousin. There is no use asking when they'll get there, wherever "there" is. It will happen when it happens, when the adults as helpless as they are, figure out what to do. In the meantime they sweat and stare. But I am not this woman anymore, not responsible for these children, some of whose intelligent faces will blank into a permanent sheen of resignation before they're five. I am a tourist in a new Plymouth Voyager, my luggage rack packed with fine camping equipment, my Minolta in my hand to snap pictures of the places I can afford to go.

When Mac suggests that we offer to help them, I am not surprised at my flat negative feeling. He doesn't know what that means, I surmise, and I don't have any way to tell him. Help them? Do you want to get anywhere today, do you have the whole afternoon? The young man's shoulders bend over the motor. He is fit and beautiful, his good torso moves knowingly but powerlessly over the heat rising from beneath the hood. I recognize him, as well as the woman. He has no job. He talks about getting off the reservation, finding work, living the dreams he still has. He'll talk this way for a few more years, then give up entirely. He drinks too much. He has nothing to do. Drinking is the only thing that makes him really laugh, and his only way to release rage. I also know that whatever else is wrong with it the car is out of gas, and that these people have no money. Okay, sure, I say to Mac, standing to one side while he asks how we can help. Close to the car now, I see that the woman is the young man's mother. These kids are his brothers and sisters.

The car is out of gas and it needs a jump. The battery is bad. The woman in the other car is the young man's aunt, who can give him a jump but has no money to give him for gas—or so she says. I know her, too. She is more prosperous than her relatives, and has learned the hard way never to give them any money because she needs it herself, and if she gives it to them she'll never see it again. She made her policy years ago, and makes it stick no matter what. She has to.

Well, then, we'll take them to the nearest gas station. Do they have a gas can? No, just a plastic washer-fluid jug with no top. Okay, that will have to do. How far is the nearest gas? Just up the road a couple of miles. But they don't have any money because they were on their way to cash his mother's unemployment check when they ran out of gas, and the town where they can do that is many miles away. So can we loan them some money for gas? We can. He gets in the front seat. I get in the back, and as we pull away from the windy parking area, I look at the woman and the kids who will be sitting in the car waiting until we return. She knows she can't figure out how soon that will be. She stares straight ahead. I don't want to catch her eye, nor will she catch mine.

Right here up this road. Mark is in his early twenties. Mac asks him questions. He is careful and restrained in his answers at first, then begins to open up. No there's no work around here. Sometimes he does a little horse breaking or fence mending for the ranchers. All the ranches here are run by whites who had the money to make the grim land yield a living. They lease it from the Lakota. Mark went away to a Job Corps camp last year, but he had to come back because his twenty-one-year-old brother died last winter, leaving his mother alone with the little ones. He froze to death. He was drinking at a party and went outside to take a leak. Mark said they figured he must have just stopped for a minute to rest, and then he fell asleep. They found him frozen in the morning. Mark had to come back home to bury his brother and help his mother with the kids.

As we bounce over the dirt road, I stare at the back of Mark's head and at his good Indian profile when he turns toward Mac to speak. He is so familiar to me that I could almost reach out to touch his black straight hair, his brown shoulder. He is my husband, he is my son. I want to give him hope. He speaks about getting out of here, going to "Rapid"—Lakota short-hand for Rapid City—and making a life. He is sick of having nothing to do, he wants work, wants an apartment. But he can't leave yet; he has to stay to help his mother. But things are going to be okay, because he has just won a hundred thousand dollars and is waiting for them to send the check.

What?

"You know the Baja Sweepstakes?" He pronounces it "Bay-jah." "Well, I won it, I think I won it, I got a letter. My little brother sent in the entry form we got with my CD club and he put my name on it, and it came back saying that I'm one of a select few chosen people who've won a hundred thousand dollars. That's what it said, it said that, and I had to scratch out the letters and if three of them matched it means I win, and they matched, and so I sent it back in and now I'm just waiting for my money. It should come pretty soon and then everything will be okay." He repeats it over and over again in the next few minutes: he's one of a select few chosen people.

As he speaks of this, his flat voice becomes animated. Slowly I begin to believe that he believes this. Whatever part of him knows better is firmly shelved for now. This hope, this belief that hundreds of thousands of dollars are on the way, is what keeps him going, what keeps him from walking out into the sky—or to the outhouse in the winter to take a leak and a nap in the snow. What will you do with the money, I ask. Well, first he is going to buy his mother and the kids a house.

The first gas stop is a little shack that's closed when we finally get there. Sandy wind and no sign of life. Miles on down the road is a small Lakota grocery store with only a few items on the shelves and a sign that reads "Stealing is not the Lakota way." Mac hands Mark a five dollar bill. You can kiss that five bucks goodbye, I say to Mac. I know, he nods. When Mark comes back out he has the gas, and also a big cup of 7-Up and a bag of nachos. You want some, he asks me? He hands Mac a buck fifty in change. On the way back I hold the gas can in the back seat, placing my hand over the opening. Despite the open windows, the van fills with fumes. My head begins to ache. I am riding in a dream of flatness, ranch fences, Mark's dark head in front of me wishing away his life, waiting for the break that takes him to Rapid. Later I learn that we are in Manderson, and this is the road where Black Elk lived.

Mark is talking about white people now. Yes, they get along okay. For "yes" he has an expression of affirmation that sounds sort of like "huh." Mari Sandoz spells it "hou" in her books on the Lakota. The Lakota are infiltrated in every way by whites, according to Mark. Lots of people in charge are white, the ranchers are white. And there's a place in Rapid called Lakota Hills, fancy houses meant for Lakotas, but whites live in them. Later it occurs to us that this is probably a development named Lakota Hills that has nothing at all to do with the Indians, but it has their name and so Mark thinks it belongs to them. I am angry for him that we borrow their name this way and paste it on our air-conditioned prosperity. I don't have anything to say to him. I lean back and close my eyes. It would be easy to be one of them again. I remember now how it's done. You just let everything flatten inside.

And when we return to Wounded Knee, the pull-off is empty. Mother, children, car, aunt, all are gone. There's nothing but wind and dust. This doesn't surprise me. Mark's mother knows better than to wait for her son's return if other help comes along. Mark means well, but maybe she has learned that sometimes it's hours before he gets back with gas—hours and a couple of six-packs if he has the chance. Now we face the prospect of driving Mark around the reservation until we can find them. I have just resigned myself to this when his aunt pulls back in and says they're broken down again a couple of miles up. We can leave now. Mark thanks us, smiles, and shyly allows us the liberty of having his aunt take a picture of all three of us. I am feeling a strange kind of shame, as though I had seen him naked, because he told us his secret and I knew it was a lie.

Unemployment, high rates of suicide and infant mortality, fetal alcohol syndrome, death by accident, and drinking related diseases such as diabetes: these are now the ways that American Indians are approaching their collective demise. Over a century ago, American whites began this destruction by displacing and killing the *pte,* the Indian name for the buffalo the Plains Indians depended upon. We herded them together in far crueler ways than they had herded the bison, whose sacredness the Indians respected even as they killed them for food and shelter. The history of our genocide is available in many historical and imaginative sources. What is still elusive, still amazingly misunderstood, is how and why the Indians seem to have participated in their own destruction by their failure to adapt to changed circumstances.

Whites can point to the phenomenal adjustments of other non-Caucasian groups in America, most recently the Asians, who were badly mistreated and who have nevertheless not only adapted but excelled. Indians even come off badly in comparison to the group in some respects most parallel to them, American blacks, whose slowness in adapting seems at first glance to have more justification. Blacks were, after all, our slaves, brought here against their will, without close cultural ties to keep them bound together in a tradition of strength; and on the whole blacks are doing better than Indians. However slowly, a black middle class is emerging in America. What's the matter with Indians? Why haven't they adjusted better as a group?

The American Indian Movement is of course strong in some areas, and Indians have articulate, tough leaders and savvy representatives of their cause who are fighting hard against the tide of despair gripping the heart of their race. But they're still losing, and they know it. Estimates of unemployment on the Pine Ridge and Rosebud reservations run as high as 85 percent. Health officials at Pine Ridge estimate that as many as 25 percent of babies born on the reservation now have fetal alcohol syndrome. This culturally lethal condition cannot be overemphasized, since it means that the next generation of Lakota are genetically as well as socioeconomically crippled; one of the consequences of fetal alcohol syndrome is not only physical disability but mental retardation. The prospects are extremely depressing for Lakota leaders whose traditional values are associated with mental acuity and imaginative wisdom. Mark is vastly ignorant and gullible, but he is intelligent enough. Many of his younger brothers and sisters are not only underprivileged and without educational advantages, but also—let the word be spoken—stupid. When the light of inquiry, curiosity, mental energy, dies out in the eyes of young Indians early in their stunted lives because they have nowhere to go and nothing to do, it is one kind of tragedy. When it is never present to die out in the first place, the magnitude of the waste and devastation is exponentially increased. Indian leaders who are now concentrating on anti-alcohol campaigns among their people are doing so for good reasons.

Indian leaders disagree about culpability at this point. Essentially the arguments become theories of genocide or suicide. On one end of the spectrum of blame is the theory that it is all the fault of white America. The evidence that can be marshaled for this point of view is massive: broken treaties, complete destruction of the Indian ways of life, welfare dependency established as the cheapest and easiest form of guilt payment, continued undermining of Indian autonomy and rights. The problem with this perspective, say others, is that it perpetuates Indian desperation and permits the easy way out—spend your life complaining that white America put you here, and drink yourself into the oblivion of martyrdom instead of taking responsibility for your own life. Some Indians say they've heard enough about white America's culpability, and prefer to transfer responsibility—not blame, but responsibility—to the shoulders of their own people. "White people aren't doing this to us—we're doing it to ourselves," said one Pine Ridge health official on National Public Radio's *Morning Edition* recently. She sees the victim stance as the lethal enemy now. The situation is as nearly hopeless as it is possible to be. Assimilation failed the first time and would fail if tried concertedly again, because Indian culture is rural and tribal and tied to open land, not urban airlessness. The Indian model is the encampment or village—the latter more recently and under duress—and not the city. Even the more stationary pueblo model is by definition not urban. The only real hope for Indian prosperity would be connected to vast tracts of land—not wasteland, but rich land. Nor are most Indians farmers in the sense that white America defines the farm. Though they might be, and have been, successful farmers under pressure, this is not their traditional milieu. Supposing that many tribes could adapt to the farming model over hunting and gathering, they would need large tracts of fine land to farm, and there are none left to grant them.

When the American government gave the Lakota 160 acres apiece and said "Farm this," they misunderstood the Indians completely; and even if Indians had been able to adapt readily—a change approximately as difficult as asking a yuppie to become a nomad moving from encampment to encampment—the land they were given was inadequate to the purpose. Grubbing a living out of the land we have given them, in what John Wesley Powell called "the arid region" west of the one hundredth meridian—takes a kind of know-how developed and perfected by white Americans, and it also takes capital. It is no coincidence that the large ranches on Pine Ridge are almost entirely leased by whites who had the initial wherewithal to make the land yield.

The Sioux were a people whose lives were shaped by a sense of seeking and vision that white America could barely understand even if we were to try, and we do not try. The life of a Sioux of a century and a half ago was framed by the Vision Quest, a search for goals, identity, purpose. One primary means of fulfillment was self-sacrifice. Now, as Royal Hassrick has written, "No longer is there anything which they can deny themselves, and so they have sacrificed themselves in pity." Whereas they were once people whose idea of being human was bound to creative self-expression, their faces now reflect what Hassrick calls "apathy and psychic emaciation." Collectively and individually they have become a people without a vision.

Why do they drink themselves into obliteration and erasure? Why not? When white America approaches the problem from within our own ethnocentric biases, we can't see why people would allow themselves to be wasted in this way, why they would not take the initiative to better themselves, to save themselves through the capitalist individuality that says, "I will make it out of this." But in fact part of their problem is that they have tried to do this, as have most Indian peoples. They've bought the American dream in part, and become greedy for money and material goods. Life on an Indian reservation—almost any reservation—is a despairing imitation of white middle-class values. In this respect Indians are like all other minority groups in ghettos in America, and this explains why Mark has a CD player instead of the more modest possessions we would not have begrudged him. If he is anything like the Indians I lived with, he also has a color TV, though he may well live in a shack or trailer without plumbing and without siding.

Their own dreams have evaded them, and so have ours. Mark and his brothers and sisters have been nourished on memories of a culture that vanished long before they were born and on the promises of a different one, from whose advantages they are forever excluded. Does Mark really believe he has won the sweepstakes? What he got was obviously one of those computer letters that invite the recipient to believe he has won something. Without the education that could teach him to read its language critically, or to read it adequately at all, he has been deceived into believing that a *deus ex machina* in the form of the Baja Sweepstakes will take him out of his despair.

In 1890, the year of the final defeat of the Sioux at Wounded Knee, the Ghost Dance was sweeping the plains. Begun by a few leaders, especially the Paiute seer Wovoka, the Ghost Dance promised its practitioners among the warriors that the buffalo would return and the white man would be defeated. Ghost Dancers believed that their ceremonial dancing and the shirts they wore would make them proof against the white man's bullets. Among the Sioux warriors at Wounded Knee, the willing suspension of disbelief was complete. It made the warriors reckless and abandoned, throwing normal caution and survival strategy to the wind.

A tragically inverted form of the self-delusion embodied in the Ghost Dance is practiced today on the Pine Ridge and other Sioux reservations. The original Ghost Dance has beauty and vitality, as well as desperation, as its sources. Now many Sioux men who would have been warriors in another time behave as though liquor and passivity will not kill them. Mark chooses to suspend his disbelief in white promises and to wait for a hundred thousand dollars to arrive in the mail.

Hank Doctor was my husband's best friend on the Seneca reservation. He was raunchy, hard drinking, outrageous in behavior and looks. His hair was long and scraggly, his nearly black eyes were genuinely wild, and his blue jeans were always caked with dust and falling down his hips. His wit was wicked, his laugh raucous, dangerous, infectious. Hank was merciless toward me, always making white-girl jokes, telling me maybe I better go home to my mama, where I'd be safe from all these dark men. He wanted me to feel a little afraid of his world, told me horrible stories about ghost-dogs that would get me on the reservation if I ventured out at night—and then he'd laugh in a way that said hey, white girl, just joking, but not entirely. He alternated his affection toward me with edgy threats, made fun of the too-white way I talked or walked, took every opportunity to make me feel foolish and out of place. He was suspicious that I was just slumming it as a temporary rebellion—maybe taking notes in my head—and that I'd probably run for home when the going got too tough. Of course he was right, even though I didn't know it at the time. I liked him a lot.

A few years ago, my son Bernie went through a period when he chose to remove himself from my world and go live in his father's, from which I'd taken him when he was three. I didn't try to stop him, even though I knew he was hanging out with people who lived dangerously. I used to lie in bed unable to go to sleep because I was wondering what tree he'd end up wrapped around with his dad. He was a minor, but I was essentially helpless to prevent this. If I'd forced the issue, it would only have made his desire to know a forbidden world more intense. He lived there for months, and I slowly learned to get to sleep at night. Mothers can't save their children. And he had a right.

The day I knew he'd ultimately be okay was when he came home and told me about Hank. He wondered if I'd known Hank. He'd never met him before because Hank had been out west for years. Now he was back home, living in a shack way out in the country, terribly crippled with diabetes and other ailments from drinking, barely able to walk. Hank would have been in his mid-forties at this time. Bernie and his dad took rabbits to Hank when they went hunting so that Hank would have something to eat. During these visits, Hank talked nonstop about the old days, reminding big Bernard of all their bar brawls, crowing to young Bernie that the two of them could beat anyone then they fought as a team, recounting the times they'd dismantled the insides of buildings at four in the morning. He told his stories in vivid, loving detail. His gift for metaphor was precise and fine, his memory perfect even if hyperbolic. He recalled the conversations leading up to fights, the way a person had leaned over the bar, and who had said what to whom just before the furniture flew.

Bernie was impressed with him, but mostly he thought it was pathetic, this not-yet-old man who looked like he was in his seventies, with nothing to remember but brawls. I told Bernie to value Hank for the way he remembered, the way he could make a night from twenty years ago intensely present again, his gift for swagger and characterization, his poetry, his laughter. In another time Hank would have been a tribal narrator, a story catcher with better exploits to recount. He would have occupied a special place in Seneca life because of his gifts.

My son left the reservation valuing and understanding important things about his father's world, but not interested in living in its grip. He lives in Florida where he's a chef in a resort, and he's going to college. A month ago his daughter, my granddaughter, was born. She is named Sequoia, after the Cherokee chief who gave his people an alphabet and a written language. Bernie took her to the reservation on his recent visit north and introduced the infant Sequoia to her great-grandmother. My husband's mother says that big Bernard is drinking again, using up her money, and she doesn't know how much more she can take. I know she'll take as much as she has to. I hope I'll see Bernard someday soon to say hello, and maybe we can bend together over our granddaughter, for whom I know we both have many hopes.

Just before we leave Wounded Knee, I walk over to Aunt Lena's Comanche and point to the tribal sign that tells the story. "It says 'Massacre' there, but it used to say something else." I ask her if she knows what it said before. She looks over my shoulder and laughs. "That's funny," she says, "I've lived here all my life, but you know, I never did read that sign." We're miles down the road before I realize that I never finished reading it myself.

CONSIDERATIONS

Thinking

What do you think George means by the "energy that vibrates on the outer reaches of cultural stability"—the energy that may have caused her to fall in love "with the idea of noble darkness in the form of an Indian carnival worker"?

What is that other kind of knowledge that George had to wait twenty years to find because it had been "spoiled" all those years by another form of knowledge?

In what ways does George find Native American culture "in its death throes"?

Connecting

Early in the essay, George makes a connection between the plight of blacks and the plight of Native Americans. Later, she says, "I lived the contrary of every white myth about Indian life, both the myths of the small-town white racists and those of the smitten hippies." What are the far-reaching implications of that claim—for George and for the rest of us in America?

When George brings up the Asians (and the blacks again), it is to substantiate her notion that "the Indians seem to have participated in their own destruction by their failure to adapt to changed circumstances." What do you think of that idea, and what do you think the reasons might be for such participation?

Writing

Write an essay about what you think George means by the "mythopoeic, self-deluding power of desire, wish, will." Explore the dark and the light side of such power, calling on experience, George's essay, and your reading.

Write an essay about what George calls the "victim stance," but do not feel compelled to concentrate only on Native Americans. Do not be quick to make up your mind about the nature of "victims"; think about why they might be justified in making such claims and why using such claims to defer action might be self-defeating.

N adine Gordimer
(b.1923)

South Africa's most widely read writer, Nadine Gordimer, was born in Springs, South Africa, and educated at the University of Witwatersrand. Since 1949, the year of publication of *Face to Face,* her first collection of stories, Gordimer has produced a steady stream of books, mostly fiction, much of which takes for its subject racial problems in South Africa.

Her essays and occasional writings have been collected in *The Essential Gesture* (1991). Although the following selection, "Where Do Whites Fit In?", was originally published in 1959, long before the recent political change to black majority rule that has occurred in South Africa, the issues Gordimer raises and the questions she asks are relevant today. Gordimer's essay is especially noteworthy for the way she honestly confronts essential problems and imagines the consequences of not resolving them.

Where Do Whites Fit In?

Where do whites fit in in the New Africa? *Nowhere,* I'm inclined to say, in my gloomier and least courageous moods; and I do believe that it is true that even the gentlest and most westernised Africans would like the emotional idea of the continent entirely without the complication of the presence of the white man for a generation or two. But *nowhere,* as an answer for us whites, is in the same category as remarks like *What's the use of living?* in the face of the threat of atomic radiation. We are living; we are in Africa. *Nowhere* is the desire to avoid painful processes and accept an ultimate and final solution (which doesn't exist in the continuous process that is life itself); the desire to have over and done with; the death wish, if not of the body, at least of the spirit.

For if we're going to fit in at all in the new Africa, it's going to be sideways, where-we-can, wherever-they'll-shift-up-for-us. This will not be comfortable; indeed, it will be hardest of all for those of us (I am one myself) who want to belong in the new Africa as we never could in the old, where our skin-colour labelled us as oppressors to the blacks and our views labelled us as traitors to the whites. We want merely to be ordinary members of a multi-coloured, any-coloured society, freed both of the privileges and the guilt of the white sins of our fathers. This seems to us perfectly reasonable and possible and, in terms of reason, it is. But belonging to a society implies two factors which are outside reason: the desire to belong, on the one part, and acceptance, on the other part. The new Africa may, with luck, grant us our legal rights, full citizenship and the vote, but I don't think it will accept us in the way we're hankering after. If ever, it will take the confidence of several generations of jealous independence before Africa will feel that she can let us belong.

There is nothing so damaging to the ego as an emotional rebuff of this kind. (More bearable by far the hate-engendered hate that the apartheiders must expect.) And you don't have to be particularly thin-skinned in order to feel this rebuff coming in Africa. Africans are prickling with the desire to be off on their own; the very fact that you welcome the new Africa almost as fervently as they do seems an intrusion in itself. They have had so much of us—let's not go through the whole list again, from tear-gas and taxes to brotherly advice—that all they crave is to have no part of us.

You'll understand that I'm not speaking in economic or even political, but purely in human or, if you prefer it, psychological terms. For the
purposes of what I have to say it may be true that in South Africa, for
example, foreign capital and skills would have to be retained, in order to
keep the mines and industry going, by wide concessions given by any
black independent government with its head screwed on the right way.
But the fact that we might go on living in our comfortable houses in the
suburbs of Johannesburg under a black republic just as we do under a
white near-republic, does not mean that we should feel ourselves
accepted as part of the homogeneous society of the new Africa. For a long
time to come any white South African must expect to find any black man,
from any African territory, considered by the black South African as more
of a brother than the white South African himself. No personal bonds of
loyalty, friendship or even love will change this; it is a nationalism of the
heart that has been brought about by suffering. There is no share in it we
can hope to have. I for one can read this already in the faces, voices and
eloquently regretful but firm handclasps of my own African friends.

Make no mistake, those moderate African political leaders who offer
us whites—with sincerity, I believe—full participation in the new life of
Africa offer us only the tangibles of existence. The intangibles that make
up emotional participation and the sense of belonging cannot be legis-
lated for.

What are we to do? Shall we go? Shall we leave Africa? For those small
white communities who are truly foreign to the African territories in which
they live, 'sent out' from a homeland in Europe for a spell of duty on
administrative jobs or as representatives of commercial firms, there can't be
much question of staying on. But in those territories, such as South Africa
and the Rhodesias, where there is a sizeable and settled white population
whose *home* is Africa, there is no easy answer; sometimes, it seems no
answer at all. I do not attempt to speak, of course, for the stubborn mass
that will continue, like a Napoleon in a mad house, to see itself as the
undisputed master and make no attempt to consider the reality of living
another role. I do not even try to guess what will happen to them; what *can*
happen to them in a situation that they find unthinkable. I can only fear
that events will deal with them grimly, as events usually do with people
who refuse to think. I speak for people like myself, who think almost too
much about the whole business and hope to arrive at an honest answer,
without self-pity for the whites or sentiment about the blacks.

Some of us in South Africa want to leave; a few of us have gone
already. And certainly, when one comes to Europe on a visit, one becomes

a little uneasy at the number of friends (well-informed friends with a good perspective on the swerves and lurches of the way the world is going) who take one aside and ask whether one isn't planning to leave Africa? Which brings me to the reasons why some people have left and why these friends in Europe think one should pack up, too. A few have left because they cannot bear the guilt and ugliness of the white man's easy lot here; a few have left because they are afraid of the black man; and most, I should say, have left because of a combination of the two. I doubt if any consciously have left for the long-term reason I have elaborated here—the growing unwelcomeness of the white man in Africa. Yet I feel that if the white man's lot were to become no better and no worse than anyone else's tomorrow and the fear of violence at the hands of the black man (which we all have) were to have been brought to the test and disproved, unwelcomeness might still remain as the factor that would, in the end, decide many of us to give up our home and quit Africa.

I myself fluctuate between the desire to be gone—to find a society for myself where my white skin will have no bearing on my place in the community—and a terrible, obstinate and fearful desire to stay. I feel the one desire with my head and the other with my guts. I know that there must be many others who feel as I do, and who realise that generally the head is the more sensible guide of the two. Those of us who stay will need to have the use of our heads in order to sustain the emotional decision that home is not necessarily where you belong ethnogenically, but rather the place you were born to, the faces you first saw around you, and the elements of the situation among your fellow men in which you found yourself and with which you have been struggling, politically, personally or artistically, all your life.

The white man who wants to fit in in the new Africa must learn a number of hard things. He'd do well to regard himself as an immigrant to a new country; somewhere he has never lived before, but to whose life he has committed himself. He'll have to forget the old impulses to leadership, and the temptation to give advice backed by the experience and culture of Western civilisation—Africa is going through a stage when it passionately prefers its own mistakes to successes (or mistakes) that are not its own. This is an absolutely necessary stage in all political, sociological and spiritual growth, but it is an uncomfortable and disillusioning one to live through. And giving up the impulse to advise and interfere and offer to resume responsibility may not be as easy as we whites think. Even those of us who don't want to be boss (or *baas*, rather) have become used to being bossy. We've been used to assuming leadership or at least tutor-

ship, even if it's only been in liberal campaigns to secure the rights of the
Africans to vote and speak for themselves. Out of our very concern to see
Africans make a go of the new Africa, we may—indeed, I know we
shall—be tempted to offer guidance when we haven't been consulted. The
facts that we'll be well-meaning and that the advice may be good and
badly-needed do not count; the sooner we drum that into our egos the
better. What counts is the need of Africa to acquire confidence through
the experience of picking itself up, dusting itself down, and starting all
over again; and the quickening marvel of often getting things right into
the bargain.

It's hard to sit quiet when you think you can tell how a problem may
be solved or a goal accomplished, but it may be even harder to give help
without recriminations or, worse, smugness when it is sought. If we want
to fit in anywhere in Africa, that is what we'll have to teach ourselves to
do; answer up, cheerfully and willingly, when we're called upon and shut
up when we're not. Already I notice that the only really happy whites I
know in Africa—the only ones who are at peace with themselves over
their place in the community—are some South African friends of mine
who have gone to live in Ghana, and who have an educational job to do
on contract from the Government. They are living as equals among the
Africans, they have no say in the affairs of the country for the Africans to
resent and they are contributing something useful and welcome to the
development of Africa. In other words, they are in the position of foreign
experts, employed at the Government's pleasure. I can positively feel my
fellow-whites in Africa swelling with indignance at this extreme picture of
the white man's future life on the continent; and it makes me feel rather
indignant myself. But I think we've got to accept the home truth of the
picture, whether we like it or not, and whether or not what we see there
seems fair. All that the new Africa will really want from us will be what
we can give as 'foreign experts'—the technical, scientific and cultural
knowledge that white civilisation has acquired many hundreds of years
before black civilisation, and on which, whether the Africans like it or
not, their own aspirations are based.

I suppose we may get over being a minority minority instead of the
majority minority we've been used to being all these past years, but I don't
know whether that valuable change of attitude will actually bring us
much nearer the integration we seek. Will intermarriage help us? It
would, of course, on a large scale, but personally I don't believe that it will
happen on a large scale in Africa. Intermarriage has always been regarded
as a social stigma by whites, even in those territories where, unlike South

Africa, it is not actually a crime, but I have never been able to find out whether, among blacks, it is regarded as a stigma or a step up in the world. (Most whites assume it is regarded as a deeply-desired privilege, of course.) I know that, for example, in South Africa many Africans who are not Bechuanas, and have nothing whatever to do with the people of Bechuanaland, have on their walls a picture of Ruth and Seretse Khama. It is difficult to say whether this means that they take pride in the fact that a white woman chose to marry an important African, or whether the picture simply gives them a chance to identify themselves with the ex-chief's successful defiance of white taboo and authority.

Once the social stigma is removed—in the new Africa marriage with an African will be marrying into the ruling class, remember, and no one can measure how much of colour-prejudice is purely class-prejudice, in a country where there has been a great gap between the living standards of black and white—and once (in the case of South Africa) there are no legal disabilities in mixed marriages, I think that intermarriage will increase at two extreme levels of the social scale, but scarcely at all in between. Intellectuals will intermarry because they feel closer to intellectuals, whatever their race or colour, than to the mass, and the humbler and poorly-adjusted fringes of both the black and white masses, who have not found acceptance in their own societies, will intermarry in order to find a home somewhere—if not within the confines of their own background, then in someone else's. But I don't think we can hope for intermarriage on an effective scale between ordinary people, and I shouldn't be surprised if independent black Africa frowned upon it, in an unofficial but firm way. Especially in a country like South Africa, where there might remain whites in sufficiently large numbers to create an unease at the possibility that they might try to close their hands once again on those possessions of power from which their fingers had been prised back one by one. It is quite likely that there will be a social stigma, among ordinary people whose sense of nationalism is well stoked up, attached to marrying whites; it may be considered un-African. (Nkrumah has set the official precedent already, by choosing not a Ruth Williams, but a girl who 'belongs' to the continent—a bride from Nasser's Egypt.) If white numbers do not dwindle in those areas of the continent which are heavily white-populated, and there is integration in schools and universities and no discrimination against white children, the picture will change in a few generations, of course. I do not see those young people as likely to regard parental race prejudice on either side as anything but fuddy-duddy. But will the whites remain, stick it out anywhere in Africa in sufficient numbers for this to come about? Isn't it much more likely that they will dwindle to small, socially isolated communities, whites in the diaspora?

If one will always have to feel white first, and African second, it would be better not to stay on in Africa. It would not be worth it for this. Yet, although I claim no mystique about Africa, I fear that like one of those oxen I sometimes read about in the Sunday papers, I might, dumped somewhere else and kindly treated, continually plod blindly back to where I came from.

CONSIDERATIONS

Thinking

Gordimer wrote this piece in 1959, yet much of what she has to say seems applicable to the South Africa of today (and tomorrow). Do you think she seems overly pessimistic about the place of whites in a South Africa controlled by blacks? Do you think Gordimer would be more optimistic today, given the recent political events in South Africa? Why or why not?

Connecting

Relate what Gordimer says about the place and position of whites in the South Africa of the future with what Cornel West says in "Race Matters" about race relations in the America of the future.

To what extent are Gordimer's observations about interracial marriage in a future South Africa relevant in America today and tomorrow?

Writing

Write an essay concerning your ambivalence about remaining in a place and leaving it. Consider, if you wish, Gordimer's ambivalence and her reasons for it in discussing your own situation.

Compare Gordimer's discussion of place and home with that of Scott Russell Sanders in "Wayland."

M ary Gordon
(b.1949)

M ary Gordon was born in Far Rockaway, New York. She graduated with a B.A. from Barnard, where she now teaches, and she has also earned an M.A. from Syracuse University. Her books include the fictional works *Final Payments* (1978), *The Company of Women* (1981), *Men and Angels* (1986), *Temporary Shelter* (1988), and *The Other Side* (1990). The following selection, "Mary Cassatt," is taken from her collection of essays, *Good Boys and Dead Girls and Other Essays* (1991).

In "Mary Cassatt," Gordon raises questions about gender, creativity, and power. She also describes a few of Cassatt's paintings, one of which can be found in the color insert. One of Gordon's achievements in this essay is her ability to direct us to aspects of Cassatt's art that are worth noticing, appreciating, and thinking about.

Mary Cassatt

When Mary Cassatt's father was told of her decision to become a painter, he said: "I would rather see you dead." When Edgar Degas saw a show of Cassatt's etchings, his response was: "I am not willing to admit that a woman can draw that well." When she returned to Philadelphia after twenty-eight years abroad, having achieved renown as an Impressionist painter and the esteem of Degas, Huysmans, Pissarro, and Berthe Morisot, the *Philadelphia Ledger* reported: "Mary Cassatt, sister of Mr. Cassatt, president of the Pennsylvania Railroad, returned from Europe yesterday. She has been studying painting in France and owns the smallest Pekingese dog in the world."

Mary Cassatt exemplified the paradoxes of the woman artist. Cut off from the experiences that are considered the entitlement of her male counterpart, she has access to a private world a man can only guess at. She has, therefore, a kind of information he is necessarily deprived of. If she has almost impossible good fortune—means, self-confidence, heroic energy and dedication, the instinct to avoid the seductions of ordinary domestic life, which so easily become a substitute for creative work—she may pull off a miracle: she will combine the skill and surety that she has stolen from the world of men with the vision she brings from the world of women.

Mary Cassatt pulled off such a miracle. But if her story is particularly female, it is also American. She typifies one kind of independent American spinster who keeps reappearing in our history in forms as various as Margaret Fuller and Katharine Hepburn. There is an astringency in such women, a fierce discipline, a fearlessness, a love of work. But they are not inhuman. At home in the world, they embrace it with a kind of aristocratic greed that knows nothing of excess. Balance, proportion, an instinct for the distant and the formal, an exuberance, a vividness, a clarity of line: the genius of Mary Cassatt includes all these elements. The details of the combination are best put down to grace; the outlines may have been her birthright.

She was one of those wealthy Americans whose parents took the children abroad for their education and medical care. The James family comes to mind and, given her father's attitude toward her career, it is remarkable that Cassatt didn't share the fate of Alice James. But she had a remarkable mother, intelligent, encouraging of her children. When her daughter wanted to study in Paris, and her husband disapproved, Mrs. Cassatt arranged to accompany Mary as her chaperone.

From her beginnings as an art student, Cassatt was determined to follow the highest standards of craftsmanship. She went first to Paris, then to Italy, where she studied in Parma with Raimondi and spent many hours climbing up scaffolding (to the surprise of the natives) to study the work of Correggio and Parmigianino. Next, she was curious to visit Spain to look at the Spanish masters and to make use of the picturesque landscape and models. Finally, she returned to Paris, where she was to make her home, and worked with Degas, her sometime friend and difficult mentor. There has always been speculation as to whether or not they were lovers; her burning their correspondence gave the rumor credence. But I believe that they were not; she was, I think, too protective of her talent to make herself so vulnerable to Degas as a lover would have to be. But I suppose I don't believe it because I cherish, instead, the notion that a man and a woman can be colleagues and friends without causing an excuse for raised eyebrows. Most important, I want to believe they were not lovers because if they were, the trustworthiness of his extreme praise grows dilute.

She lived her life until late middle age among her family. Her beloved sister, Lydia, one of her most cherished models, had always lived as a semi-invalid and died early, in Mary's flat, of Bright's disease. Mary was closely involved with her brothers and their children. Her bond with her mother was profound: when Mrs. Cassatt died, in 1895, Mary's work began to decline. At the severing of her last close familial tie, when her surviving brother died as a result of an illness he contracted when traveling with her to Egypt, she broke down entirely. "How we try for happiness, poor things, and how we don't find it. The best cure is hard work—if only one has the health for it," she said, and lived that way.

Not surprisingly, perhaps, Cassatt's reputation has suffered because of the prejudice against her subject matter. Mothers and children: what could be of lower prestige, more vulnerable to the charge of sentimentality. Yet if one looks at the work of Mary Cassatt, one sees how triumphantly she avoids the pitfalls of sentimentality because of the astringent rigor of her eye and craft. The Cassatt iconography dashes in an instant the notion of the comfortable, easily natural fit of the maternal embrace. Again and again in her work, the child's posture embodies the ambivalence of his or her dependence. In *The Family,* the mother and child exist in positions of unease; the strong diagonals created by their postures of opposition give the pictures their tense strength, a strength that renders sentimental sweetness impossible. In *Ellen Mary Cassatt in a White Coat* and *Girl in the Blue Arm Chair,* the children seem imprisoned and dwarfed by the trappings of respectable life. The lines of Ellen's coat, which create such a powerful framing device, entrap the round and living child. The sulky little girl in the armchair seems about to be swallowed up by the massive cylinders of drawing room furniture and the strong curves of emptiness that are the floor. In *The Bath,* the little girl has all the unformed charming awkwardness of a young child: the straight limbs, the loose stomach. But these are not the stuff of Gerber babies—even of the children of Millais. In this picture, the center of interest is not the relationship between the mother and the child but the strong vertical and diagonal stripes of the mother's dress, whose opposition shapes the picture with an insistence that is almost abstract.

Cassatt changed the iconography of the depiction of mothers and children. Hers do not look out into and meet the viewer's eye; neither supplicating nor seductive, they are absorbed in their own inner thoughts. Minds are at work here, a concentration unbroken by an awareness of themselves as objects to be gazed at by the world.

The brilliance of Cassatt's colors, the clarity and solidity of her forms, are the result of her love and knowledge of the masters of European painting. She had a second career as adviser to great collectors: she believed passionately that America must, for the sake of its artists, possess masterpieces, and she paid no attention to the outrage of her European friends, who felt their treasures were being sacked by barbarians. A young man visiting her in her old age noted her closed mind regarding the movement of the moderns. She thought American painters should stay home and not become "café loafers in Paris. Why should they come to Europe?" she demanded. "When I was young it was different. . . . Our Museums had not great paintings for the students to study. Now that has been corrected and something must be done to save our young over here."

One can hear the voice of the old, irascible, still splendid aunt in that comment and see the gesture of her stick toward the Left Bank. Cassatt was blinded by cataracts; the last years of her life were spent in a fog. She became ardent on the subjects of suffragism, socialism, and spiritualism; the horror of the First World War made her passionate in her conviction that mankind itself must change. She died at her country estate near Grasse, honored by the French, recipient of the Légion d'honneur, but unappreciated in America, rescued only recently from misunderstanding, really, by feminist art critics. They allowed us to begin to see her for what she is: a master of line and color whose great achievement was to take the "feminine" themes of mothers, children, women with their thoughts alone, to endow them with grandeur without withholding from them the tenderness that fits so easily alongside the rigor of her art.

CONSIDERATIONS

Thinking

Explain what Gordon means by writing that "Mary Cassatt exemplified the paradoxes of the woman artist." What "miracle," according to Gordon, did Cassatt pull off? Do you agree with Gordon about the miracle and the paradoxes? Why or why not?

Why does Gordon begin her essay with three quotations, two spoken and one written? How effective is this introductory paragraph?

Connecting

To what extent have you found that women artists (and writers) are dismissed as unimportant because of the subjects they choose to depict in their art?

Compare the ways Gordon approaches the life and work of Mary Cassatt with the approach Joan Didion takes to the life and work of Georgia O'Keeffe.

Writing

After looking at reproductions of the Cassatt paintings Gordon describes— *The Family, Ellen Mary Cassatt in a White Coat, Girl in the Blue Arm Chair*—write an essay describing what you see in the paintings.

Write an essay about an artist (any type of artist) you admire. Identify and explain the bases for your admiration of the artist's life and work.

S tephen Jay Gould (b.1941)

S tephen Jay Gould is a professor of zoology at Harvard, where he teaches biology, geology, and the history of science. His widely acclaimed works include *Ontogeny and Phylogeny, The Mismeasure of Man, Wonderful Life,* and several collections of essays, including *Ever Since Darwin, The Panda's Thumb, The Flamingo's Smile,* and *Bully for Brontosaurus.* Gould, the recipient of a MacArthur Award, writes a monthly scientific essay for *Natural History* magazine.

In "Women's Brains," he sets out to refute Paul Broca's findings that relate brain size and intelligence. In the process of exposing the limitations of Broca's findings, Gould examines a wider range of contemporary social distinctions that result from "biological labeling imposed upon members of disadvantaged groups."

Women's Brains

In the prelude to *Middlemarch*, George Eliot lamented the unfulfilled lives of talented women:

> Some have felt that these blundering lives are due to the inconvenient indefiniteness with which the Supreme Power has fashioned the natures of women: if there were one level of feminine incompetence as strict as the ability to count three and no more, the social lot of women might be treated with scientific certitude.

Eliot goes on to discount the idea of innate limitation, but while she wrote in 1872, the leaders of European anthropometry were trying to measure "with scientific certitude" the inferiority of women. Anthropometry, or measurement of the human body, is not so fashionable a field these days, but it dominated the human sciences for much of the nineteenth century and remained popular until intelligence testing replaced skull measurement as a favored device for making invidious comparisons among races, classes, and sexes. Craniometry, or measurement of the skull, commanded the most attention and respect. Its unquestioned leader, Paul Broca (1824–80), professor of clinical surgery at the Faculty of Medicine in Paris, gathered a school of disciples and imitators around himself. Their work, so meticulous and apparently irrefutable, exerted great influence and won high esteem as a jewel of nineteenth-century science.

Broca's work seemed particularly invulnerable to refutation. Had he not measured with the most scrupulous care and accuracy? (Indeed, he had. I have the greatest respect for Broca's meticulous procedure. His numbers are sound. But science is an inferential exercise, not a catalog of facts. Numbers, by themselves, specify nothing. All depends upon what you do with them.) Broca depicted himself as an apostle of objectivity, a man who bowed before facts and cast aside superstition and sentimentality. He declared that "there is no faith, however respectable, no interest, however legitimate, which must not accommodate itself to the progress of human knowledge and bend before truth." Women, like it or not, had smaller brains than men and, therefore, could not equal them in intelligence. This fact, Broca argued, may reinforce a common prejudice in male society, but it is also a scientific truth. L. Manouvrier, a black sheep in Broca's fold, rejected the inferiority of women and wrote with feeling about the burden imposed upon them by Broca's numbers:

> Women displayed their talents and their diplomas. They also invoked philosophical authorities. But they were opposed by *numbers* unknown to Condorcet or to John Stuart Mill. These numbers fell upon poor women like a sledge hammer, and they were accompanied by commentaries and sarcasms more ferocious than the most misogynist imprecations of certain church fathers. The theologians had asked if women had a soul. Several centuries later, some scientists were ready to refuse them a human intelligence.

Broca's argument rested upon two sets of data: the larger brains of men in modern societies, and a supposed increase in male superiority through time. His most extensive data came from autopsies performed personally in four Parisian hospitals. For 292 male brains, he calculated an average weight of 1,325 grams; 140 female brains averaged 1,144 grams for a difference of 181 grams, or 14 percent of the male weight. Broca understood, of course, that part of this difference could be attributed to the greater height of males. Yet he made no attempt to measure the effect of size alone and actually stated that it cannot account for the entire difference because we know, a priori, that women are not as intelligent as men (a premise that the data were supposed to test, not rest upon):

> We might ask if the small size of the female brain depends exclusively upon the small size of her body. Tiedemann has proposed this explanation. But we must not forget that women are, on the average, a little less intelligent than men, a difference which we should not exaggerate but which is, nonetheless, real. We are therefore permitted to suppose that the relatively small size of the female brain depends in part upon her physical inferiority and in part upon her intellectual inferiority.

In 1873, the year after Eliot published *Middlemarch,* Broca measured the cranial capacities of prehistoric skulls from L'Homme Mort cave. Here he found a difference of only 99.5 cubic centimeters between males and females, while modern populations range from 129.5 to 220.7. Topinard, Broca's chief disciple, explained the increasing discrepancy through time as a result of differing evolutionary pressures upon dominant men and passive women:

The man who fights for two or more in the struggle for existence, who has all the responsibility and the cares of tomorrow, who is constantly active in combating the environment and human rivals, needs more brain than the woman whom he must protect and nourish, the sedentary woman, lacking any interior occupations, whose role is to raise children, love, and be passive.

In 1879, Gustave Le Bon, chief misogynist of Broca's school, used these data to publish what must be the most vicious attack upon women in modern scientific literature (no one can top Aristotle). I do not claim his views were representative of Broca's school, but they were published in France's most respected anthropological journal. Le Bon concluded:

In the most intelligent races, as among the Parisians, there are a large number of women whose brains are closer in size to those of gorillas than to the most developed male brains. This inferiority is so obvious that no one can contest it for a moment; only its degree is worth discussion. All psychologists who have studied the intelligence of women, as well as poets and novelists, recognize today that they represent the most inferior forms of human evolution and that they are closer to children and savages than to an adult, civilized man. They excel in fickleness, inconstancy, absence of thought and logic, and incapacity to reason. Without doubt there exist some distinguished women, very superior to the average man, but they are as exceptional as the birth of any monstrosity, as, for example, of a gorilla with two heads; consequently, we may neglect them entirely.

Nor did Le Bon shrink from the social implications of his views. He was horrified by the proposal of some American reformers to grant women higher education on the same basis as men:

A desire to give them the same education, and, as a consequence, to propose the same goals for them, is a dangerous chimera. . . . The day when, misunderstanding the inferior occupations which nature has given her, women leave the home and take part in our battles; on this day a social revolution will begin, and everything that maintains the sacred ties of the family will disappear.

Sound familiar?

I have reexamined Broca's data, the basis for all this derivative pronouncement, and I find his numbers sound but his interpretation ill-founded, to say the least. The data supporting his claim for increased difference through time can be easily dismissed. Broca based his contention on the samples from L'Homme Mort alone—only seven male and six female skulls in all. Never have so little data yielded such far-ranging conclusions.

In 1888, Topinard published Broca's more extensive data on the Parisian hospitals. Since Broca recorded height and age as well as brain size, we may use modern statistics to remove their effect. Brain weight decreases with age, and Broca's women were, on average, considerably older than his men. Brain weight increases with height, and his average man was almost half a foot taller than his average woman. I used multiple regression, a technique that allowed me to assess simultaneously the influence of height and age upon brain size. In an analysis of the data for women, I found that, at average male height and age, a woman's brain would weigh 1,212 grams. Correction for height and age reduces Broca's measured difference of 181 grams by more than a third, to 113 grams.

I don't know what to make of this remaining difference because I cannot assess other factors known to influence brain size in a major way. Cause of death has an important effect: degenerative disease often entails a substantial diminution of brain size. (This effect is separate from the decrease attributed to age alone.) Eugene Schreider, also working with Broca's data, found that men killed in accidents had brains weighing, on average, 60 grams more than men dying of infectious diseases. The best modern data I can find (from American hospitals) records a full 100-gram difference between death by degenerative arteriosclerosis and by violence or accident. Since so many of Broca's subjects were very elderly women, we may assume that lengthy degenerative disease was more common among them than among the men.

More importantly, modern students of brain size still have not agreed on a proper measure for eliminating the powerful effect of body size. Height is partly adequate, but men and women of the same height do not share the same body build. Weight is even worse than height, because most of its variation reflects nutrition rather than intrinsic size—fat versus skinny exerts little influence upon the brain. Manouvrier took up this subject in the 1880s and argued that muscular mass and force should be used. He tried to measure this elusive property in various ways and found a marked difference in favor of men, even in men and women of the same height. When he corrected for what he called "sexual mass," women actually came out slightly ahead in brain size.

Thus, the corrected 113-gram difference is surely too large; the true figure is probably close to zero and may as well favor women as men. And

113 grams, by the way, is exactly the average difference between a 5 foot 4 inch and a 6 foot 4 inch male in Broca's data. We would not (especially us short folks) want to ascribe greater intelligence to tall men. In short, who knows what to do with Broca's data? They certainly don't permit any confident claim that men have bigger brains than women.

To appreciate the social role of Broca and his school, we must recognize that his statements about the brains of women do not reflect an isolated prejudice toward a single disadvantaged group. They must be weighed in the context of a general theory that supported contemporary social distinctions as biologically ordained. Women, blacks, and poor people suffered the same disparagement, but women bore the brunt of Broca's argument because he had easier access to data on women's brains. Women were singularly denigrated but they also stood as surrogates for other disenfranchised groups. As one of Broca's disciples wrote in 1881: "Men of the black races have a brain scarcely heavier than that of white women." This juxtaposition extended into many other realms of anthropological argument, particularly to claims that, anatomically and emotionally, both women and blacks were like white children—and that white children, by the theory of recapitulation, represented an ancestral (primitive) adult stage of human evolution. I do not regard as empty rhetoric the claim that women's battles are for all of us.

Maria Montessori did not confine her activities to educational reform for young children. She lectured on anthropology for several years at the University of Rome, and wrote an influential book entitled *Pedagogical Anthropology* (English edition, 1913). Montessori was no egalitarian. She supported most of Broca's work and the theory of innate criminality proposed by her compatriot Cesare Lombroso. She measured the circumference of children's heads in her schools and inferred that the best prospects had bigger brains. But she had no use for Broca's conclusions about women. She discussed Manouvrier's work at length and made much of his tentative claim that women, after proper correction of the data, had slightly larger brains than men. Women, she concluded, were intellectually superior, but men had prevailed heretofore by dint of physical force. Since technology has abolished force as an instrument of power, the era of women may soon be upon us: "In such an epoch there will really be superior human beings, there will really be men strong in morality and in sentiment. Perhaps in this way the reign of women is approaching, when the enigma of her anthropological superiority will be deciphered. Woman was always the custodian of human sentiment, morality and honor."

This represents one possible antidote to "scientific" claims for the constitutional inferiority of certain groups. One may affirm the validity of biological distinctions but argue that the data have been misinterpreted by prejudiced men with a stake in the outcome, and that disadvantaged groups are truly superior. In recent years, Elaine Morgan has followed this strategy in her *Descent of Woman,* a speculative reconstruction of human prehistory from the woman's point of view—and as farcical as more famous tall tales by and for men.

I prefer another strategy. Montessori and Morgan followed Broca's philosophy to reach a more congenial conclusion. I would rather label the whole enterprise of setting a biological value upon groups for what it is: irrelevant and highly injurious. George Eliot well appreciated the special tragedy that biological labeling imposed upon members of disadvantaged groups. She expressed it for people like herself—women of extraordinary talent. I would apply it more widely—not only to those whose dreams are flouted but also to those who never realize that they may dream—but I cannot match her prose. In conclusion, then, the rest of Eliot's prelude to *Middlemarch:*

> The limits of variation are really much wider than anyone would imagine from the sameness of women's coiffure and the favorite love stories in prose and verse. Here and there a cygnet is reared uneasily among the ducklings in the brown pond, and never finds the living stream in fellowship with its own oary-footed kind. Here and there is born a Saint Theresa, foundress of nothing, whose loving heartbeats and sobs after an unattained goodness tremble off and are dispersed among hindrances instead of centering in some long-recognizable deed.

CONSIDERATIONS

Thinking

What do you think of Gould's claim that "science is an inferential exercise, not a catalog of facts"? What exactly do you think he means by "inferential exercise"?

Identify what you think are Gould's primary aims in writing this essay.

See if you can figure out just how Gould develops his argument against Broca's theories. What, in other words, are Gould's rhetorical strategies in this essay? Are those strategies directed solely against Broca, or does Gould have other antagonists in mind?

Connecting

What is the overall effect of Gould's use of George Eliot's *Middlemarch?*

Gould brings two other women, besides Eliot, into his essay. What use does he make of Maria Montessori and Elaine Morgan?

Compare the way Gould uses scientific evidence in this essay with the way Loren Eiseley uses scientific experience in "The Dance of the Frogs." Is one use of science more effective than the other? How do you think the differences are related to the kinds of essays Gould and Eiseley are writing?

Writing

If Gould is right that "science is an inferential exercise, not a catalog of facts," how well would your formal, scientific education measure up against that definition? Write your assessment to a professor of science within your college or university.

Write an essay that examines the effect on our culture of what Gould calls "biological labeling." Consider one problem in depth, rather than making superficial generalizations about a host of problems.

E dward Hoagland
(b.1932)

E dward Hoagland splits his time between New York City, where he was born and raised, and New England country, where he attended college (Harvard) and gets in touch with nature. Although Hoagland is perhaps best known as a nature writer, he is also a novelist and travel writer. Among his books are *Red Wolves and Black Bears*, *The Tugman's Passage*, and *The Edward Hoagland Reader*, which offers a sampling of his writings in different genres.

In "The Courage of Turtles," Hoagland relates a number of stories that describe his encounters with turtles. One of the most appealing qualities of his essay is the way Hoagland characterizes the turtles he has encountered, particularly the way he endows the turtles with human qualities.

The Courage of Turtles

Turtles are a kind of bird with the governor turned low. With the same attitude of removal, they cock a glance at what is going on, as if they need only to fly away. Until recently they were also a case of virtue rewarded, at least in the town where I grew up, because, being humble creatures, there were plenty of them. Even when we still had a few bobcats in the woods the local snapping turtles, growing up to forty pounds, were the largest carnivores. You would see them through the amber water, as big as greeny wash basins at the bottom of the pond, until they faded into the inscrutable mud as if they hadn't existed at all.

When I was ten I went to Dr. Green's Pond, a two-acre pond across the road. When I was twelve I walked a mile or so to Taggart's Pond, which was lusher, had big water snakes and a waterfall; and shortly after that I was bicycling way up to the adventuresome vastness of Mud Pond, a lake-sized body of water in the reservoir system of a Connecticut city, possessed of cat-backed little islands and empty shacks and a forest of pines and hardwoods along the shore. Otters, foxes, and mink left their prints on the bank; there were pike and perch. As I got older, the estates and forgotten back lots in town were parceled out and sold for nice prices, yet, though the woods had shrunk, it seemed that fewer people walked in the woods. The new residents didn't know how to find them. Eventually, exploring, they did find them, and it required some ingenuity and doubling around on my part to go for eight miles without meeting someone. I was grown by now, I lived in New York, and that's what I wanted to do on the occasional weekends when I came out.

Since Mud Pond contained drinking water I had felt confident nothing untoward would happen there. For a long while the developers stayed away, until the drought of the mid-1960s. This event, squeezing the edges in, convinced the local water company that the pond really wasn't a necessity as a catch basin, however; so they bulldozed a hole in the earthen dam, bulldozed the banks to fill in the bottom, and landscaped the flow of water that remained to wind like an English brook and provide a domestic view for the houses which were planned. Most of the painted turtles of Mud Pond, who had been inaccessible as they sunned on their rocks, wound up in boxes in boys' closets within a matter of days. Their footsteps in the dry leaves gave them away as they wandered forlornly. The snappers and the little musk turtles, neither of whom leave the water except once a year to lay their eggs, dug into the drying mud for another siege of hot weather, which they were accustomed to doing whenever the pond got low. But this time it was low for good; the mud baked over them and slowly entombed them. As for the ducks, I couldn't stroll in the woods and not feel guilty, because they were crouched beside every stagnant pothole, or were slinking between the bushes with their heads tucked into their shoulders so that I wouldn't see them. If they decided I had, they beat their way up through the screen of trees, striking their wings dangerously, and wheeled about with that headlong, magnificent velocity to locate another poor puddle.

I used to catch possums and black snakes as well as turtles, and I kept dogs and goats. Some summers I worked in a menagerie with the big personalities of the animal kingdom, like elephants and rhinoceroses. I was twenty before these enthusiasms began to wane, and it was then that I picked turtles as the particular animal I wanted to keep in touch with. I was allergic to fur, for one thing, and turtles need minimal care and not much in the way of quarters. They're personable beasts. They see the same colors we do and they seem to see just as well, as one discovers in trying to sneak up on them. In the laboratory they unravel the twists of a maze with the hot-blooded rapidity of a mammal. Though they can't run as fast as a rat, they improve on their errors just as quickly, pausing at each crossroads to look left and right. And they rock rhythmically in place, as we often do, although they are hatched from eggs, not the womb. (A common explanation psychologists give for our pleasure in rocking quietly is that it recapitulates our mother's heartbeat *in utero.*)

Snakes, by contrast, are dryly silent and priapic. They are smooth movers, legalistic, unblinking, and they afford the humor which the humorless do. But they make challenging captives; sometimes they don't eat for months on a point of order—if the light isn't right, for instance. Alligators are sticklers too. They're like war-horses, or German shepherds, and with their bar-shaped, vertical pupils adding emphasis, they have the *idée fixe* of eating, eating, even when they choose to refuse all food and stubbornly die. They delight in tossing a salamander up towards the sky and grabbing him in their long mouths as he comes down. They're so eager that they get the jitters, and they're too much of a proposition for a casual aquarium like mine. Frogs are depressingly defenseless: that moist, extensive back, with the bones almost sticking through. Hold a frog and you're holding its skeleton. Frogs' tasty legs are the staff of life to many animals—herons, raccoons, ribbon snakes—though they themselves are hard to feed. It's not an enviable role to be the staff of life, and after frogs you descend down the evolutionary ladder a big step to fish. . . .

• • •

Turtles cough, burp, whistle, grunt and hiss, and produce social judgments. They put their heads together amicably enough, but then one drives the other back with the suddenness of two dogs who have been conversing in tones too low for an onlooker to hear. They pee in fear when they're first caught, but exercise both pluck and optimism in trying to escape, walking for hundreds of yards within the confines of their pen, carrying the weight of that cumbersome box on legs which are cruelly positioned for walking. They don't feel that the contest is unfair; they keep plugging, rolling like sailorly souls—a bobbing, infirm gait, a brave, sea-legged momentum—stopping occasionally to study the lay of the land. For me, anyway, they manage to contain the rest of the animal world. They can stretch out their necks like a giraffe, or loom underwater like an apocryphal hippo. They browse on lettuce thrown on the water like a cow moose which is partly submerged. They have a penguin's alertness, combined with a build like a brontosaurus when they rise up on tiptoe. Then they hunch and ponderously lunge like a grizzly going forward.

Baby turtles in a turtle bowl are a puzzle in geometrics. They're as decorative as pansy petals, but they are also self-directed building blocks, propping themselves on one another in different arrangements, before upending the tower. The timid individuals turn fearless, or vice versa. If one gets a bit arrogant he will push the others off the rock and afterwards climb down into the water and cling to the back of one of those he has bullied, tickling him with his hind feet until he bucks like a bronco. On the other hand, when this same milder-mannered fellow isn't exerting himself, he will stare right into the face of the sun for hours. What could be more lionlike? And he's at home in or out of the water and does lots of metaphysical tilting. He sinks and rises, with an infinity of levels to choose from; or, elongating himself, he climbs out on the land again to perambulate, sits boxed in his box, and finally slides back in the water, submerging into dreams.

I have five of these babies in a kidney-shaped bowl. The hatchling, who is a painted turtle, is not as large as the top joint of my thumb. He eats chicken gladly. Other foods he will attempt to eat but not with sufficient perseverance to succeed because he's so little. The yellow-bellied terrapin is probably a yearling, and he eats salad voraciously, but no meat, fish, or fowl. The Cumberland terrapin won't touch salad or chicken but eats fish and all of the meats except for bacon. The little snapper, with a black crenellated shell, feasts on any kind of meat, but rejects greens and fish. The fifth of the turtles is African. I acquired him only recently and don't know him well. A mottled brown, he unnerves the greener turtles, dragging their food off to his lairs. He doesn't seem to want to be green—he bites the algae off his shell, hanging meanwhile at daring, steep, head-first angles.

The snapper was a Ferdinand until I provided him with deeper water. Now he snaps at my pencil with his downturned and fearsome mouth, his swollen face like a napalm victim's. The Cumberland has an elliptical red mark on the side of his green-and-yellow head. He is benign by nature and ought to be as elegant as his scientific name (*Pseudemys scripta elegans*), except he has contracted a disease of the air bladder which has permanently inflated it; he floats high in the water at an undignified slant and can't go under. There may have been internal bleeding, too, because his carapace is stained along its ridge. Unfortunately, like flowers, baby turtles often die. Their mouths fill up with a white fungus and their lungs with pneumonia. Their organs clog up from the rust in the water, or diet troubles, and, like a dying man's, their eyes and heads become too prominent. Toward the end, the edge of the shell becomes flabby as felt and folds around them like a shroud.

While they live they're like puppies. Although they're vivacious, they would be a bore to be with all the time, so I also have an adult wood turtle about six inches long. Her top shell is the equal of any seashell for sculpturing, even a Cellini shell; it's like an old, dusty, richly engraved medallion dug out of a hillside. Her legs are salmon-orange bordered with black and protected by canted, heroic scales. Her plastron—the bottom shell—is splotched like a margay cat's coat, with black ocelli on a yellow background. It is convex to make room for the female organs inside, whereas a male's would be concave to help him fit tightly on top of her. Altogether, she exhibits every camouflage color on her limbs and shells. She has a turtleneck neck, a tail like an elephant's, wise old pachydermous hind legs, and the face of a turkey—except that when I carry her she gazes at the passing ground with a hawk's eyes and mouth. Her feet fit to the fingers of my hand, one to each one, and she rides looking down. She can walk on the floor in perfect silence, but usually she lets her plastron knock portentously, like a footstep, so that she resembles some grand, concise, slow-moving id. But if an earthworm is presented, she jerks swiftly ahead, poises above it, and strikes like a mongoose, consuming it with wild vigor. Yet she will climb on my lap to eat bread or boiled eggs.

If put into a creek, she swims like a cutter, nosing forward to intercept a strange turtle and smell him. She drifts with the current to go downstream, maneuvering behind a rock when she wants to take stock, or sinking to the nether levels, while bubbles float up. Getting out, choosing her path, she will proceed a distance and dig into a pile of humus, thrusting herself to the coolest layer at the bottom. The hole closes over her until it's as small as a mouse's hole. She's not as aquatic as a musk turtle, not quite as terrestrial as the box turtles in the same woods, but because of her versatility she's marvelous, she's everywhere. And though she breathes the way we breathe, with scarcely perceptible movements of her chest, sometimes instead she pumps her throat ruminatively, like a pipe smoker sucking and puffing. She waits and blinks, pumping her throat, turning her head, then sets off like a loping tiger in slow motion, hurdling the jungly lumber, the pea vine and twigs. She estimates angles so well that when she rides over the rocks, sliding down a drop-off with her rugged front legs extended, she has the grace of a rodeo mare.

But she's well off to be with me rather than at Mud Pond. The other turtles have fled—those that aren't baked into the bottom. Creeping up the brooks to sad, constricted marshes, burdened as they are with that box on their backs, they're walking into a setup where all their enemies move thirty times faster than they. It's like the nightmare most of us have whimpered through, where we are weighted down disastrously while trying to flee; fleeing our home ground, we try to run.

I've seen turtles in still worse straits. On Broadway, in New York, there is a penny arcade which used to sell baby terrapins that were scrawled with bon mots in enamel paint, such as KISS ME BABY. The manager turned out to be a wholesaler as well, and once I asked him whether he had any larger turtles to sell. He took me upstairs to a loft room devoted to the turtle business. There were desks for the paper work and a series of racks that held shallow tin bins atop one another, each with several hundred babies crawling around in it. He was a smudgy-complexioned, bespectacled, serious fellow and he did have a few adult terrapins, but I was going to school and wasn't actually planning to buy; I'd only wanted to see them. They were aquatic turtles, but here they went without water, presumably for weeks, lurching about in those dry bins like handicapped citizens, living on gumption. An easel where the artist worked stood in the middle of the floor. She had a palette and a clip attachment for fastening the babies in place. She wore a smock and a beret, and was homely, short, and eccentric-looking, with funny black hair, like some of the ladies who show their paintings in Washington Square in May. She had a cold, she was smoking, and her hand wasn't very steady, although she worked quickly enough. The smile that she produced for me would have looked giddy if she had been happier, or drunk. Of course the turtles' doom was sealed when she painted them, because their bodies inside would continue to grow but their shells would not. Gradually, invisibly, they would be crushed. Around us their bellies—two thousand belly shells—rubbed on the bins with a mournful, momentous hiss.

Somehow there were so many of them I didn't rescue one. Years later, however, I was walking on First Avenue when I noticed a basket of living turtles in front of a fish store. They were as dry as a heap of old bones in the sun; nevertheless, they were creeping over one another gimpily, doing their best to escape. I looked and was touched to discover that they appeared to be wood turtles, my favorites, so I bought one. In my apartment I looked closer and realized that in fact this was a diamondback terrapin, which was bad news. Diamondbacks are tidewater turtles from brackish estuaries, and I had no seawater to keep him in. He spent his days thumping interminably against the baseboards, pushing for an opening through the wall. He drank thirstily but would not eat and had none of the hearty, accepting qualities of wood turtles. He was morose, paler in color, sleeker and more Oriental in the carved ridges and rings that formed his shell. Though I felt sorry for him, finally I found his unrelenting presence exasperating. I carried him, struggling in a paper bag, across town to the Morton Street Pier on the Hudson River. It was August but gray and windy. He was very surprised when I tossed him in; for the first time in our association, I think, he was afraid. He looked afraid as he bobbed about on top of the water, looking up at me from ten feet below. Though we were both accustomed to his resistance and rigidity, seeing him still pitiful, I recognized that I must have done the wrong thing. At least the river was salty, but it was also bottomless; the waves were too rough for him, and the tide was coming in, bumping him against the pilings underneath the pier. Too late, I realized that he wouldn't be able to swim to a peaceful inlet in New Jersey, even if he could figure out which way to swim. But since, short of diving in after him, there was nothing I could do, I walked away.

CONSIDERATIONS

Thinking

What do you think Hoagland's purpose is in writing this essay? What human qualities does he associate with turtles? What do you think of these connections?

Explain what Hoagland accomplishes with his description of his pet female turtle, with the story of the painted turtles, and with the turtle story that ends his essay.

Connecting

To what extent have you shared any of the experiences Hoagland describes—with turtles or other animals he mentions? What can you link up with Hoagland's discussion that derives from your experience of having pets? How does the following passage from John Steinbeck's *Grapes of Wrath* compare with Hoagland's portrait of the turtle?

. . . The concrete highway was edged with a mat of tangled, broken, dry grass, and the grass heads were heavy with oat beards to catch on a dog's coat, and foxtails to tangle in a horse's fetlocks, and clover burrs to fasten in sheep's wool; sleeping life waiting to be spread and dispersed, every seed armed with an appliance of dispersal, twisting darts and parachutes for the wind, little spears and balls of tiny thorns, and all waiting for animals and for the wind, for a man's trouser cuff or the hem of a woman's skirt, all passive but armed with appliances of activity, still, but each possessed of the anlage of movement.

The sun lay on the grass and warmed it, and in the shade under the grass the insects moved, ants and ant lions to set traps for them, grasshoppers to jump into the air and flick their yellow wings for a second, sow bugs like little armadillos, plodding restlessly on many tender feet. And over the grass at the roadside a land turtle crawled, turning aside for nothing, dragging his high domed shell over the grass. His hard legs and yellow-nailed feet threshed slowly through the grass, not really walking, but boosting and dragging his shell along. The barley beards slid off his shell, and the clover burrs fell on him and rolled to the ground. His horny beak was partly open, and his fierce, humorous eyes, under brows like fingernails, stared straight ahead. He came over the grass leaving a beaten trail behind him, and the hill, which was the highway embankment, reared up ahead of him. For a moment he stopped, his head held high. He blinked and looked up and down. At last he started to climb the embankment. Front clawed feet reached forward but did not touch. The hind feet kicked his shell along, and it scraped on the grass, and on the gravel. As the embankment grew steeper and steeper, the more frantic were the efforts of the land turtle. Pushing hind legs strained and slipped, boosting the shell along, and the horny head protruded as far as the neck could stretch. Little by little the shell slid up the embankment until at last a parapet cut straight across its line of march, the shoulder of the road, a concrete wall four inches high. As though they worked independently the hind legs pushed the shell against the wall. The head upraised and peered over the wall to the broad smooth plain of cement. Now the hands, braced on top of the wall, strained and lifted, and the shell came slowly up and rested its front end on the wall. For a moment the turtle rested. A red ant ran into the shell, into the soft skin inside the shell, and suddenly head and legs snapped in, and the armored tail clamped in sideways. The red ant was crushed between body and legs. And one head of wild oats was clamped into the shell by a front leg. For a long moment the turtle lay still, and then the neck crept out and the old humorous frowning eyes looked about and the legs and tail came out. The back legs went to work, straining like elephant legs, and the shell tipped to an angle so that the front legs could not reach the level cement plain. But higher and higher the hind legs boosted it, until at last the center of balance was reached, the front tipped down, the front legs scratched at the

pavement, and it was up. But the head of wild oats was held by its stem around
the front legs.

Now the going was easy, and all the legs worked, and the shell boosted
along, waggling from side to side. A sedan driven by a forty-year-old woman
approached. She saw the turtle and swung to the right, off the highway, the
wheels screamed and a cloud of dust boiled up. Two wheels lifted for a moment
and then settled. The car skidded back onto the road, and went on, but more
slowly. The turtle had jerked into its shell, but now it hurried on, for the highway was burning hot.

And now a light truck approached, and as it came near, the driver saw the
turtle and swerved to hit it. His front wheel struck the edge of the shell, flipped
the turtle like a tiddly-wink, spun it like a coin, and rolled it off the highway. The
truck went back to its course along the right side. Lying on its back, the turtle
was tight in its shell for a long time. But at last its legs waved in the air, reaching for something to pull it over. Its front foot caught a piece of quartz and little
by little the shell pulled over and flopped upright. The wild oat head fell out and
three spearhead seeds stuck in the ground. And as the turtle crawled on down
the embankment, its shell dragged dirt over the seeds. The turtle entered a dust
road and jerked itself along, drawing a wavy shallow trench in the dust with its
shell. The old humorous eyes looked ahead, and the horny beak opened a little.
His yellow toe nails slipped a fraction in the dust.

Writing

Write an essay about an animal that interests or intrigues you. Try to account
for its special qualities in explaining why the animal attracts or engages you.

Compare the following poem by Robert Lowell with Hoagland's essay or the
Steinbeck passage about turtles.

Returning Turtle

Weeks hitting the road, one fasting in the bathtub,
raw hamburger mossing in the watery stoppage,
the room drenched with musk like kerosene—
no one shaved, and only the turtle washed.
He was so beautiful when we flipped him over:
greens, reds, yellows, fringe of the faded savage,
the last Sioux, old and worn, saying with weariness,
'Why doesn't the Great White Father put his red
children on wheels, and move us as he will?'
We drove to the Orland River, and watched the turtle
rush for water like rushing into marriage,
swimming in uncontaminated joy,
lovely the flies that fed that sleazy surface,
a turtle looking back at us, and blinking.

P at C. Hoy II
(b.1938)

P at C. Hoy II has taught English literature and expository writing at the U.S. Military Academy and Harvard University as well as Bergen County Community College. He is director of the expository writing program at New York University and a professor of English. He has published articles, reviews, and familiar essays on a wide range of subjects for periodicals such as *Sewanee Review, Virginia Quarterly Review, Agni,* and *Twentieth-Century Literature.*

His first book of familiar essays, *Instinct for Survival,* was published by the University of Georgia Press in 1992. In the piece that follows, taken from that collection, Hoy looks at the ways writing stabilizes his life, gives it coherence, wholeness, even permanence.

Immortality

As for writing, I want to express beauty too . . . showing all the
traces of the mind's passage through the world; & achieve in the
end, some kind of whole made of shivering fragments; to me this
seems the natural process; the flight of the mind.

VIRGINIA WOOLF

The lies of poets are lies in the service of truth.

JOHN OF SALISBURY

I sit in my office curtained behind the morning sun and tell myself that
nothing is ever finished. For the moment, that seems to be the story of
my life. And when I say those words to myself, say them over and over
as I try to arrange the countless messages and all the tasks large and small
that are laid out before me for the day's work, I wonder what that simple
story might mean if I just relax and let my mind wander over it, making
of the story what it will.

Nothing is ever finished. Nothing.

When Joan Didion reminds us that we tell ourselves stories in order
to live, she has in mind a saving act of desperation. For her, storytelling
arrests the "shifting phantasmagoria" of life, puts a stop to the movement.
Didion is on to something, of course, but I think she's a little shy of the
truth. We tell ourselves stories not so much to order the chaotic but to
reach an understanding, perhaps indirectly, of the lives we are living. Our
stories do freeze the frames of our experience, but those stories also carry
meaning as old as life itself. Embedded in each is a nugget of truth. The
truth varies, of course, according to the way we tell the stories. But without them, we are lost, alone, cut adrift. Stories provide context and continuity. Without them we begin to think there's nothing left to say, nothing left to write. With them we keep our lives at the center of our
imaginations—just where they belong.

My mother spent much of her life—about forty of her ninety years—
running a bus station in a small south Arkansas town. She went to the sta-

tion day in and day out during all those years, meeting the buses, serving the customers, entertaining friends and their children, providing a home away from home in the most unlikely place—"A place," she'd say, "where folks could sit down and take the load off their feet." She's been dead six years, and I still can't get her out of my head. Her life sits at the center of my imagination, a monument against the ravages of time. She's not at all a lifeless thing.

Today, her words about endurance come back again. "Honey," she'd say, "what can't be cured must be endured." The simplest of stories. A cliché, perhaps, out of any mouth but hers. She lost two husbands, one to cancer, the other to a wandering spirit, a son to war. She lived alone almost twenty-five years, finally gave up the bus station at eighty-five, in the aftermath of a tornado that left her hunkered under an old oak desk, rain pouring through the roof destroying her most prized possessions— the pictures and letters and cards from family and friends. But even in the nursing home, later, she managed somehow to gather about her the frag- ments, the bits and pieces from here and there that pleased her—a favorite chair from my brother, pictures, lots of pictures, on the tables, in the drawers, on the walls, cards from grandchildren, a telephone right by her head, and always a small box of stationery on the bedside table. She wrote as best she could against the palsied movement of her hand, telling her stories until almost the day she died, writing out the wisdom of her life. Even at the very end, her mind was razor sharp, memory serving her, steadying her spirit. She had a hold on things. The stories she had in her head did it for her, I suspect. Simple stories.

What can't be cured must be endured.

My father, I had thought in my younger days, couldn't be endured. He left us high and dry when I was five, and I had reason over time to resent him. There were embarrassing moments through my school days when he wouldn't come back for the big events, and there were other times when he would come bleary-eyed and a bit tipsy, glowing with false pride. I felt distanced from him then, out of touch, almost as if I didn't know him. But finally, his not being there made little difference. He hadn't been around for the daily rituals, hadn't had time for commitment. He had consumed his life living it, and nothing from the living spilled over for the rest of us.

Over the years, trying to face my own self, I have come to love and respect my father's wandering spirit. I know now how compelling the heart can be, and I imagine he had no choice but to follow his wherever it took him. But the loving spirit that led him on and gave him satisfaction also did him in. He lived a less cerebral life than I do, a life closer to the bone. He knew little, if anything, about restraint. I'm a luckier man. I sit and write and sustain myself with stories, chasing always my dad and the others I have loved. He had no knack for storytelling; never knew much about the mana of the mind. I have no idea what he thought, ever . . . and know only a little, even today, about what he did. I suspect though that memory served him ill, that he never knew the storyteller's peace, that he simply couldn't reconcile his heart to the daily grind, couldn't fit the pieces of his life together and settle his restlessness.

In the thick of middle age, I long to sit uninterrupted for lazy stretches of time or to lollygag outdoors, meandering away from people and organizations and schedules. I have to contend with a touch of my father's restlessness, but I'm more interested in solitude now than adventure. I yearn to do my wandering over a patch of ground that might bless me occasionally with surprise. I have a younger friend who has moved to the country with acres and acres of land, and she has begun to move over that bounded space, exploring its contours, observing its wildlife, learning the promise and the confinement afforded by fences and good neighbors. Today she called to tell me that she and her husband may have to give it up. The farm is one of twenty-five targeted sites for the dumping of toxic wastes. A lawyer by profession, she understands the processes that can claim her space; she knows about the laws of dominion. But the slightest prospect of personal, legal entanglements rustles her spirit, and her mind moves quickly to devise schemes of surrender that will keep her life free of legal brambles, even if it means giving up the land without a fight. She doesn't want to have to walk around the law when she roams over the fields.

Solitude is hard to come by these days, and I, like my friend, yearn for it. I need more time for the stories. Behind the urge to put all the pieces of my life together there seems to be a gathering instinct at work, something driving me back into memory and out into the world, something compelling me to bring the pieces together. It's as if I'm finally beginning to understand that going down far enough into my own soul is the same as going out into the world. I can do both simultaneously, and when I do, I begin to unearth nuggets of truth. Finding those surprises seems to be my primary business as I search for a clearer picture, hoping to find there in the images of my life the earth's treasure.

This searching may very well be a matriarchal thing. It's certainly not the kind of searching my dad did. Nor is it the kind of searching I did as a young Army officer. Eleven or so years after graduating from West Point, after my first stint with troops in Virginia and Korea after a year and a half of graduate school at the University of Pennsylvania, after three years of teaching writing and literature at West Point, after all that, I chose these representative words for the plaque the English department gave me as I left West Point to rejoin the Regular Army: "The ULTIMATE most holy form of theory is action. . . . It is not God who will save us—it is we who will save God, by battling, by creating, and by transmuting matter into spirit." I look at those words now and think of the naive and necessary heroism that lay behind my efforts. I had loved the brashness and the struggle to excel, knowing that I had to act, had to learn to stand on my own. But there came a time when action seemed less important than contemplation. When I discovered that the Army was claiming my heart and my mind and that I was losing my place beside my children, I had to face a hard and necessary fact: I would not be able to stay on that imaginary train that could take me one day to the Chief of Staff's office in Washington. I wasn't cut out for it.

What I was cut out for was teaching. During those early years in the Army, whether leading troops or working with cadets at West Point, I had been a teacher. My greatest satisfaction had not come from commanding but from developing young men who were learning to live together in a community, many for the first time. Everywhere I went, I was teaching, teaching how to prepare the Nike Hercules missile for firing, how to fire and maintain a howitzer, how to compute the firing data that would put artillery rounds on the target, how to assemble nuclear weapons, how to select and occupy field positions in a combat zone, how to keep men alive and effective in the middle of a rice paddy in Vietnam, how to coordinate and manage the activities of a battalion of artillery. Every one of those tasks required teamwork and cooperation and intensive training, and in each of those places where I worked, I was the trainer, the teacher. When the time came for graduate school and an assignment back to the West Point faculty, I chose to study literature rather than mathematics or thermodynamics, subjects the career counselor in Washington urged me to consider because they had more utility. My imagination led me to the stories. I was interested in literature as a way into life.

What I found at the University of Pennsylvania surprised me. I was not prepared for the literary historians on Penn's faculty, some of whom, even in the late sixties, were just getting to the New Critics. Only two of my teachers put the primary texts, the stories themselves, at the center of their classes. Both encouraged us to set the critics aside and read with lively imaginations. They encouraged us to reach out and connect, to imagine that there were new answers to life's old problems. They seemed to know that the stories we were reading stretched back in time and forward, and that if we read them with care and diligence, they might reveal a pearl of great value.

It was in Herbert Howarth's class that I first read *The Man Who Died,* that little novella D. H. Lawrence wrote at the end of his life on earth. Lawrence's consuming rage for understanding still fascinates me. He wanted to possess the knowledge of what it meant to be man and woman living together—in bed and in culture. Marriage was always out there in front of him, tormenting, leading, beckoning him toward understanding, and he never tired of the search that compelled him to fit the pieces together. In *The Man Who Died,* he tells us about the life of Christ following the resurrection, insisting that the resurrection story has no meaning unless Christ comes back flesh and blood, back into life a man, freed of his own consuming urge to save God by battling, by creating, by transmuting flesh into spirit. Lawrence insists on bringing Christ back resurrected, erect and upright, a living man.

The resurrection itself required a woman; it always does. Coming back from the dead is serious business, too serious, I suspect, to leave to the men . . . even in Lawrence's imagination. As the foundation for his story, Lawrence turned to the Egyptian myth of Isis and Osiris. There he found the image of a woman who could take the broken body of Christ and resurrect it; she could bring him back to life. Isis twice had her husband taken away, each time by a jealous brother, Seth. When Isis found Osiris's body the first time and returned it to Egypt, Seth cut it into fourteen pieces and scattered them throughout Egypt. Again Isis lovingly and dutifully went after Osiris, this time seeking to gather all the pieces and reassemble her husband's body. She found all of him except the genitals and therefore had to make an image of the phallus, fashioning it out of wax and spices. Having put the severed parts of Osiris's body together again, she resuscitated him long enough to conceive Horus who would revenge their suffering.

What interests me, and what interested Lawrence, about this story is not Osiris's heroic kingship but Isis's loving devotion, her configuring imagination, and her defiance in the face of established order. In the end, she had the gods granting her favors. Like Lawrence, I am intrigued by her persistence, by her relentless effort to search for and find, to collect and reassemble, the lost or scattered parts of her husband's body. Were I to be blessed by a goddess in my life, I would wish her to be Isis. In her search, I find the story of my life, the meaning at the very heart of things. I find there the key to my life as teacher and writer.

Writing has always been for me an act of collecting and reconfiguring, imagining and reconceiving, a reaching out into life and libraries to find meaning. I have, like searching Isis, been trying to find the pieces that would make life whole—a task that's never finished. The search itself carries over to my classroom, where day after day and year after year I try to set in motion searches like that of the mythic woman who's always hovering in the back of my mind. I want my students to be grasped by a single necessity that will set their minds in motion and engender the gathering instinct. I want them to know that the search has no value unless they aim to unearth the mythic nuggets, the stories and the ideas that give us bearing, connecting us with our past and leading us into the future.

Each year as a prelude to more formal, academic writing, I try to put students in an exploratory frame of mind, setting them free to follow what my friend Sam Pickering calls the "vagaries of their own willful curiosities." I send them back into memory, asking only that they retrieve a fragment from their past. What I want them to find, of course, is not some lifeless thing, but a story stolen out of time, a story that reverberates and plays on their imaginations. I want the students to be able to pluck that initial fragment out of memory so that they can set it beside other fragments and begin to make sense of things . . . if only temporarily.

It's not just a simple matter of telling a story. The stories constitute the foundation, but their inherent truths are not always self-evident. Only the writer can bring them together, arranging and shaping them to reveal the missing part, the *idea* itself. That idea must be configured, must be imagined. The stories generate it, but the writer, having gathered the stories together, must decide, finally, what they mean. Meaning, however elusive and changing, is the hidden nugget, that treasure the imagination seeks. Behind that never-ending search is the urge to understand, the human need to make things whole, to create something lasting.

About a year ago, when I was writing an essay about soldiering, I asked my students how young men and women at Harvard might be heroic, suggesting to them at the outset that my own notions about heroism had changed over time, that acts of physical grandeur now seem far less important to me than acts of mind. I wanted them to think a little bit about the never-ending struggle for self-definition. I was hoping too that I would be able to get them to think about how some of our heroic urges carry over into the latter stages of life, depriving us of solace. I wanted them to think about what a hero is supposed to do when the spaces on the map have been charted, when there is no longer a home to protect, a family to nurture, a beast to slay, a war to win. How do men and women

sustain themselves when the tasks have been completed or when there is
no cultural need for the old heroics? I gave the briefest sketch of what I
had in mind, and discovered very quickly that my own middle-aged disease didn't interest them.

My students had notions of heroism that differed markedly from
mine, differed even from those I had when I was their age. Many spoke of
their struggle to develop a voice that could meet the voice behind the
lectern in their classroom. They spoke of the enormous difficulty of facing day after day the respected voices of authority all over the university.
They talked too of the importance of thinking hard enough, struggling
actually, to utter a response, to say something finally that would make
them feel satisfied with themselves. One young woman, having listened
long enough to the men in the room, spoke of the difficulty at Harvard of
being smart and being pretty. She said that in the minds of the men, it was
impossible to be both. You couldn't be both and be a Harvard woman. To
try was to be heroic. A pall fell over the room as she adjusted herself in
the chair, tucked her legs up into the seat beneath her skirt, and faced
them.

Following close order on the heels of that discussion, Elizabeth began
a new essay. Intrigued by Ingres's *La Grande Odalisque,* she saw in the
painting a woman whose "fluid" body is "anatomically impossible: the
back and arm are far too long and her legs cross over each other in what
would be a highly uncomfortable position for anyone with solid bones."
She saw this woman as an "enigma," just as she saw something "fraudulent" about Rita Hayworth's *Gilda* who "was a whore and a virtuous
woman . . . two women inhabiting a beautiful shell whose two sides
were irreconcilable." Elizabeth thought of these two women in terms of an
ideal woman of her own, one she occasionally drew in the margins of her
notebook. She brought all these women together in her essay, placing
them alongside scenes from her life that accentuated her own struggle to
control her weight, to make her body thin by following a "regimen" that
alternated days of eating "enormous amounts" with days of fasting.

In junior high school, Elizabeth turned to "self-induced vomiting" to
maintain her own façade. In my class, she turned to Yeats to clarify her
idea about beauty:

> There is a line in Yeats' "Adam's Curse" that cries bitterness—
>> To be born woman is to know—
>> Although they do not talk of it at school—
>> That we must labour to be beautiful

> I have only just discovered that I have been misquoting these lines
> for years. In my mind the last line, though essentially the same, has
> always had a slightly different nuance. . . . . We must suffer to be beau-
> tiful.

Therein lies the story of Elizabeth's heroism: We must suffer to be beautiful. Turning to Yeats, she turns away from the autobiographical details of
her life to the idea itself. Her story gives us insight, reminds us about the
perils of beauty, and asks us indirectly to think about how we create those
perils. The essay itself is deeply rooted in the particularity of Elizabeth's
own experiences—her stories as well as her treasures from the art
museum—but she tells her tale in such a way that it links us all together.
Leaving her essay, we know that Elizabeth will have to endure forever in
a culture where beauty inflicts intense pain. The rest of us, because of her
tale, will probably never see beauty again in the same light.

Virginia Woolf once reminded us that emotion is also form. She had
in mind something other than the architectonic scaffolding Percy Lubbock
thought of as structure. Woolf saw through that surface order to something much deeper, something emotional, something deeply felt, that sets
in motion the play of our mind on paper. That movement of mind, that
grounded search, leads to the mythic nuggets—the larger, more comprehensive treasure we fashion out of the waxy substance of our imaginations, those ideas that give meaning to our struggles.

At the very beginning of *The Unbearable Lightness of Being,* Milan Kundera expresses concern that each generation seems destined to relive the
same old stories. He wonders quite simply what the myth of the eternal
return might "signify." According to Kundera's reckoning, "We must live
our lives without knowing in advance the answer to life's most troubling
questions. And what can life be worth," he asks, "if the first rehearsal for
life is life itself?" Yet in the end, Kundera seems to take comfort in the
happiness his characters find against the sad fact of recurrence. The lives
that Thomas, Sabina, and Tereza live are no more perfect than the lives
any of us live, and yet, in Kundera's mind, there is happiness.

"The sadness was the form," he says, "the happiness content."

Kundera, like Didion, I think, is a little shy of the truth. We do
indeed tell ourselves stories in order to live; the stories themselves order
our lives and record our occasional happiness. So be it. But we also tell
ourselves stories to satisfy a restless and insatiable urge to understand why
we are living. Stories give us bearing, stabilize us . . . momentarily. They

also record our legacy; they are the human trace we spread across the world, recording our movement from generation to generation. If we lay those generational stories side by side, we find the history of our progress and our failure.

Kundera's modern mind, looking at the story of the eternal return asks, in a thoroughly modern way, what the myth can *signify* . . . as if he's afraid of the old-fashioned word meaning, as if he can't risk an intellectual foray into *meaning* itself. Yet there's something old-fashioned and traditional in his question, no matter how he chooses to frame it. Kundera is not, after all, "nothing but a devouring flame of thought" like Matthew Arnold's Empedocles, who was compelled in the face of the modern dilemma to *take* his life as a retreat from "despondency and gloom." For Kundera, there is at least the content that is happiness.

But there is more. There is possibility and promise in those stories we tell ourselves. If the stories never change, if we are destined to repeat them over and over, generation after generation, it is because we fail to read them as if our very lives depend on them. If we see in them a pattern that compels us to live as our forebears have always lived, they bequeath a burden that is unbearably heavy. But if, occasionally, we can look beneath the surface into the form that is emotion, we might just catch a glimpse of the very impulses that set our lives in motion. We may discover that there are indeed new possibilities, new ways to live out the impulses. We may find that the old heroics no longer seem worthy of our imaginations . . . or our lives.

As I continue to gather the fragments of my own life, I like to think that the stories I tell myself have something to do with other lives, that my story could be everyone's. I know of course that the larger story I'm trying to tell will not be finished. Nothing ever is. As I give in to my own needs, wandering and looking for solitude so that I can find time to let my gathering instinct reveal new secrets to me, as I sit and wait and try to open myself to the wisdom of the stories themselves, I am sustained by a rhythm of involvement that binds me to those I love and chase in my imagination, whether they be the living or the dead. And like my mom, I continue to write. The smaller stories steady me against the ravages of time; they teach me about endurance and quell my wandering spirit, reminding me to sit still, telling me that this is the only life I'll ever live. From them, on the best of occasions, I relax into life's complexities, and I garner, if only for a moment, the storyteller's peace, the revelation that even the fragments of my own life can shiver into wholeness.

CONSIDERATIONS

Thinking

Explain why Hoy refers to Joan Didion near the beginning and end of his essay. How does he make use of her ideas?

Why does Hoy think the kind of searching he does is a "matriarchal thing"?

What do you suppose Virginia Woolf means when she claims that emotion is also form?

Connecting

Where in the essay do you find hints of the epigraph—Woolf's quotation about "some kind of whole made of shivering fragments"?

What is the relationship between the story about Osiris and Hoy's notions about writing?

Read Elizabeth MacDonald's essay "Odalisque." Explain how Hoy makes use of that essay in "Immortality." Why does he include it?

Writing

Tell a story (write it out) that has something to do with immortality. Then question that story to see what it tells you about your ideas concerning death.

Write an essay of your own about immortality that makes use of your story and other stories from your experience that seem to be related to the idea you want to develop.

L angston Hughes
(1902–1967)

L angston Hughes was born in Joplin, Missouri. As a young man, he worked as a merchant seaman and traveled widely, living for a time in Paris and Rome. He published his first volume of poems, *The Weary Blues* (1926), three years before he graduated from Lincoln University, where he had won a scholarship. A major figure of the Harlem Renaissance, Hughes wrote prolifically, producing fiction and folklore, drama, song lyrics, essays, memoirs, and children's books as well as many poems.

His nonfiction prose is best represented by his autobiographical writing, from which the following essay, "Salvation," is drawn. In it, Hughes displays a talent for re-creating and dramatizing experience, giving it a quality of life, as if encountered directly and lived intensely.

Salvation

I was saved from sin when I was going on thirteen. But not really saved. It happened like this. There was a big revival at my Auntie Reed's church. Every night for weeks there had been much preaching, singing, praying, and shouting, and some very hardened sinners had been brought to Christ, and the membership of the church had grown by leaps and bounds. Then just before the revival ended, they held a special meeting for children, "to bring the young lambs to the fold." My aunt spoke of it for days ahead. That night I was escorted to the front row and placed on the mourners' bench with all the other young sinners, who had not yet been brought to Jesus.

My aunt told me that when you were saved you saw a light, and something happened to you inside! And Jesus came into your life! And God was with you from then on! She said you could see and hear and feel Jesus in your soul. I believed her. I had heard a great many old people say the same thing and it seemed to me they ought to know. So I sat there calmly in the hot, crowded church, waiting for Jesus to come to me.

The preacher preached a wonderful rhythmical sermon, all moans and shouts and lonely cries and dire pictures of hell, and then he sang a song about the ninety and nine safe in the fold, but one little lamb was left out in the cold. Then he said: "Won't you come? Won't you come to Jesus? Young lambs, won't you come?" And he held out his arms to all us young sinners there on the mourners' bench. And the little girls cried. And some of them jumped up and went to Jesus right away. But most of us just sat there.

A great many old people came and knelt around us and prayed, old women with jet-black faces and braided hair, old men with work-gnarled hands. And the church sang a song about the lower lights are burning, some poor sinners to be saved. And the whole building rocked with prayer and song.

Still I kept waiting to see Jesus.

Finally all the young people had gone to the altar and were saved, but one boy and me. He was a rounder's son named Westley. Westley and I were surrounded by sisters and deacons praying. It was very hot in the church, and getting late now. Finally Westley said to me in a whisper:

"God damn! I'm tired o' sitting here. Let's get up and be saved." So he got up and was saved.

Then I was left all alone on the mourners' bench. My aunt came and knelt at my knees and cried, while prayers and song swirled all around me in the little church. The whole congregation prayed for me alone, in a mighty wail of moans and voices. And I kept waiting serenely for Jesus, waiting, waiting—but he didn't come. I wanted to see him, but nothing happened to me. Nothing! I wanted something to happen to me, but nothing happened.

I heard the songs and the minister saying: "Why don't you come? My dear child, why don't you come to Jesus? Jesus is waiting for you. He wants you. Why don't you come? Sister Reed, what is this child's name?"

"Langston," my aunt sobbed.

"Langston, why don't you come? Why don't you come and be saved? Oh, Lamb of God! Why don't you come?"

Now it was really getting late. I began to be ashamed of myself, holding everything up so long. I began to wonder what God thought about Westley, who certainly hadn't seen Jesus either, but who was now sitting proudly on the platform, swinging his knickerbockered legs and grinning down at me, surrounded by deacons and old women on their knees praying. God had not struck Westley dead for taking his name in vain or for lying in the temple. So I decided that maybe to save further trouble, I'd better lie, too, and say that Jesus had come, and get up and be saved.

So I got up.

Suddenly the whole room broke into a sea of shouting, as they saw me rise. Waves of rejoicing swept the place. Women leaped in the air. My aunt threw her arms around me. The minister took me by the hand and led me to the platform.

When things quieted down, in a hushed silence, punctuated by a few ecstatic "Amens," all the new young lambs were blessed in the name of God. Then joyous singing filled the room.

That night, for the first time in my life but one—for I was a big boy twelve years old—I cried. I cried, in bed alone, and couldn't stop. I buried my head under the quilts, but my aunt heard me. She woke up and told my uncle I was crying because the Holy Ghost had come into my life, and because I had seen Jesus. But I was really crying because I couldn't bear to tell her that I had lied, that I had deceived everybody in the church, that I hadn't seen Jesus, and that now I didn't believe there was a Jesus anymore, since he didn't come to help me.

CONSIDERATIONS

Thinking

To what extent is Hughes's essay about faith? About the loss of belief? About communal pressure to conform—to see and think as others do?

Why does Hughes begin with what seems like a contradiction: "I was saved from sin when I was going on thirteen. But not really saved"? Why do you think he uses two sentences instead of one for these words?

Connecting

Compare the way Hughes brings his scenes to life with the way Alice Walker does in "Beauty: When the Other Dancer Is the Self."

Consider your own experience in connection with Hughes's. To what extent have you accepted, rejected, or qualified the religious faith(s) you have been exposed to?

Writing

Write an essay in which you explore a turning point in your attitude toward religion and faith.

Compare the pressures toward conforming described in "Salvation" with those Didion describes in "Georgia O'Keeffe."

Zora Neale Hurston (1902–1960)

Zora Neale Hurston was born in Eatonville, Florida, where she spent her early years. She attended Howard University and in 1925, went to New York City, becoming involved in cultural activities in Harlem. There she met Langston Hughes, who, like Hurston, was interested in the folk elements of African American culture, particularly as reflected in southern life.

Hurston wrote books based on her study of folkways, including *Mules and Men* (1935). She also wrote novels, the best known of which is *Their Eyes Were Watching God* (1937). These and other works, including her essays, were rediscovered and reappreciated as a result of the women's movement and in conjunction with an upsurge in the study of African American literature.

In "How It Feels to Be Colored Me," Hurston discusses her blackness as an aspect of race and of her cultural, social, and personal identity. The essay's tone is confident and upbeat as Hurston celebrates herself as a modern African American woman who knows her worth even when others do not.

How It Feels to Be Colored Me

I am colored but I offer nothing in the way of extenuating circumstances except the fact that I am the only Negro in the United States whose grandfather on the mother's side was *not* an Indian chief.

I remember the very day that I became colored. Up to my thirteenth year I lived in the little Negro town of Eatonville, Florida. It is exclusively a colored town. The only white people I knew passed through the town going to or coming from Orlando. The native whites rode dusty horses, the Northern tourists chugged down the sandy village road in automobiles. The town knew the Southerners and never stopped cane chewing when they passed. But the Northerners were something else again. They were peered at cautiously from behind curtains by the timid. The more venturesome would come out on the porch to watch them go past and got just as much pleasure out of the tourists as the tourists got out of the village.

The front porch might seem a daring place for the rest of the town, but it was a gallery seat for me. My favorite place was atop the gate-post. Proscenium box for a born first-nighter. Not only did I enjoy the show, but I didn't mind the actors knowing that I liked it. I usually spoke to them in passing. I'd wave at them and when they returned my salute, I would say something like this: "Howdy-do-well-I-thank-you-where-you-goin'?" Usually automobile or the horse paused at this, and after a queer exchange of compliments, I would probably "go a piece of the way" with them, as we say in farthest Florida. If one of my family happened to come to the front in time to see me, of course negotiations would be rudely broken off. But even so, it is clear that I was the first "welcome-to-our-state" Floridian, and I hope the Miami Chamber of Commerce will please take notice.

During this period, white people differed from colored to me only in that they rode through town and never lived there. They liked to hear me "speak pieces" and sing and wanted to see me dance the parse-me-la, and gave me generously of their small silver for doing these things, which seemed strange to me for I wanted to do them so much that I needed bribing to stop. Only they didn't know it. The colored people gave no dimes. They deplored any joyful tendencies in me, but I was their Zora

337

nevertheless. I belonged to them, to the nearby hotels, to the county—everybody's Zora.

But changes came in the family when I was thirteen, and I was sent to school in Jacksonville. I left Eatonville, the town of the oleanders, as Zora. When I disembarked from the river-boat at Jacksonville, she was no more. It seemed that I had suffered a sea change. I was not Zora of Orange County any more, I was now a little colored girl. I found it out in certain ways. In my heart as well as in the mirror, I became a fast brown—warranted not to rub nor run.

But I am not tragically colored. There is no great sorrow dammed up in my soul, nor lurking behind my eyes. I do not mind at all. I do not belong to the sobbing school of Negrohood who hold that nature somehow has given them a lowdown dirty deal and whose feelings are all hurt about it. Even in the helter-skelter skirmish that is my life, I have seen that the world is to the strong regardless of a little pigmentation more or less. No, I do not weep at the world—I am too busy sharpening my oyster knife.

Someone is always at my elbow reminding me that I am the granddaughter of slaves. It fails to register depression with me. Slavery is sixty years in the past. The operation was successful and the patient is doing well, thank you. The terrible struggle that made me an American out of a potential slave said "On the line!" The Reconstruction said "Get set!"; and the generation before said "Go!" I am off to a flying start and I must not halt in the stretch to look behind and weep. Slavery is the price I paid for civilization, and the choice was not with me. It is a bully adventure and worth all that I have paid through my ancestors for it. No one on earth ever had a greater chance for glory. The world to be won and nothing to be lost. It is thrilling to think—to know that for any act of mine, I shall get twice as much praise or twice as much blame. It is quite exciting to hold the center of the national stage, with the spectators not knowing whether to laugh or to weep.

The position of my white neighbor is much more difficult. No brown specter pulls up a chair beside me when I sit down to eat. No dark ghost thrusts its leg against mine in bed. The game of keeping what one has is never so exciting as the game of getting.

I do not always feel colored. Even now I often achieve the unconscious Zora of Eatonville before the Hegira. I feel most colored when I am thrown against a sharp white background.

For instance at Barnard. "Beside the waters of the Hudson" I feel my race. Among the thousand white persons, I am a dark rock surged upon, and overswept, but through it all, I remain myself. When covered by the waters, I am; and the ebb but reveals me again.

Sometimes it is the other way around. A white person is set down in our midst, but the contrast is just as sharp for me. For instance, when I sit in the drafty basement that is The New World Cabaret with a white person, my color comes. We enter chatting about any little nothing that we have in common and are seated by the jazz waiters. In the abrupt way that jazz orchestras have, this one plunges into a number. It loses no time in circumlocutions, but gets right down to business. It constricts the thorax and splits the heart with its tempo and narcotic harmonies. This orchestra grows rambunctious, rears on its hind legs and attacks the tonal veil with primitive fury, rending it, clawing it until it breaks through to the jungle beyond. I follow those heathen—follow them exultingly. I dance wildly inside myself; I yell within, I whoop; I shake my assegai above my head, I hurl it true to the mark *yeeeeooww!* I am in the jungle and living in the jungle way. My face is painted red and yellow and my body is painted blue. My pulse is throbbing like a war drum. I want to slaughter something—give pain, give death to what, I do not know. But the piece ends. The men of the orchestra wipe their lips and rest their fingers. I creep back slowly to the veneer we call civilization with the last tone and find the white friend sitting motionless in his seat, smoking calmly.

"Good music they have here," he remarks, drumming the table with his fingertips.

Music. The great blobs of purple and red emotion have not touched him. He has only heard what I felt. He is far away and I see him but dimly across the ocean and the continent that have fallen between us. He is so pale with his whiteness then and I am *so* colored.

At certain times I have no race, I am *me*. When I set my hat at a certain angle and saunter down Seventh Avenue, Harlem City, feeling as snooty as the lions in front of the Forty-Second Street Library, for instance. So far as my feelings are concerned, Peggy Hopkins Joyce on the Boule Mich with her gorgeous raiment, stately carriage, knees knocking together in a most aristocratic manner, has nothing on me. The cosmic Zora emerges. I belong to no race nor time. I am the eternal feminine with its string of beads.

I have no separate feeling about being an American citizen and colored. I am merely a fragment of the Great Soul that surges within the boundaries. My country, right or wrong.

Sometimes, I feel discriminated against, but it does not make me angry. It merely astonishes me. How *can* any deny themselves the pleasure of my company? It's beyond me.

But in the main, I feel like a brown bag of miscellany propped against a wall. Against a wall in company with other bags, white, red and yellow. Pour out the contents, and there is discovered a jumble of small things priceless and worthless. A first-water diamond, an empty spool, bits of broken glass, lengths of string, a key to a door long since crumbled away, a rusty knife-blade, old shoes saved for a road that never was and never will be, a nail bent under the weight of things too heavy for any nail, a dried flower or two still a little fragrant. In your hand is the brown bag. On the ground before you is the jumble it held—so much like the jumble in the bags, could they be emptied, that all might be dumped in a single heap and the bags refilled without altering the content of any greatly. A bit of colored glass more or less would not matter. Perhaps that is how the Great Stuffer of Bags filled them in the first place—who knows?

CONSIDERATIONS

Thinking

Hurston presents herself as happy with who she is, especially with her race. Do you think her experience and attitude are characteristic of most people? Why or why not?

What does Hurston see as the advantages for her of being "colored"?

Connecting

To what extent can Hurston's celebration of herself as a black woman be applied by any reader regardless of race, ethnicity, or gender? Why?

Consider Hurston's discussion of racial difference in connection with that of James Baldwin in "Stranger in the Village."

Writing

Write an essay in which you explore your identity in terms of gender, race, class, or ethnicity. Try to account for times when you feel this aspect of your identity most acutely and times when it seems invisible or unimportant.

Discuss Hurston's presentation of herself as a black woman in conjunction with June Jordan's images of black women in "Many Rivers to Cross."

J une Jordan
(b.1936)

J une Jordan was born in Harlem and raised in the Bedford-Stuyvesant section of Brooklyn. She has taught at City College of the City University of New York, Sarah Lawrence College, and Yale University, and she has held professorships at the State University of New York, Stony Brook, and at the University of California, Berkeley. In addition to three volumes of essays, she has published fourteen volumes of poetry, drama, and biography. Her work has appeared in such publications as *The New York Times, The Village Voice,* and *The New Republic.* Her awards include a Rockefeller Grant in creative writing, the American Library Association's award for the best book of the year, *The New York Times* award for outstanding book of the year, and the Prix de Rome in environmental design. She has also been a National Book Award finalist and a fellow of the National Education Association.

Jordan worries in many of her essays about the struggle for self-respect and self-love, seeing it as a struggle against despair. In "Many Rivers to Cross," she gives us a sense of how difficult it may have been for her and for other women to gain that self-respect.

Many Rivers to Cross

When my mother killed herself I was looking for a job. That was fifteen years ago. I had no money and no food. On the pleasure side I was down to my last pack of Pall Malls plus half a bottle of J & B. I needed to find work because I needed to be able fully to support myself and my eight-year-old son, very fast. My plan was to raise enough big bucks so that I could take an okay apartment inside an acceptable public school district, by September. That deadline left me less than three months to turn my fortunes right side up.

It seemed that I had everything to do at once. Somehow, I must move all of our things, mostly books and toys, out of the housing project before the rent fell due, again. I must do this without letting my neighbors know because destitution and divorce added up to personal shame, and failure. Those same neighbors had looked upon my husband and me as an ideal young couple, in many ways: inseparable, doting, ambitious. They had kept me busy and laughing in the hard weeks following my husband's departure for graduate school in Chicago; they had been the ones to remember him warmly through teasing remarks and questions all that long year that I remained alone, waiting for his return while I became the "temporary," sole breadwinner of our peculiar long-distance family by telephone. They had been the ones who kindly stopped the teasing and the queries when the year ended and my husband, the father of my child, did not come back. They never asked me and I never told them what that meant, altogether. I don't think I really knew.

I could see how my husband would proceed more or less naturally from graduate school to a professional occupation of his choice, just as he had shifted rather easily from me, his wife, to another man's wife— another woman. What I could not see was how I should go forward, now, in any natural, coherent way. As a mother without a husband, as a poet without a publisher, a freelance journalist without assignment, a city planner without a contract, it seemed to me that several incontestable and conflicting necessities had suddenly eliminated the whole realm of choice from my life.

My husband and I agreed that he would have the divorce that he wanted, and I would have the child. This ordinary settlement is, as millions of women will testify, as absurd as saying, "I'll give you a call, you handle everything else." At any rate, as my lawyer explained, the law then was the same as the law today; the courts would surely award me a reasonable amount of the father's income as child support, but the courts would also insist that they could not enforce their own decree. In other words, according to the law, what a father owes to his child is not serious compared to what a man owes to the bank for a car, or a vacation. Hence, as they say, it is extremely regrettable but nonetheless true that the courts cannot garnish a father's salary, nor freeze his account, nor seize his property on behalf of his children, in our society. Apparently this is because a child is not a car or a couch or a boat. (I would suppose this is the very best available definition of the difference between an American child and a car.)

Anyway, I wanted to get out of the projects as quickly as possible. But I was going to need help because I couldn't bend down and I couldn't carry anything heavy and I couldn't let my parents know about these problems because I didn't want to fight with them about the reasons behind the problems—which was the same reason I couldn't walk around or sit up straight to read or write without vomiting and acute abdominal pain. My parents would have evaluated that reason as a terrible secret compounded by a terrible crime; once again an unmarried woman, I had, nevertheless, become pregnant. What's more I had tried to interrupt this pregnancy even though this particular effort required not only one but a total of three abortions— each of them illegal and amazingly expensive, as well as, evidently, somewhat poorly executed.

My mother, against my father's furious rejections of me and what he viewed as my failure, offered what she could; she had no money herself but there was space in the old brownstone of my childhood. I would live with them during the summer while I pursued my crash schedule for cash, and she would spend as much time with Christopher, her only and beloved grandchild, as her worsening but partially undiagnosed illness allowed.

After she suffered a stroke, her serenely imposing figure had shrunk into an unevenly balanced, starved shell of chronic disorder. In the last two years, her physical condition had forced her retirement from nursing, and she spent most of her days on a makeshift cot pushed against the wall of the dining room next to the kitchen. She could do very few things for herself, besides snack on crackers, or pour ready-made juice into a cup and then drink it.

In June, 1966, I moved from the projects into my parents' house with the help of a woman named Mrs. Hazel Griffin. Since my teens, she had been my hairdresser. Every day, all day, she stood on her feet, washing and straightening hair in her crowded shop, the Arch of Beauty. Mrs. Griffin had never been married, had never finished high school, and she ran the Arch of Beauty with an imperturbable and contagious sense of success. She had a daughter as old as I who worked alongside her mother, coddling customer fantasy into confidence. Gradually, Mrs. Griffin and I became close; as my own mother became more and more bedridden and demoralized, Mrs. Griffin extended herself—dropping by my parents' house to make dinner for them, or calling me to wish me good luck on a special freelance venture, and so forth. It was Mrs. Griffin who closed her shop for a whole day and drove all the way from Brooklyn to my housing project apartment in Queens. It was Mrs. Griffin who packed me up, so to speak, and carried me and the boxes back to Brooklyn, back to the house of my parents. It was Mrs. Griffin who ignored my father standing hateful at the top of the stone steps of the house and not saying a word of thanks and not once relieving her of a single load she wrestled up the stairs and past him. My father hated Mrs. Griffin because he was proud and because she was a stranger of mercy. My father hated Mrs. Griffin because he was like that sometimes: hateful and crazy.

My father alternated between weeping bouts of self-pity and storm explosions of wrath against the gods apparently determined to ruin him. These were his alternating reactions to my mother's increasing enfeeblement, her stoic depression. I think he was scared; who would take care of him? Would she get well again and make everything all right again?

This is how we organized the brownstone: I fixed a room for my son on the top floor of the house. I slept on the parlor floor in the front room. My father slept on the same floor, in the back. My mother stayed downstairs.

About a week after moving in, my mother asked me about the progress of my plans. I told her things were not terrific but that there were two different planning jobs I hoped to secure within a few days. One of them involved a study of new towns in Sweden and the other one involved an analysis of the social consequences of a huge hydro-electric dam under construction in Ghana. My mother stared at me uncomprehendingly and then urged me to look for work in the local post office. We bitterly argued about what she dismissed as my "high-falutin" ideas and, I believe, that was the last substantial conversation between us.

From my first memory of him, my father had always worked at the post office. His favorite was the night shift, which brought him home usually between three and four o'clock in the morning.

It was hot. I finally fell asleep that night, a few nights after the argument between my mother and myself. She seemed to be rallying; that afternoon, she and my son had spent a long time in the backyard, oblivious to the heat and the mosquitoes. They were both tired but peaceful when they noisily re-entered the house, holding hands awkwardly.

But someone was knocking at the door to my room. Why should I wake up? It would be impossible to fall asleep again. It was so hot. The knocking continued. I switched on the light by the bed: 3:30 A.M. It must be my father. Furious, I pulled on a pair of shorts and a t-shirt. "What do you want? What's the matter?" I asked him, through the door. Had he gone berserk? What could he have to talk about at that ridiculous hour?

"OK, all right," I said, rubbing my eyes awake as I stepped to the door and opened it. "What?"

To my surprise, my father stood there looking very uncertain.

"It's your mother," he told me, in a burly, formal voice. "I think she's dead, but I'm not sure." He was avoiding my eyes.

"What do you mean," I answered.

"I want you to go downstairs and figure it out."

I could not believe what he was saying to me. "You want me to figure out if my mother is dead or alive?"

"I can't tell! I don't know!!" he shouted angrily.

"Jesus Christ," I muttered, angry and beside myself.

I turned and glanced about my room, wondering if I could find anything to carry with me on this mission; what do you use to determine a life or a death? I couldn't see anything obvious that might be useful.

"I'll wait up here," my father said. "You call up and let me know."

I could not believe it; a man married to a woman more than forty years and he can't tell if she's alive or dead and he wakes up his kid and tells her, "You figure it out."

I was at the bottom of the stairs. I halted just outside the dining room where my mother slept. Suppose she really was dead? Suppose my father was not just being crazy and hateful? "Naw." I shook my head and confidently entered the room.

"Momma?!" I called, aloud. At the edge of the cot, my mother was leaning forward, one arm braced to hoist her body up. She was trying to stand up! I rushed over. "Wait. Here, I'll help you!" I said.

And I reached out my hands to give her a lift. The body of my mother was stiff. She was not yet cold, but she was stiff. Maybe I had come downstairs just in time! I tried to loosen her arms, to change her position, to ease her into lying down.

"Momma!" I kept saying. "Momma, listen to me! It's OK! I'm here and everything. Just relax. Relax! Give me a hand, now. I'm trying to help you lie down!"

Her body did not relax. She did not answer me. But she was not cold. Her eyes were not shut.

From upstairs my father was yelling, "Is she dead? Is she dead?"

"No!" I screamed at him. "No! She's not dead!"

At this, my father tore down the stairs and into the room. Then he braked.

"Milly?" he called out, tentative. Then he shouted at me and banged around the walls. "You damn fool. Don't you see now she's gone. Now she's gone!" We began to argue.

"She's alive! Call the doctor!"

"No!"

"Yes!"

At last my father left the room to call the doctor.

I straightened up. I felt completely exhausted from trying to gain a response from my mother. There she was, stiff on the edge of her bed, just about to stand up. Her lips were set, determined. She would manage it, but by herself. I could not help. Her eyes fixed on some point below the floor.

"Momma!" I shook her hard as I could to rouse her into focus. Now she fell back on the cot, but frozen and in the wrong position. It hit me that she might be dead. She might be dead.

My father reappeared at the door. He would not come any closer. "Dr. Davis says he will come. And he call the police."

The police? Would they know if my mother was dead or alive? Who would know?

I went to the phone and called my aunt. "Come quick," I said. "My father thinks Momma has died but she's here but she's stiff."

Soon the house was weird and ugly and crowded and I thought I was losing my mind.

Three white policemen stood around telling me my mother was dead. "How do you know?" I asked, and they shrugged and then they repeated themselves. And the doctor never came. But my aunt came and my uncle and they said she was dead.

After a conference with the cops, my aunt disappeared and when she came back she held a bottle in one of her hands. She and the police whispered together some more. Then one of the cops said, "Don't worry about it. We won't say anything." My aunt signalled me to follow her into the hallway where she let me understand that, in fact, my mother had committed suicide.

I could not assimilate this information: suicide.

I broke away from my aunt and ran to the telephone. I called a friend of mine, a woman who talked back loud to me so that I could realize my growing hysteria, and check it. Then I called my cousin Valerie who lived in Harlem; she woke up instantly and urged me to come right away.

I hurried to the top floor and stood my sleeping son on his feet. I wanted to get him out of this house of death more than I ever wanted anything. He could not stand by himself so I carried him down the two flights to the street and laid him on the backseat and then took off.

At Valerie's, my son continued to sleep, so we put him to bed, closed the door, and talked. My cousin made me eat eggs, drink whiskey, and shower. She would take care of Christopher, she said. I should go back and deal with the situation in Brooklyn.

When I arrived, the house was absolutely full of women from the church dressed as though they were going to Sunday communion. It seemed to me they were, every one of them, wearing hats and gloves and drinking coffee and solemnly addressing invitations to a funeral and I could not find my mother anywhere and I could not find an empty spot in the house where I could sit down and smoke a cigarette.

My mother was dead.

Feeling completely out of place, I headed for the front door, ready to leave. My father grabbed my shoulder from behind and forcibly spun me around.

"You see this?" He smiled, waving a large document in the air. "This am insurance paper for you!" He waved it into my face. "Your mother, she left you insurance, see?"

I watched him.

"But I gwine burn it in the furnace before I give it you to t'row away on trash!"

"Is that money?" I demanded. "Did my mother leave me money?"

"Eh-heh!" he laughed. "And you don't get it from me. Not today, not tomorrow. Not until I dead and buried!"

My father grabbed for my arm and I swung away from him. He hit me on my head and I hit back. We were fighting.

Suddenly, the ladies from the church bustled about and pushed, horrified, between us. This was a sin, they said, for a father and a child to fight in the house of the dead and the mother not yet in the ground! Such a good woman she was, they said. She was a good woman, a good woman, they all agreed. Out of respect for the memory of this good woman, in deference to my mother who had committed suicide, the ladies shook their hats and insisted we should not fight; I should not fight with my father.

Utterly disgusted and disoriented, I went back to Harlem. By the time I reached my cousin's place I had begun to bleed, heavily. Valerie said I was hemorrhaging so she called up her boyfriend and the two of them hobbled me into Harlem Hospital.

I don't know how long I remained unconscious, but when I opened my eyes I found myself on the women's ward, with an intravenous setup feeding into my arm. After a while, Valerie showed up. Christopher was fine, she told me; my friends were taking turns with him. Whatever I did, I should not admit I'd had an abortion or I'd get her into trouble, and myself in trouble. Just play dumb and rest. I'd have to stay on the ward for several days. My mother's funeral was tomorrow afternoon. What did I want her to tell people to explain why I wouldn't be there? She meant, what lie?

I thought about it and I decided I had nothing to say; if I couldn't tell the truth then the hell with it.

I lay in that bed at Harlem Hospital, thinking and sleeping. I wanted to get well.

I wanted to be strong. I never wanted to be weak again as long as I lived. I thought about my mother and her suicide and I thought about how my father could not tell whether she was dead or alive.

I wanted to get well and what I wanted to do as soon as I was strong again, actually, what I wanted to do was I wanted to live my life so that people would know unmistakably that I am alive, so that when I finally die people will know the difference for sure between my living and my death.

And I thought about the idea of my mother as a good woman and I rejected that, because I don't see why it's a good thing when you give up, or when you cooperate with those who hate you or when you polish and iron and mend and endlessly mollify for the sake of the people who love the way that you kill yourself day by day silently.

And I think all of this is really about women and work. Certainly this is all about me as a woman and my life work. I mean I am not sure my mother's suicide was something extraordinary. Perhaps most women must deal with a similar inheritance, the legacy of a woman whose death you cannot possibly pinpoint because she died so many, many times and because, even before she became your mother, the life of that woman was taken; I say it was taken away.

And really it was to honor my mother that I did fight with my father, that man who could not tell the living from the dead.

And really it is to honor Mrs. Hazel Griffin and my cousin Valerie and all the women I love, including myself, that I am working for the courage to admit the truth that Bertolt Brecht has written; he says, "It takes courage to say that the good were defeated not because they were good, but because they were weak."

I cherish the mercy and the grace of women's work. But I know there is new work that we must undertake as well: that new work will make defeat detestable to us. That new women's work will mean we will not die trying to stand up: we will live that way: standing up.

I came too late to help my mother to her feet.

By way of everlasting thanks to all of the women who have helped me to stay alive I am working never to be late again.

CONSIDERATIONS

Thinking

In what ways might "Many Rivers to Cross" be considered an essay about betrayal?

Why does Jordan want to honor her cousin Valerie and Mrs. Hazel Griffin?

What are the implications of that one-sentence paragraph near the end of the essay, "I came too late to help my mother to her feet"?

Connecting

After reading this essay, what would you guess is Jordan's attitude about men? As a writer, how does she use the two men in her essay?

How does Jordan use the image of her mother trying to get up from her cot? What does that image have to do with Jordan's central idea?

Writing

Write a short essay about the importance of feminism at your college or in your local community.

Select a powerful image from your own experience and reconstruct it. Set it aside for a few days; then go back to see what you find there in the recorded image. When you go back to the image, write a few paragraphs about what the image means to you.

Jamaica Kincaid
(b.1949)

Jamaica Kincaid was born in Antigua and immigrated to the United States, where she has been a contributor and staff writer for *The New Yorker*, served on the Harvard faculty, and won distinction for her three books: *Annie John, A Small Place,* and *Lucy.* Her collection of stories *At the Bottom of the River* won the Morton Dauwen Zabel Award from the American Academy and Institute of Arts and Letters. Her work has appeared in *The New Yorker, Rolling Stone,* and *Paris Review.*

In "On Seeing England for the First Time," Kincaid reveals the difference between the England she inherited and the England she found in reality, as she invites us to think about the "space between the idea of something and its reality"—that space that is always "wide and deep and dark."

On Seeing England
for the First Time

When I saw England for the first time, I was a child in school sitting at a desk. The England I was looking at was laid out on a map gently, beautifully, delicately, a very special jewel; it lay on a bed of sky blue—the background of the map—its yellow form mysterious, because though it looked like a leg of mutton, it could not really look like anything so familiar as a leg of mutton because it was England—with shadings of pink and green, unlike any shadings of pink and green I had seen before, squiggly veins of red running in every direction. England was a special jewel all right, and only special people got to wear it. The people who got to wear England were English people. They wore it well and they wore it everywhere: in jungles, in deserts, on plains, on top of the highest mountains, on all the oceans, on all the seas, in places where they were not welcome, in places they should not have been. When my teacher had pinned this map up on the blackboard, she said, "This is England"—and she said it with authority, seriousness, and adoration, and we all sat up. It was as if she had said, "This is Jerusalem, the place you will go to when you die but only if you have been good." We understood then—we were meant to understand then—that England was to be our source of myth and the source from which we got our sense of reality, our sense of what was meaningful, our sense of what was meaningless—and much about our own lives and much about the very idea of us headed that last list.

At the time I was a child sitting at my desk seeing England for the first time, I was already very familiar with the greatness of it. Each morning before I left for school, I ate a breakfast of half a grapefruit, an egg, bread and butter and a slice of cheese, and a cup of cocoa; or half a grapefruit, a bowl of oat porridge, bread and butter and a slice of cheese, and a cup of cocoa. The can of cocoa was often left on the table in front of me. It had written on it the name of the company, the year the company was established, and the words "Made in England." Those words, "Made in England," were written on the box the oats came in too. They would also have been written on the box the shoes I was wearing came in; a bolt of gray linen cloth lying on the shelf of a store from which my mother had

351

bought three yards to make the uniform that I was wearing had written along its edge those three words. The shoes I wore were made in England; so were my socks and cotton undergarments and the satin ribbons I wore tied at the end of two plaits of my hair. My father, who might have sat next to me at breakfast, was a carpenter and cabinet maker. The shoes he wore to work would have been made in England, as were his khaki shirt and trousers, his underpants and undershirt, his socks and brown felt hat. Felt was not the proper material from which a hat that was expected to provide shade from the hot sun should be made, but my father must have seen and admired a picture of an Englishman wearing such a hat in England, and this picture that he saw must have been so compelling that it caused him to wear the wrong hat for a hot climate most of his long life. And this hat—a brown felt hat—became so central to his character that it was the first thing he put on in the morning as he stepped out of bed and the last thing he took off before he stepped back into bed at night. As we sat at breakfast a car might go by. The car, a Hillman or a Zephyr, was made in England. The very idea of the meal itself, breakfast, and its substantial quality and quantity was an idea from England; we somehow knew that in England they began the day with this meal called breakfast and a proper breakfast was a big breakfast. No one I knew liked eating so much food so early in the day; it made us feel sleepy, tired. But this breakfast business was Made in England like almost everything else that surrounded us, the exceptions being the sea, the sky, and the air we breathed.

At the time I saw this map—seeing England for the first time—I did not say to myself, "Ah, so that's what it looks like," because there was no longing in me to put a shape to those three words that ran through every part of my life, no matter how small; for me to have had such a longing would have meant that I lived in a certain atmosphere, an atmosphere in which those three words were felt as a burden. But I did not live in such an atmosphere. My father's brown felt hat would develop a hole in its crown, the lining would separate from the hat itself, and six weeks before he thought that he could not be seen wearing it—he was a very vain man—he would order another hat from England. And my mother taught me to eat my food in the English way: the knife in the right hand, the fork in the left, my elbows held still close to my side, the food carefully balanced on my fork and then brought up to my mouth. When I had finally mastered it, I overheard her saying to a friend, "Did you see how nicely she can eat?" But I knew then that I enjoyed my food more when I ate it with my bare hands, and I continued to do so when she wasn't looking.

And when my teacher showed us the map, she asked us to study it carefully, because no test we would ever take would be complete without this statement: "Draw a map of England."

I did not know then that the statement "Draw a map of England" was something far worse than a declaration of war, for in fact a flat-out declaration of war would have put me on alert, and again in fact, there was no need for war—I had long ago been conquered. I did not know then that this statement was part of a process that would result in my erasure, not my physical erasure, but my erasure all the same. I did not know then that this statement was meant to make me feel in awe and small whenever I heard the word "England": awe at its existence, small because I was not from it. I did not know very much of anything then— certainly not what a blessing it was that I was unable to draw a map of England correctly.

After that there were many times of seeing England for the first time. I saw England in history. I knew the names of all the kings of England. I knew the names of their children, their wives, their disappointments, their triumphs, the names of people who betrayed them; I knew the dates on which they were born and the dates they died. I knew their conquests and was made to feel glad if I figured in them; I knew their defeats. I knew the details of the year 1066 (the Battle of Hastings, the end of the reign of the Anglo-Saxon kings) before I knew the details of the year 1832 (the year slavery was abolished). It wasn't as bad as I make it sound now; it was worse. I did like so much hearing again and again how Alfred the Great, traveling in disguise, had been left to watch cakes, and because he wasn't used to this the cakes got burned, and Alfred burned his hands pulling them out of the fire, and the woman who had left him to watch the cakes screamed at him. I loved King Alfred. My grandfather was named after him; his son, my uncle, was named after King Alfred; my brother is named after King Alfred. And so there are three people in my family named after a man they have never met, a man who died over ten centuries ago. The first view I got of England then was not unlike the first view received by the person who named my grandfather.

This view, though—the naming of the kings, their deeds, their disappointments—was the vivid view, the forceful view. There were other views, subtler ones, softer, almost not there—but these were the ones that made the most lasting impression on me, these were the ones that made me really feel like nothing. "When morning touched the sky" was one phrase, for no morning touched the sky where I lived. The mornings where I lived came on abruptly, with a shock of heat and loud noises.

"Evening approaches" was another, but the evenings where I lived did not approach; in fact, I had no evening—I had night and I had day and they came and went in a mechanical way: on, off; on, off. And then there were gentle mountains and low blue skies and moors over which people took walks for nothing but pleasure, when where I lived a walk was an act of labor, a burden, something only death or the automobile could relieve. And there were things that a small turn of a head could convey—entire worlds, whole lives would depend on this thing, a certain turn of a head. Everyday life could be quite tiring, more tiring than anything I was told not to do. I was told not to gossip, but they did that all the time. And they ate so much food, violating another of those rules they taught me: do not indulge in gluttony. And the foods they ate actually: if only sometime I could eat cold cuts after theater, cold cuts of lamb and mint sauce, and Yorkshire pudding and scones, and clotted cream, and sausages that came from up-country (imagine, "up-country"). And having troubling thoughts at twilight, a good time to have troubling thoughts, apparently; and servants who stole and left in the middle of a crisis, who were born with a limp or some other kind of deformity, not nourished properly in their mother's womb (that last part I figured out for myself; the point was, oh to have an untrustworthy servant); and wonderful cobbled streets onto which solid front doors opened; and people whose eyes were blue and who had fair skins and who smelled only of lavender, or sometimes sweet pea or primrose. And those flowers with those names: delphiniums, fox-gloves, tulips, daffodils, floribunda, peonies; in bloom, a striking display, being cut and placed in large glass bowls, crystal, decorating rooms so large twenty families the size of mine could fit in comfortably but used only for passing through. And the weather was so remarkable because the rain fell gently always, only occasionally in deep gusts, and it colored the air various shades of gray, each an appealing shade for a dress to be worn when a portrait was being painted; and when it rained at twilight, wonderful things happened: people bumped into each other unexpectedly and that would lead to all sorts of turns of events—a plot, the mere weather caused plots. I saw that people rushed: they rushed to catch trains, they rushed toward each other and away from each other; they rushed and rushed and rushed. That word: rushed! I did not know what it was to do that. It was too hot to do that, and so I came to envy people who would rush, even though it had no meaning to me to do such a thing. But there they are again. They loved their children; their children were sent to their own rooms as a punishment, rooms larger than my entire house. They were special, everything about them said so, even their clothes; their clothes rustled, swished, soothed. The world was theirs, not mine; everything told me so.

If now as I speak of all this I give the impression of someone on the outside looking in, nose pressed up against a glass window, that is wrong. My nose was pressed up against a glass window all right, but there was an iron vise at the back of my neck forcing my head to stay in place. To avert my gaze was to fall back into something from which I had been rescued, a hole filled with nothing, and that was the word for everything about me, nothing. The reality of my life was conquests, subjugation, humiliation, enforced amnesia. I was forced to forget. Just for instance, this: I lived in a part of St. John's, Antigua, called Ovals. Ovals was made up of five streets, each of them named after a famous English seaman—to be quite frank, an officially sanctioned criminal: Rodney Street (after George Rodney), Nelson Street (after Horatio Nelson), Drake Street (after Francis Drake), Hood Street, and Hawkins Street (after John Hawkins). But John Hawkins was knighted after a trip he made to Africa, opening up a new trade, the slave trade. He was then entitled to wear as his crest a Negro bound with a cord. Every single person living on Hawkins Street was descended from a slave. John Hawkins's ship, the one in which he transported the people he had bought and kidnapped, was called *The Jesus*. He later became the treasurer of the Royal Navy and rear admiral.

Again, the reality of my life, the life I led at the time I was being shown these views of England for the first time, for the second time, for the one-hundred-millionth time, was this: the sun shone with what sometimes seemed to be a deliberate cruelty; we must have done something to deserve that. My dresses did not rustle in the evening air as I strolled to the theater (I had no evening, I had no theater; my dresses were made of a cheap cotton, the weave of which would give way after not too many washings). I got up in the morning, I did my chores (fetched water from the public pipe for my mother, swept the yard), I washed myself, I went to a woman to have my hair combed freshly every day (because before we were allowed into our classroom our teachers would inspect us, and children who had not bathed that day, or had dirt under their fingernails, or whose hair had not been combed anew that day, might not be allowed to attend class). I ate that breakfast. I walked to school. At school we gathered in an auditorium and sang a hymn, "All Things Bright and Beautiful," and looking down on us as we sang were portraits of the Queen of England and her husband; they wore jewels and medals and they smiled. I was a Brownie. At each meeting we would form a little group around a flagpole, and after raising the Union Jack, we would say, "I promise to do my best, to do my duty to God and the Queen, to help other people every day and obey the scouts' law."

Who were these people and why had I never seen them, I mean really seen them, in the place where they lived? I had never been to England. No one I knew had ever been to England, or I should say, no one I knew had ever been and returned to tell me about it. All the people I knew who had gone to England had stayed there. Sometimes they left behind them their small children, never to see them again. England! I had seen England's representatives. I had seen the governor general at the public grounds at a ceremony celebrating the Queen's birthday. I had seen an old princess and I had seen a young princess. They had both been extremely not beautiful, but who of us would have told them that? I had never seen England, really seen it, I had only met a representative, seen a picture, read books, memorized its history. I had never set foot, my own foot, in it.

The space between the idea of something and its reality is always wide and deep and dark. The longer they are kept apart—idea of thing, reality of thing—the wider the width, the deeper the depth, the thicker and darker the darkness. This space starts out empty, there is nothing in it, but it rapidly becomes filled up with obsession or desire or hatred or love— sometimes all of these things, sometimes some of these things, sometimes only one of these things. The existence of the world as I came to know it was a result of this: idea of thing over here, reality of thing way, way over there. There was Christopher Columbus, an unlikable man, an unpleasant man, a liar (and so, of course, a thief) surrounded by maps and schemes and plans, and there was the reality on the other side of that width, that depth, that darkness. He became obsessed, he became filled with desire, the hatred came later, love was never a part of it. Eventually, his idea met the longed-for reality. That the idea of something and its reality are often two completely different things is something no one ever remembers; and so when they meet and find that they are not compatible, the weaker of the two, idea or reality, dies. That idea Christopher Columbus had was more powerful than the reality he met, and so the reality he met died.

And so finally, when I was a grown-up woman, the mother of two children, the wife of someone, a person who resides in a powerful country that takes up more than its fair share of a continent, the owner of a house with many rooms in it and of two automobiles, with the desire and will (which I very much act upon) to take from the world more than I give back to it, more than I deserve, more than I need, finally then, I saw England, the real England, not a picture, not a painting, not through a story in a book, but England, for the first time. In me, the space between the idea of it and its reality had become filled with hatred, and so when at last I saw it I wanted to take it into my hands and tear it into little pieces and then crumble it up as if it were clay, child's clay. That was impossible, and so I could only indulge in not-favorable opinions.

There were monuments everywhere; they commemorated victories, battles fought between them and the people who lived across the sea from them, all vile people, fought over which of them would have dominion over the people who looked like me. The monuments were useless to them now, people sat on them and ate their lunch. They were like markers on an old useless trail, like a piece of old string tied to a finger to jog the memory, like old decoration in an old house, dirty, useless, in the way. Their skins were so pale, it made them look so fragile, so weak, so ugly. What if I had the power to simply banish them from their land, send boat after boatload of them on a voyage that in fact had no destination, force them to live in a place where the sun's presence was a constant? This would rid them of their pale complexion and make them look more like me, make them look more like the people I love and treasure and hold dear, and more like the people who occupy the near and far reaches of my imagination, my history, my geography, and reduce them and everything they have ever known to figurines as evidence that I was in divine favor, what if all this was in my power? Could I resist it? No one ever has.

And they were rude, they were rude to each other. They didn't like each other very much. They didn't like each other in the way they didn't like me, and it occurred to me that their dislike for me was one of the few things they agreed on.

I was on a train in England with a friend, an English woman. Before we were in England she liked me very much. In England she didn't like me at all. She didn't like the claim I said I had on England, she didn't like the views I had of England. I didn't like England, she didn't like England, but she didn't like me not liking it too. She said, "I want to show you my England, I want to show you the England that I know and love." I had told her many times before that I knew England and I didn't want to love it anyway. She no longer lived in England; it was her own country, but it had not been kind to her, so she left. On the train, the conductor was rude to her; she asked something, and he responded in a rude way. She became ashamed. She was ashamed at the way he treated her; she was ashamed at the way he behaved. "This is the new England," she said. But I liked the conductor being rude; his behavior seemed quite appropriate. Earlier this had happened: we had gone to a store to buy a shirt for my husband; it was meant to be a special present, a special shirt to wear on special occasions. This was a store where the Prince of Wales has his shirts made, but the shirts sold in this store are beautiful all the same. I found a shirt I thought my husband would like and I wanted to buy him a tie to go with it. When I couldn't decide which one to choose, the salesman showed me a new set. He was very pleased with these, he said, because they bore the crest of the Prince of Wales, and the Prince of Wales had never allowed his crest to decorate an article of clothing before. There was something in the way he said it; his tone was slavish, reverential, awed. It made me feel angry; I wanted to hit him. I didn't do that. I said, my husband and I hate princes, my husband would never wear anything that had a prince's anything on it. My friend stiffened. The salesman stiffened. They both drew themselves in, away from me. My friend told me that the prince was a symbol of her Englishness, and I could see that I had caused offense. I looked at her. She was an English person, the sort of English person I used to know at home, the sort who was nobody in England but somebody when they came to live among the people like me. There were many people I could have seen England with; that I was seeing it with this particular person, a person who reminded me of the people who showed me England long ago as I sat in church or at my desk, made me feel silent and afraid, for I wondered if, all these years of our friendship, I had had a friend or had been in the thrall of a racial memory.

I went to Bath—we, my friend and I, did this, but though we were together, I was no longer with her. The landscape was almost as familiar as my own hand, but I had never been in this place before, so how could that be again? And the streets of Bath were familiar, too, but I had never walked on them before. It was all those years of reading, starting with Roman Britain. Why did I have to know about Roman Britain? It was of no real use to me, a person living on a hot, drought-ridden island, and it is of no use to me now, and yet my head is filled with this nonsense, Roman Britain. In Bath, I drank tea in a room I had read about in a novel written in the eighteenth century. In this very same room, young women wearing those dresses that rustled and so on danced and flirted and sometimes disgraced themselves with young men, soldiers, sailors, who were on their way to Bristol or someplace like that, so many places like that where so many adventures, the outcome of which was not good for me, began. Bristol, England. A sentence that began "That night the ship sailed from Bristol, England" would end not so good for me. And then I was driving through the countryside in an English motorcar, on narrow winding roads, and they were so familiar, though I had never been on them before; and through little villages the names of which I somehow knew so well though I had never been there before. And the countryside did have all those hedges and hedges, fields hedged in. I was marveling at all the toil of it, the planting of the hedges to begin with and then the care of it, all that clipping, year after year of clipping, and I wondered at the lives of the people who would have to do this, because wherever I see and feel the hands that hold up the world, I see and feel myself and all the people who look like me. And I said, "Those hedges" and my friend said that someone, a woman named Mrs. Rothchild, worried that the hedges weren't being taken care of properly; the farmers couldn't afford or find the help to keep up the hedges, and often they replaced them with wire fencing. I might have said to that, well if Mrs. Rothchild doesn't like the wire fencing, why doesn't she take care of the hedges herself, but I didn't. And then in those fields that were now hemmed in by wire fencing that a privileged woman didn't like was planted a vile yellow flowering bush that produced an oil, and my friend said that Mrs. Rothchild didn't like this either; it ruined the English countryside, it ruined the traditional look of the English countryside.

It was not at that moment that I wished every sentence, everything I knew, that began with England would end with "and then it all died; we don't know how, it just all died." At that moment, I was thinking, who are these people who forced me to think of them all the time, who forced me to think that the world I knew was incomplete, or without substance, or did not measure up because it was not England; that I was incomplete, or without substance, and did not measure up because I was not English. Who were these people? The person sitting next to me couldn't give me a clue; no one person could. In any case, if I had said to her, I find England ugly, I hate England; the weather is like a jail sentence, the English are a very ugly people, the food in England is like a jail sentence, the hair of English people is so straight, so dead looking, the English have an unbearable smell so different from the smell of people I know, real people of course, she would have said that I was a person full of prejudice. Apart from the fact that it is I—that is, the people who look like me—who made her aware of the unpleasantness of such a thing, the idea of such a thing, prejudice, she would have been only partly right, sort of right: I may be capable of prejudice, but my prejudices have no weight to them, my prejudices have no force behind them, my prejudices remain opinions, my prejudices remain my personal opinion. And a great feeling of rage and disappointment came over me as I looked at England, my head full of personal opinions that could not have public, my public, approval. The people I come from are powerless to do evil on grand scale.

The moment I wished every sentence, everything I knew, that began with England would end with "and then it all died, we don't know how, it just all died" was when I saw the white cliffs of Dover. I had sung hymns and recited poems that were about a longing to see the white cliffs of Dover again. At the time I sang the hymns and recited the poems, I could really long to see them again because I had never seen them at all, nor had anyone around me at the time. But there we were, groups of people longing for something we had never seen. And so there they were, the white cliffs, but they were not that pearly majestic thing I used to sing about, that thing that created such a feeling in these people that when they died in the place where I lived they had themselves buried facing a direction that would allow them to see the white cliffs of Dover when they were resurrected, as surely they would be. The white cliffs of Dover, when finally I saw them, were cliffs, but they were not white; you would only call them that if the word "white" meant something special to you; they were dirty and they were steep; they were so steep, the correct height from which all my views of England, starting with the map before me in my classroom and ending with the trip I had just taken, should jump and die and disappear forever.

CONSIDERATIONS

Thinking

What does England mean for Kincaid? To what extent is her view of England a product of her early education? To what extent is it affected by the world of cultural difference she inhabits?

What does the phrase "made in England" come to mean in the essay? With what does Kincaid contrast things "made in England"? Toward what point and with what effect? Why does the command "Draw a map of England" resonate so powerfully in Kincaid's memory and imagination?

Connecting

Kincaid sets up a number of contrasts between England and her Caribbean island home. Identify two different types of these, and explain what Kincaid conveys by emphasizing such differences.

What ironies does Kincaid point up in her discussion of street names in St. John's, Antigua? How does her discussion of Christopher Columbus tie in with her discussion of England?

Writing

Write an essay in which you explore what Kincaid calls "the space between the idea of something and its reality." It may be a place, a situation, an anticipated experience, a person. Whatever you write about, consider the extent to which the weaker of the two, the idea or the reality of the thing, diminishes when the two conflict.

Write an essay exploring the various views of England Kincaid presents. Consider what she says about the white cliffs of Dover in her final paragraph.

M artin Luther King, Jr. (1929–1968)

M artin Luther King, Jr., won the Nobel Peace Prize in 1964 for his indefatigable effort to secure the blessings of liberty for his people—especially black Americans living in the south. He challenged unfair laws, stood up against demagogues, led peaceful demonstrations through the south, and argued persuasively for change all across America. His successful efforts cost him his life. He was assassinated in Memphis, Tennessee, on April 4, 1968.

"Letter from Birmingham Jail" was written to a group of Christian ministers who had criticized King's effort to integrate restaurants by staging sit-ins at luncheon counters in Birmingham, Alabama. It is an argument against injustice and delay—an urgent appeal to grant African Americans their freedom and independence.

Letter from Birmingham Jail

April 16, 1963

My Dear Fellow Clergymen:

While confined here in the Birmingham city jail, I came across your recent statement calling my present activities "unwise and untimely." Seldom do I pause to answer criticism of my work and ideas. If I sought to answer all the criticisms that cross my desk, my secretaries would have little time for anything other than such correspondence in the course of the day, and I would have no time for constructive work. But since I feel that you are men of genuine good will and that your criticisms are sincerely set forth, I want to try to answer your statement in what I hope will be patient and reasonable terms.

I think I should indicate why I am here in Birmingham, since you have been influenced by the view which argues against "outsiders coming in." I have the honor of serving as president of the Southern Christian Leadership Conference, an organization operating in every southern state, with headquarters in Atlanta, Georgia. We have some eighty-five affiliated organizations across the South, and one of them is the Alabama Christian Movement for Human Rights. Frequently we share staff, educational and financial resources with our affiliates. Several months ago the affiliate here in Birmingham asked us to be on call to engage in a nonviolent direct-action program if such were deemed necessary. We readily consented, and when the hour came we lived up to our promise. So I, along with several members of my staff, am here because I was invited here. I am here because I have organizational ties here.

But more basically, I am in Birmingham because injustice is here. Just as the prophets of the eighth century B.C. left their villages and carried their "thus saith the Lord" far beyond the boundaries of their home towns, and just as the Apostle Paul left his village of Tarsus and carried the gospel of Jesus Christ to the far corners of the Greco-Roman world, so am I compelled to carry the gospel of freedom beyond my own home town. Like Paul, I must constantly respond to the Macedonian call for aid.

Moreover, I am cognizant of the interrelatedness of all communities and states. I cannot sit idly by in Atlanta and not be concerned about what happens in Birmingham. Injustice anywhere is a threat to justice everywhere. We are caught in an inescapable network of mutuality, tied in a single garment of destiny. Whatever affects one directly, affects all indirectly. Never again can we afford to live with the narrow, provincial "outside agitator" idea. Anyone who lives inside the United States can never be considered an outsider anywhere within its bounds.

You deplore the demonstrations taking place in Birmingham. But your statement, I am sorry to say, fails to express a similar concern for the conditions that brought about the demonstrations. I am sure that none of you would want to rest content with the superficial kind of social analysis that deals merely with effects and does not grapple with underlying causes. It is unfortunate that demonstrations are taking place in Birmingham, but it is even more unfortunate that the city's white power structure left the Negro community with no alternative.

In any nonviolent campaign there are four basic steps: collection of the facts to determine whether injustices exist; negotiation; self-purification; and direct action. We have gone through all these steps in Birmingham. There can be no gainsaying the fact that racial injustice engulfs this community. Birmingham is probably the most thoroughly segregated city in the United States. Its ugly record of brutality is widely known. Negroes have experienced grossly unjust treatment in the courts. There have been more unsolved bombings of Negro homes and churches in Birmingham than in any other city in the nation. These are the hard brutal facts of the case. On the basis of these conditions, Negro leaders sought to negotiate with the city fathers. But the latter consistently refused to engage in good-faith negotiation.

Then, last September, came the opportunity to talk with leaders of Birmingham's economic community. In the course of the negotiations, certain promises were made by the merchants—for example, to remove the stores' humiliating racial signs. On the basis of these promises, the Reverend Fred Shuttlesworth and the leaders of the Alabama Christian Movement for Human Rights agreed to a moratorium on all demonstrations. As the weeks and months went by, we realized that we were the victims of a broken promise. A few signs, briefly removed, returned; the others remained.

As in so many past experiences, our hopes had been blasted, and the shadow of deep disappointment settled upon us. We had no alternative except to prepare for direct action, whereby we would present our very bodies as a means of laying our case before the conscience of the local and the national community. Mindful of the difficulties involved, we decided to undertake a process of self-purification. We began a series of workshops on nonviolence, and we repeatedly asked ourselves: "Are you able to accept blows without retaliating?" "Are you able to endure the ordeal of jail?" We decided to schedule our direct-action program for the Easter season, realizing that except for Christmas, this is the main shopping period of the year. Knowing that a strong economic-withdrawal program would be the by-product of direct action, we felt that this would be the best time to bring pressure to bear on the merchants for the needed change.

Then it occurred to us that Birmingham's mayoralty election was coming up in March, and we speedily decided to postpone action until after election day. When we discovered that the Commissioner of Public Safety, Eugene "Bull" Connor, had piled up enough votes to be in the run-off, we decided again to postpone action until the day after the run-off so that the demonstrations could not be used to cloud the issues. Like many others, we waited to see Mr. Connor defeated, and to this end we endured postponement after postponement. Having aided in this community need, we felt that our direct-action program could be delayed no longer.

You may well ask: "Why direct action? Why sit-ins, marches and so forth? Isn't negotiation a better path?" You are quite right in calling for negotiation. Indeed, this is the very purpose of direct action. Nonviolent direct action seeks to create such a crisis and foster such a tension that a community which has constantly refused to negotiate is forced to confront the issue. It seeks so to dramatize the issue that it can no longer be ignored. My citing the creation of tension as part of the work of the nonviolent-resister may sound rather shocking. But I must confess that I am not afraid of the word "tension." I have earnestly opposed violent tension, but there is a type of constructive nonviolent tension which is necessary for growth. Just as Socrates felt that it was necessary to create a tension in the mind so that individuals could rise from the bondage of myths and half-truths to the unfettered realm of creative analysis and objective appraisal, so must we see the need for nonviolent gadflies to create the kind of tension in society that will help men rise from the dark depths of prejudice and racism to the majestic heights of understanding and brotherhood.

The purpose of our direct-action program is to create a situation so crisis-packed that it will inevitably open the door to negotiation. I therefore concur with you in your call for negotiation. Too long has our beloved Southland been bogged down in a tragic effort to live in monologue rather than dialogue.

One of the basic points in your statement is that the action that I and my associates have taken in Birmingham is untimely. Some have asked: "Why didn't you give the new city administration time to act?" The only answer that I can give to this query is that the new Birmingham administration must be prodded about as much as the outgoing one, before it will act. We are sadly mistaken if we feel that the election of Albert Boutwell as mayor will bring the millennium to Birmingham. While Mr. Boutwell is a much more gentle person than Mr. Connor, they are both segregationists, dedicated to maintenance of the status quo. I have hope that Mr. Boutwell will be reasonable enough to see the futility of massive resistance to desegregation. But he will not see this without pressure from devotees of civil rights. My friends, I must say to you that we have not made a single gain in civil rights without determined legal and nonviolent pressure. Lamentably, it is an historical fact that privileged groups seldom give up their privileges voluntarily. Individuals may see the moral light and voluntarily give up their unjust posture; but, as Reinhold Niebuhr has reminded us, groups tend to be more immoral than individuals.

We know through painful experience that freedom is never voluntarily given by the oppressor; it must be demanded by the oppressed. Frankly, I have yet to engage in a direct-action campaign that was "well timed" in the view of those who have not suffered unduly from the disease of segregation. For years now I have heard the word "Wait!" It rings in the ear of every Negro with piercing familiarity. This "Wait" has almost always meant "Never." We must come to see, with one of our distinguished jurists, that "justice too long delayed is justice denied."

We have waited for more than 340 years for our constitutional and Godgiven rights. The nations of Asia and Africa are moving with jet-like speed toward gaining political independence, but we still creep at horse-and-buggy pace toward gaining a cup of coffee at a lunch counter. Perhaps it is easy for those who have never felt the stinging darts of segregation to say, "Wait." But when you have seen vicious mobs lynch your mothers and fathers at will and drown your sisters and brothers at whim; when you have seen hate-filled policemen curse, kick and even kill your black brothers and sisters; when you see the vast majority of your twenty million Negro brothers smothering in an airtight cage of poverty in the midst of an affluent society; when you suddenly find your tongue twisted and your speech stammering as you seek to explain to your six-year-old daughter why she can't go to the public amusement park that has just been advertised on television, and see tears welling up in her eyes when she is told that Funtown is closed to colored children, and see ominous clouds of inferiority beginning to form in her little mental sky, and see her beginning to distort her personality by developing an unconscious bitterness toward white people; when you have to concoct an answer for a five-year-old son who is asking: "Daddy, why do white people treat colored people so mean?"; when you take a cross-country drive and find it necessary to sleep night after night in the uncomfortable corners of your automobile because no motel will accept you; when you are humiliated day in and day out by nagging signs reading "white" and "colored"; when your first name becomes "nigger," your middle name becomes "boy" (however old you are) and your last name becomes "John," and your wife and mother are never given the respected title "Mrs."; when you are harried by day and haunted by night by the fact that you are a Negro, living constantly at tiptoe stance, never quite knowing what to expect next, and are plagued with inner fears and outer resentments; when you are forever fighting a degenerating sense of "nobodiness"—then you will understand why we find it difficult to wait. There comes a time when the cup of endurance runs over, and men are no longer willing to be plunged into the abyss of despair. I hope, sirs, you can understand our legitimate and unavoidable impatience.

You express a great deal of anxiety over our willingness to break laws. This is certainly a legitimate concern. Since we so diligently urge people to obey the Supreme Court's decision of 1954 outlawing segregation in the public schools, at first glance it may seem rather paradoxical for us consciously to break laws. One may well ask: "How can you advocate breaking some laws and obeying others?" The answer lies in the fact that there are two types of laws: just and unjust. I would be the first to advocate obeying just laws. One has not only a legal but a moral responsibility to obey just laws. Conversely, one has a moral responsibility to disobey unjust laws. I would agree with St. Augustine that "an unjust law is no law at all."

Now, what is the difference between the two? How does one determine whether a law is just or unjust? A just law is a man-made code that squares with the moral law or the law of God. An unjust law is a code that is out of harmony with the moral law. To put it in the terms of St. Thomas Aquinas: An unjust law is a human law that is not rooted in eternal law and natural law. Any law that uplifts human personality is just. Any law that degrades human personality is unjust. All segregation statutes are unjust because segregation distorts the soul and damages the personality. It gives the segregator a false sense of superiority and the segregated a false sense of inferiority. Segregation, to use the terminology of the Jewish philosopher Martin Buber, substitutes an "I-it" relationship for an "I-thou" relationship and ends up relegating persons to the status of things. Hence segregation is not only politically, economically and sociologically unsound, it is morally wrong and sinful. Paul Tillich has said that sin is separation. Is not segregation an existential expression of man's tragic separation, his awful estrangement, his terrible sinfulness? Thus it is that I can urge men to obey the 1954 decision of the Supreme Court, for it is morally right; and I can urge them to disobey segregation ordinances, for they are morally wrong.

Let us consider a more concrete example of just and unjust laws. An unjust law is a code that a numerical or power majority group compels a minority group to obey but does not make binding on itself. This is *difference* made legal. By the same token, a just law is a code that a majority compels a minority to follow and that it is willing to follow itself. This is *sameness* made legal.

Let me give another explanation. A law is unjust if it is inflicted on a minority that, as a result of being denied the right to vote, had no part in enacting or devising the law. Who can say that the legislature of Alabama which set up that state's segregation laws was democratically elected? Throughout Alabama all sorts of devious methods are used to prevent Negroes from becoming registered voters, and there are some counties in which even though Negroes constitute a majority of the population, not a single Negro is registered. Can any law enacted under such circumstances be considered democratically structured?

Sometimes a law is just on its face and unjust in its application. For instance, I have been arrested on a charge of parading without a permit. Now, there is nothing wrong in having an ordinance which requires a permit for a parade. But such an ordinance becomes unjust when it is used to maintain segregation and to deny citizens the First-Amendment privilege of peaceful assembly and protest.

I hope you are able to see the distinction I am trying to point out. In no sense do I advocate evading or defying the law, as would the rabid segregationist. That would lead to anarchy. One who breaks an unjust law must do so openly, lovingly, and with a willingness to accept the penalty. I submit that an individual who breaks a law that conscience tells him is unjust, and who willingly accepts the penalty of imprisonment in order to arouse the conscience of the community over its injustice, is in reality expressing the highest respect for law.

Of course, there is nothing new about this kind of civil disobedience. It was evidenced sublimely in the refusal of Shadrach, Meshach and

Abednego to obey the laws of Nebuchadnezzar, on the ground that a higher moral law was at stake. It was practiced superbly by the early Christians, who were willing to face hungry lions and the excruciating pain of chopping blocks rather than submit to certain unjust laws of the Roman Empire. To a degree, academic freedom is a reality today because Socrates practiced civil disobedience. In our own nation, the Boston Tea Party represented a massive act of civil disobedience.

We should never forget that everything Adolf Hitler did in Germany was "legal" and everything the Hungarian freedom fighters did in Hungary was "illegal." It was "illegal" to aid and comfort a Jew in Hitler's Germany. Even so, I am sure that, had I lived in Germany at the time, I would have aided and comforted my Jewish brothers. If today I lived in a Communist country where certain principles dear to the Christian faith are suppressed, I would openly advocate disobeying that country's anti-religious laws.

I must make two honest confessions to you, my Christian and Jewish brothers. First, I must confess that over the past few years I have been gravely disappointed with the white moderate. I have almost reached the regrettable conclusion that the Negro's great stumbling block in his stride toward freedom is not the White Citizen's Counciler or the Ku Klux Klanner, but the white moderate, who is more devoted to "order" than to justice; who prefers a negative peace which is the absence of tension to a positive peace which is the presence of justice; who constantly says: "I agree with you in the goal you seek, but I cannot agree with your methods of direct action"; who paternalistically believes he can set the timetable for another man's freedom; who lives by a mythical concept of time and who constantly advises the Negro to wait for a "more convenient season." Shallow understanding from people of good will is more frustrating than absolute misunderstanding from people of ill will. Lukewarm acceptance is much more bewildering than outright rejection.

I had hoped that the white moderate would understand that law and order exist for the purpose of establishing justice and that when they fail in this purpose they become the dangerously structured dams that block the flow of social progress. I had hoped that the white moderate would understand that the present tension in the South is a necessary phase of the transition from an obnoxious negative peace, in which the Negro passively accepted his unjust plight, to a substantive and positive peace, in which all men will respect the dignity and worth of human personality. Actually, we who engage in nonviolent direct action are not the creators of tension. We merely bring to the surface the hidden tension that is already alive. We bring it out in the open, where it can be seen and dealt with. Like a boil that can never be cured so long as it is covered up but must be opened with all its ugliness to the natural medicines of air and light, injustice must be exposed, with all the tension its exposure creates, to the light of human conscience and the air of national opinion before it can be cured.

In your statement you assert that our actions, even though peaceful, must be condemned because they precipitate violence. But is this a logical assertion? Isn't this like condemning a robbed man because his possession of money precipitated the evil act of robbery? Isn't this like condemning Socrates because his unswerving commitment to truth and his philosophical inquires precipitated the act by the misguided populace in which they made him drink hemlock? Isn't this like condemning Jesus because his unique God-consciousness and never-ceasing devotion to God's will precipitated the evil act of crucifixion? We must come to see that, as the federal courts have consistently affirmed, it is wrong to urge an individual to cease his efforts to gain his basic constitutional rights because the quest may precipitate violence. Society must protect the robbed and punish the robber.

I had also hoped that the white moderate would reject the myth concerning time in relation to the struggle for freedom. I have just received a letter from a white brother in Texas. He writes: "All Christians know that the colored people will receive equal rights eventually, but it is possible that you are in too great a religious hurry. It has taken Christianity almost two thousand years to accomplish what it has. The teachings of Christ take time to come to earth." Such an attitude stems from a tragic misconception of time, from the strangely irrational notion that there is something in the very flow of time that will inevitably cure all ills. Actually, time itself is neutral; it can be used either destructively or constructively. More and more I feel that the people of ill will have used time much more effectively than have the people of good will. We will have to repent in this generation not merely for the hateful words and actions of the bad people but for the appalling silence of the good people. Human progress never rolls in on wheels of inevitability; it comes through the tireless efforts of men willing to be co-workers with God, and without this hard work, time itself becomes an ally of the forces of social stagnation. We must use time creatively, in the knowledge that the time is always ripe to do right. Now is the time to make real the promise of democracy and transform our pending national elegy into a creative psalm of brotherhood. Now is the time to lift our national policy from the quicksand of racial injustice to the solid rock of human dignity.

You speak of our activity in Birmingham as extreme. At first I was rather disappointed that fellow clergymen would see my nonviolent efforts as those of an extremist. I began thinking about the fact that I stand in the middle of two opposing forces in the Negro community. One is a force of complacency, made up in part of Negroes who, as a result of long years of oppression, are so drained of self-respect and a sense of "somebodiness" that they have adjusted to segregation; and in part of a few middle-class Negroes who, because of a degree of academic and economic security and because in some ways they profit by segregation, have become insensitive to the problems of the masses. The other force is one of bitterness and hatred, and it comes perilously close to advocating violence. It is expressed in the various black nationalist groups that are springing up across the nation, the largest and best-known being Elijah Muhammad's Muslim movement. Nourished by the Negro's frustration over the continued existence of racial discrimination, this movement is made up of people who have lost faith in America, who have absolutely repudiated Christianity, and who have concluded that the white man is an incorrigible "devil."

I have tried to stand between these two forces, saying that we need emulate neither the "do-nothingism" of the complacent nor the hatred and despair of the black nationalist. For there is the more excellent way of love and nonviolent protest. I am grateful to God that, through the influence of the Negro church, the way of nonviolence became an integral part of our struggle.

If this philosophy had not emerged, by now many streets of the South would, I am convinced, be flowing with blood. And I am further convinced that if our white brothers dismiss as "rabble-rousers" and "outside agitators" those of us who employ nonviolent direct action, and if they refuse to support our nonviolent efforts, millions of Negroes will, out of frustration and despair, seek solace and security in black-nationalist ideologies—a development that would inevitably lead to a frightening racial nightmare.

Oppressed people cannot remain oppressed forever. The yearning for freedom eventually manifests itself, and that is what has happened to the American Negro. Something within has reminded him of his birthright of freedom, and something without has reminded him that it can be gained. Consciously or unconsciously, he has been caught up by the *Zeitgeist,* and with his black brothers of Africa and his brown and yellow brothers of Asia, South America and the Caribbean, the United States Negro is moving with a sense of great urgency toward the promised land of racial justice. If one recognizes this vital urge that has engulfed the Negro community, one should readily understand why public demonstrations are taking place. The Negro has many pent-up resentments and latent frustrations, and he must release them. So let him march; let him make prayer pilgrimages to the city hall; let him go on freedom rides—and try to understand why he must do so. If his repressed emotions are not released in nonviolent ways, they will seek expression through violence; this is not a threat but a fact of history. So I have not said to my people: "Get rid of your discontent." Rather, I have tried to say that this normal and healthy discontent can be channeled into the creative outlet of nonviolent direct action. And now this approach is being termed extremist.

But though I was initially disappointed at being categorized as an extremist, as I continued to think about the matter I gradually gained a measure of satisfaction from the label. Was not Jesus an extremist for love: "Love your enemies, bless them that curse you, do good to them that hate you, and pray for them which despitefully use you, and persecute you." Was not Amos an extremist for justice: "Let justice roll down like waters and righteousness like an ever-flowing stream." Was not Paul an extremist for the Christian gospel: "I bear in my body the marks of the Lord Jesus." Was not Martin Luther an extremist: "Here I stand; I cannot do otherwise, so help me God." And John Bunyan: "I will stay in jail to the end of my days before I make a butchery of my conscience." And Abraham Lincoln: "This nation cannot survive half slave and half free." And Thomas Jefferson: "We hold these truths to be self-evident, that all men are created equal. . . ." So the question is not whether we will be extremists, but what kind of extremists we will be. Will we be extremists for hate or for love? Will we be extremists for the preservation of injustice or for the extension of justice? In that dramatic scene on Calvary's hill three men were crucified. We must never forget that all three were crucified for the same crime—the crime of extremism. Two were extremists for immorality, and thus fell below their environment. The other, Jesus Christ, was an extremist for love, truth and goodness, and thereby rose above his environment. Perhaps the South, the nation and the world are in dire need of creative extremists.

I had hoped that the white moderate would see this need. Perhaps I was too optimistic; perhaps I expected too much. I suppose I should have realized that few members of the oppressor race can understand the deep groans and passionate yearnings of the oppressed race, and still fewer have the vision to see that injustice must be rooted out by strong, persistent and determined action. I am thankful, however, that some of our white brothers in the South have grasped the meaning of this social revolution and committed themselves to it. They are still all too few in quantity, but they are big in quality. Some—such as Ralph McGill, Lillian Smith, Harry Golden, James McBride Dabbs, Ann Braden and Sarah Patton Boyle—have written about our struggle in eloquent and prophetic terms. Others have marched with us down nameless streets of the South. They have languished in filthy, roach-infested jails, suffering the abuse and brutality of policemen who view them as "dirty nigger-lovers." Unlike so many of their moderate brothers and sisters, they have recognized the urgency of the moment and sensed the need for powerful "action" antidotes to combat the disease of segregation.

Let me take note of my other major disappointment. I have been so greatly disappointed with the white church and its leadership. Of course, there are some notable exceptions. I am not unmindful of the fact that each of you has taken some significant stands on this issue. I commend you, Reverend Stallings, for your Christian stand on this past Sunday, in welcoming Negroes to your worship service on a nonsegregated basis. I commend the Catholic leaders of this state for integrating Spring Hill College several years ago.

But despite these notable exceptions, I must honestly reiterate that I have been disappointed with the church. I do not say this as one of those negative critics who can always find something wrong with the church. I say this as a minister of the gospel, who loves the church; who was nurtured in its bosom; who has been sustained by its spiritual blessings and who will remain true to it as long as the cord of life shall lengthen.

When I was suddenly catapulted into the leadership of the bus protest in Montgomery, Alabama, a few years ago, I felt we would be supported by the white church. I felt that the white ministers, priests and rabbis of the South would be among our strongest allies. Instead, some have been outright opponents, refusing to understand the freedom movement and misrepresenting its leaders; all too many others have been more cautious than courageous and have remained silent behind the anesthetizing security of stained-glass windows.

In spite of my shattered dreams, I came to Birmingham with the hope that the white religious leadership of this community would see the justice of our cause and, with deep moral concern, would serve as the channel through which our just grievances could reach the power structure. I had hoped that each of you would understand. But again I have been disappointed.

I have heard numerous southern religious leaders admonish their worshipers to comply with a desegregation decision because it is the law, but I have longed to hear white ministers declare: "Follow this decree because integration is morally right and because the Negro is your brother." In the midst of blatant injustices inflicted upon the Negro, I have watched white churchmen stand on the sideline and mouth pious irrelevancies and sanctimonious trivialities. In the midst of a mighty struggle to rid our nation of racial and economic injustice, I have heard many ministers say: "Those are social issues, with which the gospel has no real concern." And I have watched many churches commit themselves to a completely other-worldly religion which makes a strange, un-Biblical distinction between body and soul, between the sacred and the secular.

I have traveled the length and breadth of Alabama, Mississippi and all the other southern states. On sweltering summer days and crisp autumn mornings I have looked at the South's beautiful churches with their lofty spires pointing heavenward. I have beheld the impressive outlines of her massive religious-education buildings. Over and over I have found myself asking: "What kind of people worship here? Who is their God? Where were their voices when the lips of Governor Barnett dripped with words of interposition and nullification? Where were they when Governor Wallace gave a clarion call for defiance and hatred? Where were their voices of support when bruised and weary Negro men and women decided to rise from the dark dungeons of complacency to the bright hills of creative protest?"

Yes, these questions are still in my mind. In deep disappointment I have wept over the laxity of the church. But be assured that my tears have been tears of love. There can be no deep disappointment where there is not deep love. Yes, I love the church. How could I do otherwise? I am in the rather unique position of being the son, the grandson and the great-grandson of preachers. Yes, I see the church as the body of Christ. But, oh! How we have blemished and scarred that body through social neglect and through fear of being nonconformists.

There was a time when the church was very powerful—in the time when the early Christians rejoiced at being deemed worthy to suffer for what they believed. In those days the church was not merely a thermometer that recorded the ideas and principles of popular opinion; it was a thermostat that transformed the mores of society. Whenever the early Christians entered a town, the people in power became disturbed and immediately sought to convict the Christians for being "disturbers of the peace" and "outside agitators." But the Christians pressed on, in the conviction that they were "a colony of heaven," called to obey God rather than man. Small in number, they were big in commitment. They were too

God-intoxicated to be "astronomically intimidated." By their effort and example they brought an end to such ancient evils as infanticide and gladiatorial contests.

Things are different now. So often the contemporary church is a weak, ineffectual voice with an uncertain sound. So often it is an archdefender of the status quo. Far from being disturbed by the presence of the church, the power structure of the average community is consoled by the church's silent—and often even vocal—sanction of things as they are.

But the judgment of God is upon the church as never before. If today's church does not recapture the sacrificial spirit of the early church, it will lose its authenticity, forfeit the loyalty of millions, and be dismissed as an irrelevant social club with no meaning for the twentieth century. Every day I meet young people whose disappointment with the church has turned into outright disgust.

Perhaps I have once again been too optimistic. Is organized religion too inextricably bound to the status quo to save our nation and the world? Perhaps I must turn my faith to the inner spiritual church, the church within the church, as the true ekklesia and the hope of the world. But again I am thankful to God that some noble souls from the ranks of organized religion have broken loose from the paralyzing chains of conformity and joined us as active partners in the struggle for freedom. They have left their secure congregations and walked the streets of Albany, Georgia, with us. They have gone done the highways of the South on tortuous rides for freedom. Yes, they have gone to jail with us. Some have been dismissed from their churches, have lost the support of their bishops and fellow ministers. But they have acted in the faith that right defeated is stronger than evil triumphant. Their witness has been the spiritual salt that has preserved the true meaning of the gospel in these troubled times. They have carved a tunnel of hope through the dark mountain of disappointment.

I hope the church as a whole will meet the challenge of this decisive hour. But even if the church does not come to the aid of justice, I have no despair about the future. I have no fear about the outcome of our struggle in Birmingham, even if our motives are at present misunderstood. We will reach the goal of freedom in Birmingham and all over the nation, because the goal of America is freedom. Abused and scorned though we may be, our destiny is tied up with America's destiny. Before the pilgrims landed at Plymouth, we were here. Before the pen of Jefferson etched the majestic words of the Declaration of Independence across the pages of history, we were here. For more than two centuries our forebears labored in this country without wages; they made cotton king; they built the homes of their masters while suffering gross injustice and shameful humiliation— and yet out of a bottomless vitality they continued to thrive and develop. If the inexpressible cruelties of slavery could not stop us, the opposition we now face will surely fail. We will win our freedom because the sacred heritage of our nation and the eternal will of God are embodied in our echoing demands.

Before closing I feel impelled to mention one other point in your statement that has troubled me profoundly. You warmly commended the Birmingham police force for keeping "order" and "preventing violence." I doubt that you would have so warmly commended the police force if you had seen its dogs sinking their teeth into unarmed, nonviolent Negroes. I doubt that you would so quickly commend the policemen if you were to observe their ugly and inhumane treatment of Negroes here in the city jail; if you were to watch them push and curse old Negro women and young Negro girls; if you were to see them slap and kick old Negro men and young boys; if you were to observe them, as they did on two occasions, refuse to give us food because we wanted to sing our grace together. I cannot join you in your praise of the Birmingham police department.

It is true that the police have exercised a degree of discipline in handling the demonstrators. In this sense they have conducted themselves rather "nonviolently" in public. But for what purpose? To preserve the evil system of segregation. Over the past few years I have consistently preached that nonviolence demands that the means we use must be as pure as the ends we seek. I have tried to make clear that it is wrong to use immoral means to attain moral ends. But now I must affirm that it is just as wrong, or perhaps even more so, to use moral means to preserve immoral ends. Perhaps Mr. Connor and his policemen have been rather nonviolent in public, as was Chief Pritchett in Albany, Georgia, but they have used the moral means of nonviolence to maintain the immoral end of racial injustice. As T. S. Eliot has said: "The last temptation is the greatest treason: To do the right deed for the wrong reason."

I wish you had commended the Negro sit-inners and demonstrators of Birmingham for their sublime courage, their willingness to suffer and their amazing discipline in the midst of great provocation. One day the South will recognize its real heroes. They will be the James Merediths, with the noble sense of purpose that enables them to face jeering and hostile mobs, and with the agonizing loneliness that characterizes the life of the pioneer. They will be old, oppressed, battered Negro women, symbolized in a seventy-two-year-old woman in Montgomery, Alabama, who rose up with a sense of dignity and with her people decided not to ride segregated buses, and who responded with ungrammatical profundity to one who inquired about her weariness: "My feet is tired, but my soul is at rest." They will be the young high school and college students, the young ministers of the gospel and a host of their elders, courageously and nonviolently sitting in at lunch counters and willingly going to jail for conscience's sake. One day the South will know that when these disinherited children of God sat down at lunch counters, they were in reality standing up for what is best in the American dream and for the most sacred values in our Judaeo-Christian heritage, thereby bringing our nation back to those great wells of democracy which were dug by the founding fathers in their formulation of the Constitution and the Declaration of Independence.

Never before have I written so long a letter. I'm afraid it is much too long to take your precious time. I can assure you that it would have been much shorter if I had been writing from a comfortable desk, but what else can one do when he is alone in a narrow jail cell, other than write long letters, think long thoughts and pray long prayers?

If I have said anything in this letter that overstates the truth and indicates an unreasonable impatience, I beg you to forgive me. If I have said anything that understates the truth and indicates my having a patience that allows me to settle for anything less than brotherhood, I beg God to forgive me.

I hope this letter finds you strong in the faith. I also hope that circumstances will soon make it possible for me to meet each of you, not as an integrationist or a civil-rights leader but as a fellow clergyman and a Christian brother. Let us all hope that the dark clouds of racial prejudice will soon pass away and the deep fog of misunderstanding will be lifted from our fear-drenched communities, and in some not too distant tomorrow the radiant stars of love and brotherhood will shine over our great nation with all their scintillating beauty.

Yours for the cause of Peace and Brotherhood,
Martin Luther King, Jr.

CONSIDERATIONS

Thinking

What does King mean by "a nonviolent direct-action program"? What do you think about the necessity for "tension," which, according to King, is "necessary for growth"?

What do you think of King's claim that "privileged groups seldom give up their privileges voluntarily"? Is that still true?

How can you tell when a law is "out of harmony with the moral law"?

Connecting

Turn to King's response to the clergymen's admonition to wait. Read aloud the entire passage, beginning with the words, "But when you have seen vicious mobs lynch your mothers and fathers at will and drown your sisters and brothers at whim . . ." What do you know after reading the passage aloud that you did not know when you read it silently?

In what ways might you consider King's letter historical? What are its limitations as a historical document?

Writing

Write an essay in which you assess the extent to which you think this claim of King's rings true in your community or at your college at the turn into the twenty-first century: "Anyone who lives inside the United States can never be considered an outsider anywhere within its bounds."

Write your own letter to address an injustice in your community or in your college.

L eonard Kriegel
(b.1933)

eonard Kriegel, a retired professor of English from the City College
of New York, is a novelist, short story writer, and essayist. His
work includes *Quitting Time* (a novel), *Notes for a Two-Dollar
Window* (a memoir), and *Falling into Life* (a collection of essays). His
stories and essays have appeared in *The American Scholar, Dissent, The
Sewanee Review, The Gettysburg Review, The Georgia Review, Raritan,
Partisan Review, The Nation, The New Republic,* and *The New York Times
Magazine.* He has completed a new collection of essays, *Flying Solo.*

"Falling into Life" first appeared in *The American Scholar;* it recounts
a moment from Kriegel's early bout with polio and reminds us of the
euphoria that accompanies our fall into life, and perhaps into death.

Falling into Life

It is not the actual death a man is doomed to die but the deaths his imagination anticipates that claim attention as one grows older. We are constantly being reminded that the prospect of death forcefully concentrates the mind. While that may be so, it is not a prospect that does very much else for the imagination—other than to make one aware of its limitations and imbalances.

Over the past five years, as I have moved into the solidity of middle age, my own most formidable imaginative limitation has turned out to be a surprising need for symmetry. I am possessed by a peculiar passion: I want to believe that my life has been balanced out. And because I once had to learn to fall in order to keep that life mine, I now seem to have convinced myself that I must also learn to fall into death.

Falling into life wasn't easy, and I suspect that is why I hunger for such awkward symmetry today. Having lost the use of my legs during the polio epidemic that swept across the eastern United States during the summer of 1944, I was soon immersed in a process of rehabilitation that was, at least when looked at in retrospect, as much spiritual as physical.

That was a full decade before the discovery of the Salk vaccine ended polio's reign as the disease most dreaded by America's parents and their children. Treatment of the disease had been standardized by 1944: following the initial onslaught of the virus, patients were kept in isolation for a period of ten days to two weeks. Following that, orthodox medical opinion was content to subject patients to as much heat as they could stand. Stiff paralyzed limbs were swathed in heated, coarse woolen towels known as "hot packs." (The towels were that same greenish brown as blankets issued to American GIs, and they reinforced a boy's sense of being at war.) As soon as the hot packs had baked enough pain and stiffness out of a patient's body so that he could be moved on and off a stretcher, the treatment was ended, and the patient faced a series of daily immersions in a heated pool.

I would ultimately spend two full years at the appropriately named New York State Reconstruction Home in West Haverstraw. But what I remember most vividly about the first three months of my stay there was being submerged in a hot pool six times a day, for periods of between fifteen and twenty minutes. I would lie on a stainless steel slab, my face alone out of water, while the wet heat rolled against my dead legs and the physical therapist was at my side working at a series of manipulations intended to bring my useless muscles back to health.

Each immersion was a baptism by fire in the water. While my mind pitched and reeled with memories of the "normal" boy I had been a few weeks earlier, I would close my eyes and focus not, as my therapist urged, on bringing dead legs back to life but on my strange fall from the childhood grace of the physical. Like all eleven-year-old boys, I had spent a good deal of time thinking about my body. Before the attack of the virus, however, I thought about it only in connection with my own lunge toward adolescence. Never before had my body seemed an object in itself. Now it was. And like the twenty-one other boys in the ward—all of us between the ages of nine and twelve—I sensed I would never move beyond the fall from grace, even as I played with memories of the way I once had been.

Each time I was removed from the hot water and placed on a stretcher by the side of the pool, there to await the next immersion, I was fed salt tablets. These were simply intended to make up for the sweat we lost, but salt tablets seemed to me the cruelest confirmation of my new status as spiritual debtor. Even today, more than four decades later, I still shiver at the mere thought of those salt tablets. Sometimes the hospital orderly would literally have to pry my mouth open to force me to swallow them. I dreaded the nausea the taste of salt inspired in me. Each time I was resubmerged in the hot pool, I would grit my teeth—not from the flush of heat sweeping over my body but from the thought of what I would have to face when I would again be taken out of the water. To be an eater of salt was far more humiliating than to endure pain. Nor was I alone in feeling this way. After lights-out had quieted the ward, we boys would furtively whisper from cubicle to cubicle of how we dreaded being forced to swallow salt tablets. It was that, rather than the pain we endured, that anchored our sense of loss and dread.

Any recovery of muscle use in a polio patient usually took place within three months of the disease's onset. We all knew that. But as time passed, every boy in the ward learned to recite stories of those who, like Lazarus, had witnessed their own bodily resurrection. Having fallen from physical grace, we also chose to fall away from the reality in front of us. Our therapists were skilled and dedicated, but they weren't wonder-working saints. Paralyzed legs and arms rarely responded to their manipulations. We could not admit to ourselves, or to them, that we were permanently crippled. But each of us knew without knowing that his future was tied to the body that floated on the stainless steel slab.

We sweated out the hot pool and we choked on the salt tablets, and through it all we looked forward to the promise of rehabilitation. For, once the stiffness and pain had been baked and boiled out of us, we would no longer be eaters of salt. We would not be what we once had been, but at least we would be candidates for re-entry into the world, admittedly made over to face its demands encased in leather and steel.

I suppose we might have been told that our fall from grace was permanent. But I am still grateful that no one—neither doctors nor nurses nor therapists, not even that sadistic orderly, himself a former polio patient, who limped through our lives and through our pain like some vengeful presence—told me that my chances of regaining the use of my legs were nonexistent. Like every other boy in the ward, I organized my needs around whatever illusions were available. And the illusion I needed above any other was that one morning I would simply wake up and rediscover the "normal" boy of memory, once again playing baseball in French Charley's Field in Bronx Park rather than roaming the fields of his own imagination. At the age of eleven, I needed to weather reality, not face it. And to this very day, I silently thank those who were concerned enough about me, or indifferent enough to my fate, not to tell me what they knew.

Like most boys, sick or well, I was an adaptable creature—and rehabilitation demanded adaptability. The fall from bodily grace transformed each of us into acolytes of the possible, pragmatic Americans for whom survival was method and strategy. We would learn, during our days in the New York State Reconstruction Home, to confront the world that was. We would learn to survive the way we were, with whatever the virus had left intact.

I had fallen away from the body's prowess, but I was being led toward a life measured by different standards. Even as I fantasized about the past, it disappeared. Rehabilitation, I was to learn, was ahistorical, a future devoid of any significant claim on the past. Rehabilitation was a thief's primer of compensation and deception: its purpose was to teach one how to steal a touch of the normal from an existence that would be striking in its abnormality.

When I think back to those two years in the ward, the boy who made his rehabilitation most memorable was Joey Tomashevski. Joey was the son of an upstate dairy farmer, a Polish immigrant who had come to America before the Depression and whose English was even poorer than the English of my own shtetl-bred father. The virus had left both of Joey's arms so lifeless and atrophied that I could circle where his bicep should have been with pinky and thumb and still stick the forefinger of my own hand through. And yet, Joey assumed that he would make do with whatever had been left him. He accepted without question the task of making his toes and feet over into fingers and hands. With lifeless arms encased in a canvas sling that looked like the breadbasket a European peasant might carry to market, Joey would sit up in bed and demonstrate how he could maneuver fork and spoon with his toes.

I would never have dreamed of placing such confidence in my fingers, let alone my toes. I found, as most of the other boys in the ward did, Joey's unabashed pride in the flexibility and control with which he could maneuver a forkful of mashed potatoes into his mouth a continuous indictment of my sense of the world's natural order. We boys with dead legs would gather round his bed in our wheelchairs and silently watch Joey display his dexterity with a vanity so open and naked that it seemed an invitation to being struck down yet again. But Joey's was a vanity already tested by experience. For he was more than willing to accept whatever challenges the virus threw his way. For the sake of demonstrating his skill to us, he kicked a basketball from the auditorium stage through the hoop attached to a balcony some fifty feet away. When one of our number derisively called him lucky, he proceeded to kick five of seven more balls through that same hoop.

I suspect that Joey's pride in his ability to compensate for what had been taken away from him irritated me, because I knew that, before I could pursue my own rehabilitation with such singular passion, I had to surrender myself to what was being demanded of me. And that meant I had to learn to fall. It meant that I had to learn, as Joey Tomashevski had already learned, how to transform absence into opportunity. Even though I still lacked Joey's instinctive willingness to live with the legacy of the virus, I found myself being overhauled, re-created in much the same way as a car engine is rebuilt. Nine months after I arrived in the ward, a few weeks before my twelfth birthday, I was fitted for double long-legged braces bound together by a steel pelvic band circling my waist. Lifeless or not, my legs were precisely measured, the steel carefully molded to form, screws and locks and leather joined to one another for my customized benefit alone. It was technology that would hold me up—another offering on the altar of compensation. "You get what you give," said Jackie Lyons, my closest friend in the ward. For he, too, was now a novitiate of the possible. He, too, now had to learn how to choose the road back.

Falling into life was not a metaphor; it was real, a process learned only through doing, the way a baby learns to crawl, to stand, and then to walk. After the steel bands around calves and thighs and pelvis had been covered over by the rich-smelling leather, after the braces had been precisely

fitted to allow my fear-ridden imagination the surety of their holding presence, I was pulled to my feet. For the first time in ten months, I stood.
Two middle-aged craftsmen, the hospital bracemakers who worked in a
machine shop deep in the basement, held me in place as my therapist
wedged two wooden crutches beneath my shoulders.

They stepped back, first making certain that my grip on the crutches
was firm. Filled with pride in their technological prowess, the three of
them stood in front of me, admiring their skill. Had I been created in the
laboratory of Mary Shelley's Dr. Frankenstein, I could not have felt myself
any more the creature of scientific pride. I stood on the braces, crutches
beneath my shoulders slanting outward like twin towers of Pisa. I flushed,
swallowed hard, struggled to keep from crying, struggled not to be overwhelmed by my fear of falling.

My future had arrived. The leather had been fitted, the screws had
been turned to the precise millimeter, the locks at the knees and the bush-
ings at the ankles had been properly tested and retested. That very afternoon I was taken for the first time to a cavernous room filled with barbells
and Indian clubs and crutches and walkers. I would spend an hour each
day there for the next six months. In the rehab room, I would learn how to
mount two large wooden steps made to the exact measure of a New York
City bus's. I would swing on parallel bars from one side to the other, my
arms learning how they would have to hurl me through the world. I balanced Indian clubs like a circus juggler because my therapist insisted it
would help my coordination. And I was expected to learn to fall.

I was a dutiful patient. I did as I was told because I could see no
advantage to doing anything else. I hungered for the approval of those in
authority—doctors, nurses, therapists, the two bracemakers. Again and
again, my therapist demonstrated how I was to throw my legs from the
hip. Again and again, I did as I was told. Grabbing the banister with my
left hand, I threw my leg from the hip while pushing off my right crutch.
Like some baby elephant (despite the sweat lost in the heated pool, the
months of inactivity in bed had fattened me up considerably), I dangled
from side to side on the parallel bars. Grunting with effort, I did everything demanded of me. I did it with an unabashed eagerness to please
those who had power over my life. I wanted to put myself at risk. I
wanted to do whatever was supposed to be "good" for me. I believed as
absolutely as I have ever believed in anything that rehabilitation would
finally placate the hunger of the virus.

But when my therapist commanded me to fall, I cringed. For the
prospect of falling terrified me. Every afternoon, as I worked through my

prescribed activities, I prayed that I would be able to fall when the session ended. Falling was the most essential "good" of all the "goods" held out for my consideration by my therapist. I believed that. I believed it so intensely that the belief itself was painful. Everything else asked of me was given—and given gladly. I mounted the bus stairs, pushed across the parallel bars until my arms ached with the effort, allowed the medicine ball to pummel me, flailed away at the empty air with my fists because my therapist wanted me to rid myself of the tension within. The slightest sign of approval from those in authority was enough to make me puff with pleasure. Other boys in the ward might not have taken rehabilitation seriously, but I was an eager servant cringing before the promise of approval.

Only I couldn't fall. As each session ended, I would be led to the mats that took up a full third of the huge room. "It's time," the therapist would say. Dutifully, I would follow her, step after step. Just as dutifully, I would stand on the edge of those two-inch-thick mats, staring down at them until I could feel my body quiver. "All you have to do is let go," my therapist assured me. "The other boys do it. Just let go and fall."

But the prospect of letting go was precisely what terrified me. That the other boys in the ward had no trouble in falling added to my shame and terror. I didn't need my therapist to tell me the two-inch-thick mats would keep me from hurting myself. I knew there was virtually no chance of injury when I fell, but that knowledge simply made me more ashamed of a cowardice that was as monumental as it was unexplainable. Had it been able to rid me of my sense of my own cowardice, I would happily have settled for bodily harm. But I was being asked to surrender myself to the emptiness of space, to let go and crash down to the mats below, to feel myself suspended in air when nothing stood between me and the vacuum of the world. *That* was the prospect that overwhelmed me. *That* was what left me sweating with rage and humiliation. The contempt I felt was for my own weakness.

I tried to justify what I sensed could never be justified. Why should I be expected to throw myself into emptiness? Was this sullen terror the price of compensation, the badge of normality? Maybe my refusal to fall embodied some deeper thrust than I could then understand. Maybe I had unconsciously seized upon some fundamental resistance to the forces that threatened to overwhelm me. What did it matter that the ground was covered by the thick mats? The tremors I feared were in my heart and soul.

Shame plagued me—and shame is the older brother to disease. Flushing with shame, I would stare down at the mats. I could feel myself want-

ing to cry out. But I shriveled at the thought of calling more attention to my cowardice. I would finally hear myself whimper, "I'm sorry. But
I can't. I can't let go."

Formless emptiness. A rush of air through which I would plummet
toward obliteration. As my "normal" past grew more and more distant, I
reached for it more and more desperately, recalling it like some movie
whose plot has long since been forgotten but whose scenes continue to
comfort through images disconnected from anything but themselves. I
remembered that there had been a time when the prospect of falling
evoked not terror but joy: football games on the rain-softened autumn
turf of Mosholu Parkway, belly-flopping on an American Flyer down its
snow-covered slopes in winter, rolling with a pack of friends down one of
the steep hills in Bronx Park. Free falls from the past, testifying not to a
loss of the self but to an absence of barriers.

My therapist pleaded, ridiculed, cajoled, threatened, bullied. I was
sighed over and railed at. But I couldn't let go and fall. I couldn't sell my
terror off so cheaply. Ashamed as I was, I wouldn't allow myself to be bullied out of terror.

A month passed—a month of struggle between me and my therapist.
Daily excursions to the rehab room, daily practice runs through the future
that was awaiting me. The daily humiliation of discovering that one's own
fear had been transformed into a public issue, a subject of discussion
among the other boys in the ward, seemed unending.

And then, terror simply evaporated. It was as if I had served enough
time in that prison. I was ready to move on. One Tuesday afternoon, as my
session ended, the therapist walked resignedly alongside me toward the
mats. "All right, Leonard. It's time again. All you have to do is let go and
fall." Again, I stood above the mats. Only this time, it was as if something
beyond my control or understanding had decided to let my body's fall from
grace take me down for good. I was not seized by the usual paroxysm of
fear. I didn't feel myself break out in a terrified sweat. It was over.

I don't mean that I suddenly felt myself spring into courage. That
wasn't what happened at all. The truth was I had simply been worn down
into letting go, like a boxer in whose eyes one recognizes not the flicker
of defeat—that issue never having been in doubt—but the acceptance of
defeat. Letting go no longer held my imagination captive. I found myself
quite suddenly faced with a necessary fall—a fall into life.

So it was that I stood above the mat and heard myself sigh and then
felt myself let go, dropping through the quiet air, crutches slipping off to

the sides. What I didn't feel this time was the threat of my body slipping into emptiness, so mummified by the terror before it that the touch of air pre-empted even death. I dropped. I did not crash. I dropped. I did not collapse. I dropped. I did not plummet. I felt myself enveloped by a curiously gentle moment in my life. In that sliver of time before I hit the mat, I was kissed by space.

My body absorbed the slight shock and I rolled onto my back, braced legs swinging like unguided missiles into the free air, crutches dropping away to the sides. Even as I fell through the air, I could sense the shame and fear drain from my soul, and I knew that my sense of my own cowardice would soon follow. In falling, I had given myself a new start, a new life.

"That's it!" my therapist triumphantly shouted. "You let go! And there it is!"

You let go! And there it is! Yes, and you discover not terror but the only self you are going to be allowed to claim anyhow. You fall free, and then you learn that those padded mats hold not courage but the unclaimed self. And if it turned out to be not the most difficult of tasks, did that make my sense of jubilation any less?

From that moment, I gloried in my ability to fall. Falling became an end in itself. I lost sight of what my therapist had desperately been trying to demonstrate for me—that there was a purpose in learning how to fall. For she wanted to teach me through the fall what I would have to face in the future. She wanted to give me a wholeness I could not give myself. For she knew that mine would be a future so different from what confronts the "normal" that I had to learn to fall into life in order not to be overwhelmed.

From that day, she urged me to practice falling as if I were a religious disciple being urged by a master to practice spiritual discipline. Letting go meant allowing my body to float into space, to turn at the direction of the fall and follow the urgings of emptiness. For her, learning to fall was learning the most essential of American lessons: how to turn incapacity into capacity.

"You were afraid of hurting yourself," she explained to me. "But that's the beauty of it. When you let go, you can't hurt yourself."

An echo of the streets and playgrounds I called home until I met the virus. American slogans: go with the flow, roll with the punch, slide with the threat until it is no longer a threat. They were simply slogans, and they were all intended to create strength from weakness, a veritable world's fair of compensation.

I returned to the city a year later. By that time, I was a willing convert, one who now secretly enjoyed demonstrating his ability to fall. I enjoyed the surprise that would greet me as I got to my feet, unscathed and undamaged. However perverse it may seem, I felt a certain pleasure when, as I walked with a friend, I felt a crutch slip out of my grasp. Watching the thrust of concern darken his features, I felt myself in control of my own capacity. For falling had become the way my body sought out its proper home. It was an earthbound body, and mine would be an earthbound life. My quest would be for the solid ground beneath me. Falling with confidence, I fell away from terror and fear.

Of course, some falls took me unawares, and I found myself letting go too late or too early. Bruised in ego and sometimes in body, I would pull myself to my feet to consider what had gone wrong. Yet I was essentially untroubled. Such defeats were part of the game, even when they confined me to bed for a day or two afterward. I was an accountant of pain, and sometimes heavier payment was demanded. In my mid-thirties, I walked my two-year-old son's babysitter home, tripped on the curbstone, and broke my wrist. At forty-eight, an awkward fall triggered by a carelessly unlocked brace sent me smashing against the bathtub and into surgery for a broken femur. It took four months for me to learn to walk on the crutches all over again. But I learned. I already knew how to fall.

I knew such accidents could be handled. After all, pain was not synonymous with mortality. In fact, pain was insurance against an excessive consciousness of mortality. Pain might validate the specific moment in time, but it didn't have very much to do with the future. I did not yet believe that falling into life had anything to do with falling into death. It was simply a way for me to exercise control over my own existence.

It seems to me today that, when I first let my body fall to those mats, I was somehow giving myself the endurance I would need to survive in this world. In a curious way, falling became a way of celebrating what I had lost. My legs were lifeless, useless, but their loss had created a dancing image in whose shadowy gyrations I recognized a strange but potentially interesting new self. I would survive. I knew that now. I could let go, I could fall, and, best of all, I could get up.

To create an independent self, a man had to rid himself of both the myths that nurtured him and the myths that held him back. Learning to fall had been the first lesson in how I yet might live successfully as a cripple. Even disease had its inviolate principles. I understood that the most dangerous threat to the sense of self I needed was an inflated belief in my own capacity. Falling rid a man of excess baggage; it taught him how each of us is dependent on balance.

But what really gave falling legitimacy was the knowledge that I could get to my feet again. That was what taught me the rules of survival. As long as I could pick myself up and stand on my own two feet, brace-bound and crutch-propped as I was, the fall testified to my ability to live in the here and now, to stake my claim as an American who had turned incapacity into capacity. For such a man, falling might well be considered the language of everyday achievement.

But the day came, as I knew it must come, when I could no longer pick myself up. It was then that my passion for symmetry in endings began. On that day, spurred on by another fall, I found myself spinning into the inevitable future.

The day was actually a rainy night in November of 1983. I had just finished teaching at the City College Center for Worker Education, an off-campus degree program for working adults, and had joined some friends for dinner. All of us, I remember, were in a jovial, celebratory mood, although I no longer remember what it was we were celebrating. Perhaps it was simply the satisfaction of being good friends and colleagues at dinner together.

We ate in a Spanish restaurant on Fourteenth Street in Manhattan. It was a dinner that took on, for me at least, the intensity of a time that would assume greater and greater significance as I grew older, one of those watershed moments writers are so fond of. In the dark, rain-swept New York night, change and possibility seemed to drift like a thick fog all around us.

Our mood was still convivial when we left the restaurant around eleven. The rain had slackened off to a soft drizzle and the street glistened beneath the play of light on the wet black creosote. At night, rain in the city has a way of transforming proportion into optimism. The five of us stood around on the slicked-down sidewalk, none of us willing to be the first to break the richness of the mood by leaving.

Suddenly, the crutch in my left hand began to slip out from under me, slowly, almost deliberately, as if the crutch had a mind of its own and had not yet made the commitment that would send me down. Apparently, I had hit a slick patch of city sidewalk, some nub of concrete worn smooth as medieval stone by thousands of shoppers and panhandlers and tourists and students who daily pounded the bargain hustlings of Fourteenth Street.

Instinctively, I at first tried to fight the fall, to seek for balance by pushing off from the crutch in my right hand. But as I recognized that the fall was inevitable, I simply went slack—and for the thousandth time my body sought vindication in its ability to let go and drop. These good friends had seen me fall before. They knew my childish vanities, understood that I still thought of falling as a way to demonstrate my control of the traps and uncertainties that lay in wait for us all.

Thirty-eight years earlier, I had discovered that I could fall into life simply by letting go. Now I made a different discovery—that I could no longer get to my feet by myself. I hit the wet ground and quickly turned over and pushed up, trying to use one of the crutches as a prop to boost myself to my feet, as I had been taught to do as a boy of twelve.

But try as hard as I could, I couldn't get to my feet. It wasn't that I lacked physical strength. I knew that my arms were as powerful as ever as I pushed down on the wet concrete. It had nothing to do with the fact that the street was wet, as my friends insisted later. No, it had to do with a subtle, if mysterious, change in my own sense of rhythm and balance. My body had decided—*and decided on its own, autonomously*—that the moment had come for me to face the question of endings. It was the body that chose its time of recognition.

It was, it seems to me now, a distinctively American moment. It left me pondering limitations and endings and summations. It left me with the curiously buoyant sense that mortality had quite suddenly made itself a felt presence rather than the rhetorical strategy used by the poets and novelists I taught to my students. This was what writers had in mind when they spoke of the truly common fate, this sense of ending coming to one unbidden. This had brought with it my impassioned quest for symmetry. As I lay on the wet ground—no more than a minute or two—all I could think of was how much I wanted my life to balance out. It was as if I were staring into a future in which time itself had evaporated.

Here was a clear, simple perception, and there was nothing mystical about it. There are limitations we recognize and those that recognize us. My friends, who had nervously been standing around while I tried to get to my feet, finally asked if they could help me up. "You'll have to," I said. "I can't get up any other way."

Two of them pulled me to my feet while another jammed the crutches beneath my arms, as the therapist and the two bracemakers had done almost four decades earlier. When I was standing, they proceeded to joke about my sudden incapacity in that age-old way men of all ages have, as if words might codify loss and change and time's betrayal. I joined in the joking. But what I really wanted was to go home and contemplate this latest fall in the privacy of my apartment. The implications were clear: I would never again be an eater of salt, I would also never again get to my feet on my own. A part of my life had ended. But that didn't depress me. In fact, I felt almost as exhilarated as I had thirty-eight years earlier, when my body surrendered to the need to let go and I fell into life.

Almost four years have passed since I fell on the wet sidewalk of Fourteenth Street. I suppose it wasn't a particularly memorable fall. It wasn't even particularly significant to anyone who had not once fallen into life. But it was inevitable, the first time I had let go into a time when it would no longer even be necessary to let go.

It was a fall that left me with the knowledge that I could no longer pick myself up. That meant I now needed the help of others as I had not needed their help before. It was a fall that left me burning with this strange passion for symmetry, this desire to balance my existence out. When the day comes, I want to be able to fall into my death as nakedly as I once had to fall into my life.

Do not misunderstand me. I am not seeking a way out of mortality, for I believe in nothing more strongly than I believe in the permanency of endings. I am not looking for a way out of this life, a life I continue to find immensely enjoyable—even if I can no longer pull myself to my own two feet. Of course, a good deal in my life has changed. For one thing, I am increasingly impatient with those who claim to have no use for endings of any sort. I am also increasingly embarrassed by the thought of the harshly critical adolescent I was, self-righteously convinced that the only way for a man to go to his end was by kicking and screaming.

But these are, I suppose, the kinds of changes any man or woman of forty or fifty would feel. Middle-aged skepticism is as natural as adolescent acne. In my clearer, less passionate moments, I can even laugh at my need for symmetry in beginnings and endings as well as my desire to see my own eventual death as a line running parallel to my life. Even in mathematics, let alone life, symmetry is sometimes too neat, too closed off from the way things actually work. After all, it took me a full month before I could bring myself to let go and fall into life.

I no longer talk about how one can seize a doctrine of compensation from disease. I don't talk about it, but it still haunts me. In my heart, I believe it offers a man the only philosophy by which he can actually live. It is the only philosophy that strips away both spiritual mumbo jumbo and the procrustean weight of existential anxiety. In the final analysis, a man really is what a man does.

Believing as I do, I wonder why I so often find myself trying to frame a perspective that will prove adequate to a proper sense of ending. Perhaps that is why I find myself sitting in a bar with a friend, trying to explain to him all that I have learned from falling. "There must be a time," I hear myself tell him, "when a man has the right to stop thinking about falling."

"Sure," my friend laughs. "Four seconds before he dies."

CONSIDERATIONS

Thinking

What does it mean in a more normal life than that of Kriegel's boyhood to organize one's needs "around whatever illusions were available." In what ways was that necessity of Kriegel's every adolescent's necessity?

What do you think Kriegel means when he says that his friend Jackie Lyons was a "novitiate of the possible"?

Why do you suppose it was more difficult for Kriegel than for the other boys simply to "surrender [himself] to the emptiness of space," to let himself fall onto those protective mats?

What do you think of the paradox of a fortunate fall? Do you think that falls often serve as a prelude to a newfound life?

Connecting

Why do you suppose Kriegel includes the story about Joey Tomashevski, the boy who was so nimble with his toes? How does his appearance in the essay help Kriegel develop his idea about falling?

Recount some moment in your own life when you were, as Kriegel was, "kissed by space"—when you finally let go and experienced something on the other side of dread.

How do you account for Kriegel's passion for symmetry? How do you suppose the fall into death will somehow balance out that earlier fall into life?

Writing

Write an essay about rehabilitation—its meaning and its application, from your perspective.

Kriegel seems primarily concerned about telling the story of learning to fall, although he attaches to that story, almost from the outset, an evolving concern, a story if you will, about falling into death. Write a three-page account of the various ideas that grow out of those two stories, along with your sense of how those ideas about life and death fit together in this essay.

D.H. Lawrence
(1885–1930)

D avid Herbert Lawrence is a prominent figure in modern British
literature. Best known as a novelist, Lawrence wrote prolifically in
other genres as well. He produced many volumes of travel writing,
letters, criticism, essays, short stories, poetry, and polemic. His works in
whatever genre he worked tended to be ahead of his time. Among his
most important novels, which most often attacked the rise of
industrialism and celebrated the role of sex in human experience, are *Sons
and Lovers* (1913), *Women in Love* (1920), and *Lady Chatterly's Lover*
(1928), which was censored and banned for what was considered
pornographic detail.

The following essay is characteristic of Lawrence's blunt assessment
of the relations between the sexes. Although cast partly in the form of
an animal fable, Lawrence's point is no less sharply delineated for its use
of analogy. One of its most interesting features is its tone.

Cocksure Women
and Hensure Men

It seems to me there are two aspects to women. There is the demure and the dauntless. Men have loved to dwell, in fiction at least, on the demure maiden whose inevitable reply is: Oh, yes, if you please, kind sir! The demure maiden, the demure spouse, the demure mother—this is still the ideal. A few maidens, mistresses and mothers *are* demure. A few pretend to be. But the vast majority are not. And they don't pretend to be. We don't expect a girl skilfully driving her car to be demure, we expect her to be dauntless. What good would demure and maidenly Members of Parliament be, inevitably responding: Oh, yes, if you please, kind sir!— Though of course there are masculine members of that kidney.—And a demure telephone girl? Or even a demure stenographer? Demureness, to be sure, is outwardly becoming, it is an outward mark of femininity, like bobbed hair. But it goes with inward dauntlessness. The girl who has got to make her way in life has got to be dauntless, and if she has a pretty, demure manner with it, then lucky girl. She kills two birds with two stones.

With the two kinds of femininity go two kinds of confidence: There are the women who are cocksure, and the women who are hensure. A really up-to-date woman is a cocksure woman. She doesn't have a doubt nor a qualm. She is the modern type. Whereas the old-fashioned demure woman was sure as a hen is sure, that is, without knowing anything about it. She went quietly and busily clucking around, laying the eggs and mothering the chickens in a kind of anxious dream that still was full of sureness. But not mental sureness. Her sureness was a physical condition, very soothing, but a condition out of which she could easily be startled or frightened.

It is quite amusing to see the two kinds of sureness in chickens. The cockerel is, naturally, cocksure. He crows because he is *certain* it is day. Then the hen peeps out from under her wing. He marches to the door of the hen-house and pokes out his head assertively: *Ah ha! daylight, of course, just as I said!*—and he majestically steps down the chicken ladder towards *terra firma*, knowing that the hens will step cautiously after him, drawn by his confidence. So after him, cautiously, step the hens. He crows again: *Ha-ha! here we are!*—It is indisputable, and the hens accept it entirely. He marches towards the house. From the house a person ought to appear, scattering corn. Why does the person not appear? The cock will see to it. He is cocksure. He gives a loud crow in the doorway, and the person appears. The hens are suitably impressed but immediately devote all their henny consciousness to the scattered corn, pecking absorbedly, while the cock runs and fusses, cocksure that he is responsible for it all.

So the day goes on. The cock finds a tit-bit, and loudly calls the hens. They scuffle up in henny surety, and gobble the tit-bit. But when they find a juicy morsel for themselves, they devour it in silence, hensure. Unless, of course, there are little chicks, when they most anxiously call the brood. But in her own dim surety, the hen is really much surer than the cock, in a different way. She marches off to lay her egg, she secures obstinately the nest she wants, she lays her egg at last, then steps forth again with prancing confidence, and gives that most assured of all sounds, the hensure cackle of a bird who has laid her egg. The cock, who is never so sure about anything as the hen is about the egg she has laid, immediately starts to cackle like the female of his species. He is pining to be hensure, for hensure is so much surer than cocksure.

Nevertheless, cocksure is boss. When the chicken-hawk appears in the sky, loud are the cockerel's calls of alarm. Then the hens scuffle under the verandah, the cock ruffles his feathers on guard. The hens are numb with fear, they say: Alas, there is no health in us! How wonderful to be a cock so bold!—And they huddle, numbed. But their very numbness is hensurety.

Just as the cock can cackle, however, as if he had laid the egg, so can the hen bird crow. She can more or less assume his cocksureness. And yet she is never so easy, cocksure, as she used to be when she was hensure. Cocksure, she is cocksure, but uneasy. Hensure, she trembles, but is easy.

It seems to me just the same in the vast human farmyard. Only nowadays all the cocks are cackling and pretending to lay eggs, and all the hens are crowing and pretending to call the sun out of bed. If women today are cocksure, men are hensure. Men are timid, tremulous, rather soft and submissive, easy in their very henlike tremulousness. They only want to be spoken to gently. So the women step forth with a good loud *cock-a-doodle-do!*

The tragedy about cocksure women is that they are more cocky, in their assurance, than the cock himself. They never realize that when the cock gives his loud crow in the morning, he listens acutely afterwards, to hear if some other wretch of a cock dare crow defiance, challenge. To the cock, there is always defiance, challenge, danger and death on the clear air; or the possibility thereof.

But alas, when the hen crows, she listens for no defiance or challenge. When she says *cock-a-doodle-do!* then it is unanswerable. The cock listens for an answer, alert. But the hen knows she is unanswerable. *Cock-a-doodle-do!* and there it is, take it or leave it!

And it is this that makes the cocksureness of women so dangerous, so devastating. It is really out of scheme, it is not in relation to the rest of things. So we have the tragedy of cocksure women. They find, so often, that instead of having laid an egg, they have laid a vote, or an empty ink-bottle, or some other absolutely unhatchable object, which means nothing to them.

It is the tragedy of the modern woman. She becomes cocksure, she puts all her passion and energy and years of her life into some effort or assertion, without ever listening for the denial which she ought to take into count. She is cocksure, but she is a hen all the time. Frightened of her own henny self, she rushes to mad lengths about votes, or welfare, or sports, or business: she is marvellous, out-manning the man. But alas, it is all fundamentally disconnected. It is all an attitude, and one day the attitude will become a weird cramp, a pain, and then it will collapse. And when it has collapsed, and she looks at the eggs she has laid, votes, or miles of typewriting, years of business efficiency—suddenly, because she is a hen and not a cock, all she has done will turn into pure nothingness to her. Suddenly it all falls out of relation to her basic henny self, and she realizes she has lost her life. The lovely henny surety, the hensureness which is the real bliss of every female, has been denied her: she had never had it. Having lived her life with such utmost strenuousness and cocksureness, she has missed her life altogether. Nothingness!

CONSIDERATIONS

Thinking

What is the effect of Lawrence's couching his views about modern women in an animal fable? Does Lawrence's description of the barnyard seem accurate? To what extent is his analogy accurate? Why?

Do you agree with Lawrence's contention that each sex has its own gender-specific type of certainty—what Lawrence calls "cocksureness" and "hensureness"? Do you agree with what Lawrence sees as the hen's problem in trying to attain cocksureness instead of hensureness? Explain.

Connecting

To what extent does Lawrence's barnyard analogy for relations between the sexes hold for the men and women of today? To what extent have cultural attitudes regarding women changed since this essay was written (1929)?

Compare Lawrence's characterization of the relation between the sexes with that of Katherine Anne Porter in "The Necessary Enemy."

Writing

Write an essay supporting, refuting, or qualifying Lawrence's views as expressed in "Cocksure Women and Hensure Men." Be sure to cite specific passages from Lawrence's essay in yours.

Write an animal fable or an essay that includes an animal fable to reveal a perspective on modern men.

B*arry Lopez*
(b.1945)

B arry Lopez—born in New York, raised in southern California, educated at the University of Notre Dame—has taught at the University of Iowa and at Carlton College and served as an editor at *Harper's* and *The North American Review.* Lopez is best known as a writer whose passionate commitment to history and preservation has brought him into touch with knowledge often hidden from those who fail to see how our ideas and our perceptions are gifts bestowed on us by a world that reveals its secrets only when we have the patience, interest, and experience to discern them. His books include *Of Wolves and Men, Artic Dreams, Crossing Open Ground, Coyote Love,* and *The Rediscovery of North America.* He has received the John Burroughs Medal and an award in literature from the American Academy and Institute of Arts and Letters.

"The Stone Horse" recounts a moment of awareness, when Lopez was able to feel intensely and then reflect on his own (our own) connection with a past that is in danger of slipping away from us; he was moved by a stone horse.

The Stone Horse

I

The deserts of southern California, the high, relatively cooler and wetter Mojave and the hotter, dryer Sonoran to the south of it, carry the signatures of many cultures. Prehistoric rock drawings in the Mojave's Coso Range, probably the greatest concentration of petroglyphs in North America, are at least three thousand years old. Big-game-hunting cultures that flourished six or seven thousand years before that are known from broken spear tips, choppers, and burins left scattered along the shores of great Pleistocene lakes, long since evaporated. Weapons and tools discovered at China Lake may be thirty thousand years old; and worked stone from a quarry in the Calico Mountains is, some argue, evidence that human beings were here more than 200,000 years ago.

Because of the long-term stability of such arid environments, much of this prehistoric stone evidence still lies exposed on the ground, accessible to anyone who passes by—the studious, the acquisitive, the indifferent, the merely curious. Archaeologists do not agree on the sequence of cultural history beyond about twelve thousand years ago, but it is clear that these broken bits of chalcedony, chert, and obsidian, like the animal drawings and geometric designs etched on walls of basalt throughout the desert, anchor the earliest threads of human history, the first record of human endeavor here.

Western man did not enter the California desert until the end of the eighteenth century, 250 years after Coronado brought his soldiers into the Zuni pueblos in a bewildered search for the cities of Cibola. The earliest appraisals of the land were cursory, hurried. People traveled *through* it, en route to Santa Fe or the California coastal settlements. Only miners tarried. In 1823 what had been Spain's became Mexico's, and in 1848 what had been Mexico's became America's; but the bare, jagged mountains and dry lake beds, the vast and uniform plains of creosote bush and yucca plants, remained as obscure as the northern Sudan until the end of the nineteenth century.

Before 1940 the tangible evidence of twentieth-century man's passage here consisted of very little—the hard tracery of travel corridors; the widely scattered, relatively insignificant evidence of mining operations; and the fair expanse of irrigated fields at the desert's periphery. In the space of a hundred years or so the wagon roads were paved, railroads were laid down, and canals and high-tension lines were built to bring water and electricity across the desert to Los Angeles from the Colorado River. The dark mouths of gold, talc, and tin mines yawned from the bony flanks of desert ranges. Dust-encrusted chemical plants stood at work on the lonely edges of dry lake beds. And crops of grapes, lettuce, dates, alfalfa, and cotton covered the Coachella and Imperial valleys, north and south of the Salton Sea, and the Palo Verde Valley along the Colorado.

These developments proceeded with little or no awareness of earlier human occupations by cultures that preceded those of the historic Indians—the Mohave, the Chemehuevi, the Quechan. (Extensive irrigation began actually to change the climate of the Sonoran Desert, and human settlements, the railroads, and farming introduced many new, successful plants into the region.)

During World War II, the American military moved into the desert in great force, to train troops and to test equipment. They found the clear weather conducive to year-round flying, the dry air and isolation very attractive. After the war, a complex of training grounds, storage facilities, and gunnery and test ranges was permanently settled on more than three million acres of military reservations. Few perceived the extent or significance of the destruction of the aboriginal sites that took place during tank maneuvers and bombing runs or in the laying out of highways, railroads, mining districts, and irrigated fields. The few who intuited that something like an American Dordogne Valley lay exposed here were (only) amateur archaeologists; even they reasoned that the desert was too vast for any of this to matter.

After World War II, people began moving out of the crowded Los Angeles basin into homes in Lucerne, Apple, and Antelope valleys in the western Mojave. They emigrated as well to a stretch of resort land at the foot of the San Jacinto Mountains that included Palm Springs, and farther out to old railroad and military towns like Twentynine Palms and Barstow. People also began exploring the desert, at first in military-surplus jeeps and then with a variety of all-terrain and off-road vehicles that became available in the 1960s. By the mid-1970s, the number of people using such vehicles for desert recreation had increased exponentially. Most came and went in innocent curiosity; the few who didn't wreaked a havoc all out of proportion to their numbers. The disturbance of previously isolated archaeological sites increased by an order of magnitude. Many sites were vandalized before archaeologists, themselves late to the desert, had any firm grasp of the bounds of human history in the desert. It was as though in the same moment an Aztec library had been discovered intact various lacunae had begun to appear.

The vandalism was of three sorts: the general disturbance usually caused by souvenir hunters and by the curious and the oblivious; the wholesale stripping of a place by professional thieves for black-market sale and trade; and outright destruction, in which vehicles were actually used to ram and trench an area. By 1980, the Bureau of Land Management estimated that probably 35 percent of the archaeological sites in the desert had been vandalized. The destruction at some places by rifles and shotguns, or by power winches mounted on vehicles, was, if one cared for history, demoralizing to behold.

In spite of public education, land closures, and stricter law enforcement in recent years, the BLM estimates that, annually, about 1 percent of the archaeological record in the desert continues to be destroyed or stolen.

II

A BLM archaeologist told me, with understandable reluctance, where to find the intaglio. I spread my Automobile Club of Southern California map of Imperial County out on his desk, and he traced the route with a pink felt-tip pen. The line crossed Interstate 8 and then turned west along the Mexican border.

"You can't drive any farther than about here," he said, marking a small X. "There's boulders in the wash. You walk up past them."

On a separate piece of paper he drew a route in a smaller scale that would take me up the arroyo to a certain point where I was to cross back east, to another arroyo. At its head, on higher ground just to the north, I would find the horse.

"It's tough to spot unless you know it's there. Once you pick it up . . ." He shook his head slowly, in a gesture of wonder at its existence.

I waited until I held his eye. I assured him I would not tell anyone else how to get there. He looked at me with stoical despair, like a man who had been robbed twice, whose belief in human beings was offered without conviction.

I did not go until the following day because I wanted to see it at dawn. I ate breakfast at four A.M. in El Centro and then drove south. The route was easy to follow, though the last section of road proved difficult, broken and drifted over with sand in some spots. I came to the barricade of boulders and parked. It was light enough by then to find my way over the ground with little trouble. The contours of the landscape were stark, without any masking vegetation. I worried only about rattlesnakes.

I traversed the stone plain as directed, but, in spite of the frankness of the land, I came on the horse unawares. In the first moment of recognition I was without feeling. I recalled later being startled, and that I held my breath. It was laid out on the ground with its head to the east, three times life size. As I took in its outline I felt a growing concentration of all my senses, as though my attentiveness to the pale rose color of the morning sky and other peripheral images had now ceased to be important. I was aware that I was straining for sound in the windless air, and I felt the uneven pressure of the earth hard against my feet. The horse, outlined in a standing profile on the dark ground, was as vivid before me as a bed of tulips.

I've come upon animals suddenly before, and felt a similar tension, a precipitate heightening of the senses. And I have felt the inexplicable but sharply boosted intensity of a wild moment in the bush, where it is not until some minutes later that you discover the source of electricity—the warm remains of a grizzly bear kill, or the still moist tracks of a wolverine.

But this was slightly different. I felt I had stepped into an unoccupied corridor. I had no familiar sense of history, the temporal structure in which to think: This horse was made by Quechan people three hundred years ago. I felt instead a headlong rush of images: people hunting wild horses with spears on the Pleistocene veld of southern California; Cortés riding across the causeway into Montezuma's Tenochtitlán; a short-legged Comanche, astride his horse like some sort of ferret, slashing through cavalry lines of young men who rode like farmers; a hood exploding past my face one morning in a corral in Wyoming. These images had the weight and silence of stone.

When I released my breath, the images softened. My initial feeling, of facing a wild animal in a remote region, was replaced with a calm sense of antiquity. It was then that I became conscious, like an ordinary tourist, of what was before me, and thought: this horse was probably laid out by Quechan people. But when? I wondered. The first horses they saw, I knew, might have been those that came north from Mexico in 1692 with Father Eusebio Kino. But Cocopa people, I recalled, also came this far north on occasion, to fight with their neighbors, the Quechan. And they could have seen horses with Melchior Díaz, at the mouth of the Colorado

River in the fall of 1540. So, it could be four hundred years old. (No one in fact knows.)

I still had not moved. I took my eyes off the horse for a moment to look south over the desert plain into Mexico, to look east past its head at the brightening sunrise, to situate myself. Then, finally, I brought my trailing foot slowly forward and stood erect. Sunlight was running like a thin sheet of water over the stony ground and it threw the horse into relief. It looked as though no hand had ever disturbed the stones that gave it its form.

The horse had been brought to life on ground called desert pavement, a tight, flat matrix of small cobbles blasted smooth by sand-laden winds. The uniform, monochromatic blackness of the stones, a patina of iron and magnesium oxides called desert varnish, is caused by long-term exposure to the sun. To make this type of low-relief ground glyph, or intaglio, the artist either selectively turns individual stones over to their lighter side or removes areas of stone to expose the lighter soil underneath, creating a negative image. This horse, about eighteen feet from brow to rump and eight feet from withers to hoof, had been made in the latter way, and its outline was bermed at certain points with low ridges of stone a few inches high to enhance its three-dimensional qualities. (The left side of the horse was in full profile; each leg was extended at 90 degrees to the body and fully visible, as though seen in three-quarter profile.)

I was not eager to move. The moment I did I would be back in the flow of time, the horse no longer quivering in the same way before me. I did not want to feel again the sequence of quotidian events—to be drawn off into deliberation and analysis. A human being, a four-footed animal, the open land. That was all that was present—and a "thoughtless" understanding of the very old desires bearing on this particular animal: to hunt it, to render it, to fathom it, to subjugate it, to honor it, to take it as a companion.

What finally made me move was the light. The sun now filled the shallow basin of the horse's body. The weighted line of the stone berm created the illusion of a mane and the distinctive roundness of an equine belly. The change in definition impelled me. I moved to the left, circling past its rump, to see how the light might flesh the horse out from various points of view. I circled it completely before squatting on my haunches. Ten or fifteen minutes later I chose another view. The third time I moved, to a point near the rear hooves, I spotted a stone tool at my feet. I stared at it a long while, more in awe than disbelief, before reaching out to pick it up. I turned it over in my left palm and took it between my fingers to feel its cutting edge. It is always difficult, especially with something so portable, to rechannel the desire to steal.

I spent several hours with the horse. As I changed positions and as the angle of the light continued to change I noticed a number of things. The angle at which the pastern carried the hoof away from the ankle was perfect. Also, stones had been placed within the image to suggest at precisely the right spot the left shoulder above the foreleg. The line that joined thigh and hock was similarly accurate. The muzzle alone seemed distorted—but perhaps these stones had been moved by a later hand. It was an admirably accurate representation, but not what a breeder would call perfect conformation. There was the suggestion of a bowed neck and an undershot jaw, and the tail, as full as a winter coyote's, did not appear to be precisely to scale.

The more I thought about it, the more I felt I was looking at an individual horse, a unique combination of generic and specific detail. It was easy to imagine one of Kino's horses as a model, or a horse that ran off from one of Coronado's columns. What kind of horses would these have been? I wondered. In the sixteenth century the most sought-after horses in Europe were Spanish, the offspring of Arabian stock and Barbary horses that the Moors brought to Iberia and bred to the older, eastern European strains brought in by the Romans. The model for this horse, I speculated, could easily have been a palomino, or a descendant of horses trained for lion hunting in North Africa.

A few generations ago, cowboys, cavalry quartermasters, and draymen would have taken this horse before me under consideration and not let up their scrutiny until they had its heritage fixed to their satisfaction. Today, the distinction between draft and harness horses is arcane knowledge, and no image may come to mind for a blue roan or a claybank horse. The loss of such refinement in everyday conversation leaves me unsettled. People praise the Eskimo's ability to distinguish among forty types of snow but forget the skill of others who routinely differentiate between overo and tobiano pintos. Such distinctions are made for the same reason. You have to do it to be able to talk clearly about the world.

For parts of two years I worked as a horse wrangler and packer in Wyoming. It is dim knowledge now; I would have to think to remember if a buckskin was a kind of dun horse. And I couldn't throw a double-diamond hitch over a set of panniers—the packer's basic tie-down—without guidance. As I squatted there in the desert, however, these more personal memories seemed tenuous in comparison with the sweep of this animal in human time. My memories had no depth. I thought of the Hittite cavalry riding against the Syrians 3,500 years ago. And the first of the Chinese emperors, Ch'in Shih Huang, buried in Shensi Province in 210 B.C. with thousands of life-size horses and soldiers, a terra-cotta guardian army. What could I know of what was in the mind of whoever made this horse? Was there some racial memory of it as an animal that had once fed the artist's ancestors and then disappeared from North America? And then returned in this strange alliance with another race of men?

Certainly, whoever it was, the artist had observed the animal very closely. Certainly the animal's speed had impressed him. Among the first things the Quechan would have learned from an encounter with Kino's horses was that their own long-distance runners—men who could run down mule deer—were no match for this animal.

From where I squatted I could look far out over the Mexican plain. Juan Bautista de Anza passed this way in 1774, extending El Camino Real into Alta California from Sinaloa. He was followed by others, all of them astride the magical horse; *gente de razón,* the people of reason, coming into the country of *los primitivos.* The horse, like the stone animals of Egypt, urged these memories upon me. And as I drew them up from some forgotten corner of my mind—huge horses carved in the white chalk downs of southern England by an Iron Age people; Spanish horses rearing and wheeling in fear before alligators in Florida—the images seemed tethered before me. With this sense of proportion, a memory of my own—the morning I almost lost my face to a horse's hoof—now had somewhere to fit.

I rose up and began to walk slowly around the horse again. I had taken the first long measure of it and was now looking for a way to depart, a new angle of light, a fading of the image itself before the rising sun, that would break its hold on me. As I circled, feeling both heady and serene at the encounter, I realized again how strangely vivid it was. It had been created on a barren bajada between two arroyos, as nondescript a place as one could imagine. The only plant life here was a few wands of ocotillo cactus. The ground beneath my shoes was so hard it wouldn't take the print of a heavy animal even after a rain. The only sounds I heard here were the voices of quail.

The archaeologist had been correct. For all its forcefulness, the horse is inconspicuous. If you don't care to see it you can walk right past it. That pleases him, I think. Unmarked on the bleak shoulder of the plain, the site signals to no one; so he wants no protective fences here, no informative plaque, to act as beacons. He would rather take a chance that no motorcyclist, no aimless wanderer with a flair for violence and a depth of ignorance, will ever find his way here.

The archaeologist had given me something before I left his office that now seemed peculiar—an aerial photograph of the horse. It is widely believed that an aerial view of an intaglio provides a fair and accurate depiction. It does not. In the photograph the horse looks somewhat crudely constructed; from the ground it appears far more deftly rendered. The photograph is of a single moment, and in that split second the horse seems vaguely impotent. I watched light pool in the intaglio at dawn; I imagine you could watch it withdraw at dusk and sense the same animation I did. In those prolonged moments its shape and so, too, its general character changed—noticeably. The living quality of the image, its immediacy to the eye, was brought out by the light-in-time, not, at least here, in the camera's frozen instant.

Intaglios, I thought, were never meant to be seen by gods in the sky above. They were meant to be seen by people on the ground, over a long period of shifting light. This could even be true of the huge figures on the Plain of Nazca in Peru, where people could walk for the length of a day beside them. It is our own impatience that leads us to think otherwise.

This process of abstraction, almost unintentional, drew me gradually away from the horse. I came to a position of attention at the edge of the sphere of its influence. With a slight bow I paid my respects to the horse, its maker, and the history of us all, and departed.

III

A short distance away I stopped the car in the middle of the road to make a few notes. I could not write down what I was thinking when I was with the horse. It would have seemed disrespectful, and it would have required another kind of attention. So now I patiently drained my memory of the details it had fastened itself upon. The road I'd stopped on was adjacent to the All American Canal, the major source of water for the Imperial and Coachella valleys. The water flowed west placidly. A disjointed flock of coots, small, dark birds with white bills, was paddling against the current, foraging in the rushes.

I was peripherally aware of the birds as I wrote, the only movement in the desert, and of a series of sounds from a village a half-mile away. The first sounds from this collection of ramshackle houses in a grove of cottonwoods were the distracted dawn voices of dogs. I heard them intermingled with the cries of a rooster. Later, the high-pitched voices of children calling out to each other came disembodied through the dry desert air. Now, a little after seven, I could hear someone practicing on the trumpet, the same rough phrases played over and over. I suddenly remembered how as children we had tried to get the rhythm of a galloping horse with hands against our thighs, or by fluttering our tongues against the roofs of our mouths.

After the trumpet, the impatient calls of adults summoning children. Sunday morning. Wood smoke hung like a lens in the trees. The first car starts—a cold eight-cylinder engine, of Chrysler extraction perhaps, goosed to life, then throttled back to murmur through dual mufflers, the obbligato music of a shade-tree mechanic. The rote bark of mongrel dogs at dawn, the jagged outcries of men and women, an engine coming to life. Like a thousand villages from West Virginia to Guadalajara.

I finished my notes—where was I going to find a description of the horses that came north with the conquistadors? Did their manes come forward prominently over the brow, like this one's, like the forelocks of Blackfeet and Assiniboin men in nineteenth-century paintings? I set the notes on the seat beside me.

The road followed the canal for a while and then arced north, toward Interstate 8. It was slow driving and I fell to thinking how the desert had changed since Anza had come through. New plants and animals—the MacDougall cottonwood, the English house sparrow, the chukar from India—have about them now the air of the native born. Of the native species, some—no one knows how many—are extinct. The populations of many others, especially the animals, have been sharply reduced. The idea of a desert impoverished by agricultural poisons and varmint hunters, by off-road vehicles and military operations, did not seem as disturbing to me, however, as this other horror, now that I had been those hours with the horse. The vandals, the few who crowbar rock art off the desert's walls, who dig up graves, who punish the ground that holds intaglios, are people who devour history. Their self-centered scorn, their disrespect for ideas and images beyond their ken, create the awful atmosphere of loose ends in which totalitarianism thrives, in which the past is merely curious or wrong.

I thought about the horse sitting out there on the unprotected plain. I enumerated its qualities in my mind until a sense of its vulnerability receded and it became an anchor for something else. I remembered that history, a history like this one, which ran deeper than Mexico, deeper than the Spanish, was a kind of medicine. It permitted the great breadth of human expression to reverberate, and it did not urge you to locate its apotheosis in the present.

Each of us, individuals and civilizations, has been held upside down like Achilles in the River Styx. The artist mixing his colors in the dim light of Altamira; an Egyptian ruler lying still now, wrapped in his byssus, stored against time in a pyramid; the faded Dorset culture of the Arctic; the Hmong and Samburu and Walbiri of historic time; the modern nations. This great, imperfect stretch of human expression is the clarification and encouragement, the urging and the reminder, we call history. And it is inscribed everywhere in the face of the land, from the mountain passes of the Himalayas to a nameless bajada in the California desert.

Small birds rose up in the road ahead, startled, and flew off. I prayed no infidel would ever find that horse.

CONSIDERATIONS

Thinking

How does the horse serve as a "kind of medicine" for Lopez? How can it be medicinal for the rest of us? What is our illness?

What is an intaglio? Does Lopez manage to convince you that a photograph of an intaglio might not be good enough to give you a sense of the thing itself?

Connecting

Read the entire essay a second time, looking for what Lopez reveals about the nature and the power of images. Codify it.

How can Loren Eiseley's "The Dance of the Frogs" help you understand the relationship between Lopez and that image of the horse, or should we say, between Lopez and the horse?

Writing

Write a two- or three-page analysis of the way in which the three parts of the essay—the historical section, the actual encounter with the horse, and the reflective aftermath—work together to reveal Lopez's central idea.

In "The Achievement of Desire" Richard Rodriguez frets over the connection between reading and learning. Write Rodriguez a letter explaining how Lopez "reads" the horse, how he first pushes reflections out of the way as he stands in the presence of the horse and then, later, brings historical knowledge to bear on what he has experienced.

N ancy Mairs
(b.1943)

N ancy Mairs is a teacher, essayist, and prize-winning poet who has also worked as a technical editor at the Smithsonian Astrophysical Observatory, the MIT Press, and the Harvard Law School. Her books include *Plaintext, Carnal Acts, Remembering the Bone House* (autobiography), and *All the Rooms of the Yellow House* (poems).

In "On Being a Cripple," Mairs describes her struggle with multiple sclerosis. She raises important questions about what those with disabling diseases wish to call themselves and what they wish others to describe them. One especially striking feature of this remarkable essay is its honesty, particularly in its concern with using language that accurately characterizes Mairs's physical condition.

On Being a Cripple

To escape is nothing. Not to escape is nothing.

Louise Bogan

The other day I was thinking of writing an essay on being a cripple. I was thinking hard in one of the stalls of the women's room in my office building, as I was shoving my shirt into my jeans and tugging up my zipper. Preoccupied, I flushed, picked up my book bag, took my cane down from the hook, and unlatched the door. So many movements unbalanced me, and as I pulled the door open I fell over backward, landing fully clothed on the toilet seat with my legs splayed in front of me: the old beetle-on-its-back routine. Saturday afternoon, the building deserted, I was free to laugh aloud as I wriggled back to my feet, my voice bouncing off the yellowish tiles from all directions. Had anyone been there with me, I'd have been still and faint and hot with chagrin. I decided that it was high time to write the essay.

First, the matter of semantics. I am a cripple. I choose this word to name me. I choose from among several possibilities, the most common of which are "handicapped" and "disabled." I made the choice a number of years ago, without thinking, unaware of my motives for doing so. Even now, I'm not sure what those motives are, but I recognize that they are complex and not entirely flattering. People—crippled or not—wince at the word "cripple," as they do not at "handicapped" or "disabled." Perhaps I want them to wince. I want them to see me as a tough customer, one to whom the fates/gods/viruses have not been kind, but who can face the brutal truth of her existence squarely. As a cripple, I swagger.

But, to be fair to myself, a certain amount of honesty underlies my choice. "Cripple" seems to me a clean word, straightforward and precise. It has an honorable history, having made its first appearance in the Lindisfarne Gospel in the tenth century. As a lover of words, I like the accuracy with which it describes my condition: I have lost the full use of my limbs. "Disabled," by contrast, suggests any incapacity, physical or mental. And I certainly don't like "handicapped," which implies that I have deliberately been put at a disadvantage, by whom I can't imagine (my God is

not a Handicapper General), in order to equalize chances in the great race
of life. These words seem to me to be moving away from my condition, to
be widening the gap between word and reality. Most remote is the recently
coined euphemism "differently abled," which partakes of the same semantic hopefulness that transformed countries from "undeveloped" to "under-
developed," then to "less developed," and finally to "developing" nations.
People have continued to starve in those countries during the shift. Some
realities do not obey the dictates of language.

Mine is one of them. Whatever you call me, I remain crippled. But I
don't care what you call me, so long as it isn't "differently abled," which
strikes me as pure verbal garbage designed, by its ability to describe anyone, to describe no one. I subscribe to George Orwell's thesis that "the
slovenliness of our language makes it easier for us to have foolish
thoughts." And I refuse to participate in the degeneration of the language
to the extent that I deny that I have lost anything in the course of this
calamitous disease; I refuse to pretend that the only differences between
you and me are the various ordinary ones that distinguish any one person
from another. But call me "disabled" or "handicapped" if you like. I have
long since grown accustomed to them; and if they are vague, at least they
hint at the truth. Moreover, I use them myself. Society is no readier to
accept crippledness than to accept death, war, sex, sweat, or wrinkles. I
would never refer to another person as a cripple. It is the word I use to
name only myself.

I haven't always been crippled, a fact for which I am soundly grateful. To be whole of limb is, I know from experience, infinitely more
pleasant and useful than to be crippled; and if that knowledge leaves me
open to bitterness at my loss, the physical soundness I once enjoyed
(though I did not enjoy it half enough) is well worth the occasional stab
of regret. Though never any good at sports, I was a normally active child
and young adult. I climbed trees, played hopscotch, jumped rope,
skated, swam, rode my bicycle, sailed. I despised team sports, spending
some of the wretchedest afternoons of my life, sweaty and humiliated,
behind a field-hockey stick and under a basketball hoop. I tramped
alone for miles along the bridle paths that webbed the woods behind the
house I grew up in. I swayed through countless dim hours in the arms
of one man or another under the scattered shot of light from mirrored
balls, and gyrated through countless more as Tab Hunter and Johnny
Mathis gave way to the Rolling Stones, Creedence Clearwater Revival,
Cream. I walked down the aisle. I pushed baby carriages, changed tires
in the rain, marched for peace.

When I was twenty-eight I started to trip and drop things. What at first seemed my natural clumsiness soon became too pronounced to shrug off. I consulted a neurologist, who told me that I had a brain tumor. A battery of tests, increasingly disagreeable, revealed no tumor. About a year and a half later I developed a blurred spot in one eye. I had, at last, the episodes "disseminated in space and time" requisite for a diagnosis: multiple sclerosis. I have never been sorry for the doctor's initial misdiagnosis, however. For almost a week, until the negative results of the tests were in, I thought that I was going to die right away. Every day for the past nearly ten years, then, has been a kind of gift. I accept all gifts.

Multiple sclerosis is a chronic degenerative disease of the central nervous system, in which the myelin that sheathes the nerves is somehow eaten away and scar tissue forms in its place, interrupting the nerves' signals. During its course, which is unpredictable and uncontrollable, one may lose vision, hearing, speech, the ability to walk, control of bladder and/or bowels, strength in any or all extremities, sensitivity to touch, vibration, and/or pain, potency, coordination of movements—the list of possibilities is lengthy and, yes, horrifying. One may also lose one's sense of humor. That's the easiest to lose and the hardest to survive without.

In the past ten years, I have sustained some of these losses. Characteristic of MS are sudden attacks, called exacerbations, followed by remissions, and these I have not had. Instead, my disease has been slowly progressive. My left leg is now so weak that I walk with the aid of a brace and a cane; and for distances I use an Amigo, a variation on the electric wheelchair that looks rather like an electrified kiddie car. I no longer have much use of my left hand. Now my right side is weakening as well. I still have the blurred spot in my right eye. Overall, though, I've been lucky so far. My world has, of necessity, been circumscribed by my losses, but the terrain left me has been ample enough for me to continue many of the activities that absorb me: writing, teaching, raising children and cats and plants and snakes, reading, speaking publicly about MS and depression, even playing bridge with people patient and honorable enough to let me scatter cards every which way without sneaking a peek.

Lest I begin to sound like Pollyanna, however, let me say that I don't like having MS. I hate it. My life holds realities—harsh ones, some of them—that no right-minded human being ought to accept without grumbling. One of them is fatigue. I know of no one with MS who does not complain of bone-weariness; in a disease that presents an astonishing variety of symptoms, fatigue seems to be a common factor. I wake up in the morning feeling the way most people do at the end of a bad day, and

I take it from there. As a result, I spend a lot of time *in extremis* and, impatient with limitation, I tend to ignore my fatigue until my body breaks down in some way and forces rest. Then I miss picnics, dinner parties, poetry readings, the brief visits of old friends from out of town. The offspring of a puritanical tradition of exceptional venerability, I cannot view these lapses without shame. My life often seems a series of small failures to do as I ought.

I lead, on the whole, an ordinary life, probably rather like the one I would have led had I not had MS. I am lucky that my predilections were already solitary, sedentary, and bookish—unlike the world-famous French cellist I have read about, or the young woman I talked with one long afternoon who wanted only to be a jockey. I had just begun graduate school when I found out something was wrong with me, and I have remained, interminably, a graduate student. Perhaps I would not have if I'd thought I had the stamina to return to a full-time job as a technical editor; but I've enjoyed my studies.

In addition to studying, I teach writing courses. I also teach medical students how to give neurological examinations. I pick up freelance editing jobs here and there. I have raised a foster son and sent him into the world, where he has made me two grandbabies, and I am still escorting my daughter and son through adolescence. I go to Mass every Saturday. I am a superb, if messy, cook. I am also an enthusiastic laundress, capable of sorting a hamper full of clothes into five subtly differentiated piles, but a terrible housekeeper. I can do italic writing and, in an emergency, bathe an oil-soaked cat. I play a fiendish game of Scrabble. When I have the time and the money, I like to sit on my front steps with my husband, drinking Amaretto and smoking a cigar, as we imagine our counterparts in Leningrad and make sure that the sun gets down once more behind the sharp childish scrawl of the Tucson Mountains.

This lively plenty has its bleak complement, of course, in all the things I can no longer do. I will never run again, except in dreams, and one day I may have to write that I will never walk again. I like to go camping, but I can't follow George and the children along the trails that wander out of a campsite through the desert or into the mountains. In fact, even on the level I've learned never to check the weather or try to hold a coherent conversation: I need all my attention for my wayward feet. Of late, I have begun to catch myself wondering how people can propel themselves without canes. With only one usable hand, I have to select my clothing with care not so much for style as for ease of ingress and egress, and even so, dressing can be laborious. I can no longer do fine stitchery, pick up babies, play the piano, braid my hair. I am immobilized by acute attacks of depression, which may or may not be physiologically related to MS but are certainly its logical concomitant.

These two elements, the plenty and the privation, are never pure, nor are the delight and wretchedness that accompany them. Almost every pickle that I get into as a result of my weakness and clumsiness—and I get into plenty—is funny as well as maddening and sometimes painful. I recall one May afternoon when a friend and I were going out for a drink after finishing up at school. As we were climbing into opposite sides of my car, chatting, I tripped and fell, flat and hard, onto the asphalt parking lot, my abrupt departure interrupting him in mid-sentence. "Where'd you go?" he called as he came around the back of the car to find me hauling myself up by the door frame. "Are you all right?" Yes, I told him, I was fine, just a bit rattly, and we drove off to find a shady patio and some beer. When I got home an hour or so later, my daughter greeted me with "What have you done to yourself?" I looked down. One elbow of my white turtleneck with the green froggies, one knee of my white trousers, one white kneesock were blood-soaked. We peeled off the clothes and inspected the damage, which was nasty enough but not alarming. That part wasn't funny: The abrasions took a long time to heal, and one got a little infected. Even so, when I think of my friend talking earnestly, suddenly, to the hot thin air while I dropped from his view as though through a trap door, I find the image as silly as something from a Marx Brothers movie.

I may find it easier than other cripples to amuse myself because I live propped by the acceptance and the assistance and, sometimes, the amusement of those around me. Grocery clerks tear my checks out of my checkbook for me, and sales clerks find chairs to put into dressing rooms when I want to try on clothes. The people I work with make sure I teach at times when I am least likely to be fatigued, in places I can get to, with the materials I need. My students, with one anonymous exception (in an end-of-the-semester evaluation), have been unperturbed by my disability. Some even like it. One was immensely cheered by the information that I paint my own fingernails; she decided, she told me, that if I could go to such trouble over fine details, she could keep on writing essays. I suppose I became some sort of bright-fingered muse. She wrote good essays, too.

The most important struts in the framework of my existence, of course, are my husband and children. Dismayingly few marriages survive the MS test, and why should they? Most twenty-two- and nineteen-year-olds, like George and me, can vow in clear conscience, after a childhood of chickenpox and summer colds, to keep one another in sickness and in health so long as they both shall live. Not many are equipped for catastrophe: the dismay, the depression, the extra work, the boredom that a degenerative disease can insinuate into a relationship. And our society, with its emphasis on fun and its association of fun with physical performance, offers little encouragement for a whole spouse to stay with a crippled partner. Children experience similar stresses when faced with a crippled parent, and they are more helpless, since parents and children can't usually get divorced. They hate, of course, to be different from their peers, and the child whose mother is tacking down the aisle of a school auditorium packed with proud parents like a Cape Cod dinghy in a stiff breeze jolly well stands out in a crowd. Deprived of legal divorce, the child can at least deny the mother's disability, even her existence, forgetting to tell her about recitals and PTA meetings, refusing to accompany her to stores or church or the movies, never inviting friends to the house. Many do.

But I've been limping along for ten years now, and so far George and the children are still at my left elbow, holding tight. Anne and Matthew vacuum floors and dust furniture and haul trash and rake up dog droppings and button my cuffs and bake lasagne and Toll House cookies with just enough grumbling so I know that they don't have brain fever. And far from hiding me, they're forever dragging me by racks of fancy clothes or through teeming school corridors, or welcoming gaggles of friends while I'm wandering through the house in Anne's filmy pink babydoll pajamas. George generally calls before he brings someone home, but he does just as many dumb thankless chores as the children. And they all yell at me, laugh at some of my jokes, write me funny letters when we're apart—in short, treat me as an ordinary human being for whom they have some use. I think they like me. Unless they're faking. . . .

Faking. There's the rub. Tugging at the fringes of my consciousness always is the terror that people are kind to me only because I'm a cripple. My mother almost shattered me once, with that instinct mothers have— blind, I think, in this case, but unerring nonetheless—for striking blows along the fault-lines of their children's hearts, by telling me, in an attack on my selfishness, "We all have to make allowances for you, of course, because of the way you are." From the distance of a couple of years, I have to admit that I haven't any idea just what she meant, and I'm not sure that she knew either. She was awfully angry. But at the time, as the words thudded home, I felt my worst fear, suddenly realized. I could bear being called selfish: I am. But I couldn't bear the corroboration that those around me were doing in fact what I'd always suspected them of doing, professing fondness while silently putting up with me because of the way I am. A cripple. I've been a little cracked ever since.

Along with this fear that people are secretly accepting shoddy goods comes a relentless pressure to please—to prove myself worth the burdens I impose, I guess, or to build a substantial account of goodwill against which I may write drafts in times of need. Part of the pressure arises from social expectations. In our society, anyone who deviates from the norm had better find some way to compensate. Like fat people, who are expected to be jolly, cripples must bear their lot meekly and cheerfully. A grumpy cripple isn't playing by the rules. And much of the pressure is self-generated. Early on I vowed that, if I had to have MS, by God I was going to do it well. This is a class act, ladies and gentlemen. No tears, no recriminations, no faint-heartedness.

One way and another, then, I wind up feeling like Tiny Tim, peering over the edge of the table at the Christmas goose, waving my crutch, piping down God's blessing on us all. Only sometimes I don't want to play Tiny Tim. I'd rather be Caliban, a most scurvy monster. Fortunately, at home no one much cares whether I'm a good cripple or a bad cripple as long as I make vichyssoise with fair regularity. One evening several years ago, Anne was reading at the dining-room table while I cooked dinner. As I opened a can of tomatoes, the can slipped in my left hand and juice spattered me and the counter with bloody spots. Fatigued and infuriated, I bellowed, "I'm so sick of being crippled!" Anne glanced at me over the top of her book. "There now," she said, "do you feel better?" "Yes," I said, "yes, I do." She went back to her reading. I felt better. That's about all the attention my scurviness ever gets.

Because I hate being crippled, I sometimes hate myself for being a cripple. Over the years I have come to expect—even accept—attacks of violent self-loathing. Luckily, in general our society no longer connects deformity and disease directly with evil (though a charismatic once told me that I have MS because a devil is in me) and so I'm allowed to move largely at will, even among small children. But I'm not sure that this revision of attitude has been particularly helpful. Physical imperfection, even freed of moral disapprobation, still defies and violates the ideal, especially for women, whose confinement in their bodies as objects of desire is far from over. Each age, of course, has its ideal, and I doubt that ours is any better or worse than any other. Today's ideal woman, who lives on the glossy pages of dozens of magazines, seems to be between the ages of eighteen and twenty-five; her hair has body, her teeth flash white, her breath smells minty, her underarms are dry; she has a career but is still a fabulous cook, especially of meals that take less than twenty minutes to prepare; she does not ordinarily appear to have a husband or children; she is trim and deeply tanned; she jogs, swims, plays tennis, rides a bicycle, sails, but does not bowl; she travels widely, even to out-of-the-way places like Finland and Samoa, always in the company of the ideal man, who possesses a nearly identical set of characteristics. There are a few exceptions. Though usually white and often blonde, she may be black, Hispanic, Asian, or Native American, so long as she is unusually sleek. She may be old, provided she is selling a laxative or is Lauren Bacall. If she is selling a detergent, she may be married and have a flock of strikingly messy children. But she is never a cripple.

Like many women I know, I have always had an uneasy relationship with my body. I was not a popular child, largely, I think now, because I was peculiar: intelligent, intense, moody, shy, given to unexpected actions and inexplicable notions and emotions. But as I entered adolescence, I believed myself unpopular because I was homely: my breasts too flat, my mouth too wide, my hips too narrow, my clothing never quite right in fit or style. I was not, in fact, particularly ugly, old photographs inform me, though I was well off the ideal; but I carried this sense of self-alienation with me into adulthood, where it regenerated in response to the depredations of MS. Even with my brace I walk with a limp so pronounced that, seeing myself on the videotape of a television program on the disabled, I couldn't believe that anything but an inchworm could make progress humping along like that. My shoulders droop and my pelvis thrusts forward as I try to balance myself upright, throwing my frame into a bony S. As a result of contractures, one shoulder is higher than the other and I carry one arm bent in front of me, the fingers curled into a claw. My left arm and leg have wasted into pipe-stems, and I try always to keep them covered. When I think about how my body must look to others, especially to men, to whom I have been trained to display myself, I feel ludicrous, even loathsome.

At my age, however, I don't spend much time thinking about my appearance. The burning egocentricity of adolescence, which assures one that all the world is looking all the time, has passed, thank God, and I'm generally too caught up in what I'm doing to step back, as I used to, and watch myself as though upon a stage. I'm also too old to believe in the accuracy of self-image. I know that I'm not a hideous crone, that in fact, when I'm rested, well dressed, and well made up, I look fine. The self-loathing I feel is neither physically nor intellectually substantial. What I hate is not me but a disease.

I am not a disease.

And a disease is not—at least not singlehandedly—going to determine who I am, though at first it seemed to be going to. Adjusting to a chronic incurable illness, I have moved through a process similar to that outlined by Elizabeth Kübler-Ross in *On Death and Dying*. The major difference—and it is far more significant than most people recognize—is that I can't be sure of the outcome, as the terminally ill cancer patient can. Research studies indicate that, with proper medical care, I may achieve a "normal" life span. And in our society, with its vision of death as the ultimate evil, worse even than decrepitude, the response to such news is, "Oh well, at least you're not going to *die*." Are there worse things than dying? I think that there may be.

I think of two women I know, both with MS, both enough older than I to have served me as models. One took to her bed several years ago and has been there ever since. Although she can sit in a high-backed wheelchair, because she is incontinent she refuses to go out at all, even though incontinence pants, which are readily available at any pharmacy, could protect her from embarrassment. Instead, she stays at home and insists that her husband, a small quiet man, a retired civil servant, stay there with her except for a quick weekly foray to the supermarket. The other woman, whose illness was diagnosed when she was eighteen, a nursing student engaged to a young doctor, finished her training, married her doctor, accompanied him to Germany when he was in the service, bore three sons and a daughter, now grown and gone. When she can, she travels with her husband; she plays bridge, embroiders, swims regularly; she works, like me, as a symptomatic-patient instructor of medical students in neurology. Guess which woman I hope to be.

At the beginning, I thought about having MS almost incessantly. And because of the unpredictable course of the disease, my thoughts were always terrified. Each night I'd get into bed wondering whether I'd get out again the next morning, whether I'd be able to see, to speak, to hold a pen between my fingers. Knowing that the day might come when I'd be physically incapable of killing myself, I thought perhaps I ought to do so right away, while I still had the strength. Gradually I came to understand that the Nancy who might one day lie inert under a bedsheet, arms and legs paralyzed, unable to feed or bathe herself, unable to reach out for a gun, a bottle of pills, was not the Nancy I was at present, and that I could not presume to make decisions for that future Nancy, who might well not want in the least to die. Now the only provision I've made for the future Nancy is that when the time comes—and it is likely to come in the form of pneumonia, friend to the weak and the old—I am not to be treated with machines and medications. If she is unable to communicate by then, I hope she will be satisfied with these terms.

Thinking all the time about having MS grew tiresome and intrusive, especially in the large and tragic mode in which I was accustomed to considering my plight. Months and even years went by without catastrophe (at least without one related to MS), and really I was awfully busy, what with George and children and snakes and students and poems, and I hadn't the time, let alone the inclination, to devote myself to being a disease. Too, the richer my life became, the funnier it seemed, as though there were some connection between largesse and laughter, and so my tragic stance began to waver until, even with the aid of a brace and a cane, I couldn't hold it for very long at a time.

After several years I was satisfied with my adjustment. I had suffered my grief and fury and terror, I thought, but now I was at ease with my lot. Then one summer day I set out with George and the children across the desert for a vacation in California. Part way to Yuma I became aware that my right leg felt funny. "I think I've had an exacerbation," I told George. "What shall we do?" he asked. "I think we'd better get the hell to California," I said, "because I don't know whether I'll ever make it again." So we went on to San Diego and then to Orange, up the Pacific Coast Highway to Santa Cruz, across to Yosemite, down to Sequoia and Joshua Tree, and so back over the desert to home. It was a fine two-week trip, filled with friends and fair weather, and I wouldn't have missed it for the world, though I did in fact make it back to California two years later. Nor would there have been any point in missing it, since in MS, once the symptoms have appeared, the neurological damage has been done, and there's no way to predict or prevent that damage.

The incident spoiled my self-satisfaction, however. It renewed my grief and fury and terror, and I learned that one never finishes adjusting to MS. I don't know now why I thought one would. One does not, after all, finish adjusting to life, and MS is simply a fact of my life—not my favorite fact, of course—but as ordinary as my nose and my tropical fish and my yellow Mazda station wagon. It may at any time get worse, but no amount of worry or anticipation can prepare me for a new loss. My life is a lesson in losses. I learn one at a time.

And I had best be patient in the learning, since I'll have to do it like it or not. As any rock fan knows, you can't always get what you want. Particularly when you have MS. You can't, for example, get cured. In recent years researchers and the organizations that fund research have started to pay MS some attention even though it isn't fatal; perhaps they have begun to see that life is something other than a quantitative phenomenon, that one may be very much alive for a very long time in a life that isn't worth living. The researchers have made some progress toward understanding the mechanism of the disease: It may well be an autoimmune reaction triggered by a slow-acting virus. But they are nowhere near its prevention, control, or cure. And most of us want to be cured. Some, unable to accept incurability, grasp at one treatment after another, no matter how bizarre: megavitamin therapy, gluten-free diet, injections of cobra venom, hypothermal suits, lymphocytopharesis, hyperbaric chambers. Many treatments are probably harmless enough, but none are curative.

The absence of a cure often makes MS patients bitter toward their doctors. Doctors are, after all, the priests of modern society, the new shamans, whose business is to heal, and many an MS patient roves from one to another, searching for the "good" doctor who will make him well. Doctors too think of themselves as healers, and for this reason many have trouble dealing with MS patients, whose disease in its intransigence defeats their aims and mocks their skills. Too few doctors, it is true, treat their patients as whole human beings, but the reverse is also true. I have always tried to be gentle with my doctors, who often have more at stake in terms of ego than I do. I may be frustrated, maddened, depressed by the incurability of my disease, but I am not diminished by it, and they are. When I push myself up from my seat in the waiting room and stumble toward them, I incarnate the limitation of their powers. The least I can do is refuse to press on their tenderest spots.

This gentleness is part of the reason that I'm not sorry to be a cripple. I didn't have it before. Perhaps I'd have developed it anyway—how could I know such a thing?—and I wish I had more of it, but I'm glad of what I have. It has opened and enriched my life enormously, this sense that my frailty and need must be mirrored in others, that in searching for and shaping a stable core in a life wrenched by change and loss, change and loss, I must recognize the same process, under individual conditions, in the lives around me. I do not deprecate such knowledge, however I've come by it.

All the same, if a cure were found, would I take it? In a minute. I may be a cripple, but I'm only occasionally a loony and never a saint. Anyway, in my brand of theology God doesn't give bonus points for a limp. I'd take a cure; I just don't need one. A friend who also has MS startled me once by asking, "Do you ever say to yourself, 'Why me, Lord?'" "No, Michael, I don't," I told him, "because whenever I try, the only response I can think of is 'Why not?'" If I could make a cosmic deal, who would I put in my place? What in my life would I give up in exchange for sound limbs and a thrilling rush of energy? No one. Nothing. I might as well do the job myself. Now that I'm getting the hang of it.

CONSIDERATIONS

Thinking

Why does Mairs insist on referring to herself as a "cripple" rather than as "handicapped" or "disabled"? What is Mairs's objection to newly coined euphemistic terms such as "differently abled"?

What does Mairs mean by saying, "I'd take a cure; I just don't need one"? To what extent are her identity and her image of herself bound up with her disease? What can we learn about Mairs from the metaphors she uses to describe herself as a person with multiple sclerosis?

Connecting

Consider Mairs's discussion of female beauty midway through the essay. Does her description of the ideal of American female beauty seem accurate? How is it related to images of beauty presented in the media?

Compare the image of female beauty presented in Mairs's essay with that presented in Maxine Hong Kingston's "No Name Woman." Compare the way Mairs describes her relation to her multiple sclerosis with the way Alice Walker describes her scarred eye in "Beauty: When the Other Dancer Is the Self."

Writing

Write an essay about your own attempts to come to terms with some kind of imperfection—physical, social, intellectual. Try to account for the extent to which this imperfection and your efforts to deal (or live) with it affect your self-image, your attitudes, or your behavior.

Do some research on multiple sclerosis, and write an essay presenting your findings. Link your research to Mairs's descriptions of her disease.

N. Scott Momaday
(b.1934)

N. Scott Momaday was born in Oklahoma in 1934 and was educated at New Mexico University and at Stanford, where he earned a Ph.D. and now teaches. Momaday won the 1969 Pulitzer Prize for his novel *House Made of Dawn*. He is also the author of a children's book, *Owl in the Cedar Tree,* two volumes of poetry, and an autobiographical memoir, *The Way to Rainy Mountain*. Recent work includes *The Ancient Child* (1989) and *In the Presence of the Sun* (1991).

The essay that follows was published in the popular magazine *National Geographic* in 1976. In it, Momaday describes the sacredness of the land in language that is at once simple and elegant.

A First American Views His Land

First Man
behold:
the earth
glitters
with leaves;
the sky
glistens
with rain.
Pollen
is borne
on winds
that low
and lean
upon
mountains.
Cedars
blacken
the slopes—
and pines.

One hundred centuries ago There is a wide, irregular landscape in what is now northern New Mexico. The sun is a dull white disk, low in the south; it is a perfect mystery, a deity whose coming and going are inexorable. The gray sky is curdled, and it bears very close upon the earth. A cold wind runs along the ground, dips and spins, flaking drift from a pond in the bottom of a ravine. Beyond the wind the silence is acute. A man crouches in the ravine, in the darkness there, scarcely visible. He moves not a muscle; only the wind lifts a lock of his hair and lays it back along his neck. He wears skins and carries a spear. These things in particular mark his human intelligence and distinguish him as the lord of the universe. And for him the universe is especially *this* landscape; for him the landscape is an element like the air. The vast, virgin wilderness is by and large his whole context. For him there is no possibility of existence elsewhere.

Directly there is a blowing, a rumble of breath deeper than the wind, above him, where some of the hard clay of the bank is broken off and the clods roll down into the water. At the same time there appears on the sky-line the massive head of a long-horned bison, then the hump, then the whole beast, huge and black on the sky, standing to a height of seven feet at the hump, with horns that extend six feet across the shaggy crown. For a moment it is poised there; then it lumbers obliquely down the bank to the pond. Still the man does not move, though the beast is now only a few steps upwind. There is no sign of what is about to happen; the beast meanders; the man is frozen in repose.

Then the scene explodes. In one and the same instant the man springs to his feet and bolts forward, his arm cocked and the spear held high, and the huge animal lunges in panic, bellowing, its whole weight thrown violently into the bank, its hooves churning and chipping earth into the air, its eyes gone wide and wild and white. There is a moment in which its awful, frenzied motion is wasted, and it is mired and helpless in its fear, and the man hurls the spear with his whole strength, and the point is driven into the deep, vital flesh, and the bison in its agony staggers and crashes down and dies.

This ancient drama of the hunt is enacted again and again in the landscape. The man is preeminently a predator, the most dangerous of all. He hunts in order to survive; his very existence is simply, squarely established upon that basis. But he hunts also because he can, because he has the means; he has the ultimate weapon of his age, and his prey is plentiful. His relationship to the land has not yet become a moral equation.

But in time he will come to understand that there is an intimate, vital link between the earth and himself, a link that implies an intricate network of rights and responsibilities. In some unimagined future he will understand that he has the ability to devastate and perhaps destroy his environment. That moment will be one of extreme crisis in his evolution.

The weapon is deadly and efficient. The hunter has taken great care in its manufacture, especially in the shaping of the flint point, which is an extraordinary thing. A larger flake has been removed from each face, a groove that extends from the base nearly to the tip. Several hundred pounds of pressure, expertly applied, were required to make these grooves. The hunter then is an artisan, and he must know how to use rudimentary tools. His skill, manifest in the manufacture of this artifact, is unsurpassed for its time and purpose. By means of this weapon is the Paleo-Indian hunter eminently able to exploit his environment.

Thousands of years later, about the time that Columbus begins his first voyage to the New World, another man, in the region of the Great Lakes, stands in the forest shade on the edge of a sunlit brake. In a while a deer enters into the pool of light. Silently the man fits an arrow to a bow, draws aim, and shoots. The arrow zips across the distance and strikes home. The deer leaps and falls dead.

But this latter-day man, unlike his ancient predecessor, is only incidentally a hunter; he is also a fisherman, a husbandman, even a physician. He fells trees and builds canoes; he grows corn, squash, and beans, and he gathers fruits and nuts; he uses hundreds of species of wild plants for food, medicine, teas, and dyes. Instead of one animal, or two or three, he hunts many, none to extinction as the Paleo-Indian may have done. He has fitted himself far more precisely into the patterns of the wilderness than did his ancient predecessor. He lives on the land; he takes his living from it; but he does not destroy it. This distinction supports the fundamental ethic that we call conservation today. In principle, if not yet in name, this man is a conservationist.

These two hunting sketches are far less important in themselves than is that long distance between them, that whole possibility within the dimension of time. I believe that in that interim there grew up in the mind of man an idea of the land as sacred.

> At dawn
> eagles
> lie and
> hover
> above
> the plain
> where light
> gathers
> in pools.
> Grasses
> shimmer
> and shine.
> Shadows
> withdraw
> and lie
> away
> like smoke.

"The earth is our mother. The sky is our father." This concept of nature, which is at the center of the Native American world view, is familiar to us all. But it may well be that we do not understand entirely what the concept is in its ethical and philosophical implications.

I tell my students that the American Indian has a unique investment in the American landscape. It is an investment that represents perhaps thirty thousand years of habitation. That tenure has to be worth something in itself—a great deal, in fact. The Indian has been here a long time; he is at home here. That simple and obvious truth is one of the most important realities of the Indian world, and it is integral in the Indian mind and spirit.

How does such a concept evolve? Where does it begin? Perhaps it begins with the recognition of beauty, the realization that the physical world is beautiful. We don't know much about the ancient hunter's sensibilities. It isn't likely that he had leisure in his life for the elaboration of an aesthetic ideal. And yet the weapon he made was beautiful as well as functional. It has been suggested that much of the minute chipping along the edges of his weapon served no purpose but that of aesthetic satisfaction.

A good deal more is known concerning that man of the central forests. He made beautiful boxes and dishes out of elm and birch bark, for example. His canoes were marvelous, delicate works of art. And this aesthetic perception was a principle of the whole Indian world of his time, as indeed it is of our time. The contemporary Native American is a man whose strong aesthetic perceptions are clearly evident in his arts and crafts, in his religious ceremonies, and in the stories and songs of his rich oral tradition. This, in view of the pressures that have been brought to bear upon the Indian world and the drastic changes that have been effected in its landscape, is a blessing and an irony.

Consider for example the Navajos of the Four Corners area. In recent years an extensive coal-mining operation has mutilated some of their most sacred land. A large power plant in that same region spews a contamination into the sky that is visible for many miles. And yet, as much as any people of whom I have heard, the Navajos perceive and celebrate the beauty of the physical world.

There is a Navajo ceremonial song that celebrates the sounds that are made in the natural world, the particular voices that beautify the earth:

> Voice above,
> Voice of thunder,
> Speak from the
> dark of clouds;
> Voice below,
> Grasshopper voice,
> Speak from the
> green of plants;
> So may the earth
> be beautiful.

There is in the motion and meaning of this song a comprehension of the world that is peculiarly native, I believe, that is integral in the Native American mentality. Consider: The singer stands at the center of the natural world, at the source of its sound, of its motion, of its life. Nothing of that world is inaccessible to him or lost upon him. His song is filled with reverence, with wonder and delight, and with confidence as well. He knows something about himself and about the things around him—and he knows that he knows. I am interested in what he sees and hears; I am interested in the range and force of his perception. Our immediate impression may be that his perception is narrow and deep—vertical. After all, "voice above . . . voice below," he sings. But is it vertical only? At each level of his expression there is an extension of his awareness across the whole landscape. The voice above is the voice of thunder, and thunder rolls. Moreover, it issues from the impalpable dark clouds and runs upon their horizontal range. It is a sound that integrates the whole of the atmosphere. And even so, the voice below, that of the grasshopper, issues from the broad plain and multiplicity of plants. And of course the singer is mindful of much more than thunder and insects; we are given in his song the wide angle of his vision and his hearing—and we are given the testimony of his dignity, his trust, and his deep belief.

This comprehension of the earth and air is surely a matter of morality, for it brings into account not only man's instinctive reaction to his environment but the full realization of his humanity as well, the achievement of his intellectual and spiritual development as an individual and as a race.

In my own experience I have seen numerous examples of this regard for nature. My grandfather Mammedaty was a farmer in his mature years; his grandfather was a buffalo hunter. It was not easy for Mammedaty to be a farmer; he was a Kiowa, and the Kiowas never had an agrarian tradition. Yet he had to make his living, and the old, beloved life of roaming the plains and hunting the buffalo was gone forever. Even so, as much as any man before him, he fitted his mind and will and spirit to the land; there was nothing else. He could not have conceived of living apart from the land.

In *The Way to Rainy Mountain* I set down a small narrative that belongs in the oral tradition of my family. It indicates something essential about the Native American attitude toward the land:

"East of my grandmother's house, south of the pecan grove, there is buried a woman in a beautiful dress. Mammedaty used to know where she is buried, but now no one knows. If you stand on the front porch of the house and look eastward towards Carnegie, you know that the woman is buried somewhere within the range of your vision. But her grave is unmarked. She was buried in a cabinet, and she wore a beautiful dress. How beautiful it was! It was one of those fine buckskin dresses, and it was decorated with elk's teeth and beadwork. That dress is still there, under the ground."

It seems to me that this statement is primarily a declaration of love for the land, in which the several elements—the woman, the dress, and this plain—are at last become one reality, one expression of the beautiful in nature. Moreover, it seems to me a peculiarly Native American expression in this sense: that the concentration of things that are explicitly remembered—the general landscape, the simple, almost abstract nature of the burial, above all the beautiful dress, which is wholly singular in kind (as well as in its function within the narrative)—is especially Indian in character. The things that are *not* explicitly remembered—the woman's name, the exact location of her grave—are the things that matter least in the special view of the storyteller. What matters here is the translation of the woman into the landscape, a translation particularly signified by means of the beautiful and distinctive dress, an *Indian* dress.

When I was a boy, I lived for several years at Jemez Pueblo, New Mexico. The Pueblo Indians are perhaps more obviously invested in the land than are other people. Their whole life is predicated upon a thorough perception of the physical world and its myriad aspects. When I first went there to live, the cacique, or chief, of the Pueblos was a venerable old man with long, gray hair and bright, deep-set eyes. He was entirely dignified and imposing—and rather formidable in the eyes of a boy. He excited my imagination a good deal. I was told that this old man kept the calendar of the tribe, that each morning he stood on a certain spot of ground near the center of the town and watched to see where the sun appeared on the skyline. By means of this solar calendar did he know and announce to his people when it was time to plant, to harvest, to perform this or that ceremony. This image of him in my mind's eye—the old man gazing each morning after the ranging sun—came to represent for me the epitome of that real harmony between man and the land that signifies the Indian world.

One day when I was riding my horse along the Jemez River, I looked up to see a long caravan of wagons and people on horseback and on foot. Men, women, and children were crossing the river ahead of me, moving out to the west, where most of the cultivated fields were, the farmland of the town. It was a wonderful sight to see, this long procession, and I was immediately deeply curious. I wanted to investigate, but it was not in me to do so at once, for that racial reserve, that sense of propriety that is deep-seated in Native American culture, stayed me, held me up. Then I saw someone coming toward me on horseback, galloping. It was a friend of mine, a boy of my own age. "Come on," he said. "Come with us," "Where are you going?" I asked casually. But he would not tell me. He simply laughed and urged me to come along, and of course I was very glad to do so. It was a bright spring morning, and I had a good horse under me, and the prospect of adventure was delicious. We moved far out across the eroded plain to the farthest fields at the foot of a great red mesa, and there we planted two large fields of corn. And afterward, on the edge of the fields, we sat on blankets and ate a feast in the shade of a cottonwood grove. Later I learned it was the cacique's fields we planted. And this is an ancient tradition at Jemez. The people of the town plant and tend and harvest the cacique's fields, and in the winter the hunters give to him a portion of the meat that they bring home from the mountains. It is as if the cacique is himself the translation of man, every man, into the landscape.

I have not forgotten that day, nor shall I forget it. I remember the warm earth of the fields, the smooth texture of seeds in my hands, and the brown water moving slowly and irresistibly among the rows. Above all I remember the spirit in which the procession was made, the work was done, and the feasting was enjoyed. It was a spirit of communion, of the life of each man in relation to the life of the planet and of the infinite distance and silence in which it moves. We made, in concert, an appropriate expression of that spirit.

One afternoon an old Kiowa woman talked to me, telling me of the place in Oklahoma in which she had lived for a hundred years. It was the place in which my grandparents, too, lived; and it is the place where I was born. And she told me of a time even further back, when the Kiowas came down from the north and centered their culture in the red earth of the southern plains. She told wonderful stories, and as I listened, I began to feel more and more sure that her voice proceeded from the land itself. I asked her many things concerning the Kiowas, for I wanted to understand all that I could of my heritage. I told the old woman that I had come there to learn from her and from people like her, those in whom the old ways were preserved. And she said simply: "It is good that you have come here." I believe that her word "good" meant many things; for one thing it meant *right*, or *appropriate*. And indeed it was appropriate that she should speak of the land. She was eminently qualified to do so. She had a great reverence for the land, and an ancient perception of it, a perception that it acquired only in the course of many generations.

It is this notion of the appropriate, along with that of the beautiful, that forms the Native American perspective on the land. In a sense these considerations are indivisible; Native American oral tradition is rich with songs and tales that celebrate natural beauty, the beauty of the natural world. What is more appropriate to our world than that which is beautiful:

> At noon
> turtles
> enter
> slowly
> into
> the warm
> dark loam.
> Bees hold
> the swarm.
> Meadows
> recede
> through planes
> of heat
> and pure
> distance.

Very old in the Native American world view is the conviction that the earth is vital, that there is a spiritual dimension to it, a dimension in which man rightly exists. It follows logically that there are ethical imperatives in this matter. I think: Inasmuch as I am in the land, it is appropriate that I should affirm myself in the spirit of the land. I shall celebrate my life in the world and the world in my life. In the natural order man invests himself in the landscape and at the same time incorporates the landscape into his own most fundamental experience. This trust is sacred.

The process of investment and appropriation is, I believe, preeminently a function of the imagination. It is accomplished by means of an act of the imagination that is especially ethical in kind. We are what we imagine ourselves to be. The Native American is someone who thinks of himself, imagines himself in a particular way. By virtue of his experience his idea of himself comprehends his relationship to the land.

And the quality of this imagining is determined as well by racial and cultural experience. The Native American's attitudes toward this landscape have been formulated over a long period of time, a span that reaches back to the end of the Ice Age. The land, *this* land, is secure in his racial memory.

In our society as a whole we conceive of the land in terms of ownership and use. It is a lifeless medium of exchange; it has for most of us, I
suspect, no more spirituality than has an automobile, say, or a refrigerator. And our laws confirm us in this view, for we can buy and sell the
land, we can exclude each other from it, and in the context of ownership
we can use it as we will. Ownership implies use, and use implies con-
sumption.

But this way of thinking of the land is alien to the Indian. His cultural
intelligence is opposed to these concepts; indeed, for him they are all but
inconceivable quantities. This fundamental distinction is easier to understand with respect to ownership than to use, perhaps. For obviously the
Indian does use, and has always used, the land and the available resources
in it. The point is that *use* does not indicate in any real way his idea of the
land. "Use" is neither his word nor his idea. As an Indian I think: "You say
that I *use* the land, and I reply, yes, it is true; but it is not the first truth.
The first truth is that I *love* the land; I see that it is beautiful; I delight in
it; I am alive in it."

In the long course of his journey from Asia and in the realization of
himself in the New World, the Indian has assumed a deep ethical regard
for the earth and sky, a reverence for the natural world that is antipodal
to that strange tenet of modern civilization that seemingly has it that man
must destroy his environment. It is this ancient ethic of the Native American that must shape our efforts to preserve the earth and the life upon
and within it.

> At dusk
> the gray
> foxes
> stiffen
> in cold;
> blackbirds
> are fixed
> in white
> branches.
> Rivers
> follow
> the moon,
> the long
> white track
> of the
> full moon.

CONSIDERATIONS

Thinking

What are some implications of Momaday's expression of the Native American world view concerning what he describes as the earth's spiritual dimension? What do you think he means by suggesting that there are "ethical imperatives" for human beings in their relationship with the earth?

What aspect of Momaday's Native American perspective does he put in counterpoint to looking at the earth in terms of "ownership and use"? Why?

Connecting

How does each of the stories Momaday introduces into his essay fit in with the ideas and cultural perspectives he develops? What does the poem he includes contribute to the essay?

Compare Momaday's discussion of the Native American perspective toward nature and the land with that of Leslie Marmon Silko in "Landscape, History, and the Pueblo Imagination."

Writing

Write an essay in which you explore the implications of what it means to "love the land" in Momaday's terms.

Write an analysis of the poem that Momaday includes in his essay. Discuss the image of nature the poem conveys.

T oni Morrison (b.1931)

T oni Morrison, a novelist, won the Nobel Prize in literature in 1993. Her novels include *Song of Solomon, Sula, The Bluest Eye, Jazz,* and *Beloved.* She has an unerring instinct about the plight of African Americans and a remarkable talent for reconstructing their inner lives.

"The Site of Memory" was a talk given at the New York Public Library. In it, Morrison reveals her own process of transforming slave narratives into fiction—telling how she tracks "an image from picture to meaning to text." Her aim is also to "throw into relief the differences between self-recollection (memoir) and fiction."

The Site of Memory

My inclusion in a series of talks on autobiography and memoir is not entirely a misalliance. Although it's probably true that a fiction writer thinks of his or her work as alien in that company, what I have to say may suggest why I'm not completely out of place here. For one thing, I might throw into relief the differences between self-recollection (memoir) and fiction, and also some of the similarities—the places where those two crafts embrace and where that embrace is symbiotic.

But the authenticity of my presence here lies in the fact that a very large part of my own literary heritage is the autobiography. In this country the print origins of black literature (as distinguished from the oral origins) were slave narratives. These book-length narratives (autobiographies, recollections, memoirs), of which well over a hundred were published, are familiar texts to historians and students of black history. They range from the adventure-packed life of Olaudah Equiano's *The Interesting Narrative of the Life of Olaudah Equiano, or Gustavus Vassa, the African, Written by Himself* (1769) to the quiet desperation of *Incidents in the Life of a Slave Girl: Written by Herself* (1861), in which Harriet Jacob ("Linda Brent") records hiding for seven years in a room too small to stand up in; from the political savvy of Frederick Douglass's *Narrative of the Life of Frederick Douglass, an American Slave, Written by Himself* (1845) to the subtlety and modesty of Henry Bibb, whose voice, in *Life and Adventures of Henry Bibb, an American Slave, Written by Himself* (1849), is surrounded by ("loaded with" is a better phrase) documents attesting to its authenticity. Bibb is careful to note that his formal schooling (three weeks) was short, but that he was "educated in the school of adversity, whips, and chains." Born in Kentucky, he put aside his plans to escape in order to marry. But when he learned that he was the father of a slave and watched the degradation of his wife and child, he reactivated those plans.

Whatever the style and circumstances of these narratives, they were written to say principally two things. One: "This is my historical life—my singular, special example that is personal, but that also represents the race." Two: "I write this text to persuade other people—you, the reader, who is probably not black—that we are human beings worthy of God's grace and the immediate abandonment of slavery." With these two missions in mind, the narratives were clearly pointed.

In Equiano's account, the purpose is quite up-front. Born in 1745 near the Niger River and captured at the age of ten, he survived the Middle Passage, American plantation slavery, wars in Canada and the Mediterranean; learned navigation and clerking from a Quaker named Robert King, and bought his freedom at twenty-one. He lived as a free servant, traveling widely and living most of his latter life in England. Here he is speaking to the British without equivocation: "I hope to have the satisfaction of seeing the renovation of liberty and justice resting on the British government. . . . I hope and expect the attention of gentlemen of power. . . . May the time come—at least the speculation is to me pleasing—when the sable people shall gratefully commemorate the auspicious era of extensive freedom." With typically eighteenth-century reticence he records his singular and representative life for one purpose: to change things. In fact, he and his co-authors *did* change things. Their works gave fuel to the fires that abolitionists were setting everywhere.

More difficult was getting the fair appraisal of literary critics. The writings of church martyrs and confessors are and were read for the eloquence of their message as well as their experience of redemption, but the American slaves' autobiographical narratives were frequently scorned as "biased," "inflammatory" and "improbable." These attacks are particularly difficult to understand in view of the fact that it was extremely important, as you can imagine, for the writers of these narratives to appear as objective as possible—not to offend the reader by being too angry, or by showing too much outrage, or by calling the reader names. As recently as 1966, Paul Edwards, who edited and abridged Equiano's story, praises the narrative for its refusal to be "inflammatory."

"As a rule," Edwards writes, "he [Equiano] puts no emotional pressure on the reader other than that which the situation itself contains—his language does not strain after our sympathy, but expects it to be given naturally and at the proper time. This quiet avoidance of emotional display produces many of the best passages in the book." Similarly, an 1836 review of Charles Bell's *Life and Adventures of a Fugitive Slave,* which appeared in the "Quarterly Anti-Slavery Magazine," praised Bell's account for its objectivity. "We rejoice in the book the more, because it is not a partisan work. . . . It broaches no theory in regard to [slavery], nor proposes any mode or time of emancipation."

As determined as these black writers were to persuade the reader of the evil of slavery, they also complimented him by assuming his nobility of heart and his high-mindedness. They tried to summon up his finer nature in order to encourage him to employ it. They knew that their readers were the people who could make a difference in terminating slavery. Their stories—of brutality, adversity and deliverance—had great popularity in spite of critical hostility in many quarters and patronizing sympathy in others. There was a time when the hunger for "slave stories" was difficult to quiet, as sales figures show. Douglass's *Narrative* sold five thousand copies in four months; by 1847 it had sold eleven thousand copies. Equiano's book had thirty-six editions between 1789 and 1850. Moses Roper's book had ten editions from 1837 to 1856; William Wells Brown's was reprinted four times in its first year. Solomon Northrop's book sold twenty-seven thousand copies before two years had passed. A book by Josiah Henson (argued by some to be the model for the "Tom" of Harriet Beecher Stowe's *Uncle Tom's Cabin*) had a pre-publication sale of five thousand.

In addition to using their own lives to expose the horrors of slavery, they had a companion motive for their efforts. The prohibition against teaching a slave to read and write (which in many Southern states carried severe punishment) and against a slave's learning to read and write had to be scuttled at all costs. These writers knew that literacy was power. Voting, after all, was inextricably connected to the ability to read; literacy was a way of assuming and proving the "humanity" that the Constitution denied them. That is why the narratives carry the subtitle "written by himself," or "herself," and include introductions and prefaces by white sympathizers to authenticate them. Other narratives, "edited by" such well-known anti-slavery figures as Lydia Maria Child and John Greenleaf Whittier, contain prefaces to assure the reader how little editing was needed. A literate slave was supposed to be a contradiction in terms.

One has to remember that the climate in which they wrote reflected not only the Age of Enlightenment but its twin, born at the same time, the Age of Scientific Racism. David Hume, Immanuel Kant and Thomas Jefferson, to mention only a few, had documented their conclusions that blacks were incapable of intelligence. Frederick Douglass knew otherwise, and he wrote refutations of what Jefferson said in "Notes on the State of Virginia": "Never yet could I find that a black had uttered a thought above the level of plain narration, never see even an elementary trait of painting or sculpture." A sentence that I have always thought ought to be engraved at the door to the Rockefeller Collection of African Art. Hegel, in 1813, had said that Africans had no "history" and couldn't write in modern languages. Kant disregarded a perceptive observation by a black man by saying, "This fellow was quite black from head to foot, a clear proof that what he said was stupid."

Yet no slave society in the history of the world wrote more—or more thoughtfully—about its own enslavement. The milieu, however, dictated the purpose and the style. The narratives are instructive, moral and obviously representative. Some of them are patterned after the sentimental novel that was in vogue at the time. But whatever the level of eloquence or the form, popular taste discouraged the writers from dwelling too long or too carefully on the more sordid details of their experience. Whenever there was an unusually violent incident, or a scatological one, or something "excessive," one finds the writer taking refuge in the literary conventions of the day. "I was left in a state of distraction not to be described" (Equiano). "But let us now leave the rough usage of the field . . . and turn our attention to the less repulsive slave life as it existed in the house of my childhood" (Douglass). "I am not about to harrow the feelings of my readers by a terrific representation of the untold horrors of that fearful system of oppression. . . . It is not my purpose to descend deeply into the dark and noisome caverns of the hell of slavery" (Henry Box Brown).

Over and over, the writers pull the narrative up short with a phrase such as, "But let us drop a veil over these proceedings too terrible to relate." In shaping the experience to make it palatable to those who were in a position to alleviate it, they were silent about many things, and they "forgot" many other things. There was a careful selection of the instances that they would record and a careful rendering of those that they chose to describe. Lydia Maria Child identified the problem in her introduction to "Linda Brent's" tale of sexual abuse: "I am well aware that many will accuse me of indecorum for presenting these pages to the public; for the experiences of this intelligent and much-injured woman belong to a class which some call delicate subjects, and others indelicate. This peculiar phase of Slavery has generally been kept veiled; but the public ought to be made acquainted with its monstrous features, and I am willing to take the responsibility of presenting them with the veil drawn [aside]."

But most importantly—at least for me—there was no mention of their interior life.

For me—a writer in the last quarter of the twentieth century, not much more than a hundred years after Emancipation, a writer who is black and a woman—the exercise is very different. My job becomes how to rip that veil drawn over "proceedings too terrible to relate." The exercise is also critical for any person who is black, or who belongs to any marginalized category, for, historically, we were seldom invited to participate in the discourse even when we were its topic.

Moving that veil aside requires, therefore, certain things. First of all, I must trust my own recollections. I must also depend on the recollections of others. Thus memory weighs heavily in what I write, in how I begin and in what I find to be significant. Zora Neale Hurston said, "Like the dead-seeming cold rocks, I have memories within that came out of the material that went to make me." These "memories within" are the subsoil of my work. But memories and recollections won't give me total access to the unwritten interior life of these people. Only the act of the imagination can help me.

If writing is thinking and discovery and selection and order and meaning, it is also awe and reverence and mystery and magic. I suppose I could dispense with the last four if I were not so deadly serious about fidelity to the milieu out of which I write and in which my ancestors actually lived. Infidelity to that milieu—the absence of the interior life, the deliberate excising of it from the records that the slaves themselves told—is precisely the problem in the discourse that proceeded without us. How I gain access to that interior life is what drives me and is the part of this talk which both distinguishes my fiction from autobiographical strategies and which also embraces certain autobiographical strategies. It's a kind of literary archeology: on the basis of some information and a little bit of guesswork you journey to a site to see what remains were left behind and to reconstruct the world that these remains imply. What makes it fiction is the nature of the imaginative act: my reliance on the image—on the remains—in addition to recollection, to yield up a kind of a truth. By "image," of course, I don't mean "symbol"; I simply mean "picture" and the feelings that accompany the picture.

Fiction, by definition, is distinct from fact. Presumably it's the product of imagination—invention—and it claims the freedom to dispense with "what really happened," or where it really happened, or when it really happened, and nothing in it needs to be publicly verifiable, although much in it can be verified. By contrast, the scholarship of the biographer and the literary critic seems to us only trustworthy when the events of fiction can be traced to some publicly verifiable fact. It's the research of the "Oh, yes, this is where he or she got it from" school, which gets its own credibility from excavating the credibility of the sources of the imagination, not the nature of the imagination.

The work that I do frequently falls, in the minds of most people, into that realm of fiction called fantastic, or mythic, or magical, or unbelievable. I'm not comfortable with these labels. I consider that my single gravest responsibility (in spite of that magic) is not to lie. When I hear someone say, "Truth is stranger than fiction," I think that old chestnut is truer than we know, because it doesn't say that truth is truer than fiction; just that it's stranger, meaning that it's odd. It may be excessive, it may be more interesting, but the important thing is that it's random—and fiction is not random.

Therefore the crucial distinction for me is not the difference between fact and fiction, but the distinction between fact and truth. Because facts can exist without human intelligence, but truth cannot. So if I'm looking to find and expose a truth about the interior life of people who didn't write it (which doesn't mean that they didn't have it); if I'm trying to fill in the blanks that the slave narratives left—to part the veil that was so frequently drawn, to implement the stories that I heard—then the approach that's most productive and most trustworthy for me is the recollection that moves from the image to the text. Not from the text to the image.

Simone de Beauvoir, in *A Very Easy Death,* says, "I don't know why I was so shocked by my mother's death." When she heard her mother's name being called at the funeral by the priest, she says, "Emotion seized me by the throat. . . . 'Françoise de Beauvoir': the words brought her to life; they summed up her history, from birth to marriage to widowhood to the grave. Françoise de Beauvoir—that retiring woman, so rarely named, became an *important* person." The book becomes an exploration both into her own grief and into the images in which the grief lay buried.

Unlike Mme. de Beauvoir, Frederick Douglass asks the reader's patience for spending about half a page on the death of his grandmother—easily the most profound loss he had suffered—and he apologizes by saying, in effect, "It really was very important to me. I hope you aren't bored by my indulgence." He makes no attempt to explore that death: its images or its meaning. His narrative is as close to factual as he can make it, which leaves no room for subjective speculation. James Baldwin, on the other hand, in *Notes of a Native Son,* says, in recording his father's life and his own relationship to his father, "All of my father's Biblical texts and songs, which I had decided were meaningless, were ranged before me at his death like empty bottles, waiting to hold the meaning which life would give them for me." And then his text fills those bottles. Like Simone de Beauvoir, he moves from the event to the image that it left. My route is the reverse: the image comes first and tells me what the "memory" is about.

I can't tell you how I felt when my father died. But I was able to write *Song of Solomon* and imagine, not him, and not his specific interior life,

but the world that he inhabited and the private or interior life of the people in it. And I can't tell you how I felt reading to my grandmother while
she was turning over and over in her bed (because she was dying, and she
was not comfortable), but I could try to reconstruct the world that she
lived in. And I have suspected, more often than not, that I *know* more
than she did, that I *know* more than my grandfather and my great-grandmother did, but I also know that I'm no wiser than they were. And whenever I have tried earnestly to diminish their vision and prove to myself
that I know more, and when I have tried to speculate on their interior life
and match it up with my own, I have been overwhelmed every time by
the richness of theirs compared to my own. Like Frederick Douglass talking about his grandmother, and James Baldwin talking about his father,
and Simone de Beauvoir talking about her mother, these people are my
access to me; they are my entrance into my own interior life. Which is
why the images that float around them—the remains, so to speak, at the
archeological site—surface first, and they surface so vividly and so compellingly that I acknowledge them as my route to a reconstruction of a
world, to an exploration of an interior life that was not written and to the
revelation of a kind of truth.

So the nature of my research begins with something as ineffable and
as flexible as a dimly recalled figure, the corner of a room, a voice. I began
to write my second book, which was called *Sula,* because of my preoccupation with a picture of a woman and the way in which I heard her name
pronounced. Her name was Hannah, and I think she was a friend of my
mother's. I don't remember seeing her very much, but what I do remember is the color around her—a kind of violet, a suffusion of something
violet—and her eyes, which appeared to be half closed. But what I
remember most is how the women said her name: how they said "Hannah Peace" and smiled to themselves, and there was some secret about her
that they knew, which they didn't talk about, at least not in my hearing,
but it seemed *loaded* in the way in which they said her name. And I suspected that she was a little bit of an outlaw but that they approved in
some way.

And then, thinking about their relationship to her and the way in
which they talked about her, the way in which they articulated her name,
made me think about friendship between women. What is it that they
forgive each other for? And what is it that is unforgivable in the world of
women? I don't want to know any more about Miss Hannah Peace, and
I'm not going to ask my mother who she really was and what did she do
and what were you laughing about and why were you smiling? Because

my experience when I do this with my mother is so crushing: she will give you *the* most pedestrian information you ever heard, and I would like to keep all of my remains and my images intact in their mystery when I begin. Later I will get to the facts. That way I can explore two worlds— the actual and the possible.

What I want to do this evening is to track an image from picture to meaning to text—a journey which appears in the novel that I'm writing now, which is called *Beloved*.

I'm trying to write a particular kind of scene, and I see corn on the cob. To "see" corn on the cob doesn't mean that it suddenly hovers; it only means that it keeps coming back. And in trying to figure out "What is all this corn doing?" I discover what it *is* doing.

I see the house where I grew up in Lorain, Ohio. My parents had a garden some distance away from our house, and they didn't welcome me and my sister there, when we were young, because we were not able to distinguish between the things that they wanted to grow and the things that they didn't, so we were not able to hoe, or weed, until much later.

I see them walking, together, away from me. I'm looking at their backs and what they're carrying in their arms: their tools, and maybe a peck basket. Sometimes when they walk away from me they hold hands, and they go to this other place in the garden. They have to cross some railroad tracks to get there.

I also am aware that my mother and father sleep at odd hours because my father works many jobs and works at night. And these naps are times of pleasure for me and my sister because nobody's giving us chores, or telling us what to do, or nagging us in any way. In addition to which, there is some feeling of pleasure in them that I'm only vaguely aware of. They're very rested when they take these naps.

And later on in the summer we have an opportunity to eat corn, which is the one plant that I can distinguish from the others, and which is the harvest that I like the best; the others are the food that no child likes—the collards, the okra, the strong, violent vegetables that I would give a great deal for now. But I do like the corn because it's sweet, and because we all sit down to eat it, and it's finger food, and it's hot, and it's even good cold, and there are neighbors in, and there are uncles in, and it's easy, and it's nice.

The picture of the corn and the nimbus of emotion surrounding it became a powerful one in the manuscript I'm now completing.

Authors arrive at text and subtext in thousands of ways, learning each time they begin anew how to recognize a valuable idea and how to render the texture that accompanies, reveals or displays it to its best advantage. The process by which this is accomplished is endlessly fascinating to me. I have always thought that as an editor for twenty years I understood writers better than their most careful critics, because in examining the manuscript in each of its subsequent stages I knew the author's process, how his or her mind worked, what was effortless, what took time, where the "solution" to a problem came from. The end result—the book—was all that the critic had to go on.

Still, for me, that was the least important aspect of the work. Because, no matter how "fictional" the account of these writers, or how much it was a product of invention, the act of imagination is bound up with memory. You know, they straightened out the Mississippi River in places, to make room for houses and livable acreage. Occasionally the river floods these places. "Floods" is the word they use, but in fact it is not flooding; it is remembering. Remembering where it used to be. All water has a perfect memory and is forever trying to get back to where it was. Writers are like that: remembering where we were, what valley we ran through, what the banks were like, the light that was there and the route back to our original place. It is emotional memory—what the nerves and the skin remember as well as how it appeared. And a rush of imagination is our "flooding."

Along with personal recollection, the matrix of the work I do is the wish to extend, fill in and complement slave autobiographical narratives. But only the matrix. What comes of all that is dictated by other concerns, not least among them the novel's own integrity. Still, like water, I remember where I was before I was "straightened out."

———

Q. I would like to ask about your point of view as a novelist. Is it a vision, or are you taking the part of the particular characters?

A. I try sometimes to have genuinely minor characters just walk through, like a walk-on actor. But I get easily distracted by them, because a novelist's imagination goes like that: every little road looks to me like an adventure, and once you begin to claim it and describe it, it looks like more, and you invent more and more and more. I don't mind doing that in my first draft, but afterward I have to cut back. I have seen myself get distracted, and people have loomed much larger than I had planned, and minor characters have seemed a little bit more interesting than they need to be for the purposes of the book. In that case I try to endow them: if there are little pieces of information that I want to reveal, I let them do some of the work. But I try not to get carried away; I try to restrain it, so that, finally, the texture is consistent and nothing is wasted; there are no words in the final text that are unnecessary, and no people who are not absolutely necessary.

As for the point of view, there should be the illusion that it's the characters' point of view, when in fact it isn't; it's really the narrator who is there but who doesn't make herself (in my case) known in that role. I like the feeling of a *told* story, where you hear a voice but you can't identify it, and you think it's your own voice. It's a comfortable voice, and it's a guiding voice, and it's alarmed by the same things that the reader is alarmed by, and it doesn't know what's going to happen next either. So you have this sort of guide. But that guide can't have a personality; it can only have a sound, and you have to feel comfortable with this voice, and then this voice can easily abandon itself and reveal the interior dialogue of a character. So it's a combination of using the point of view of various characters but still retaining the power to slide in and out, provided that when I'm "out" the reader doesn't see little fingers pointing to what's in the text.

What I really want is that intimacy in which the reader is under the impression that he isn't really reading this; that he is participating in it as he goes along. It's unfolding, and he's always two beats ahead of the characters and right on target.

Q. You have said that writing is a solitary activity. Do you go into steady seclusion when you're writing, so that your feelings are sort of contained, or do you have to get away, and go out shopping and . . . ?

A. I do all of it. I've been at this book for three years. I go out shopping, and I stare, and I do whatever. It goes away. Sometimes it's very intense and I walk—I mean, I write a sentence and I jump up and run outside or something; it sort of beats you up. And sometimes I don't. Sometimes I write long hours every day. I get up at 5:30 and just go do it, and if I don't like it the next day, I throw it away. But I sit down and do it. By now I know how to get to that place where something is working. I didn't always know; I thought every thought I had was interesting— because it was mine. Now I know better how to throw away things that are not useful. I can stand around and do other things and think about it at the same time. I don't mind not writing every minute; I'm not so terrified.

When you first start writing—and I think it's true for a lot of beginning writers—you're scared to death that if you don't get that sentence right that minute it's never going to show up again. And it isn't. But it doesn't matter—another one will, and it'll probably be better. And I don't mind writing badly for a couple of days because I know I can fix it—and fix it again and again and again, and it will be better. I don't have the hysteria that used to accompany some of those dazzling passages that I thought the world was just dying for me to remember. I'm a little more sanguine about it now. Because the best part of it all, the absolutely most delicious part, is finishing it and then doing it over. That's the thrill of a lifetime for me: if I can just get done with that first phase and then have infinite time to fix it and change it. I rewrite a lot, over and over again, so that it looks like I never did. I try to make it look like I never touched it, and that takes a lot of time and a lot of sweat.

Q. *In "Song of Solomon," what was the relationship between your memories and what you made up? Was it very tenuous?*

A. Yes, it was tenuous. For the first time I was writing a book in which the central stage was occupied by men, and which had something to do with my loss, or my perception of loss, of a man (my father) and the world that disappeared with him. (It didn't, but I *felt* that it did.) So I was re-creating a time period that was his—not biographically his life or anything in it; I use whatever's around. But it seemed to me that there was this big void after he died, and I filled it with a book that was about men because my two previous books had had women as the central characters. So in that sense it was about my memories and the need to invent. I had to do something. I was in such a rage because my father was dead. The connections between us were threads that I either mined for a lot of strength or they were purely invention. But I created a male world and inhabited it and it had this quest—a journey from stupidity to epiphany, of a man, a complete man. It was my way of exploring all that, of trying to figure out what he may have known.

CONSIDERATIONS

Thinking

Morrison tells us that "a literate slave was supposed to be a contradiction in terms." What are the implications of such a statement—in the slaves' time and in ours? Fill in the blank to fit our present-day circumstance: "A _____ is a contradiction in terms."

What do you think about Morrison's belief that she can reach truth through fiction? Do you believe in fictional truth-telling, or would you rather just have the facts? Explain.

Connecting

When Morrison describes her job as a fiction writer, she says she has first to look at slave narratives and then "rip that veil drawn over 'proceedings too terrible to relate.'" In reconstructing what the interior life of her characters must have been like, she must also trust her "own recollections," her own memories. But none of that is enough, finally: "Only the act of the imagination can help me." How do you suppose such imaginative acts are related to what Steven Jay Gould calls the "inferential acts" that characterize scientific thinking? Morrison, recall, speaks of her work as "a kind of literary archeology."

Morrison says that when she does her reconstructing, she relies on the "image—on the remains" she finds at the site. How might her notion about images help you with your writing?

Writing

Write an essay in which you explore the ramifications of Morrison's claim that "facts can exist without human intelligence, but truth cannot."

Morrison tells us that the images at the archeological site "surface first, and they surface so vividly and so compellingly that I acknowledge them as my route to a reconstruction of a world, to an exploration of an interior life that was not written and to the revelation of a kind of truth." See what happens when you follow Morrison's path. Return to an archeological site in your memory; record the image, render it, and see what it reveals to you.

J oyce Carol Oates (b.1938)

J oyce Carol Oates is perhaps America's most prolific writer. Already she has given us numerous novels, fourteen volumes of short stories, five books of literary criticism, and two books of plays. The end is nowhere in sight.

In "On Boxing," Oates's "mosaic-like essay" on the nature of masculinity, she tries to capture what others have left out in their accounts of boxing—pain, eroticism, and women, for example. Each piece of the mosaic also gives us a clearer sense of *machismo* as well as revealing glimpses into the art of writing.

On Boxing

STORIES

> Why are you a boxer, Irish featherweight champion Barry
> McGuigan was asked. He said: "I can't be a poet. I can't tell
> stories. . . ."

Each boxing match is a story—a unique and highly condensed drama without words. Even when nothing sensational happens: then the drama is "merely" psychological. Boxers are there to establish an absolute experience, a public accounting of the outermost limits of their beings; they will know, as few of us can know of ourselves, what physical and psychic power they possess—of how much, or how little, they are capable. To enter the ring near-naked and to risk one's life is to make of one's audience voyeurs of a kind: boxing is so intimate. It is to ease out of sanity's consciousness and into another, difficult to name. It is to risk, and sometimes to realize, the agony of which *agon* (Greek, "contest") is the root.

In the boxing ring there are two principal players, overseen by a shadowy third. The ceremonial ringing of the bell is a summoning to full wakefulness for both boxers and spectators. It sets into motion, too, the authority of Time.

The boxers will bring to the fight everything that is themselves, and everything will be exposed—including secrets about themselves they cannot fully realize. The physical self, the maleness, one might say, underlying the "self." There are boxers possessed of such remarkable intuition, such uncanny prescience, one would think they were somehow recalling their fights, not fighting them as we watch. There are boxers who perform skillfully, but mechanically, who cannot improvise in response to another's alteration of strategy; there are boxers performing at the peak of their talent who come to realize, mid-fight, that it will not be enough; there are boxers—including great champions—whose careers end abruptly, and irrevocably, as we watch. There has been at least one boxer possessed of an extraordinary and disquieting awareness not only of his opponent's every move and anticipated move but of the audience's keenest shifts in mood as

447

well, for which he seems to have felt personally responsible—Cassius Clay/Muhammad Ali, of course. "The Sweet Science of Bruising" celebrates the physicality of men even as it dramatizes the limitations, sometimes tragic, more often poignant, of the physical. Though male spectators identify with boxers no boxer behaves like a "normal" man when he is in the ring and no combination of blows is "natural." All is style.

Every talent must unfold itself in fighting. So Nietzsche speaks of the Hellenic past, the history of the "contest"—athletic, and otherwise—by which Greek youths were educated into Greek citizenry. Without the ferocity of competition, without, even, "envy, jealousy, and ambition" in the contest, the Hellenic city, like the Hellenic man, degenerated. If death is a risk, death is also the prize—for the winning athlete.

In the boxing ring, even in our greatly humanized times, death is always a possibility—which is why some of us prefer to watch films or tapes of fights already past, already defined as history. Or, in some instances, art. (Though to prepare for writing this mosaic-like essay I saw tapes of two infamous "death" fights of recent times: the Lupe Pintor–Johnny Owen bantamweight match of 1982, and the Ray Mancini–Duk Koo-Kim lightweight match of the same year. In both instances the boxers died as a consequence of their astonishing resilience and apparent indefatigability—their "heart," as it's known in boxing circles.) Most of the time, however, death in the ring is extremely unlikely; a statistically rare possibility like your possible death tomorrow morning in an automobile accident or in next month's headlined airline disaster or in a freak accident involving a fall on the stairs or in the bathtub, a skull fracture, subarachnoid hemorrhage. Spectators at "death" fights often claim afterward that what happened simply seemed to happen—unpredictably, in a sense accidentally. Only in retrospect does death appear to have been inevitable.

If a boxing match is a story it is an always wayward story, one in which anything can happen. And in a matter of seconds. Split seconds! (Muhammad Ali boasted that he could throw a punch faster than the eye could follow, and he may have been right.) In no other sport can so much take place in so brief a period of time, and so irrevocably.

Because a boxing match is a story without words, this doesn't mean that it has no text or no language, that it is somehow "brute," "primitive," "inarticulate," only that the text is improvised in action; the language a dialogue between the boxers of the most refined sort (one might say, as much neurological as psychological: a dialogue of split-second reflexes) in a joint response to the mysterious will of the audience which is always

that the fight be a worthy one so that the crude paraphernalia of the setting—ring, lights, ropes, stained canvas, the staring onlookers themselves—be erased, forgotten. (As in the theater or the church, settings are
erased by way, ideally, of transcendent action.) Ringside announcers give
to the wordless spectacle a narrative unity, yet boxing as performance is
more clearly akin to dance or music than narrative.

To turn from an ordinary preliminary match to a "Fight of the Century" like those between Joe Louis and Billy Conn, Joe Frazier and
Muhammad Ali, Marvin Hagler and Thomas Hearns is to turn from listening or half-listening to a guitar being idly plucked to hearing Bach's
Well-Tempered Clavier perfectly executed, and that too is part of the story's
mystery: so much happens so swiftly and with such heart-stopping subtlety you cannot absorb it except to know that something profound is
happening and it is happening in a place beyond words.

PAIN

> I hate to say it, but it's true—I only like it better when pain comes.
>
> FRANK "THE ANIMAL" FLETCHER,
> FORMER MIDDLEWEIGHT CONTENDER

Years ago in the early 1950s when my father first took me to a Golden
Gloves boxing tournament in Buffalo, New York, I asked him why the
boys wanted to fight one another, why they were willing to get hurt. As if
it were an explanation my father said, "Boxers don't feel pain quite the
way we do."

Pain, in the proper context, is something other than pain.

Consider: Gene Tunney's single defeat in a thirteen-year career of
great distinction was to a notorious fighter named Harry Greb who seems
to have been, judging from boxing lore, the dirtiest fighter in history. Greb
was infamous for his fouls—low blows, butting, "holding and hitting,"
rubbing his laces against an opponent's eyes, routine thumbing—as well
as for a frenzied boxing style in which blows were thrown from all directions. (Hence, "The Human Windmill.") Greb, who died young, was a
world middleweight champion for three years but a flamboyant presence
in boxing circles for a long time. After the first of his several fights with
Greb the twenty-two-year-old Tunney was so badly hurt he had to spend
a week in bed; he'd lost an astonishing two quarts of blood during the fif-
teen-round fight. Yet, as Tunney said some years later:

Greb gave me a terrible whipping. He broke my nose, maybe with a butt. He cut my eyes and ears, perhaps with his laces. . . . My jaw was swollen from the right temple down the cheek, along under the chin and partway up the other side. The referee, the ring itself, was full of blood. . . . But it was in that first fight, in which I lost my American light-heavyweight title, that I knew I had found a way to beat Harry eventually. I was fortunate, really. If boxing in those days had been afflicted with the Commission doctors we have today—who are always poking their noses into the ring and examining superficial wounds—the first fight with Greb would have been stopped before I learned how to beat him. It's possible, even probable, that if this had happened I would never have been heard of again.

Tunney's career, in other words, was built upon pain. Without it he would never have moved up into Dempsey's class.

Tommy Loughran, light-heavyweight champion in the years 1927–29, was a master boxer greatly admired by other boxers. He approached boxing literally as a science—as Tunney did—studying his opponents' styles and mapping out ring strategy for each fight, as boxers and their trainers commonly do today. Loughran rigged up mirrors in his basement so that he could watch himself as he worked out, for, as he said, no boxer ever sees himself quite as he appears to his opponent. He sees the opponent but not himself as an opponent. The secret of Loughran's career was that his right hand broke easily so that he was forced to use it only once each fight: for the knockout punch or nothing. "I'd get one shot then the agony of the thing would hurt me if the guy got up," Loughran said. "Anybody I ever hit with a left hook I knocked flat on his face, but I would never take a chance for fear if my [left hand] goes, I'm done for."

Both Tunney and Loughran, it is instructive to note, retired from boxing well before they were forced to retire. Tunney became a highly successful businessman, and Loughran a highly successful sugar broker on the Wall Street commodities market. (Just to suggest that boxers are not invariably stupid, illiterate, or punch-drunk.)

Then there was Carmen Basilio!—much loved for his audacious ring style, his hit-and-be-hit approach. Basilio was world middle- and welterweight champion 1953–57, stoic, determined, a slugger willing to get hit in order to deal powerful counter-punches of his own. Onlookers marveled at the punishment Basilio seemed to absorb though Basilio insisted that he didn't get hit the way people believed. And when he was hit, and hit hard—

People don't realize how you're affected by a knockout punch when you're hit on the chin. It's nerves is all it is. There's no real concussion as far as the brain is concerned. I got hit on the point of the chin [in a match with Tony DeMarco in 1955]. It was a left hook that hit the right point of my chin. What happens is it pulls your jawbone out of your socket from the right side and jams it into the left side and the nerve there paralyzed the whole left side of my body, especially my legs. My left knee buckled and I almost went down, but when I got back to my corner the bottom of my foot felt like it had needles about six inches high and I just kept stamping my foot on the floor, trying to bring it back. And by the time the bell rang it was all right.

Basilio belongs to the rough-and-tumble era of LaMotta, Graziano, Zale, Pep, Saddler; Gene Fullmer, Dick Tiger, Kid Gavilan. An era when, if two boxers wanted to fight dirty, the referee was likely to give them license, or at least not to interfere.

Of Muhammad Ali in his prime Norman Mailer observed, "He worked apparently on the premise that there was something obscene about being hit." But in fights in his later career, as with George Foreman in Zaire, even Muhammad Ali was willing to be hit, and to be hurt, in order to wear down an opponent. Brawling fighters—those with "heart" like Jake LaMotta, Rocky Graziano, Ray Mancini—have little choice but to absorb terrible punishment in exchange for some advantage (which does not in any case always come). And surely it is true that some boxers (see Jake LaMotta's autobiographical *Raging Bull*) invite injury as a means of assuaging guilt, in a Dostoyevskian exchange of physical well-being for peace of mind. Boxing is about being hit rather more than it is about hitting, just as it is about feeling pain, if not devastating psychological paralysis, more than it is about winning. One sees clearly from the "tragic" careers of any number of boxers that the boxer prefers physical pain in the ring to the absence of pain that is ideally the condition of ordinary life. If one cannot hit, one can yet be hit, and know that one is still alive.

It might be said that boxing is primarily about maintaining a body capable of entering combat against other well-conditioned bodies. Not the public spectacle, the fight itself, but the rigorous training period leading up to it demands the most discipline, and is believed to be the chief cause of the boxer's physical and mental infirmities. (As a boxer ages his sparring partners get younger, the game itself gets more desperate.)

The artist senses some kinship, however oblique and one-sided, with the professional boxer in this matter of training. This fanatic subordination of the self in terms of a wished-for destiny. One might compare the time-bound public spectacle of the boxing match (which could be as brief as an ignominious forty-five seconds—the record for a title fight!) with the publication of a writer's book. That which is "public" is but the final stage in a protracted, arduous, grueling, and frequently despairing period of preparation. Indeed, one of the reasons for the habitual attraction of serious writers to boxing (from Swift, Pope, Johnson to Hazlitt, Lord Byron, Hemingway, and our own Norman Mailer, George Plimpton, Ted Hoagland, Wilfrid Sheed, Daniel Halpern, et al.) is the sport's systematic cultivation of pain in the interests of a project, a life-goal: the willed transposing of the sensation we know as pain (physical, psychological, emotional) into its polar opposite. If this is masochism—and I doubt that it is, or that it is simply—it is also intelligence, cunning, strategy. It is an act of consummate self-determination—the constant reestablishment of the parameters of one's being. To not only accept but to actively invite what most sane creatures avoid—pain, humiliation, loss, chaos—is to experience the present moment as already, in a sense, past. *Here* and *now* are but part of the design of *there* and *then:* pain now but control, and therefore triumph, later. And pain itself is miraculously transposed by dint of its context. Indeed, it might be said that "context" is all.

The novelist George Garrett, an amateur boxer of some decades ago, reminisces about his training period:

> I learned something . . . about the brotherhood of boxers. People went into this brutal and often self-destructive activity for a rich variety of motivations, most of them bitterly antisocial and verging on the psychotic. Most of the fighters I knew of were wounded people who felt a deep, powerful urge to wound others at real risk to themselves. In the beginning. What happened was that in almost every case, there was so much self-discipline required and craft involved, so much else besides one's original motivations to concentrate on, that these motivations became at least cloudy and vague and were often forgotten, lost completely. Many good and experienced fighters (as has often been noted) become gentle and kind people. . . . They have the habit of leaving all their fight in the ring. And even there, in the ring, it is dangerous to invoke too much anger. It can be a stimulant, but is very expensive of energy. It is impractical to get mad most of the time.

Of all boxers it seems to have been Rocky Marciano (still our only undefeated heavyweight champion) who trained with the most monastic devotion; his training methods have become legendary. In contrast to reckless fighters like Harry "The Human Windmill" Greb, who kept in condition by boxing all the time, Marciano was willing to seclude himself from the world, including his wife and family, for as long as three months before a fight. Apart from the grueling physical ordeal of this period and the obsessive preoccupation with diet and weight and muscle tone, Marciano concentrated on one thing: the upcoming fight. Every minute of his life was defined in terms of the opening second of the fight. In his training camp the opponent's name was never mentioned in Marciano's hearing, nor was boxing as a subject discussed. In the final month Marciano would not write a letter since a letter related to the outside world. During the last ten days before a fight he would see no mail, take no telephone calls, meet no new acquaintances. During the week before the fight he would not shake hands. Or go for a ride in a car, however brief. No new foods! No dreaming of the morning after the fight! For all that was not *the fight* had to be excluded from consciousness. When Marciano worked out with a punching bag he saw his opponent before him, when he jogged he saw his opponent close beside him, no doubt when he slept he "saw" his opponent constantly—as the cloistered monk or nun chooses by an act of fanatical will to "see" only God.

Madness?—or merely discipline?—this absolute subordination of the self. In any case, for Marciano, it worked.

EROTICISM

Tommy Hearns was a little cocky, and I had something for him.

MARVIN HAGLER

No sport is more physical, more direct, than boxing. No sport appears more powerfully homoerotic: the confrontation in the ring—the disrobing—the sweaty heated combat that is part dance, courtship, coupling—the frequent urgent pursuit by one boxer of the other in the fight's natural and violent movement toward the "knockout": surely boxing derives much of its appeal from this mimicry of a species of erotic love in which one man overcomes the other in an exhibition of superior strength and will. The heralded celibacy of the fighter-in-training is very much a part of boxing lore: instead of focusing his energies and fantasies upon a woman the boxer focuses them upon an opponent. Where Woman has been, Opponent must be.

As Ali's Bundini Brown has said: "You got to get the hard-on, and then you got to keep it. You want to be careful not to lose the hard-on, and cautious not to come."

Most fights, however fought, end with an embrace between the boxers after the final bell—a gesture of mutual respect and apparent affection that appears to the onlooker to be more than perfunctory. Rocky Graziano sometimes kissed his opponents out of gratitude for the fight. One might wonder if the boxing match leads irresistibly to this moment: the public embrace of two men who otherwise, in public or in private, could never approach each other with such passion. Though many men are loudly contemptuous of weakness (as if eager to dissociate themselves from it: as during a boxing match when one or both boxers are unwilling to fight) a woman is struck by the admiration, amounting at times to awe, they will express for a man who has exhibited superior courage while losing his fight. And they will express tenderness for injured boxers, even if it is only by way of commentary on photographs: the picture of Ray Mancini after his second defeat by Livingstone Bramble, for instance, when Mancini's face was hideously battered (photographs in *Sports Illustrated* and elsewhere were gory, near-pornographic); the much-reprinted photograph of the defeated Thomas Hearns being carried to his corner in the arms of an enormous black man (a bodyguard, one assumes) in solemn formal attire—Hearns the "Hit Man" now helpless, semiconscious, looking very like a black Christ taken from the cross. These are powerful, haunting, unsettling images, cruelly beautiful, inextricably bound up with boxing's primordial appeal.

Yet to suggest that men might love and respect one another directly, without the violent ritual of combat, is to misread man's greatest passion—for war, not peace. Love, if there is to be love, comes second.

IN PLACE OF WOMAN

What time is it?—"Macho Time"!

HECTOR "MACHO MAN" CAMACHO,
WBC LIGHTWEIGHT CHAMPION

I don't want to knock my opponent out. I want to hit him, step away, and watch him hurt. I want his heart.

JOE FRAZIER,
FORMER HEAVYWEIGHT CHAMPION OF THE WORLD

A fairy-tale proposition: the heavyweight champion is the most dangerous man on earth: the most feared, the most manly. His proper mate is very likely the fairy-tale princess whom the mirrors declare the fairest woman on earth.

Boxing is a purely masculine activity and it inhabits a purely masculine world. Which is not to suggest that most men are defined by it: clearly, most men are not. And though there are female boxers—a fact that seems to surprise, alarm, amuse—women's role in the sport has always been extremely marginal. (At the time of this writing the most famous American woman boxer is the black champion Lady Tyger Trimiar with her shaved head and theatrical tiger-striped attire.) At boxing matches women's role is limited to that of card girl and occasional National Anthem singer: stereotypical functions usually performed in stereotypically zestful feminine ways—for women have no natural place in the spectacle otherwise. The card girls in their bathing suits and spike heels, glamour girls of the 1950s, complement the boxers in their trunks and gym shoes but are not to be taken seriously: their public exhibition of themselves involves no risk and is purely decorative. Boxing is for men, and is about men, and is men. A celebration of the lost religion of masculinity all the more trenchant for its being lost.

In this world, strength of a certain kind—matched of course with intelligence and tirelessly developed skills—determines masculinity. Just as a boxer is his body, a man's masculinity is his use of his body. But it is also his triumph over another's use of his body. The Opponent is always male, the Opponent is the rival for one's own masculinity, most fully and combatively realized. Sugar Ray Leonard speaks of coming out of retirement to fight one man, Marvin Hagler: "I want Hagler. I need that man." Thomas Hearns, decisively beaten by Hagler, speaks of having been obsessed with him: "I want the rematch badly . . . there hasn't been a minute or an hour in any day that I haven't thought about it." Hence women's characteristic repugnance for boxing per se coupled with an intense interest in and curiosity about men's fascination with it. Men fighting men to determine worth (i.e., masculinity) excludes women as completely as the female experience of childbirth excludes men. And is there, perhaps, some connection?

In any case, raw aggression is thought to be the peculiar province of men, as nurturing is the peculiar province of women. (The female boxer violates this stereotype and cannot be taken seriously—she is parody, she is cartoon, she is monstrous. Had she an ideology, she is likely to be a feminist.) The psychologist Erik Erikson discovered that while little girls playing with blocks generally create pleasant interior spaces and attractive entrances, little boys are inclined to pile up the blocks as high as they can and then watch them fall down: "the contemplation of ruins," Erikson observes, "is a masculine specialty." No matter the mesmerizing grace and beauty of a great boxing match, it is the catastrophic finale for which everyone waits, and hopes: the blocks piled as high as they can possibly be piled, then brought spectacularly down. Women, watching a boxing match, are likely to identify with the losing, or hurt, boxer; men are likely to identify with the winning boxer. There is a point at which male spectators are able to identify with the fight itself as, it might be said, a Platonic experience abstracted from its particulars; if they have favored one boxer over the other, and that boxer is losing, they can shift their loyalty to the winner—or, rather, "loyalty" shifts, apart from conscious volition. In that way the ritual of fighting is always honored. The high worth of combat is always affirmed.

Boxing's very vocabulary suggests a patriarchal world taken over by adolescents. This world is young. Its focus is youth. Its focus is of course *macho—machismo* raised beyond parody. To enter the claustrophobic world of professional boxing even as a spectator is to enter what appears to be a distillation of the masculine world, empty now of women, its fantasies, hopes, and stratagems magnified as in a distorting mirror, or a dream.

Here, we find ourselves through the looking-glass. Values are reversed, evaginated: a boxer is valued not for his humanity but for being a "killer," a "mauler," a "hit-man," an "animal," for being "savage," "merciless," "devastating," "ferocious," "vicious," "murderous." Opponents are not merely defeated as in a game but are "decked," "stiffed," "starched," "iced," "destroyed," "annihilated." Even the veteran sportswriters of so respectable a publication as *The Ring* are likely to be pitiless toward a boxer who has been beaten. Much of the appeal of Roberto Durán for intellectual boxing *aficionados* no less than for those whom one might suppose his natural constituency was that he seemed truly to want to kill his opponents: in his prime he was the "baby-faced assassin" with the "dead eyes" and "deadpan" expression who once said, having knocked out an opponent named Ray Lampkin, that he hadn't trained for the fight—next time he would kill the man. (According to legend Durán once felled a horse with a single blow.) Sonny Liston was another champion lauded for his menace, so different in spirit from Floyd Patterson as to seem to belong to another subspecies; to watch Liston overcome Patterson in tapes of their fights in the early 1960s is to watch the defeat of "civilization" by something so elemental and primitive it cannot be named. Masculinity in these terms is strictly hierarchical—two men cannot occupy the same space at the same time.

At the present time twenty-year-old Mike Tyson, Cus D'Amato's much-vaunted protégé, is being groomed as the most dangerous man in the heavyweight division. He is spoken of with awe as a "young bull"; his strength is prodigious, at least as demonstrated against fairly hapless, stationary opponents; he enters the arena robeless—"I feel more like a warrior"—and gleaming with sweat. He does not even wear socks. His boxing model is not Muhammad Ali, the most brilliant heavyweight of modern times, but Rocky Marciano, graceless, heavy-footed, indomitable, the man with the massive right-hand punch who was willing to absorb five blows in the hope of landing one. It was after having broken Jesse Ferguson's nose in a recent match that Tyson told reporters that it was his strategy to try to drive the bone back into the brain. . . .

The names of boxers! *Machismo* as sheer poetry.

Though we had, in another era, "Gentleman Jim" Corbett (world heavyweight champion, 1892–97); and the first black heavyweight champion, Jack Johnson (1908–15) called himself "Li'l Arthur" as a way of commenting playfully on his powerful physique and savage ring style. (Johnson was a white man's nightmare: the black man who mocked his white opponents as he humiliated them with his fists.) In more recent times we had "Sugar Ray" Robinson and his younger namesake "Sugar Ray" Leonard. And Tyrone Crawley, a thinking man's boxer, calls himself "The Butterfly." But for the most part a boxer's ring name is chosen to suggest something more ferocious: Jack Dempsey of Manassa, Colorado, was "The Manassa Mauler"; the formidable Harry Greb was "The Human Windmill"; Joe Louis was, of course, "The Brown Bomber"; Rocky Marciano, "The Brockton Blockbuster"; Jake LaMotta, "The Bronx Bull"; Tommy Jackson, "Hurricane" Jackson; Roberto Durán, "Hands of Stone" and "The Little Killer" variously. More recent are Ray "Boom-Boom" Mancini, Thomas "Hit-Man" Hearns, James "Hard Rock" Green, Al "Earthquake" Carter, Frank "The Animal" Fletcher, Donald "The Cobra" Curry, Aaron "The Hawk" Pryor, "Terrible" Tim Witherspoon, "Bonecrusher" Smith, Johnny "Bump City" Bumphus, Lonnie "Lightning" Smith, Barry "The Clones Cyclone" McGuigan, Gene "Mad Dog" Hatcher, Livingstone "Pit Bull" Bramble, Hector "Macho Man" Camacho. "Marvelous" Marvin Hagler changed his name legally to Marvelous Marvin Hagler before his fight with Thomas Hearns brought him to national prominence.

It was once said by José Torres that the *machismo* of boxing is a condition of poverty. But it is not, surely, a condition uniquely of poverty? Or
even of adolescence? I think of it as the obverse of the feminine, the
denial of the feminine-in-man that has its ambiguous attractions for all
men, however "civilized." It is a remnant of another, earlier era when the
physical being was primary and the warrior's masculinity its highest
expression.

CONSIDERATIONS

Thinking

Oates believes that "each boxing match is a story—a unique and highly condensed drama without words." She believes as well that "boxing as performance
is more clearly akin to dance or music than narrative." What do you suppose she
means by that kinship?

To what extent do you agree with the broader implications of Oates's suggestion about the finale of the boxing match: "One might wonder if the boxing
match leads irresistibly to this moment: the public embrace of two men who otherwise, in public or in private, could never approach each other with such passion."

Connecting

Recall a moment in your life when you either experienced or observed someone else experiencing pain as "something other than pain."

Besides sports and writing, account for other activities that call for the "systematic cultivation of pain in the interests of a project, a life-goal: the willed transposing of the sensation we know as pain (physical, psychological, emotional) into
its polar opposite."

Writing

In a few paragraphs, develop Oates's notion that boxing is more akin to
music or dance than to narrative. Call on your own experience and your imagination to help you develop Oates's notion.

Write an essay about competition. In the essay, develop your judgment about
competition, keeping in mind Oates's claim that "without the ferocity of competition, without, even, 'envy, jealousy, and ambition' in the context, the Hellenic city,
like the Hellenic man, degenerated."

Go to the library and read "On Boxing" in its entirety. As you read, try to figure out what Oates means by the "primitive" or "primordial" aspects of boxing.
Write a short essay accounting for what you find. Cite Oates in your essay to justify your interpretation.

T im O'Brien (b.1946)

Tim O'Brien was born in Austin, Minnesota. After attending Macalaster College and Harvard University, he was drafted into the Army during the Vietnamese war, in which he fought and was wounded. O'Brien's work often combines elements of fiction and nonfiction, as for example, the pieces in his first book, *If I Die in a Combat Zone, Box Me Up and Ship Me Home* (1973), for which he coined the term *autofiction* to indicate their blend of fiction and autobiography.

His more recent collection, *The Things They Carried*, while largely fiction, also contains pieces such as "How to Tell a True War Story" that read more like essays. This piece, in fact, calls attention to its factuality, inviting readers to consider the way fact and fiction intersect and diverge, fade in and out of one another. The piece is noteworthy as well for the striking stories it includes and for the way it depends on the storyteller's distinctive voice.

How to Tell a True War Story

This is true.

I had a buddy in Vietnam. His name was Bob Kiley, but everybody called him Rat.

A friend of his gets killed, so about a week later Rat sits down and writes a letter to the guy's sister. Rat tells her what a great brother she had, how together the guy was, a number one pal and comrade. A real soldier's soldier, Rat says. Then he tells a few stories to make the point, how her brother would always volunteer for stuff nobody else would volunteer for in a million years, dangerous stuff, like doing recon or going out on these really badass night patrols. Stainless steel balls, Rat tells her. The guy was a little crazy, for sure, but crazy in a good way, a real daredevil, because he liked the challenge of it, he liked testing himself, just man against gook. A great, great guy, Rat says.

Anyway, it's a terrific letter, very personal and touching. Rat almost bawls writing it. He gets all teary telling about the good times they had together, how her brother made the war seem almost fun, always raising hell and lighting up villes and bringing smoke to bear every which way. A great sense of humor, too. Like the time at this river when he went fishing with a whole damn crate of hand grenades. Probably the funniest thing in world history, Rat says, all that gore, about twenty zillion dead gook fish. Her brother, he had the right attitude. He knew how to have a good time. On Halloween, this real hot spooky night, the dude paints up his body all different colors and puts on this weird mask and hikes over to a ville and goes trick-or-treating almost stark naked, just boots and balls and an M-16. A tremendous human being, Rat says. Pretty nutso sometimes, but you could trust him with your life.

And then the letter gets very sad and serious. Rat pours his heart out. He says he loved the guy. He says the guy was his best friend in the world. They were like soul mates, he says, like twins or something, they had a whole lot in common. He tells the guy's sister he'll look her up when the war's over.

So what happens?

Rat mails the letter. He waits two months. The dumb cooze never writes back.

460

A true war story is never moral. It does not instruct, nor encourage virtue, nor suggest models of proper human behavior, nor restrain men from doing the things men have always done. If a story seems moral, do not believe it. If at the end of a war story you feel uplifted, or if you feel that some small bit of rectitude has been salvaged from the larger waste, then you have been made the victim of a very old and terrible lie. There is no rectitude whatsoever. There is no virtue. As a first rule of thumb, there-fore, you can tell a true war story by its absolute and uncompromising allegiance to obscenity and evil. Listen to Rat Kiley. Cooze, he says. He does not say bitch. He certainly does not say woman, or girl. He says cooze. Then he spits and stares. He's nineteen years old—it's too much for him—so he looks at you with those big sad gentle killer eyes and says *cooze,* because his friend is dead, and because it's so incredibly sad and true: she never wrote back.

You can tell a true war story if it embarrasses you. If you don't care for obscenity, you don't care for the truth; if you don't care for the truth, watch how you vote. Send guys to war, they come home talking dirty.

Listen to Rat: "Jesus Christ, man, I write this beautiful fuckin' letter, I slave over it, and what happens? The dumb cooze never writes back."

The dead guy's name was Curt Lemon. What happened was, we crossed a muddy river and marched west into the mountains, and on the third day we took a break along a trail junction in deep jungle. Right away, Lemon and Rat Kiley started goofing. They didn't understand about the spooki-ness. They were kids; they just didn't know. A nature hike, they thought, not even a war, so they went off into the shade of some giant trees—quadruple canopy, no sunlight at all—and they were giggling and calling each other yellow mother and playing a silly game they'd invented. The game involved smoke grenades, which were harmless unless you did stu-pid things, and what they did was pull out the pin and stand a few feet apart and play catch under the shade of those huge trees. Whoever chick-ened out was a yellow mother. And if nobody chickened out, the grenade would make a light popping sound and they'd be covered with smoke and they'd laugh and dance around and then do it again.

It's all exactly true.

It happened to *me,* nearly twenty years ago, and I still remember that trail junction and those giant trees and a soft dripping sound somewhere beyond the trees. I remember the smell of moss. Up in the canopy there were tiny white blossoms, but no sunlight at all, and I remember the shadows spreading out under the trees where Curt Lemon and Rat Kiley were playing catch with smoke grenades. Mitchell Sanders sat flipping his yo-yo. Norman Bowker and Kiowa and Dave Jensen were dozing, or half dozing, and all around us were those ragged green mountains.

Except for the laughter things were quiet.

At one point, I remember, Mitchell Sanders turned and looked at me, not quite nodding, as if to warn me about something, as if he already *knew*, then after a while he rolled up his yo-yo and moved away.

It's hard to tell you what happened next.

They were just goofing. There was a noise, I suppose, which must've been the detonator, so I glanced behind me and watched Lemon step from the shade into bright sunlight. His face was suddenly brown and shining. A handsome kid, really. Sharp gray eyes, lean and narrow-waisted, and when he died it was almost beautiful, the way the sunlight came around him and lifted him up and sucked him high into a tree full of moss and vines and white blossoms.

In any war story, but especially a true one, it's difficult to separate what happened from what seemed to happen. What seems to happen becomes its own happening and has to be told that way. The angles of vision are skewed. When a booby trap explodes, you close your eyes and duck and float outside yourself. When a guy dies, like Curt Lemon, you look away and then look back for a moment and then look away again. The pictures get jumbled; you tend to miss a lot. And then afterward, when you go to tell about it, there is always that surreal seemingness, which makes the story seem untrue, but which in fact represents the hard and exact truth as it *seemed*.

*   *   *

In many cases a true war story cannot be believed. If you believe it, be skeptical. It's a question of credibility. Often the crazy stuff is true and the normal stuff isn't, because the normal stuff is necessary to make you believe the truly incredible craziness.

In other cases you can't even tell a true war story. Sometimes it's just beyond telling.

I heard this one, for example, from Mitchell Sanders. It was near dusk and we were sitting at my foxhole along a wide muddy river north of Quang Ngai. I remember how peaceful the twilight was. A deep pinkish red spilled out on the river, which moved without sound, and in the morning we would cross the river and march west into the mountains. The occasion was right for a good story.

"God's truth," Mitchell Sanders said. "A six-man patrol goes up into the mountains on a basic listening-post operation. The idea's to spend a week up there, just lie low and listen for enemy movement. They've got a radio along, so if they hear anything suspicious—anything—they're supposed to call in artillery or gunships, whatever it takes. Otherwise they keep strict field discipline. Absolute silence. They just listen."

Sanders glanced at me to make sure I had the scenario. He was playing with his yo-yo, dancing it with short, tight little strokes of the wrist.

His face was blank in the dusk.

"We're talking regulation, by-the-book LP. These six guys, they don't say boo for a solid week. They don't got tongues. *All* ears."

"Right," I said.

"Understand me?"

"Invisible."

Sanders nodded.

"Affirm," he said. "Invisible. So what happens is, these guys get themselves deep in the bush, all camouflaged up, and they lie down and wait and that's all they do, nothing else, they lie there for seven straight days and just listen. And man, I'll tell you—it's spooky. This is mountains. You don't *know* spooky till you been there. Jungle, sort of, except it's way up in the clouds and there's always this fog—like rain, except it's not raining—everything's all wet and swirly and tangled up and you can't see jack, you can't find your own pecker to piss with. Like you don't even have a body. Serious spooky. You just go with the vapors—the fog sort of takes you in . . . And the sounds, man. The sounds carry forever. You hear stuff nobody should *ever* hear."

Sanders was quiet for a second, just working the yo-yo, then he smiled at me.

"So after a couple days the guys start hearing this real soft, kind of wacked-out music. Weird echoes and stuff. Like a radio or something, but it's not a radio, it's this strange gook music that comes right out of the rocks. Faraway, sort of, but right up close, too. They try to ignore it. But it's a listening post, right? So they listen. And every night they keep hearing that crazyass gook concert. All kinds of chimes and xylophones. I mean, this is wilderness—no way, it can't be real—but there it *is*, like the mountains are tuned in to Radio fucking Hanoi. Naturally they get nervous. One guy sticks Juicy Fruit in his ears. Another guy almost flips. Thing is, though, they can't report music. They can't get on the horn and call back to base and say, 'Hey, listen, we need some firepower, we got to blow away this weirdo gook rock band.' They can't do that. It wouldn't go down. So they lie there in the fog and keep their mouths shut. And what makes it extra bad, see, is the poor dudes can't horse around like normal. Can't joke it away. Can't even talk to each other except maybe in whispers, all hush-hush, and that just revs up the willies. All they do is listen."

Again there was some silence as Mitchell Sanders looked out on the river. The dark was coming on hard now, and off to the west I could see the mountains rising in silhouette, all the mysteries and unknowns.

"This next part," Sanders said quietly, "you won't believe."

"Probably not," I said.

"You won't. And you know why?" He gave me a long, tired smile. "Because it happened. Because every word is absolutely dead-on true."

Sanders made a sound in his throat, like a sigh, as if to say he didn't care if I believed him or not. But he did care. He wanted me to feel the truth, to believe by the raw force of feeling. He seemed sad, in a way.

"These six guys," he said, "they're pretty fried out by now, and one night they start hearing voices. Like at a cocktail party. That's what it sounds like, this big swank gook cocktail party somewhere out there in the fog. Music and chitchat and stuff. It's crazy, I know, but they hear the champagne corks. They hear the actual martini glasses. Real hoity-toity, all very civilized, except this isn't civilization. This is Nam.

"Anyway, the guys try to be cool. They just lie there and groove, but after a while they start hearing—you won't believe this—they hear chamber music. They hear violins and cellos. They hear this terrific mama-san soprano. Then after a while they hear gook opera and a glee club and the Haiphong Boys Choir and a barbershop quartet and all kinds of weird chanting and Buddha-Buddha stuff. And the whole time, in the background, there's still that cocktail party going on. All these different voices. Not human voices, though. Because it's the mountains. Follow me? The rock—it's *talking*. And the fog, too, and the grass and the goddamn mongooses. Everything talks. The trees talk politics, the monkeys talk religion. The whole country. Vietnam. The place talks. It talks. Understand? Nam—it truly *talks*.

"The guys can't cope. They lose it. They get on the radio and report enemy movement—a whole army, they say—and they order up the firepower. They get arty and gunships. They call in air strikes. And I'll tell you, they fuckin' crash that cocktail party. All night long, they just smoke those mountains. They make jungle juice. They blow away trees and glee clubs and whatever else there is to blow away. Scorch time. They walk napalm up and down the ridges. They bring in the Cobras and F-4s, they use Willie Peter and HE and incendiaries. It's all fire. They make those mountains burn.

"Around dawn things finally get quiet. Like you never even *heard* quiet before. One of those real thick, real misty days—just clouds and fog, they're off in this special zone—and the mountains are absolutely dead-flat silent. Like Brigadoon—pure vapor, you know? Everything's all sucked up inside the fog. Not a single sound, except they still *hear* it.

"So they pack up and start humping. They head down the mountain, back to base camp, and when they get there they don't say diddly. They don't talk. Not a word, like they're deaf and dumb. Later on this fat bird colonel comes up and asks what the hell happened out there. What'd they hear? Why all the ordnance? The man's ragged out, he gets down tight on their case. I mean, they spent six trillion dollars on firepower, and this fatass colonel wants answers, he wants to know what the fuckin' story is.

"But the guys don't say zip. They just look at him for a while, sort of funny like, sort of amazed, and the whole war is right there in that stare. It says everything you can't ever say. It says, man, you got *wax* in your ears. It says, poor bastard, you'll never know—wrong frequency—you don't *even* want to hear this. Then they salute the fucker and walk away, because certain stories you don't ever tell."

You can tell a true war story by the way it never seems to end. Not then, not ever. Not when Mitchell Sanders stood up and moved off into the dark.

It all happened.

Even now, at this instant, I remember that yo-yo. In a way, I suppose, you had to be there, you had to hear it, but I could tell how desperately Sanders wanted me to believe him, his frustration at not quite getting the details right, not quite pinning down the final and definitive truth.

And I remember sitting at my foxhole that night, watching the shadows of Quang Ngai, thinking about the coming day and how we would cross the river and march west into the mountains, all the ways I might die, all the things I did not understand.

Late in the night Mitchell Sanders touched my shoulder.

"Just came to me," he whispered. "The moral, I mean. Nobody listens. Nobody hears nothin'. Like that fatass colonel. The politicians, all the civilian types. Your girlfriend. My girlfriend. Everybody's sweet little virgin girlfriend. What they need is to go out on LP. The vapors, man. Trees and rocks—you got to *listen* to your enemy."

And then again, in the morning, Sanders came up to me. The platoon was preparing to move out, checking weapons, going through all the little rituals that preceded a day's march. Already the lead squad had crossed the river and was filing off toward the west.

"I got a confession to make," Sanders said. "Last night, man, I had to make up a few things."

"I know that."

"The glee club. There wasn't any glee club."

"Right."

"No opera."

"Forget it, I understand."

"Yeah, but listen, it's still true. Those six guys, they heard wicked sound out there. They heard sound you just plain won't believe."

Sanders pulled on his rucksack, closed his eyes for a moment, then almost smiled at me. I knew what was coming.

"All right," I said, "what's the moral?"

"Forget it."

"No, go ahead."

For a long while he was quiet, looking away, and the silence kept stretching out until it was almost embarrassing. Then he shrugged and gave me a stare that lasted all day.

"Hear that quiet, man?" he said. "That quiet—just listen. There's your moral."

In a true war story, if there's a moral at all, it's like the thread that makes the cloth. You can't tease it out. You can't extract the meaning without unraveling the deeper meaning. And in the end, really, there's nothing much to say about a true war story, except maybe "Oh."

True war stories do not generalize. They do not indulge in abstraction or analysis.

For example: War is hell. As a moral declaration the old truism seems perfectly true, and yet because it abstracts, because it generalizes, I can't believe it with my stomach. Nothing turns inside.

It comes down to gut instinct. A true war story, if truly told, makes the stomach believe.

*   *   *

This one does it for me. I've told it before—many times, many versions—but here's what actually happened.

We crossed that river and marched west into the mountains. On the third day, Curt Lemon stepped on a booby-trapped 105 round. He was playing catch with Rat Kiley, laughing, and then he was dead. The trees were thick; it took nearly an hour to cut an LZ for the dustoff.

Later, higher in the mountains, we came across a baby VC water buffalo. What it was doing there I don't know—no farms or paddies—but we chased it down and got a rope around it and led it along to a deserted village where we set up for the night. After supper Rat Kiley went over and stroked its nose.

He opened up a can of C rations, pork and beans, but the baby buffalo wasn't interested.

Rat shrugged.

He stepped back and shot it through the right front knee. The animal did not make a sound. It went down hard, then got up again, and Rat took careful aim and shot off an ear. He shot it in the hindquarters and in the little hump at its back. He shot it twice in the flanks. It wasn't to kill; it was to hurt. He put the rifle muzzle up against the mouth and shot the mouth away. Nobody said much. The whole platoon stood there watching, feeling all kinds of things, but there wasn't a great deal of pity for the baby water buffalo. Curt Lemon was dead. Rat Kiley had lost his best friend in the world. Later in the week he would write a long personal letter to the guy's sister, who would not write back, but for now it was a question of pain. He shot off the tail. He shot away chunks of meat below the ribs. All around us there was the smell of smoke and filth and deep greenery, and the evening was humid and very hot. Rat went to automatic. He shot randomly, almost casually, quick little spurts in the belly and butt. Then he reloaded, squatted down, and shot it in the left front knee. Again the animal fell hard and tried to get up, but this time it couldn't quite make it. It wobbled and went down sideways. Rat shot it in the nose. He bent forward and whispered something, as if talking to a pet, then he shot it in the throat. All the while the baby buffalo was silent, or almost silent, just a light bubbling sound where the nose had been. It lay very still. Nothing moved except the eyes, which were enormous, the pupils shiny black and dumb.

Rat Kiley was crying. He tried to say something, but then cradled his rifle and went off by himself.

The rest of us stood in a ragged circle around the baby buffalo. For a time no one spoke. We had witnessed something essential, something brand-new and profound, a piece of the world so startling there was not yet a name for it.

Somebody kicked the baby buffalo.

It was still alive, though just barely, just in the eyes.

"Amazing," Dave Jensen said. "My whole life, I never seen anything like it."

"Never?"

"Not hardly. Not once."

Kiowa and Mitchell Sanders picked up the baby buffalo. They hauled it across the open square, hoisted it up, and dumped it in the village well.

Afterward, we sat waiting for Rat to get himself together.

"Amazing," Dave Jensen kept saying. "A new wrinkle. I never seen it before."

Mitchell Sanders took out his yo-yo. "Well, that's Nam," he said. "Garden of Evil. Over here, man, every sin's real fresh and original."

How do you generalize?

War is hell, but that's not the half of it, because war is also mystery and terror and adventure and courage and discovery and holiness and pity and despair and longing and love. War is nasty; war is fun. War is thrilling; war is drudgery. War makes you a man; war makes you dead.

The truths are contradictory. It can be argued, for instance, that war is grotesque. But in truth war is also beauty. For all its horror, you can't help but gape at the awful majesty of combat. You stare out at tracer rounds unwinding through the dark like brilliant red ribbons. You crouch in ambush as a cool, impassive moon rises over the nighttime paddies. You admire the fluid symmetries of troops on the move, the harmonies of sound and shape and proportion, the great sheets of metal-fire streaming down from a gunship, the illumination rounds, the white phosphorus, the purply orange glow of napalm, the rocket's red glare. It's not pretty, exactly. It's astonishing. It fills the eye. It commands you. You hate it, yes, but your eyes do not. Like a killer forest fire, like cancer under a microscope, any battle or bombing raid or artillery barrage has the aesthetic purity of absolute moral indifference—a powerful, implacable beauty—and a true war story will tell the truth about this, though the truth is ugly.

To generalize about war is like generalizing about peace. Almost everything is true. Almost nothing is true. At its core, perhaps, war is just another name for death, and yet any soldier will tell you, if he tells the truth, that proximity to death brings with it a corresponding proximity to life. After a firefight, there is always the immense pleasure of aliveness. The trees are alive. The grass, the soil—everything. All around you things are purely living, and you among them, and the aliveness makes you tremble. You feel an intense, out-of-the-skin awareness of your living self—your truest self, the human being you want to be and then become by the force of wanting it. In the midst of evil you want to be a good man. You want decency. You want justice and courtesy and human concord, things you never knew you wanted. There is a kind of largeness to it, a kind of godliness. Though it's odd, you're never more alive than when you're almost dead. You recognize what's valuable. Freshly, as if for the first time, you love what's best in yourself and in the world, all that might be lost. At the hour of dusk you sit at your foxhole and look out on a wide river turning pinkish red, and at the mountains beyond, and although in the morning you must cross the river and go into the mountains and do terrible things and maybe die, even so, you find yourself studying the fine colors on the river, you feel wonder and awe at the setting of the sun, and you are filled with a hard, aching love for how the world could be and always should be, but now is not.

Mitchell Sanders was right. For the common soldier, at least, war has the feel—the spiritual texture—of a great ghostly fog, thick and permanent. There is no clarity. Everything swirls. The old rules are no longer binding, the old truths no longer true. Right spills over into wrong. Order blends into chaos, love into hate, ugliness into beauty, law into anarchy, civility into savagery. The vapors suck you in. You can't tell where you are, or why you're there, and the only certainty is overwhelming ambiguity.

In war you lose your sense of the definite, hence your sense of truth itself, and therefore it's safe to say that in a true war story nothing is ever absolutely true.

Often in a true war story there is not even a point, or else the point doesn't hit you until twenty years later, in your sleep, and you wake up and shake your wife and start telling the story to her, except when you get to the end you've forgotten the point again. And then for a long time you lie there watching the story happen in your head. You listen to your wife's breathing. The war's over. You close your eyes. You smile and think, Christ, what's the *point?*

This one wakes me up.

In the mountains that day, I watched Lemon turn sideways. He laughed and said something to Rat Kiley. Then he took a peculiar half step, moving from shade into bright sunlight, and the booby-trapped 105 round blew him into a tree. The parts were just hanging there, so Dave Jensen and I were ordered to shinny up and peel him off. I remember the white bone of an arm. I remember pieces of skin and something wet and yellow that must've been the intestines. The gore was horrible, and stays with me. But what wakes me up twenty years later is Dave Jensen singing "Lemon Tree" as we threw down the parts.

You can tell a true war story by the questions you ask. Somebody tells a story, let's say, and afterward you ask, "Is it true?" and if the answer matters, you've got your answer.

For example, we've all heard this one. Four guys go down a trail. A grenade sails out. One guy jumps on it and takes the blast and saves his three buddies.

Is it true?

The answer matters.

You'd feel cheated if it never happened. Without the grounding reality, it's just a trite bit of puffery, pure Hollywood, untrue in the way all such stories are untrue. Yet even if it did happen—and maybe it did, anything's possible—even then you know it can't be true, because a true war story does not depend upon that kind of truth. Absolute occurrence is irrelevant. A thing may happen and be a total lie; another thing may not happen and be truer than the truth. For example: Four guys go down a trail. A grenade sails out. One guy jumps on it and takes the blast, but it's a killer grenade and everybody dies anyway. Before they die, though, one of the dead guys says, "The fuck you do *that* for?" and the jumper says, "Story of my life, man," and the other guy starts to smile but he's dead.

That's a true story that never happened.

Twenty years later, I can still see the sunlight on Lemon's face. I can see him turning, looking back at Rat Kiley, then he laughed and took that curious half step from shade into sunlight, his face suddenly brown and shining, and when his foot touched down, in that instant, he must've thought it was the sunlight that was killing him. It was not the sunlight. It was a rigged 105 round. But if I could ever get the story right, how the sun seemed to gather around him and pick him up and lift him high into a tree, if I could somehow re-create the fatal whiteness of that light, the quick glare, the obvious cause and effect, then you would believe the last thing Curt Lemon believed, which for him must've been the final truth.

Now and then, when I tell this story, someone will come up to me afterward and say she liked it. It's always a woman. Usually it's an older woman of kindly temperament and humane politics. She'll explain that as a rule she hates war stories; she can't understand why people want to wallow in all the blood and gore. But this one she liked. The poor baby buffalo, it made her sad. Sometimes, even, there are little tears. What I should do, she'll say, is put it all behind me. Find new stories to tell.

I won't say it but I'll think it.

I'll picture Rat Kiley's face, his grief, and I'll think, *You dumb cooze.* Because she wasn't listening.

It *wasn't* a war story. It was a *love* story.

But you can't say that. All you can do is tell it one more time, patiently, adding and subtracting, making up a few things to get at the real truth. No Mitchell Sanders, you tell her. No Lemon, no Rat Kiley. No trail junction. No baby buffalo. No vines or moss or white blossoms. Beginning to end, you tell her, it's all made up. Every goddamn detail—the mountains and the river and especially that poor dumb baby buffalo. None of it happened. *None* of it. And even if it did happen, it didn't happen in the mountains, it happened in this little village on the Batangan Peninsula, and it was raining like crazy, and one night a guy named Stink Harris woke up screaming with a leech on his tongue. You can tell a true war story if you just keep on telling it.

And in the end, of course, a true war story is never about war. It's about sunlight. It's about the special way that dawn spreads out on a river when you know you must cross the river and march into the mountains and do things you are afraid to do. It's about love and memory. It's about sorrow. It's about sisters who never write back and people who never listen.

CONSIDERATIONS

Thinking

What, according to O'Brien, are the characteristics of a true war story? What do you think might characterize untrue or false war stories? Is this a true war story? Why or why not?

What do you think of the examples of war stories O'Brien includes to illustrate the characteristics of a true war story?

Connecting

Use a few of O'Brien's characteristics of true war stories to evaluate any war story you have heard or read.

Compare the way O'Brien approaches the truth of stories with Lee K. Abbott's approach to telling stories and getting at truth in "The True Story of Why I Do What I Do."

In telling his final war story, O'Brien says, "That's a true story that never happened." What does he mean? Can a writer of true stories make up "a few things to get at the real truth"? Why or why not?

Writing

Select one passage you find especially engaging in O'Brien's piece and write a few pages reacting to and commenting upon what is said or shown there.

Discuss the extent to which the following comment from Philip Caputo's *A Rumor of War* corroborates what O'Brien suggests about war in "How to Tell a True War Story."

Writing about this kind of warfare is not a simple task. Repeatedly, I have found myself wishing that I had been the veteran of a conventional war, with dramatic campaigns and historic battles for subject matter instead of a monotonous succession of ambushes and fire-fights. But there were no Normandies or Gettysburgs for us, no epic clashes that decided the fates of armies or nations. The war was mostly a matter of enduring weeks of expectant waiting and, at random intervals, of conducting vicious manhunts through jungles and swamps where snipers harassed us constantly and booby traps cut us down one by one.

The tedium was occasionally relieved by a large-scale search-and-destroy operation, but the exhilaration of riding the lead helicopter into a landing zone was usually followed by more of the same hot walking, with the mud sucking at our boots and the sun thudding against our helmets while an invisible enemy shot at us from distant tree lines. The rare instances when the VC chose to fight a set-piece battle provided the only excitement; not ordinary excitement, but the manic ecstasy of contact. Weeks of bottled-up tensions would be released in a few minutes of orgiastic violence, men screaming and shouting obscenities above the explosions of grenades and the rapid, rippling bursts of automatic rifles.

Beyond adding a few more corpses to the weekly body count, none of these encounters achieved anything; none will ever appear in military histories or be studied by cadets at West Point. Still, they changed us and taught us, the men who fought in them; in those obscure skirmishes we learned the old lessons about fear, cowardice, courage, suffering, cruelty, and comradeship. Most of all, we learned about death at an age when it is common to think of oneself as immortal. Everyone loses that illusion eventually, but in civilian life it is lost in installments over the years. We lost it all at once and, in the span of months, passed from boyhood through manhood to a premature middle age. The knowledge of death, of the implacable limits placed on a man's existence, severed us from our youth as irrevocably as a surgeon's scissors had once severed us from the womb. And yet, few of us were past twenty-five. We left Vietnam peculiar creatures, with young shoulders that bore rather old heads.

George Orwell (1903–1950)

George Orwell is the pen name of Eric Blair, born in 1903 to English parents in Bengal, India. Orwell was educated in England, at Crossgates School, and at Eton as a King's Scholar. After declining the university, he went to Burma, where he served as a subdivisional officer in the Indian Imperial Police.

Best known for his fictional allegories *Animal Farm* and *1984*, Orwell has also written remarkable nonfiction, including both books and essays. *Homage to Catalonia* (1938) provides an eyewitness account of the Spanish Civil War, in which Orwell served as a soldier on the Republican side. *The Road to Wigan Pier* (1937) provides an angry account of mining conditions in northern England.

In "Marrakech," Orwell presents an account of a visit to the north African city in Morocco. He organizes his essay as a series of vignettes—brief descriptions of different places around the city, each of which conveys through carefully selected details and artfully constructed incidents an idea about the people who inhabit Marrakech.

Marrakech

As the corpse went past the flies left the restaurant table in a cloud and rushed after it, but they came back a few minutes later.

The little crowd of mourners—all men and boys, no women—threaded their way across the market-place between the piles of pomegranates and the taxis and the camels, wailing a short chant over and over again. What really appeals to the flies is that the corpses here are never put into coffins, they are merely wrapped in a piece of rag and carried on a rough wooden bier on the shoulders of four friends. When the friends get to the burying-ground they hack an oblong hole a foot or two deep, dump the body in it and fling over it a little of the dried-up, lumpy earth, which is like broken brick. No gravestone, no name, no identifying mark of any kind. The burying-ground is merely a huge waste of hummocky earth, like a derelict building-lot. After a month or two no one can even be certain where his own relatives are buried.

When you walk through a town like this—two hundred thousand inhabitants, of whom at least twenty thousand own literally nothing except the rags they stand up in—when you see how the people live, and still more how easily they die, it is always difficult to believe that you are walking among human beings. All colonial empires are in reality founded upon that fact. The people have brown faces—besides, there are so many of them! Are they really the same flesh as yourself? Do they even have names? Or are they merely a kind of undifferentiated brown stuff, about as individual as bees or coral insects? They rise out of the earth, they sweat and starve for a few years, and then they sink back into the nameless mounds of the graveyard and nobody notices that they are gone. And even the graves themselves soon fade back into the soil. Sometimes, out for a walk, as you break your way through the prickly pear, you notice that it is rather bumpy underfoot, and only a certain regularity in the bumps tells you that you are walking over skeletons.

I was feeding one of the gazelles in the public gardens.

Gazelles are almost the only animals that look good to eat when they are still alive, in fact, one can hardly look at their hindquarters without thinking of mint sauce. The gazelle I was feeding seemed to know that this thought was in my mind, for though it took the piece of bread I was holding out it obviously did not like me. It nibbled rapidly at the bread, then lowered its head and tried to butt me, then took another nibble and then butted again. Probably its idea was that if it could drive me away the bread would somehow remain hanging in mid-air.

An Arab navvy working on the path nearby lowered his heavy hoe and sidled towards us. He looked from the gazelle to the bread and from the bread to the gazelle, with a sort of quiet amazement, as though he had never seen anything quite like this before. Finally he said shyly in French:

"I could eat some of that bread."

I tore off a piece and he stowed it gratefully in some secret place under his rags. This man is an employee of the Municipality.

When you go through the Jewish quarters you gather some idea of what the medieval ghettoes were probably like. Under their Moorish rulers the Jews were only allowed to own land in certain restricted areas, and after centuries of this kind of treatment they have ceased to bother about overcrowding. Many of the streets are a good deal less than six feet wide, the houses are completely windowless, and sore-eyed children cluster everywhere in unbelievable numbers, like clouds of flies. Down the centre of the street there is generally running a little river of urine.

In the bazaar huge families of Jews, all dressed in the long black robe and little black skull-cap, are working in dark fly-infested booths that look like caves. A carpenter sits cross-legged at a prehistoric lathe, turning chair-legs at lightning speed. He works the lathe with a bow in his right hand and guides the chisel with his left foot, and thanks to a lifetime of sitting in this position his left leg is warped out of shape. At his side his grandson, aged six, is already starting on the simpler parts of the job.

I was just passing the coppersmiths' booths when somebody noticed that I was lighting a cigarette. Instantly, from the dark holes all round, there was a frenzied rush of Jews, many of them old grandfathers with flowing grey beards, all clamouring for a cigarette. Even a blind man somewhere at the back of one of the booths heard a rumour of cigarettes and came crawling out, groping in the air with his hand. In about a minute I had used up the whole packet. None of these people, I suppose, works less than twelve hours a day, and every one of them looks on a cigarette as a more or less impossible luxury.

As the Jews live in self-contained communities they follow the same trades as the Arabs, except for agriculture. Fruit-sellers, potters, silversmiths, blacksmiths, butchers, leather-workers, tailors, water-carriers, beggars, porters—whichever way you look you see nothing but Jews. As a matter of fact there are thirteen thousand of them, all living in the space of a few acres. A good job Hitler isn't here. Perhaps he is on his way, however. You hear the usual dark rumours about the Jews, not only from the Arabs but from the poorer Europeans.

"Yes, *mon vieux,* they took my job away from me and gave it to a Jew. The Jews! They're the real rulers of this country, you know. They've got all the money. They control the banks, finance—everything."

"But," I said, "isn't it a fact that the average Jew is a labourer working for about a penny an hour?"

"Ah, that's only for show! They're all moneylenders really. They're cunning, the Jews."

In just the same way, a couple of hundred years ago, poor old women used to be burned for witchcraft when they could not even work enough magic to get themselves a square meal.

All people who work with their hands are partly invisible, and the more important the work they do, the less visible they are. Still, a white skin is always fairly conspicuous. In northern Europe, when you see a labourer ploughing a field, you probably give him a second glance. In a hot country, anywhere south of Gibraltar or east of Suez, the chances are that you don't even see him. I have noticed this again and again. In a tropical landscape one's eye takes in everything except the human beings. It takes in the dried-up soil, the prickly pear, the palm-tree and the distant mountain, but it always misses the peasant hoeing at his patch. He is the same colour as the earth, and a great deal less interesting to look at.

It is only because of this that the starved countries of Asia and Africa are accepted as tourist resorts. No one would think of running cheap trips to the Distressed Areas. But where the human beings have brown skins their poverty is simply not noticed. What does Morocco mean to a Frenchman? An orange-grove or a job in government service. Or to an Englishman? Camels, castles, palm-trees, Foreign Legionnaires, brass trays and bandits. One could probably live here for years without noticing that for nine-tenths of the people the reality of life is an endless, back-breaking struggle to wring a little food out of an eroded soil.

Most of Morocco is so desolate that no wild animal bigger than a hare can live on it. Huge areas which were once covered with forest have turned into a treeless waste where the soil is exactly like broken-up brick. Nevertheless a good deal of it is cultivated, with frightful labour. Everything is done by hand. Long lines of women, bent double like inverted capital Ls, work their way slowly across the field, tearing up the prickly weeds with their hands, and the peasant gathering lucerne for fodder pulls it up stalk by stalk instead of reaping it, thus saving an inch or two on each stalk. The plough is a wretched wooden thing, so frail that one can easily carry it on one's shoulder, and fitted underneath with a rough iron spike which stirs the soil to a depth of about four inches. This is as much as the strength of the animals is equal to. It is usual to plough with a cow and a donkey yoked together. Two donkeys would not be quite strong enough, but on the other hand two cows would cost a little more to feed. The peasants possess no harrows, they merely plough the soil several times over in different directions, finally leaving it in rough furrows, after which the whole field has to be shaped with hoes into small oblong patches, to conserve water. Except for a day or two after the rare rainstorms there is never enough water. Along the edges of the fields channels are hacked out to a depth of thirty or forty feet to get at the tiny trickles which run through the subsoil.

Every afternoon a file of very old women passes down the road outside my house, each carrying a load of firewood. All of them are mummified with age and the sun, and all of them are tiny. It seems to be generally the case in primitive communities that the women, when they get beyond a certain age, shrink to the size of children. One day a poor old creature who could not have been more than four feet tall crept past me under a vast load of wood. I stopped her and put a five-sou piece (a little more than a farthing) into her hand. She answered with a shrill wail, almost a scream, which was partly gratitude but mainly surprise. I suppose that from her point of view, by taking any notice of her, I seemed almost to be violating a law of nature. She accepted her status as an old woman, that is to say as a beast of burden. When a family is travelling it is quite usual to see a father and a grown-up son riding ahead on donkeys, and an old woman following on foot, carrying the baggage.

But what is strange about these people is their invisibility. For several weeks, always at about the same time of day, the file of old women had hobbled past the house with their firewood, and though they had registered themselves on my eyeballs I cannot truly say that I had seen them. Firewood was passing—that was how I saw it. It was only that one day I happened to be walking behind them, and the curious up-and-down motion of a load of wood drew my attention to the human being underneath it. Then for the first time I noticed the poor old earth-coloured bodies, bodies reduced to bones and leathery skin, bent double under the crushing weight. Yet I suppose I had not been five minutes on Moroccan soil before I noticed the overloading of the donkeys and was infuriated by it. There is no question that the donkeys are damnably treated. The Moroccan donkey is hardly bigger than a St Bernard dog, it carries a load which in the British army would be considered too much for a fifteen-hands mule, and very often its pack-saddle is not taken off its back for weeks together. But what is peculiarly pitiful is that it is the most willing creature on earth, it follows its master like a dog and does not need either bridle or halter. After a dozen years of devoted work it suddenly drops dead, whereupon its master tips it into the ditch and the village dogs have torn its guts out before it is cold.

This kind of thing makes one's blood boil, whereas—on the whole—the plight of the human beings does not. I am not commenting, merely pointing to a fact. People with brown skins are next door to invisible. Anyone can be sorry for the donkey with its galled back, but it is generally owing to some kind of accident if one even notices the old woman under her load of sticks.

As the storks flew northward the Negroes were marching southward—a long, dusty column, infantry, screw-gun batteries and then more infantry, four or five thousand men in all, winding up the road with a clumping of boots and a clatter of iron wheels.

They were Senegalese, the blackest Negroes in Africa, so black that sometimes it is difficult to see whereabouts on their necks the hair begins. Their splendid bodies were hidden in reach-me-down khaki uniforms, their feet squashed into boots that looked like blocks of wood, and every tin hat seemed to be a couple of sizes too small. It was very hot and the men had marched a long way. They slumped under the weight of their packs and the curiously sensitive black faces were glistening with sweat.

As they went past a tall, very young Negro turned and caught my eye. But the look he gave me was not in the least the kind of look you might expect. Not hostile, not contemptuous, not sullen, not even inquisitive. It was the shy, wide-eyed Negro look, which actually is a look of profound respect. I saw how it was. This wretched boy, who is a French citizen and has therefore been dragged from the forest to scrub floors and catch syphilis in garrison towns, actually has feelings of reverence before a white skin. He has been taught that the white race are his masters, and he still believes it.

But there is one thought which every white man (and in this connection it doesn't matter twopence if he calls himself a Socialist) thinks when

he sees a black army marching past. "How much longer can we go on kid-
ding these people? How long before they turn their guns in the other
direction?"

It was curious, really. Every white man there has this thought stowed
somewhere or other in his mind. I had it, so had the other onlookers, so
had the officers on their sweating chargers and the white NCOs marching
in the ranks. It was a kind of secret which we all knew and were too
clever to tell; only the Negroes didn't know it. And really it was almost
like watching a flock of cattle to see the long column, a mile or two miles
of armed men, flowing peacefully up the road, while the great white birds
drifted over them in the opposite direction, glittering like scraps of paper.

CONSIDERATIONS

Thinking

This essay says something about Marrakech and about its people. What
political point does Orwell make in describing both the place and the people?

To make his point, Orwell relies on incident, illustration, and analogy. In the
gazelle episode, for example, a brief scenario is described and a bit of conversation included. What is implied by the man's remark, "I could eat some of that
bread"? What is implied by his act of putting the bread in his clothes?

Connecting

In the essay overall, Orwell presents a series of scenes—the burial ground,
the zoo, the ghetto, the women carrying firewood, the Senegalese troops—all to
convey his view of Marrakech. What does each scene imply, and how are the
scenes related?

You might think of the section that begins "When you go through the Jewish
quarters" as a miniature version of the essay as a whole. This section contains a
series of vignettes, each of which suggests an idea. Identify the scenes and explain
what they have in common.

Writing

Write an advertisement or travel poster inviting Americans to vacation in
Marrakech, either Orwell's Marrakech or the Marrakech of today. You might think
of yourself as a representative for public relations for the Morrocan government.
Or you might write as a member of a United Nations committee on world brotherhood.

Describe your neighborhood or campus by selecting a series of locations for
brief descriptive vignettes. Try to suggest rather than explicitly state your overall
view of the place the vignettes convey.

Cynthia Ozick
(b.1928)

Cynthia Ozick was born in New York City, the daughter of a pharmacist. After receiving a B.A. from New York University and an M.A. from Ohio State University, she began writing fiction, publishing her first novel, *Trust,* in 1966. She has subsequently published additional novels, novellas, and short stories. In addition to her fiction, Ozick has published two collections of essays, *Art and Ardor* (1983) and *Metaphor and Memory* (1988).

In "The Seam of the Snail," her talent is amply evident—in a richness of language including a profusion of details and a persistence in working out the implications of her most important and striking images. Her essay, which celebrates the contrast between her and her mother's styles of being alive, is itself full of energy, passion, and vitality.

The Seam of the Snail

In my Depression childhood, whenever I had a new dress, my cousin Sarah would get suspicious. The nicer the dress was, and especially the more expensive it looked, the more suspicious she would get. Finally she would lift the hem and check the seams. This was to see if the dress had been bought or if my mother had sewed it. Sarah could always tell. My mother's sewing had elegant outsides, but there was something catch-as-catch-can about the insides. Sarah's sewing, by contrast, was as impeccably finished inside as out; not one stray thread dangled.

My uncle Jake built meticulous grandfather clocks out of rosewood; he was a perfectionist, and sent to England for the clockworks. My mother built serviceable radiator covers and a serviceable cabinet, with hinged doors, for the pantry. She built a pair of bookcases for the living room. Once, after I was grown and in a house of my own, she fixed the sewer pipe. She painted ceilings, and also landscapes; she reupholstered chairs. One summer she planted a whole yard of tall corn. She thought herself capable of doing anything, and did everything she imagined. But nothing was perfect. There was always some clear flaw, never visible head-on. You had to look underneath where the seams were. The corn thrived, though not in rows. The stalks elbowed one another like gossips in a dense little village.

"Miss Brrrroooobaker," my mother used to mock, rolling her Russian *r*s, whenever I crossed a *t* she had left uncrossed, or corrected a word she had misspelled, or became impatient with a *v* that had tangled itself up with a *w* in her speech. ("Vvventriloquist," I would say. "Vvventriloquist," she would obediently repeat. And the next time it would come out "wiolinist.") Miss Brubaker was my high school English teacher, and my mother invoked her name as an emblem of raging finical obsession. "Miss Brrrroooobaker," my mother's voice hoots at me down the years, as I go on casting and recasting sentences in a tiny handwriting on monomaniacally uniform paper. The loops of my mother's handwriting—it was the Palmer Method—were as big as hoops, spilling generous splashy ebullience. She could pull off, at five minutes' notice, a satisfying dinner for 10 concocted out of nothing more than originality and panache. But the napkin would be folded a little off-center, and the spoon might be on the wrong side of the knife. She was an optimist who ignored trifles; for her, God was not in the details but in the intent. And all these culinary and agricultural efflorescences were extracurricular, accomplished in the crevices and niches of a 14-hour business day. When she scribbled out her family memoirs, in heaps of dog-eared notebooks, or on the backs of old bills, or on the margins of last year's calendar, I would resist typing them; in the speed of the chase she often omitted words like "the," "and," "will." The same flashing and bountiful hand fashioned and fired ceramic pots, and painted brilliant autumn views and vases of imaginary flowers and ferns, and decorated ordinary Woolworth platters with lavish enameled gardens. But bits of the painted petals would chip away.

Lavish: my mother was as lavish as nature. She woke early and saturated the hours with work and inventiveness, and read late into the night. She was all profusion, abundance, fabrication. Angry at her children, she would run after us whirling the cord of the electric iron, like a lasso or a whip; but she never caught us. When, in the seventh grade, I was afraid of failing the Music Appreciation final exam because I could not tell the difference between "To a Wild Rose" and "Barcarolle," she got the idea of sending me to school with a gauze sling rigged up on my writing arm, and an explanatory note that was purest fiction. But the sling kept slipping off. My mother gave advice like mad—she boiled over with so much passion for the predicaments of strangers that they turned into permanent cronies. She told intimate stories about people I had never heard of.

Despite the gargantuan Palmer loops (or possibly because of them), I have always known that my mother's was a life of—intricately abashing word!—excellence: insofar as excellence means ripe generosity. She burgeoned, she proliferated; she was endlessly leafy and flowering. She wore red hats, and called herself a gypsy. In her girlhood she marched with the suffragettes and for Margaret Sanger* and called herself a Red. She made me laugh, she was so varied: like a tree on which lemons, pomegranates, and prickly pears absurdly all hang together. She had the comedy of prodigality.

My own way is a thousand times more confined. I am a pinched perfectionist, the ultimate fruition of Miss Brubaker; I attend to crabbed minutiae and am self-trammeled through taking pains. I am a kind of human snail, locked in and condemned by my own nature. The ancients believed that the moist track left by the snail as it crept was the snail's own essence, depleting its body little by little; the farther the snail toiled, the

*(1883–1966) American leader in the birth control movement.

smaller it became, until it finally rubbed itself out. That is how perfectionists are. Say to us Excellence, and we will show you how we use up our substance and wear ourselves away, while making scarcely any progress at all. The fact that I am an exacting perfectionist in a narrow strait only, and nowhere else, is hardly to the point, since nothing matters to me so much as a comely and muscular sentence. It is my narrow strait, this snail's road: the track of the sentence I am writing now; and when I have eked out the wet substance, ink or blood, that is its mark, I will begin the next sentence. Only in reading out sentences am I perfectionist; but then there is nothing else I know how to do, or take much interest in. I miter every pair of abutting sentences as scrupulously as Uncle Jake fitted one strip of rosewood against another. My mother's worldly and bountiful hand has escaped me. The sentence I am writing is my cabin and my shell, compact, self-sufficient. It is the burnished horizon—a merciless planet where flawlessness is the single standard, where even the inmost seams, however hidden from a laxer eye, must meet perfection. Here "excellence" is not strewn casually from a tipped cornucopia, here disorder does not account for charm, here trifles rule like tyrants.

I measure my life in sentences, and my sentences are superior to my mother's, pressed out, line by line, like the lustrous ooze on the underside of the snail, the snail's secret open seam, its wound, leaking attar. My mother was too mettlesome to feel the force of a comma. She scorned minutiae. She measured her life according to what poured from the horn of plenty, which was her ample, cascading, elastic, susceptible, inexact heart. My narrower heart rides between the tiny horns of the snail, dwindling as it goes.

And out of this thinnest thread, this ink-wet line of words, must rise a visionary fog, a mist, a smoke, forging cities, histories, sorrows, quagmires, entanglements, lives of sinners, even the life of my furnace-hearted mother: so much wilderness, waywardness, plentitude on the head of the precise and impeccable snail, between the horns.

CONSIDERATIONS

Thinking

Which do you think is a better title for this essay, "The Seam of the Snail" or "Excellence"? Why? How does Ozick characterize her mother? How does she present herself in relation to her mother? To what extent does Ozick integrate or harmonize the different tendencies each embodies?

Connecting

To what extent do you share characteristics that Ozick possesses? To what extent do you share (or prefer) her mother's way of being?

Identify two metaphors or analogies Ozick uses to describe herself, her mother, or each of them. Explain what Ozick conveys with her metaphors or analogies and what she gains by employing them.

Writing

Write an essay in which you define yourself by contrasting yourself with another.

Compare Ozick's depiction of her mother with June Jordan's portrayal of hers in "Many Rivers to Cross."

S am Pickering (b.1941)

S am Pickering is a professor of English at the University of Connecticut at Storrs, where his classes are oversubscribed, his students happy, and his colleagues bemused. Pickering doesn't try to live up to the fact that he is the prototype for Mr. Keating in *The Dead Poet's Society*, but he manages to do so nevertheless. He is a noted scholar of children's literature but is best known for the familiar essays that he writes about the small, commonplace details of our lives. He has published six collections of essays, among them *Let It Ride, Still Life, The Right Distance,* and most recently, *Trespassing*.

In "Trespassing," Pickering explains his own need to trespass—to cross boundaries, leap fences marked "Do Not Enter," and violate conventions of propriety. In the course of telling stories about his own forms of trespassing, Pickering raises questions about its pleasures and its dangers.

Trespassing

A heavy gate blocked the dirt road. Made from pipes painted white and banded with red warning stripes, the gate hung on two iron bars. Bolted to the middle of the gate was a white metal sign stamped with black letters. "STATE PROPERTY," it read, "NO TRESPASSING." I took the black racer I found on the road and after wedging its mouth open with a thick twig stretched it through the pipes so that the head gaped over the NO blocking two legs of the N from sight. No longer did the snake resemble a flattened branch. On the fence its body seemed to expand, coiling quick into odor and mood. Flies landed on the snake, and after perching for a moment on the twig in the snake's mouth, one crawled down the throat. Virginia creeper grew along the bank beside the fence. I broke off a bunch of new leaves and ground them into my palms washing off the smell of road and waste. I rubbed my hands up and down my thighs, drying them on my jeans, and then smiling, walked around the gate into the STATE PROPERTY.

For years I have trespassed. For me a closed gate is an open invitation to explore. Writers, of course, forever trespass, wandering beyond the margins of good behavior into off limits and then converting private property into public page. Indeed much of the attraction of writing is that it opens life. A writer must stray from path and turnpike, and so I roam days, clambering over fences and pushing through pasture and wood. Occasionally I snag trousers on a barb, but the cuts never tear the rich fabric of my hours. I can find snakes at the edges of woods, and I know where muskrats live. On Monday I brought a wood turtle home to show Eliza, and so far this July I have picked six quarts of wild raspberries. They grow in the field beyond the no trespassing sign, not only red and black raspberries but a third kind which seems a hybrid of the first two. The canes billow around a small rise in the field in thick green tufts, and in the sun berries glisten by the bushel, not by the quart. Yet I am the only human picker, gate and sign, I suppose, deterring other people.

Much as I pay little attention to fences and signs so I ignore those of decorum and push unseen into conversations. In June I traveled to Cape Cod and at a banquet for honors students talked about curiosity. Arriving early at my hotel I ordered a seafood Caesar salad at "The Pub." At a

486

nearby table three lawyers discussed opponents in a recent case. "They have gone the sleaze route together for thirty years," one said. "Yes," the man at his left answered, "They'll stoop to anything. Phony documents, you name it, anything." Two weeks ago at six-thirty in the morning I drove to Manchester to have the brakes repaired on the Mazda. While the rear shoes were being replaced, I walked up Center Street to The Whole Donut. After I ordered a medium-sized cup of coffee and a chocolate doughnut frosted with coconut, I sat at a booth and taking out an orange pencil and a small CVS spiral notebook began to eavesdrop. Cars and dogs dominated conversation. A man in a blue tee-shirt with "SUPERCREW" printed across the front wanted to get rid of a white labrador puppy. His landlord disliked dogs and had hit the puppy with a rake. A young woman working behind the counter was interested. Her boyfriend owned "a greyhound and black lab mix." The dog was dopey and roamed the shore of a pond near where they lived, searching for dead fish. When he found a fish, the dog picked it up and walked around all day with it in his mouth. The white labrador appealed to her, the girl explained, because her sister once owned "a fuzzy white dog that was mostly Spitz." One afternoon when she was driving near Colchester, the sister saw a man throw a bag from a car window. Curious, she stopped. Inside was the Spitz. "It was a good dog," the girl recalled, "we had it six or seven years, and then one day it ran into the road and got kind of squished." "My puppy is good, too," the man said; "I have raised her right. She eats out of a stainless steel bowl. I don't believe animals should eat off plastic. With the dog," he continued, "I'll give you the bowl, her braided rope, a rawhide bone, some Puppy Chow, and a bottle of Pepto-Bismol. She has a little diarrhea, and every morning I give her a dose of Pepto-Bismol."

"You and the puppy," a bearded man said to the girl, "would look good in my Camaro." "Is it a four-door?" the girl asked; "I hate four-doors. The first car I had was a Lynx that my father bought me for three thousand dollars. It had four doors." A man driving a gray pickup with a red bug shield in front of the radiator bought a cup of coffee and the day's special pastry, a cherry doughnut. Sitting down across the aisle from me, he entered the conversation, saying, "Cars ain't that cheap any more." "I ought to know. I just spent two hundred and one dollars getting mine fixed," a woman smoking a cigarette burst out; "I didn't have the money and had to borrow from my mother." The doughnut shop was without fences, and people jumped in and out of conversations. Maybe the real attraction of trespassing is that it confines one to the present. Alert to the moment, people don't dig up the past, as the saying goes, or tote the future. "Working?" the bearded man asked a man in shorts who was drinking coffee and eating a squat doughnut filled with Boston Creme. "I worked my ass off yesterday," the man said; "I ripped a roof off, ply-wooded and shingled it in twelve hours. Just me and a kid. Of course it was a small roof, only seven squares, but, by God, we worked." "Did we get our hearing aids this morning?" one of the girls behind the counter asked. "I haven't seen them," the other girl replied, "or the two titsy rolls."

Many customers were in a hurry and did not talk. Often, though, their shirts spoke for them, advertising "Bob's Stores" or "The World's Largest Source of Natural Gas." Written across the chest of somebody's hall monitor was the declaration "Teachers Have Class." Above the letters stretched a line of eight ripe apples, each topped by a sprig of green leaves. Two women sat in the booth in front of me. They dressed similarly, wearing white trousers, white socks, and white sneakers. While one woman had removed the laces from her shoes, the other kept the laces in but left them untied. Both wore black tee-shirts. Printed in white up the right side from waist to armpit was "Narnia 1992." Stamped on the front of the shirt was the face of Aslan, the hero of C. S. Lewis's inspirational novels describing the imaginary kingdom Narnia. Instead of a great and terrifying lion, however, Aslan resembled a rumpled furry slipper. Although the women often laughed, they talked in a whisper. Still, I heard the phrase "fourth world missions." "Find people who believe in your vision," one said. The other nodded and said something I did not under-stand after which she added, "it's sort of lunar." "Yes," the other replied, "yes, yes."

I stayed at The Whole Donut for an hour. Then I returned to the garage. My car was still on the rack, and so I went to the waiting room. A small man, his stomach bulging like a gourd, sat on a sofa reading the morning paper. He smiled, and I nodded and sat in a plastic chair. A cof-fee machine gasped, and the hostess of a television show gurgled from a set high on the wall. I drank too much coffee at the doughnut shop, and the television program bored me, the hostess appearing to be one of the missing titsy rolls. Eavesdropping determined my mood, and I could not sit quietly. I wanted to hoist myself over a gate and swing uninvited through a conversation. The opportunity soon arose. A tall, white-haired man with blue eyes and a hooked nose entered the room and sat on the sofa. "What's wrong with your car?" he asked the short man. Before the man could put down his newspaper and reply, the tall man continued, providing a joint by joint, gear by gear mechanical history of his 1982 Ford. Diagnosis of the car's sundry ailments always proved difficult, and this, he informed the short man, was the eighth garage to which he had brought the Ford. The speaker was a supply house of automotive information. Having replaced most of the accessories on his car, he next described stores where one could buy the cheapest parts in eastern Connecticut, places that sold lights, radios, mufflers, oil filters, alternators, and carburetors. "Last week," he said, "I found a place that will mount tires free." "Dear God," I interrupted, "who would want to do that for free? Why," I exclaimed, "I would not mount a tire for money, not even one of those cute steel-belted radials." For a moment the white-haired man paused, his eyes cloudy with incomprehension. Finally, awareness spread like the open sky over his brow, and he blinked and said, "No, I didn't mean. . . ." "I know what you meant," I said. "I wouldn't mount a tire, not even one wearing chains and studs," I continued, standing and opening the door to leave the room. "The very idea."

The conventional, particularly when it is detailed into the soporific, provokes the fence-climber in my nature. In May I spoke at Rock Valley College in Rockford, Illinois. Resembling great mills, pentecostal churches cover downtown blocks, their chapels, schools, community centers, and nursing homes blocking out the sun. At the beginning of my talk I alluded to the local fervor. "Never," I began, "have I seen such big churches." They were so large, I continued, that I was giving "serious thought to moving to town and opening one of God's own businesses, a rattlesnake farm, so that true believers would never run short of serpents to toss around on Sunday mornings." Such remarks are the beginning of story, and I say them, in part, because I hope others will slide under sharp propriety and follow me to tale and observation. Of course, the truth is probably that I say such things because I am a foolish and impatient person. That aside, however, rarely do people trail after me into the forbidden brush, and such tales as I fashion are always episodic and their casts of characters thin, limited to myself and a series of flat, cartoon-like individuals. In April I visited my old college Sewanee. On the road outside Murfreesboro I stopped at the Firecracker Warehouse and bought a box of block busters. The box contained forty packs of firecrackers, each pack loaded with sixteen one-and-a-half-inch "Super Charged Flashlight Crackers." That night at one o'clock I set off the firecrackers. The noise flushed students from their rooms, many of them resembling the picture on the front of the box of Crackers: a blue dragon with yellow eyes, snorting fire and smoke, its red hair curling like a nest of angry worms. Wearing pajamas I mingled with the newly awakened and nodded in agreement whenever anyone expressed disgust at "such a silly undergraduate prank." Few people delighted in the disturbance, and fashioning the next episode was left to me alone. I did not disappoint myself. At a literary gathering the following afternoon a distinguished poet gave a public lecture. Before the poet spoke, however, I introduced him. I had done extensive research, and the introduction was detailed. The June bug was, I informed listeners, the poet's favorite insect. He drove a four-door Chevrolet Celebrity "with no bumper stickers." He owned four cats: Wanda Fay, Sammy Ray, Wayne Dwayne, and Rosebud Sue Ann. The redbud was his favorite tree, and the raccoon his preferred animal, these last being particularly fond of the cornbread the poet put out for them under his bird feeder. The poet himself fancied cornbread, and no meal made him smack his chops louder than cornbread, turnip greens, and a pot of pinto beans. At such a devouring little pleased the poet more than listening to music, especially his favorite pop songs, "Run Around Sue" and "Breaking Up Is Hard To Do." "Yes," I told the crowd, "the poet is a man of taste, discretion, and personality," although this last, I noted, "occasionally comes on a bit strong." "He is," I continued, "slightly addicted to fireworks as some of you may have heard last night. For that lapse he has nevertheless, apologized to both me and the administration of this college. We accepted his apology willingly, and we urge you to do the same. Allowance must always be made for true genius, for like a fly it only falls upon ordure to imbibe new life."

Rarely am I asked to make introductions. The form itself is so circumscribed by convention that it resembles a pasture, fenced and far from the sharp tooth of plough and man. Acquaintances know that if I introduce someone I am liable to batter at the structure of the form and then burst into the pasture and, as the saying goes, put my foot in it. No man is consistent however. While I forgive my own trespasses, thinking they have a boyish charm, I do not tolerate the trespasses of boys themselves. I have aged, and when I climb a fence, I do so with care, unlike rude, hormonal youth. When a student says "no problem" to me when he should say "thank you" or, better yet, "thank you great teacher," I immediately think of several problems to which I would like to subject him, most, I should add, of the high Aztec or Mohawk variety. In May I found a message in my box in the English department. A student who missed the final examination left his telephone number and asked me to call. I did so immediately. "May I please speak to Jim Watkins," I said when a boy picked up the telephone. "This is," the boy answered. The absence of *he* after *is* so trespassed against what I know to be polite form that I cared little for the boy's plight. Instead of murmuring long and sympathetically, I said crisply, "You must talk to the dean. The matter is out of my hands. Have a nice day. Good-bye."

In his first letter home from camp, Francis wrote that one of his counselors used "inappropriate language" and provided two scouring examples. On a camping trip the same counselor burned a leech, even though Francis asked him not to. "It wiggled around and suffered," Francis wrote, "then grew fat and wiggled one last time in agony before dying." Three minutes after reading the letter I talked to the director of the camp. In my conversation I used the expression "this is." Unlike the student, however, I forged past the verb and piled a mound of *in* and *im* words around the counselor's trespasses, words like insensitive, improper, and inappropriate. Thirty years ago I was a counselor at the same camp, and although boyish I did not use harsh language to children or harm the small things of this earth. The camp is a fine place, one fenced in by propriety and all those *no* signs I think necessary for the happiness of my little boys. "Bill," Francis wrote in his next letter, "is better. He is almost a different person."

To write a person must observe, and observation often provokes questions, turning one into a crank if not a trespasser. At a recent meeting of the school board an administrator stated that dealing with a particular matter "has been a time-management issue." "If you had said 'took a lot of time,'" I interjected, "you would have saved not only time but letters, twelve letters in fact, the difference between fourteen and twenty-six. And," I continued, "the angels rejoice in heaven whenever a letter is saved. They don't give a happy damn about people, but they are eager to convert alphas and omegas." Not only do cranks read and worry about children's letters, but they know leeches are annelids, members of a marvelous family of creatures including, among some fourteen thousand others, earth and blood worms and from the seashore bristleworms, the bodies of these last divided into more than a hundred segments. For the person willing to trespass far enough to marvel at the ordinary, days are a series of small joys, and life itself is wondrous. Late in May Vicki, the children, and I hiked up West Ridge Trail to the top of Cardigan Mountain, near Canaan, New Hampshire. The day was muggy, and in the woods black flies spun around us like cars rushing into a rotary, buzzing and sharp. I hardly noticed the flies, though, for I wandered from the path to look at flowers: Clintonia, wake robin, painted trillium, trout lilies, Canada mayflower, hobblebush, and then rose twisted stalk, its stem jutting out in jags and its flowers small pink bells. "The flies were bad," Edward said when we reached the top of the mountain, "but the view is great, and this is the high point of my life." "Yes," I answered, "three thousand, one hundred and twenty-one feet high." "No, Daddy," Edward said, "I climbed higher than that and so did you, looking at flowers."

Observance determines remembrance. Like a fence, detail protects experience from the hurly-burly of happenings that trample event out of memory. Oddly, in wandering beyond convention the trespasser preserves not a pasture or wood lot but his own life, and, against their wills, sometimes the lives of those nearest him. Along with wayside flowers I observe the doings of my children, locking what will become their remembered pasts behind a gate of words. Because I have described the cards they gave me the children will never be free to revisit this past Father's Day and trespassing against detail create memory. While Francis forgot Father's Day, Edward made a card, one and a half inches square. On the front Edward sketched a baseball diamond. Stick men wearing gloves played the positions. Despite the small size of the card Edward created motion; the catcher leaned forward behind the plate and the pitcher rolled toward him off the mound. The drawing was not centered, though, and Edward didn't have room to draw the right fielder. Consequently my team has only eight players. "To Dad. Happy Fathers Day. From Ed," Edward wrote in pencil, neglecting to put the apostrophe between the r and the s in Father's. Eliza's card was bigger, five and a half by four and a half inches. "To Dad," she wrote in red ink, "I hope you will like your moskita kalectsin." Drawn on the card were two insects, the first resembling a small beetle leaping into flight and spreading its front wings or elytra, the other a fat, goofy fly with a long snout and antennae thicker than sheaves of wheat. Pasted below the drawings were the leggy remains of stilt bugs that Eliza found beneath the storm windows in the upstairs bathroom.

Although Father's Day slipped his mind, Francis will remember this year's picnic at Northwest School. The day was wet, and the picnic was held in the auditorium. A mime performed, first by himself then with children. The mime selected Francis to play an imaginary baseball game. The mime was not successful. "A ball," Francis said later; "I thought he was throwing logs at me, and I pretended to split them, lifting the maul over my head then swinging it toward the ground." If Francis's acting mystified both mime and audience, my performance clearly irked Vicki. The first two acts went well and conventionally with grinder, potato chip, and fudge cake. Then at the beginning of the third act the woman sitting next to me said, "Oh, you're the famous Sam Pickering. I know," she said, smiling and thinking of the movie *Dead Poets Society,* "that you must get tired of people asking you." She got no further. "You're damn right I'm tired of it," I broke out; "the whole thing drives me crazy." And right here, alas, I vaulted over the gate and began to whoop and flap my arms, my voice rising like that of an owl on the *o*'s and falling with a spluttering *ploop* on the *p*'s. "You went too far again," Vicki said later, flicking her eyes at me like a snake's tongue; "I don't know why I ever married you." Vicki married me, of course, because when she sensed the time was right for her to marry I was the only person who asked her. And, in truth, she may have married because I trespassed. The old adage, "faint heart ne'er won fair lady," may be the bounder's motto, but it contains wisdom.

From a distance or before marriage trespassers appeal to people who chafe at convention and hope that their lives will differ from those led by parents and acquaintances. Young dreamers, though, are not alone in hankering after trespassers. Trustees of colleges often look back upon their student days fondly, to be sure with chagrin for some of their foolishness but mostly with admiration for the boyish doings of those few years before they became corporate. Thus when trustees begin searches for college presidents they will, at first, say they are looking for someone to exert moral authority or provide cultural and intellectual leadership. What lies behind the statement is the memory of a favorite teacher, both memory and man scrubbed and buffed by time. In the flesh, however, even the polished seem tarnished, and when a real teacher appears, he rarely shines. The real teacher educates himself by wandering and encourages others to do the same. Only platitudes come easily, and as the real teacher struggles to think for himself and fumbles through inappropriate words attempting to describe those thoughts, he makes others uncomfortable. In grasping for understanding he loses dignity and often seems a buffoon. Even worse, the attempt to be truthful can anger. Honesty threatens the fictions people erect to make social life possible. Belief, whether right or wrong, supports culture, and if people begin to wander from accepted paths and tear down *no* signs, community shatters. Then all those things done or accomplished past boyhood suddenly seem silly. In private, in an essay, one acknowledges the foolishness of accomplishment, maybe even the meaninglessness of life itself. In public one rallies to structure and buttresses the old fictions. My own explorations don't go far. Although I have tossed words over hedges, I have never really pushed through briars at the side of a path. I have not dug up a thought; instead I have wandered soft glades, places not visited by everyone but places familiar to people who read. And, of course, I have hammered *no* signs throughout my children's days. I want my babies to be happy. If they stick to well-trod thoroughfares, life will be easier for them, and maybe kinder to them, and so I batter them into correct grammar and appropriate language. Yet when they are asleep, sometimes I go into their bedrooms, kiss them, and whisper, "I'm sorry."

In my ambivalent behavior I resemble college trustees. Instead of the real teacher they select the easy manager, a person comfortable with budgets and platitudes. In May Hampden-Sydney College began looking for a president. An all-male school with a thousand students, Hampden-Sydney is located near Farmville, Virginia. Founded in 1776 the school has enjoyed a long history of modest aspirations and quiet successes. Still, its reputation is parochial. Few people beyond Virginia know its name, and those friends to whom I mentioned the college confused it with Hampton University near Norfolk. The trustees wanted their school to be more than local, and in May I was asked to apply for the presidency. Reputation is often only bunting, and I applied not because I thought making the school better known was important but because I have a sentimental attachment to Virginia. Mother grew up in Richmond, and I spent many summers in Hanover Courthouse. I also thought my family would like the rural south and that I might be able to lead others, not to make their school "outstanding" but to help it rise from third or fourth rank to second. Dominated by extravagant claim and promise, most educational talk smacks of advertising, and I realized that modest intention would brand me a trespasser, someone not fit to "transform" a college. Nevertheless I flew to Virginia for interviews. In driving through Richmond I passed the building which housed my grandfather's store at the corner of Grace and Fifth. It was now a woman's shop called Hit or Miss. Both the surrounding streets and the store itself were empty, and the business seemed a miss much as I reckoned my interviews would be. Still, the premonition did not bother me, and I looked forward to seeing great-aunt Elizabeth and my cousin Sherry. At Aunt Elizabeth's house Chinese chestnuts bloomed in long fingers. On a rock a river otter groomed itself. At Cumberland Courthouse I ate a lunch that the poet would have envied: snap beans, black-eyed peas, turnip greens, and cornbread. I talked to one of mother's bridesmaids. She told me what she knew about Hampden-Sydney then asked about my children. "They are doing wonderfully," I said. "Of course they are," she said; "they are Katharine's grandchildren."

The people who interviewed me were gracious and generous, and I had fun. When asked what my personal goals were, I told the truth, saying that goals were for the young and that aside from seduction I had not had a goal since I was seventeen, adding that I wanted only to get through the rest of my days with a remnant of decorum and maybe live a little longer than an acquaintance or two. "Also I hope I won't be found out, but that," I said, "is a pipedream." On being asked over cocktails if I liked horses, I said I preferred gerbils and hamsters. A trustee took me to a picnic, and I changed clothes in a pasture. Under the trousers to my suit I wore boxer shorts decorated with small green cats. On seeing the shorts the man said, "I have seen it all now." "You've seen most of it," I responded, "but certainly not all." Or at least that's what I tell friends I said. What the truth is I don't know. I exaggerate so much that not only friends but even I think the truths I tell fiction. Indeed as I age, reality itself grows progressively vague and mysterious. Sometimes I think the things which have happened to me since my boyish days are just the dreams of a few moments. Instead of sitting at a card table writing, I know that I am stretched out dying in a ditch, my body crushed in a car wreck, and the events of the last thirty years are figments of a disordered imagination. Other people have similar thoughts. "Daddy," Eliza said to me as we walked toward Mirror Lake holding hands, "life goes by so fast. I can't really believe this is my life. It goes by so fast that you don't really notice it."

Occasionally I think imagined life more real than actual life. I know that I telephoned Prince Edward Academy, a private school in Farmville, and asked about tuition, in the process learning that Latin had been dropped from the curriculum. But did I really say I would not accept the presidency unless the trustees gave Vicki a West Highland terrier? Did the man to whom I was talking answer, "Dog? Why not a Porsche? You'd like a Porsche." And did I say, "Porsche, hell! They are too low to the ground. Every time I got in and out I'd fart." What I do know is that I daydreamed about Hampden-Sydney. In my mind I roamed the campus running my hands raw across the red brick. Not only did I learn the names of all the trees on campus but I climbed some. I wrote speeches and presented honorary degrees to people whom I admired: to Mr. Rogers, heart of the host neighborhood on television, and to John Sawhill, head of the Nature Conservancy. I also awarded a degree to Little Richard because he makes me smile. Little Richard did not deliver a speech at graduation. Instead he sang "Tutti Frutti," and I joined him. Dreaming, of course, is done alone. Maybe the real trespasser is a solitary, and genuine trespassing is interior, wandering mind instead of hill and field. "Sam is too free a spirit to become a college president," a dean said to a friend recently. The dean was right. In part I trespass because I want to be alone, a desire, I am afraid, that has been passed along to the children. In June Eliza began day camp. "I don't want to make any friends," she told me before camp; "if I don't make any, I won't miss them when camp is over." "Oh, Eliza," I began. "But daddy," she continued, "sometimes I want to be solitary."

To be in the middle of life maybe one has to be solitary or at least drift from crowds and thoroughfares. Beyond "No Trespassing" wonder thrives, and after a walk I wrestle with language, not shaping phrases to win or fool but to celebrate. "You have had no administrative experience," a trustee said to me. "What makes you think you could manage Hampden-Sydney?" "Arrogance, sheer arrogance," I answered. What I almost said was that maybe the key to happiness lay in avoiding managing. Instead of channeling words into distortion perhaps the successful person allows himself to be managed, rolling with the pitch of hill and creek, following the rain and then standing silent like a root in a field, feeling sunlight clap warm through the air. For an essayist a college presidency would be a long mistake, and so I say odd things in order to remain free to wander the woods. From a worldly point of view I would have been a successful president, one of those admirable people remembered by portrait and building. In being tacked into substance by convention, though, I would have lost the ability to escape others, and myself. "Sam," Vicki said when Hampden-Sydney fell through, "I don't know whether you are a sap or not. Sometimes I think you are a jackass; other times I think you are a little right, maybe even smart, especially," she added, pausing, "when you find raspberries."

On the kitchen table was a blue bowl filled with more wild raspberries. I discovered them growing in an abandoned field. With them and the earlier quarts I picked, I brought home a peck of seasonal impressions. For the first two weeks in July I spent part of every day wandering beyond signs. For the first time I noticed moosewood or striped maple, its trunk streaked with green and its leaves big as hams and almost tropical. In the middle of a wood I found a dead white pine. The needles had turned pink, and bursts of long, thick flames flickered through the half-light. Seeds hung from ashes in gouts, each pod a drop of water streaming upward, not down, the wing of the seed dangling behind like a damp khaki trail. At the corner of a pasture stood two old apple trees, the green fruits gnarled as character, bumpy and bent, their sides sucked inward and wrinkled into ridges. May and June were cool, and flowers bloomed late this year. Several mornings I stood in a meadow amid fleabane high as my chest, the frayed blossoms pouring around me like milk. Winter cress had gone to seed, and the pods curled up in hangers like old-fashioned coat racks. Throughout the meadow Canada thistle bloomed, its blossoms gentle above the fleabane but its leaves spiny and tearing. Vervain rose in pitchforks, the square stems green and soft in the middle but hard and molded by red on the edges. Against the light the tines on the forks seemed sharp until they bloomed and blue flowers wrapped them in aprons. In the damp, Joe Pye weed was waist high. Starting at the tips, the new purple leaves turned green around creamy bundles of blossoms. Tall meadow rue grew frail along the Fenton River. In a breeze the stamens of each flower swayed like a squad of long soldiers, white and straight in parade dress, yellow bonnets on their heads.

The ringing of bees rose above milkweed while on the leaves red milkweed beetles doubled themselves. From the leaf axils of nettles green flowers tumbled out in cowlicks. In the abandoned bell of hornet's nest a nursery web spider clutched a white egg. Above the fleabane white butterflies spun upward in cylinders of air. A blackwinged damselfly wobbled through an elderberry, and like salt and pepper shakers twelve-spotted dragonflies turned white and black above the beaver pond. A wren bubbled as it darted from a tree to hunt bugs in brush. In a sandy field birdfoot trefoil bloomed in yellow puddles, and ground beetles hid under rocks. Along a creek skunk cabbage splayed out and melted into the ground. The ribbed leaves of false hellebore collapsed and turned yellow then brown. I picked flowers for Vicki, bundles so big that she did not arrange them in vases but set them around the house in buckets. I found a robin's egg for Eliza and mailed snake skins to the boys at camp. One morning I spent two hours kneeling on a rock in the middle of the Fenton River watching gnats swim through the air in currents, just above the stream. Around me water hurried and dug between rocks like screws twisting through soft wood. Beside the bank quiet basins resembled wishing wells, their bottoms coppery with rocks bright as pennies. Over them royal fern swayed yellow in the light. A towhee landed on a limb and began calling. The feathers on his head resembled a black cap, and the inside of his tail a white morning suit edged with black. For a moment I thought him a barrister, rising stuffy in a British court and incessantly saying "to whit."

Rooms and words can confine. Inside I often listen to myself and occasionally have thought I sounded knowledgeable. Outside amid the quiet of bird, leaf, and stream, I know better. I decided to learn the names of grasses. How could I swell so pompous about moral authority and cultural leadership, I thought, when I didn't recognize the grasses I saw every day? "Daddy, you are very nice-looking," Eliza said one afternoon when I returned from the woods, "but very old looking." Although wandering brightened my days, I was tired, and I limited myself to a handful of grasses. Next summer, I told myself, I could wander farther afield. Like a pink mist, red top hovered near the ground by the fence and ran along the road slicing up the side of Horsebarn Hill. Timothy bloomed lavender in the sun, its minute anthers dangling and shaking like purple clappers. By a wetland reed canary grass was shoulder high. The long panicle had expanded, and sharp purple lines cut through it like washes down a breaking slope. Smooth brome grass grew around a corn field. Like a series of ridges rising sharp above yet shadowing those below, sandy triangles climbed the tight spikelet. From the side of ray grass spikelets jutted stiffly out, their light green anthers yellow in the sun. Although I recognized deer-tongue, rarely did I mow through panic grasses to recognition. Much as they draw streams, wetlands pulled me, and for the first time I looked closely at rushes and sedges. With their spikelets clustered and joined by stems, the tops of meadow bulrush reminded me of bristly tinker toys. While the flowers of wool grass burst out in great sprays from the top of the stalk those of bog rush fell from the side. On my last walk I brought sedges home—hop, bog, and fringed sedge—and put them in a pitcher on my desk. I left them in the pitcher for several days, and Eliza asked when I was going to replace them. "Not for a while, honey," I said; "I'm resting."

Despite what I told Eliza, I won't rest much longer. Monkey flower and panicled tick-trefoil are about to bloom. Goldenrod is yellow, and I want to pick peppermint and bouncing bet for Vicki. Soon butterflies will hang on the big pasture thistles. Behind Unnamed Pond blackberries are swelling beyond green into red. By the time the boys return home from camp the berries will be black. Nailed to a tree on a hill above the blackberries is a red metal sign. Stamped on it in white letters is the warning. "TRESPASSERS WILL BE PROSECUTED." Someone sprayed black paint over the last word, and from a distance the sign seems to say "Trespassers Will Be." I thought about writing something over the black paint, but the words I considered seemed inadequate: FOOLISH, DISAPPOINTED, HAPPY, JOYFUL. At a time when no signs so stifle that people retreat from character into platitude, maybe it is enough just to assert that trespassers WILL BE.

CONSIDERATIONS

Thinking

What does Pickering mean by "trespassing"? What kinds of trespassing does he touch on in this essay? What kinds of trespassing does he exclude from consideration?

What, according to Pickering, are the dangers of trespassing? Why does he seem to be ambivalent about trespassing? Where does that ambivalence show itself most forcefully? Why?

Connecting

At a number of points, Pickering connects trespassing with writing. To what extent are writers trespassers? What aspects of writing can lead to writerly trespassing? Why?

To what extent have you shared Pickering's impulse to trespass? Have you ever gone against the grain of convention or leaped the fence of propriety? If so, on what occasion(s) and for what purpose? If not, why haven't you?

Consider Pickering's ideas about trespassing in connection with one or more of the following essays: Lee K. Abbott's "The True Story of Why I Do What I Do," Gloria Anzuldúa's "How to Tame a Wild Tongue," James Baldwin's "Stranger in the Village," Annie Dillard's "Living Like Weasels," and Jamaica Kincaid's "On Seeing England for the First Time."

Writing

Write an essay about your own attitude toward one or another form of trespassing. In the course of your exploration, tell a couple of stories about times you trespassed or thought about trespassing without following through and explain your decisions.

After isolating the appeals and dangers of trespassing from Pickering's essay, write an essay that supports, qualifies, or contests what Pickering has to say about the subject.

Katherine Anne Porter (1890–1980)

Katherine Anne Porter was born at Indian Creek, Texas, and received her childhood education at Catholic schools in Texas and California. She moved to New York in her thirties and worked as an actress and ballad singer after serving as a news reporter in Chicago, Denver, and Fort Worth. Primarily a writer of short stories, Porter published one novel, *Ship of Fools* (1962). In 1967, she was awarded a Pulitzer Prize and a National Book Award for her *Collected Stories.*

In "The Necessary Enemy," from her *Collected Essays and Occasional Writings,* Porter explores the relations between the sexes, presenting an incisive analysis of the idea of romantic love. The essay is noteworthy for its toughmindedness and its scrupulous honesty.

The Necessary Enemy

She is a frank, charming, fresh-hearted young woman who married for love. She and her husband are one of those gay, good-looking young pairs who ornament this modern scene rather more in profusion perhaps than ever before in our history. They are handsome, with a talent for finding their way in their world, they work at things that interest them, their tastes agree and their hopes. They intend in all good faith to spend their lives together, to have children and do well by them and each other—to be happy, in fact, which for them is the whole point of their marriage. And all in stride, keeping their wits about them. Nothing romantic, mind you; their feet are on the ground.

Unless they were this sort of person, there would be not much point to what I wish to say; for they would seem to be an example of the high-spirited, right-minded young whom the critics are always invoking to come forth and do their duty and practice all those sterling old-fashioned virtues which in every generation seem to be falling into disrepair. As for virtues, these young people are more or less on their own, like most of their kind; they get very little moral or other aid from their society; but after three years of marriage this very contemporary young woman finds herself facing the oldest and ugliest dilemma of marriage.

She is dismayed, horrified, full of guilt and foreboding because she is finding out little by little that she is capable of hating her husband, whom she loves faithfully. She can hate him at times as fiercely and mysteriously, indeed in terribly much the same way, as often she hated her parents, her brothers and sisters, whom she loves, when she was a child. Even then it had seemed to her a kind of black treacherousness in her, her private wickedness that, just the same, gave her her only private life. That was one thing her parents never knew about her, never seemed to suspect. For it was never given a name. They did and said hateful things to her and to each other as if by right, as if in them it was a kind of virtue. But when they said to her, "Control your feelings," it was never when she was amiable and obedient, only in the black times of her hate. So it was her secret, a shameful one. When they punished her, sometimes for the strangest reasons, it was, they said, only because they loved her—it was for her good. She did not believe this, but she thought herself guilty of something worse than ever they had punished her for. None of this really frightened her: the real fright came when she discovered that at times her father and mother hated each other; this was like standing on the doorsill of a familiar room and seeing in a lightning flash that the floor was gone, you were on the edge of a bottomless pit. Sometimes she felt that both of them hated her, but that passed, it was simply not a thing to be thought of, much less believed. She thought she had outgrown all this, but here it was again, an element in her own nature she could not control, or feared she could not. She would have to hide from her husband, if she could, the same spot in her feelings she had hidden from her parents, and for the same no doubt disreputable, selfish reason: she wants to keep his love.

Above all, she wants him to be absolutely confident that she loves him, for that is the real truth, no matter how unreasonable it sounds, and no matter how her own feelings betray them both at times. She depends recklessly on his love; yet while she is hating him, he might very well be hating her as much or even more, and it would serve her right. But she does not want to be served right, she wants to be loved and forgiven— that is, to be sure he would forgive her anything, if he had any notion of what she had done. But best of all she would like not to have anything in her love that should ask for forgiveness. She doesn't mean about their quarrels—they are not so bad. Her feelings are out of proportion, per- haps. She knows it is perfectly natural for people to disagree, have fits of temper, fight it out; they learn quite a lot about each other that way, and not all of it disappointing either. When it passes, her hatred seems quite unreal. It always did.

Love. We are early taught to say it. I love you. We are trained to the thought of it as if there were nothing else, or nothing else worth having without it, or nothing worth having which it could not bring with it. Love is taught, always by precept, sometimes by example. Then hate, which no one meant to teach us, comes of itself. It is true that if we say I love you, it may be received with doubt, for there are times when it is hard to believe. Say I hate you, and the one spoken to believes it instantly, once for all.

Say I love you a thousand times to that person afterward and mean it every time, and still it does not change the fact that once we said I hate you, and meant that too. It leaves a mark on that surface love had worn so smooth with its eternal caresses. Love must be learned, and learned again and again; there is no end to it. Hate needs no instruction, but waits only to be provoked . . . hate, the unspoken word, the unacknowledged presence in the house, that faint smell of brimstone among the roses, that invisible tongue-tripper, that unkempt finger in every pie, that sudden oh-so-curiously *chilling* look—could it be boredom?—on your dear one's features, making them quite ugly. Be careful: love, perfect love, is in danger.

If it is not perfect, it is not love, and if it is not love, it is bound to be hate sooner or later. This is perhaps a not too exaggerated statement of the extreme position of Romantic Love, more especially in America, where we are all brought up on it, whether we know it or not. Romantic Love is changeless, faithful, passionate, and its sole end is to render the two lovers happy. It has no obstacles save those provided by the hazards of fate (that is to say, society), and such sufferings as the lovers may cause each other are only another word for delight: exciting jealousies, thrilling uncertainties, the ritual dance of courtship within the charmed closed circle of their secret alliance; all *real* troubles come from without, they face them unitedly in perfect confidence. Marriage is not the end but only the beginning of true happiness, cloudless, changeless to the end. That the candidates for this blissful condition have never seen an example of it, nor ever knew anyone who had, makes no difference. That is the ideal and they will achieve it.

How did Romantic Love manage to get into marriage at last, where it was most certainly never intended to be? At its highest it was tragic; the love of Héloïse and Abélard. At its most graceful, it was the homage of the trouvère for his lady. In its most popular form, the adulterous strayings of solidly married couples who meant to stray for their own good reasons, but at the same time do nothing to upset the property settlements or the line of legitimacy; at its most trivial, the pretty trifling of shepherd and shepherdess.

This was generally condemned by church and state and a word of fear to honest wives whose mortal enemy it was. Love within the sober, sacred realities of marriage was a matter of personal luck, but in any case, private feelings were strictly a private affair having, at least in theory, no bearing whatever on the fixed practice of the rules of an institution never intended as a recreation ground for either sex. If the couple discharged their religious and social obligations, furnished forth a copious progeny, kept their troubles to themselves, maintained public civility and died under the same roof, even if not always on speaking terms, it was rightly regarded as a successful marriage. Apparently this testing ground was too severe for all but the stoutest spirits; it too was based on an ideal, as impossible in its way as the ideal Romantic Love. One good thing to be said for it is that society took responsibility for the conditions of marriage, and the sufferers within its bonds could always blame the system, not themselves. But Romantic Love crept into the marriage bed, very stealthily, by centuries, bringing its absurd notions about love as eternal springtime and marriage as a personal adventure meant to provide personal happiness. To a Western romantic such as I, though my views have been much modified by painful experience, it still seems to me a charming work of the human imagination, and it is a pity its central notion has been taken too literally and has hardened into a convention as cramping and enslaving as the older one. The refusal to acknowledge the evils in ourselves which therefore are implicit in any human situation is as extreme and unworkable a proposition as the doctrine of total depravity; but somewhere between them, or maybe beyond them, there does exist a possibility for reconciliation between our desires for impossible satisfactions and the simple unalterable fact that we also desire to be unhappy and that we create our own sufferings; and out of these sufferings we salvage our fragments of happiness.

Our young woman who has been taught that an important part of her human nature is not real because it makes trouble and interferes with her peace of mind and shakes her self-love, has been very badly taught; but she has arrived at a most important stage of her re-education. She is afraid her marriage is going to fail because she has not love enough to face its difficulties; and this because at times she feels a painful hostility toward her husband, and cannot admit its reality because such an admission would damage in her own eyes her view of what love should be, an absurd view, based on her vanity of power. Her hatred is real as her love is real, but her hatred has the advantage at present because it works on a blind instinctual level, it is lawless; and her love is subjected to a code of ideal conditions, impossible by their very nature of fulfillment, which prevents its free growth and deprives it of its right to recognize its human limitations and come to grips with them. Hatred is natural in a sense that love, as she conceives it, a young person brought up in the tradition of Romantic Love, is not natural at all. Yet it did not come by hazard, it is the very imperfect expression of the need of the human imagination to create beauty and harmony out of chaos, no matter how mistaken its notion of these things may be, nor how clumsy its methods. It has conjured love out of the air, and seeks to preserve it by incantations; when she spoke a vow to love and honor her husband until death, she did a very reckless thing, for it is not possible by an act of the will to fulfill such an engagement. But it was the necessary act of faith performed in defense of a mode of feeling, the statement of honorable intention to practice as well as she is able the noble, acquired faculty of love, that very mysterious overtone to sex which is the best thing in it. Her hatred is part of it, the necessary enemy and ally.

CONSIDERATIONS

Thinking

What is the relationship between love and hatred as suggested by Porter in this essay? How do you see their relationship?

Do the woman's feelings of hatred and her strategy for concealing that hatred from her husband and others seem plausible? Why or why not?

Connecting

How does what Porter says about love and hate in paragraphs 5 and 6 connect with your own experience?

To what extent does Porter's description of "Romantic Love" coincide with images of romance employed in popular novels, films, and television shows?

Writing

Write an essay on love, hate, or their interrelationship. You can use Porter's essay to support your views, you can refute her, or you can ignore her.

Read Porter's story "Rope" and discuss its situation in relation to your understanding of "The Necessary Enemy."

R oy Reed
(b.1930)

R oy Reed was national and foreign correspondent for *The New York Times* following a long stint with the *Arkansas Gazette*. Reed recently retired as a professor of journalism at the University of Arkansas and is a farmer in the hills around Fayetteville. He is at work on a biography of Orval Faubus, a former governor of Arkansas.

"Spring Comes to Hogeye" is from Reed's book of essays, *Looking for Hogeye*. In this essay, Reed focuses on Ira Solenberger, an aging farmer, who is waiting for the late arrival of spring. With Solenberger's help, Reed raises some interesting questions about the mysteries of plowing and planting as he looks deep into the ebb and flow of the seasons.

Spring Comes to Hogeye

Spring was late in the Ozark Mountains. The first week of April had passed, and the oaks and maples were only then risking a few pale green shoots, tentative little leaves that would not constitute much of a loss if another frost stole in at night on the villainous northwest air.

Ira Solenberger was also late. Practically everybody else in Hogeye had braved the hazard of frost and had planted corn, onions, English peas and Irish potatoes. A few, emulating the bold dogwood and redbud trees, which for more than a week had been blooming bright white and purple against the dark hills, had gone so far as to put out beans, squash and even tender tomato plants.

But Mr. Solenberger, who was regarded as the best gardener in Washington County, had not plowed a furrow or planted a seed. Like the craggy maple in front of his house (itself one of the oldest things in Hogeye, a relic of the Butterfield Stage era), he found that his sap was slow to rise that spring. It had not occurred to him to blame it on his eighty-six years.

"It's that old flu," he said. "Got it back in the winter and can't get rid of it. First time I've had it since 19 and 18."

He opened the door of his heating stove and threw another chunk of wood on the fire. He closed it a little sharply and glanced out the window toward his empty garden.

Every April, the main thing going on in the rural South is vegetable gardening. A farmer might take an hour to talk politics or help a cow give birth, but the really urgent business for him, his wife and all of the children who are old enough to keep their feet off the onion sets is getting seeds and plants in the ground to take advantage of the warming days. With a little luck, the sweet corn planted in early April will have roasting ears ("roashnears," they are called) by the middle of June.

This is a pursuit that seeks every year to outwit the awful force that pushes the shoots from the oak's branches, and that turns Seth Timmons's meadow from brown to green, and impels swallows to build nests in weathered barns.

It was the same force, that spring, that pushed Ira Solenberger out the door in a hat and coat, hunched against the biting bright air blowing up

507

from the Illinois River, to kick the dirt and study the sky, and then retreat
to the house to throw another chunk of wood on the fire.

There is still a poet up the road at Fayetteville who, in those days,
drove into the hills every April to study the hills and watch for Robert
Frost's signs—the gold that is nature's first evidence, "her hardest hue to
hold"—and for private signs of his own that stirred his spirit.

Ira Solenberger's mind ran less to poetry than to science. He was an
amateur magician, and he performed magic with plants as well as cards.

"Summer before last, I grafted some tomatoes on some poke stalks."

Why?

"Just to see if they would grow."

But when he talked of nature and growth, he used words that Frost
might have used, or Thoreau.

"Plow deep. There's one acre right under another acre. I plow both of
them."

"Phosphorous makes things grow roots. If you get roots, you're going
to get something else."

"I farm with a tractor. But when it gets rowed up and a-growing, I use
a roan horse."

He was now in the April sun, away from the stove. His eye scanned
the three and a half acres where, just a year earlier—unencumbered by
the flu—he had planted rhubarb, corn, tomatoes, squash, sweet potatoes,
Irish potatoes, okra, green beans, cantaloupes, radishes, onions, cucum-
bers and strawberries. He had harvested a bumper crop of everything. He
had eaten what he wanted and sold the rest at the farmers' market on the
square at Fayetteville.

He pointed to a fallow patch and said, "That's where I had my watermelons last year." He spoke in a loud, professorial voice, as if addressing
the cows at the top of the hill.

"They told me I raised the biggest watermelons in Northwest
Arkansas. One of them weighed eighty-three pounds.

"I've had people ask me, 'What's your secret for raising watermelons?'
I tell them, 'I ain't got no secret.'"

Then, still addressing the cows, he proceeded to tell the secret. Plow
the ground deep. Watermelons need more air than water, and deep plowing lets in air.

"I plow turrible deep. Eight or ten inches." He grinned with private
satisfaction and moved on to a strawberry patch.

Mr. Solenberger believed in humus. He produced it by placing mulch
between the rows. I once knew a Mississippi liberal who enjoyed a minor

reputation as a gardener by mulching old copies of *The New York Times*. Mr. Solenberger did not take the *Times*. He used dead crab grass.

"Make sure it's rotten," he said, jabbing the air with an open pocket knife. "If you plow under something that ain't rotten, it's a detriment to you for the first season."

Many of his neighbors planted by the moon, and still do. Mr. Solenberger did not.

"I don't pay any attention to the moon, and I'll tell you why. I've got a neighbor that plants by the moon, and I asked him a question one day that he couldn't answer. I said, 'You plant a seed in dry ground, when the moon is right, and it won't come up. Then ten days later it comes a rain and that seed sprouts and comes up. But by then the sign of the moon is wrong. How do you account for that?' He couldn't answer that. I don't plant by the moon. I plant by the ground."

He was troubled, though, by another phenomenon, and he was a little reluctant to talk about it. He said the frosts seemed to come later each spring, just as the force that drove him to the plow seemed to have arrived late that year.

"The timber's awful slow a-leafing out." He cast a blue eye toward the hill across the road. "When I was a boy, we weren't bothered with frost. When spring come, it come. Our spring's almost a month later than it used to be."

I asked him what he thought the reason was. He glanced at my face to see whether I was ready to accept what he had to say. He decided to risk it.

"Well, sir, I believe the world twists a little bit. You know, everything that grows twists around to the right. Follows the sun. Even our storms that come out of the Gulf, they twist to the right. It's just nature."

Why was a man of eighty-six still involved every April with the earth's greening, as if it were his own? He passed the question off quickly. He indicated that it was merely the same motive that led him to do card tricks and tell jokes and graft tomatoes to poke weed.

"I just like to be doing things."

He returned to the question later, however, sidling up to it so as not to sound too serious. He began by confessing that spring was his favorite season. I asked him why, and he said, "Life is at a high ebb in the spring."

He leaned his chair back against the porch wall and hooked his shoe heels over the lower rung. He studied the trees on the hill across the road, and then he said, "People who are getting up in years, more of them die in the winter when the days are short, and in the hours after midnight.

Life is at a low ebb after midnight and in the short days. Did you know that? And the shorter the days, the lower the ebb."

Thus it was the lengthening days that sent Ira Solenberger to the garden, and he could no more resist than the hapless oak bud could resist becoming a leaf.

He was also right about the other. He thrived for one more season of the high ebb. He made one more garden. Then he died in the winter, during the short days.

CONSIDERATIONS

Thinking

Why do you suppose Mr. Solenberger is impatient about the coming of spring? What are the outward signs of his impatience?

What is Reed's attitude toward Mr. Solenberger? How do you know?

Does Mr. Solenberger seem wise to you, or does he seem like a fool? How can you tell?

Connecting

What do you think this question of Reed's has to do with the rest of his essay: "Why was a man of eighty-six still involved every April with the earth's greening, as if it were his own?"

Why does Reed include the paragraph about the "poet up the road at Fayetteville"? Why are Robert Frost's words important in that paragraph?

Writing

Begin by writing a character sketch about someone you know who is interesting. Interview the person, if possible, or interview someone who knows that person well.

Use the character sketch as the basis for writing an essay like "Spring Comes to Hogeye." Bring character sketch and idea together to create the essay. If appropriate, add other stories to those about your character, stories that help you illustrate and develop your idea.

Richard Rodriguez
(b.1944)

R ichard Rodriguez, born in San Francisco, the son of Mexican immigrants, earned his B.A. from Stanford University and his Ph.D. from the University of California at Berkeley. His essays and articles have appeared in *Harper's, Saturday Review, American Scholar, The New York Times,* and the *Los Angeles Times.* His books include *Hunger of Memory: The Education of Richard Rodriguez* and *Days of Obligation: An Argument with My Mexican Father.* He has received a Fulbright Fellowship and a National Endowment for the Humanities Fellowship.

"The Achievement of Desire," a chapter from *Hunger of Memory,* reveals the perils of an education founded on principles of imitation rather than on originality and creativity; it suggests how nostalgia can serve as a counterpoise for the isolating weight of such an education.

The Achievement of Desire

I stand in the ghetto classroom—"the guest speaker"—attempting to lecture on the mystery of the sounds of our words to rows of diffident students. "Don't you hear it? Listen! The music of our words. *'Sumer is icumen in. . . .'* And songs on the car radio. We need Aretha Franklin's voice to fill plain words with music—her life." In the face of their empty stares, I try to create an enthusiasm. But the girls in the back row turn to watch some boy passing outside. There are flutters of smiles, waves. And someone's mouth elongates heavy, silent words through the barrier of glass. Silent words—the lips straining to shape each voiceless syllable: *"Meet meee late errr."* By the door, the instructor smiles at me, apparently hoping that I will be able to spark some enthusiasm in the class. But only one student seems to be listening. A girl, maybe fourteen. In this gray room her eyes shine with ambition. She keeps nodding and nodding at all that I say; she even takes notes. And each time I ask a question, she jerks up and down in her desk like a marionette, while her hand waves over the bowed heads of her classmates. It is myself (as a boy) I see as she faces me now (a man in my thirties).

The boy who first entered a classroom barely able to speak English, twenty years later concluded his studies in the stately quiet of the reading room in the British Museum. Thus with one sentence I can summarize my academic career. It will be harder to summarize what sort of life connects the boy to the man.

With every award, each graduation from one level of education to the next, people I'd meet would congratulate me. Their refrain always the same: "Your parents must be very proud." Sometimes then they'd ask me how I managed it—my "success." (How?) After a while, I had several quick answers to give in reply. I'd admit, for one thing, that I went to an excellent grammar school. (My earliest teachers, the nuns, made my success their ambition.) And my brother and both my sisters were very good students. (They often brought home the shiny school trophies I came to want.) And my mother and father always encouraged me. (At every graduation they were behind the stunning flash of the camera when I turned to look at the crowd.)

As important as these factors were, however, they account inadequately for my academic advance. Nor do they suggest what an odd success I managed. For although I was a very good student, I was also a very bad student. I was a "scholarship boy," a certain kind of scholarship boy. Always successful, I was always unconfident. Exhilarated by my progress. Sad. I became the prized student—anxious and eager to learn. Too eager, too anxious—an imitative and unoriginal pupil. My brother and two sisters enjoyed the advantages I did, and they grew to be as successful as I, but none of them ever seemed so anxious about their schooling. A second-grade student, I was the one who came home and corrected the "simple" grammatical mistakes of our parents. ("Two negatives make a positive.") Proudly I announced—to my family's startled silence—that a teacher had said I was losing all trace of a Spanish accent. I was oddly annoyed when I was unable to get parental help with a homework assignment. The night my father tried to help me with an arithmetic exercise, he kept reading the instructions, each time more deliberately, until I pried the textbook out of his hands, saying, "I'll try to figure it out some more by myself."

When I reached the third grade, I outgrew such behavior. I became more tactful, careful to keep separate the two very different worlds of my day. But then, with ever-increasing intensity, I devoted myself to my studies. I became bookish, puzzling to all my family. Ambition set me apart. When my brother saw me struggling home with stacks of library books, he would laugh, shouting: "Hey, Four Eyes!" My father opened a closet one day and was startled to find me inside, reading a novel. My mother would find me reading when I was supposed to be asleep or helping around the house or playing outside. In a voice angry or worried or just curious, she'd ask: "What do you see in your books?" It became the family's joke. When I was called and wouldn't reply, someone would say I must be hiding under my bed with a book.

(How did I manage my success?)

What I am about to say to you has taken me more than twenty years to admit: *A primary reason for my success in the classroom was that I couldn't forget that schooling was changing me and separating me from the life I enjoyed before becoming a student.* That simple realization! For years I never spoke to anyone about it. Never mentioned a thing to my family or my teachers or classmates. From a very early age, I understood enough, just enough about my classroom experiences to keep what I knew repressed, hidden beneath layers of embarrassment. Not until my last months as a graduate student, nearly thirty years old, was it possible for me to think much about the reasons for my academic success. Only then. At the end of my schooling, I needed to determine how far I had moved from my past. The adult finally confronted, and now must publicly say, what the child shuddered from knowing and could never admit to himself or to those many faces that smiled at his every success. ("Your parents must be very proud. . . .")

I

At the end, in the British Museum (too distracted to finish my dissertation) for weeks I read, speed-read, books by modern educational theorists, only to find infrequent and slight mention of students like me. (Much more is written about the more typical case, the lower-class student who barely is helped by his schooling.) Then one day, leafing through Richard Hoggart's *The Uses of Literacy,* I found, in his description of the scholarship boy, myself. For the first time I realized that there were other students like me, and so I was able to frame the meaning of my academic success, its consequent price—the loss.

Hoggart's description is distinguished, at least initially, by deep understanding. What he grasps very well is that the scholarship boy must move between environments, his home and the classroom, which are at cultural extremes, opposed. With his family, the boy has the intense pleasure of intimacy, the family's consolation in feeling public alienation. Lavish emotions texture home life. *Then,* at school, the instruction bids him to trust lonely reason primarily. Immediate needs set the pace of his parents' lives. From his mother and father the boy learns to trust spontaneity and non-rational ways of knowing. *Then,* at school, there is mental calm. Teachers emphasize the value of a reflectiveness that opens a space between thinking and immediate action.

Years of schooling must pass before the boy will be able to sketch the cultural differences in his day as abstractly as this. But he senses those differences early. Perhaps as early as the night he brings home an assignment from school and finds the house too noisy for study.

> He has to be more and more alone, if he is going to "get on." He will have, probably unconsciously, to oppose the ethos of the hearth, the intense gregariousness of the working-class family group. Since everything centres upon the living-room, there is unlikely to be a room of his own; the bedrooms are cold and inhospitable, and to warm them or the front room, if there is one, would not only be expensive, but would require an imaginative leap—out of the tradition—which most families are not capable of making. There is a corner of the living-room table. On

the other side Mother is ironing, the wireless is on, someone is singing a snatch of song or Father says intermittently whatever comes into his head. The boy has to cut himself off mentally, so as to do his homework, as well as he can.[1]

The next day, the lesson is as apparent at school. There are even rows of desks. Discussion is ordered. The boy must rehearse his thoughts and raise his hand before speaking out in a loud voice to an audience of classmates. And there is time enough, and silence, to think about ideas (big ideas) never considered at home by his parents.

Not for the working-class child alone is adjustment to the classroom difficult. Good schooling requires that any student alter early childhood habits. But the working-class child is usually least prepared for the change. And, unlike many middle-class children, he goes home and sees in his parents a way of life not only different but starkly opposed to that of the classroom. (He enters the house and hears his parents talking in ways his teachers discourage.)

Without extraordinary determination and the great assistance of others—at home and at school—there is little chance for success. Typically most working-class children are barely changed by the classroom. The exception succeeds. The relative few become scholarship students. Of these, Richard Hoggart estimates, most manage a fairly graceful transition. Somehow they learn to live in the two very different worlds of their day. There are some others, however, those Hoggart pejoratively terms "scholarship boys," for whom success comes with special anxiety. Scholarship boy: good student, troubled son. The child is "moderately endowed," intellectually mediocre, Hoggart supposes—though it may be more pertinent to note the special qualities of temperament in the child. High-strung child. Brooding. Sensitive. Haunted by the knowledge that one *chooses* to become a student. (Education is not an inevitable or natural step in growing up.) Here is a child who cannot forget that his academic success distances him from a life he loved, even from his own memory of himself.

Initially, he wavers, balances allegiance. ("The boy is himself [until he reaches, say, the upper forms] very much of *both* the worlds of home and school. He is enormously obedient to the dictates of the world of school, but emotionally still strongly wants to continue as part of the family circle.") Gradually, necessarily, the balance is lost. The boy needs to spend more and more time studying, each night enclosing himself in the silence permitted and required by intense concentration. He takes his first step toward academic success, away from his family.

From the very first days, through the years following, it will be with his parents—the figures of lost authority, the persons toward whom he feels deepest love—that the change will be most powerfully measured. A separation will unravel between them. Advancing in his studies, the boy notices that his mother and father have not changed as much as he. Rather, when he sees them, they often remind him of the person he once was and the life he earlier shared with them. He realizes what some Romantics also know when they praise the working class for the capacity for human closeness, qualities of passion and spontaneity, that the rest of us experience in like measure only in the earliest part of our youth. For the Romantic, this doesn't make working-class life childish. Working-class life challenges precisely because it is an *adult* way of life.

The scholarship boy reaches a different conclusion. He cannot afford to admire his parents. (How could he and still pursue such a contrary life?) He permits himself embarrassment at their lack of education. And to evade nostalgia for the life he has lost, he concentrates on the benefits education will bestow upon him. He becomes especially ambitious. Without the support of old certainties and consolations, almost mechanically, he assumes the procedures and doctrines of the classroom. The kind of allegiance the young student might have given his mother and father only days earlier, he transfers to the teacher, the new figure of authority. "[The scholarship boy] tends to make a father-figure of his form-master," Hoggart observes.

But Hoggart's calm prose only makes me recall the urgency with which I came to idolize my grammar school teachers. I began by imitating their accents, using their diction, trusting their every direction. The very first facts they dispensed, I grasped with awe. Any book they told me to read, I read—then waited for them to tell me which books I enjoyed. Their every casual opinion I came to adopt and to trumpet when I returned home. I stayed after school "to help"—to get my teacher's undivided attention. It was the nun's encouragement that mattered most to me. (She understood exactly what—my parents never seemed to appraise so well—all my achievements entailed.) Memory gently caressed each word of praise bestowed in the classroom so that compliments teachers paid me years ago come quickly to mind even today.

The enthusiasm I felt in second-grade classes I flaunted before both my parents. The docile, obedient student came home a shrill and precocious son who insisted on correcting and teaching his parents with the remark: "My teacher told us. . . ."

I intended to hurt my mother and father. I was still angry at them for having encouraged me toward classroom English. But gradually this anger was exhausted, replaced by guilt as school grew more and more attractive to me. I grew increasingly successful, a talkative student. My hand was raised in the classroom; I yearned to answer any question. At home, life was less noisy than it had been. (I spoke to classmates and teachers more often each day than to family members.) Quiet at home, I sat with my papers for hours each night. I never forgot that schooling had irretrievably changed my family's life. That knowledge, however, did not weaken ambition. Instead, it strengthened resolve. Those times I remembered the loss of my past with regret, I quickly reminded myself of all the things my teachers could give me. (They could make me an educated man.) I tightened my grip on pencil and books. I evaded nostalgia. Tried hard to forget. But one does not forget by trying to forget. One only remembers. I remembered too well that education had changed my family's life. I would not have become a scholarship boy had I not so often remembered.

Once she was sure that her children knew English, my mother would tell us, "You should keep up your Spanish." Voices playfully groaned in response. "¡Pochos!" my mother would tease. I listened silently.

After a while, I grew more calm at home. I developed tact. A fourth-grade student, I was no longer the show-off in front of my parents. I became a conventionally dutiful son, politely affectionate, cheerful enough, even—for reasons beyond choosing—my father's favorite. And much about my family life was easy then, comfortable, happy in the rhythm of our living together: hearing my father getting ready for work; eating the breakfast my mother had made me; looking up from a novel to hear my brother or one of my sisters playing with friends in the backyard; in winter, coming upon the house all lighted up after dark.

But withheld from my mother and father was any mention of what most mattered to me: the extraordinary experience of first-learning. Late afternoon: in the midst of preparing dinner, my mother would come up behind me while I was trying to read. Her head just over mine, her breath warmly scented with food. "What are you reading?" Or, "Tell me all about your new courses." I would barely respond, "Just the usual things, nothing special." (A half smile, then silence. Her head moving back in the silence. Silence! Instead of the flood of intimate sounds that had once flowed smoothly between us, there was this silence.) After dinner, I would rush to a bedroom with papers and books. As often as possible, I resisted parental pleas to "save lights" by coming to the kitchen to work. I kept so much, so often, to myself. Sad. Enthusiastic. Troubled by the excitement of coming upon new ideas. Eager. Fascinated by the promising texture of a brand-new book. I hoarded the pleasures of learning. Alone for hours.

Enthralled. Nervous. I rarely looked away from my books—or back on my memories. Nights when relatives visited and the front rooms were warmed by Spanish sounds, I slipped quietly out of the house.

It mattered that education was changing me. It never ceased to matter. My brother and sisters would giggle at our mother's mispronounced words. They'd correct her gently. My mother laughed girlishly one night, trying not to pronounce *sheep* as *ship*. From a distance I listened sullenly. From that distance, pretending not to notice on another occasion, I saw my father looking at the title pages of my library books. That was the scene on my mind when I walked home with a fourth-grade companion and heard him say that his parents read to him every night. (A strange-sounding book—*Winnie the Pooh*.) Immediately, I wanted to know, "What is it like?" My companion, however, thought I wanted to know about the plot of the book. Another day, my mother surprised me by asking for a "nice" book to read. "Something not too hard you think I might like." Carefully I chose one, Willa Cather's *My Ántonia*. But when, several weeks later, I happened to see it next to her bed unread except for the first few pages, I was furious and suddenly wanted to cry. I grabbed up the book and took it back to my room and placed it in its place, alphabetically on my shelf.

"Your parents must be very proud of you." People began to say that to me about the time I was in sixth grade. To answer affirmatively, I'd smile. Shyly I'd smile, never betraying my sense of the irony: I was not proud of my mother and father. I was embarrassed by their lack of education. It was not that I ever thought they were stupid, though stupidly I took for granted their enormous native intelligence. Simply, what mattered to me was that they were not like my teachers.

But, "Why didn't you tell us about the award?" my mother demanded, her frown weakened by pride. At the grammar school ceremony several weeks after, her eyes were brighter than the trophy I'd won. Pushing back the hair from my forehead, she whispered that I had "shown" the *gringos*. A few minutes later, I heard my father speak to my teacher and felt ashamed of his labored, accented words. Then guilty for the shame. I felt such contrary feelings. (There is no simple road-map through the heart of the scholarship boy.) My teacher was so soft-spoken and her words were edged sharp and clean. I admired her until it seemed to me that she spoke too carefully. Sensing that she was condescending to them, I became nervous. Resentful. Protective. I tried to move my parents away. "You both must be very proud of Richard," the nun said. They responded quickly.

(They were proud.) "We are proud of all our children." Then this after-thought: "They sure didn't get their brains from us." They all laughed. I smiled.

Tightening the irony into a knot was the knowledge that my parents were always behind me. They made success possible. They evened the path. They sent their children to parochial schools because the nuns "teach better." They paid a tuition they couldn't afford. They spoke English to us.

For their children my parents wanted chances they never had—an easier way. It saddened my mother to learn that some relatives forced their children to start working right after high school. To *her* children she would say, "Get all the education you can." In schooling she recognized the key to job advancement. And with the remark she remembered her past.

As a girl new to America my mother had been awarded a high school diploma by teachers too careless or busy to notice that she hardly spoke English. On her own, she determined to learn how to type. That skill got her jobs typing envelopes in letter shops, and it encouraged in her an optimism about the possibility of advancement. (Each morning when her sisters put on uniforms, she chose a bright-colored dress.) The years of young womanhood passed, and her typing speed increased. She also became an excellent speller of words she mispronounced. "And I've never been to college," she'd say, smiling, when her children asked her to spell words they were too lazy to look up in a dictionary.

Typing, however, was dead-end work. Finally frustrating. When her youngest child started high school, my mother got a full-time office job once again. (Her paycheck combined with my father's to make us—in fact—what we had already become in our imagination of ourselves—middle class.) She worked then for the (California) state government in numbered civil service positions secured by examinations. The old ambition of her youth was rekindled. During the lunch hour, she consulted bulletin boards for announcements of openings. One day she saw mention of something called an "anti-poverty agency." A typing job. A glamorous job, part of the governor's staff. "A knowledge of Spanish required." Without hesitation she applied and became nervous only when the job was suddenly hers.

"Everyone comes to work all dressed up," she reported at night. And didn't need to say more than that her co-workers wouldn't let her answer the phones. She was only a typist, after all, albeit a very fast typist. And an excellent speller. One morning there was a letter to be sent to a Washington cabinet officer. On the dictating tape, a voice referred to urban guerrillas. My mother typed (the wrong word, correctly): "gorillas." The mistake horrified the anti-poverty bureaucrats who shortly after arranged to have her returned to her previous position. She would go no further. So she willed her ambition to her children. "Get all the education you can; with an education you can do anything." (With a good education *she* could have done anything.)

When I was in high school, I admitted to my mother that I planned to become a teacher someday. That seemed to please her. But I never tried to explain that it was not the occupation of teaching I yearned for as much as it was something more elusive: I wanted to *be* like my teachers, to possess their knowledge, to assume their authority, their confidence, even to assume a teacher's persona.

In contrast to my mother, my father never verbally encouraged his children's academic success. Nor did he often praise us. My mother had to remind him to "say something" to one of his children who scored some academic success. But whereas my mother saw in education the opportunity for job advancement, my father recognized that education provided an even more startling possibility: it could enable a person to escape from a life of mere labor.

In Mexico, orphaned when he was eight, my father left school to work as an "apprentice" for an uncle. Twelve years later, he left Mexico in frustration and arrived in America. He had great expectations then of becoming an engineer. ("Work for my hands and my head.") He knew a Catholic priest who promised to get him money enough to study full time for a high school diploma. But the promises came to nothing. Instead there was a dark succession of warehouse, cannery, and factory jobs. After work he went to night school along with my mother. A year, two passed. Nothing much changed, except that fatigue worked its way into the bone; then everything changed. He didn't talk anymore of becoming an engineer. He stayed outside on the steps of the school while my mother went inside to learn typing and shorthand.

By the time I was born, my father worked at "clean" jobs. For a time he was a janitor at a fancy department store. ("Easy work; the machines do it all.") Later he became a dental technician. ("Simple.") But by then he was pessimistic about the ultimate meaning of work and the possibility of ever escaping its claims. In some of my earliest memories of him, my father already seems aged by fatigue. (He has never really grown old like my mother.) From boyhood to manhood, I have remembered him in a single image: seated, asleep on the sofa, his head thrown back in a hideous corpselike grin, the evening newspaper spread out before him. "But look at all you've accomplished," his best friend said to him once. My father said nothing. Only smiled.

It was my father who laughed when I claimed to be tired by reading and writing. It was he who teased me for having soft hands. (He seemed to sense that some great achievement of leisure was implied by my papers and books.) It was my father who became angry while watching on television some woman at the Miss America contest tell the announcer that she was going to college. ("Majoring in fine arts.") "College!" he snarled. He despised the trivialization of higher education, the inflated grades and cheapened diplomas, the half education that so often passed as mass education in my generation.

It was my father again who wondered why I didn't display my awards on the wall of my bedroom. He said he liked to go to doctors' offices and see their certificates and degrees on the wall. ("Nice.") My citations from school got left in closets at home. The gleaming figure astride one of my trophies was broken, wingless, after hitting the ground. My medals were placed in a jar of loose change. And when I lost my high school diploma, my father found it as it was about to be thrown out with the trash. Without telling me, he put it away with his own things for safekeeping.

These memories slammed together at the instant of hearing that refrain familiar to all scholarship students: "Your parents must be proud. . . ." Yes, my parents were proud. I knew it. But my parents regarded my progress with more than mere pride. They endured my early precocious behavior—but with what private anger and humiliation? As their children got older and would come home to challenge ideas both of them held, they argued before submitting to the force of logic or superior factual evidence with the disclaimer, "It's what we were taught in our time to believe." These discussions ended abruptly, though my mother remembered them on other occasions when she complained that our "big ideas" were going to our heads. More acute was her complaint that the family wasn't close anymore, like some others she knew. Why weren't we close, "more in the Mexican style"? Everyone is so private, she added. And she mimicked the yes and no answers she got in reply to her questions. Why didn't we talk more? (My father never asked.) I never said.

I was the first in my family who asked to leave home when it came time to go to college. I had been admitted to Stanford, one hundred miles away. My departure would only make physically apparent the separation that had occurred long before. But it was going too far. In the months preceding my leaving, I heard the question my mother never asked except indirectly. In the hot kitchen, tired at the end of her workday, she demanded to know, "Why aren't the colleges here in Sacramento good enough for you? They are for your brother and sister." In the middle of a car ride, not turning to face me, she wondered, "Why do you need to go so far away?" Late at night, ironing, she said with disgust, "Why do you have to put us through this big expense? You know your scholarship will never cover it all." But when September came there was a rush to get everything ready. In a bedroom that last night I packed the big brown valise, and my mother sat nearby sewing initials onto the clothes I would take. And she said no more about my leaving.

Months later, two weeks of Christmas vacation: the first hours home were the hardest. ("What's new?") My parents and I sat in the kitchen for a conversation. (But, lacking the same words to develop our sentences and to shape our interests, what was there to say? What could I tell them of the term paper I had just finished on the "universality of Shakespeare's appeal"?) I mentioned only small, obvious things: my dormitory life; weekend trips I had taken; random events. They responded with news of their own. (One was almost grateful for a family crisis about which there was much to discuss.) We tried to make our conversation seem like more than an interview.

II

From an early age I knew that my mother and father could read and write both Spanish and English. I had observed my father making his way through what, I now suppose, must have been income tax forms. On other occasions I waited apprehensively while my mother read onion-paper letters airmailed from Mexico with news of a relative's illness or death. For both my parents, however, reading was something done out of necessity and as quickly as possible. Never did I see either of them read an entire book. Nor did I see them read for pleasure. Their reading consisted of work manuals, prayer books, newspaper, recipes.

Richard Hoggart imagines how, at home,

> . . . [the scholarship boy] sees strewn around, and reads regularly himself, magazines which are never mentioned at school, which seem not to belong to the world to which the school introduces him; at school he

hears about and reads books never mentioned at home. When he brings those books into the house they do not take their place with other books which the family are reading, for often there are none or almost none; his books look, rather, like strange tools.

In our house each school year would begin with my mother's careful instruction: "Don't write in your books so we can sell them at the end of the year." The remark was echoed in public by my teachers, but only in part: "Boys and girls, don't write in your books. You must learn to treat them with great care and respect."

OPEN THE DOORS OF YOUR MIND WITH BOOKS, read the red and white poster over the nun's desk in early September. It soon was apparent to me that reading was the classroom's central activity. Each course had its own book. And the information gathered from a book was unquestioned. READ TO LEARN, the sign on the wall advised in December. I privately wondered: What was the connection between reading and learning? Did one learn something only by reading it? Was an idea only an idea if it could be written down? In June, CONSIDER BOOKS YOUR BEST FRIENDS. Friends? Reading was, at best, only a chore. I needed to look up whole paragraphs of words in a dictionary. Lines of type were dizzying, the eye having to move slowly across the page, then down, and across. . . . The sentences of the first books I read were coolly impersonal. Toned hard. What most bothered me, however, was the isolation reading required. To console myself for the loneliness I'd feel when I read, I tried reading in a very soft voice. Until: "Who is doing all that talking to his neighbor?" Shortly after, remedial reading classes were arranged for me with a very old nun.

At the end of each school day, for nearly six months, I would meet with her in the tiny room that served as the school's library but was actually only a storeroom for used textbooks and a vast collection of *National Geographics*. Everything about our sessions pleased me: the smallness of the room; the noise of the janitor's broom hitting the edge of the long hallway outside the door; the green of the sun, lighting the wall; and the old woman's face blurred white with a beard. Most of the time we took turns. I began with my elementary text. Sentences of astonishing simplicity seemed to me lifeless and drab: "The boys ran from the rain . . . She wanted to sing . . . The kite rose in the blue." Then the old nun would read from her favorite books, usually biographies of early American presidents. Playfully she ran through complex sentences, calling the words alive with her voice, making it seem that the author somehow was speaking directly to me. I smiled just to listen to her. I sat there and sensed for the very first time some possibility of fellowship between a reader and a writer, a communication, never *intimate* like that I heard spoken words at home convey, but one nonetheless *personal.*

One day the nun concluded a session by asking me why I was so reluctant to read by myself. I tried to explain; said something about the way written words made me feel all alone—almost, I wanted to add but didn't, as when I spoke to myself in a room just emptied of furniture. She studied my face as I spoke; she seemed to be watching more than listening. In an uneventful voice she replied that I had nothing to fear. Didn't I realize that reading would open up whole new worlds? A book could open doors for me. It could introduce me to people and show me places I never imagined existed. She gestured toward the bookshelves. (Bare-breasted African women danced, and the shiny hubcaps of automobiles on the back covers of the *Geographic* gleamed in my mind.) I listened with respect. But her words were not very influential. I was thinking then of another consequence of literacy, one I was too shy to admit but nonetheless trusted. Books were going to make me "educated." *That* confidence enabled me, several months later, to overcome my fear of the silence.

In fourth grade I embarked upon a grandiose reading program. "Give me the names of important books," I would say to startled teachers. They soon found out that I had in mind "adult books." I ignored their suggestion of anything I suspected was written for children. (Not until I was in college, as a result, did I read *Huckleberry Finn* or *Alice's Adventures in Wonderland.*) Instead, I read *The Scarlet Letter* and Franklin's *Autobiography.* And whatever I read I read for extra credit. Each time I finished a book, I reported the achievement to a teacher and basked in the praise my effort earned. Despite my best efforts, however, there seemed to be more and more books I needed to read. At the library I would literally tremble as I came upon whole shelves of books I hadn't read. So I read and I read and I read: *Great Expectations;* all the short stories of Kipling; *The Babe Ruth Story;* the entire first volume of the *Encyclopedia Britannica* (A–ANSIEY); the *Iliad; Moby Dick; Gone with the Wind; The Good Earth; Ramona; Forever Amber; The Lives of the Saints; Crime and Punishment; The Pearl. . . .* Librarians who initially frowned when I checked out the maximum ten books at a time started saving books they thought I might like. Teachers would say to the rest of the class, "I only wish the rest of you took reading as seriously as Richard obviously does."

But at home I would hear my mother wondering, "What do you see in your books?" (Was reading a hobby like her knitting? Was so much reading even healthy for a boy? Was it the sign of "brains"? Or was it just a convenient excuse for not helping about the house on Saturday mornings?) Always, "What do you see . . . ?"

What *did* I see in my books? I had the idea that they were crucial for my academic success, though I couldn't have said exactly how or why. In the sixth grade I simply concluded that what gave a book its value was some major idea or theme it contained. If that core essence could be mined and memorized, I would become learned like my teachers. I decided to record in a notebook the themes of the books that I read. After reading *Robinson Crusoe,* I wrote that its theme was "the value of learning to live by oneself." When I completed *Wuthering Heights,* I noted the danger of "letting emotions get out of control." Rereading these brief moralistic appraisals usually left me disheartened. I couldn't believe that they were really the source of reading's value. But for many more years, they constituted the only means I had of describing to myself the educational value of books.

In spite of my earnestness, I found reading a pleasurable activity. I came to enjoy the lonely good company of books. Early on weekday mornings, I'd read in my bed. I'd feel a mysterious comfort then, reading in the dawn quiet—the blue-gray silence interrupted by the occasional churning of the refrigerator motor a few rooms away or the more distant sounds of a city bus beginning its run. On weekends I'd go to the public library to read, surrounded by old men and women. Or, if the weather was fine, I would take my books to the park and read in the shade of a tree. A warm summer evening was my favorite reading time. Neighbors would leave for vacation and I would water their lawns. I would sit through the twilight on the front porches or in backyards, reading to the cool, whirling sounds of the sprinklers.

I also had favorite writers. But often those writers I enjoyed most I was least able to value. When I read William Saroyan's *The Human Comedy,* I was immediately pleased by the narrator's warmth and the charm of his story. But as quickly I became suspicious. A book so enjoyable to read couldn't be very "important." Another summer I determined to read all the novels of Dickens. Reading his fat novels, I loved the feeling I got—after the first hundred pages—of being at home in a fictional world where I knew the names of the characters and cared about what was going to happen to them. And it bothered me that I was forced away at the conclusion, when the fiction closed tight, like a fortune-teller's fist—the futures of all the major characters neatly resolved. I never knew how to take such feelings seriously, however. Nor did I suspect that these experiences could be part of a novel's meaning. Still, there were pleasures to sustain me after I'd finish my books. Carrying a volume back to the library, I would be pleased by its weight. I'd run my fingers along the edge of the pages and marvel at the breadth of my achievement. Around my room, growing stacks of paperback books reenforced my assurance.

I entered high school having read hundreds of books. My habit of reading made me a confident speaker and writer of English. Reading also enabled me to sense something of the shape, the major concerns, of Western thought. (I was able to say something about Dante and Descartes and Engels and James Baldwin in my high school term papers.) In these various ways, books brought me academic success as I hoped that they would. But I was not a good reader. Merely bookish, I lacked a point of view when I read. Rather, I read in order to acquire a point of view. I vacuumed books for epigrams, scraps of information, ideas, themes—anything to fill the hollow within me and make me feel educated. When one of my teachers suggested to his drowsy tenth-grade English class that a person could not have a "complicated idea" until he had read at least two thousand books, I heard the remark without detecting either its irony or its very complicated truth. I merely deter-mined to compile a list of all the books I had ever read. Harsh with myself, I included only once a title I might have read several times. (How, after all, could one read a book more than once?) And I included only those books over a hundred pages in length. (Could anything shorter be a book?)

There was yet another high school list I compiled. One day I came across a newspaper article about the retirement of an English professor at a nearby state college. The article was accompanied by a list of the "hundred most important books of Western Civilization." "More than anything else in my life," the professor told the reporter with finality, "these books have made me all that I am." That was the kind of remark I couldn't ignore. I clipped out the list and kept it for the several months it took me to read all of the titles. Most books, of course, I barely under-stood. While reading Plato's *Republic,* for instance, I needed to keep looking at the book jacket comments to remind myself what the text was about. Nevertheless, with the special patience and superstition of a scholarship boy, I looked at every word of the text. And by the time I reached the last word, relieved, I convinced myself that I had read *The Republic.* In a ceremony of great pride, I solemnly crossed Plato off my list.

III

The scholarship boy pleases most when he is young—the working-class child struggling for academic success. To his teachers, he offers great satisfaction; his success is their proudest achievement. Many other persons offer to help him. A businessman learns the boy's story and promises to underwrite part of the cost of his college education. A woman leaves him her entire library of several hundred books when she moves. His progress is featured in a newspaper article. Many people seem happy for him. They marvel. "How did you manage so fast?" From all sides, there is lavish praise and encouragement.

In his grammar school classroom, however, the boy already makes students around him uneasy. They scorn his desire to succeed. They scorn him for constantly wanting the teacher's attention and praise. "Kiss Ass," they call him when his hand swings up in response to every question he hears. Later, when he makes it to college, no one will mock him aloud. But he detects annoyance on the faces of some students and even some teachers who watch him. It puzzles him often. In college, then in graduate school, he behaves much as he always has. If anything is different about him it is that he dares to anticipate the successful conclusion of his studies. At last he feels that he belongs in the classroom, and this is exactly the source of the dissatisfaction he causes. To many persons around him, he appears too much the academic. There may be some things about him that recall his beginnings—his shabby clothes; his persistent poverty; or his dark skin (in those cases when it symbolizes his parents' disadvantaged condition)—but they only make clear how far he has moved from his past. He has used education to remake himself.

It bothers his fellow academics to face this. They will not say why exactly. (They sneer.) But their expectations become obvious when they are disappointed. They expect—they want—a student less changed by his schooling. If the scholarship boy, from a past so distant from the classroom, could remain in some basic way unchanged, he would be able to prove that it is possible for anyone to become educated without basically changing from the person one was.

Here is no fabulous hero, no idealized scholar-worker. The scholarship boy does not straddle, cannot reconcile, the two great opposing cultures of his life. His success is unromantic and plain. He sits in the classroom and offers those sitting beside him no calming reassurance about their own lives. He sits in the seminar room—a man with brown skin, the son of working-class Mexican immigrant parents. (Addressing the professor at the head of the table, his voice catches with nervousness.) There is no trace of his parents' in his speech. Instead he approximates the accents of teachers and classmates. Coming from *him* those sounds seem suddenly odd. Odd too is the effect produced when *he* uses academic jargon—bubbles at the tip of his tongue: "*Topos* . . . negative capability . . . vegetation imagery in Shakespearean comedy." He lifts an opinion from Coleridge, takes something else from Frye or Empson or Leavis. He even repeats exactly his professor's earlier comment. All his ideas are clearly borrowed. He seems to have no thought of his own. He chatters while his listeners smile—their look one of disdain.

When he is older and thus when so little of the person he was survives, the scholarship boy makes only too apparent his profound lack of *self*-confidence. This is the conventional assessment that even Richard Hoggart repeats:

> [The scholarship boy] tends to over-stress the importance of examinations, of the piling-up of knowledge and of received opinions. He discovers a technique of apparent learning, of the acquiring of facts rather than of the handling and use of facts. He learns how to receive a purely literate education, one using only a small part of the personality and challenging only a limited area of his being. He begins to see life as a ladder, as permanent examination with some praise and some further exhortation at each stage. He becomes an expert imbiber and doler-out; his competence will vary, but will rarely be accompanied by genuine enthusiasms. He rarely feels the reality of knowledge, of other men's thoughts and imaginings, on his own pulses. . . . He has something of the blinkered pony about him.

But this is criticism more accurate than fair. The scholarship boy is a very bad student. He is the great mimic; a collector of thoughts, not a thinker; the very last person in class who ever feels obliged to have an opinion of his own. In large part, however, the reason he is such a bad student is because he realizes more often and more acutely than most other students—than Hoggart himself—that education requires radical self-reformation. As a very young boy, regarding his parents, as he struggles with an early homework assignment, he knows this too well. That is why he lacks self-assurance. He does not forget that the classroom is responsible for remaking him. He relies on his teacher, depends on all that he hears in the classroom and reads in his books. He becomes in every obvious way the worst student, a dummy mouthing the opinions of others. But he would not be so bad—nor would he become so successful, a *scholarship* boy—if he did not accurately perceive that the best synonym for primary "education" is "imitation."

Those who would take seriously the boy's success—and his failure— would be forced to realize how great is the change any academic under- goes, how far one must move from one's past. It is easiest to ignore such considerations. So little is said about the scholarship boy in pages and pages of educational literature. Nothing is said of the silence that comes to separate the boy from his parents. Instead, one hears proposals for increasing the self-esteem of students and encouraging early intellectual independence. Paragraphs glitter with a constellation of terms like *creativity* and *originality*. (Ignored altogether is the function of imitation in a student's life.) Radical educationalists meanwhile complain that ghetto schools "oppress" students by trying to mold them, stifling native charac- teristics. The truer critique would be just the reverse: not that schools change ghetto students too much, but that while they might promote the occasional scholarship student, they change most students barely at all.

From the story of the scholarship boy there is no specific pedagogy to glean. There is, however, a much larger lesson. His story makes clear that education is a long, unglamorous, even demeaning process—*a nurturing never natural to the person one was before one entered a classroom.* At once different from most other students, the scholarship boy is also the arche- typal "good student." He exaggerates the difficulty of being a student, but his exaggeration reveals a general predicament. Others are changed by their schooling as much as he. They too must re-form themselves. They must develop the skill of memory long before they become truly critical thinkers. And when they read Plato for the first several times, it will be with awe more than deep comprehension.

The impact of schooling on the scholarship boy is only more appar- ent to the boy himself and to others. Finally, although he may be laugh- able—a blinkered pony—the boy will not let his critics forget their own change. He ends up too much like them. When he speaks, they hear themselves echoed. In his pedantry, they trace their own. His ambitions are theirs. If his failure were singular, they might readily pity him. But he is more troubling than that. They would not scorn him if this were not so.

IV

Like me, Hoggart's imagined scholarship boy spends most of his years in the classroom afraid to long for his past. Only at the very end of his schooling does the boy-man become nostalgic. In this sudden change of heart, Richard Hoggart notes:

> He longs for the membership he lost, "he pines for some Nameless Eden where he never was." The nostalgia is the stronger and the more ambiguous because he is really "in quest of his own absconded self yet scared to find it." He both wants to go back and yet thinks he has gone beyond his class, feels himself weighted with knowledge of his own and their situation, which hereafter forbids him the simpler pleasures of his father and mother.

According to Hoggart, the scholarship boy grows nostalgic because he remains the uncertain scholar, bright enough to have moved from his past, yet unable to feel easy, a part of a community of academics.

This analysis, however, only partially suggests what happened to me in my last year as a graduate student. When I traveled to London to write a dissertation on English Renaissance literature, I was finally confident of membership in a "community of scholars." But the pleasure that confidence gave me faded rapidly. After only two or three months in the reading room of the British Museum, it became clear that I had joined a lonely community. Around me each day were dour faces eclipsed by large piles of books. There were the regulars, like the old couple who arrived every morning, each holding a loop of the shopping bag which contained all their notes. And there was the historian who chattered madly to herself. ("Oh dear! Oh! Now, what's this? What? Oh, my!") There were also the faces of young men and women worn by long study. And everywhere eyes turned away the moment our glance accidentally met. Some persons I sat beside day after day, yet we passed silently at the end of the day, strangers. Still, we were united by a common respect for the written word and for scholarship. We did form a union, though one in which we remained distant from one another.

More profound and unsettling was the bond I recognized with those writers whose books I consulted. Whenever I opened a text that hadn't been used for years, I realized that my special interests and skills united me to a mere handful of academics. We formed an exclusive—eccentric!—society, separated from others who would never care or be able to share our concerns. (The pages I turned were stiff like layers of dead skin.) I began to wonder: Who, beside my dissertation director and a few faculty members, would ever read what I wrote? And: Was my dissertation much more than an act of social withdrawal? These questions went unanswered in the silence of the Museum reading room. They remained to trouble me after I'd leave the library each afternoon and feel myself shy—unsteady, speaking simple sentences at the grocer's or the butcher's on my way back to my bed-sitter.

Meanwhile my file cards accumulated. A professional, I knew exactly how to search a book for pertinent information. I could quickly assess and summarize the usability of the many books I consulted. But whenever I started to write, I knew too much (and not enough) to be able to write anything but sentences that were overly cautious, timid, strained brittle under the heavy weight of footnotes and qualifications. I seemed unable to dare a passionate statement. I felt drawn by professionalism to the edge of sterility, capable of no more than pedantic, lifeless, unassailable prose.

Then nostalgia began.

After years spent unwilling to admit its attractions, I gestured nostalgically toward the past. I yearned for that time when I had not been so alone. I became impatient with books. I wanted experience more immediate. I feared the library's silence. I silently scorned the gray, timid faces around me. I grew to hate the growing pages of my dissertation on genre and Renaissance literature. (In my mind I heard relatives laughing as they tried to make sense of its title.) I wanted something—I couldn't say exactly what. I told myself that I wanted a more passionate life. And a life less thoughtful. And above all, I wanted to be less alone. One day I heard some Spanish academics whispering back and forth to each other, and their sounds seemed ghostly voices recalling my life. Yearning became preoccupation then. Boyhood memories beckoned, flooded my mind. (Laughing intimate voices. Bounding up the front steps of the porch. A sudden embrace inside the door.)

For weeks after, I turned to books by educational experts. I needed to learn how far I had moved from my past—to determine how fast I would be able to recover something of it once again. But I found little. Only a chapter in a book by Richard Hoggart. . . . I left the reading room and the circle of faces.

I came home. After the year in England, I spent three summer months living with my mother and father, relieved by how easy it was to be home. It no longer seemed very important to me that we had little to say. I felt easy sitting and eating and walking with them. I watched them, nevertheless, looking for evidence of those elastic, sturdy strands that bind generations in a web of inheritance. I thought as I watched my mother one night: Of course a friend had been right when she told me that I gestured and laughed just like my mother. Another time I saw for myself: my father's eyes were much like my own, constantly watchful.

But after the early relief, this return, came suspicion, nagging until I realized that I had not neatly sidestepped the impact of schooling. My desire to do so was precisely the measure of how much I remained an academic. *Negatively* (for that is how this idea first occurred to me): my need to think so much and so abstractly about my parents and our relationship was in itself an indication of my long education. My father and mother did not pass their thinking about the cultural meanings of their experience. It was I who described their daily lives with airy ideas. And yet, *positively:* the ability to consider experience so abstractly allowed me to shape into desire what would otherwise have remained indefinite, meaningless longing in the British Museum. If, because of my schooling, I had grown culturally separated from my parents, my education finally had given me ways of speaking and caring about that fact.

My best teachers in college and graduate school, years before, had tried to prepare me for this conclusion, I think, when they discussed texts of aristocratic pastoral literature. Faithfully, I wrote down all that they said. I memorized it: "The praise of the unlettered by the highly educated is one of the primary themes of 'elitist' literature." But, "the importance of the praise given the unsolitary, richly passionate and spontaneous life is that it simultaneously reflects the value of a reflective life." I heard it all. But there was no way for any of it to mean very much to me. I was a scholarship boy at the time, busily laddering my way up the rungs of education. To pass an examination, I copied down exactly what my teachers told me. It would require many more years of schooling (an inevitable miseducation) in which I came to trust the silence of reading and the habit of abstracting from immediate experience—moving away from a life of closeness and immediacy I remembered with my parents, growing older—before I turned unafraid to desire the past, and thereby achieved what had eluded me for so long—the end of education.

Notes

[1]All quotations in this essay are from Richard Hoggart, *The Uses of Literacy* (London: Chatto and Windus, 1957), chapter 10. [Author's note]

CONSIDERATIONS

Thinking

There is a feeling throughout this essay that Rodriguez is not pleased with being a "scholarship boy." Where do you first detect that uneasiness? Where do you begin to understand it?

What do you suppose Rodriguez has in mind when he talks about "some possibility of fellowship between a reader and a writer"?

What do you imagine Rodriguez means in the last sentence of the essay when he speaks of "the end of education"?

Connecting

Are you a "good reader"? Or do you, too, "read in order to acquire a point of view"? What comes first, an idea to guide your reading or reading itself? Explain.

Distinguish two of your own college experiences—one that involved creativity and originality and one that was nothing more than imitation. What do you make of those two experiences?

What happens, according to Rodriguez, when finally you can connect nostalgia with your accumulated reading and imitating?

Is a scholarship boy a product only of working-class families?

Writing

Write an essay that tries to answer Rodriguez's questions: "What was the connection between reading and learning? Did one learn something only by reading it? Was an idea only an idea if it could be written down?"

Write an essay on what you consider to be the "consequences of literacy," as you know them.

Phyllis Rose
(b.1942)

Phyllis Rose, a professor of English at Wesleyan University, has written essays and reviews for a wide variety of periodicals, including *Vogue, The Atlantic Monthly, The Washington Post,* and *The New York Times.* She has published biographies of Josephine Baker and Virginia Woolf, written a study of five Victorian marriages *(Parallel Lives),* and published two collections of essays—*Writing About Women* (1985) and *Never Say Goodbye* (1990).

In "Tools of Torture," Rose explores some surprising connections between beauty and pain. The essay is noteworthy for its striking comparisons and its easy and casual manner.

Tools of Torture: An Essay on Beauty and Pain

In a gallery off the rue Dauphine, near the *parfumerie* where I get my massage, I happened upon an exhibit of medieval torture instruments. It made me think that pain must be as great a challenge to the human imagination as pleasure. Otherwise there's no accounting for the number of torture instruments. One would be quite enough. The simple pincer, let's say, which rips out flesh. Or the head crusher, which breaks first your tooth sockets, then your skull. But in addition I saw tongs, thumbscrews, a rack, a ladder, ropes and pulleys, a grill, a garrote, a Spanish horse, a Judas cradle, an iron maiden, a cage, a gag, a strappado, a stretching table, a saw, a wheel, a twisting stork, an inquisitor's chair, a breast breaker, and a scourge. You don't need complicated machinery to cause incredible pain. If you want to saw your victim down the middle, for example, all you need is a slightly bigger than usual saw. If you hold the victim upside down so the blood stays in his head, hold his legs apart and start sawing at the groin, you can get as far as the navel before he loses consciousness.

Even in the Middle Ages, before electricity, there were many things you could do to torment a person. You could tie him up in an iron belt that held the arms and legs up to the chest and left no point of rest, so that all his muscles went into spasm within minutes and he was driven mad within hours. This was the twisting stork, a benign-looking object. You could stretch him out backward over a thin piece of wood so that his whole body weight rested on his spine, which pressed against the sharp wood. Then you could stop up his nostrils and force water into his stomach through his mouth. Then, if you wanted to finish him off, you and your helper could jump on his stomach, causing internal hemorrhage. This torture was called the rack. If you wanted to burn someone to death without hearing him scream, you could use a tongue lock, a metal rod between the jaw and collarbone that prevented him from opening his mouth. You could put a person in a chair with spikes on the seat and arms, tie him down against the spikes, and beat him, so that every time he flinched from the beating he drove his own flesh deeper onto the spikes. This was the inquisitor's chair. If you wanted to make it

535

worse, you could heat the spikes. You could suspend a person over a pointed wooden pyramid and whenever he started to fall asleep, you could drop him onto the point. If you were Ippolito Marsili, the inventor of this torture, known as the Judas cradle, you could tell yourself you had invented something humane, a torture that worked without burning flesh or breaking bones. For the torture here was supposed to be sleep deprivation.

The secret of torture, like the secret of French cuisine, is that nothing is unthinkable. The human body is like a foodstuff, to be grilled, pounded, filleted. Every opening exists to be stuffed, all flesh to be carved off the bone. You take an ordinary wheel, a heavy wooden wheel with spokes. You lay the victim on the ground with blocks of wood at strategic points under his shoulders, legs, and arms. You use the wheel to break every bone in his body. Next you tie his body onto the wheel. With all its bones broken, it will be pliable. However, the victim will not be dead. If you want to kill him, you hoist the wheel aloft on the end of a pole and leave him to starve. Who would have thought to do this with a man and a wheel? But, then, who would have thought to take the disgusting snail, force it to render its ooze, stuff it in its own shell with garlic butter, bake it, and eat it?

Not long ago I had a facial—only in part because I thought I needed one. It was research into the nature and function of pleasure. In a dark booth at the back of the beauty salon, the aesthetician put me on a table and applied a series of ointments to my face, some cool, some warmed. After a while she put something into my hand, cold and metallic. "Don't be afraid, madame," she said. "It is an electrode. It will not hurt you. The other end is attached to two metal cylinders, which I roll over your face. They break down the electricity barrier on your skin and allow the moisturizers to penetrate deeply." I didn't believe this hocus-pocus. I didn't believe in the electricity barrier or in the ability of these rollers to break it down. But it all felt very good. The cold metal on my face was a pleasant change from the soft warmth of the aesthetician's fingers. Still, since Algeria it's hard to hear the word "electrode" without fear. So when she left me for a few minutes with a moist, refreshing cheesecloth over my face, I thought, What if the goal of her expertise had been pain, not moisture? What if the electrodes had been electrodes in the Algerian sense? What if the cheesecloth mask were dipped in acid?

In Paris, where the body is so pampered, torture seems particularly sinister, not because it's hard to understand but because—as the dark side of sensuality—it seems so easy. Beauty care is among the glories of Paris. *Soins esthétiques* include makeup, facials, massages (both relaxing and reducing), depilations (partial and complete), manicures, pedicures, and tanning, in addition to the usual run of *soins* for the hair: cutting, brushing, setting, waving, styling, blowing, coloring, and streaking. In Paris the state of your skin, hair, and nerves is taken seriously, and there is little of the puritanical thinking that tries to persuade us that beauty comes from within. Nor do the French think, as Americans do, that beauty should be offhand and low-maintenance. Spending time and money on *soins esthétiques* is appropriate and necessary, not self-indulgent. Should that loving attention to the body turn malevolent, you have torture. You have the procedure—the aesthetic, as it were—of torture, the explanation for the rich diversity of torture instruments, but you do not have the cause.

Historically torture has been a tool of legal systems, used to get information needed for a trial or, more directly, to determine guilt or innocence. In the Middle Ages confession was considered the best of all proofs, and torture was the way to produce a confession. In other words, torture didn't come into existence to give vent to human sadism. It is not always private and perverse but sometimes social and institutional, vetted by the government and, of course, the Church. (There have been few bigger fans of torture than Christianity and Islam.) Righteousness, as much as viciousness, produces torture. There aren't squads of sadists beating down the doors to the torture chambers begging for jobs. Rather, as a recent book on torture by Edward Peters says, the institution of torture creates sadists; the weight of a culture, Peters suggests, is necessary to recruit torturers. You have to convince people that they are working for a great goal in order to get them to overcome their repugnance to the task of causing physical pain to another person. Usually the great goal is the preservation of society, and the victim is presented to the torturer as being in some way out to destroy it.

From another point of view, what's horrifying is how easily you can persuade someone that he is working for the common good. Perhaps the most appalling psychological experiment of modern times, by Stanley Milgram, showed that ordinary, decent people in New Haven, Connecticut, could be brought to the point of inflicting (as they thought) severe electric shocks on other people in obedience to an authority and in pursuit of a goal, the advancement of knowledge, of which they approved. Milgram used—some would say abused—the prestige of science and the university to make his point, but his point is chilling nonetheless. We can cluck over torture, but the evidence at least suggests that with intelligent handling most of us could be brought to do it ourselves.

In the Middle Ages, Milgram's experiment would have had no point. It would have shocked no one that people were capable of cruelty in the interest of something they believed in. That was as it should be. Only recently in the history of human thought has the avoidance of cruelty moved to the forefront of ethics. "Putting cruelty first," as Judith Shklar says in *Ordinary Vices,* is comparatively new. The belief that the "pursuit of happiness" is one of man's inalienable rights, the idea that "cruel and unusual punishment" is an evil in itself, the Benthamite notion that behavior should be guided by what will produce the greatest happiness for the greatest number—all these principles are only two centuries old. They were born with the eighteenth-century democratic revolutions. And in two hundred years they have not been universally accepted. Wherever people believe strongly in some cause, they will justify torture—not just the Nazis, but the French in Algeria.

Many people who wouldn't hurt a fly have annexed to fashion the imagery of torture—the thongs and spikes and metal studs—hence reducing it to the frivolous and transitory. Because torture has been in the mainstream and not on the margins of history, nothing could be healthier. For torture to be merely kinky would be a big advance. Exhibitions like the one I saw in Paris, which presented itself as educational, may be guilty of pandering to the tastes they deplore. Solemnity may be the wrong tone. If taking one's goals too seriously is the danger, the best discouragement of torture may be a radical hedonism that denies that any goal is worth the means, that refuses to allow the nobly abstract to seduce us from the sweetness of the concrete. Give people a good croissant and a good cup of coffee in the morning. Give them an occasional facial and a plate of escargots. Marie Antoinette picked a bad moment to say "Let them eat cake," but I've often thought she was on the right track.

All of which brings me back to Paris, for Paris exists in the imagination of much of the world as the capital of pleasure—of fun, food, art, folly, seduction, gallantry, and beauty. Paris is civilization's reminder to itself that nothing leads you less wrong than your awareness of your own pleasure and a genial desire to spread it around. In that sense the myth of Paris constitutes a moral touchstone, standing for the selfish frivolity that helps keep priorities straight.

CONSIDERATIONS

Thinking

Do you think Rose is correct in her assertion that "wherever people believe strongly in some cause, they will justify torture"? Why or why not? Do you think torture is ever justified?

Do you agree with Rose that the Milgrim experiment she refers to is "perhaps the most appalling psychological experiment of modern times"? Why or why not?

Connecting

Summarize the connections Rose identifies between torture and French cuisine. What is your reaction to the analogies she draws between torture and cooking?

What connections does Rose make between the beauty parlor and the torture chamber?

Can Rose's speculations and analogies be further extended to the health and fitness club? Why or why not?

Writing

Write a letter to Phyllis Rose responding to those parts of her essay that struck you more forcibly—whether you like or dislike what she has to say.

Track down Stanley Milgram's description of his experiment on obedience to authority. Discuss your response to Milgram's experiment and his results.

S harman Apt Russell (b.1945)

S harman Apt Russell teaches writing at Western New Mexico University. Her work has appeared in *The Missouri Review, The Threepenny Review,* and *Quarterly West.* "Homebirth" is from her collection of essays, *Songs of the Fluteplayer: Seasons of Life in the Southwest.*

In "Homebirth," Russell looks closely at the practice of giving birth at home in the company of family and midwives, and contrasts it with delivery in a hospital under the charge of paternalistic male physicians.

Homebirth

Her clinic is a tiny whitewashed adobe blazoned with turquoise paint on the door and window sills. Turquoise is a popular color here in Silver City; in Mexican folklore, it has the power to ward off witches. Outside, posted on the minuscule lawn, a neat hand-lettered sign reads Licensed Midwife and then again, underneath, *Partera Registrada*. Inside is a waiting room with three chairs, a box of children's toys, and a decor that leans toward primitive art. A large bulletin board shows a collage of colorful snapshots: euphoric mothers holding newborn babies, euphoric fathers holding newborn babies, babies themselves with eyes squeezed shut and hands upraised in gestures of peace. In a number of photos is the midwife herself, looking tired and pleased.

I am here to pick up a friend, a fellow teacher, who is six months pregnant. A former student of mine, Angelica Gutierrez, waits on the chair beside me. I have been teaching writing skills at the nearby university for nine years, and I see my former students everywhere: at the bank, at the grocery store, at the park with our mutual children. I am not surprised now to see Angelica, and instead of flipping through the magazines provided, we talk about her births.

In 1984 Angelica was sixteen when she had her first baby in the hospital. "Awful, awful, awful," she says of that. They didn't let her husband be with her during labor. They shaved her pubic hair. They took the baby away afterwards. When she was nineteen and pregnant again, Angelica couldn't afford to go to the hospital and so approached, with trepidation, a local midwife. Today Angelica is having her third child. Her husband's new insurance would cover a team of specialists. But Angelica is in love with the homebirth experience. Her friends think she is crazy. "Aren't you scared?" they ask. "No, I'm happy," she says. "Listen to me. This is wonderful."

Angelica's children are being born in the same house that their grandfather and great-uncles and great-aunts were born in. Up into the 1950s, most babies in Grant County were born at home, attended by a registered and licensed midwife. Thirty years later, homebirth accounts for only two percent of national births, a figure true for this area as well. In this clinic, the midwife averages two births a month, although she would like to do more. Her clients range from teenagers to thirty-five-year-old "teacher types." Forty percent are Hispanic, an ethnic group that makes up over 60 percent of the county's population. About half of her customers are on Medicaid. Of these, those who are having a homebirth only to save money almost always, the midwife says, find some last minute, last ditch way to the hospital.

In any discussion of homebirth, ideas of safety—"Aren't you afraid?"—usually come up. In New Mexico, the statistics of midwives and their homebirths are consistently better or similar to hospital births. Indeed, studies across the country and across the world confirm the reasonableness of having a baby at home; the World Health Organization has even urged the United States to support midwives as a way of reducing our high infant mortality rate. For people in the homebirth movement, this is all very old news. Safety is a priority. It is not, necessarily, the heart of the matter.

In 1984, the year Angelica went to the hospital for her first child, I was having my first child in an adobe house thirty miles from town. Like Angelica, I did not choose homebirth intuitively. In truth, I probably would not have had one if most of my friends had not. More bluntly, I did it because they did. Peer pressure may not seem a good reason for this or any decision of importance. In reality, it is exactly why we do so many important things, from getting married to wearing clothes on a hot summer's day. Normalcy is defined by what people are normally doing around you, and the majority of my friends—teacher types, ex-hippies, and one computer consultant—were birthing at home.

My acceptance of a homebirth was also influenced by my husband. Together, we had sweated and strained to build a single adobe room, fifteen-by-twenty feet large. We had made each brick, hammered in each nail, and rolled up the vigas onto the roof by the brute strength of our arms. Although the choice was mine to make, it was clear that a birth in this, our home, followed truly and cleanly from the vision that had brought us here. A homebirth was another way of claiming this house and land as our own. It was a root sinking into the ground. It appealed to my husband's imagination, and in our constructed lives, imagination was a potent force.

Finally, not least, there was my midwife. As she had impressed Angelica on their first meeting, so she impressed me. She is a beautiful Anglo woman, with long golden hair and green eyes, who at the age of twenty-eight projected the authority of someone much older. Those who do not find beauty powerful are possibly around it too much or have never seen it at all. I don't know what this gift did to or for my midwife. I know only that she appeared tremendously competent, forthright, and self-assured. In her presence I felt it would be too gauche, too life-denying, to feel anything but trust in whatever she believed in. (I would realize, years later, that I had obscurely and pre-adolescently fallen in love with her.)

My midwife's assumption that I was also forthright, competent, and self-assured more or less corresponded with my own self-image. At the same time, I had doubts that I never revealed in our biweekly and then weekly sessions. There were moments in which I hoped for some physical problem that would rule out homebirth at the last minute. Under a licensed midwife, the list of these is long, for the integrity of homebirth lies in its restriction to a low-risk pregnancy. If, for example, my baby was too large, too small, too late, too early—then I would go to the hospital.

I had never stayed overnight in a hospital before. Now, suddenly, my picture of that experience grew increasingly benign. Hospital beds seemed so cool and inviting. Hospital white was such a clean color. I knew that such whiteness had its price. The most respected obstetrician in town had once smirked at me and let loose the Freudian slip, "I'd love to have your baby for you, Sharman." Still, secretly, I yearned to lay down the burden of having a child and to lay it precisely in the hands of someone who *was* paternal and overbearing. Let an obstetrician take the credit of birth, as long as he also took the blame. Let him lead me blindfolded through this valley of uncertainty. Let the drugs contract my uterus and the forceps extract the child. If the unspeakable happened, if horror struck and the baby died or was damaged, I believed—I rationalized—that I would be safer in the hospital. I did not mean physically. I meant emotionally. I would not have to feel as much there. A passive figure, wheeled on a metal table, strapped in, drugged, catheterized, fed through an IV, hooked to a machine: I would not be myself. I would not be responsible.

With inverse psychology, these feelings also led me home. The more I yearned for an outside authority, the more I guessed what was to be gained in not relinquishing my own. Something messy, bloody, and intensely personal lay ahead. It must be important if I was afraid of it. It must be, I reasoned, too important to give away.

Desired and even orchestrated, my first pregnancy had its share of inauspicious omens. As I drove home with the good news, a truck turning left accordioned my fender into the passenger's seat. Three days later, a doctor gave me Progesterone to "prevent miscarriage." In my vulnerable state,

I still roused myself to protest. "Don't take it," the man said classically, "if you don't care about your baby." Soon after I learned that Progesterone was a known cause of birth defects. When I rushed to confirm this with another doctor, he spoke of "heart holes" and "limb reductions" and noted, in a kindly way, that his office did abortions. My third appointment was with a specialist who dismissed the whole affair. In his opinion, if my husband and I were not willing to risk this pregnancy, we were not willing to risk pregnancy at all.

At this point, four weeks after conception, I settled into being an expectant mother. My initiation was fairly typical. Most pregnant women I know have either had a true scare or have concocted one. Growing a baby is the most exotic of lands, bordered by joy, fraught with a sense of danger, and beset by internal politics. Nine months is barely enough time for us to drain these emotions to their last bittersweet dregs. By the end, discomfort compels us. Like adventurers cast on some Pacific isle, we are ready to sail back to civilization.

Thirty-year-old women often have a long first labor, and I was no exception. The amniotic sac ruptured at four o'clock Tuesday morning and as I jumped from the bed to let the water gush from my body, I felt very young, like a child who had gotten up too early on Christmas. For two weeks, I had kept prepared the bag of things my midwife required of me. These included disposable surgical gloves, a bottle of Betadine, a suction for the baby's nose, a thermometer, a large pan, sanitary napkins, three towels, three sheets, and a dozen clean rags. The last three items had to be sterilized, a feat accomplished by placing them in a brown paper bag in a hot oven for two hours. The "sterilization" lasted two weeks, and I had re-sterilized everything a few days ago. Smugly, a good girl, I returned to bed and a fitful sleep.

In the morning, I called my midwife. By late afternoon she had arrived with her assistant, also a licensed midwife, in a big red van. As the summer evening darkened our south facing wall of windows, my contractions began seriously. By nine o'clock, they lasted a minute and were two to three minutes apart. My husband set out dinner, a friend came over to help, music was played, and happy talk eddied about the room. I began to pace up and down from the bed to the table to the rocking chair that symbolized our future. My route followed no particular pattern but traced the cement grouting of a floor covered with yellow and orange Mexican tile. As each contraction heightened, my steps slowed, and I counted the tiles, and counted my steps.

By midnight, people were taking shifts. My midwife was herself seven months pregnant and had fallen asleep in the big red van. Her assistant lay on a cot outside, under the dramatic sweep of the Milky Way. Earlier she had impressed us by picking out constellations like Perseus and Lacerta. For three hours, my friend stayed with me and then woke my husband who, for the rest of the night, read aloud *The Yearling* by Marjorie Kinnan Rawlings. I listened to his voice, not the words, and continued to pace the floor, slowly, slavishly, like some ancient Chinese woman with bound feet.

Tedium is a word to describe that labor. The contractions went on, and on, a kneading and cramping meant to stretch and pull open the circular muscles around the cervix. This dilation, measured in centimeters, is complete at the magical number of ten: at that point, the baby is ready to be pushed down the birth canal. Periodically through the night, the midwife or her assistant would check the baby's heartbeat with a stethoscope on my belly. They also checked inside me for an update on the cervix, and for most of that interminable Wednesday, the update was disappointing. At 1:00 A.M., I was three centimeters. At 7:00 A.M., I was four.

At that time, our little adobe had no hot water, and as a way of "making it happen" we all trooped over to a neighbor's house so that I could take a shower and enema. Now, in the few minutes between contractions, I dozed in the hallucinatory way that causes the head to snap upright just as the soul touches the coastline of sleep. There in the shower I saw the pink porcelain tile come alarmingly close. I snapped awake and did not fall. A few hours later, back home again, I had dilated to five.

It was a bold bright afternoon and the southern glass wall of which we were so proud framed the lengthening shadows of yuccas on grama grass. My water had broken a day and a half before, and I had been in moderate to hard labor for fifteen hours. I asked my midwife why it was taking so long. She may have replied that a mother can lengthen labor out of fear or rejection of the child. More probably, she did not say this at all. More probably, it was only an idea rattling about in my head, and I suspected, in the heads of those around me. It was an idea that made me angry. I wasn't afraid! I wanted the baby! I asked my midwife if there was something I could do.

"Get mad," she suggested. "Tell your body you're ready."

That fit my mood well and so I began to mutter, "I'm mad! I'm ready!" as I wandered in my slow and crazy way about the room.

Next I asked the midwife if crying ever helped.

"Oh yes," she assured me, brightening a little. We were both lovers of strategy—of scientific reasoning, technique, and causation. Who knew what chemicals a good cry might stimulate?

Strategically then, my husband and I went off for a car ride on the bumpy road that leads from our house to the black-topped highway. When we reached its flat expanse, we went on driving and in the car, between contractions, as the scenery unrolled, I cried.

In hindsight, the comic moment occurred when we stopped at a trailhead into the Gila National Forest and Gila Wilderness Area. The path follows the sparkling Sapillo Creek, and my husband thought that a short hike along this creek, in the beauty of the woods, would be a good idea. Protesting, I stumbled from the car and leaned heavily on his arm. As we hobbled a few steps down the path, a backpacker emerged from what must have been a first trip or a long one. Spying us, he broke into a grin. We were the first human beings he had seen for days, and eagerly he began the hail-well-met exchange that hikers luxuriate in. He did not get the expected reply. Instead, a huge woman moaned in his face, turned her husband around, and labored back to the car before ever reaching the scenic Sapillo. The backpacker's face remains with me today: young, acne marked, shocked at my inappropriateness.

An hour later, at the house, the midwife's assistant lay tanning on her cot and flipping the last pages of a murder mystery. The midwife sat inside, doing nothing, in a straight-backed chair. She had circles under her eyes, and her own pregnant stomach bloomed uncomfortably beneath her folded hands. "You know," she said, as I began once more to whine and pace the floor. "The pains are only going to get worse."

I stared at her, devastated. They were? At that moment they felt pretty bad. Was this a hint? A move to the hospital? The latter had not occurred to me, for my doubts about homebirth had vanished at the onset of a labor that was long and tedious but never fearful. Now I felt admonished and betrayed. "I'm really mad now," I muttered to my body, to my uterus, to the baby itself. "I'm really ready!"

Later still, we checked my dilation. By this time, I think, I was too tired to feel hopeful. "Oh, you're going to love this," the midwife said. The room's ceiling of pine vigas glowed with the golden light of freshly cut wood. In fact, the ceiling always glowed like this but I rarely noticed it. "You're at nine centimeters. You're almost there!" She laughed, I laughed, and suddenly everyone but me began to move with a bustle and wonderful sense of purpose. Water started boiling. I heard the joyful clink of instruments. I got up from the bed, but no. For the first time, after twenty hours of walking, I wanted only to lie down. From the windows I could see the tip of Cooke's Peak turning to lavender. The hills below were silhouetted against a royal blue in which a single planet shone. Another evening, another night, was at hand.

It took an hour more of waiting and three of pushing before anyone was born. In that time, I learned a lot. As a child, I had never been an athlete in competitive sports, had never understood about concentration or team effort. Once in the sixth grade I did make the "B" team, where my idea of playing baseball was to daydream in the outfield until the ball came to me, by which time it was almost always too late to catch it. In my twenties, for exercise, I became a runner and let my mind and body go their separate ways. Now, here, lying naked in a quilted bed, was what I imagined the best kind of athleticism to be about—about pushing yourself to the limit, about believing in yourself, trying again, moving through the pain, listening to your coach, and trying again.

You can do it! The baby was posterior, lying against my back, and that made it harder. You can do it! I had no urge to push, I didn't know how, and that made it harder. You can do it! My squad of cheerleaders—midwife, assistant, husband, friend—rallied me again and again with that cry. You can do it, they said, and when they forgot to cheer me on, I reminded them to, for I depended on their enthusiasm. I followed their instructions. I used their energy. This was a group effort and, for the first time in my life, I was at the center of it. I was the focal point, concentrating, intent, working, only sometimes scared. Can I do it? I asked them. You can, they said. And I did. It felt great. (My husband has his own story to tell. The pine vigas glowed. Darkness lapped at the window. He had never felt so connected to his life.)

As seven pounds of newborn spilled into the world, I heard the assistant say "It's a blondie!" and then, in a moment, "Oh, what a temper." Gently, they put the amazingly solid baby on my stomach. My husband and I drew close together and stared: our daughter looked floppy, distracted, radiantly pink. It was one minute past midnight, slightly chilly, and someone bundled her into a blanket. My husband cut the cord and we squabbled briefly over who would hold her first. "Maria!" I breathed into her tiny ear. She turned to me, dazed and uncomprehending. Then she held still and took my breast.

As the placenta slithered out, the midwife kneaded my stomach. When I continued to bleed, she gave me a shot of Pitocin to control hemorrhage. By then, the baby had already been given its one and five minute rating on the Apgar scale, where she scored high. As in a hospital, silver nitrate would be applied to her eyes to prevent infection and she would be given a dose of Vitamin K. Because I am Rh negative, a sample of the cord blood would be sent to the hospital. Meanwhile the midwife was sewing up a small tear in my perineum, and my friend, as she is wont to do, went quietly about the business of washing dishes and cleaning house. My husband sat and rocked his child. Outside, the darkness had the eerie expectant sheen of early morning. The birds were still asleep. The birth was over. I felt tremendously energized.

The word *midwife* literally means "with woman" and this quality of withness is perhaps the midwife's greatest virtue. Withness implies empathy, equality, and, in practical terms, a willingness to stay with a laboring mother for as long as it takes. During Hippocrates' time, in Western society, midwives were an honored class. But in the Dark Ages, this feminine profession became increasingly devalued. The idea that witches, acting as midwives, killed unbaptized babies and used them in Satanic rites seemed logical to the Church. As potential sources of birth control and abortion techniques, midwives were doubly damned—and occasionally burned.

By the sixteenth century, tradesmen called barber-surgeons were being brought in for cases of obstructed childbirth. These men brought a bag of perforators and metal hooks used to drag a child from the womb whole or piecemeal. The later refinement of forceps was a major breakthrough in obstetrics. But like other tools of science they were seen as distinctly masculine. At this point, the use of instruments in delivery can be seen as a rough dividing line, with women on one side and men on the other.

The rest of Western midwifery is marked by a struggle between the sexes to gain control of the birth process. By 1850, a part of life historically dominated by women was being successfully usurped. At first, midwives fought back, accusing doctors even then of using instruments unnecessarily to avoid "the onerous chore of staying up throughout the night." Playing hardball, they also brought in the specter of lust: what other motive could explain such "frequent examinations with the finger and the hand?" In response, physicians encouraged the idea that even a normal delivery was so dangerous as to override any embarrassment, suspicion, or pain on the part of the patient. By the twentieth century, pregnancy had evolved, philosophically, into a life-threatening disease.

Starting in the 1920s with the beatific-sounding Twilight Sleep—morphine followed by a hallucinogen coupled with ether or chloroform—mothers could be completely removed from the birth of their children. In 1950, my mother fondly remembers being given a shot, blankness, and then waiting in bed while the nurses took care of my sister. For other women, the hospital experience was anything but beatific, and the horror stories of these years are well known: the isolation of labor, the leather straps, the high metal stirrups. In this setting, the woman was seen, from a technician's point of view, as a birthing machine that required service. Usually the machine also required tinkering. Oxytocyn to start up a "slow" uterus, pain relievers to ease the artificial and unnaturally strong contractions, synthetic hormones again as the drugs impaired the mother's ability to push. Babies were born "blue" from a drug-induced lack of oxygen. The Cesarean rate skyrocketed. And in 1980, American hospitals had more infant deaths due to birth injuries and respiratory diseases than almost any other industrialized nation.

There was opposition. As we learned about the dangers of drugs, both mothers and doctors came to see them as less desirable. Husbands and family members were allowed in the delivery room. Certain medical routines—induced labor, intravenous feeding, and the episiotomy— became less routine. In remote areas, progress, as usual, moved in fits and starts. Still, in 1987 when I was pregnant with my second child, a progressive family-care doctor had just opened her office, nurse-midwives worked at the hospital, and the hospital itself touted a "birthing room" with homey atmosphere and wooden cradle for the baby. Even the most respected obstetrician in town had adopted a different, if still paternal, stance. One friend reported with dismay that he would not let her have the painkiller she requested. "Wait it out," he cajoled her cheerfully. "Just a few more minutes. You can do it."

In part because my options were greater, my decision to have a second homebirth was not automatic. In some ways I felt more conservative than before and, to my surprise, so did my midwife. After three more years of catching babies, she had a greater respect for her relationship to statistics. If only 1 percent of mothers hemorrhage dangerously after labor, the midwife who sees a hundred mothers will see the one who does. If only a fraction of cords are looped too tightly about the baby's neck, it's still a significant number; in one year my midwife had three such babies. That she could handle these emergencies was not in question. But her natural optimism had tempered, and she no longer did births more than twenty minutes from the hospital. For my husband and me, she would make an exception. But she also suggested we have the birth in town, at a friend's house, say, or—as one couple did—at a nearby hotel.

This time, my husband and I even visited the hospital's new birthing room. There was nothing wrong with it, exactly. The pink pillows matched the pink coverlet, the baby's cradle had been varnished to a shine, and a poster of trees covered one entire wall. Best of all, as the nurse showed us, was the mechanical bed that rose up and down and let the woman actually sit up during delivery. In the tour, we went on to examine the traditional labor room next door. Here was the flat white table with its heavy stirrups, surrounded by the decor of machinery and plastic. Of course, our guide said, there was no guarantee I would get the birthing room. I would get on a list, and it was first-come, first-served. There was no guarantee I would not wind up flat on my back on the white table, a position which, short of being hanged upside down, is perhaps the worst one for delivery. There was no guarantee I would get the pink coverlet.

In the end, as I went home and thought about it, the pink coverlet didn't even look that good. Naturally I would come to the hospital if I needed to. I would even have the birth in town so as to be closer to its services. But as for the bed that rose up and down—as though I couldn't rise up and down by myself! as though the privilege of being able to sit up was the best I could hope for, a privilege granted by the pulleys of a mechanical bed—as for first-come, first-served and stirrups to place my feet, no, I thought, not for me. I was grateful for the hospital. It was an important aid to birth. But it was not a replacement.

My intuition, at long last, had started to kick in.

In retrospect, it seems my ambiguity concerning homebirth vanished for the rest of that pregnancy. In truth, I don't think it did until the beginning of labor. Then, as before, all my doubts disappeared and I was where I needed to be, focusing on the task at hand.

In this birth, events moved so rapidly that my focus blurred a little. Labor started with strong contractions at 12:30 A.M. and ended with a ten-pound baby boy six hours later. In this birth, I didn't try to be stoic. This one hurt more. This time, too, my husband's and midwife's reassurances rang a bit perfunctory. We were all surprised at the speed of dilation. We were all a bit more businesslike and a bit less magical. No golden *vigas* glowed over our heads, for we were at a friend's house, in a modern room with walls made of sheetrock. This time, when the baby's large head began to crown, I screamed in outrage. I hollered out my midwife's name, not caring who heard me or what they might think. My friend, her husband, their two young sons, and my three-year-old daughter were sitting in the middle of the room, watching me with considerable interest. Something in their position, crosslegged on the floor, made me feel like a television set. In a small but well-lit clearing of my mind, I realized that I had a choice. I could grit my teeth or scream unbecomingly. What does it matter? I remember thinking. Perhaps in this instance, screaming was the better strategy.

After all the fuss, our son emerged with a headful of brown hair and a mouth screwed only slightly in irritation. His Apgar scores were nearly perfect, his wrists and ankles rolled with fat. Flopped on my stomach, he stared up at me peacefully in the morning light. For a few minutes, the assistant took the baby and busied herself verifying his patently healthy condition. Peacefully I delivered the placenta and continued to bleed. My midwife gave me a dose of Pitocin and then another. Because large babies are associated with diabetes, she also telephoned our pediatrician. Outside the window, the sky trailed banners of celebratory pink. Relieved and euphoric, I submitted to the medical procedures: my blood pressure taken, some slight stitching up. Because I had hemorrhaged, the midwife measured the iron in my blood with a small hand-held device, and my husband was impressed with this bit of gadgetry. Within an hour, a friend came by and took pictures. In all of these, my daughter holds her new brother. While the rest of us look obediently at the camera, she and he gaze with complete concentration into each other's eyes.

My daughter is nearly five now. Recently, in a seminar at work, I was asked to remember a time when I had felt powerful. Instantly I saw Maria's birth. I did not, of course, see a baby's head crowning. Instead I saw my own naked thighs and knees spread unnaturally apart. I saw, at the periphery of vision, the blurred hands and faces of my husband and friends. I saw the colors of my grandmother's quilt glowing intensely. It seemed that one of my legs was streaked with blood. It would seem that I had never been so vulnerable, so dependent in all my life. Yet I remember this, a physical memory, lodged deep in the body, as a moment of power. In my second homebirth, I remember as well the unabashed decision to shriek. I remember, still, feeling at the center.

As my friend emerges from her appointment with the midwife, I say goodbye to Angelica Gutierrez. I also say hello to the midwife, who stops to tell me about a homebirth-related case headed for the Supreme Court. This class action suit will determine if women have a constitutional right to choose their place of giving birth and if midwives have a constitutional right to practice their profession. My midwife is passionate about the subject. So am I. It appalls me that homebirth is illegal in some states. I am aghast that Arizona midwives can not carry Pitocin. All of us, all the women in this room, feel the flare of anger. It dies quickly and, eager to start their private communion, the midwife and Angelica disappear into the office.

On my way out, I touch the door and tell my friend that turquoise is the color to ward off witches. "Oh," she says, lulled and euphoric by her visit to the midwife, "it's my favorite color too."

Her big belly, taut and firm, pushes out into the late afternoon air. Life is swimming inside her. A child dreams beneath the skin. Briefly she rests a hand on the highest point of her curved stomach, where I would like, very much, to put my hand as well.

CONSIDERATIONS

Thinking

At the beginning of her essay, Russell tells us that "safety is a priority" for those involved with homebirth but that "it is not, necessarily, the heart of the matter." What do you think Russell sees as the heart of the matter?

What do you consider the essential difference between Russell's husband and the other men mentioned in this essay?

If you were having a baby or attending a birth, where would you want to be, in a home or in a hospital? How does Russell's essay affect your decision?

Connecting

How does the competitive sports analogy help Russell render her account of the birth of her first child? What do you learn about homebirth from that analogy?

What connections does Russell make in her essay to suggest how "pregnancy had evolved, philosophically, into a life-threatening disease" by the twentieth century?

What is the relationship between witches and male doctors in this essay?

Writing

When Russell speaks of the beautiful Anglo woman who was her midwife, she tells us, "Those who do not find beauty powerful are possibly around it too much or have never seen it at all." Write an essay in which you deepen our understanding of Russell's claim. Use your own experience—including your reading—to help you clarify your thoughts.

Recall a moment when you felt powerful. Write an essay that reveals the meaning and significance of that moment—and of any other moments that you include in your essay to help you with your revelation.

S cott Russell Sanders
(b.1945)

S cott Russell Sanders's many books include *The Paradise of Bombs, In Limestone Country, Secrets of the Universe, Staying Put,* and *Writing from the Center.* His essays have appeared in literary and popular magazines such as *North American Review, Georgia Review, Sewanee Review, Omni,* and *New Dimensions.* He has been a Woodrow Wilson Fellow, a Marshall Scholar, a Bennett Fellow in creative writing, and a National Endowment for the Arts Fellow.

In "Wayland," Sanders traces a voyage he made back to his childhood home after a twenty-five-year absence; it was a journey back to bedrock values.

Wayland

Two blacktop roads, broken by frost and mended with tar, running from nowhere to nowhere, cross at right angles in the rumpled farm country of northeastern Ohio. The neighborhood where they intersect is called Wayland—not a village, not even a hamlet, only a cluster of barns and silos and frame houses and a white steepled Methodist church. Just north of Wayland, the Army fenced in fifty square miles of ground for a bomb factory, and just to the south the Corps of Engineers built a dam and flooded even more square miles for a reservoir. I grew up behind those government fences in the shadows of bunkers, and on farms that have since vanished beneath those government waters. Family visits to church began carrying me to Wayland when I was five, romance was carrying me there still at seventeen, and in the years between I was drawn there often by duty or desire. Thus it happened that within shouting distance of the Wayland crossroads I met seven of the great mysteries.

Even as a boy, oblivious much of the time to all save my own sensations, I knew by the tingle in my spine when I had bumped into something utterly new. I groped for words to describe what I had felt, as I grope still. Since we give labels to all that puzzles us, as we name every blank space on the map, I could say that what I stumbled into in Wayland were the mysteries of death, life, beasts, food, mind, sex, and God. But these seven words are only tokens, worn coins that I drop onto the page, hoping to bribe you, coins I finger as reminders of those awful encounters.

The roads that cross at Wayland are too humble to show on the Ohio map, too small even to wear numbers. And yet, without maps or mistakes, without quite meaning to, I recently found my way back there from half a thousand miles away, after an absence of twenty-five years, led along the grooves of memory.

The grooves are deep, and they set me vibrating well before I reached the place, as the spiral cuts in phonograph records will shake music from a needle. I was heading toward Cleveland when I took a notion to veer off the interstate and see what had become of Akron, which led me to see what had become of Kent, which led me to Ravenna, the seat of Portage County. Nothing aside from stoplights made me pause. Not sure what I was looking for, I drove east from the county seat along a highway hurtling with trucks. Soon the rusted chain link fence of the Ravenna Arsenal came whipping by on my left and the raised bed of the Baltimore & Ohio tracks surged by on the right. Then I realized where I was going. My knuckles whitened on the steering wheel as I turned from the highway, put my back toward the trucks and bombs, and passed under the railroad through a concrete arch. Beyond the arch, the woods and fields and houses of Wayland shimmered in the October sunlight, appearing to my jealous eye scarcely changed after a quarter of a century.

I knew the place had changed, of course, if only because in the years since I had come here last—drawn in those days like a moth to the flame of a girl—the population of the earth had nearly doubled. Every crossroads, every woods, every field on the planet is warping under the pressure of our terrible hunger. So I knew that Wayland had changed, for all its pastoral shimmer in the autumn light. Yet I was grateful that on the surface it so much resembled my childhood memories, for in my effort to live adequately in the present, I had come here to conduct some business with the past. What had brought me back to Wayland was a need to dig through the fluff and debris of ordinary life, down to some bedrock of feeling and belief.

I left my car in the graveled parking lot of the church and set out walking. Without planning my steps, I meandered where memory led, and where it led was from station to station of my childhood astonishment. Not yet ready for the church, I went next door to the parsonage, where I had first caught a whiff of death. The white clapboard house, a two-story box with a porch across the front and a green hipped roof, could have belonged to any of the neighboring farms. That was appropriate, for the ministers who succeeded one another in the house often preached as though they were farmers, weeding out sins, harvesting souls.

The minister whom I knew first was the Reverend Mr. Knipe, a bulky man sunken with age, his hair as white as the clapboards on the parsonage, his voice like the cooing of pigeons in the barn. Much in life amused him. Whenever he told you something that struck him as funny, he would cover his mouth with a hand to hide his smile. Despite the raised hand, often his laugh burst free and rolled over you. I began listening to him preach and pray and lead hymns when I was five, and for the next two years I heard Reverend Knipe every Sunday, until his voice became for me that of the Bible itself, even the voice of God. Then one Sunday when I was seven, I shook his great hand after the service as usual, suffering him to bend down and pat my head, and I went home to my dinner and he went home to his. While his wife set the table in the parsonage, Reverend Knipe rested on the front porch in his caned rocking chair, drifted off to sleep, and never woke up.

When Mother told me of this, the skin prickled on my neck. To sleep and never wake! To be a white-haired man with a voice like a barnful of pigeons, and the next minute to be nothing at all! Since my parents considered me too young to attend the funeral, I could only imagine what had become of his body, and I imagined not decay but evaporation—the flesh dispersing into thin air like morning mist from a pond.

The following Sunday, while a visitor preached, I stole from church and crept over to the parsonage. I drew to the edge of the porch, wrapped my fingers around the spindles of the railing, and stared at the empty rocker. Reverend Knipe will never sit in that chair again, I told myself. Never, never, never. I tried to imagine how long forever would last. I tried to imagine how it would feel to be nothing. No thing. Suddenly chair and house and daylight vanished, and I was gazing into a dark hole, I was falling, I was gone. I caught a whiff of death, the damp earthy smell seeping from beneath the porch. It was also the smell of mud, of leaping grass, of spring. Clinging to that sensation, I pulled myself up out of the hole. There was the house again, the chair. I let go of the railing, swung away, and ran back to the church, chanting to myself: *He was old and I am young. He was old and I am young.*

Nights, often, and sometimes in the broad light of day, I still have to scrabble up out of that hole. We all do. Sometime in childhood, each of us bangs head-on into the blank fact we call death. Once that collision takes place, the shock of it never wears off. We may find ourselves returning to the spot where it occurred as to the scene of an accident, the way I found myself drawn, half a lifetime later, to the front steps of this parsonage. I was a stranger to the family who lived there now. Not wishing to intrude on them, I paused by the steps and surveyed the porch. Vinyl siding had covered the clapboard. An aluminum folding chair had replaced the rocker. I squatted by the railing, lowering my face to the height of a seven-year-old, closed my eyes against the shadows, and sniffed. From below the sill of the porch came the earth's dank perennial breath, fetid and fertile. Yes, I thought, filling myself with the smell: this abides, this is real; no matter the name we give it, life or death, it is a fact as rough and solid as a stone squeezed in the palm of the hand.

A dog yapped inside the parsonage. I stood up hurriedly and backed away, before anyone could appear at the door to ask me what in tarnation I was looking for under that porch.

Still following the grooves of memory, I crossed the road to stand in the driveway of another white frame house. It was not so much the house that drew me as it was the side yard, where, about this time each fall, we brought our apples for pressing. The old press with its wooden vat and iron gears used to balance on concrete blocks in the shade of a willow. We would pick apples in the military reservation, from orchards that had been allowed to go wild after the government bulldozed the farmsteads. Unsprayed, blotched and wormy, these apples were also wonderfully sweet. We kept them in bushel baskets and cardboard boxes in the cellar, their fragrance filling the house, until we had accumulated enough to load our station wagon. Then we drove here, parked beside the willow, and fed our fruit into the press.

On this mild October day, the willow looked as I remembered it, thick in the trunk and gold in the leaves. There was no sign of a press, but that did not keep me from remembering what it was like to squeeze apples. First we pulped them in a mill, then we wrapped them in cheese-cloth and tamped them down, layer by layer, into the slotted wooden vat. To mash them, we spun a cast iron wheel. It was easy to begin with, so easy that my brother and sister and I could make the spokes whirl. Later, the cranking would become too hard for us, and our mother would take her turn, then our father, then both of them together. The moment that set me trembling, however, came early on, while my hand was still on the iron wheel, the moment when cider began to ooze through the cheese-cloth, between the slats, and down the spout into a waiting bucket. Out of the dirt, out of the gnarled trunks and wide-flung branches, out of the ripe red fruit had come this tawny juice. When my arms grew tired, I held a Mason jar under the spout, caught a glassful, and drank it down. It was as though we had squeezed the planet and out had poured sweetness.

What came back to me, musing there by the willow all these years later, was the sound of cider trickling into the bucket, the honeyed taste of it, and my bewilderment that rain and wood and dirt and sun had yielded this juice. Amazing, that we can drink the earth! Amazing, that it quenches our thirst, answers our hunger! Who would have predicted such an outlandish thing? Who, having sipped, can forget that it is the earth we swallow?

Well, I had forgotten; or at least I had buried under the habits of casual eating that primal awareness of the meaning of food. And so here was another fundamental perception, renewed for me by my sojourn in Wayland. This image of cider gushing from a spout was my cornucopia, proof of the dazzling abundance that sustains us.

From the cider house I walked downhill to the crossroads. One corner was still a pasture, browsed by three horses, another was a scrubby field grown up in brush and weeds, and the other two corners were expansive lawns. Through the brushy field meandered a creek where I used to hunt frogs with a flashlight and bucket. As in all the Octobers I could remember, the maples in the yards were scarlet, the pasture oaks were butterscotch, and the sycamores along the creek were stripped down to their voluptuous white limbs. Yellow mums and bright red pokers of salvia were still thriving in flowerbeds. A portly older man on a riding mower was cutting one of the lawns, while from a stump beside the driveway an older woman observed his progress, a hand shading her eyes. I knew them from childhood, but their names would not come. I waved, and they waved back. That was conversation enough. I had no desire to speak with them or with anyone in Wayland, since I would have been hard put to explain who I was or why I had come back. Maybe I also wanted to keep the past pure, unmixed with the present.

Because the crossroads are laid out on the grid of survey lines, the blacktop runs due north and south, east and west. The roads were so little traveled that I could stand in the intersection, the tar gummy beneath my boots, and gaze along the pavement in each of the cardinal directions. I had just come from the south, where the church gleamed on its hill. My view to the north was cut off by the railroad, except for the arched opening of the underpass, through which I could see the rusted fence of the Arsenal. Memories of a girl I had courted were beckoning from the west; but less feverish memories beckoned from the opposite direction, and that is where I chose to go next.

A quarter mile east of the crossroads I came to a farm where the Richards family used to breed and board and train horses. Although the name on the mailbox had changed, ten or twelve horses were grazing, as before, in a paddock beside the barn. I leaned against the fence and admired them.

In boyhood I had raised and ridden horses of my own, a stocky mixture of Shetland pony and the high-stepping carriage breed known as hackney. They all came out of a single ornery mare called Belle, and they all had her color, a sorrel coat that grew sleek in summer and shaggy in winter. We used to bring Belle here to the Richards place for mating with a hackney stallion. Years before the voltage of sex began to make my own limbs jerk, I had been amazed by the stallion's urgency and the mare's skittishness. He nipped and nuzzled and pursued her; she danced and wheeled. Their energy seemed too great for the paddock to hold. Surely the fence would give way, the barn itself would fall! Then at length Belle shivered to a standstill and allowed the stallion to lift his forelegs onto her rump, his back legs jigging, hoofs scrambling for purchase, her legs opening to his dark pizzle, the two of them momentarily one great plunging beast. And then, if luck held, twelve months later Belle would open her legs once more and drop a foal. Within minutes of entering the world, the foal would be tottering about on its wobbly stilts, drunk on air, and it would be ramming its muzzle into Belle's belly in search of milk. What a world, that the shivering union of mare and stallion in the barnyard should lead to this new urgency!

Musing there by the paddock on this October afternoon, I felt toward the grazing horses a huge affection. Each filled its hide so gloriously. I gave a low whistle. Several massive heads bobbed up and swung toward me, jaws working on grass, ears pricked forward. Their black eyes regarded me soberly, then all but one of the heads returned to grazing. The exception was a palomino gelding, who tossed his white mane, switched his white tail, and started ambling in my direction. As he drew near, I stretched my right arm toward him, palm open. Had I known I would be coming here, I would have brought apples or sugar cubes. My father would have pulled a cigarette from his pocket and offered that. But all I had to offer was the salt on my skin. The palomino lowered his muzzle to my palm, sniffed cautiously, then curled out his rasping red tongue and licked.

I knew that sandpapery stroke on my hand as I knew few other sensations. Just so, my own horses had nibbled oats and sugar and sweat from my palm. The pressure of their tongues made my whole body sway. There by the fence, past and present merged, and I was boy and man, swaying. I reveled in the muscular touch, animal to animal. Contact! It assured me that I was not alone in the world. I was a creature among creatures.

When the palomino lost interest in my right hand, I offered my left. He sniffed idly, and, finding it empty, turned back to the greater temptation of grass. But the rasp of his tongue on my palm stayed with me, another clean, hard fact, another piece of bedrock on which to build a life.

*   *   *

The field across the road from the Richards place was grown up into a young woods, mostly staghorn sumac and cedar and oak. When I had seen it last, twenty-five years earlier, this had been a meadow luxuriant with grasses and wildflowers. Back where the far edge of the field ran up against the sinuous line of willows bordering the creek, there had been a cottage, low and brown, moss growing on the roof, weeds lapping at the windows, a place that looked from a distance more like a forgotten wood-pile than a house. Today, no cottage showed above the vigorous trees. But near my feet I could see the twin ruts of the dirt track that used to lead back to the place. I followed them, my boots knocking seeds from thistle and wild rye.

I knew the meadow and the cottage because the woman who used to live here was my science teacher in high school. Fay Givens must have been in her early sixties when I met her in my freshman year. Many students mocked her for being so unthinkably old, for looking like a schoolmarm, for loving science, for trembling when she spoke about nature. She would gaze fervently into a beaker as though an entire galaxy spun before her. She grew so excited while recounting the habits of molecules that she would skip about the lab and clap her spotted hands. She would weep for joy over what swam before her in a microscope. Mrs. Givens wept easily, more often than not because of a wisecrack or prank from one of the students. Our cruelty was a defense against the claim she made on us. For she was inviting us to share her passionate curiosity. She called us to hunger and thirst after knowledge of the universe.

I would not join the others in mocking her. I supposed it was pity that held me back, or an ingrained respect for my elders. Only in the fall of my freshman year, on a day when Mrs. Givens brought us here to this field for a botany class, did I realize that I could not mock her because I loved her. She led us through her meadow, naming every plant, twirling the bright fallen leaves, telling which birds ate which berries, opening milkweed pods, disclosing the burrows of groundhogs, parting the weeds to reveal caterpillars and crickets, showing where mice had severed blades of grass. Much of the meadow she had planted, with seeds carried in her pockets from the neighboring countryside. Every few years she burned it, as the Indians had burned the prairies, to keep the woods from reclaiming it.

While Mrs. Givens told us these things in her quavery voice, students kept sidling away to smoke or joke or dabble their hands in the creek, until there were only three of us following her. I stayed with her not from a sense of obedience but from wonder. To know this patch of land, I dimly realized, would be the work of a lifetime. But in knowing it deeply, right down to the foundations, you would comprehend a great deal more, perhaps everything. As she touched the feathery plants of her meadow, as she murmured the names and histories of the creatures who shared the place with her, I came to feel that this was holy ground. And if the meadow was holy, why not the entire earth?

At one point, Mrs. Givens knelt amid the bristly spikes of a tall russet grass. "You see why it's called foxtail, don't you?" she said. "Livestock won't eat it, but you can twist the stalks together and make a fair rope. Farmers used to bind up corn fodder with hanks of foxtail." She grasped one of the spikes, and, with a rake of her thumb, brushed seeds into her palm. She poured a few seeds into my hand and a few into the hands of the other two students who had remained with her. "Now what do you have there?" she asked us.

We stared at the barbed grains in our palms. "Seeds," one of us replied.

"That's the universe unfolding," she told us, "right there in your hands. The same as in every cell of our bodies. Now *why*? That's the question I can't ever get behind. Why should the universe be alive? Why does it obey laws? And why these particular laws? For that matter, why is there a universe at all?" She gave a rollicking laugh. "And isn't it curious that there should be creatures like us who can walk in this beautiful field and puzzle over things?"

She asked her questions gaily, and I have carried them with me all these years in the same spirit. They rose in me again on this October afternoon as I followed the dirt track to the spot where her cottage used to be. Stones marked the cellar hole and the front stoop. Brush grew up through the space left by her death. The woods had reclaimed her meadow. Yet the ground still felt holy. Her marveling gaze had disclosed for me the force and shapeliness of things, and that power survived her passing. She taught me that genius is not in our looking but in what we see. If only we could be adequate to the given world, we need not dream of paradise.

Reversing my steps, I walked back to the crossroads and kept going west for a hundred yards or so, until I fetched up before the house where, as a simmering teenager, I had wooed a girl. Let me call her Veronica. She and her family moved from Wayland soon after the Army Corps of Engineers built that needless dam, and so on this October day her house was for me another shell filled only with memory. The present kept abrading the past, however, because during the few minutes while I stood there a grown man in a go-cart kept zooming around the yard, following a deeply gouged path. Every time he roared past, he peered at me from beneath his crash helmet. I nodded, assuming the look of one who is infatuated with loud machines, and that appeared to satisfy him.

Veronica had the face of a queen on the deck of cards with which I learned to play poker, a face I considered perfect. Words tumbled from her lush lips, impulsively, like rabbits fleeing a burrow. Black wavy hair tumbled down her back, twitching nearly to her slender hips. Having learned in marriage what it means to love a woman, I cannot say that what I felt for Veronica was quite love. Nor was it simply lust, although for much of my seventeenth year the mere thought of her set me aching. At that age, I would have been reluctant to see myself as the urgent stallion and Veronica as the skittish mare. Later, I would realize that horseflesh and humanflesh dance to the same ardent music, even though our human dance is constrained by rules that horses never know. During the season of our affection, Veronica was a chased girl but also a chaste one, and I was a polite boy, both of us keenly aware of boundaries.

In her backyard there was a sycamore tree that loomed high over the house, its fat trunk a patchwork of peeling bark and its crooked upper branches as creamy as whole milk. Wooden crossbars nailed to the trunk formed a ladder up to a treehouse. Veronica and I often sat beneath the sycamore on a stone bench, talking and falling silent, aware of parental eyes watching us from the kitchen. With our backs to the house, our sides pressed together, I could risk brushing a hand over her knee, she could run a fingernail under my chin. But even a kiss, our mouths so visibly meeting, would have prompted a visit from the kitchen.

One October day, a day very like this one of my return to Wayland, Veronica and I were sitting on the bench, hunting for words to shape our confusion, when suddenly she leapt to her feet and said, "Let's go up to the treehouse."

"We'll get filthy," I said. I glanced with misgiving at my white knit shirt and chino pants, so carefully pressed. Her lemony blouse was protected by a green corduroy jumper.

"It'll wash out," she said, tugging me by the hand.

I stood. Without waiting for me, she kicked off her shoes and clambered up the wooden rungs, but instead of halting at the rickety platform of the treehouse, she kept on, swaying from limb to limb. I watched until the flashing of her bare legs made me look away. When she had gone as high as she dared, high enough to escape the view from the kitchen, she balanced on a branch and called to me, "Come on up! Are you afraid?"

I was afraid—but not of the tree. I stepped onto a crossbrace and started climbing, and as I climbed there was nowhere else to look but up, and there was nothing else to see above me except those white legs parted within the green hoop of her skirt. Her creamy forked limbs and the creamy forked limbs of the sycamore merged in my sight, as they merge now in memory, and I was drawn upward into the pale shadows between her thighs. My knowledge of what I was climbing toward would remain abstract for a number of years. I understood only that where her legs joined there was an opening, a gateway for life coming and going. When I reached Veronica I put my hand, briefly, where my gaze had gone, just far enough to feel the surprising warmth of that secret, satiny place. Then I withdrew my hand and she smoothed her skirt, neither of us risking a word, and we teetered there for a hundred heartbeats on those swaying branches, shaken by inner as well as outer winds. Then the kitchen door creaked open and her mother's voice inquired as to our sanity, and we climbed down. I went first, as though to catch Veronica should she fall, my eyes toward the ground.

The buzzing of the go-cart eventually wore through the husk of memory, and my lungs filled with the present. I became again what I was, a man long married, a man with a daughter the age Veronica had been on that day of our climb into the tree. The sycamore still rose behind the house, twenty-five years taller, crisp brown leaves rattling in the wind, the pale upper limbs as pale and silky as ever.

I had a choice of returning to the church by the road or across the stubble of a cornfield. I chose the field. All the way, I could see the white steepled box gleaming on its rise. The only car in the parking lot was mine. Beyond a treeline to the southwest, beyond the annihilating waters of the reservoir that I could not bear to look at, the sun wallowed down toward dusk. The church might already be locked, I thought, so late on a weekday afternoon. Still I did not hurry. My boots scuffed the ridges where corn had stood. Raccoons and crows would find little to feast on in this stubble, for the harvester had plucked it clean. I recalled the biblical injunction to farmers, that they leave the margins of their fields unpicked, for the poor and the beasts. I thought of the margins in a life, in my life, the untended zones beyond the borders of clarity, the encircling wilderness out of which new powers and visions come.

A cornfield is a good approach to a church, for you arrive with dirt on your boots, the smell of greenery in your nostrils, dust on your tongue. The door would be locked, I figured, and the main door was, the broad entrance through which the Methodist women carried their piety and their pies, through which men carried mortgages and mortality, through which children like myself carried headfuls of questions. But the rear door was unlocked. I left my boots on the stoop and went inside.

The back room I entered had the familiarity of a place one returns to in dream: the squeaky pine boards of the floor, the dwarf tables where children would sit on Sundays to color pictures of Jesus, the brass hooks where the choir would hang their robes and the minister his hat, the folding chairs collapsed into a corner, the asthmatic furnace, and on a counter the stack of lathe-turned walnut plates for the offering.

Every few paces I halted, listening. The joints of the church cricked as the sun let go. Birds fussed beyond the windows. But no one else was about; this relieved me, for here least of all was I prepared to explain myself. I had moved too long in circles where to confess an interest in religious things marked one as a charlatan, a sentimentalist, or a fool. No doubt I have all three qualities in my character. But I also have another quality, and that is an unshakable hunger to know who I am, where I am, and into what sort of cosmos I have been so briefly and astonishingly sprung. Whatever combination of shady motives might have led me here, the impulse that shook me right then was a craving to glimpse the very source and circumference of things.

I made my way out through the choir door into the sanctuary. Cushionless pews in somber ranks, uncarpeted floor, exposed beams in the vault overhead and whitewashed plaster on the walls: it was a room fashioned by men and women who knew barns, for preachers who lived out of saddlebags, in honor of a God who cares nothing for ornament. No tapestries, no shrines, no racks of candles, no gold on the altar, no bragging memorials to vanished patrons. The window glass, unstained, let in the plain light of day.

I sat in a pew midway along the central aisle and looked out through those clear windows. My reasons for coming here were entwined with that sky full of light. As a boy I had looked out, Sunday after Sunday, to see corn grow and clouds blow, to watch crows bustle among the tops of trees, to follow hawks, unmindful of the Sabbath, on their spiraling hunts, and to sense in all this radiant surge the same rush I felt under my fingers when I pressed a hand to my throat. There was no gulf between outside and inside. We gathered in this room not to withdraw, but more fully to enter the world.

On this day of my return, I kept watching the sky as the light thinned and the darkness thickened. I became afraid. Afraid of dying, yes, but even more of not having lived, afraid of passing my days in a stupor, afraid of squandering my moment in the light. I gripped the pew in front of me to still my trembling. I wanted to dive down to the center of being, touch bedrock, open my eyes and truly, finally, unmistakably see. I shifted my gaze from the darkening window to the altar, to the wooden cross, to the black lip of the Bible showing from the pulpit. But those were only props for a play that was forever in rehearsal, the actors clumsy, the script obscure. I was myself one of the actors, sustained in my own clumsy efforts by the hope that one day the performance would be perfect, and everything would at last come clear.

One cannot summon grace with a whistle. The pew beneath me, the air around me, the darkening windows did not turn to fire. The clouds of unknowing did not part. I sat there for a long while, and then I rose and made my way down the aisle, past the organ, through the choir door and back room, out into the freshening night. On the stoop I drew on my boots and laced them up. The chrome latch of my car was already cool. I drove back through the crossroads with headlights glaring, alert for animals that might dash before me in the confusion of dusk.

There is more to be seen at any crossroads than one can see in a lifetime of looking. My return visit to Wayland was less than two hours long. Once again half a thousand miles distant from that place, making this model from slippery words, I cannot be sure where the pressure of mind has warped the surface of things. If you were to go there, you would not find every detail exactly as I have described it. How could you, bearing as you do a past quite different from mine? No doubt my memory, welling up through these lines, has played tricks with time and space.

What memory is made of I cannot say; my body, at least, is made of atoms on loan from the earth. How implausible, that these atoms should have gathered to form this *I*, this envelope of skin that walks about and strokes horses and tastes apples and trembles with desire in the branches of a sycamore and gazes through the windows of a church at the ordinary sky. Certain moments in one's life cast their influence forward over all the moments that follow. My encounters in Wayland shaped me first as I lived through them, then again as I recalled them during my visit, and now as I write them down. That is of course why I write them down. The self is a fiction. I make up the story of myself with scraps of memory, sensation, reading, and hearsay. It is a tale I whisper against the dark. Only in rare moments of luck or courage do I hush, forget myself entirely, and listen to the silence that precedes and surrounds and follows all speech.

If you have been keeping count, you may have toted up seven mysteries, or maybe seven times seven, or maybe seven to the seventh power. My hunch is that, however we count, there is only one mystery.

In our nearsightedness, we merely glimpse the light scintillating off the numberless scales of Leviathan, and we take each spark for a separate wonder.

Could we bear to see all the light at once? Could we bear the roar of infinite silence? I sympathize with science, where, in order to answer a question, you limit the variables. You draw a circle within which everything can be measured, and you shut out the rest of the universe. But every enclosure is a makeshift, every boundary an illusion. With great ingenuity, we decipher some of the rules that govern this vast shining dance, but all our efforts could not change the least of them.

Nothing less than the undivided universe can be our true home. Yet how can one speak or even think about the whole of things? Language is of only modest help. Every sentence is a wispy net, capturing a few flecks of meaning. The sun shines without vocabulary. The salmon has no name for the desire that drives it upstream. The newborn groping for the nipple knows hunger long before it knows a single word. Even with an entire dictionary in one's head, one eventually comes to the end of words. Then what? Then drink deep like the baby, swim like the salmon, burn like any brief star.

CONSIDERATIONS

Thinking

Early in the essay, Sanders uses seven words to, as he says, "bribe you" to follow him into his stumble into "the mysteries of death, life, beasts, food, mind, sex, and God." To what extent do you think he succeeds in communicating his experience of those mysteries?

Toward the end of "Wayland," Sanders says that if you visit the place described you would not find it just as he has described it—not so much because it has changed but because of how memory plays "tricks with time and space." What does Sanders mean, and how is what he says about memory related to his comment that "the self is a fiction. I make up the story of myself"?

Connecting

Compare what Sanders says about returning to a place after you have been away for a while with your experience of returning to places you have moved away from. Consider, for example, your experience of returning to an old neighborhood or a school you once attended.

Compare the way Sanders writes about returning to Wayland with the way N. Scott Momaday writes about his ancestral homeland in "A First American Views His Land."

Writing

Write an essay about your return to a place after being away for some time. Try to show your readers how the place differed and how it remained the same. Explain how your perceptions of it at the different times may have been affected by who you were at those times.

Write Sanders a letter responding to this claim of his: "With great ingenuity, we decipher some of the rules that govern this vast shining dance [of ours through life], but all our efforts could not change the least of them." Do you agree with Sanders? Do you think he believes what he says? Explain.

R ichard Selzer
(b.1928)

R ichard Selzer was born in Troy, New York, and educated at Union College, Albany Medical College, and Yale University. Selzer began writing at age forty, amid the rigors of medical responsibilities as a surgeon and a professor of surgery at Yale; he recently retired to devote himself full time to writing. Throughout his medical career, Selzer led a second life as an essayist and storyteller, publishing six books, beginning with *Rituals of Surgery* (1974). His most recent books are *Down from Troy* (1992), an autobiography, and *Raising the Dead* (1993), a work that blends history, autobiography, and fiction.

In "A Mask on the Face of Death," which appeared in *Best American Essays 1988*, Selzer describes the AIDS situation in Haiti. His essay is notable for its precise rendering of place and for its distinctive presentation of character, as Selzer employs techniques of the fiction writer in conveying ideas and perspectives.

A Mask on the Face of Death

It is ten o'clock at night as we drive up to the Copacabana, a dilapidated brothel on the rue Dessalines in the red-light district of Port-au-Prince. My guide is a young Haitian, Jean-Bernard. Ten years before, J-B tells me, at the age of fourteen, "like every good Haitian boy" he had been brought here by his older cousins for his *rite de passage*. From the car to the entrance, we are accosted by a half dozen men and women for sex. We enter, go down a long hall that breaks upon a cavernous room with a stone floor. The cubicles of the prostitutes, I am told, are in an attached wing of the building. Save for a red-purple glow from small lights on the walls, the place is unlit. Dark shapes float by, each with a blindingly white stripe of teeth. Latin music is blaring. We take seats at the table farthest from the door. Just outside, there is the rhythmic lapping of the Caribbean Sea. About twenty men are seated at the tables or lean against the walls. Brightly dressed women, singly or in twos or threes, stroll about, now and then exchanging banter with the men. It is as though we have been deposited in act two of Bizet's *Carmen*. If this place isn't Lillas Pastia's tavern, what is it?

Within minutes, three light-skinned young women arrive at our table. They are very beautiful and young and lively. Let them be Carmen, Mercedes and Frasquita.

"I want the old one," says Frasquita, ruffling my hair. The women laugh uproariously.

"Don't bother looking any further," says Mercedes. "We are the prettiest ones."

"We only want to talk," I tell her.

"Aaah, aaah," she crows. "*Massissi*. You are *massissi*." It is the contemptuous Creole term for homosexual. If we want only to talk, we must be gay. Mercedes and Carmen are slender, each weighing one hundred pounds or less. Frasquita is tall and hefty. They are dressed for work: red taffeta, purple chiffon and black sequins. Among them a thousand gold bracelets and earrings multiply every speck of light. Their bare shoulders are like animated lamps gleaming in the shadowy room. Since there is as yet no business, the women agree to sit with us. J-B orders beer and cigarettes. We pay each woman $10.

"Where are you from?" I begin.

"We are Dominican."

"Do you miss your country?"

"Oh, yes, we do." Six eyes go muzzy with longing. "Our country is the most beautiful in the world. No country is like the Dominican. And it doesn't stink like this one."

"Then why don't you work there? Why come to Haiti?"

"Santo Domingo has too many whores. All beautiful, like us. All light-skinned. The Haitian men like to sleep with light women."

"Why is that?"

"Because always, the whites have all the power and the money. The black men can imagine they do, too, when they have us in bed."

Eleven o'clock. I looked around the room that is still sparsely peopled with men.

"It isn't getting any busier," I say. Frasquita glances over her shoulder. Her eyes drill the darkness.

"It is still early," she says.

"Could it be that the men are afraid of getting sick?" Frasquita is offended.

"Sick! They do not get sick from us. We are healthy, strong. Every week we go for a checkup. Besides, we know how to tell if we are getting sick."

"I mean sick with AIDS." The word sets off a hurricane of taffeta, chiffon and gold jewelry. They are all gesticulation and fury. It is Carmen who speaks.

"AIDS!" Her lips curl about the syllable. "There is no such thing. It is a false disease invented by the American government to take advantage of the poor countries. The American President hates poor people, so now he makes up AIDS to take away the little we have." The others nod vehemently.

"*Mira, mon cher.* Look, my dear," Carmen continues. "One day the police came here. Believe me, they are worse than the *tonton macoutes* with their submachine guns. They rounded up one hundred and five of us and they took our blood. That was a year ago. None of us have died, you see? We are all still here. *Mira,* we sleep with all the men and we are not sick."

"But aren't there some of you who have lost weight and have diarrhea?"

"One or two, maybe. But they don't eat. That is why they are weak."

"Only the men die," says Mercedes. "They stop eating, so they die. It is hard to kill a woman."

"Do you eat well?"

"Oh, yes, don't worry, we do. We eat like poor people, but we eat." There is a sudden scream from Frasquita. She points to a large rat that has emerged from beneath our table.

"My God!" she exclaims. "It is big like a pig." They burst into laughter. For a moment the women fall silent. There is only the restlessness of their many bracelets. I give them each another $10.

"Are many of the men here bisexual?"

"Too many. They do it for money. Afterward, they come to us." Carmen lights a cigarette and looks down at the small lace handkerchief she has been folding and unfolding with immense precision on the table. All at once she turns it over as though it were the ace of spades.

"*Mira, blanc . . .* look, white man," she says in a voice suddenly full of foreboding. Her skin too seems to darken to coincide with the tone of her voice.

"*Mira,* soon many Dominican women will die in Haiti!"

"Die of what?"

She shrugs. "It is what they do to us."

"Carmen," I say, "if you knew that you had AIDS, that your blood was bad, would you still sleep with men?" Abruptly, she throws back her head and laughs. It is the same laughter with which Frasquita had greeted the rat at our feet. She stands and the others follow.

"*Méchant!* You wicked man," she says. Then, with terrible solemnity, "You don't know anything."

"But you are killing the Haitian men," I say.

"As for that," she says, "everyone is killing everyone else." All at once, I want to know everything about these three—their childhood, their dreams, what they do in the afternoon, what they eat for lunch.

"Don't leave," I say. "Stay a little more." Again, I reach for my wallet. But they are gone, taking all the light in the room with them—Mercedes and Carmen to sit at another table where three men have been waiting. Frasquita is strolling about the room. Now and then, as if captured by the music, she breaks into a few dance steps, snapping her fingers, singing to herself.

Midnight. And the Copacabana is filling up. Now it is like any other seedy nightclub where men and women go hunting. We get up to leave. In the center a couple are dancing a *méringue.* He is the most graceful dancer I have ever watched; she, the most voluptuous. Together they seem to be riding the back of the music as it gallops to a precisely sexual beat. Closer up, I see that the man is short of breath, sweating. All at once, he collapses into a chair. The woman bends over him, coaxing, teasing, but he is through. A young man with a long polished stick blocks my way.

"I come with you?" he asks. "Very good time. You say yes? Ten dollars? Five?"

I have been invited by Dr. Jean William Pape to attend the AIDS clinic of which he is the director. Nothing from the outside of the low whitewashed structure would suggest it as a medical facility. Inside, it is divided into many small cubicles and a labyrinth of corridors. At nine A.M. the hallways are already full of emaciated silent men and women, some sitting on the few benches, the rest leaning against the walls. The only sounds are subdued moans of discomfort interspersed with coughs. How they eat us with their eyes as we pass.

The room where Pape and I work is perhaps ten feet by ten. It contains a desk, two chairs and a narrow wooden table that is covered with a sheet that will not be changed during the day. The patients are called in one at a time, asked how they feel and whether there is any change in their symptoms, then examined on the table. If the patient is new to the clinic, he or she is questioned about sexual activities.

A twenty-seven-year-old man whose given name is Miracle enters. He is wobbly, panting, like a groggy boxer who has let down his arms and is waiting for the last punch. He is neatly dressed and wears, despite the heat, a heavy woolen cap. When he removes it, I see that his hair is thin, dull reddish and straight. It is one of the signs of AIDS in Haiti, Pape tells me. The man's skin is covered with a dry itchy rash. Throughout the interview and examination he scratches himself slowly, absentmindedly. The rash is called prurigo. It is another symptom of AIDS in Haiti. This man has had diarrhea for six months. The laboratory reports that the diarrhea is due to an organism called cryptosporidium, for which there is no treatment. The telltale rattling of the tuberculous moisture in his chest is audible without a stethoscope. He is like a leaky cistern that bubbles and froths. And, clearly, exhausted.

"Where do you live?" I ask.

"Kenscoff." A village in the hills above Port-au-Prince.

"How did you come here today?"

"I came on the *tap-tap*." It is the name given to the small buses that swarm the city, each one extravagantly decorated with religious slogans, icons, flowers, animals, all painted in psychedelic colors. I have never seen a *tap-tap* that was not covered with passengers as well, riding outside and hanging on. The vehicles are little masterpieces of contagion, if not of AIDS then of the multitude of germs which Haitian flesh is heir to. Miracle is given a prescription for a supply of Sera, which is something like Gatorade, and told to return in a month.

"*Mangé kou bêf,*" says the doctor in farewell. "Eat like an ox." What can he mean? The man has no food or money to buy any. Even had he food, he has not the appetite to eat or the ability to retain it. To each departing patient the doctor will say the same words—"*Mangé kou bêf.*" I see that it is his way of offering a hopeful goodbye.

"Will he live until his next appointment?" I ask.

"No." Miracle leaves to catch the *tap-tap* for Kenscoff.

Next is a woman of twenty-six who enters holding her right hand to her forehead in a kind of permanent salute. In fact, she is shielding her eye from view. This is her third visit to the clinic. I see that she is still quite well nourished.

"Now, you'll see something beautiful, tremendous," the doctor says. Once seated upon the table, she is told to lower her hand. When she does, I see that her right eye and its eyelid are replaced by a huge fungating ulcerated tumor, a side product of her AIDS. As she turns her head, the cluster of lymph glands in her neck to which the tumor has spread is thrown into relief. Two years ago she received a blood transfusion at a time when the country's main blood bank was grossly contaminated with AIDS. It has since been closed down. The only blood available in Haiti is a small supply procured from the Red Cross.

"Can you give me medicine?" the woman wails.

"No."

"Can you cut it away?"

"No."

"Is there radiation therapy?" I ask.

"No."

"Chemotherapy?" The doctor looks at me in what some might call weary amusement. I see that there is nothing to do. She has come here because there is nowhere else to go.

"What will she do?"

"Tomorrow or the next day or the day after that she will climb up into the mountains to seek relief from the *houngan,* the voodoo priest, just as her slave ancestors did two hundred years ago."

Then comes a frail man in his thirties, with a strangely spiritualized face, like a child's. Pus runs from one ear onto his cheek, where it has dried and caked. He has trouble remembering, he tells us. In fact, he seems confused. It is from toxoplasmosis of the brain, an effect of his AIDS. This man is bisexual. Two years ago he engaged in oral sex with foreign men for money. As I palpate the swollen glands of his neck, a mosquito flies between our faces. I swat at it, miss. Just before coming to Haiti I had read that the AIDS virus had been isolated from a certain mosquito. The doctor senses my thought.

"Not to worry," he says. "So far as we know there has never been a case transmitted by insects."

"Yes," I say. "I see."

And so it goes until the last, the thirty-sixth AIDS patient has been seen. At the end of the day I am invited to wash my hands before leaving. I go down a long hall to a sink. I turn on the faucets but there is no water.

"But what about *you?*" I ask the doctor. "You are at great personal risk here—the tuberculosis, the other infections, no water to wash . . ." He shrugs, smiles faintly and lifts his hands palm upward.

We are driving up a serpiginous steep road into the barren mountains above Port-au-Prince. Even in the bright sunshine the countryside has the bloodless color of exhaustion and indifference. Our destination is the Baptist Mission Hospital, where many cases of AIDS have been reported. Along the road there are slow straggles of schoolchildren in blue uniforms who stretch out their hands as we pass and call out, "Give me something." Already a crowd of outpatients has gathered at the entrance to the mission compound. A tour of the premises reveals that in contrast to the aridity outside the gates, this is an enclave of productivity, lush with fruit trees and poinsettia.

The hospital is clean and smells of creosote. Of the forty beds, less than a third are occupied. In one male ward of twelve beds, there are two patients. The chief physician tells us that last year he saw ten cases of AIDS each week. Lately the number has decreased to four or five.

"Why is that?" we want to know.

"Because we do not admit them to the hospital, so they have learned not to come here."

"Why don't you admit them?"

"Because we would have nothing but AIDS here then. So we send them away."

"But I see that you have very few patients in bed."

"That is also true."

"Where do the AIDS patients go?"

"Some go to the clinic in Port-au-Prince or the general hospital in the city. Others go home to die or to the voodoo priest."

"Do the people with AIDS know what they have before they come here?"

"Oh, yes, they know very well, and they know there is nothing to be done for them."

Outside, the crowd of people is dispersing toward the gate. The clinic has been canceled for the day. No one knows why. We are conducted to the office of the reigning American pastor. He is a tall, handsome Midwesterner with an ecclesiastical smile.

"It is voodoo that is the devil here." He warms to his subject. "It is a demonic religion, a cancer on Haiti. Voodoo is worse than AIDS. And it is one of the reasons for the epidemic. Did you know that in order for a man to become a *houngan* he must perform anal sodomy on another man? No, of course you didn't. And it doesn't stop there. The *houngans* tell the men that in order to appease the spirits they too must do the same thing. So you have ritualized homosexuality. That's what is spreading the AIDS." The pastor tells us of a nun who witnessed two acts of sodomy in a provincial hospital where she came upon a man sexually assaulting a houseboy and another man mounting a male patient in his bed.

"Fornication," he says. "It is Sodom and Gomorrah all over again, so what can you expect from these people?" Outside his office we are shown a cage of terrified, cowering monkeys to whom he coos affectionately. It is clear that he loves them. At the car, we shake hands.

"By the way," the pastor says, "what is your religion? Perhaps I am a kinsman?"

"While I am in Haiti," I tell him, "it will be voodoo or it will be nothing at all."

Abruptly, the smile breaks. It is as though a crack had suddenly appeared in the face of an idol.

From the mission we go to the general hospital. In the heart of Port-au-Prince, it is the exact antithesis of the immaculate facility we have just left—filthy, crowded, hectic and staffed entirely by young interns and residents. Though it is associated with a medical school, I do not see any members of the faculty. We are shown around by Jocelyne, a young intern in a scrub suit. Each bed in three large wards is occupied. On the floor about the beds, hunkered in the posture of the innocent poor, are family members of the patients. In the corridor that constitutes the emergency room, someone lies on a stretcher receiving an intravenous infusion. She is hardly more than a cadaver.

"Where are the doctors in charge?" I ask Jocelyne. She looks at me questioningly.

"We are in charge."

"I mean your teachers, the faculty."

"They do not come here."

"What is wrong with that woman?"

"She has had diarrhea for three months. Now she is dehydrated." I ask the woman to open her mouth. Her throat is covered with the white plaques of thrush, a fungus infection associated with AIDS.

"How many AIDS patients do you see here?"

"Three or four a day. We send them home. Sometimes the families abandon them, then we must admit them to the hospital. Every day, then, a relative comes to see if the patient has died. They want to take the body. That is important to them. But they know very well that AIDS is contagious and they are afraid to keep them at home. Even so, once or twice a week the truck comes to take away the bodies. Many are children. They are buried in mass graves."

"Where do the wealthy patients go?"

"There is a private hospital called Canapé Vert. Or else they go to Miami. Most of them, rich and poor, do not go to the hospital. Most are never diagnosed."

"How do you know these people have AIDS?"

"We don't know sometimes. The blood test is inaccurate. There are many false positives and false negatives. Fifteen percent of those with the disease have negative blood tests. We go by their infections—tuberculosis, diarrhea, fungi, herpes, skin rashes. It is not hard to tell."

"Do they know what they have?"

"Yes. They understand at once and they are prepared to die."

"Do the patients know how AIDS is transmitted?"

"They know, but they do not like to talk about it. It is taboo. Their memories do not seem to reach back to the true origins of their disaster. It is understandable, is it not?"

"Whatever you write, don't hurt us any more than we have already been hurt." It is a young Haitian journalist with whom I am drinking a rum punch. He means that any further linkage of AIDS and Haiti in the media would complete the economic destruction of the country. The damage was done early in the epidemic when the Centers for Disease Control in

Atlanta added Haitians to the three other high-risk groups—hemophili-acs, intravenous drug users and homosexual and bisexual men. In fact, Haitians are no more susceptible to AIDS than anyone else. Although the CDC removed Haitians from special scrutiny in 1985, the lucrative tourism on which so much of the country's economy was based was crip-pled. Along with tourism went much of the foreign business investment. Worst of all was the injury to the national pride. Suddenly Haiti was indicted as the source of AIDS in the western hemisphere.

What caused the misunderstanding was the discovery of a large num-ber of Haitian men living in Miami with AIDS antibodies in their blood. They denied absolutely they were homosexuals. But the CDC investiga-tors did not know that homosexuality is the strongest taboo in Haiti and that no man would ever admit to it. Bisexuality, however, is not uncom-mon. Many married men and heterosexually oriented males will occa-sionally seek out other men for sex. Further, many, if not most, Haitian men visit female prostitutes from time to time. It is not difficult to see that once the virus was set loose in Haiti, the spread would be swift through both genders.

Exactly how the virus of AIDS arrived is not known. Could it have been brought home by the Cuban soldiers stationed in Angola and thence to Haiti, about fifty miles away? Could it have been passed on by the thousands of Haitians living in exile in Zaire, who later returned home or immigrated to the United States? Could it have come from the American and Canadian homosexual tourists, and, yes, even some U.S. diplomats who have traveled to the island to have sex with impoverished Haitian men all too willing to sell themselves to feed their families? Throughout the international gay community Haiti was known as a good place to go for sex.

On a private tip from an official at the Ministry of Tourism, J-B and I drive to a town some fifty miles from Port-au-Prince. The hotel is owned by two Frenchmen who are out of the country, one of the staff tells us. He is a man of about thirty and clearly he is desperately ill. Tottering, short of breath, he shows us about the empty hotel. The furnishings are opu-lent and extreme—tiger skins on the wall, a live leopard in the garden, a bedroom containing a giant bathtub with gold faucets. Is it the heat of the day or the heat of my imagination that makes these walls echo with the painful cries of pederasty?

The hotel where we are staying is in Pétionville, the fashionable suburb of Port-au-Prince. It is the height of the season but there are no tourists, only a dozen or so French and American businessmen. The swimming pool is used once or twice a day by a single person. Otherwise, the water remains undisturbed until dusk, when the fruit bats come down to drink in midswoop. The hotel keeper is an American. He is eager to set me straight on Haiti.

"What did and should attract foreign investment is a combination of reliable weather, an honest and friendly populace, low wages and multilingual managers."

"What spoiled it?"

"Political instability and a bad American press about AIDS." He pauses, then adds: "To which I hope you won't be contributing."

"What about just telling the truth?" I suggest.

"Look," he says, "there is no more danger of catching AIDS in Haiti than in New York or Santo Domingo. It is not where you are but what you do that counts." Agreeing, I ask if he had any idea that much of the tourism in Haiti during the past few decades was based on sex.

"No idea whatsoever. It was only recently that we discovered that that was the case."

"How is it that you hoteliers, restaurant owners and the Ministry of Tourism did not know what *tout* Haiti knew?"

"Look. All I know is that this is a middle-class, family-oriented hotel. We don't allow guests to bring women, or for that matter men, into their rooms. If they did, we'd ask them to leave immediately."

At five A.M. the next day the telephone rings in my room. A Creole-accented male voice.

"Is the lady still with you, sir?"

"There is no lady here."

"In your room, sir, the lady I allowed to go up with a package?"

"There is no lady here, I tell you."

At seven A.M. I stop at the front desk. The clerk is a young man.

"Was it you who called my room at five o'clock?"

"Sorry," he says with a smile. "It was a mistake, sir. I meant to ring the room next door to yours." Still smiling, he holds up his shushing finger.

Next to Dr. Pape, director of the AIDS clinic, Bernard Liautaud, a dermatologist, is the most knowledgeable Haitian physician on the subject of the epidemic. Together, the two men have published a dozen articles on AIDS in international medical journals. In our meeting they present me with statistics:

- There are more than one thousand documented cases of AIDS in Haiti, and as many as one hundred thousand carriers of the virus.
- Eighty-seven percent of AIDS is now transmitted heterosexually. While it is true that the virus was introduced via the bisexual community, that route has decreased to 10 percent or less.
- Sixty percent of the wives or husbands of AIDS patients tested positive for the antibody.
- Fifty percent of the prostitutes tested in the Port-au-Prince area are infected.
- Eighty percent of the men with AIDS have had contact with prostitutes.
- The projected number of active cases in four years is ten thousand. (Since my last visit, the Haitian Medical Association broke its silence on the epidemic by warning that one million of the country's six million people could be carriers by 1992.)

The two doctors have more to tell. "The crossing over of the plague from the homosexual to the heterosexual community will follow in the United States within two years. This, despite the hesitation to say so by those who fear to sow panic among your population. In Haiti, because bisexuality is more common, there was an early crossover into the general population. The trend, inevitably, is the same in the two countries."

"What is there to do, then?"

"Only education, just as in America. But here the Haitians reject the use of condoms. Only the men who are too sick to have sex are celibate."

"What is to be the end of it?"

"When enough heterosexuals of the middle and upper classes die, perhaps there will be the panic necessary for the people to change their sexual lifestyles."

This evening I leave Haiti. For two weeks I have fastened myself to this lovely fragile land like an ear pressed to the ground. It is a country to break a traveler's heart. It occurs to me that I have not seen a single jogger. Such a public expenditure of energy while everywhere else strength is ebbing—it would be obscene. In my final hours, I go to the Cathédral of Sainte Trinité, the inner walls of which are covered with murals by Haiti's most renowned artists. Here are all the familiar Bible stories depicted in naïveté and piety, and all in such an exuberance of color as to tax the capacity of the retina to receive it, as though all the vitality of Haiti had been turned to paint and brushed upon these walls. How to explain its efflorescence at a time when all else is lassitude and inertia? Perhaps one day the plague will be rendered in poetry, music, painting, but not now. Not now.

CONSIDERATIONS

Thinking

What images of AIDS does Selzer present? Taken together, what do those images suggest about the disease?

What attitudes about AIDS are conveyed by the people Selzer talks with— the prostitutes, the pastor, the journalist, the hotel manager, the doctors?

Connecting

Examine each of the essay's six scenes. Identify the focus of each and consider how the scenes are related.

Consider what Selzer shows about AIDS in light of what Susan Sontag and Randy Shilts say about it in "AIDS and Its Metaphors" and "Talking AIDS to Death."

Writing

Analyze Selzer's essay to identify and explain the techniques he uses to convey the essay's idea. You might consider Selzer's use of dialogue, details, imagery, metaphor and analogy, and scene.

Compare Selzer's technique of scenic description with that of George Orwell in "Marrakech" and Alice Walker in "Beauty: When the Other Dancer Is the Self."

R andy Shilts
(1951–1994)

W hen Randy Shilts died in 1994, he was national correspondent
of the *San Francisco Chronicle* and the author of three best-
selling books: *The Mayor of Castro Street: The Life and Times of
Harvey Milk,* about gay political power in San Francisco; *And the Band
Played On: Politics, People, and the AIDS Epidemic,* an international bestseller naming the government and the public health and scientific
establishments as culprits in the AIDS crisis; and *Conduct Unbecoming,* a
searching inquiry into gay life, frustration, and torment in the military.
Shilts was named Outstanding Author of 1988 by the American Society
of Authors and Journalists for *And the Band Played On.*

"Talking AIDS to Death" is a provocative familiar essay in which Shilts
reveals his frustration over being an AIDS celebrity and still being unable
to effect significant change at the national level to combat the crisis that
was killing his friends . . . and that eventually killed him as well.

Talking AIDS to Death

I'm talking to my friend Kit Herman when I notice a barely perceptible spot on the left side of his face. Slowly, it grows up his cheekbone, down to his chin, and forward to his mouth. He talks on cheerfully, as if nothing is wrong, and I'm amazed that I'm able to smile and chat on, too, as if nothing were there. His eyes become sunken; his hair turns gray; his ear is turning purple now, swelling into a carcinomatous cauliflower, and still we talk on. He's dying in front of me. He'll be dead soon if nothing is done.

Dead soon if nothing is done.

"Excuse me, Mr. Shilts, I asked if you are absolutely sure, if you can categorically state that you definitely can*not* get AIDS from a mosquito."

I forget the early-morning nightmare and shift into my canned response. All my responses are canned now. I'm an AIDS talk-show juke-box. Press the button, any button on the AIDS question list, and I have my canned answer ready. Is this Chicago or Detroit?

"Of course you can get AIDS from a mosquito," I begin.

Here I pause for dramatic effect. In that brief moment, I can almost hear the caller murmur, "I *knew* it."

"If you have unprotected anal intercourse with an infected mosquito, you'll get AIDS," I continue. "Anything short of that and you won't."

The talk-show host likes the answer. All the talk-show hosts like my answers because they're short, punchy, and to the point. Not like those boring doctors with long recitations of scientific studies so overwritten with maybes and qualifiers that they frighten more than they reassure an AIDS-hysteric public. I give good interviews, talk-show producers agree. It's amazing, they say, how I always stay so cool and never lose my temper.

"Mr. Shilts, has there ever been a case of anyone getting AIDS from a gay waiter?"

"In San Francisco, I don't think they allow heterosexuals to be waiters. This fact proves absolutely that if you could get AIDS from a gay waiter, all northern California would be dead by now."

I gave that same answer once on a Bay Area talk show, and my caller, by the sound of her a little old lady, quickly rejoined, "What if that gay waiter took my salad back into the kitchen and ejaculated into my salad dressing? Couldn't I get AIDS then?"

I didn't have a pat answer for that one, and I still wonder at what this elderly caller thought went on in the kitchens of San Francisco restaurants. Fortunately, this morning's phone-in—in Chicago, it turned out—is not as imaginative.

"You know, your question reminds me of a joke we had in California a couple of years back," I told the caller. "How many heterosexual waiters in San Francisco does it take to screw in a light bulb? The answer is both of them."

The host laughs, the caller is silent. Next comes the obligatory question about whether AIDS can be spread through coughing.

I had written a book to change the world, and here I was on talk shows throughout America, answering questions about mosquitoes and gay waiters.

This wasn't exactly what I had envisioned when I began writing *And the Band Played On*. I had hoped to effect some fundamental changes. I really believed I could alter the performance of the institutions that had allowed AIDS to sweep through America unchecked.

AIDS had spread, my book attested, because politicians, particularly those in charge of federal-level response, had viewed the disease as a political issue, not an issue of public health—they deprived researchers of anything near the resources that were needed to fight it. AIDS had spread because government health officials consistently lied to the American people about the need for more funds, being more concerned with satisfying their political bosses and protecting their own jobs than with telling the truth and protecting the public health. And AIDS had spread because indolent news organizations shunned their responsibility to provide tough, adversarial reportage, instead basing stories largely on the Official Truth of government press releases. The response to AIDS was never even remotely commensurate with the scope of the problem.

I figured the federal government, finally exposed, would stumble over itself to accelerate the pace of AIDS research and put AIDS prevention programs on an emergency footing. Once publicly embarrassed by the revelations of its years of shameful neglect, the media would launch serious investigative reporting on the epidemic. Health officials would step forward and finally lay bare the truth about how official disregard had cost this country hundreds of thousands of lives. And it would never happen again.

I was stunned by the "success" of my book. I quickly acquired all the trappings of bestsellerdom: *60 Minutes* coverage of my "startling" revelations, a Book-of-the-Month Club contract, a miniseries deal with NBC, translation into six languages, book tours on three continents, featured roles in movie-star-studded AIDS fund raisers, regular appearances on network news shows, and hefty fees on the college lecture circuit. A central figure in my book became one of *People* magazine's "25 Most Intriguing People of 1987," even though he had been dead for nearly four years, and the *Los Angeles Herald Examiner* pronounced me one of the "in" authors of 1988. The mayor of San Francisco even proclaimed my birthday last year "Randy Shilts Day."

And one warm summer day as I was sunning at a gay resort in the redwoods north of San Francisco, a well-toned, perfectly tanned young man slid into a chaise next to me and offered the ultimate testimony to my fifteen minutes of fame. His dark eyelashes rising and falling shyly, he whispered, "When I saw you on *Good Morning America* a couple weeks ago, I wondered what it would be like to go to bed with you."

"You're the world's first AIDS celebrity," enthused a friend at the World Health Organization, after hearing one of WHO's most eminent AIDS authorities say he would grant me an interview on one condition— that I autograph his copy of my book. "It must be great," he said.

It's not so great.

The bitter irony is, my role as an AIDS celebrity just gives me a more elevated promontory from which to watch the world make the same mistakes in the handling of the AIDS epidemic that I had hoped my work would help to change. When I return from network tapings and celebrity glad-handing, I come back to my home in San Francisco's gay community and see friends dying. The lesions spread from their cheeks to cover their faces, their hair falls out, they die slowly, horribly, and sometimes suddenly, before anybody has a chance to know they're sick. They die in my arms and in my dreams, and nothing at all has changed.

Never before have I succeeded so well; never before have I failed so miserably.

I gave my first speech on the college lecture circuit at the University of California at Los Angeles in January 1988. I told the audience that there were 50,000 diagnosed AIDS cases in the United States as of that week and that within a few months there would be more people suffering from this deadly disease in the United States than there were Americans killed during the Vietnam War. There were audible gasps. During the question-

and-answer session, several students explained that they had heard that the number of AIDS cases in America was leveling off.

In the next speech, at the University of Tennessee, I decided to correct such misapprehension by adding the federal government's projections—the 270,000 expected to be dead or dying from AIDS in 1991, when the disease would kill more people than any single form of cancer, more than car accidents. When I spoke at St. Cloud State University in Minnesota three months later, I noted that the number of American AIDS cases had that week surpassed the Vietnam benchmark. The reaction was more a troubled murmur than a gasp.

By the time I spoke at New York City's New School for Social Research in June and there were 65,000 AIDS cases nationally, the numbers were changing so fast that the constant editing made my notes difficult to read. By then as many as 1,000 Americans a week were learning that they, too, had AIDS, or on the average, about one every fourteen minutes. There were new government projections to report, too: by 1993, some 450,000 Americans would be diagnosed with AIDS. In that year, one American will be diagnosed with the disease every thirty-six seconds. Again, I heard the gasps.

For my talk at a hospital administrators' conference in Washington in August, I started using little yellow stick-ons to update the numbers on my outline. That made it easier to read; there were now 72,000 AIDS cases. Probably this month, or next, I'll tell another college audience that the nation's AIDS case load has topped 100,000, and there will be gasps again.

The gasps always amaze me. Why are they surprised? In epidemics, people get sick and die. That's what epidemics do to people and that's why epidemics are bad.

When Kit Herman was diagnosed with AIDS on May 13, 1986, his doctor leaned over his hospital bed, took his hand, and assured him, "Don't worry, you're in time for AZT." The drug worked so well that all Kit's friends let themselves think he might make it. And we were bolstered by the National Institutes of Health's assurance that AZT was only the first generation of AIDS drugs, and that the hundreds of millions of federal dollars going into AIDS treatment research meant there would soon be a second and third generation of treatments to sustain life beyond AZT's effectiveness. Surely nothing was more important, considering the federal government's own estimates that between 1 and 1.5 million Americans were infected with the Human Immunodeficiency Virus (HIV), and virtually all would die within the next decade if nothing was done. The new drugs, the NIH assured everyone, were "in the pipeline," and government scientists were working as fast as they possibly could.

Despite my nagging, not one of dozens of public-affairs-show producers chose to look seriously into the development of those long-sought second and third generations of AIDS drugs. In fact, clinical trials of AIDS drugs were hopelessly stalled in the morass of bureaucracy at the NIH, but this story tip never seemed to cut it with producers. Clinical trials were not sexy. Clinical trials were boring.

I made my third *Nightline* appearance in January 1988 because new estimates had been released revealing that one in sixty-one babies born in New York City carried antibodies to the AIDS virus. And the link between those babies and the disease was intravenous drug use by one or both parents. Suddenly, junkies had become the group most likely to catch and spread AIDS through the heterosexual community. Free needles to junkies—now there was a sizzling television topic. I told the show's producers I'd talk about that, but that I was much more interested in the issue of AIDS treatments—which seemed most relevant to the night's program, since Ted Koppel's other guest was Dr. Anthony Fauci, associate NIH director for AIDS, and the Reagan administration's most visible AIDS official.

After fifteen minutes of talk on the ins and outs and pros and cons of free needles for intravenous drug users, I raised the subject of the pressing need for AIDS treatments. Koppel asked Fauci what was happening. The doctor launched into a discussion of treatments "in the pipeline" and how government scientists were working as fast as they possibly could.

I'd heard the same words from NIH officials for three years: drugs were in the pipeline. Maybe it was true, but when were they going to come out of their goddamn pipeline? Before I could formulate a polite retort to Fauci's stall, however, the segment was over, Ted was thanking us, and the red light on the camera had blipped off. Everyone seemed satisfied that the government was doing everything it possibly could to develop AIDS treatments.

Three months later, I was reading a week-old *New York Times* in Kit's room in the AIDS ward at San Francisco General Hospital. It was April, nearly two years after my friend's AIDS diagnosis. AZT had given him two years of nearly perfect health, but now its effect was wearing off, and Kit had suffered his first major AIDS-related infection since his original bout with pneumonia—cryptococcal meningitis. The meningitis could be treated, we all knew, but the discovery of this insidious brain infection meant more diseases were likely to follow. And the long-promised second and third generations of AIDS drugs were still nowhere on the horizon.

While perusing the worn copy of the *Times*, I saw a story about Dr. Fauci's testimony at a congressional hearing. After making Fauci swear an oath to tell the truth, a subcommittee headed by Congressman Ted Weiss of New York City asked why it was taking so long to get new AIDS treatments into testing at a time when Congress was putting hundreds of millions of dollars into NIH budgets for just such purposes. At first Fauci talked about unavoidable delays. He claimed government scientists were working as fast as they could. Pressed harder, he finally admitted that the problem stemmed "almost exclusively" from the lack of staffing in his agency. Congress had allocated funds, it was true, but the Reagan administration had gotten around spending the money by stingily refusing to let Fauci hire anybody. Fauci had requested 127 positions to speed the development of AIDS treatments; the administration had granted him eleven. And for a year, he had not told anyone. For a year, this spokesman for the public health answered reporters that AIDS drugs were in the pipeline and that government scientists had all the money they needed. It seemed that only when faced with the penalty of perjury would one of the administration's top AIDS officials tell the truth. That was the real story, I thought, but for some reason nobody else had picked up on it.

At the international AIDS conference in Stockholm two months later, the other reporters in "the AIDS pack" congratulated me on my success and asked what I was working on now. I admitted that I was too busy promoting the British and German release of my book to do much writing myself, and next month I had the Australian tour. But if I *were* reporting, I added with a vaguely conspiratorial tone, *I'd* look at the *scandal* in the NIH. Nobody had picked up that *New York Times* story from a few months ago about staffing shortages on AIDS clinical trials. The lives of 1.5 million HIV-infected Americans hung in the balance, and the only way you could get a straight answer out of an administration AIDS official was to put him under oath and make him face the charge of perjury. Where I went to journalism school, *that* was a news story.

One reporter responded to my tip with the question "But who's going to play *you* in the miniseries?"

A few minutes later, when Dr. Fauci came into the press room, the world's leading AIDS journalists got back to the serious business of transcribing his remarks. Nobody asked him if he was actually telling the truth, or whether they should put him under oath to ensure a candid response to questions about when we'd get AIDS treatments. Most of the subsequent news accounts of Dr. Fauci's comments faithfully reported that many AIDS treatments were in the pipeline. Government scientists, he said once more, were doing all they possibly could.

The producer assured my publisher that Morton Downey, Jr., would be "serious" about AIDS. "He's not going to play games on this issue," the producer said, adding solemnly, "His brother has AIDS. He understands the need for compassion." The abundance of Mr. Downey's compassion was implicit in the night's call-in poll question: "Should all people with AIDS be quarantined?"

Downey's first question to me was, "You *are* a homosexual, aren't you?"

He wasn't ready for my canned answer: "Why do you ask? Do you want a date or something?"

The show shifted into an earnest discussion of quarantine. In his television studio, Clearasil-addled high school students from suburban New Jersey held up MORTON DOWNEY FAN CLUB signs and cheered aggressively when the truculent, chain-smoking host appeared to favor a kind of homespun AIDS Auschwitz. The youths shouted down any audience member who stepped forward to defend the rights of AIDS sufferers, their howls growing particularly vitriolic if the speakers were gay. These kids were the ilk from which Hitler drew his Nazi youth. In the first commercial break, the other guest, an AIDS activist, and I told Downey we would walk off the show if he didn't tone down his gay-baiting rhetoric. Smiling amiably, Downey took a long drag on his cigarette and assured us, "Don't worry, I have a fallback position."

That comment provided one of the most lucid moments in my year as an AIDS celebrity. Downey's "fallback position," it was clear, was the opposite of what he was promoting on the air. Of course, he didn't *really* believe that people with AIDS, people like his brother, should all be locked up. This was merely a deliciously provocative posture to exploit the working-class resentments of people who needed someone to hate. AIDS sufferers and gays would do for this week. Next week, if viewership dropped and Downey needed a new whipping boy, maybe he'd move on to Arabs, maybe Jews. It didn't seem to matter much to him, since he didn't believe what he was saying anyway. For Morton Downey, Jr., talking about AIDS was not an act of conscience; it was a ratings ploy. He knew it, he let his guests know it, his producers certainly knew it, and his television station knew it. The only people left out of the joke were his audience.

The organizers of the Desert AIDS Project had enlisted actor Kirk Douglas and CBS morning anchor Kathleen Sullivan to be honorary co-chairs of the Palm Springs fund raiser. The main events would include a celebrity tennis match pitting Douglas against Mayor Sonny Bono, and a $1,500-a-head dinner at which I would receive a Lucite plaque for my contributions to the fight against AIDS. The next morning I would fly to L.A. to speak at still another event, this one with Shirley MacLaine, Valerie Harper, and Susan Dey of *L.A. Law.*

The desert night was exquisite. There were 130 dinner guests, the personification of elegance and confidence, who gathered on a magnificent patio of chocolate-brown Arizona flagstone at the home of one of Palm Springs's most celebrated interior designers. A lot of people had come simply to see what was regarded as one of the most sumptuous dwellings in this sumptuous town.

When I was called to accept my reward, I began with the same lineup of jokes I use on talk shows and on the college lecture circuit. They work every time.

I told the crowd about how you get AIDS from a mosquito.

Kirk Douglas laughed; everybody laughed.

Next, I did the how-many-gay-waiters joke.

Kirk Douglas laughed; everybody laughed.

Then I mentioned the woman who asked whether she could get AIDS from a waiter ejaculating in her salad dressing.

That one always has my college audiences rolling in the aisles, so I paused for the expected hilarity.

But in the utter stillness of the desert night air, all that could be heard was the sound of Kirk Douglas's steel jaw dropping to the magnificent patio of chocolate-brown Arizona flagstone. The rest was silence.

"You've got to remember that most of these people came because they're my clients," the host confided later. "You said that, and all I could think was how I'd have to go back to stitching slipcovers when this was done."

It turned out that there was more to my lead-balloon remark than a misjudged audience. Local AIDS organizers told me that a year earlier, a rumor that one of Palm Springs's most popular restaurants was owned by a homosexual, and that most of its waiters were gay, had terrified the elite community. Patronage at the eatery quickly plummeted, and it had nearly gone out of business. Fears that I dismissed as laughable were the genuine concerns of my audience, I realized. My San Francisco joke was a Palm Springs fable.

As I watched the busboys clear the tables later that night, I made a mental note not to tell that joke before dinner again. Never had I seen so many uneaten salads, so much wasted iceberg lettuce.

A friend had just tested antibody positive, and I was doing my best to cheer him up as we ambled down the sidewalk toward a Castro Street restaurant a few blocks from where I live in San Francisco. It seems most of my conversations now have to do with who has tested positive or lucked out and turned up negative, or who is too afraid to be tested. We had parked our car near Coming Home, the local hospice for AIDS patients and others suffering from terminal illnesses, and as we stepped around a nondescript, powder-blue van that blocked our path, two men in white uniforms emerged from the hospice's side door. They carried a stretcher, and on the stretcher was a corpse, neatly wrapped in a royal-blue blanket and secured with navy-blue straps. My friend and I stopped walking. The men quickly guided the stretcher into the back of the van, climbed in the front doors, and drove away. We continued our walk but didn't say anything.

I wondered if the corpse was someone I had known. I'd find out Thursday when the weekly gay paper came out. Every week there are at least two pages filled with obituaries of the previous week's departed. Each week, when I turn to those pages, I hold my breath, wondering whose picture I'll see. It's the only way to keep track, what with so many people dying.

Sometimes I wonder if an aberrant mother or two going to mass at the Most Holy Redeemer Church across the street from Coming Home Hospice has ever warned a child, "That's where you'll end up it you don't obey God's law." Or whether some youngster, feeling that first awareness of a different sexuality, has looked at the doorway of this modern charnel house with an awesome, gnawing dread of annihilation.

"Is the limousine here? Where are the dancers?"

The room fell silent. Blake Rothaus had sounded coherent until that moment, but he was near death now and his brain was going. We were gathered around his bed in a small frame house on a dusty street in Oklahoma City. The twenty-four-year-old was frail and connected to life through a web of clear plastic tubing. He stared up at us and seemed to recognize from our looks that he had lapsed into dementia. A friend broke the uncomfortable silence.

"Of course, we all brought our dancing shoes," he said. "Nice fashionable pumps at that. I wouldn't go out without them."

Everyone laughed and Blake Rothaus was lucid again.

Blake had gone to high school in a San Francisco suburb. When he was a sophomore, he told us, he and his best friend sometimes skipped school, sneaking to the city to spend their afternoons in the gay neighborhood around Castro Street.

It's a common sight, suburban teenagers playing hooky on Castro Street. I could easily imagine him standing on a corner not far from my house. But back in 1982, when he was eighteen, I was already writing about a mysterious, unnamed disease that had claimed 330 victims in the United States.

Blake moved back to Oklahoma City with his family after he graduated from high school. When he fell ill with AIDS, he didn't mope. Instead, he started pestering Oklahoma health officials with demands to educate people about this disease and to provide services for the sick. The state health department didn't recoil. At the age of twenty-two, Blake Rothaus had become the one-man nucleus for Oklahoma's first AIDS patient services. He was the hero of the Sooner State's AIDS movement and something of a local legend.

Though the state had reported only 250 AIDS cases, Oklahoma City had a well-coordinated network of religious leaders, social workers, health-care providers, gay-rights advocates, state legislators, and businessmen, all committed to providing a sane and humane response to this frightening new disease.

"I think it's the old Dust Bowl mentality," suggested one AIDS organizer. "When the hard times come, people pull together."

My past year's travels to twenty-nine states and talks with literally thousands of people have convinced me of one thing about this country and AIDS: most Americans want to do the right thing about this epidemic. Some might worry about mosquitoes and a few may be suspicious of their salad dressing. But beyond these fears is a reservoir of compassion and concern that goes vastly underreported by a media that needs conflict and heartlessness to fashion a good news hook.

In Kalamazoo, Michigan, when I visited my stepmother, I was buttonholed by a dozen middle-aged women who wondered anxiously whether we were any closer to a vaccine or a long-term treatment. One mentioned a hemophiliac nephew. Another had a gay brother in Chicago. A third went to a gay hairdresser who, she quickly added, was one of the finest people you'd ever meet. When I returned to my conservative hometown of Aurora, Illinois, nestled among endless fields of corn and soy, the local health department told me they receive more calls than they know what to do with from women's groups, parishes, and community organizations that want to do something to help. In New Orleans, the archconservative, pro-nuke, anti-gay bishop had taken up the founding of an AIDS hospice as a personal mission because, he said, when people are sick, you've got to help them out.

Scientists, reporters, and politicians privately tell me that of course *they* want to do more about AIDS, but they have to think about the Morton Downeys of the world, who argue that too much research or too much news space or too much official sympathy is being meted out to a bunch of miscreants. They do as much as they can, they insist; more would rile the resentments of the masses. So the institutions fumble along, convinced they must pander to the lowest common denominator, while the women and men of America's heartland pull me aside to fret about a dying cousin or co-worker and to plead, "When will there be a cure? When will this be over?"

"I think I'll make it through this time," Kit said to me, "but I don't have it in me to go through it again."

We were in room 3 in San Francisco General Hospital's ward 5A, the AIDS ward. The poplar trees outside Kit's window were losing their leaves, and the first winter's chill was settling over the city. I was preparing to leave for my fourth and, I hoped, final media tour, this time for release of the book in paperback and on audiocassette; Kit was preparing to die.

The seizures had started a week earlier, indicating he was suffering either from toxoplasmosis, caused by a gluttonous protozoa that sets up housekeeping in the brain; or perhaps it was a relapse of cryptococcal meningitis; or, another specialist guessed, it could be one of those other nasty brain infections that nobody had seen much of until the past year. Now that AIDS patients were living longer, they fell victim to even more exotic infections than in the early days. But the seizures were only part of it. Kit had slowly been losing the sight in his left eye to a herpes infection. And the Kaposi's sarcoma lesions that had scarred his face were beginning to coat the inside of his lungs. When Kit mentioned he'd like to live until Christmas, the doctors said he might want to consider having an early celebration this year, because he wasn't going to be alive in December.

"I can't take another infection," Kit said.

"What does that mean?"

"Morphine," Kit answered, adding mischievously, "lots of it."

We talked briefly about the mechanics of suicide. We both knew people who'd made a mess of it, and people who had done it right. It was hardly the first time the subject had come up in conversation for either of us. Gay men facing AIDS now exchange formulas for suicide as casually as housewives swap recipes for chocolate-chip cookies.

Kit was released from the hospital a few days later. He had decided to take his life on a Tuesday morning. I had to give my first round of interviews in Los Angeles that day, so I stopped on the way to the airport to say goodbye on Monday. All day Tuesday, while I gave my perfectly formed sound bites in a round of network radio appearances, I wondered: Is this the moment he's slipping out of consciousness and into that perfect darkness? When I called that night, it turned out he'd delayed his suicide until Thursday to talk to a few more relatives. I had to give a speech in Portland that day, so on the way to the airport I stopped again. He showed me the amber-brown bottle with the bubble-gum-pink morphine syrup, and we said another goodbye.

The next morning, Kit drank his morphine and fell into a deep sleep. That afternoon, he awoke and drowsily asked what time it was. When told it was five hours later, he murmured, "That's amazing. I should have been dead hours ago."

And then he went back to sleep.

That night, Kit woke up again.

"You know what they say about near-death experiences?" he asked. "Going toward the light?"

Shaking his head, he sighed. "No light. Nothing."

His suicide attempt a failure, Kit decided the timing of his death would now be up to God. I kept up on the bizarre sequence of events by phone and called as soon as I got back to San Francisco. I was going to tell Kit that his theme song should be "Never Can Say Goodbye," but then the person on the other end of the phone told me that Kit had lapsed into a coma.

The next morning, he died.

Kit's death was like everything about AIDS—anticlimactic. By the time he actually did die, I was almost beyond feeling.

The next day, I flew to Boston for the start of the paperback tour, my heart torn between rage and sorrow. All week, as I was chauffeured to my appearances on *Good Morning America, Larry King Live,* and various CNN shows, I kept thinking, It's all going to break. I'm going to be on a TV show with some officious government health spokesman lying to protect his job, and I'm going to start shouting, "You lying son of a bitch. Don't you know there are people, real people, people I love out there dying?" Or I'll be on a call-in show and another mother will phone about her thirty-seven-year-old son who just died and it will hit me all at once, and I'll start weeping.

But day after day as the tour went on, no matter how many official lies I heard and how many grieving mothers I talked to, the crack-up never occurred. All my answers came out rationally in tight little sound bites about institutional barriers to AIDS treatments and projections about 1993 case loads.

By the last day of the tour, when a limousine picked me up at my Beverly Hills hotel for my last round of satellite TV interviews, I knew I had to stop. In a few weeks I'd return to being national correspondent for the *Chronicle,* and it was time to get off the AIDS celebrity circuit, end the interviews and decline the invitations to the star-studded fund raisers, and get back to work as a newspaper reporter. That afternoon, there was just one last radio interview to a call-in show in the San Fernando Valley, and then it would be over.

The first caller asked why his tax money should go toward funding an AIDS cure when people got the disease through their own misdeeds.

I used my standard jukebox answer about how most cancer cases are linked to people's behavior but that nobody ever suggested we stop trying to find a cure for cancer.

A second caller phoned to ask why her tax money should go to finding an AIDS cure when these people clearly deserved what they got.

I calmly put a new spin on the same answer, saying in America you usually don't sentence people to die for having a different lifestyle from yours.

Then a third caller phoned in to say that he didn't care if all those queers and junkies died, as did a fourth and fifth and sixth caller. By then I was shouting, "You stupid bigot. You just want to kill off everybody you don't like. You goddamn Nazi."

The talk-show host sat in stunned silence. She'd heard I was so *reasonable.* My anger baited the audience further, and the seventh and eighth callers began talking about "you guys," as if only a faggot like myself could give a shit about whether AIDS patients all dropped dead tomorrow.

In their voices, I heard the reporters asking polite questions of NIH officials. Of course, they had to be polite to the government doctors; dying queers weren't anything to lose your temper over. I heard the dissembling NIH researchers go home to their wives at night, complain about the lack of personnel, and shrug; this was just how it was going to have to be for a while. They'd excuse their inaction by telling themselves that if they went public and lost their jobs, worse people would replace them. It was best to go along. But how would they feel if *their* friends, *their* daughters, were dying of this disease? Would they be silent—or would they shout? Maybe they'll forgive me for suspecting they believed that ultimately a bunch of fags weren't worth losing a job over. And when I got home, I was going to have to watch my friends get shoved into powder-blue vans, and it wasn't going to change.

The history of the AIDS epidemic, of yesterday and of today, was echoing in the voices of those callers. And I was screaming at them, and the show host just sat there stunned, and I realized I had rendered myself utterly and completely inarticulate.

I stopped, took a deep breath, and returned to compound-complex sentences about the American tradition of compassion and the overriding need to overcome institutional barriers to AIDS treatments.

When I got home to San Francisco that night, I looked over some notes I had taken from a conversation I'd had with Kit during his last stay in the hospital. I was carping about how frustrated I was at the prospect of returning to my reporting job. If an internationally acclaimed best seller hadn't done shit to change the world, what good would mere newspaper stories do?

"The limits of information," Kit said. "There's been a lot written on it."

"Oh," I said.

Kit closed his eyes briefly and faded into sleep while plastic tubes fed him a cornucopia of antibiotics. After five minutes, he stirred, looked up, and added, as if we had never stopped talking, "But you don't really have a choice. You've got to keep on doing it. What else are you going to do?"

CONSIDERATIONS

Thinking

At the beginning and at the end of his essay, Shilts sounds a note of deep concern about what happens in the AIDS epidemic "if nothing is done." How does he make you respond to that concern?

How would you characterize Shilts' sense of humor? How does he use it to further his cause? Does he ever misuse it?

What happened when, during a radio interview to a call-in show, Shilts stopped talking "rationally in tight little sound bites"? What are the broader implications of losing control while waging a frustrating war against indifference, ignorance, and an epidemic?

Connecting

What does the evidence in this essay suggest about the relationship between death, laughter, and courage in the gay community?

In what ways does Richard Selzer's essay "A Mask on the Face of Death" help you understand the magnitude of the problems Shilts writes about?

Writing

Write a couple of paragraphs about the ironic implications of the essay's title: "Talking AIDS to Death." What do you think Shilts had in mind when he chose that title?

Write an essay about "the limits of information," that phrase Shilts' friend Kit mentioned near the end of the essay. Your essay need not focus on AIDS; choose any subject area that interests you. Develop your essay through research or through anecdote and recollected experience, or through both research and experience.

L eslie Marmon Silko (b.1948)

L eslie Marmon Silko, poet, essayist, and storyteller, was born in New Mexico of Laguna parentage. Silko spent her childhood on the Laguna Pueblo Indian Reservation. She has published a volume of poetry, *Laguna Woman* (1974); a collection of short stories, *Storyteller* (1981); and two novels, *Ceremony* (1977) and *Almanac of the Dead* (1991). She has been the recipient of a MacArthur Fellowship as well as other awards.

In "Landscape, History, and the Pueblo Imagination," Silko explains the relationship between nature and people. She also explains the significance of Pueblo burial customs, and she encourages people to develop an attitude toward the land based on harmony, respect, and connectedness.

Landscape, History, and the Pueblo Imagination

FROM A HIGH ARID PLATEAU IN NEW MEXICO

You see that after a thing is dead, it dries up. It might take weeks or years, but eventually if you touch the thing, it crumbles under your fingers. It goes back to dust. The soul of the thing has long since departed. With the plants and wild game the soul may have already been borne back into bones and blood or thick green stalk and leaves. Nothing is wasted. What cannot be eaten by people or in some way used must then be left where other living creatures may benefit. What domestic animals or wild scavengers can't eat will be fed to the plants. The plants feed on the dust of these few remains.

The ancient Pueblo people buried the dead in vacant rooms or partially collapsed rooms adjacent to the main living quarters. Sand and clay used to construct the roof make layers many inches deep once the roof has collapsed. The layers of sand and clay make for easy gravedigging. The vacant room fills with cast-off objects and debris. When a vacant room has filled deep enough, a shallow but adequate grave can be scooped in a far corner. Archaeologists have remarked over formal burials complete with elaborate funerary objects excavated in trash middens of abandoned rooms. But the rocks and adobe mortar of collapsed walls were valued by the ancient people. Because each rock had been carefully selected for size and shape, then chiseled to an even face. Even the pink clay adobe melting with each rainstorm had to be prayed over, then dug and carried some distance. Corn cobs and husks, the rinds and stalks and animal bones were not regarded by the ancient people as filth or garbage. The remains were merely resting at a midpoint in their journey back to dust. Human remains are not so different. They should rest with the bones and rinds where they all may benefit living creatures—small rodents and insects—until their return is completed. The remains of things—animals and plants, the clay and the stones—were treated with respect. Because for the ancient people all these things had spirit and being.

The antelope merely consents to return home with the hunter. All phases of the hunt are conducted with love. The love the hunter and the people have for the Antelope People. And the love of the antelope who agree to give up their meat and blood so that human beings will not starve. Waste of meat or even the thoughtless handling of bones cooked bare will offend the antelope spirits. Next year the hunters will vainly search the dry plains for antelope. Thus it is necessary to return carefully the bones and hair, and the stalks and leaves to the earth who first created them. The spirits remain close by. They do not leave us.

The dead become dust, and in this becoming they are once more joined with the Mother. The ancient Pueblo people called the earth the Mother Creator of all things in this world. Her sister, the Corn Mother, occasionally merges with her because all succulent green life rises out of the depths of the earth.

Rocks and clay are part of the Mother. They emerge in various forms, but at some time before, they were smaller particles or great boulders. At a later time they may again become what they once were. Dust.

A rock shares this fate with us and with animals and plants as well. A rock has being or spirit, although we may not understand it. The spirit may differ from the spirit we know in animals or plants or in ourselves. In the end we all originate from the depths of the earth. Perhaps this is how all beings share in the spirit of the Creator. We do not know.

FROM THE EMERGENCE PLACE

Pueblo potters, the creators of petroglyphs and oral narratives, never conceived of removing themselves from the earth and sky. So long as the human consciousness remains *within* the hills, canyons, cliffs, and the plants, clouds, and sky, the term *landscape,* as it has entered the English language, is misleading. "A portion of territory the eye can comprehend in a single view" does not correctly describe the relationship between the human being and his or her surroundings. This assumes the viewer is somehow *outside* or *separate from* the territory he or she surveys. Viewers are as much a part of the landscape as the boulders they stand on. There is no high mesa edge or mountain peak where one can stand and not immediately be part of all that surrounds. Human identity is linked with all the elements of Creation through the clan: you might belong to the Sun Clan or the Lizard Clan or the Corn Clan or the Clay Clan.[1] Standing deep within the natural world, the ancient Pueblo understood the thing as it was—the squash blossom, grasshopper, or rabbit itself could never be created by the human hand. Ancient Pueblos took the modest view that the thing itself (the landscape) could not be improved upon. The ancients did not presume to tamper with what had already been created. Thus *realism,* as we now recognize it in painting and sculpture, did not catch the imaginations of Pueblo people until recently.

The squash blossom itself is *one thing:* itself. So the ancient Pueblo potter abstracted what she saw to be the key elements of the squash blossom—the four symmetrical petals, with four symmetrical stamens in the center. These key elements, while suggesting the squash flower, also link it with the four cardinal directions. By representing only its intrinsic form, the squash flower is released from a limited meaning or restricted identity. Even in the most sophisticated abstract form, a squash flower or a cloud or a lightning bolt became intricately connected with a complex system of relationships which the ancient Pueblo people maintained with each other, and with the populous natural world they lived within. A bolt of lightning is itself, but at the same time it may mean much more. It may be a messenger of good fortune when summer rains are needed. It may deliver death, perhaps the result of manipulations by the Gunnadeyahs, destructive necromancers. Lightning may strike down an evil-doer. Or lightning may strike a person of good will. If the person survives, lightning endows him or her with heightened power.

Pictographs and petroglyphs of constellations or elk or antelope draw their magic in part from the process wherein the focus of all prayer and concentration is upon the thing itself, which, in its turn, guides the hunter's hand. Connection with the spirit dimensions requires a figure or form which is all-inclusive. A "lifelike" rendering of an elk is too restrictive. Only the elk *is* itself. A *realistic* rendering of an elk would be only one particular elk anyway. The purpose of the hunt rituals and magic is to make contact with *all* the spirits of the Elk.

The land, the sky, and all that is within them—the landscape— includes human beings. Interrelationships in the Pueblo landscape are complex and fragile. The unpredictability of the weather, the aridity and harshness of much of the terrain in the high plateau country explain in large part the relentless attention the ancient Pueblo people gave the sky and the earth around them. Survival depended upon harmony and cooperation not only among human beings, but among all things—the animate and the less animate, since rocks and mountains were known to move, to travel occasionally.

The ancient Pueblos believed the Earth and the Sky were sisters (or sister and brother in the post-Christian version). As long as good family relations are maintained, then the Sky will continue to bless her sister, the Earth, with rain, and the Earth's children will continue to survive. But the old stories recall incidents in which troublesome spirits or beings threaten the earth. In one story, a malicious ka'tsina, called the Gambler, seizes the Shiwana, or Rainclouds, the Sun's beloved children.[2] The Shiwana are snared in magical power late one afternoon on a high mountain top. The Gambler takes the Rainclouds to his mountain stronghold where he locks them in the north room of his house. What was his idea? The Shiwana were beyond value. They brought life to all things on earth. The Gambler wanted a big stake to wager in his games of chance. But such greed, even on the part of only one being, had the effect of threatening the survival of all life on earth. Sun Youth, aided by old Grandmother Spider, outsmarts the Gambler and the rigged game, and the Rainclouds are set free. The drought ends, and once more life thrives on earth.

THROUGH THE STORIES WE HEAR WHO WE ARE

All summer the people watch the west horizon, scanning the sky from south to north for rain clouds. Corn must have moisture at the time the tassels form. Otherwise pollination will be incomplete, and the ears will be stunted and shriveled. An inadequate harvest may bring disaster. Stories told at Hopi, Zuni, and at Acoma and Laguna describe drought and starvation as recently as 1900. Precipitation in west-central New Mexico averages fourteen inches annually. The western Pueblos are located at altitudes over 5,600 feet above sea level, where winter temperatures at night fall below freezing. Yet evidence of their presence in the high desert plateau country goes back ten thousand years. The ancient Pueblo people not only survived in this environment, but many years they thrived. In A.D. 1100 the people at Chaco Canyon had built cities with apartment buildings of stone five stories high. Their sophistication as sky-watchers was surpassed only by Mayan and Inca astronomers. Yet this vast complex of knowledge and belief, amassed for thousands of years, was never recorded in writing.

Instead, the ancient Pueblo people depended upon collective memory through successive generations to maintain and transmit an entire culture, a world view complete with proven strategies for survival. The oral narrative, or "story," became the medium in which the complex of Pueblo knowledge and belief was maintained. Whatever the event or the subject, the ancient people perceived the world and themselves within that world as part of an ancient continuous story composed of innumerable bundles of other stories.

The ancient Pueblo vision of the world was inclusive. The impulse was to leave nothing out. Pueblo oral tradition necessarily embraced all levels of human experience. Otherwise, the collective knowledge and beliefs comprising ancient Pueblo culture would have been incomplete. Thus stories about the Creation and Emergence of human beings and animals into this World continue to be retold each year for four days and four nights during the winter solstice. The "humma-hah" stories related events from the time long ago when human beings were still able to communicate with animals and other living things. But, beyond these two preceding categories, the Pueblo oral tradition knew no boundaries. Accounts of the appearance of the first Europeans in Pueblo country or of the tragic encounters between Pueblo people and Apache raiders were no more and no less important than stories about the biggest mule deer ever taken or adulterous couples surprised in cornfields and chicken coops. Whatever happened, the ancient people instinctively sorted events and details into a loose narrative structure. Everything became a story.

Traditionally everyone, from the youngest child to the oldest person, was expected to listen and to be able to recall or tell a portion, if only a small detail, from a narrative account or story. Thus the remembering and retelling were a communal process. Even if a key figure, an elder who knew much more than others, were to die unexpectedly, the system would remain intact. Through the efforts of a great many people, the community was able to piece together valuable accounts and crucial information that might otherwise have died with an individual.

Communal storytelling was a self-correcting process in which listeners were encouraged to speak up if they noted an important fact or detail omitted. The people were happy to listen to two or three different versions of the same event or the same humma-hah story. Even conflicting versions of an incident were welcomed for the entertainment they provided. Defenders of each version might joke and tease one another, but seldom were there any direct confrontations. Implicit in the Pueblo oral tradition was the awareness that loyalties, grudges, and kinship must always influence the narrator's choices as she emphasizes to listeners this is the way *she* has always heard the story told. The ancient Pueblo people sought a communal truth, not an absolute. For them this truth lived somewhere within the web of differing versions, disputes over minor points, outright contradictions tangling with old feuds and village rivalries.

A dinner-table conversation, recalling a deer hunt forty years ago when the largest mule deer ever was taken, inevitably stimulates similar memories in listeners. But hunting stories were not merely after-dinner entertainment. These accounts contained information of critical importance about behavior and migration patterns of mule deer. Hunting stories carefully described key landmarks and locations of fresh water. Thus a deer-hunt story might also serve as a "map." Lost travelers, and lost piñon-nut gatherers, have been saved by sighting a rock formation they recognize only because they once heard a hunting story describing this rock formation.

The importance of cliff formations and water holes does not end with hunting stories. As offspring of the Mother Earth, the ancient Pueblo people could not conceive of themselves within a specific landscape. Location, or "place," nearly always plays a central role in the Pueblo oral narratives. Indeed, stories are most frequently recalled as people are passing by a specific geographical feature or the exact place where a story takes place. The precise date of the incident often is less important than the place or location of the happening. "Long, long ago," "a long time ago," "not too long ago," and "recently" are usually how stories are classified in terms of time. But the places where the stories occur are precisely located, and prominent geographical details recalled, even if the landscape is well-known to listeners. Often because the turning point in the narrative involved a peculiarity or special quality of a rock or tree or plant found only at that place. Thus, in the case of many of the Pueblo narratives, it is impossible to determine which came first: the incident or the geographical feature which begs to be brought alive in a story that features some unusual aspect of this location.

There is a giant sandstone boulder about a mile north of Old Laguna, on the road to Paguate. It is ten feet tall and twenty feet in circumference. When I was a child, and we would pass this boulder driving to Paguate village, someone usually made reference to the story about Kochininako, Yellow Woman, and the Estrucuyo, a monstrous giant who nearly ate her. The Twin Hero Brothers saved Kochininako, who had been out hunting rabbits to take home to feed her mother and sisters. The Hero Brothers had heard her cries just in time. The Estrucuyo had cornered her in a cave too small to fit its monstrous head. Kochininako had already thrown to the Estrucuyo all her rabbits, as well as her moccasins and most of her clothing. Still the creature had not been satisfied. After killing the Estruc-uyo with their bows and arrows, the Twin Hero Brothers slit open the Estrucuyo and cut out its heart. They threw the heart as far as they could. The monster's heart landed there, beside the old trail to Paguate village, where the sandstone boulder rests now.

It may be argued that the existence of the boulder precipitated the creation of a story to explain it. But sandstone boulders and sandstone formations of strange shapes abound in the Laguna Pueblo area. Yet most of them do not have stories. Often the crucial element in a narrative is the terrain—some specific detail of the setting.

A high dark mesa rises dramatically from a grassy plain fifteen miles southeast of Laguna, in an area known as Swanee. On the grassy plain one hundred and forty years ago, my great-grandmother's uncle and his brother-in-law were grazing their herd of sheep. Because visibility on the plain extends for over twenty miles, it wasn't until the two sheepherders came near the high dark mesa that the Apaches were able to stalk them. Using the mesa to obscure their approach, the raiders swept around from both ends of the mesa. My great-grandmother's relatives were killed, and the herd lost. The high dark mesa played a critical role: the mesa had compromised the safety which the openness of the plains had seemed to assure. Pueblo and Apache alike relied upon the terrain, the very earth herself, to give them protection and aid. Human activities or needs were maneuvered to fit the existing surroundings and conditions. I imagine the last afternoon of my distant ancestors as warm and sunny for late September. They might have been traveling slowly, bringing the sheep closer to Laguna in preparation for the approach of colder weather. The grass was tall and only beginning to change from green to a yellow which matched the late-afternoon sun shining off it. There might have been comfort in the warmth and the sight of the sheep fattening on good pasture which lulled my ancestors into their fatal inattention. They might have had a rifle whereas the Apaches had only bows and arrows. But there would have been four or five Apache raiders, and the surprise attack would have canceled any advantage the rifles gave them.

Survival in any landscape comes down to making the best use of all available resources. On that particular September afternoon, the raiders made better use of the Swanee terrain than my poor ancestors did. Thus the high dark mesa and the story of the two lost Laguna herders became inextricably linked. The memory of them and their story resides in part with the high black mesa. For as long as the mesa stands, people within the family and clan will be reminded of the story of that afternoon long ago. Thus the continuity and accuracy of the oral narratives are reinforced by the landscape—and the Pueblo interpretation of that landscape is *maintained.*

THE MIGRATION STORY: AN INTERIOR JOURNEY

The Laguna Pueblo migration stories refer to specific places—mesas, springs, or cottonwood trees—not only locations which can be visited still, but also locations which lie directly on the state highway route linking Paguate village with Laguna village. In traveling this road as a child with older Laguna people I first heard a few of the stories from that much larger body of stories linked with the Emergence and Migration.[3] It may be coincidental that Laguna people continue to follow the same route which, according to the Migration story, the ancestors followed south from the Emergence Place. It may be that the route is merely the shortest and best route for car, horse, or foot traffic between Laguna and Paguate villages. But if the stories about boulders, springs, and hills are actually remnants from a ritual that retraces the creation and emergence of the Laguna Pueblo people as a culture, as the people they became, then continued use of that route creates a unique relationship between the ritual-mythic world and the actual, everyday world. A journey from Paguate to Laguna down the long incline of Paguate Hill retraces the original journey from the Emergence Place, which is located slightly north of the Paguate village. Thus the landscape between Paguate and Laguna takes on a deeper significance: the landscape resonates the spiritual or mythic dimension of the Pueblo world even today.

Although each Pueblo culture designates a specific Emergence Place—usually a small natural spring edged with mossy sandstone and full of cattails and wild watercress—it is clear that they do not agree on any single location or natural spring as the one and only true Emergence Place. Each Pueblo group recounts its own stories about Creation, Emergence, and Migration, although they all believe that all human beings, with all the animals and plants, emerged at the same place and at the same time.[4]

Natural springs are crucial sources of water for all life in the high desert plateau country. So the small spring near Paguate village is literally the source and continuance of life for the people in the area. The spring also functions on a spiritual level, recalling the original Emergence Place and linking the people and the spring water to all other people and to that moment when the Pueblo people became aware of themselves as they are even now. The Emergence was an emergence into a precise cultural identity. Thus the Pueblo stories about the Emergence and Migration are not to be taken as literally as the anthropologists might wish. Prominent geographical features and landmarks which are mentioned in the narratives exist for ritual purposes, not because the Laguna people actually journeyed south for hundreds of years from Chaco Canyon or Mesa Verde, as the archaeologists say, or eight miles from the site of the natural springs at Paguate to the sandstone hilltop at Laguna.

The eight miles, marked with boulders, mesas, springs, and river crossings, are actually a ritual circuit or path which marks the interior journey the Laguna people made: a journey of awareness and imagination in which they emerged from being within the earth and from everything included in earth to the culture and people they became, differentiating themselves for the first time from all that had surrounded them, always aware that interior distances cannot be reckoned in physical miles or in calendar years.

The narratives linked with prominent features of the landscape between Paguate and Laguna delineate the complexities of the relationship which human beings must maintain with the surrounding natural world if they hope to survive in this place. Thus the journey was an interior process of the imagination, a growing awareness that being human is somehow different from all other life—animal, plant, and inanimate. Yet we are all from the same source: the awareness never deteriorated into Cartesian duality, cutting off the human from the natural world.

The people found the opening into the Fifth World too small to allow them or any of the animals to escape. They had sent a fly out through the small hole to tell them if it was the world which the Mother Creator had promised. It was, but there was the problem of getting out. The antelope tried to butt the opening to enlarge it, but the antelope enlarged it only a little. It was necessary for the badger with her long claws to assist the antelope, and at last the opening was enlarged enough so that all the people and animals were able to emerge up into the Fifth World. The human beings could not have emerged without the aid of antelope and badger. The human beings depended upon the aid and charity of the animals. Only through interdependence could the human beings survive. Families belonged to clans, and it was by clan that the human being joined with the animal and plant world. Life on the high arid plateau became viable when the human beings were able to imagine themselves as sisters and brothers to the badger, antelope, clay, yucca, and sun. Not until they could find a viable relationship to the terrain, the landscape they found themselves in, could they *emerge*. Only at the moment the requisite balance between human and *other* was realized could the Pueblo people become a culture, a distinct group whose population and survival remained stable despite the vicissitudes of climate and terrain.

Landscape thus has similarities with dreams. Both have the power to seize terrifying feelings and deep instincts and translate them into images—visual, aural, tactile—into the concrete where human beings may more readily confront and channel the terrifying instincts or powerful emotions into rituals and narratives which reassure the individual while reaffirming cherished values of the group. The identity of the individual as a part of the group and the greater Whole is strengthened, and the terror of facing the world alone is extinguished.

Even now, the people at Laguna Pueblo spend the greater portion of social occasions recounting recent incidents or events which have occurred in the Laguna area. Nearly always, the discussion will precipitate the retelling of older stories about similar incidents or other stories connected with a specific place. The stories often contain disturbing or provocative material, but are nonetheless told in the presence of children and women. The effect of these inter-family or inter-clan exchanges is the reassurance for each person that she or he will never be separated or apart from the clan, no matter what might happen. Neither the worst blunders or disasters nor the greatest financial prosperity and joy will ever be permitted to isolate anyone from the rest of the group. In the ancient times, cohesiveness was all that stood between extinction and survival, and, while the individual certainly was recognized, it was always as an individual simultaneously bonded to family and clan by a complex bundle of custom and ritual. You are never the first to suffer a grave loss or profound humiliation. You are never the first, and you understand that you will probably not be the last to commit or be victimized by a repugnant act. Your family and clan are able to go on at length about others now passed on, others older or more experienced than you who suffered similar losses.

The wide deep arroyo near the Kings Bar (located across the reservation borderline) has over the years claimed many vehicles. A few years ago, when a Viet Nam veteran's new red Volkswagen rolled backwards into the arroyo while he was inside buying a six-pack of beer, the story of his loss joined the lively and large collection of stories already connected with that big arroyo. I do not know whether the Viet Nam veteran was consoled when he was told the stories about the other cars claimed by the ravenous arroyo. All his savings of combat pay had gone for the red Volkswagen. But this man could not have felt any worse than the man who, some years before, had left his children and mother-in-law in his station wagon with the engine running. When he came out of the liquor store his station wagon was gone. He found it and its passengers upside down in the big arroyo. Broken bones, cuts and bruises, and a total wreck of the car. The big arroyo has a wide mouth. Its existence needs no explanation. People in the area regard the arroyo much as they might regard a living being, which has a certain character and personality. I seldom drive past that wide deep arroyo without feeling a familiarity with and even a strange affection for this arroyo. Because as treacherous as it may be, the arroyo maintains a strong connection between human beings and the earth. The arroyo demands from us the caution and attention that constitute respect. It is this sort of respect the old believers have in mind when they tell us we must respect and love the earth.

Hopi Pueblo elders have said that the austere and, to some eyes, barren plains and hills surrounding their mesa-top villages actually help to nurture the spirituality of the Hopi *way*. The Hopi elders say the Hopi people might have settled in locations far more lush where daily life would not have been so grueling. But there on the high silent sandstone mesas that overlook the sandy arid expanses stretching to all horizons, the Hopi elders say the Hopi people must "live by their prayers" if they are to survive. The Hopi way cherishes the intangible: the riches realized from interaction and interrelationships with all beings above all else. Great abundances of material things, even food, the Hopi elders believe, tend to lure human attention away from what is most valuable and important. The views of the Hopi elders are not much different from those elders in all the Pueblos.

The bare vastness of the Hopi landscape emphasizes the visual impact of every plant, every rock, every arroyo. Nothing is overlooked or taken for granted. Each ant, each lizard, each lark is imbued with great value simply because the creature is there, simply because the creature is alive in a place where any life at all is precious. Stand on the mesa edge at Walpai and look west over the bare distances toward the pale blue outlines of the San Francisco peaks where the ka'tsina spirits reside. So little lies between you and the sky. So little lies between you and the earth. One look and you know that simply to survive is a great triumph, that every possible resource is needed, every possible ally—even the most humble insect or reptile. You realize you will be speaking with all of them if you intend to last out the year. Thus it is that the Hopi elders are grateful to the landscape for aiding them in their quest as spiritual people.

OUT UNDER THE SKY

My earliest memories are of being outside, under the sky. I remember climbing the fence when I was three years old, and heading for the plaza in the center of Laguna village because other children passing by had told me there were ka'tsinas there dancing with pieces of wood in their mouths. A neighbor woman retrieved me before I ever saw the wood-swallowing ka'tsinas, but from an early age I knew that I wanted to be outside. Outside walls and fences.

My father had wandered all the hills and mesas around Laguna when he was a child. Because the Indian School and the taunts of the other children did not set well with him. It had been difficult in those days to be part Laguna and part white, or *amedicana*. It was still difficult when I attended the Indian School at Laguna. Our full-blooded relatives and clanspeople assured us we were theirs and that we belonged there because we had been born and reared there. But the racism of the wider world we call America had begun to make itself felt years before. My father's response was to head for the mesas and hills with his older brother, their dog, and .22 rifles. They retreated to the sandstone cliffs and juniper forests. Out in the hills they were not lonely because they had all the living creatures of the hills around them, and, whatever the ambiguities of racial heritage, my father and my uncle understood what the old folks had taught them: the earth loves all of us regardlessly, because we are her children.

I started roaming those same mesas and hills when I was nine years old. At eleven I rode away on my horse, and explored places my father and uncle could not have reached on foot. I was never afraid or lonely, although I was high in the hills, many miles from home. Because I carried with me the feeling I'd acquired from listening to the old stories, that the land all around me was teeming with creatures that were related to human beings and to me. The stories had also left me with a feeling of familiarity and warmth for the mesas and hills and boulders where the incidents or action in the stories had taken place. I felt as if I had actually been to those places, although I had only heard stories about them. Somehow the stories had given a kind of being to the mesas and hills, just as the stories had left me with the sense of having spent time with the people in the stories, although they had long since passed on.

It is unremarkable to sense the presence of those long passed at the locations where their adventures took place. Spirits range without boundaries of any sort. Spirits may be called back in any number of ways. The method used in the calling also determines how the spirit manifests itself. I think a spirit may or may not choose to remain at the site of its passing or death. I think they might be in a number of places at the same time. Storytelling can procure fleeting moments to experience who they were and how life felt long ago. What I enjoyed most as a child was standing at the site of an incident recounted in one of the ancient stories Aunt Susie had told us as girls. What excited me was listening to old Aunt Susie tell us an old-time story and then for me to realize that I was familiar with a certain mesa or cave that figured as the central location of the story she was telling. That was when the stories worked best. Because then I could sit there listening and be able to visualize myself as being located *within* the story being told, within the landscape. Because the storytellers did not just tell the stories, they would in their way act them out. The storyteller would imitate voices for vast dialogues between the various figures in the story. So we sometimes say the moment is alive again within us, within our imaginations and our memory, as we listen.

Aunt Susie once told me how it had been when she was a child and her grandmother agreed to tell the children stories. The old woman would always ask the youngest child in the room to go open the door. "Go open the door," her grandmother would say. "Go open the door so our esteemed ancestors may bring us the precious gift of their stories." Two points seem clear: the spirits could be present and the stories were valuable because they taught us how we were the people we believed we were. The myth, the web of memories and ideas that create an identity, a part of oneself. This sense of identity was intimately linked with the surrounding terrain, to the landscape which has often played a significant role in a story or in the outcome of a conflict.

The landscape sits in the center of Pueblo belief and identity. Any narratives about the Pueblo people necessarily give a great deal of attention and detail to all aspects of a landscape. For this reason, the Pueblo people have always been extremely reluctant to relinquish their land for dams or highways. For this reason, Taos Pueblo fought from 1906 until 1973 to win back their sacred Blue Lake, which was illegally taken from them by the creation of Taos National Forest. For this reason, the decision in the early 1950s to begin open-pit mining of the huge uranium deposits north of Laguna, near Paguate village, has had a powerful psychological impact upon the Laguna people. Already a large body of stories has grown up around the subject of what happens to people who disturb or destroy the earth. I was a child when the mining began and the apocalyptic warning stories were being told. And I have lived long enough to begin hearing the stories which verify the earlier warnings.

All that remains of the gardens and orchards that used to grow in the sandy flats southeast of Paguate village are the stories of the lovely big peaches and apricots the people used to grow. The Jackpile Mine is an open pit that has been blasted out of the many hundreds of acres where the orchards and melon patches once grew. The Laguna people have not witnessed changes to the land without strong reactions. Descriptions of the landscape *before* the mine are as vivid as any description of the present-day destruction by the open-pit mining. By its very ugliness and by the violence it does to the land, the Jackpile Mine insures that from now on it, too, will be included in the vast body of narratives which make up the history of the Laguna people and the Pueblo landscape. And the description of what that landscape looked like *before* the uranium mining began will always carry considerable impact.

LANDSCAPE AS A CHARACTER IN FICTION

Drought or the disappearance of game animals may signal disharmony or even witchcraft. When the rain clouds fail to appear in time to help the corn plants, or the deer are suddenly scarce, then we know the very sky and earth are telling human beings that all is not well. A deep arroyo continues to claim victims.

When I began writing I found that the plots of my short stories very often featured the presence of elements out of the landscape, elements which directly influenced the outcome of events. Nowhere is landscape more crucial to the outcome than in my short story, "Storyteller." The site is southwest Alaska, near the village of Bethel, on the Kushokwim River. Tundra country. Here the winter landscape can suddenly metamorphize into a seamless blank white so solid that pilots in aircraft without electronic instruments lose their bearings and crash their planes straight into the frozen tundra, believing down to be up. Here on the Alaska tundra, in mid-February, not all the space-age fabrics, electronics, or engines can ransom human beings from the restless shifting forces of the winter sky and winter earth.

The young Yupik Eskimo woman works out an elaborate yet subconscious plan to avenge the deaths of her parents. After months of baiting the trap, she lures the murderer onto the river ice where he falls through to his death. The murderer is a white man who operates the village trading post. For years the murderer has existed like a parasite, exploiting not only the fur-bearing animals and the fish, but the Yupik people themselves. When the Yupik woman kills him, the white trader has just finished cashing in on the influx of workers for the petroleum exploration and pipeline who have suddenly come to the tiny village. For the Yupik people, souls deserving punishment spend varying lengths of time in a place of freezing. The Yupik see the world's end coming with ice, not fire. Although the white trader possesses every possible garment, insulation, heating fuel, and gadget ever devised to protect him from the frozen tundra environment, he still dies, drowning under the freezing river ice. Because the white man had not reckoned with the true power of that landscape, especially not the power which the Yupik woman understood instinctively and which she used so swiftly and efficiently. The white man had reckoned with the young woman and determined he could overpower her. But the white man failed to account for the conjunction of the landscape with the woman. The Yupik woman had never seen herself as anything but a part of that sky, that frozen river, that tundra. The river ice and the blinding white are her accomplices, and yet the Yupik woman never for a moment misunderstands her own relationship with that landscape. After the white trader has crashed through the river ice, the young woman finds herself a great distance from either shore of the treacherous frozen river. She can see nothing but the whiteness of the sky swallowing the earth. But far away in the distance, on the side of her log and tundra sod cabin, she is able to see the spot of bright red. A bright red marker she had nailed up weeks earlier because she was intrigued by the contrast between all that white and the spot of brilliant red. The Yupik woman knows the appetite of the frozen river. She realizes that the ice and the fog, the tundra and the snow seek constantly to be reunited with the living beings which skitter across it. The Yupik woman knows that inevitably she and all things will one day lie in those depths. But the woman is young and her instinct is to live. The Yupik woman knows how to do this.

Inside the small cabin of logs and tundra sod, the old Storyteller is mumbling the last story he will ever tell. It is the story of the hunter stalking a giant polar bear the color of blue glacier ice. It is a story which the old Storyteller has been telling since the young Yupik woman began to arrange the white trader's death. But a sudden storm develops. The hunter finds himself on an ice floe off shore. Visibility is zero, and the scream of the wind blots out all sound. Quickly the hunter realizes he is being stalked. Hunted by all the forces, by all the elements of the sky and earth around him. When at last the hunter's own muscles spasm and cause the jade knife to fall and shatter the ice, the hunter's death in the embrace of the giant ice blue bear is the foretelling of the world's end. When humans have blasted and burned the last bit of life from the earth, an immeasurable freezing will descend with a darkness that obliterates the sun.

Notes

[1]Clan—A social unit composed of families sharing common ancestors who trace their lineage back to the Emergence where their ancestors allied themselves with certain plants or animals or elements.

[2]Ka'tsina—Ka'tsinas are spirit beings who roam the earth and who inhabit kachina masks worn in Pueblo ceremonial dances.

[3]The Emergence—All human beings, animals, and life which had been created emerged from the four worlds below when the earth became habitable. The Migration— The Pueblo people emerged in the Fifth World, but they had already been warned they would have to travel and search before they found the place they were meant to live.

[4]Creation—Tse'itsi'nako, Thought Woman, the Spider, thought about it, and everything she thought came into being. First she thought of three sisters for herself, and they helped her think of the rest of the Universe, including the Fifth World and the four worlds below. The Fifth World is the world we are living in today. There are four previous worlds below this world.

CONSIDERATIONS

Thinking

What is the relationship between a Pueblo and the landscape?

How do stories incorporate features of the landscape? To what end do they do so? In what way do Pueblo stories become mythic?

What do you suppose is Silko's sense of the spiritual?

Connecting

Compare the images of the house and the earth at the beginning and ending of Silko's essay. What do those images have to do with Silko's central ideas?

What do you think is the central idea that Silko associates with the creation story she tells, the story about coming out of the earth into the Fifth World?

Writing

Analyze how Silko uses various images of the gaping hole to develop her ideas about the Pueblo people.

Compare Silko's treatment of Native Americans with that of Diana Hume George in "Wounded Chevy at Wounded Knee." As a coda to your comparison, give your readers a sense of what you think these two women might have to say to one another about the plight of Native Americans.

$\int$ usan Sontag (b.1933)

O ne of America's foremost intellectuals, Susan Sontag has been intimately involved in the world of ideas all her life. After studying at the University of California at Berkeley, she earned a B.A. in philosophy from the University of Chicago at the age of eighteen. After studying religion at Union Theological Seminary in New York, she studied philosophy and literature at Harvard, receiving master's degrees in both fields. She has also studied at Oxford and the Sorbonne. From the other side of the desk, Sontag has taught and lectured extensively at many universities, but especially at Rutgers and Columbia.

The subjects of Sontag's books and essays range widely, though two of her books explore ways of thinking about disease—*Illness as Metaphor* (1978) and *AIDS and Its Metaphors* (1989), from which the selection reprinted here has been taken. This piece reveals Sontag's erudition as well as here capacity for incisive analysis. These intellectual qualities Sontag puts in the service of understanding, especially of understanding how our ways of talking about AIDS reflect our deepest fears.

AIDS and Its Metaphors

"Plague" is the principal metaphor by which the AIDS epidemic is understood. And because of AIDS, the popular misidentification of cancer as an epidemic, even a plague, seems to be receding: AIDS has banalized cancer.

Plague, from the Latin *plaga* (stroke, wound), has long been used metaphorically as the highest standard of collective calamity, evil, scourge—Procopius, in his masterpiece of calumny, *The Secret History,* called the Emperor Justinian worse than the plague ("fewer escaped")—as well as being a general name for many frightening diseases. Although the disease to which the word is permanently affixed produced the most lethal of recorded epidemics, being experienced as a pitiless slayer is not necessary for a disease to be regarded as plague-like. Leprosy, very rarely fatal now, was not much more so when at its greatest epidemic strength, between about 1050 and 1350. And syphilis has been regarded as a plague—Blake speaks of "the youthful Harlot's curse" that "blights with plagues the Marriage hearse"—not because it killed often, but because it was disgracing, disempowering, disgusting.

It is usually epidemics that are thought of as plagues. And these mass incidences of illness are understood as inflicted, not just endured. Considering illness as a punishment is the oldest idea of what causes illness, and an idea opposed by all attention to the ill that deserves the noble name of medicine. Hippocrates, who wrote several treatises on epidemics, specifically ruled out "the wrath of God" as a cause of bubonic plague. But the illnesses interpreted in antiquity as punishments, like the plague in *Oedipus,* were not thought to be shameful, as leprosy and subsequently syphilis were to be. Diseases, insofar as they acquired meaning, were collective calamities, and judgments on a community. Only injuries and disabilities, not diseases, were thought of as individually merited. For an analogy in the literature of antiquity to the modern sense of a shaming, isolating disease, one would have to turn to Philoctetes and his stinking wound.

The most feared diseases, those that are not simply fatal but transform the body into something alienating, like leprosy and syphilis and cholera and (in the imagination of many) cancer, are the ones that seem particularly susceptible to promotion to "plague." Leprosy and syphilis were the first illnesses to be consistently described as repulsive. It was syphilis that, in the earliest descriptions by doctors at the end of the fifteenth century, generated a version of the metaphors that flourish around AIDS: of a disease that was not only repulsive and retributive but collectively invasive. Although Erasmus, the most influential European pedagogue of the early sixteenth century, described syphilis as "nothing but a kind of leprosy" (by 1529 he called it "something worse than leprosy"), it had already been understood as something different, because sexually transmitted. Paracelsus speaks (in Donne's paraphrase) of "that foule contagious disease which then had invaded mankind in a few places, and since overflowes in all, that for punishment of generall licentiousnes God first inflicted that disease." Thinking of syphilis as a punishment for an individual's transgression was for a long time, virtually until the disease became easily curable, not really distinct from regarding it as retribution for the licentiousness of a community—as with AIDS now, in the rich industrial countries. In contrast to cancer, understood in a modern way as a disease incurred by (and revealing of) individuals, AIDS is understood in a premodern way, as a disease incurred by people both as individuals and as members of a "risk group"—that neutral-sounding, bureaucratic category which also revives the archaic idea of a tainted community that illness has judged.

Not every account of plague or plague-like diseases, of course, is a vehicle for lurid stereotypes about illness and the ill. The effort to think critically, historically, about illness (about disaster generally) was attempted throughout the eighteenth century: say, from Defoe's *A Journal of the Plague Year* (1722) to Alessandro Manzoni's *The Betrothed* (1827). Defoe's historical fiction, purporting to be an eyewitness account of bubonic plague in London in 1665, does not further any understanding of the plague as punishment or, a later part of the script, as a transforming experience. And Manzoni, in his lengthy account of the passage of plague through the duchy of Milan in 1630, is avowedly committed to presenting a more accurate, less reductive view than his historical sources. But even these two complex narratives reinforce some of the perennial, simplifying ideas about plague.

One feature of the usual script for plague: The disease invariably comes from somewhere else. The names for syphilis, when it began its epidemic sweep through Europe in the last decade of the fifteenth century, are an exemplary illustration of the need to make a dreaded disease foreign.[1] It was the "French pox" to the English, *morbus Germanicus* to the Parisians, the Naples sickness to the Florentines, the Chinese disease to the Japanese. But what may seem like a joke about the inevitability of chauvinism reveals a more important truth: that there is a link between imagining disease and imagining foreignness. It lies perhaps in the very concept of wrong, which is archaically identical with the non-us, the alien. A polluting person is always wrong, as Mary Douglas has observed. The inverse is also true: A person judged to be wrong is regarded as, at least potentially, a source of pollution.

The foreign place of origin of important illnesses, as of drastic changes in the weather, may be no more remote than a neighboring country. Illness is a species of invasion, and indeed is often carried by soldiers. Manzoni's account of the plague of 1630 (chapters 31 to 37) begins:

> The plague which the Tribunal of Health had feared might enter the Milanese provinces with the German troops had in fact entered, as is well known; and it is also well known that it did not stop there, but went on to invade and depopulate a large part of Italy.

Defoe's chronicle of the plague of 1665 begins similarly, with a flurry of ostentatiously scrupulous speculation about its foreign origin:

> It was about the beginning of September, 1664, that I, among the rest of my neighbours, heard in ordinary discourse that the plague was returned again in Holland; for it had been very violent there, and particularly at Amsterdam and Rotterdam, in the year 1663, whither, they say, it was brought, some said from Italy, others from the Levant, among some goods which were brought home by their Turkey fleet; others said it was brought from Candia; others from Cyprus. It mattered not from whence it came; but all agreed it was come into Holland again.

The bubonic plague that reappeared in London in the 1720s had arrived from Marseilles, which was where plague in the eighteenth century was usually thought to enter Western Europe: brought by seamen, then transported by soldiers and merchants. By the nineteenth century the foreign origin was usually more exotic, the means of transport less specifically imagined, and the illness itself had become phantasmagorical, symbolic.

At the end of *Crime and Punishment* Raskolnikov dreams of plague: "He dreamt that the whole world was condemned to a terrible new strange plague that had come to Europe from the depths of Asia." At the beginning of the sentence it is "the whole world," which turns out by the end of the sentence to be "Europe," afflicted by a lethal visitation from Asia. Dostoevsky's model is undoubtedly cholera, called Asiatic cholera, long endemic in Bengal, which had rapidly become and remained through most of the nineteenth century a worldwide epidemic disease. Part of the centuries-old conception of Europe as a privileged cultural entity is that it is a place which is colonized by lethal diseases coming from elsewhere. Europe is assumed to be by rights free of disease. (And Europeans have been astoundingly callous about the far more devastating extent to which they—as invaders, as colonists—have introduced *their* lethal diseases to the exotic, "primitive" world: Think of the ravages of smallpox, influenza, and cholera on the aboriginal populations of the Americas and Australia.) The tenacity of the connection of exotic origin with dreaded disease is one reason why cholera, of which there were four great outbreaks in Europe in the nineteenth century, each with a lower death toll than the preceding one, has continued to be more memorable than smallpox, whose ravages increased as the century went on (half a million died in the European smallpox pandemic of the early 1870s) but which could not be construed as, plague-like, a disease with a non-European origin.

Plagues are no longer "sent," as in Biblical and Greek antiquity, for the question of agency has blurred. Instead, peoples are "visited" by plagues. And the visitations recur, as is taken for granted in the subtitle of Defoe's narrative, which explains that it is about that "which happened in London during the Last Great Visitation in 1665." Even for non-Europeans, lethal disease may be called a visitation. But a visitation on "them" is invariably described as different from one on "us." "I believe that about one half of the whole people was carried off by this visitation," wrote the English traveler Alexander Kinglake, reaching Cairo at a time of the bubonic plague (sometimes called "oriental plague"). "The Orientals, however, have more quiet fortitude than Europeans under afflictions of this sort." Kinglake's influential book *Eothen* (1844)—suggestively subtitled "Traces of Travel Brought Home from the East"—illustrates many of the enduring Eurocentric presumptions about others, starting from the fantasy that peoples with little reason to expect exemption from misfortune have a lessened capacity to *feel* misfortune. Thus it is believed that Asians (or the poor, or blacks, or Africans, or Moslems) don't suffer or don't grieve as Europeans (or whites) do. The fact that illness is associated with the poor—who are, from the perspective of the privileged, aliens in one's midst—reinforces the association of illness with the foreign: with an exotic, often primitive place.

Thus, illustrating the classic script for plague, AIDS is thought to have started in the "dark continent," then spread to Haiti, then to the United

States and to Europe, then . . . It is understood as a tropical disease: another infestation from the so-called Third World, which is after all where most people in the world live, as well as a scourge of the *tristes tropiques*. Africans who detect racist stereotypes in much of the speculation about the geographical origin of AIDS are not wrong. (Nor are they wrong in thinking that depictions of Africa as the cradle of AIDS must feed anti-African prejudices in Europe and Asia.) The subliminal connection made to notions about a primitive past and the many hypotheses that have been fielded about possible transmission from animals (a disease of green monkeys? African swine fever?) cannot help but activate a familiar set of stereotypes about animality, sexual license, and blacks. In Zaire and other countries in Central Africa where AIDS is killing tens of thousands, the counterreaction has begun. Many doctors, academics, journalists, government officials, and other educated people believe that the virus was sent to Africa from the United States, an act of bacteriological warfare (whose aim was to decrease the African birth rate) which got out of hand and has returned to afflict its perpetrators. A common African version of this belief about the disease's provenance has the virus fabricated in a CIA-Army laboratory in Maryland, sent from there to Africa, and brought back to its country of origin by American homosexual missionaries returning from Africa to Maryland.[2]

At first it was assumed that AIDS must become widespread elsewhere in the same catastrophic form in which it has emerged in Africa, and those who still think this will eventually happen invariably invoke the Black Death. The plague metaphor is an essential vehicle of the most pessimistic reading of the epidemiological prospects. From classic fiction to the latest journalism, the standard plague story is of inexorability, inescapability. The unprepared are taken by surprise; those observing the recommended precautions are struck down as well. *All* succumb when the story is told by an omniscient narrator, as in Poe's parable "The Masque of the Red Death" (1842), inspired by an account of a ball held in Paris during the cholera epidemic of 1832. Almost all—if the story is told from the point of view of a traumatized witness, who will be a benumbed survivor, as in Jean Giono's Stendhalian novel *Horseman on the Roof* (1951), in which a young Italian nobleman in exile wanders through cholera-stricken southern France in the 1830s.

Plagues are invariably regarded as judgments on society, and the metaphoric inflation of AIDS into such a judgment also accustoms people to the inevitability of global spread. This is a traditional use of sexually transmitted diseases: to be described as punishments not just of individuals but of a group ("generall licentiousnes"). Not only venereal diseases have been used in this way, to identify transgressing or vicious populations. Interpreting any catastrophic epidemic as a sign of moral laxity or political decline was as common until the later part of the last century as associating dreaded diseases with foreignness. (Or with despised and feared minorities.) And the assignment of fault is not contradicted by cases that do not fit. The Methodist preachers in England who connected the cholera epidemic of 1832 with drunkenness (the temperance movement was just starting) were not understood to be claiming that *everybody* who got cholera was a drunkard: There is always room for "innocent victims" (children, young women). Tuberculosis, in its identity as a disease of the poor (rather than of the "sensitive"), was also linked by late-nineteenth-century reformers to alcoholism. Responses to illnesses associated with sinners and the poor invariably recommended the adoption of middle-class values: the regular habits, productivity, and emotional self-control to which drunkenness was thought the chief impediment.[3] Health itself was eventually identified with these values, which were religious as well as mercantile, health being evidence of virtue as disease was of depravity. The dictum that cleanliness is next to godliness is to be taken quite literally. The succession of cholera epidemics in the nineteenth century shows a steady waning of religious interpretations of the disease; more precisely, these increasingly coexisted with other explanations. Although, by the time of the epidemic of 1866, cholera was commonly understood not simply as a divine punishment but as the consequence of remediable defects of sanitation, it was still regarded as the scourge of the sinful. A writer in the *New York Times* declared (April 22, 1866): "Cholera is especially the punishment of neglect of sanitary laws; it is the curse of the dirty, the intemperate, and the degraded."[4]

That it now seems unimaginable for cholera or a similar disease to be regarded in this way signifies not a lessened capacity to moralize about diseases but only a change in the kind of illnesses that are used didactically. Cholera was perhaps the last major epidemic disease fully qualifying for plague status for almost a century. (I mean cholera as a European and American, therefore a nineteenth-century, disease; until 1817 there had never been a cholera epidemic outside the Far East.) Influenza, which would seem more plague-like than any other epidemic in this century if loss of life were the main criterion, and which struck as suddenly as cholera and killed as quickly, usually in a few days, was never viewed metaphorically as a plague. Nor was a more recent epidemic, polio. One reason why plague notions were not invoked is that these epidemics did not have enough of the attributes perenially ascribed to plagues. (For instance, polio was construed as typically a disease of children—of the innocent.) The more important reason is that there has been a shift in the focus of the moralistic exploitation of illness. This shift, to diseases that can be interpreted as judgments on the individual, makes it harder to use epidemic disease as such. For a long time cancer was the illness that best fitted this secular culture's need to blame and punish and censor through the imagery of disease. Cancer was a disease of an individual, and understood as the result not of an action but rather of a failure to act (to be prudent, to exert proper self-control, or to be properly expressive). In the twentieth century it has become almost impossible to moralize about epidemics except those which are transmitted sexually.

The persistence of the belief that illness reveals, and is a punishment for, moral laxity or turpitude can be seen in another way, by noting the persistence of descriptions of disorder or corruption as a disease. So indispensable has been the plague metaphor in bringing summary judgments about social crisis that its use hardly abated during the era when collective diseases were no longer treated so moralistically—the time between the influenza and encephalitis pandemics of the early and mid-1920s and the acknowledgment of a new, mysterious epidemic illness in the early 1980s—and when great infectious epidemics were so often and confidently proclaimed a thing of the past.[5] The plague metaphor was common in the 1930s as a synonym for social and psychic catastrophe. Evocations of plague of this type usually go with rant, with antiliberal attitudes: Think of Artaud on theater and plague, of Wilhelm Reich on "emotional plague." And such a generic "diagnosis" necessarily promotes antihistorical thinking. A theodicy as well as a demonology, it not only stipulates something emblematic of evil but makes this the bearer of a rough, terrible justice. In Karel Čapek's The White Plague (1937), the loathsome pestilence that has appeared in a state where fascism has come to power afflicts only those over the age of forty, those who could be held morally responsible.

Written on the eve of the Nazi takeover of Czechoslovakia, Čapek's allegorical play is something of an anomaly—the use of the plague metaphor to convey the menace of what is defined as barbaric by a mainstream European liberal. The play's mysterious, grisly malady is something like leprosy, a rapid, invariably fatal leprosy that is supposed to have come, of course, from Asia. But Čapek is not interested in identifying political evil with the incursion of the foreign. He scores his didactic points by focusing not on the disease itself but on the management of information about it by scientists, journalists, and politicians. The most famous specialist in the disease harangues a reporter ("The disease of the hour, you might say. A good five million have died of it to date, twenty million have it and at least three times as many are going about their business, blithely unaware of the marble-like, marble-sized spots on their bodies"); chides a fellow doctor for using the popular terms, "the white plague" and "Peking leprosy," instead of the scientific name, "the Cheng Syndrome"; fantasizes about how his clinic's work on identifying the new virus and finding a cure ("every clinic in the world has an intensive research program") will add to the prestige of science and win a Nobel Prize for its discoverer; revels in hyperbole when it is thought a cure has been found ("it was the most dangerous disease in all history, worse than the bubonic plague"); and outlines plans for sending those with symptoms to well-guarded detention camps ("Given that every carrier of the disease is a potential spreader of the disease, we *must* protect the uncontaminated from the contaminated. All sentimentality in this regard is fatal and therefore criminal"). However cartoonish Čapek's ironies may seem, they are a not improbable sketch of catastrophe (medical, ecological) as a managed public event in modern mass society. And however conventionally he deploys the plague metaphor, as an agency of retribution (in the end the plague strikes down the dictator himself), Čapek's feel for public relations leads him to make explicit in the play the understanding of disease *as* a metaphor. The eminent doctor declares the accomplishments of science to be as nothing compared with the merits of the dictator, about to launch a war, "who has averted a far worse scourge: the scourge of anarchy, the leprosy of corruption, the epidemic of barbaric liberty, the plague of social disintegration fatally sapping the organism of our nation."

Camus's *The Plague,* which appeared a decade later, is a far less literal use of plague by another great European liberal, as subtle as Čapek's *The White Plague* is schematic. Camus's novel is not, as is sometimes said, a political allegory in which the outbreak of bubonic plague in a Mediterranean port city represents the Nazi occupation. This plague is not retributive. Camus is not protesting anything, not corruption or tyranny, not even mortality. The plague is no more or less than an exemplary event, the irruption of death that gives life its seriousness. His use of plague, more epitome than metaphor, is detached, stoic, aware—it is not about bringing judgment. But, as in Čapek's play, characters in Camus's novel declare how unthinkable it is to have a plague in the twentieth century . . . as if the belief that such a calamity could not happen, could not happen *anymore,* means that it must.

Notes

[1]As noted in the first accounts of the disease: "This malady received from different peoples whom it affected different names," writes Giovanni di Vigo in 1514. Like earlier treatises on syphilis, written in Latin—by Nicolo Leoniceno (1497) and by Juan Almenar (1502)—the one by di Vigo calls it *morbus Gallicus,* the French disease. (Excerpts from this and other accounts of the period, including *Syphilis: Or a Poetical History of the French Disease* [1530] by Girolamo Fracastoro, who coined the name that prevailed, are in *Classic Descriptions of Disease,* edited by Ralph H. Major [1932].) Moralistic explanations abounded from the beginning. In 1495, a year after the epidemic started, the Emperor Maximilian issued an edict declaring syphilis to be an affliction from God for the sins of men.

The theory that syphilis came from even farther than a neighboring country, that it was an entirely new disease in Europe, a disease of the New World brought back to the Old by sailors of Columbus who had contracted it in America, became the accepted explanation of the origin of syphilis in the sixteenth century and is still widely credited. It is worth noting that the earliest medical writers on syphilis did not accept the dubious theory. Leoniceno's *Libellus de Epidemia, quam vulgo morbum Gallicum vocant* starts by taking up the question of whether "the French disease under another name was common to the ancients," and says he believes firmly that it was.

[2]The rumor may not have originated as a KGB-sponsored "disinformation" campaign, but it received a crucial push from Soviet propaganda specialists. In October 1985 the Soviet weekly *Literaturnaya Gazeta* published an article alleging that the AIDS virus had been engineered by the U.S. government during biological-warfare research at Fort Detrick, Maryland, and was being spread abroad by U.S. servicemen who had been used as guinea pigs. The source cited was an article in the Indian newspaper *Patriot.* Repeated on Moscow's "Radio Peace and Progress" in English, the story was taken up by newspapers and magazines throughout the world. A year later it was featured on the front page of London's conservative, mass-circulation *Sunday Express.* ("The killer AIDS virus was artificially created by American scientists during laboratory experiments which went disastrously wrong—and a massive cover-up has kept the secret from the world until today.") Though ignored by most American newspapers, the *Sunday Express* story was recycled in virtually every other country. As recently as the summer of 1987, it appeared in newspapers in Kenya, Peru, Sudan, Nigeria, Senegal, and Mexico. Gorbachev-era policies have since produced an official denial of the allegations by two eminent members of the Soviet Academy of Sciences, which was published in *Izvestia* in late October 1987. But the story is still being repeated—from Mexico to Zaire, from Australia to Greece.

[3]According to the more comprehensive diagnosis favored by secular reformers, cholera was the result of poor diet and "indulgence in irregular habits." Officials of the Central Board of Health in London warned that there were no specific treatments for the disease, and advised paying attention to fresh air and cleanliness, though "the true preventatives are a healthy body and a cheerful, unruffled mind." Quoted in R. J. Morris, *Cholera 1832* (1976).

[4]Quoted in Charles E. Rosenberg, *The Cholera Years: The United States in 1832, 1849, and 1866* (1962).

[5]As recently as 1983, the historian William H. McNeill, author of *Plagues and Peoples,* started his review of a new history of the Black Death by asserting: "One of the things that separate us from our ancestors and make contemporary experience profoundly different from that of other ages is the disappearance of epidemic disease as a serious factor in human life" (*The New York Review of Books,* July 21, 1983). The Eurocentric presumption of this and many similar statements hardly needs pointing out.

CONSIDERATIONS

Thinking

What are the connotations of the word *plague?* To what extent, according to Sontag, is AIDS viewed as a plague by the general population? Why do you think Sontag focuses on the causes of plague, on who or what is seen as ultimately responsible for its spreading?

Why do you think Sontag spends time discussing literary representations of plague such as Daniel Defoe's *A Journal of the Plague Year?* What do her literary and historical references and discussion add to her argument about AIDS?

Connecting

What connections between medieval bubonic plague and AIDS does Sontag consider? What is her view of the comparisons made between the two diseases?

Consider Sontag's view of AIDS in terms of what Randy Shilts says about the disease in his "Talking AIDS to Death."

Writing

Write an essay in which you identify three or four essential facets of Sontag's argument about AIDS and what an understanding of the disease in her terms would mean for how we should think about AIDS and respond to it.

Identify and explore the most prominent and pervasive metaphors that have been used to characterize AIDS. Follow Sontag's lead in thinking about the implications of those metaphors for national health policy and for the responses of those who do not have the disease to those who do.

B rent Staples
(b.1951)

B rent Staples is a journalist who earned his B.A. from Widener University and his Ph.D. from the University of Chicago. His work has appeared in *Harpers, New York Woman, The New York Times Magazine, Chicago Magazine,* and *Down Beat.* He has recently published his autobiography, *Parallel Time: Growing Up in Black and White.*

"Just Walk on By" first appeared in 1986. In this essay, Staples examines his "unwieldy inheritance . . . the ability to alter public space in ugly ways." In the essay, he is a "youngish black man."

Just Walk on By:
A Black Man Ponders His Power
to Alter Public Space

My first victim was a woman—white, well dressed, probably in her early twenties. I came upon her late one evening on a deserted street in Hyde Park, a relatively affluent neighborhood in an otherwise mean, impoverished section of Chicago. As I swung onto the avenue behind her, there seemed to be a discreet, uninflammatory distance between us. Not so. She cast back a worried glance. To her, the youngish black man—a broad six feet two inches with a beard and billowing hair, both hands shoved into the pockets of a bulky military jacket—seemed menacingly close. After a few more quick glimpses, she picked up her pace and was soon running in earnest. Within seconds she disappeared into a cross street.

That was more than a decade ago. I was twenty-two years old, a graduate student newly arrived at the University of Chicago. It was in the echo of that terrified woman's footfalls that I first began to know the unwieldy inheritance I'd come into—the ability to alter public space in ugly ways. It was clear that she thought herself the quarry of a mugger, a rapist, or worse. Suffering a bout of insomnia, however, I was stalking sleep, not defenseless wayfarers. As a softy who is scarcely able to take a knife to a raw chicken—let alone hold it to a person's throat—I was surprised, embarrassed, and dismayed all at once. Her flight made me feel like an accomplice in tyranny. It also made it clear that I was indistinguishable from the muggers who occasionally seeped into the area from the surrounding ghetto. That first encounter, and those that followed, signified that a vast, unnerving gulf lay between nighttime pedestrians—particularly women—and me. And I soon gathered that being perceived as dangerous is a hazard in itself. I only needed to turn a corner into a dicey situation, or crowd some frightened, armed person in a foyer somewhere, or make an errant move after being pulled over by a policeman. Where fear and weapons meet—and they often do in urban America—there is always the possibility of death.

In that first year, my first away from my hometown, I was to become thoroughly familiar with the language of fear. At dark, shadowy intersections in Chicago, I could cross in front of a car stopped at a traffic light and elicit the *thunk, thunk, thunk* of the driver—black, white, male, or female—hammering down the door locks. On less traveled streets after dark, I grew accustomed to but never comfortable with people who crossed to the other side of the street rather than pass me. Then there were the standard unpleasantries with police, doormen, bouncers, cabdrivers, and others whose business is to screen out troublesome individuals *before* there is any nastiness.

I moved to New York nearly two years ago and I have remained an avid night walker. In central Manhattan, the near-constant crowd cover minimizes tense one-on-one street encounters. Elsewhere—visiting friends in SoHo, where sidewalks are narrow and tightly spaced buildings shut out the sky—things can get very taut indeed.

Black men have a firm place in New York mugging literature. Norman Podhoretz in his famed (or infamous) 1963 essay, "My Negro Problem—And Ours," recalls growing up in terror of black males; they "were tougher than we were, more ruthless," he writes—and as an adult on the Upper West Side of Manhattan, he continues, he cannot constrain his nervousness when he meets black men on certain streets. Similarly, a decade later, the essayist and novelist Edward Hoagland extols a New York where once "Negro bitterness bore down mainly on other Negroes." Where some see mere panhandlers, Hoagland sees "a mugger who is clearly screwing up his nerve to do more than just *ask* for money." But Hoagland has "the New Yorker's quick-hunch posture for broken-field maneuvering," and the bad guy swerves away.

I often witness that "hunch posture," from women after dark on the warrenlike streets of Brooklyn where I live. They seem to set their faces on neutral and, with their purse straps strung across their chests bandolier style, they forge ahead as though bracing themselves against being tackled. I understand, of course, that the danger they perceive is not a hallucination. Women are particularly vulnerable to street violence, and young black males are drastically overrepresented among the perpetrators of that violence. Yet these truths are no solace against the kind of alienation that comes of being ever the suspect, against being set apart, a fearsome entity with whom pedestrians avoid making eye contact.

It is not altogether clear to me how I reached the ripe old age of twenty-two without being conscious of the lethality nighttime pedestrians attributed to me. Perhaps it was because in Chester, Pennsylvania, the

small, angry industrial town where I came of age in the 1960s, I was
scarcely noticeable against a backdrop of gang warfare, street knifings,
and murders. I grew up one of the good boys, had perhaps a half-dozen
fistfights. In retrospect, my shyness of combat has clear sources.

Many things go into the making of a young thug. One of those things
is the consummation of the male romance with the power to intimidate.
An infant discovers that random flailings send the baby bottle flying out
of the crib and crashing to the floor. Delighted, the joyful babe repeats
those motions again and again, seeking to duplicate the feat. Just so, I
recall the points at which some of my boyhood friends were finally
seduced by the perception of themselves as tough guys. When a mark
cowered and surrendered his money without resistance, myth and reality
merged—and paid off. It is, after all, only manly to embrace the power to
frighten and intimidate. We, as men, are not supposed to give an inch of
our lane on the highway; we are to seize the fighter's edge in work and in
play and even in love; we are to be valiant in the face of hostile forces.

Unfortunately, poor and powerless young men seem to take all this
nonsense literally. As a boy, I saw countless tough guys locked away; I
have since buried several, too. They were babies, really—a teenage
cousin, a brother of twenty-two, a childhood friend in his midtwenties—
all gone down in episodes of bravado played out in the streets. I came to
doubt the virtues of intimidation early on. I chose, perhaps even unconsciously, to remain a shadow—timid, but a survivor.

The fearsomeness mistakenly attributed to me in public places often
has a perilous flavor. The most frightening of these confusions occurred in
the late 1970s and early 1980s when I worked as a journalist in Chicago.
One day, rushing into the office of a magazine I was writing for with a
deadline story in hand, I was mistaken for a burglar. The office manager
called security and, with an ad hoc posse, pursued me through the
labyrinthine halls, nearly to my editor's door. I had no way of proving
who I was. I could only move briskly toward the company of someone
who knew me.

Another time I was on assignment for a local paper and killing time
before an interview. I entered a jewelry store on the city's affluent Near
North Side. The proprietor excused herself and returned with an enormous red Doberman pinscher straining at the end of a leash. She stood,
the dog extended toward me, silent to my questions, her eyes bulging
nearly out of her head. I took a cursory look around, nodded, and bade
her good night. Relatively speaking, however, I never fared as badly as
another black male journalist. He went to nearby Waukegan, Illinois, a

couple of summers ago to work on a story about a murderer who was born there. Mistaking the reporter for the killer, police hauled him from his car at gunpoint and but for his press credentials would probably have tried to book him. Such episodes are not uncommon. Black men trade tales like this all the time.

In "My Negro Problem—And Ours," Podhoretz writes that the hatred he feels for blacks makes itself known to him through a variety of avenues—one being his discomfort with that "special brand of paranoid touchiness" to which he says blacks are prone. No doubt he is speaking here of black men. In time, I learned to smother the rage I felt at so often being taken for a criminal. Not to do so would surely have led to madness—via that special "paranoid touchiness" that so annoyed Podhoretz at the time he wrote the essay.

I began to take precautions to make myself less threatening. I move about with care, particularly late in the evening. I give a wide berth to nervous people on subway platforms during the wee hours, particularly when I have exchanged business clothes for jeans. If I happen to be entering a building behind some people who appear skittish, I may walk by, letting them clear the lobby before I return, so as not to seem to be following them. I have been calm and extremely congenial on those rare occasions when I've been pulled over by the police.

And on late-evening constitutionals along streets less traveled by, I employ what has proved to be an excellent tension-reducing measure: I whistle melodies from Beethoven and Vivaldi and the more popular classical composers. Even steely New Yorkers hunching toward nighttime destinations seem to relax, and occasionally they even join in the tune. Virtually everybody seems to sense that a mugger wouldn't be warbling bright, sunny selections from Vivaldi's *Four Seasons*. It is my equivalent of the cowbell that hikers wear when they know they are in bear country.

CONSIDERATIONS

Thinking

What is the chief way that Staples wins your confidence in this essay? Why might he not be able to win your confidence the same way on the street? Think of reasons other than appearance.

What do you think of the precautions Staples takes to "make [himself] less threatening"? Should he have to take such precautions?

Connecting

Staples writes about two white men—Norman Podhoretz and Edward Hoagland—who write about black men. What use does Staples make of those two writers and their ideas? What is his attitude about them? How can you tell?

Go to the library and read Norman Mailer's essay "The White Negro" in *Advertisements for Myself.* What do you think Staples would have to say about the effect that essay might have on his ability to walk serenely down the streets of New York minding his own business? In what other ways might Mailer's attempt to romanticize the "Negro" complicate the lives of African Americans?

Writing

Tell a story of your own that illustrates what Staples calls "the male romance with the power to intimidate." Let that story serve as a departure for a closer examination of your attitude toward such a romance.

Write Staples a letter exploring the complications involved in taking him or any other man at face value on the streets of an American city, late at night when you are alone.

M ark Strand (b.1934)

M ark Strand was born to American parents on Prince Edward Island, Canada. He was educated at Antioch College, Yale University, and the University of Iowa. He has taught at various universities, including Princeton, Virginia, and Utah, whose creative writing program he directs. His published work includes fiction, translations, and children's books as well as poetry and essays. His most recent book is *Hopper* (1994).

Before becoming a writer, Strand studied painting. The following selection about the American painter Edward Hopper reflects Strand's interest in the estrangement displayed in Hopper's art. One of the essay's most engaging features is its directness in addressing issues Hopper's paintings raise for thoughtful viewers.

Crossing the Tracks to Hopper's World

The blank concrete walls and steel constructions of modern industry, midsummer streets with the acid green of close-cut lawns, the dusty Fords and gilded movies—all the sweltering, tawdry life of the American small town, and behind all, the sad desolation of our suburban landscape. He derives daily stimulus from these, that others flee from or pass with indifference.

Edward Hopper wrote the preceding words about Charles Burchfield, but he might just as well have been writing about himself. He is the painter of American life at its most hopeless and provincial. Yet he has rescued it from the workaday rhythms in which it is demeaned and has given it a preserving character. Buildings, people and natural objects take on, in his work, an emblematic or pictorial unity. The formal properties of offices, hotel rooms and bleak tenement interiors reinforce the isolation of his people who seem always in the act of entering a meaningless future—meaningless because it is anticipated in the sterility of the present.

The remarkable number of roads, highways, and railroad tracks in his paintings speak for Hopper's fascination with passage. Often, while looking at his work, we are made to feel like transients, momentary visitors to a scene that will endure without us and that suffers our presence with aggressive reticence. His famous painting at the Museum of Modern Art, *The House by the Railroad Tracks*, is a good example of what I mean.

Separated from the house by tracks, we *feel* separated by change, by progress, by motion, and ultimately by the conditions our own mortality imposes. The house glares at us from what seems like an enormous distance. It appears so withdrawn, in fact, that it stands as an emblem of refusal, a monument to the idea of enclosure. And Hopper's famous statement of his aims—"What I wanted to do was paint sunlight on the side of a house"—seems misleading in its simplicity, for the sunlight in his paintings illuminates the secretive without penetrating it. Thus we feel separated from something essential and, as a consequence, our lives seem

632

frivolous. When we look at his paintings we are made to feel, more than we care to, like time's creatures. Each of us would have to cross the tracks to inhabit that Victorian mansion with its coffin-like finality. And across the tracks is Hopper's forbidden land, where the present is lived eternally, where the moment is without moment, where it is always just after and just before—in this case, just after the train has passed, just before the train will arrive.

Hopper's use of light is almost always descriptive of time. In many of his paintings, duration is given a substantial and heroic geometry. In *Rooms by the Sea,* for example, an enormous trapezoid of light fills a room, denying the moment its temporality. Hopper's ability to use space convincingly as a metaphor for time is extraordinary. It demonstrates the ratio between stillness and emptiness, so that we are able to experience the emptiness of moments, hours, a whole lifetime.

His paintings frequently take place at dawn or in late afternoon in a twilight of few or no people. Again, the focus is the transitional. The times which combine elements of night and day paradoxically give the world greater solidity than it has when it is fully illuminated. Night and day in their more local manifestations as shadows and light are so arranged that they dramatize and give extra significance to buildings or parts of buildings we would otherwise take for granted. Such significance is heightened in those paintings where a house, say, stands next to trees or woods. Hopper's trees are strangely opaque; we never enter the woods in his work, nor does light. Their mystery is preserved, acting as an ominous reminder of how fragile our world of measured verticals and horizontals is.

The current show at the Whitney of selections from the Hopper Bequest is fascinating. There is not one painting in it that ranks with his masterpieces and only a few that manage to communicate that quality of loneliness and desolation we associate with many of his best known works. One of those that does is *Stairway* (no date given), a small, eerie painting which looks down a stairway leading to an open door and a dark massing of trees or hills directly outside. Not as rigorously defined spatially as his more mature paintings, it nevertheless mystifies in the same way. The open door becomes not merely a passage connecting inside and outside, but the disturbing link between nowhere and nowhere, or, again, the spatial and tangible restoration of a moment that exists between events, the events of leavetaking or arrival.

Even in the early paintings, there are a great number of roads and embankments, though they do not have the weight they will have later. *El Station* (1908) is typical Hopper subject matter, but quite insubstantial.

The people, merely indicated in a few strokes, do not emerge as presences; the sunlight, convincing as itself, is without psychological depth or effect. Another painting which appears to have much in common with other, better known Hoppers is *Cape Cod Sunset* (1934), but it lacks their solidity, their monumental reticence and, in fact, displays an uncharacteristic frailty. There are a few handsome paintings of Cobb's barns and house in Truro, but these, too, lack the forcefulness we usually associate with Hopper.

The most important aspect of the show is the watercolors, prints and drawings. Many of the watercolors move beyond being mere notation, hurried and perfunctory in gesture, and take on the strangeness, the involved quiet, of his oils. The prints also have qualities in common with the major oils. Though less austere and surely less compelling, such prints as *Evening Wind* and *American Landscape* already incorporate themes that will appear again in future Hoppers. Also exhibited are sketches and preparatory drawings for many of his well-known paintings. These more than anything else in the show bring us close to his greatest work. Something of the same quality is transmitted—an oddness, a disturbing quiet, a sense of being in a room with a man who insists on being with us, but always with his back turned.

CONSIDERATIONS

Thinking

What does Strand find admirable about Hopper's painting? To what extent do you think Hopper's art reflects aspects of the American experience?

How helpful do you find Strand's explanation of Hopper's work? To what extent do you find the epigraph helpful? Why?

Connecting

In what ways is Strand's approach to Hopper similar to and different from Mary Gordon's essay "Mary Cassatt" or Joan Didion's essay "Georgia O'Keeffe"?

To what extent can you link to your own experience either what Strand says about Hopper's work or what you see in it yourself?

Writing

Compare two of Hopper's paintings, drawing out similarities to arrive at some common features. Or compare one of Hopper's paintings with a work by another artist, perhaps an artist whose work is reproduced in this book.

Or write an essay about an aspect of your experience into which you introduce the work of an artist. (See Elizabeth MacDonald's "Odalisque.")

A my Tan (b.1952)

A my Tan was born and raised in Stockton, California. After her father's death, she moved with her mother to Switzerland, where she attended high school. She attended college in Oregon before taking a job with IBM as a writer of computer manuals. A few years later, having been inspired by Louise Erdrich's interlocked stories about Native American (Chippewa) life in her book *Love Medicine,* Tan began writing the interlocking stories that soon became her best-selling novel, *The Joy Luck Club* (1989).

Like the stories in *The Joy Luck Club* and those in her later novel, *The Kitchen God's Wife,* the essay that follows concerns Tan's exploration of cultural difference and cultural connectedness through language. Tan conveys through description and example how using different kinds of English leads to widely differing results.

Mother Tongue

I am not a scholar of English or literature. I cannot give you much more than personal opinions on the English language and its variations in this country or others.

I am a writer. And by that definition, I am someone who has always loved language. I am fascinated by language in daily life. I spend a great deal of my time thinking about the power of language—the way it can evoke an emotion, a visual image, a complex idea, or a simple truth. Language is the tool of my trade. And I use them all—all the Englishes I grew up with.

Recently, I was made keenly aware of the different Englishes I do use. I was giving a talk to a large group of people, the same talk I had already given to half a dozen other groups. The nature of the talk was about my writing, my life, and my book, *The Joy Luck Club*. The talk was going along well enough, until I remembered one major difference that made the whole talk sound wrong. My mother was in the room. And it was perhaps the first time she had heard me give a lengthy speech, using the kind of English I have never used with her. I was saying things like "The intersection of memory upon imagination" and "There is an aspect of my fiction that relates to thus-and-thus"—a speech filled with carefully wrought grammatical phrases, burdened, it suddenly seemed to me, with nominalized forms, past perfect tenses, conditional phrases, all the forms of standard English that I had learned in school and through books, the forms of English I did not use at home with my mother.

Just last week, I was walking down the street with my mother, and I again found myself conscious of the English I was using, the English I do use with her. We were talking about the price of new and used furniture and I heard myself saying this: "Not waste money that way." My husband was with us as well, and he didn't notice any switch in my English. And then I realized why. It's because over the twenty years we've been together I've often used that same kind of English with him, and sometimes he even uses it with me. It has become our language of intimacy, a different sort of English that relates to family talk, the language I grew up with.

So you'll have some idea of what this family talk I heard sounds like, I'll quote what my mother said during a recent conversation which I videotaped and then transcribed. During this conversation, my mother was talking about a political gangster in Shanghai who had the same last name as her family's, Du, and how the gangster in his early years wanted to be adopted by her family, which was rich by comparison. Later, the gangster became more powerful, far richer than my mother's family, and one day showed up at my mother's wedding to pay his respects. Here's what she said in part:

"Du Yusong having business like fruit stand. Like off the street kind. He is Du like Du Zong—but not Tsung-ming Island people. The local people call putong, the river east side, he belong to that side local people. That man want to ask Du Zong father take him in like become own family. Du Zong father wasn't look down on him, but didn't take seriously, until that man big like become a mafia. Now important person, very hard to inviting him. Chinese way, came only to show respect, don't stay for dinner. Respect for making big celebration, he shows up. Mean gives lots of respect. Chinese custom. Chinese social life that way. If too important won't have to stay too long. He come to my wedding. I didn't see, I heard it. I gone to boy's side, they have YMCA dinner. Chinese age I was nineteen."

You should know that my mother's expressive command of English belies how much she actually understands. She reads the *Forbes* report, listens to *Wall Street Week*, converses daily with her stockbroker, reads all of Shirley MacLaine's books with ease—all kinds of things I can't begin to understand. Yet some of my friends tell me they understand 50 percent of what my mother says. Some say they understand 80 to 90 percent. Some say they understand none of it, as if she were speaking pure Chinese. But to me, my mother's English is perfectly clear, perfectly natural. It's my mother tongue. Her language, as I hear it, is vivid, direct, full of observation and imagery. That was the language that helped shape the way I saw things, expressed things, made sense of the world.

Lately, I've been giving more thought to the kind of English my mother speaks. Like others, I have described it to people as "broken" or "fractured" English. But I wince when I say that. It has always bothered me that I can think of no other way to describe it other than "broken," as if it were damaged and needed to be fixed, as if it lacked a certain wholeness and soundness. I've heard other terms used, "limited English," for example. But they seem just as bad, as if everything is limited, including people's perceptions of the limited English speaker.

I know this for a fact, because when I was growing up, my mother's "limited" English limited *my* perception of her. I was ashamed of her English. I believed that her English reflected the quality of what she had to say. That is, because she expressed them imperfectly her thoughts were imperfect. And I had plenty of empirical evidence to support me: the fact that people in department stores, at banks, and at restaurants did not take her seriously, did not give her good service, pretended not to understand her, or even acted as if they did not hear her.

My mother has long realized the limitations of her English as well. When I was fifteen, she used to have me call people on the phone to pretend I was she. In this guise, I was forced to ask for information or even to complain and yell at people who had been rude to her. One time it was a call to her stockbroker in New York. She had cashed out her small portfolio and it just so happened we were going to go to New York the next week, our very first trip outside California. I had to get on the phone and say in an adolescent voice that was not very convincing, "This is Mrs. Tan."

And my mother was standing in the back whispering loudly, "Why he don't send me check, already two weeks late. So mad he lie to me, losing me money."

And then I said in perfect English, "Yes, I'm getting rather concerned. You had agreed to send the check two weeks ago, but it hasn't arrived."

Then she began to talk more loudly. "What he want, I come to New York tell him front of his boss, you cheating me?" And I was trying to calm her down, make her be quiet, while telling the stockbroker, "I can't tolerate any more excuses. If I don't receive the check immediately, I am going to have to speak to your manager when I'm in New York next week." And sure enough, the following week there we were in front of this astonished stockbroker, and I was sitting there red-faced and quiet, and my mother, the real Mrs. Tan, was shouting at his boss in her impeccable broken English.

We used a similar routine just five days ago, for a situation that was far less humorous. My mother had gone to the hospital for an appointment, to find out about a benign brain tumor a CAT scan had revealed a month ago. She said she had spoken very good English, her best English, no mistakes. Still, she said, the hospital did not apologize when they said they had lost the CAT scan and she had come for nothing. She said they did not seem to have any sympathy when she told them she was anxious to know the exact diagnosis, since her husband and son had both died of brain tumors. She said they would not give her any more information until the next time and she would have to make another appointment for that. So she said she would not leave until the doctor called her daughter.

She wouldn't budge. And when the doctor finally called her daughter, me, who spoke in perfect English—lo and behold—we had assurances the CAT scan would be found, promises that a conference call on Monday would be held, and apologies for any suffering my mother had gone through for a most regrettable mistake.

I think my mother's English almost had an effect on limiting my possibilities in life as well. Sociologists and linguists probably will tell you that a person's developing language skills are more influenced by peers. But I do think that the language spoken in the family, especially in immigrant families which are more insular, plays a large role in shaping the language of the child. And I believe that it affected my results on achievement tests, IQ tests, and the SAT. While my English skills were never judged as poor, compared to math, English could not be considered my strong suit. In grade school I did moderately well, getting perhaps B's, sometimes B-pluses, in English and scoring perhaps in the sixtieth or seventieth percentile on achievement tests. But those scores were not good enough to override the opinion that my true abilities lay in math and science, because in those areas I achieved A's and scored in the ninetieth percentile or higher.

This was understandable. Math is precise; there is only one correct answer. Whereas, for me at least, the answers on English tests were always a judgment call, a matter of opinion and personal experience. Those tests were constructed around items like fill-in-the-blank sentence completion, such as "Even though Tom was _____, Mary thought he was _____." And the correct answer always seemed to be the most bland combinations of thoughts, for example, "Even though Tom was shy, Mary thought he was charming," with the grammatical structure "even though" limiting the correct answer to some sort of semantic opposites, so you wouldn't get answers like, "Even though Tom was foolish, Mary thought he was ridiculous." Well, according to my mother, there were very few limitations as to what Tom could have been and what Mary might have thought of him. So I never did well on tests like that.

The same was true with word analogies, pairs of words in which you were supposed to find some sort of logical, semantic relationship—for example, "Sunset is to nightfall as _____ is to _____." And here you would be presented with a list of four possible pairs, one of which showed the same kind of relationship: red is to stoplight, bus is to arrival, chills is to fever, yawn is to boring. Well, I could never think that way. I knew what the tests were asking, but I could not block out of my mind the images already created by the first pair, "sunset is to nightfall"—and I would see a burst of colors against a darkening sky, the moon rising, the lowering of a curtain of stars. And all the other pairs of words—red, bus, stoplight, boring—just threw up a mass of confusing images, making it impossible for me to sort out something as logical as saying: "A sunset precedes nightfall" is the same as "a chill precedes a fever." The only way I would have gotten that answer right would have been to imagine an associative situation, for example, my being disobedient and staying out past sunset, catching a chill at night, which turns into feverish pneumonia as punishment, which indeed did happen to me.

I have been thinking about all this lately, about my mother's English, about achievement tests. Because lately I've been asked, as a writer, why there are not more Asian Americans represented in American literature. Why are there few Asian Americans enrolled in creative writing programs? Why do so many Chinese students go into engineering? Well, these are broad sociological questions I can't begin to answer. But I have noticed in surveys—in fact, just last week—that Asian students, as a whole, always do significantly better on math achievement tests than in English. And this makes me think that there are other Asian-American students whose English spoken in the home might also be described as "broken" or "limited." And perhaps they also have teachers who are steering them away from writing and into math and science, which is what happened to me.

Fortunately, I happen to be rebellious in nature and enjoy the challenge of disproving assumptions made about me. I became an English major my first year in college, after being enrolled as pre-med. I started writing nonfiction as a freelancer the week after I was told by my former boss that writing was my worst skill and I should hone my talents toward account management.

But it wasn't until 1985 that I finally began to write fiction. And at first I wrote using what I thought to be wittily crafted sentences, sentences that would finally prove I had mastery over the English language. Here's an example from the first draft of a story that later made its way into *The Joy Luck Club,* but without this line: "That was my mental quandary in its nascent state." A terrible line, which I can barely pronounce.

Fortunately, for reasons I won't get into today, I later decided I should envision a reader for the stories I would write. And the reader I decided upon was my mother, because these were stories about mothers. So with this reader in mind—and in fact she did read my early drafts—I began to write stories using all the Englishes I grew up with: the English I spoke to my mother, which for lack of a better term might be described as "simple"; the English she used with me, which for lack of a better term might be described as "broken"; my translation of her Chinese, which could certainly be described as "watered down"; and what I imagined to be her translation of her Chinese if she could speak in perfect English, her internal language, and for that I sought to preserve the essence, but neither an English nor a Chinese structure. I wanted to capture what language ability tests can never reveal: her intent, her passion, her imagery, the rhythms of her speech, and the nature of her thoughts.

Apart from what any critic had to say about my writing, I knew I had succeeded where it counted when my mother finished reading my book and gave me her verdict: "So easy to read."

CONSIDERATIONS

Thinking

Why does Tan reject terms such as limited, broken, or fractured to describe her mother's spoken English? Do you agree with her? Why or why not?

Why is Tan's mother's English so important to Amy Tan herself?

Connecting

Tan describes how the English she uses with her mother and her husband differs from the language she uses with others in public. To what extent do you use language differently with different people or different groups?

Have you ever been ashamed of your own use of English or of another's? Why or why not?

Compare Tan's attitude toward her mother's English with that of Richard Rodriguez toward his parents' English in "The Achievement of Desire."

Compare your response to Tan's ideas with your response to David Reich's ideas in "'Mother Tongue' and Standard English."

Writing

Write an essay about an occasion (or occasions) when your use of language had a significant effect on something that happened to you or that affected someone else's feelings.

Discuss Tan's contention that "language spoken in the family, especially in immigrant families . . . plays a large role in shaping the language of the child."

L ewis Thomas
(1913–1993)

L ewis Thomas, born in New York, was educated at Princeton and
Harvard. He served as president of Memorial Sloan-Kettering
Cancer Center from 1973 to 1980. Earlier, he had worked as a
research pathologist and as a medical administrator in the South Pacific
during World War II, at the Rockefeller Institute, Tulane University, the
University of Minnesota, New York University, and the Yale University
School of Medicine. He is the author of a number of collections of essays,
including *The Youngest Science, The Medusa and the Snail, The Lives of a Cell*
(National Book Award winner), and *Late Night Thoughts on Listening to
Mahler's Ninth Symphony*.

"The Corner of the Eye" suggests that much of importance lies just
on the periphery of our vision, or barely audible in the corners of our
minds. The essay also speaks of the earth's secrets.

The Corner of the Eye

There are some things that human beings can see only out of the corner of the eye. The niftiest examples of this gift, familiar to all children, are small, faint stars. When you look straight at one such star, it vanishes; when you move your eyes to stare into the space nearby, it reappears. If you pick two faint stars, side by side, and focus on one of the pair, it disappears and now you can see the other in the corner of your eye, and you can move your eyes back and forth, turning off the star in the center of your retina and switching the other one on. There is a physiological explanation for the phenomenon: we have more rods, the cells we use for light perception, at the periphery of our retinas, more cones, for perceiving color, at the center.

Something like this happens in music. You cannot really hear certain sequences of notes in a Bach fugue unless at the same time there are other notes being sounded, dominating the field. The real meaning in music comes from tones only audible in the corner of the mind.

I used to worry that computers would become so powerful and sophisticated as to take the place of human minds. The notion of Artificial Intelligence used to scare me half to death. Already, a large enough machine can do all sorts of intelligent things beyond our capacities: calculate in a split second the answers to mathematical problems requiring years for a human brain, draw accurate pictures from memory, even manufacture successions of sounds with a disarming resemblance to real music. Computers can translate textbooks, write dissertations of their own for doctorates, even speak in machine-tooled, inhuman phonemes any words read off from a printed page. They can communicate with one another, holding consultations and committee meetings of their own in networks around the earth.

Computers can make errors, of course, and do so all the time in small, irritating ways, but the mistakes can be fixed and nearly always are. In this respect they are fundamentally inhuman, and here is the relaxing thought: computers will not take over the world, they cannot replace us, because they are not designed, as we are, for ambiguity.

Imagine the predicament faced by a computer programmed to make language, not the interesting communication in sounds made by vervets or in symbols by brilliant chimpanzee prodigies, but real human talk. The grammar would not be too difficult, and there would be no problem in constructing a vocabulary of etymons, the original, pure, unambiguous words used to name real things. The impossibility would come in making the necessary mistakes we humans make with words instinctively, intuitively, as we build our kinds of language, changing the meanings to imply quite different things, constructing and elaborating the varieties of ambiguity without which speech can never become human speech.

Look at the record of language if you want to glimpse the special qualities of the human mind that lie beyond the reach of any machine. Take, for example, the metaphors we use in everyday speech to tell ourselves who we are, where we live, and where we come from.

The earth is a good place to begin. The word "earth" is used to name the ground we walk on, the soil in which we grow plants or dig clams, and the planet itself; we also use it to describe all of humanity ("the whole earth responds to the beauty of a child," we say to each other).

The earliest word for earth in our language was the Indo-European root *dhghem,* and look what we did with it. We turned it, by adding suffixes, into *humus* in Latin; today we call the complex polymers that hold fertile soil together "humic" acids, and somehow or other the same root became "humility." With another suffix the word became "human." Did the earth become human, or did the human emerge from the earth? One answer may lie in that nice cognate word "humble." "Humane" was built on, extending the meaning of both the earth and ourselves. In ancient Hebrew, *adamha* was the word for earth, *adam* for man. What computer could run itself through such manipulations as those?

We came at the same system of defining ourselves from the other direction. The word *wiros* was the first root for man; it took us in our vanity on to "virile" and "virtue," but also turned itself into the Germanic word *weraldh,* meaning the life of man, and thence in English to our word "world."

There is a deep hunch in this kind of etymology. The world of man derives from this planet, shares origin with the life of the soil, lives in humility with all the rest of life. I cannot imagine programming a computer to think up an idea like that, not a twentieth-century computer, anyway.

The world began with what it is now the fashion to call the "Big Bang." Characteristically, we have assigned the wrong words for the very beginning of the earth and ourselves, in order to evade another term that would cause this century embarrassment. It could not, of course, have been a bang of any sort, with no atmosphere to conduct the waves of sound, and no ears. It was something else, occurring in the most absolute silence we can imagine. It was the Great Light.

We say it had been chaos before, but it was not the kind of place we use the word "chaos" for today, things tumbling over each other and bumping around. Chaos did not have that meaning in Greek; it simply meant empty.

We took it, in our words, from chaos to cosmos, a word that simply meant order, cosmetic. We perceived the order in surprise, and our cosmologists and physicists continue to find new and astonishing aspects of the order. We made up the word "universe" from the whole affair, meaning literally turning everything into one thing. We used to say it was a miracle, and we still permit ourselves to refer to the whole universe as a marvel, holding in our unconscious minds the original root meaning of these two words, miracle and marvel—from the ancient root word *smei,* signifying a smile. It immensely pleases a human being to see something never seen before, even more to learn something never known before, most of all to think something never thought before. The rings of Saturn are the latest surprise. All my physicist friends are enchanted by this phenomenon, marveling at the small violations of the laws of planetary mechanics, shocked by the unaccountable braids and spokes stuck there among the rings like graffiti. It is nice for physicists to see something new and inexplicable; it means that the laws of nature are once again about to be amended by a new footnote.

The greatest surprise of all lies within our own local, suburban solar system. It is not Mars; Mars was surprising in its way but not flabbergasting; it was a disappointment not to find evidences of life, and there was some sadness in the pictures sent back to earth from the Mars Lander, that lonely long-legged apparatus poking about with its jointed arm, picking up sample after sample of the barren Mars soil, looking for any flicker of life and finding none; the only sign of life on Mars was the Lander itself, an extension of the human mind all the way from earth to Mars, totally alone.

Nor is Saturn the great surprise, nor Jupiter, nor Venus, nor Mercury, nor any of the glimpses of the others.

The overwhelming astonishment, the queerest structure we know about so far in the whole universe, the greatest of all cosmological scientific puzzles, confounding all our efforts to comprehend it, is the earth. We are only now beginning to appreciate how strange and splendid it is, how it catches the breath, the loveliest object afloat around the sun, enclosed in its own blue bubble of atmosphere, manufacturing and breathing its own oxygen, fixing its own nitrogen from the air into its own soil, generating its own weather at the surface of its rain forests, constructing its own carapace from living parts: chalk cliffs, coral reefs, old fossils from earlier forms of life now covered by layers of new life meshed together around the globe, Troy upon Troy.

Seen from the right distance, from the corner of the eye of an extraterrestrial visitor, it must surely seem a single creature, clinging to the round warm stone, turning in the sun.

CONSIDERATIONS

Thinking

Why is the title—"The Corner of the Eye"—so important to Thomas?

What is Thomas really trying to tell us about the earth? Where does he make that point most clearly?

Connecting

Why do you suppose Thomas tells us that he used to worry about computers' becoming too powerful? Why are "ambiguity" and "surprise" so crucial to our understanding of Thomas' idea?

What is hidden in the "record of language" that interests Thomas so much?

Writing

Select and describe one instance of seeing something out of the corner of your eye or detecting something out of the corner of your mind. Is there some logical explanation for what you saw or heard? Explain.

Go to the library and read two more essays from Thomas' books of essays. On the basis of those two essays and the one in this anthology, try to characterize what you think of as a preoccupation, central to Thomas' way of thinking.

B
arbara Tuchman
(1912–1989)

O ne of America's most accomplished popular historians, Barbara Tuchman was born and raised in New York City and spent vacations at her family's estate in Connecticut. She was educated at Radcliffe and in 1936 joined the staff of *The Nation,* a political journal, for which she covered the Spanish Civil War. That experience led to her first book, *The Lost British Policy* (1938), a study of British foreign policy toward Spain. Many other books followed, including *The Guns of August* (1962), a Pulitzer Prize–winning account of the initial month of World War I; *The Proud Tower* (1966), a study of the decades that preceded that war; *Stillwell and the American Experience in China* (1970), for which she was awarded her second Pulitzer Prize; and *A Distant Mirror,* a history of the social and cultural life of the fourteenth century.

Tuchman's essays appear in a number of volumes, including *The March of Folly* (1984) and *Practicing History* (1981), from which the following essay has been taken. In "History by the Ounce," Tuchman advances an argument for the necessity of what she calls "corroborative detail," by which she means any detail, however small, that provides evidence in support of a claim. Her essay itself is filled with such corroborative details, which is one of its strongest qualities. It is also written in a language far removed from the jargon of many academic historians.

History by the Ounce

A
t a party given for its reopening last year, the Museum of Modern Art in New York served champagne to five thousand guests. An alert reporter for the *Times,* Charlotte Curtis, noted that there were eighty cases, which, she informed her readers, amounted to 960 bottles or 7,680 three-ounce drinks. Somehow through this detail the Museum's party at once becomes alive; a fashionable New York occasion. One sees the crush, the women eyeing each other's clothes, the exchange of greetings, and feels the gratifying sense of elegance and importance imparted by champagne—even if, at one and a half drinks per person, it was not on an exactly riotous scale. All this is conveyed by Miss Curtis' detail. It is, I think, the way history as well as journalism should be written. It is what Pooh-Bah, in *The Mikado,* meant when, telling how the victim's head stood on its neck and bowed three times to him at the execution of Nanki-Poo, he added that this was "corroborative detail intended to give artistic verisimilitude to an otherwise bald and unconvincing narrative." Not that Miss Curtis' narrative was either bald or unconvincing; on the contrary, it was precise, factual, and a model in every way. But what made it excel, made it vivid and memorable, was her use of corroborative detail.

Pooh-Bah's statement of the case establishes him in my estimate as a major historian or, at least, as the formulator of a major principle of historiography. True, he invented his corroborative detail, which is cheating if you are a historian and fiction if you are not; nevertheless, what counts is his recognition of its importance. He knew that it supplies verisimilitude, that without it a narrative is bald and unconvincing. Neither he nor I, of course, discovered the principle; historians have for long made use of it, beginning with Thucydides, who insisted on details of topography, "the appearance of cities and localities, the description of rivers and harbors, the peculiar features of seas and countries and their relative distances."

Corroborative detail is the great corrective. Without it historical narrative and interpretation, both, may slip easily into the invalid. It is a disciplinarian. It forces the historian who uses and respects it to cleave to the truth, or as much as he can find out of the truth. It keeps him from soaring off the ground into theories of his own invention. On those Toynbeean heights the air is stimulating and the view is vast, but people and houses down below are too small to be seen. However persuaded the historian may be of the validity of the theories he conceives, if they are not supported and illustrated by corroborative detail they are of no more value as history than Pooh-Bah's report of the imagined execution.

It is wiser, I believe, to arrive at theory by way of the evidence rather than the other way around, like so many revisionists today. It is more rewarding, in any case, to assemble the facts first and, in the process of arranging them in narrative form, to discover a theory or a historical generalization emerging of its own accord. This to me is the excitement, the built-in treasure hunt, of writing history. In the book I am working on now, which deals with the twenty-year period before 1914 (and the reader must forgive me if all my examples are drawn from my own work, but that, after all, is the thing one knows best), I have been writing about a moment during the Dreyfus Affair in France when on the day of the reopening of Parliament everyone expected the Army to attempt a *coup d'état*. English observers predicted it, troops were brought into the capital, the Royalist pretender was summoned to the frontier, mobs hooted and rioted in the streets, but when the day had passed, nothing had happened; the Republic still stood. By this time I had assembled so much corroborative detail pointing to a *coup d'état* that I had to explain why it had not occurred. Suddenly I had to stop and think. After a while I found myself writing, "The Right lacked that necessary chemical of a coup—a leader. It had its small, if loud, fanatics; but to upset the established government in a democratic country requires either foreign help or the stuff of a dictator." That is a historical generalization, I believe; a modest one, to be sure, but my size. I had arrived at it out of the necessity of the material and felt immensely pleased and proud. These moments do not occur every day; sometimes no more than one a chapter, if that, but when they do they leave one with a lovely sense of achievement.

I am a disciple of the ounce because I mistrust history in gallon jugs whose purveyors are more concerned with establishing the meaning and purpose of history than with what happened. Is it necessary to insist on a purpose? No one asks the novelist why he writes novels or the poet what is his purpose in writing poems. The lilies of the field, as I remember, were not required to have a demonstrable purpose. Why cannot history be studied and written and read for its own sake, as the record of human behavior, the most fascinating subject of all? Insistence on a purpose turns the historian into a prophet—and that is another profession.

To return to my own: Corroborative detail will not produce a generalization every time, but it will often reveal a historical truth, besides keeping one grounded in historical reality. When I was investigating General Mercier, the Minister of War who was responsible for the original condemnation of Dreyfus and who in the course of the Affair became the hero of the Right, I discovered that at parties of the *haut monde* ladies rose to their feet when General Mercier entered the room. That is the kind of detail which to me is worth a week of research. It illustrates the society, the people, the state of feeling at the time more vividly than anything I could write and in shorter space, too, which is an additional advantage. It epitomizes, it crystallizes, it visualizes. The reader can see it; moreover, it sticks in his mind; it is memorable.

The same is true, verbally though not visually, of a statement by President Eliot of Harvard in 1896 in a speech on international arbitration, a great issue of the time. In this chapter I was writing about the founding tradition of the United States as an anti-militarist, anti-imperialist nation, secure within its own shores, having nothing to do with the wicked armaments and standing armies of Europe, setting an example of unarmed strength and righteousness. Looking for material to illustrate the tradition, I found in a newspaper report these words of Eliot, which I have not seen quoted by anyone else: "The building of a navy," he said, "and the presence of a large standing army mean . . . the abandonment of what is characteristically American. . . . The building of a navy and particularly of battleships is English and French policy. It should never be ours."

How superb that is! Its assurance, its conviction, its Olympian authority—what does it not reveal of the man, the time, the idea? In those words I saw clearly for the first time the nature and quality of the American anti-militarist tradition, of what has been called the American dream—it was a case of detail not merely corroborating but revealing an aspect of history.

Failing to know such details, one can be led astray. In 1890 Congress authorized the building of the first three American battleships and, two years later, a fourth. Shortly thereafter, in 1895, this country plunged into a major quarrel with Great Britain, known as the Venezuelan crisis, in which there was much shaking of fists and chauvinist shrieking for war. Three years later we were at war with Spain. She was no longer a naval power equal to Britain, of course, but still not negligible. One would like to know what exactly was American naval strength at the time of both these crises. How many, if any, of the battleships authorized in 1890 were actually at sea five years later? When the jingoes were howling for war in

1895, what ships did we have to protect our coasts, much less to take the offensive? It seemed to me this was a piece of information worth knowing. To my astonishment, on looking for the answer in textbooks on the period, I could not find it. The historians of America's rise to world power, of the era of expansion, of American foreign policy, or even of the navy have not concerned themselves with what evidently seems to them an irrelevant detail. It was hardly irrelevant to policymakers of the time who bore the responsibility for decisions of peace or war. Text after text in American history is published every year, each repeating on this question more or less what his predecessor has said before, with no further enlightenment. To find the facts I finally had to write to the Director of Naval History at the Navy Department in Washington.

My point is not how many battleships we had on hand in 1895 and '98 (which I now know) but why this hard, physical fact was missing from the professional historians' treatment. "Bald and unconvincing," said Pooh-Bah of narrative without fact, a judgment in which I join.

When I come across a generalization or a general statement in history unsupported by illustration I am instantly on guard; my reaction is, "Show me." If a historian writes that it was raining heavily on the day war was declared, that is a detail corroborating a statement, let us say, that the day was gloomy. But if he writes merely that it was a gloomy day without mentioning the rain, I want to know what is his evidence; what made it gloomy. Or if he writes, "The population was in a belligerent mood," or, "It was a period of great anxiety," he is indulging in general statements which carry no conviction to me if they are not illustrated by some evidence. I write, for example, that fashionable French society in the 1890s imitated the English in manners and habits. Imagining myself to be my own reader—a complicated fugue that goes on all the time at my desk— my reaction is of course, "Show me." The next two sentences do. I write, "The Greffulhes and Breteuils were intimates of the Prince of Wales, le betting was the custom at Longchamps, le Derby was held at Chantilly, le steeplechase at Auteuil and an unwanted member was black-boulé at the Jockey Club. Charles Haas, the original of Swann, had 'Mr' engraved on his calling cards."

Even if corroborative detail did not serve a valid historical purpose, its use makes a narrative more graphic and intelligible, more pleasurable to read, in short more readable. It assists communication, and communication is, after all, the major purpose. History written in abstract terms communicates nothing to me. I cannot comprehend the abstract and since a writer tends to create the reader in his own image, I assume my reader cannot comprehend it either. No doubt I underestimate him. Certainly many serious thinkers write in the abstract and many people read them with interest and profit and even, I suppose, pleasure. I respect this ability, but I am unable to emulate it.

My favorite visible detail in *The Guns of August,* for some inexplicable reason, is the one about the Grand Duke Nicholas, who was so tall (six foot six) that when he established headquarters in a railroad car his aide pinned up a fringe of white paper over the doorway to remind him to duck his head. Why this insignificant item, after several years' work and out of all the material crammed into a book of 450 pages, should be the particular one to stick most sharply in my mind I cannot explain, but it is. I was so charmed by the white paper fringe that I constructed a whole paragraph describing Russian headquarters at Baranovici in order to slip it in logically.

In another case the process failed. I had read that the Kaiser's birthday gift to his wife was the same every year: twelve hats selected by himself which she was obliged to wear. There you see the value of corroborative detail in revealing personality; this one is worth a whole book about the Kaiser—or even about Germany. It represents, however, a minor tragedy of *The Guns,* for I never succeeded in working it in at all. I keep my notes on cards, and the card about the hats started out with those for the first chapter. Not having been used, it was moved forward to a likely place in Chapter 2, missed again, and continued on down through all the chapters until it emerged to a final resting place in a packet marked "Unused."

A detail about General Sir Douglas Haig, equally revealing of personality or at any rate of contemporary customs and conditions in the British officer corps, did find a place. This was the fact that during the campaign in the Sudan in the nineties he had "a camel laden with claret" in the personal pack train that followed him across the desert. Besides being a vivid bit of social history, the phrase itself, "a camel laden with claret," is a thing of beauty, a marvel of double and inner alliteration. That, however, brings up another whole subject, the subject of language, which needs an article of its own for adequate discussion.

Having inadvertently reached it, I will only mention that the independent power of words to affect the writing of history is a thing to be watched out for. They have an almost frightening autonomous power to produce in the mind of the reader an image or idea that was not in the mind of the writer. Obviously they operate this way in all forms of writing, but history is particularly sensitive because one has a duty to be accurate, and careless use of words can leave a false impression one had not intended. Fifty percent at least of the critics of *The Guns* commented on what they said was my exposé of the stupidity of the generals. Nothing of the kind was in my mind when I wrote. What I meant to convey was that the generals were in the trap of the circumstances, training, ideas, and national impulses of their time and their individual countries. I was not trying to convey stupidity but tragedy, fatality. Many reviewers understood this, clearly intelligent perceptive persons (those who understand one always are), but too many kept coming up with the word "stupidity" to my increasing dismay.

This power of words to escape from a writer's control is a fascinating problem which, since it was not what I started out to discuss, I can only hint at here. One more hint before I leave it: For me the problem lies in the fact that the art of writing interests me as much as the art of history (and I hope it is not provocative to say that I think of history as an art, not a science). In writing I am seduced by the sound of words and by the interaction of their sound and sense. Recently at the start of a paragraph I wrote, "Then occurred the intervention which irretrievably bent the twig of events." It was intended as a kind of signal to the reader. (Every now and then in a historical narrative, after one has been explaining a rather complicated background, one feels the need of waving a small red flag that says, "Wake up, Reader; something is going to happen.") Unhappily, after finishing the paragraph, I was forced to admit that the incident in question had *not* irretrievably bent the twig of events. Yet I hated to give up such a well-made phrase. Should I leave it in because it was good writing or take it out because it was not good history? History governed and it was lost to posterity (although, you notice, I have rescued it here). Words are seductive and dangerous material, to be used with caution. Am I writer first or am I historian? The old argument starts inside my head. Yet there need not always be dichotomy or dispute. The two functions need not be, in fact should not be, at war. The goal is fusion. In the long run the best writer is the best historian.

In quest of that goal I come back to the ounce. The most effective ounce of visual detail is that which indicates something of character or circumstance in addition to appearance. Careless clothes finished off by drooping white socks corroborate a description of Jean Jaurès as looking like the expected image of a labor leader. To convey both the choleric looks and temper and the cavalry officer's snobbism of Sir John French, it helps to write that he affected a cavalryman's stock in place of collar and tie, which gave him the appearance of being perpetually on the verge of choking.

The best corroborative detail I ever found concerned Lord Shaftes-
bury, the eminent Victorian social reformer, author of the Factory Act and
child-labor laws, who appeared in my first book, *Bible and Sword*. He was
a man, wrote a contemporary, of the purest, palest, stateliest exterior in
Westminster, on whose classic head "every separate dark lock of hair
seemed to curl from a sense of duty." For conveying both appearance and
character of a man and the aura of his times, all in one, that line is
unequaled.

Novelists have the advantage that they can invent corroborative
detail. Wishing to portray, let us say, a melancholy introspective character,
they make up physical qualities to suit. The historian must make do with
what he can find, though he may sometimes point up what he finds by
calling on a familiar image in the mental baggage of the reader. To say that
General Joffre looked like Santa Claus instantly conveys a picture which
struck me as peculiarly apt when I wrote it. I was thinking of Joffre's massive paunch, fleshy face, white mustache, and bland and benevolent
appearance, and I forgot that Santa Claus wears a beard, which Joffre, of
course, did not. Still, the spirit was right. One must take care to choose a
recognizable image for this purpose. In my current book I have a melancholy and introspective character, Lord Salisbury, Prime Minister in 1895,
a supreme, if far from typical, product of the British aristocracy, a heavy
man with a curly beard and big, bald forehead, of whom I wrote that he
was called the Hamlet of English politics and looked like Karl Marx. I
must say that I was really rather pleased with that phrase, but my editor
was merely puzzled. It developed that he did not know what Karl Marx
looked like, so the comparison conveyed no image. If it failed its first test,
it would certainly not succeed with the average reader and so, sadly, I cut
it out.

Sources of corroborative detail must of course be contemporary with
the subject. Besides the usual memoirs, letters, and autobiographies, do
not overlook novelists and newspapers. The inspired bit about the ladies
rising to their feet for General Mercier comes from Proust, as do many
other brilliant details; for instance, that during the Affair ladies had *"A bas
les juifs"* printed on their parasols. Proust is invaluable not only because
there is so much of him but because it is all confined to a narrow segment
of society which he knew personally and intimately; it is like a woman
describing her own living room. On the other hand, another novel set in
the same period, *Jean Barois* by Roger Martin du Gard, considered a major
work of fiction on the Affair, gave me nothing I could use, perhaps
because visual detail—at least the striking and memorable detail—was

missing. It was all talk and ideas, interesting, of course, but for source material I want something I can *see*. When you have read Proust you can see Paris of the nineties, horse cabs and lamplight, the clubman making his calls in white gloves stitched in black and gray top hat lined in green leather.

Perhaps this illustrates the distinction between a major and a less gifted novelist which should hold equally true, I believe, for historians. Ideas alone are not flesh and blood. Too often, scholarly history is written in terms of ideas rather than acts; it tells what people wrote instead of what they performed. To write, say, a history of progressivism in America or of socialism in the era of the Second International by quoting the editorials, books, articles, speeches, and so forth of the leading figures is easy. They were the wordiest people in history. If, however, one checks what they said and wrote against what actually was happening, a rather different picture emerges. At present I am writing a chapter on the Socialists and I feel like someone in a small rowboat under Niagara. To find and hold on to anything hard and factual under their torrent of words is an epic struggle. I suspect the reason is that people out of power always talk more than those who have power. The historian must be careful to guard against this phenomenon—weight it, as the statisticians say—lest his result be unbalanced.

Returning to novels as source material, I should mention *The Edwardians* by V. Sackville-West, which gave me precise and authoritative information on matters on which the writers of memoirs remain discreet. Like Proust, this author was writing of a world she knew. At the great house parties, one learns, the hostess took into consideration established liaisons in assigning the bedrooms and each guest had his name on a card slipped into a small brass frame outside his door. The poets too serve. Referring in this chapter on Edwardian England to the central role of the horse in the life of the British aristocracy, and describing the exhilaration of the hunt, I used a line from a sonnet by Wilfrid Scawen Blunt, "My horse a thing of wings, myself a god." Anatole France supplied, through the mouth of a character in *M. Bergeret,* the words to describe a Frenchman's feeling about the Army at the time of the Affair, that it was "all that is left of our glorious past. It consoles us for the present and gives us hope of the future." Zola expressed the fear of the bourgeoisie for the working class through the manager's wife in *Germinal,* who, watching the march of the striking miners, saw "the red vision of revolution . . . when on some somber evening at the end of the century the people, unbridled at last, would make the blood of the middle class flow." In *The Guns* there is a description of the retreating French Army after the Battle of the Frontiers with their red trousers faded to the color of pale brick, coats ragged and torn, cavernous eyes sunk in unshaven faces, gun carriages with once-new gray paint now blistered and caked with mud. This came from Blasco Ibáñez's novel *The Four Horsemen of the Apocalypse.* From H. G. Wells's *Mr. Britling Sees It Through* I took the feeling in England at the outbreak of war that it contained an "enormous hope" of something better afterward, a chance to end war, a "tremendous opportunity" to remake the world.

I do not know if the professors would allow the use of such sources in a graduate dissertation, but I see no reason why a novelist should not supply as authentic material as a journalist or a general. To determine what may justifiably be used from a novel, one applies the same criterion as for any nonfictional account: If a particular item fits with what one knows of the time, the place, the circumstances, and the people, it is acceptable; otherwise not. For myself, I would rather quote Proust or Sackville-West or Zola than a professional colleague as is the academic habit. I could never see any sense whatever in referring to one's neighbor in the next university as a source. To me that is no source at all; I want to know where a given fact came from originally, not who used it last. As for referring to an earlier book of one's own as a source, this seems to me the ultimate absurdity. I am told that graduate students are required to cite the secondary historians in order to show they are familiar with the literature, but if I were granting degrees I would demand primary familiarity with primary sources. The secondary histories are necessary when one starts out ignorant of a subject and I am greatly in their debt for guidance, suggestion, bibliography, and outline of events, but once they have put me on the path I like to go the rest of the way myself. If I were a teacher I would disqualify anyone who was content to cite a secondary source as his reference for a fact. To trace it back oneself to its origin means to discover all manner of fresh material from which to make one's own selection instead of being content to re-use something already selected by someone else.

Though it is far from novels, I would like to say a special word for *Who's Who.* For one thing, it is likely to be accurate because its entries are written by the subjects themselves. For another, it shows them as they wish to appear and thus often reveals character and even something of the times. H. H. Rogers, a Standard Oil partner and business tycoon of the 1890s, listed himself simply and succinctly as "Capitalist," obviously in his own eyes a proud and desirable thing to be. The social history of a period is contained in that self-description. Who would call himself by that word today?

As to newspapers, I like them for period flavor perhaps more than for factual information. One must be wary in using them for facts, because an event reported one day in a newspaper is usually modified or denied or turns out to be rumor on the next. It is absolutely essential to take nothing from a newspaper without following the story through for several days or until it disappears from the news. For period flavor, however, newspapers are unsurpassed. In the *New York Times* for August 10, 1914, I read an account of the attempt by German officers disguised in British uniforms to kidnap General Leman at Liège. The reporter wrote that the General's staff, "maddened by the dastardly violation of the rules of civilized warfare, spared not but slew."

This sentence had a tremendous effect on me. In it I saw all the difference between the world before 1914 and the world since. No reporter could write like that today, could use the word "dastardly," could take as a matter of course the concept of "civilized warfare," could write unashamedly, "spared not but slew." Today the sentence is embarrassing; in 1914 it reflected how people thought and the values they believed in. It was this sentence that led me back to do a book on the world before the war.

Women are a particularly good source for physical detail. They seem to notice it more than men or at any rate to consider it more worth reporting. The contents of the German soldier's knapsack in 1914, including thread, needles, bandages, matches, chocolate, tobacco, I found in the memoirs of an American woman living in Germany. The Russian moose who wandered over the frontier to be shot by the Kaiser at Rominten came from a book by the English woman who was governess to the Kaiser's daughter. Lady Warwick, mistress for a time of the Prince of Wales until she regrettably espoused socialism, is indispensable for Edwardian society, less for gossip than for habits and behavior. Princess Daisy of Pless prattles endlessly about the endless social rounds of the nobility, but every now and then supplies a dazzling nugget of information. One, which I used in *The Zimmermann Telegram,* was her description of how the Kaiser complained to her at dinner of the ill-treatment he had received over the *Daily Telegraph* affair and of how, in the excess of his emotion, "a tear fell on his cigar." In the memoirs of Edith O'Shaughnessy, wife of the First Secretary of the American Embassy in Mexico, is the description of the German Ambassador, von Hintze, who dressed and behaved in all things like an Englishman except that he wore a large sapphire ring on his little finger which gave him away. No man would have remarked on that.

In the end, of course, the best place to find corroborative detail is on the spot itself, if it can be visited, as Herodotus did in Asia Minor or Parkman on the Oregon Trail. Take the question of German atrocities in 1914. Nothing requires more careful handling because, owing to post-war disillusions, "atrocity" came to be a word one did not believe in. It was supposed because the Germans had not, after all, cut off the hands of Belgian babies, neither had they shot hostages nor burned Louvain. The results of this disbelief were dangerous because when the Germans became Nazis people were disinclined to believe they were as bad as they seemed and appeasement became the order of the day. (It strikes me that here is a place to put history to use and that a certain wariness might be in order today.) In writing of German terrorism in Belgium in 1914 I was at pains to use only accounts by Germans themselves or in a few cases by Americans, then neutral. The most telling evidence, however, was that which I saw forty-five years later: the rows of gravestones in the churchyard of a little Belgian village on the Meuse, each inscribed with a name and a date and the legend *"fusillé par les Allemands."* Or the stone marker on the road outside Senlis, twenty-five miles from Paris, engraved with the date September 2, 1914, and the names of the mayor and six other civilian hostages shot by the Germans. Somehow the occupations engraved opposite the names—baker's apprentice, stonemason, *garçon de café*—carried extra conviction. This is the verisimilitude Pooh-Bah and I too have been trying for.

The desire to find the significant detail plus the readiness to open his mind to it and let it report to him are half the historian's equipment. The other half, concerned with idea, point of view, the reason for writing, the "Why" of history, has been left out of this discussion although I am not unconscious that it looms in the background. The art of writing is the third half. If that list does not add up, it is because history is human behavior, not arithmetic.

CONSIDERATIONS

Thinking

Why does Tuchman object to generalizations without corroborating, supporting, or illustrative details? What, according to Tuchman, is the value of using specific details in historical writing?

What types of sources does Tuchman value most? Why?

Connecting

Relate what Tuchman says about details to what Stephen Jay Gould says in "Women's Brains" about science being more than "a catalog of facts."

Consider what Tuchman says about the value of corroborating detail for your own writing—course papers, reports, essays in the various disciplines. How necessary is it for you to use detail in your academic writing?

How can you prevent your writing from becoming simply a catalog or accumulation of details?

Writing

Look back over one or two papers you have written for your courses. Identify places where you could have, perhaps should have, supplied corroborating details. Supply them.

Use Tuchman's approach to historical writing to assess the historical writing of Guy Davenport in "The Geography of the Imagination."

A lice Walker (b.1944)

A lice Walker has written poetry, fiction, and essays. Her novel *The Color Purple*, which won both a Pulitzer Prize and an American Book Award, was made into a feature film. Her essays and speeches have been collected in two volumes—*Living by the Word* (1988) and *In Search of Our Mothers' Gardens* (1983), from which the following selection has been taken.

In "Beauty: When the Other Dancer Is the Self," Walker describes a childhood incident that left her blind in one eye. The essay is remarkable for the images Walker uses to convey the complexity of her feelings and the richness of her experience. The essay is also noteworthy for its handling of the passage of time and for the way Walker dramatizes the immediacy of her experience.

Beauty:
When the Other Dancer
Is the Self

It is a bright summer day in 1947. My father, a fat, funny man with beautiful eyes and a subversive wit, is trying to decide which of his eight children he will take with him to the county fair. My mother, of course, will not go. She is knocked out from getting most of us ready: I hold my neck stiff against the pressure of her knuckles as she hastily completes the braiding and the beribboning of my hair.

My father is the driver for the rich old white lady up the road. Her name is Miss Mey. She owns all the land for miles around, as well as the house in which we live. All I remember about her is that she once offered to pay my mother thirty-five cents for cleaning her house, raking up piles of her magnolia leaves, and washing her family's clothes, and that my mother—she of no money, eight children, and a chronic earache—refused it. But I do not think of this in 1947. I am two-and-a-half years old. I want to go everywhere my daddy goes. I am excited at the prospect of riding in a car. Someone has told me fairs are fun. That there is room in the car for only three of us doesn't faze me at all. Whirling happily in my starchy frock, showing off my biscuit-polished patent-leather shoes and lavender socks, tossing my head in a way that makes my ribbons bounce, I stand, hands on hips, before my father. "Take me, Daddy," I say with assurance; "I'm the prettiest!"

Later, it does not surprise me to find myself in Miss Mey's shiny black car, sharing the back seat with the other lucky ones. Does not surprise me that I thoroughly enjoy the fair. At home that night I tell the unlucky ones all I can remember about the merry-go-round, the man who eats live chickens, and the teddy bears, until they say: that's enough, baby Alice. Shut up now, and go to sleep.

It is Easter Sunday, 1950. I am dressed in a green, flocked, scalloped-hem dress (handmade by my adoring sister, Ruth) that has its own smooth satin petticoat and tiny hot-pink roses tucked into each scallop.

My shoes, new T-strap patent leather, again highly biscuit-polished. I am six years old and have learned one of the longest Easter speeches to be heard that day, totally unlike the speech I said when I was two: "Easter lilies/pure and white/blossom in/the morning light." When I rise to give my speech I do so on a great wave of love and pride and expectation. People in the church stop rustling their new crinolines. They seem to hold their breath. I can tell they admire my dress, but it is my spirit, bordering on sassiness (womanishness), they secretly applaud.

"That girl's a little *mess*," they whisper to each other, pleased.

Naturally I say my speech without stammer or pause, unlike those who stutter, stammer, or, worst of all, forget. This is before the word "beautiful" exists in people's vocabulary, but "Oh, isn't she the *cutest* thing!" frequently floats my way. "And got so much sense!" they gratefully add . . . for which thoughtful addition I thank them to this day.

It was great fun being cute. But then, one day, it ended.

I am eight years old and a tomboy. I have a cowboy hat, cowboy boots, checkered shirt and pants, all red. My playmates are my brothers, two and four years older than I. Their colors are black and green, the only difference in the way we are dressed. On Saturday nights we all go to the picture show, even my mother; Westerns are her favorite kind of movie. Back home, "on the ranch," we pretend we are Tom Mix, Hopalong Cassidy, Lash LaRue (we've even named one of our dogs Lash LaRue); we chase each other for hours rustling cattle, being outlaws, delivering damsels from distress. Then my parents decide to buy my brothers guns. These are not "real" guns. They shoot BBs, copper pellets my brothers say will kill birds. Because I am a girl, I do not get a gun. Instantly I am relegated to the position of Indian. Now there appears a great distance between us. They shoot and shoot at everything with their new guns. I try to keep up with my bow and arrows.

One day while I am standing on top of our makeshift "garage"— pieces of tin nailed across some poles—holding my bow and arrow and looking out toward the fields, I feel an incredible blow in my right eye. I look down just in time to see my brother lower his gun.

Both brothers rush to my side. My eye stings, and I cover it with my hand. "If you tell," they say, "we will get a whipping. You don't want that to happen, do you?" I do not. "Here is a piece of wire," says the older brother, picking it up from the roof; "say you stepped on one end of it and the other flew up and hit you." The pain is beginning to start. "Yes," I say. "Yes, I will say that is what happened." If I do not say this is what happened, I know my brothers will find ways to make me wish I had. But now I will say anything that gets me to my mother.

Confronted by our parents we stick to the lie agreed upon. They place me on a bench on the porch and I close my left eye while they examine the right. There is a tree growing from underneath the porch that climbs past the railing to the roof. It is the last thing my right eye sees. I watch as its trunk, its branches, and then its leaves are blotted out by the rising blood.

I am in shock. First there is intense fever, which my father tries to break using lily leaves bound around my head. Then there are chills: my mother tries to get me to eat soup. Eventually, I do not know how, my parents learn what has happened. A week after the "accident" they take me to see a doctor. "Why did you wait so long to come?" he asks, looking into my eye and shaking his head. "Eyes are sympathetic," he says. "If one is blind, the other will likely become blind too."

This comment of the doctor's terrifies me. But it is really how I look that bothers me most. Where the BB pellet struck there is a glob of whitish scar tissue, a hideous cataract, on my eye. Now when I stare at people—a favorite pastime, up to now—they will stare back. Not at the "cute" little girl, but at her scar. For six years I do not stare at anyone, because I do not raise my head.

Years later, in the throes of a mid-life crisis, I ask my mother and sister whether I changed after the "accident." "No," they say, puzzled. "What do you mean?"

What do I mean?

I am eight, and, for the first time, doing poorly in school, where I have been something of a whiz since I was four. We have just moved to the place where the "accident" occurred. We do not know any of the people around us because this is a different county. The only time I see the friends I knew is when we go back to our old church. The new school is the former state penitentiary. It is a large stone building, cold and drafty, crammed to overflowing with boisterous, ill-disciplined children. On the third floor there is a huge circular imprint of some partition that has been torn out.

"What used to be here?" I ask a sullen girl next to me on our way past it to lunch.

"The electric chair," says she.

At night I have nightmares about the electric chair, and about all the people reputedly "fried" in it. I am afraid of the school, where all the students seem to be budding criminals.

"What's the matter with your eye?" they ask, critically.

When I don't answer (I cannot decide whether it was an "accident" or not), they shove me, insist on a fight.

My brother, the one who created the story about the wire, comes to my rescue. But then brags so much about "protecting" me, I become sick.

After months of torture at the school, my parents decide to send me back to our old community, to my old school. I live with my grandparents and the teacher they board. But there is no room for Phoebe, my cat. By the time my grandparents decide there is room, and I ask for my cat, she cannot be found. Miss Yarborough, the boarding teacher, takes me under her wing, and begins to teach me to play the piano. But soon she marries an African—a "prince," she says—and is whisked away to his continent.

At my old school there is at least one teacher who loves me. She is the teacher who "knew me before I was born" and bought my first baby clothes. It is she who makes life bearable. It is her presence that finally helps me turn on the one child at the school who continually calls me "one-eyed bitch." One day I simply grab him by his coat and beat him until I am satisfied. It is my teacher who tells me my mother is ill.

My mother is lying in bed in the middle of the day, something I have never seen. She is in too much pain to speak. She has an abscess in her ear. I stand looking down on her, knowing that if she dies, I cannot live. She is being treated with warm oils and hot bricks held against her cheek. Finally a doctor comes. But I must go back to my grandparents' house. The weeks pass but I am hardly aware of it. All I know is that my mother might die, my father is not so jolly, my brothers still have their guns, and I am the one sent away from home.

"You did not change," they say.

Did I imagine the anguish of never looking up?

I am twelve. When relatives come to visit I hide in my room. My cousin Brenda, just my age, whose father works in the post office and whose mother is a nurse, comes to find me. "Hello," she says. And then she asks, looking at my recent school picture, which I did not want taken, and on which the "glob," as I think of it, is clearly visible, "You still can't see out of that eye?"

"No," I say, and flop back on the bed over my book.

That night, as I do almost every night, I abuse my eye. I rant and rave at it, in front of the mirror. I plead with it to clear up before morning. I tell it I hate and despise it. I do not pray for sight. I pray for beauty.

"You did not change," they say.

I am fourteen and baby-sitting for my brother Bill, who lives in Boston. He is my favorite brother and there is a strong bond between us. Understanding my feelings of shame and ugliness he and his wife take me to a local hospital, where the "glob" is removed by a doctor named O. Henry. There is still a small bluish crater where the scar tissue was, but the ugly white stuff is gone. Almost immediately I become a different person from the girl who does not raise her head. Or so I think. Now that I've raised my head I win the boyfriend of my dreams. Now that I've raised my head I have plenty of friends. Now that I've raised my head classwork comes from my lips as faultlessly as Easter speeches did, and I leave high school as valedictorian, most popular student, and *queen*, hardly believing my luck. Ironically, the girl who was voted most beautiful in our class (and was) was later shot twice through the chest by a male companion, using a "real" gun, while she was pregnant. But that's another story in itself. Or is it?

"You did not change," they say.

It is now thirty years since the "accident." A beautiful journalist comes to visit and to interview me. She is going to write a cover story for her magazine that focuses on my latest book. "Decide how you want to look on the cover," she says. "Glamorous, or whatever."

Never mind "glamorous," it is the "whatever" that I hear. Suddenly all I can think of is whether I will get enough sleep the night before the photography session: If I don't, my eye will be tired and wander, as blind eyes will.

At night in bed with my lover I think up reasons why I should not appear on the cover of a magazine. "My meanest critics will say I've sold out," I say. "My family will now realize I write scandalous books."

"But what's the real reason you don't want to do this?" he asks.

"Because in all probability," I say in a rush, "my eye won't be straight."

"It will be straight enough," he says. Then, "Besides, I thought you'd made your peace with that."

And I suddenly remember that I have.

I remember:

I am talking to my brother Jimmy, asking if he remembers anything unusual about the day I was shot. He does not know I consider that day the last time my father, with his sweet home remedy of cool lily leaves, chose me, and that I suffered and raged inside because of this. "Well," he says, "all I remember is standing by the side of the highway with Daddy, trying to flag down a car. A white man stopped, but when Daddy said he needed somebody to take his little girl to the doctor, he drove off."

I remember:

I am in the desert for the first time. I fall totally in love with it. I am so overwhelmed by its beauty, I confront for the first time, consciously, the meaning of the doctor's words years ago: "Eyes are sympathetic. If one is blind, the other will likely become blind too." I realize I have dashed about the world madly, looking at this, looking at that, storing up images against the fading of the light. *But I might have missed seeing the desert!* The shock of that possibility—and gratitude for over twenty-five years of sight—sends me literally to my knees. Poem after poem comes—which is perhaps how poets pray.

On Sight

I am so thankful I have seen
The Desert
And the creatures in the desert
And the desert Itself.

The desert has its own moon
Which I have seen
With my own eye.
There is no flag on it.

Trees of the desert have arms
All of which are always up
That is because the moon is up
The sun is up
Also the sky
The Stars
Clouds
None with flags.

If there were flags, I doubt
the trees would point.
Would you?

But mostly, I remember this:

I am twenty-seven, and my baby daughter is almost three. Since her birth I have worried about her discovery that her mother's eyes are different from other people's. Will she be embarrassed? I think. What will she say? Every day she watches a television program called *Big Blue Marble*. It begins with a picture of the earth as it appears from the moon. It is bluish, a little battered-looking, but full of light, with whitish clouds swirling around it. Every time I see it I weep with love, as if it is a picture of Grandma's house. One day when I am putting Rebecca down for her nap, she suddenly focuses on my eye. Something inside me cringes, gets ready to try to protect myself. All children are cruel about physical differences, I know from experience, and that they don't always mean to be is another matter. I assume Rebecca will be the same.

But no-o-o-o She studies my face intently as we stand, her inside and me outside her crib. She even holds my face maternally between her dimpled little hands. Then, looking every bit as serious and lawyerlike as her father, she says, as if it may just possibly have slipped my attention: "Mommy, there's a *world* in your eye." (As in, "Don't be alarmed, or do anything crazy.") And then, gently, but with great interest: "Mommy, where did you *get* that world in your eye?"

For the most part, the pain left then. (So what, if my brothers grew up to buy even more powerful pellet guns for their sons and to carry real guns themselves. So what, if a young "Morehouse man" once nearly fell off the steps of Trevor Arnett Library because he thought my eyes were blue.) Crying and laughing I ran to the bathroom, while Rebecca mumbled and sang herself to sleep. Yes indeed, I realized, looking into the mirror. There *was* a world in my eye. And I saw that it was possible to love it: that in fact, for all it had taught me of shame and anger and inner vision, I *did* love it. Even to see it drifting out of orbit in boredom, or rolling up out of fatigue, not to mention floating back at attention in excitement (bearing witness, a friend has called it), deeply suitable to my personality, and even characteristic of me.

That night I dream I am dancing to Stevie Wonder's song "Always" (the name of the song is really "As," but I hear it as "Always"). As I dance, whirling and joyous, happier than I've ever been in my life, another bright-faced dancer joins me. We dance and kiss each other and hold each other through the night. The other dancer has obviously come through all right, as I have done. She is beautiful, whole, and free. And she is also me.

CONSIDERATIONS

Thinking

Consider the extent to which Walker's injury affected her self-image. How important is it that Walker's injury was facial? Why?

Why does Walker's attitude toward her old injury and its consequences change? Explain what Walker learns during her trip to the desert and as a result of her daughter's observation, "Mommy, there's a *world* in your eye."

Connecting

Relate Walker's presentation of her self as a young girl with her self-presentation as a young woman.

Consider the extent to which Walker's essay illustrates familiar conventional attitudes about women's beauty.

Writing

Describe a time when an accident or other turn of events damaged your self-image, made you feel insecure or unhappy with yourself. Explain how you came to terms with your situation and what the consequences for your later life have been—or might yet be.

Analyze Walker's use of imagery to convey the meaning and feeling of her experience.

Compare Walker's description of her injury and response to it with Leonard Kriegel's in "Falling into Life."

C ornel West
(b.1953)

C ornel West grew up in Tulsa, Oklahoma. He graduated from Harvard and Princeton Universities and taught at Union Theological Seminary and the Yale University Divinity School. He has also taught at Harvard and the University of Paris and is presently director of the Afro-American studies department at Princeton.

His many books include *Breaking Bread: Insurgent Black Intellectual Life* (1991) and *Race Matters* (1993), for which the following essay serves as an introduction. West urges his readers to understand the causes of racism and appeals to their sense of justice and wisdom to resolve the hitherto intractable problems that could destroy American society. His tone is measured and his language carefully balanced to avoid excessive passion.

Race Matters

Since the beginning of the nation, white Americans have suffered from a deep inner uncertainty as to who they really are. One of the ways that has been used to simplify the answer has been to seize upon the presence of black Americans and use them as a marker, a symbol of limits, a metaphor for the "outsider." Many whites could look at the social position of blacks and feel that color formed an easy and reliable gauge for determining to what extent one was or was not American. Perhaps that is why one of the first epithets that many European immigrants learned when they got off the boat was the term "nigger"—it made them feel instantly American. But this is tricky magic. Despite his racial difference and social status, something indisputably American about Negroes not only raised doubts about the white man's value system but aroused the troubling suspicion that whatever else the true American is, he is also somehow black.

RALPH ELLISON
"What America Would Be Like without Blacks" (1970)

What happened in Los Angeles in April of 1992 was neither a race riot nor a class rebellion. Rather, this monumental upheaval was a multiracial, trans-class, and largely male display of justified social rage. For all its ugly, xenophobic resentment, its air of adolescent carnival, and its downright barbaric behavior, it signified the sense of powerlessness in American society. Glib attempts to reduce its meaning to the pathologies of the black underclass, the criminal actions of hoodlums, or the political revolt of the oppressed urban masses miss the mark. Of those arrested, only 36 percent were black, more than a third had full-time jobs, and most claimed to shun political affiliation. What we witnessed in Los Angeles was the consequence of a lethal linkage of economic decline, cultural decay, and political lethargy in American life. Race was the visible catalyst, not the underlying cause.

670

The meaning of the earthshaking events in Los Angeles is difficult to grasp because most of us remain trapped in the narrow framework of the dominant liberal and conservative views of race in America, which with its worn-out vocabulary leaves us intellectually debilitated, morally disempowered, and personally depressed. The astonishing disappearance of the event from public dialogue is testimony to just how painful and distressing a serious engagement with race is. Our truncated public discussions of race suppress the best of who and what we are as a people because they fail to confront the complexity of the issue in a candid and critical manner. The predictable pitting of liberals against conservatives, Great Society Democrats against self-help Republicans, reinforces intellectual parochialism and political paralysis.

The liberal notion that more government programs can solve racial problems is simplistic—precisely because it focuses *solely* on the economic dimension. And the conservative idea that what is needed is a change in the moral behavior of poor black urban dwellers (especially poor black men, who, they say, should stay married, support their children, and stop committing so much crime) highlights immoral actions while ignoring public responsibility for the immoral circumstances that haunt our fellow citizens.

The common denominator of these views of race is that each still sees black people as a "problem people," in the words of Dorothy I. Height, president of the National Council of Negro Women, rather than as fellow American citizens with problems. Her words echo the poignant "unasked question" of W. E. B. Du Bois, who, in *The Souls of Black Folk* (1903), wrote:

> They approach me in a half-hesitant sort of way, eye me curiously or compassionately, and then instead of saying directly, How does it feel to be a problem? they say, I know an excellent colored man in my town. . . . Do not these Southern outrages make your blood boil? At these I smile, or am interested, or reduce the boiling to a simmer, as the occasion may require. To the real question, How does it feel to be a problem? I answer seldom a word.

Nearly a century later, we confine discussions about race in America to the "problems" black people pose for whites rather than consider what this way of viewing black people reveals about us as a nation.

This paralyzing framework encourages liberals to relieve their guilty consciences by supporting public funds directed at "the problems"; but at the same time, reluctant to exercise principled criticism of black people, liberals deny them the freedom to err. Similarly, conservatives blame the "problems" on black people themselves—and thereby render black social misery invisible or unworthy of public attention.

Hence, for liberals, black people are to be "included" and "integrated" into "our" society and culture, while for conservatives they are to be "well behaved" and "worthy of acceptance" by "our" way of life. Both fail to see that the presence and predicaments of black people are neither additions to nor defections from American life, but rather *constitutive elements of that life*.

To engage in a serious discussion of race in America, we must begin not with the problems of black people but with the flaws of American society—flaws rooted in historic inequalities and longstanding cultural stereotypes. How we set up the terms for discussing racial issues shapes our perception and response to these issues. As long as black people are viewed as a "them," the burden falls on blacks to do all the "cultural" and "moral" work necessary for healthy race relations. The implication is that only certain Americans can define what it means to be American—and the rest must simply "fit in."

The emergence of strong black-nationalist sentiments among blacks, especially among young people, is a revolt against this sense of having to "fit in." The variety of black-nationalist ideologies, from the moderate views of Supreme Court Justice Clarence Thomas in his youth to those of Louis Farrakhan today, rest upon a fundamental truth: White America has been historically weak-willed in ensuring racial justice and has continued to resist fully accepting the humanity of blacks. As long as double standards and differential treatment abound—as long as the rap performer Ice-T is harshly condemned while former Los Angeles Police Chief Daryl F. Gates's antiblack comments are received in polite silence, as long as Dr. Leonard Jeffries's anti-Semitic statements are met with vitriolic outrage while presidential candidate Patrick J. Buchanan's anti-Semitism receives a genteel response—black nationalisms will thrive.

Afrocentrism, a contemporary species of black nationalism, is a gallant yet misguided attempt to define an African identity in a white society perceived to be hostile. It is gallant because it puts black doings and sufferings, not white anxieties and fears, at the center of discussion. It is misguided because—out of fear of cultural hybridization and through silence on the issue of class, retrograde views on black women, gay men, and lesbians, and a reluctance to link race to the common good—it reinforces the narrow discussions about race.

To establish a new framework, we need to begin with a frank acknowledgment of the basic humanness and Americanness of each of us. And we must acknowledge that as a people—*E Pluribus Unum*—we are on a slippery slope toward economic strife, social turmoil, and cultural chaos. If we go down, we go down together. The Los Angeles upheaval forced us to see not only that we are not connected in ways we would like to be but also, in a more profound sense, that this failure to connect binds us even more tightly together. The paradox of race in America is that our common destiny is more pronounced and imperiled precisely when our divisions are deeper. The Civil War and its legacy speak loudly here. And our divisions are growing deeper. Today, eighty-six percent of white suburban Americans live in neighborhoods that are less than one percent black, meaning that the prospects for the country depend largely on how its cities fare in the hands of a suburban electorate. There is no escape from our interracial interdependence, yet enforced racial hierarchy dooms us as a nation to collective paranoia and hysteria—the unmaking of any democratic order.

The verdict in the Rodney King case which sparked the incidents in Los Angeles was perceived to be wrong by the vast majority of Americans. But whites have often failed to acknowledge the widespread mistreatment of black people, especially black men, by law enforcement agencies, which helped ignite the spark. The verdict was merely the occasion for deep-seated rage to come to the surface. This rage is fed by the "silent" depression ravaging the country—in which real weekly wages of all American workers since 1973 have declined nearly twenty percent, while at the same time wealth has been upwardly distributed.

The exodus of stable industrial jobs from urban centers to cheaper labor markets here and abroad, housing policies that have created "chocolate cities and vanilla suburbs" (to use the popular musical artist George Clinton's memorable phrase), white fear of black crime, and the urban influx of poor Spanish-speaking and Asian immigrants—all have helped erode the tax base of American cities just as the federal government has cut its supports and programs. The result is unemployment, hunger, homelessness, and sickness for millions.

And a pervasive spiritual impoverishment grows. The collapse of meaning in life—the eclipse of hope and absence of love of self and others, the breakdown of family and neighborhood bonds—leads to the social deracination and cultural denudement of urban dwellers, especially children. We have created rootless, dangling people with little link to the supportive networks—family, friends, school—that sustain some sense of

purpose in life. We have witnessed the collapse of the spiritual communities that in the past helped Americans face despair, disease, and death and
that transmit through the generations dignity and decency, excellence and
elegance.

The result is lives of what we might call "random nows," of fortuitous
and fleeting moments preoccupied with "getting over"—with acquiring
pleasure, property, and power by any means necessary. (This is not what
Malcolm X meant by this famous phrase.) Post-modern culture is more
and more a market culture dominated by gangster mentalities and self-
destructive wantonness. This culture engulfs all of us—yet its impact on
the disadvantaged is devastating, resulting in extreme violence in everyday life. Sexual violence against women and homicidal assaults by young
black men on one another are only the most obvious signs of this empty
quest for pleasure, property, and power.

Last, this rage is fueled by a political atmosphere in which images,
not ideas, dominate, where politicians spend more time raising money
than debating issues. The functions of parties have been displaced by
public polls, and politicians behave less as thermostats that determine the
climate of opinion than as thermometers registering the public mood.
American politics has been rocked by an unleashing of greed among
opportunistic public officials—who have followed the lead of their counterparts in the private sphere, where, as of 1989, one percent of the population owned thirty-seven percent of the wealth and ten percent of the
population owned eighty-six percent of the wealth—leading to a profound cynicism and pessimism among the citizenry.

And given the way in which the Republican Party since 1968 has
appealed to popular xenophobic images—playing the black, female, and
homophobic cards to realign the electorate along race, sex, and sexual-
orientation lines—it is no surprise that the notion that we are all part of
one garment of destiny is discredited. Appeals to special interests rather
than to public interests reinforce this polarization. The Los Angeles
upheaval was an expression of utter fragmentation by a powerless citizenry that includes not just the poor but all of us.

What is to be done? How do we capture a new spirit and vision to
meet the challenges of the post-industrial city, post-modern culture, and
post-party politics?

First, we must admit that the most valuable sources for help, hope,
and power consist of ourselves and our common history. As in the ages of

Lincoln, Roosevelt, and King, we must look to new frameworks and languages to understand our multilayered crisis and overcome our deep malaise.

Second, we must focus our attention on the public square—the common good that undergirds our national and global destinies. The vitality of any public square ultimately depends on how much we *care* about the quality of our lives together. The neglect of our public infrastructure, for example—our water and sewage systems, bridges, tunnels, highways, subways, and streets—reflects not only our myopic economic policies, which impede productivity, but also the low priority we place on our common life.

The tragic plight of our children clearly reveals our deep disregard for public well-being. About one out of every five children in this country lives in poverty, including one out of every two black children and two out of every five Hispanic children. Most of our children—neglected by overburdened parents and bombarded by the market values of profit-hungry corporations—are ill-equipped to live lives of spiritual and cultural quality. Faced with these facts, how do we expect ever to constitute a vibrant society?

One essential step is some form of large-scale public intervention to ensure access to basic social goods—housing, food, health care, education, child care, and jobs. We must invigorate the common good with a mixture of government, business, and labor that does not follow any existing blueprint. After a period in which the private sphere has been sacralized and the public square gutted, the temptation is to make a fetish of the public square. We need to resist such dogmatic swings.

Last, the major challenge is to meet the need to generate new leadership. The paucity of courageous leaders—so apparent in the response to the events in Los Angeles—requires that we look beyond the same elites and voices that recycle the older frameworks. We need leaders—neither saints nor sparkling television personalities—who can situate themselves within a larger historical narrative of this country and our world, who can grasp the complex dynamics of our peoplehood and imagine a future grounded in the best of our past, yet who are attuned to the frightening obstacles that now perplex us. Our ideals of freedom, democracy, and equality must be invoked to invigorate all of us, especially the landless, propertyless, and luckless. Only a visionary leadership that can motivate "the better angels of our nature," as Lincoln said, and activate possibilities for a freer, more efficient, and stable America—only that leadership deserves cultivation and support.

This new leadership must be grounded in grass-roots organizing that highlights democratic accountability. Whoever *our* leaders will be as we approach the twenty-first century, their challenge will be to help Americans determine whether a genuine multiracial democracy can be created and sustained in an era of global economy and a moment of xenophobic frenzy.

Let us hope and pray that the vast intelligence, imagination, humor, and courage of Americans will not fail us. Either we learn a new language of empathy and compassion, or the fire this time will consume us all.

CONSIDERATIONS

Thinking

What, according to West, is "the paradox of race in America"? What does he believe is required for the problems of racial tension to be resolved? Has he omitted anything of importance? What cultural values animate his argument?

Connecting

West begins by referring to the Los Angeles riots of April 1992. How did you respond to learning about those riots in the media? Why?

Compare the argument West makes here—especially what he says about the inadequacies of liberal and conservative positions—with the argument Martin Luther King, Jr., makes in "Letter from Birmingham Jail."

Writing

Write an essay in which you explore your own thoughts and feelings about race in America. You may wish to tell a personal story (or more than one). You may prefer to refer to events such as the Los Angeles riots, civil rights marches or demonstrations of an earlier time, or some other significant public events.

Compare what West says about race in America with what Ralph Ellison suggests about racial difference in the epigraph to West's essay.

T om Wolfe (b.1931)

om Wolfe began his career as an academic, earning a doctorate in American studies at Yale. But his inclination was more journalistic than academic, and he began working as a reporter for *The Washington Post* and later as a magazine writer for the now defunct *New York Herald-Tribune*.

Wolfe has written articles and essays on trends in popular culture, many of them later collected in books such as *The Kandy-Kolored Tangerine-Flake Streamline Baby* (1965), *The Pump House Gang* (1968), and *Mauve Gloves and Madmen, Clutter and Vine* (1976). His book about the space program, *The Right Stuff* (1979), was made into a movie, as was his only novel, *Bonfire of the Vanities* (1988).

In the following chapter from *The Right Stuff*, Wolfe describes the qualities men require to become successful test pilots and astronauts. He describes the community of men who strive to join an even more special fraternity—those with "the right stuff" for success. The selection demonstrates Wolfe's stylistic daring, his verbal pyrotechnics and high jinks.

The Right Stuff

A young man might go into military flight training believing that he was entering some sort of technical school in which he was simply going to acquire a certain set of skills. Instead, he found himself all at once enclosed in a fraternity. And in this fraternity, even though it was military, men were not rated by their outward rank as ensigns, lieutenants, commanders, or whatever. No, herein the world was divided into those who had it and those who did not. This quality, this *it*, was never named, however, nor was it talked about in any way.

As to just what this ineffable quality was . . . well, it obviously involved bravery. But it was not bravery in the simple sense of being willing to risk your life. The idea seemed to be that any fool could do that, if that was all that was required, just as any fool could throw away his life in the process. No, the idea here (in the all-enclosing fraternity) seemed to be that a man should have the ability to go up in a hurtling piece of machinery and put his hide on the line and then have the moxie, the reflexes, the experience, the coolness, to pull it back in the last yawning moment—and then to go up again *the next day,* and the next day, and every next day, even if the series should prove infinite—and, ultimately, in its best expression, do so in a cause that means something to thousands, to a people, a nation, to humanity, to God. Nor was there *a test* to show whether or not a pilot had this righteous quality. There was, instead, a seemingly infinite series of tests. A career in flying was like climbing one of those ancient Babylonian pyramids made up of a dizzy progression of steps and ledges, a ziggurat, a pyramid extraordinarily high and steep; and the idea was to prove at every foot of the way up that pyramid that you were one of the elected and anointed ones who had *the right stuff* and could move higher and higher and even—ultimately, God willing, one day—that you might be able to join that special few at the very top, that elite who had the capacity to bring tears to men's eyes, the very Brotherhood of the Right Stuff itself.

None of this was to be mentioned, and yet it was acted out in a way that a young man could not fail to understand. When a new flight (i.e., a class) of trainees arrived at Pensacola, they were brought into an auditorium for a little lecture. An officer would tell them: "Take a look at the man on either side of you." Quite a few actually swiveled their heads this way and that, in the interest of appearing diligent. Then the officer would say: "One of the three of you is not going to make it!"—meaning, not get his wings. That was the opening theme, the *motif* of primary training. We already know that one-third of you do not have the right stuff—it only remains to find out who.

Furthermore, that was the way it turned out. At every level in one's progress up that staggeringly high pyramid, the world was once more divided into those men who had the right stuff to continue the climb and those who had to be *left behind* in the most obvious way. Some were eliminated in the course of the opening classroom work, as either not smart enough or not hardworking enough, and were left behind. Then came the basic flight instruction in single-engine, propeller-driven trainers, and a few more—even though the military tried to make this stage easy—were washed out and left behind. Then came more demanding levels, one after the other, formation flying, instrument flying, jet training, all-weather flying, gunnery, and at each level more were washed out and left behind. By this point easily a third of the original candidates had been, indeed, eliminated . . . from the ranks of those who might prove to have the right stuff.

In the Navy, in addition to the stages that Air Force trainees went through, the neophyte always had waiting for him, out in the ocean, a certain grim gray slab; namely, the deck of an aircraft carrier; and with it perhaps the most difficult routine in military flying, carrier landings. He was shown films about it, he heard lectures about it, and he knew that carrier landings were hazardous. He first practiced touching down on the shape of a flight deck painted on an airfield. He was instructed to touch down and gun right off. This was safe enough—the shape didn't move, at least—but it could do terrible things to, let us say, the gyroscope of the soul. *That shape!—it's so damned small!* And more candidates were washed out and left behind. Then came the day, without warning, when those who remained were sent out over the ocean for the first of many days of reckoning with the slab. The first day was always a clear day with little wind and a calm sea. The carrier was so steady that it seemed, from up there in the air, to be resting on pilings, and the candidate usually made his first carrier landing successfully, with relief and even *élan.* Many young candidates looked like terrific aviators up to that very point—and it was not until they were actually standing on the carrier deck that they first began to wonder if they had the proper stuff, after all. In the training film the flight deck was a grand piece of gray geometry, perilous, to be sure, but an amazing abstract shape as one looks down upon it on the screen. And yet once the newcomer's two feet were on it . . . *Geometry*—my God, man, this is a . . . skillet! It *heaved,* it moved up and down underneath his feet, it pitched up, it pitched down, it rolled to port (this great beast *rolled!*) and it rolled to starboard, as the ship moved into the wind and, therefore, into the waves, and the wind kept sweeping across, sixty feet up in the air out in the open sea, and there were no railings whatsoever. This was a *skillet!*—a frying pan!—a short-order grill!—not gray but black, smeared with skid marks from one end to the other and glistening with pools of hydraulic fluid and the occasional jet-fuel slick, all of it still hot, sticky, greasy, runny, virulent from God knows what traumas—still ablaze!—consumed in detonations, explosions, flames, combustion, roars, shrieks, whines, blasts, horrible shudders, fracturing impacts, as little men in screaming red and yellow and purple and green shirts with black Mickey Mouse helmets over their ears skittered about on the surface as if for their very lives (you've said it now!), hooking fighter planes onto the catapult shuttles so that they can explode their afterburners and be slung off the deck in a red-mad fury with a *kaboom!* that pounds through the entire deck—a procedure that seems absolutely controlled, orderly, sublime, however, compared to what he is about to watch as aircraft return to the ship for what is known in the engineering stoicisms of the military as "recovery and arrest." To say that an F–4 was coming back onto this heaving barbecue from out of the sky at a speed of 135 knots . . . that might have been the truth in the training lecture, but it did not begin to get across the idea of what the newcomer saw from the deck itself, because it created the notion that perhaps the plane was gliding in. On the deck one knew differently! As the aircraft came closer and the carrier heaved on into the waves and the plane's speed did not diminish and the deck did not grow steady—indeed, it pitched up and down five or ten feet per greasy heave—one experienced a neural alarm that no lecture could have prepared him for: This is not an *airplane* coming toward me, it is a brick with some poor sonofabitch riding it (*someone much like myself!*), and it is not *gliding,* it is *falling,* a thirty-thousand-pound brick, headed not for a stripe on the deck but for *me*—and with a horrible *smash!* it hits the skillet, and with a blur of momentum as big as a freight train's it hurtles toward the far end of the deck—another blinding storm!—another roar as the pilot pushes the throttle up to full military power and another smear of rubber screams out over the skillet—and this is nominal!—quite okay!—for a wire stretched across the deck has grabbed the hook on the end of the plane as it hit the deck tail down, and the smash was the rest of the fifteen-ton brute slamming onto the deck, as it tripped up, so that it is now straining against the wire at full throttle, in case it hadn't held and the plane had "boltered" off the end of the deck and had to struggle up into the air again. And already the Mickey Mouse helmets are running toward the fiery monster . . .

And the candidate, looking on, begins to *feel* that great heaving sun-blazing deathboard of a deck wallowing in his own vestibular system—and suddenly he finds himself backed up against his own limits. He ends up going to the flight surgeon with so-called conversion symptoms. Overnight he develops blurred vision or numbness in his hands and feet or sinusitis so severe that he cannot tolerate changes in altitude. On one level the symptom is real. He really cannot see too well or use his fingers or stand the pain. But somewhere in his subconscious he knows it is a plea and a beg-off; he shows not the slightest concern (the flight surgeon notes) that the condition might be permanent and affect him in whatever life awaits him outside the arena of the right stuff.

Those who remained, those who qualified for carrier duty—and even more so those who later on qualified for *night* carrier duty—began to feel a bit like Gideon's warriors. *So many have been left behind!* The young warriors were now treated to a deathly sweet and quite unmentionable sight. They could gaze at length upon the crushed and wilted pariahs who had washed out. They could inspect those who did not have that righteous stuff.

The military did not have very merciful instincts. Rather than packing up these poor souls and sending them home, the Navy, like the Air Force and the Marines, would try to make use of them in some other role, such as flight controller. So the washout has to keep taking classes with the rest of his group, even though he can no longer touch an airplane. He sits there in the classes staring at sheets of paper with cataracts of sheer human mortification over his eyes while the rest steal looks at him . . . this man reduced to an ant, this untouchable, this poor sonofabitch. And in what test had he been found wanting? Why, it seemed to be nothing less than *manhood* itself. Naturally, this was never mentioned, either. Yet there it was. *Manliness, manhood, manly courage* . . . there was something ancient, primordial, irresistible about the challenge of this stuff, no matter what a sophisticated and rational age one might think he lived in.

Perhaps because it could not be talked about, the subject began to take on superstititous and even mystical outlines. A man either had it or he didn't! There was no such thing as having *most* of it. Moreover, it could blow at any seam. One day a man would be ascending the pyramid at a terrific clip, and the next—bingo!—he would reach his own limits in the most unexpected way. Conrad and Schirra met an Air Force pilot who had had a great pal at Tyndall Air Force Base in Florida. This man had been the budding ace of the training class; he had flown the hottest fighter-style trainer, the T–38, like a dream; and then he began the routine step of being checked out in the T–33. The T–33 was not nearly as hot an air-craft as the T–38; it was essentially the old P–80 jet fighter. It had an exceedingly small cockpit. The pilot could barely move his shoulders. It was the sort of airplane of which everybody said, "You don't get into it, you *wear* it." Once inside a T–33 cockpit this man, this budding ace, developed claustrophobia of the most paralyzing sort. He tried everything to overcome it. He even went to a psychiatrist, which was a serious mis-take for a military officer if his superiors learned of it. But nothing worked. He was shifted over to flying jet transports, such as the C–135. Very demanding and necessary aircraft they were, too, and he was still spoken of as an excellent pilot. But as everyone knew—and, again, it was never explained in so many words—only those who were assigned to fighter squadrons, the "fighter jocks," as they called each other with a self-satisfied irony, remained in the true fraternity. Those assigned to trans-ports were not humiliated like washouts—*somebody* had to fly those planes—nevertheless, they, too, had been *left behind* for lack of the right stuff.

Or a man could go for a routine physical one fine day, feeling like a million dollars, and be grounded for *fallen arches*. It happened!—just like that! (And try raising them.) Or for breaking his wrist and losing only *part* of its mobility. Or for a minor deterioration of eyesight, or for any of hun-dreds of reasons that would make no difference to a man in an ordinary occupation. As a result all fighter jocks began looking upon doctors as their natural enemies. Going to see a flight surgeon was a no-gain propo-sition; a pilot could only hold his own or lose in the doctor's office. To be grounded for a medical reason was no humiliation, looked at objectively. But it was a humiliation, nonetheless!—for it meant you no longer had that indefinable, unutterable, integral stuff. (It could blow at *any* seam.)

All the hot young fighter jocks began trying to test the limits them-selves in a superstitious way. They were like believing Presbyterians of a century before who used to probe their own experience to see if they were truly among *the elect*. When a fighter pilot was in training, whether in the Navy or the Air Force, his superiors were continually spelling out strict rules for him, about the use of the aircraft and conduct in the sky. They repeatedly forbade so-called hot-dog stunts, such as outside loops,

buzzing, flat-hatting, hedgehopping and flying under bridges. But somehow one got the message that the man who truly *had* it could ignore those
rules—not that he should make a point of it, but that he *could*—and that
after all there was only one way to find out—and that in some strange
unofficial way, peeking through his fingers, his instructor halfway
expected him to challenge all the limits. They would give a lecture about
how a pilot should never fly without a good solid breakfast—eggs, bacon,
toast, and so forth—because if he tried to fly with his blood-sugar level
too low, it could impair his alertness. Naturally, the next day every hot
dog in the unit would get up and have a breakfast consisting of one cup
of black coffee and take off and go up into a vertical climb until the
weight of the ship exactly canceled out the upward thrust of the engine
and his air speed was zero, and he would hang there for one thick adrenal
instant—and then fall like a rock, until one of three things happened: he
keeled over nose first and regained his aerodynamics and all was well, he
went into a spin and fought his way out of it, or he went into a spin and
had to eject or crunch it, which was always supremely possible.

Likewise, "hassling"—mock dogfighting—was strictly forbidden, and
so naturally young fighter jocks could hardly wait to go up in, say, a pair
of F–100s and start the duel by making a pass at each other at 800 miles
an hour, the winner being the pilot who could slip in behind the other
one and get locked in on his tail ("wax his tail"), and it was not uncommon for some eager jock to try too tight an outside turn and have his
engine flame out, whereupon, unable to restart it, he has to eject . . . and
he shakes his fist at the victor as he floats down by parachute and his
million-dollar aircraft goes *kaboom!* on the palmetto grass or the desert
floor, and he starts thinking about how he can get together with the other
guy back at the base in time for the two of them to get their stories
straight before the investigation: "I don't know what happened, sir. I was
pulling up after a target run, and it just flamed out on me." Hassling was
forbidden, and hassling that led to the destruction of an aircraft was a
serious court-martial offense, and the man's superiors knew that the
engine hadn't *just flamed out,* but every unofficial impulse on the base
seemed to be saying: "Hell, we wouldn't give you a nickel for a pilot who
hasn't done some crazy rat-racing like that. It's all part of the right stuff."

The other side of this impulse showed up in the reluctance of the
young jocks to admit it when they had maneuvered themselves into a bad
corner they couldn't get out of. There were two reasons why a fighter pilot
hated to declare an emergency. First, it triggered a complex and very public chain of events at the field: all other incoming flights were held up,

including many of one's comrades who were probably low on fuel; the fire trucks came trundling out to the runway like yellow toys (as seen from way up there), the better to illustrate one's hapless state; and the bureaucracy began to crank up the paper monster for the investigation that always followed. And second, to declare an emergency, one first had to reach that conclusion in his own mind, which to the young pilot was the same as saying: "A minute ago I still *had* it—now I need your help!" To have a bunch of young fighter pilots up in the air thinking this way used to drive flight controllers crazy. They would see a ship beginning to drift off the radar, and they couldn't rouse the pilot on the microphone for anything other than a few meaningless mumbles, and they would know he was probably out there with engine failure at a low altitude, trying to reignite by lowering his auxilliary generator rig, which had a little propeller that was supposed to spin in the slipstream like a child's pinwheel.

"Whiskey Kilo Two Eight, do you want to declare an emergency?"

This would rouse him!—to say: "Negative, negative, Whiskey Kilo Two Eight is not declaring an emergency."

Kaboom. Believers in the right stuff would rather crash and burn.

One fine day, after he had joined a fighter squadron, it would dawn on the young pilot exactly how the losers in the great fraternal competition were now being left behind. Which is to say, not by instructors or other superiors or by failures at prescribed levels of competence, but by death. At this point the essence of the enterprise would begin to dawn on him. Slowly, step by step, the ante had been raised until he was now involved in what was surely the grimmest and grandest gamble of manhood. Being a fighter pilot—for that matter, simply taking off in a single-engine jet fighter of the Century series, such as an F–102, or any of the military's other marvelous bricks with fins on them—presented a man, on a perfectly sunny day, with more ways to get himself killed than his wife and children could imagine in their wildest fears. If he was barreling down the runway at two hundred miles an hour, completing the takeoff run, and the board started lighting up red, should he (a) abort the takeoff (and try to wrestle with the monster, which was gorged with jet fuel, out in the sand beyond the end of the runway) or (b) eject (and hope that the goddamned human cannonball trick works at zero altitude and he doesn't shatter an elbow or a kneecap on the way out) or (c) continue the takeoff and deal with the problem aloft (knowing full well that the ship may be on fire and therefore seconds away from exploding)? He would have one second to sort out the options and act, and this kind of little workaday decision came up all the time. Occasionally a man would look coldly at the binary problem he was now confronting every day—Right Stuff/Death—and decide it wasn't worth it and voluntarily shift over to transports or reconnaissance or whatever. And his comrades would wonder, for a day or so, what evil virus had invaded his soul . . . as they left him behind. More often, however, the reverse would happen. Some college graduate would enter Navy aviation through the Reserves, simply as an alternative to the Army draft, fully intending to return to civilian life, to some waiting profession or family business; would become involved in the obsessive business of ascending the ziggurat pyramid of flying; and, at the end of his enlistment, would astound everyone back home and very likely himself as well by signing up for another one. What on earth got into him? He couldn't explain it. After all, the very words for it had been amputated. A Navy study showed that two-thirds of the fighter pilots who were rated in the top rungs of their groups—i.e., the hottest young pilots—reenlisted when the time came, and practically all were college graduates. By this point, a young fighter jock was like the preacher in *Moby Dick* who climbs up into the pulpit on a rope ladder and then pulls the ladder up behind him; except the pilot could not use the words necessary to express the vital lessons. Civilian life, and even home and hearth, now seemed not only far away but far *below*, back down many levels of the pyramid of the right stuff.

A fighter pilot soon found he wanted to associate only with other fighter pilots. Who else could understand the nature of the little proposition (right stuff/death) they were all dealing with? And what other subject could compare with it? It was riveting! To talk about it in so many words was forbidden, of course. The very words *death, danger, bravery, fear* were not to be uttered except in the occasional specific instance or for ironic effect. Nevertheless, the subject could be adumbrated in *code* or *by example.* Hence the endless evenings of pilots huddled together talking about flying. On these long and drunken evenings (the bane of their family life) certain theorems would be propounded and demonstrated—and all by *code* and *example.* One theorem was: There are no *accidents* and no fatal flaws in the machines; there are only pilots with the wrong stuff. (I.e., blind Fate can't kill me.) When Bud Jennings crashed and burned in the swamps at Jacksonville, the other pilots in Pete Conrad's squadron said: *How could he have been so stupid?* It turned out that Jennings had gone up in the SNJ with his cockpit canopy opened in a way that was expressly forbidden in the manual, and carbon monoxide had been sucked in from the exhaust, and he passed out and crashed. All agreed that Bud Jennings was a good guy and a good pilot,

but his epitaph on the ziggurat was: *How could he have been so stupid?*
This seemed shocking at first, but by the time Conrad had reached the
end of that bad string at Pax River, he was capable of his own corollary
to the theorem: viz., no single factor ever killed a pilot; there was always
a chain of mistakes. But what about Ted Whelan, who fell like a rock
from 8,100 feet when his parachute failed? Well, the parachute was
merely part of the chain: first, someone should have caught the structural defect that resulted in the hydraulic leak that triggered the emergency; second, Whelan did not check out his seat-parachute rig, and
the drogue failed to separate the main parachute from the seat; but even
after those two mistakes, Whelan had fifteen or twenty seconds, as he
fell, to disengage himself from the seat and open the parachute manually.
Why just stare at the scenery coming up to smack you in the face! And
everyone nodded. (He failed—but I wouldn't have!) Once the theorem
and the corollary were understood, the Navy's statistics about one in
every four Navy aviators dying meant nothing. The figures were averages, and averages applied to those with average stuff.

A riveting subject, especially if it were one's own hide that was on the
line. Every evening at bases all over America, there were military pilots
huddled in officers clubs eagerly cutting the right stuff up in coded slices
so they could talk about it. What more compelling topic of conversation
was there in the world? In the Air Force there were even pilots who would
ask the tower for priority landing clearance so that they could make the
beer call on time, at 4 P.M. sharp, at the Officers Club. They would come
right out and state the reason. The drunken rambles began at four and
sometimes went on for ten or twelve hours. Such conversations! They
diced that righteous stuff up into little bits, bowed ironically to it, stumbled blindfolded around it, groped, lurched, belched, staggered, bawled,
sang, roared, and feinted at it with self-deprecating humor. Nevertheless!—they never mentioned it by name. No, they used the approved
codes, such as: "Like a jerk I got myself into a hell of a corner today."
They told of how they "lucked out of it." To get across the extreme peril
of his exploit, one would use certain oblique cues. He would say, "I
looked over at Robinson"—who would be known to the listeners as a
non-com who sometimes rode backseat to read radar—"and he wasn't
talking any more, he was just staring at the radar, like this, giving it that
zombie look. Then I *knew* I was in trouble!" Beautiful! Just right! For it
would also be known to the listeners that the non-coms advised one
another: "*Never* fly with a lieutenant. *Avoid* captains and majors. Hell,
man, do yourself a favor: don't fly with anybody below colonel." Which

in turn said: "Those young bucks shoot dice with death!" And yet once in the air the non-com had his own standards. He was determined to remain as outwardly cool as the pilot, so that when the pilot did something that truly petrified him, he would say nothing; instead, he would turn silent, catatonic, like a zombie. Perfect! *Zombie.* There you had it, compressed into a single word, all of the foregoing. I'm a hell of a pilot! I shoot dice with death! And now all you fellows know it! And I haven't spoken of that unspoken stuff even once!

The talking and drinking began at the beer call, and then the boys would break for dinner and come back afterward and get more wasted and more garrulous or else more quietly fried, drinking good cheap PX booze until 2 A.M. The night was young! Why not get the cars and go out for a little proficiency run? It seemed that every fighter jock thought himself an ace driver, and he would do anything to obtain a hot car, especially a sports car, and the drunker he was, the more convinced he would be about his driving skills, as if the right stuff, being indivisible, carried over into any enterprise whatsoever, under any conditions. A little proficiency run, boys! (There's only one way to find out!) And they would roar off in close formation from, say, Nellis Air Force Base, down Route 15, into Las Vegas, barreling down the highway, ratracing, sometimes four abreast, jockeying for position, piling into the most listless curve in the desert flats as if they were trying to root each other out of the groove at the Rebel 500—and then bursting into downtown Las Vegas with a rude fraternal roar like the Hell's Angels—and the natives chalked it up to youth and drink and the bad element that the Air Force attracted. They knew nothing about the right stuff, of course.

More fighter pilots died in automobiles than in airplanes. Fortunately, there was always some kindly soul up the chain to certify the papers "line of duty," so that the widow could get a better break on the insurance. That was okay and only proper because somehow the system itself had long ago said *Skol!* and *Quite right!* to the military cycle of Flying & Drinking and Drinking & Driving, as if there were no other way. Every young fighter jock knew the feeling of getting two or three hours' sleep and then waking up at 5:30 A.M. and having a few cups of coffee, a few cigarettes, and then carting his poor quivering liver out to the field for another day of flying. There were those who arrived not merely hungover but still drunk, slapping oxygen tank cones over their faces and trying to burn the alcohol out of their systems, and then going up, remarking later: "I don't *advise* it, you understand, but it *can* be done." (Provided you have the right stuff, you miserable pudknocker.)

Air Force and Navy airfields were usually on barren or marginal stretches of land and would have looked especially bleak and Low Rent to an ordinary individual in the chilly light of dawn. But to a young pilot there was an inexplicable bliss to coming out to the flight line while the sun was just beginning to cook up behind the rim of the horizon, so that the whole field was still in shadow and the ridges in the distance were in silhouette and the flight line was a monochrome of Exhaust Fume Blue, and every little red light on top of the water towers or power stanchions looked dull, shriveled, congealed, and the runway lights, which were still on, looked faded, and even the landing lights on a fighter that had just landed and was taxiing in were no longer dazzling, as they would be at night, and looked instead like shriveled gobs of candlepower out there— and yet it was beautiful, exhilarating!—for he was revved up with adrenalin, anxious to take off before the day broke, to burst up into the sunlight over the ridges before all those thousands of comatose souls down there, still dead to the world, snug in home and hearth, even came to their senses. To take off in an F–100 at dawn and cut in the afterburner and hurtle twenty-five thousand feet up into the sky so suddenly that you felt not like a bird but like a trajectory, yet with full control, full control of *five tons* of thrust, all of which flowed from your will and through your fingertips, with the huge engine right beneath you, so close that it was as if you were riding it bareback, until you leveled out and went supersonic, an event registered on earth by a tremendous cracking boom that shook windows, but up here only by the fact that you now felt utterly free of the earth—to describe it, even to wife, child, near ones and dear ones, seemed impossible. So the pilot kept it to himself, along with an even more indescribable . . . an even more sinfully inconfessable . . . feeling of superiority, appropriate to him and to his kind, lone bearers of the right stuff.

From *up here* at dawn the pilot looked down upon poor hopeless Las Vegas (or Yuma, Corpus Christi, Meridian, San Bernardino, or Dayton) and began to wonder: How can all of them down there, those poor souls who will soon be waking up and trudging out of their minute rectangles and inching along their little noodle highways toward whatever slots and grooves make up their everyday lives—how could they live like that, with such earnestness, if they had the faintest idea of what it was like up here in this righteous zone?

But of course! Not only the washed-out, grounded, and dead pilots had been left behind—but also all of those millions of sleepwalking souls who never even attempted the great gamble. The entire world below . . .

left behind. Only at this point can one begin to understand just how big, how titanic, the ego of the military pilot could be. The world was used to enormous egos in artists, actors, entertainers of all sorts, in politicians, sports figures, and even journalists, because they had such familiar and convenient ways to show them off. But that slim young man over there in uniform, with the enormous watch on his wrist and the withdrawn look on his face, that young officer who is so shy that he can't even open his mouth unless the subject is flying—that young pilot—well, my friends, his ego is even *bigger!*—so big, it's *breathtaking!* Even in the 1950's it was difficult for civilians to comprehend such a thing, but *all* military officers and many enlisted men tended to feel superior to civilians. It was really quite ironic, given the fact that for a good thirty years the rising business classes in the cities had been steering their sons away from the military, as if from a bad smell, and the officer corps had never been held in lower esteem. Well, career officers returned the contempt in trumps. They looked upon themselves as men who lived by higher standards of behavior than civilians, as men who were the bearers and protectors of the most important values of American life, who maintained a sense of discipline while civilians abandoned themselves to hedonism, who maintained a sense of honor while civilians lived by opportunism and greed. Opportunism and greed: there you had your much-vaunted corporate business world. Khrushchev was right about one thing: when it came time to hang the capitalist West, an American businessman would sell him the rope. When the showdown came—and the showdowns always came—not all the wealth in the world or all the sophisticated nuclear weapons and radar and missile systems it could buy would take the place of those who had the uncritical willingness to face danger, those who, in short, had the right stuff.

In fact, the feeling was so righteous, so exalted, it could become religious. Civilians seldom understood this, either. There was no one to teach them. It was no longer the fashion for serious writers to describe the glories of war. Instead, they dwelt upon its horrors, often with cynicism or disgust. It was left to the occasional pilot with a literary flair to provide a glimpse of the pilot's self-conception in its heavenly or spiritual aspect. When a pilot named Robert Scott flew his P–43 over Mount Everest, quite a feat at the time, he brought his hand up and snapped a salute to his fallen adversary. He thought he had *defeated* the mountain, surmounting all the forces of nature that had made it formidable. And why not? "God is my co-pilot," he said—that became the title of his book—and he meant it. So did the most gifted of all the pilot authors, the Frenchman Antoine

de Saint-Exupéry. As he gazed down upon the world . . . from up there
. . . during transcontinental flights, the good Saint-Ex saw civilization as
a series of tiny fragile patches clinging to the otherwise barren rock of
Earth. He felt like a lonely sentinel, a protector of those vulnerable little
oases, ready to lay down his life in their behalf, if necessary; a saint, in
short, true to his name, flying up here at the right hand of God. The good
Saint-Ex! And he was not the only one. He was merely the one who put
it into words most beautifully and anointed himself before the altar of the
right stuff.

CONSIDERATIONS

Thinking

What qualities and attributes, according to Wolfe, are necessary for success
as a military test pilot? Why? Do you agree? Why or why not?

To what extent does the fact that pilots see themselves as members of an "all-
enclosing fraternity" affect their view of themselves and influence their behavior?

Why do you think Wolfe presents two sides of the test pilots—the official
and the unofficial? Do we need to see both sides? Why or why not?

Connecting

Compare Wolfe's analysis of military test pilots with Paul Fussell's of race car
drivers in "Indy" or Joyce Carol Oates' of boxers in "On Boxing."

To what extent can the qualities and attitudes of the pilots be compared with
those of professional athletes—hockey or football players, golf or tennis stars, for
example?

Writing

Interview half a dozen athletes, teachers, musicians, scholars, students who
have what you think of as "the right stuff." Write an essay presenting a composite picture of what the right stuff is for that group.

Read one or both of the following, and then write an essay on some aspect
of military life and your idea about it: Tim O'Brien's "How to Tell a True War
Story," or Diane Hume George's "Wounded Chevy at Wounded Knee."

Virginia Woolf
(1882–1941)

Virginia Woolf was a brilliant novelist, a distinguished essayist, and an astute critic of literature and of British culture. Her novels include *Jacob's Room, Mrs. Dalloway, To the Lighthouse,* and *The Waves.* There are also five volumes of essays. *Roger Fry: A Biography; Moments of Being,* a collection of autobiographical writings; and *A Room of One's Own,* an expansive exploration about women, writing, and dire circumstance, attest to Woolf's interest in other genres and confirm her genius.

"Old Mrs. Grey" takes us into the land of terror and gives us glimpses of the possibility of peace in death. It conveys its idea through a single story replete with poignant images that inform the idea.

Old Mrs. Grey

There are moments even in England, now, when even the busiest, most contented suddenly let fall what they hold—it may be the week's washing. Sheets and pyjamas crumble and dissolve in their hands, because, though they do not state this in so many words, it seems silly to take the washing round to Mrs. Peel when out there over the fields over the hills, there is no washing; no pinning of clotheslines; mangling and ironing; no work at all, but boundless rest. Stainless and boundless rest; space unlimited; untrodden grass; wild birds flying; hills whose smooth uprise continues that wild flight.

Of all this however only seven foot by four could be seen from Mrs. Grey's corner. That was the size of her front door which stood wide open, though there was a fire burning in the grate. The fire looked like a small spot of dusty light feebly trying to escape from the embarrassing pressure of the pouring sunshine.

Mrs. Grey sat on a hard chair in the corner looking—but at what? Apparently at nothing. She did not change the focus of her eyes when visitors came in. Her eyes had ceased to focus themselves; it may be that they had lost the power. They were aged eyes, blue, unspectacled. They could see, but without looking. She had never used her eyes on anything minute and difficult; merely upon faces, and dishes and fields. And now at the age of ninety-two they saw nothing but a zigzag of pain wriggling across the door, pain that twisted her legs as it wriggled; jerked her body to and fro like a marionette. Her body was wrapped round the pain as a damp sheet is folded over a wire. The wire was spasmodically jerked by a cruel invisible hand. She flung out a foot, a hand. Then it stopped. She sat still for a moment.

In that pause she saw herself in the past at ten, at twenty, at twenty-five. She was running in and out of a cottage with eleven brothers and sisters. The line jerked. She was thrown forward in her chair.

'All dead. All dead,' she mumbled. 'My brothers and sisters. And my husband gone. My daughter too. But I go on. Every morning I pray God to let me pass.'

The morning spread seven foot by four green and sunny. Like a fling of grain the birds settled on the land. She was jerked again by another tweak of the tormenting hand.

'I'm an ignorant old woman. I can't read or write, and every morning when I crawls downstairs, I say I wish it were night; and every night, when I crawls up to bed, I say I wish it were day. I'm only an ignorant old woman. But I prays to God: O let me pass. I'm an ignorant old woman— I can't read or write.'

So when the colour went out of the doorway, she could not see the other page which is then lit up; or hear the voices that have argued, sung, talked for hundreds of years.

The jerked limbs were still again.

'The doctor comes every week. The parish doctor now. Since my daughter went, we can't afford Dr. Nicholls. But he's a good man. He says he wonders I don't go. He says my heart's nothing but wind and water. Yet I don't seem able to die.'

So we—humanity—insist that the body shall still cling to the wire. We put out the eyes and the ears; but we pinion it there, with a bottle of medicine, a cup of tea, a dying fire, like a rook on a barn door; but a rook that still lives, even with a nail through it.

CONSIDERATIONS

Thinking

What is this essay's implicit argument?

Why do you suppose Woolf lets us hear Mrs. Grey talk?

Why does Woolf take us inside Mrs. Grey's house and let us see the "morning spread seven foot by four green and sunny"?

Connecting

Make a list of the images in the essay. How do those images help you understand Woolf's idea?

Go to the library and find a reproduction of René Magritte's painting The Human Condition I. How does that painting help you understand Mrs. Grey's condition?

Writing

Write a short, speculative account of what you think Woolf would have "us" do about the Mrs. Greys of the world.

Visit someone in the hospital or in a nursing home; then write an essay about that person's predicament.

Write an essay in which you argue for or against euthanasia.

*T*wo *Professional Writers;*
Related Student Essays

One advantage of reading more than a single essay by a writer is
that you can see how a writer approaches different subjects and
how that writer varies his or her approach to the same subject.
We have selected three essays each by Maxine Hong Kingston
and E. B. White, both of whom write about their experiences.
Kingston describes her cultural experience as an Asian American
woman of Chinese ancestry. Relevant also is the fact that she is a
woman writing about women. E. B. White describes episodes
from his life that lead him to reflect on issues of time and change
and mortality. Both writers use personal experience as evidence
in developing their ideas.

Both Kingston and White explore in their essays issues and
questions that haunt them. Even though Kingston's three pieces
have different topics, their concern with race, gender, and
culture overlap. And even though White's three essays appear
completely different at first, they too contain overlapping ideas
and concerns that echo and reverberate from one essay to
another. In fact, one way of reading both Kingston's and White's
prose pieces is to look for ways each piece of each writer's work
echoes and speaks to other pieces.

For both of these writers, we have written an introduction
that sets their pieces in the context of their lives and their writing.
Following the essays by Kingston and White are student essays
based on the work of the two professionals—three analytical
essays based on Maxine Hong Kingston's "On Discovery" and two
research essays based on the writings of E. B. White.

Maxine Hong Kingston (b.1940)

Although she had a novel published in 1989 (*Tripmaster Monkey: His Fake Book*), Maxine Hong Kingston is best known for her earlier mixed-genre works, *The Woman Warrior* (1976) and *China Men* (1980), winner of the American Book Award. Kingston has described the earlier work as the book of her mother since it is filled with stories her mother told her, stories about Chinese women, her Asian ancestors whom Kingston describes as the ghosts of her girlhood. *China Men*, by contrast, is her father's book since it tells the stories of her male ancestors, including her father and grandfathers—though she learned these male stories too from women, especially from her mother. Both books are filled with stories. Both mix fact and fiction, autobiography and legend, combining in imaginative ways family history with fictional invention.

Kingston's books are, thus, difficult to classify. They refuse to sit still and accept the tidy categories we devise for prose narrative. The selections excerpted here from these two family chronicles reflect the curious and striking effects Kingston achieves throughout them with her blending of myth and legend with autobiography and family history. Moreover, in addition to their provocative combinations of fact and fiction, the two books possess another striking quality: their compelling voices. Kingston's narratives retell heard stories, stories told *by* her and stories told *to* her. Her stories derive from an oral tradition—the "talk story"—sustained largely by Chinese women. Kingston thus simultaneously inherits this oral narrative tradition and participates in it. Perhaps even more importantly, however, by inscribing her mother's stories and imagining her own variants of them, Kingston marks that tradition with her own distinctive imaginative imprint. In doing so, she demonstrates the power of these stories to enthrall readers outside the Chinese cultural tradition.

Maxine Hong Kingston was born and raised in Stockton, California, where her immigrant parents operated a laundry. She graduated from the University of California at Berkeley in 1962, and she has taught high school and college English, primarily in Hawaii, where she lived for seventeen years before moving to Oakland, California.

Kingston's autobiographical impulse appears strongly in "Silence," an excerpt from *The Woman Warrior.* In "Silence," we see Kingston begin to negotiate the struggle between the Chinese culture she inherited and the American culture she was born into. Her silence powerfully illustrates her uncertainty about how to invoke one cultural perspective without revoking or violating the other.

Kingston's versatility in letting the voices of others speak through her is powerfully manifested in "No Name Woman," the opening section of *The Woman Warrior.* As Esther Schor has pointed out in *Women's Voices,* the first voice we hear in "No Name Woman" is the voice of her mother, who "ironically . . . admonishes the daughter to silence even as she nourishes her with stories." Kingston's instincts as a writer are revealed not only in the stories she chooses to tell, but in the voices she creates to tell them. This is as true for the multiple voices we hear in "No Name Woman" as for the singularly different voices that sound in the other tales Kingston narrates in both books, including the brief parable, "On Discovery," which turns gender role and power inside out.

To some extent, Kingston is a woman's writer precisely because she gives public voice to what women had spoken only in private or what they had to keep silent. To some extent, she is also an ethnic writer, one who transmits stories of her Cantonese heritage. Her artistry and imaginative sympathy, however, transcend the limits of both gender and culture, as Kingston invents a world and constructs a self that appear both strange and familiar, at once "other" and recognizably our own.

No Name Woman

"You must not tell anyone," my mother said, "what I am about to tell you. In China your father had a sister who killed herself. She jumped into the family well. We say that your father has all brothers because it is as if she had never been born.

"In 1924 just a few days after our village celebrated seventeen hurry-up weddings—to make sure that every young man who went 'out on the road' would responsibly come home—your father and his brothers and your grandfather and his brothers and your aunt's new husband sailed for America, the Gold Mountain. It was your grandfather's last trip. Those lucky enough to get contracts waved good-bye from the decks. They fed and guarded the stowaways and helped them off in Cuba, New York, Bali, Hawaii. 'We'll meet in California next year,' they said. All of them sent money home.

"I remember looking at your aunt one day when she and I were dressing; I had not noticed before that she had such a protruding melon of a stomach. But I did not think, 'She's pregnant,' until she began to look like other pregnant women, her shirt pulling and the white tops of her black pants showing. She could not have been pregnant, you see, because her husband had been gone for years. No one said anything. We did not discuss it. In early summer she was ready to have the child, long after the time when it could have been possible.

"The village had also been counting. On the night the baby was to be born the villagers raided our house. Some were crying. Like a great saw, teeth strung with lights, files of people walked zigzag across our land, tearing the rice. Their lanterns doubled in the disturbed black water, which drained away through the broken bunds. As the villagers closed in, we could see that some of them, probably men and women we knew well, wore white masks. The people with long hair hung it over their faces. Women with short hair made it stand up on end. Some had tied white bands around their foreheads, arms, and legs.

"At first they threw mud and rocks at the house. Then they threw eggs and began slaughtering our stock. We could hear the animals scream their deaths—the roosters, the pigs, a last great roar from the ox. Familiar wild heads flared in our night windows; the villagers encircled us. Some of the faces stopped to peer at us, their eyes rushing like searchlights. The hands flattened against the panes, framed heads, and left red prints.

"The villagers broke in the front and the back doors at the same time, even though we had not locked the doors against them. Their knives dripped with the blood of our animals. They smeared blood on the doors and walls. One woman swung a chicken, whose throat she had slit, splattering blood in red arcs about her. We stood together in the middle of our house, in the family hall with the pictures and tables of the ancestors around us, and looked straight ahead.

"At that time the house had only two wings. When the men came back we would build two more to enclose our courtyard and a third one to begin a second courtyard. The villagers pushed through both wings, even your grandparents' rooms, to find your aunt's, which was also mine until the men returned. From this room a new wing for one of the younger families would grow. They ripped up her clothes and shoes and broke her combs, grinding them underfoot. They tore her work from the loom. They scattered the cooking fire and rolled the new weaving in it. We could hear them in the kitchen breaking our bowls and banging the pots. They overturned the great waist-high earthenware jugs; duck eggs, pickled fruits, vegetables burst out and mixed in acrid torrents. The old woman from the next field swept a broom through the air and loosed the spirits-of-the-broom over our heads. 'Pig.' 'Ghost.' 'Pig,' they sobbed and scolded while they ruined our house.

"When they left, they took sugar and oranges to bless themselves. They cut pieces from the dead animals. Some of them took bowls that were not broken and clothes that were not torn. Afterward we swept up the rice and sewed it back up into sacks. But the smells from the spilled preserves lasted. Your aunt gave birth in the pigsty that night. The next morning when I went up for the water, I found her and the baby plugging up the family well.

"Don't let your father know that I told you. He denies her. Now that you have started to menstruate, what happened to her could happen to you. Don't humiliate us. You wouldn't like to be forgotten as if you had never been born. The villagers are watchful."

Whenever she had to warn us about life, my mother told stories that ran like this one, a story to grow up on. She tested our strength to establish realities. Those in the emigrant generations who could not reassert brute survival died young and far from home. Those of us in the first American generations have had to figure out how the invisible world the emigrants built around our childhoods fit in solid America.

The emigrants confused the gods by diverting their curses, misleading them with crooked streets and false names. They must try to confuse their offspring as well, who, I suppose, threaten them in similar ways— always trying to get things straight, always trying to name the unspeakable. The Chinese I know hide their names; sojourners take new names when their lives change and guard their real names with silence.

Chinese-Americans, when you try to understand what things in you are Chinese, how do you separate what is peculiar to childhood, to poverty, insanities, one family, your mother who marked your growing with stories, from what is Chinese? What is Chinese tradition and what is the movies?

If I want to learn what clothes my aunt wore, whether flashy or ordinary, I would have to begin, "Remember Father's drowned-in-the-well sister?" I cannot ask that. My mother has told me once and for all the useful parts. She will add nothing unless powered by Necessity, a riverbank that guides her life. She plants vegetable gardens rather than lawns; she carries the odd-shaped tomatoes home from the fields and eats food left for the gods.

Whenever we did frivolous things, we used up energy; we flew high kites. We children came up off the ground over the melting cones our parents brought home from work and the American movie on New Years' Day—*Oh, You Beautiful Doll* with Betty Grable one year, and *She Wore a Yellow Ribbon* with John Wayne another year. After the one carnival ride each, we paid in guilt; our tired father counted his change on the dark walk home.

Adultery is extravagance. Could people who hatch their own chicks and eat the embryos and the heads for delicacies and boil the feet in vinegar for party food, leaving only the gravel, eating even the gizzard lining—could such people engender a prodigal aunt? To be a woman, to have a daughter in starvation time was a waste enough. My aunt could not have been the lone romantic who gave up everything for sex. Women in the old China did not choose. Some man had commanded her to lie with him and be his secret evil. I wonder whether he masked himself when he joined the raid on her family.

Perhaps she encountered him in the fields or on the mountain where the daughters-in-law collected fuel. Or perhaps he first noticed her in the marketplace. He was not a stranger because the village housed no strangers. She had to have dealings with him other than sex. Perhaps he worked an adjoining field, or he sold her the cloth for the dress she sewed and wore. His demand must have surprised, then terrified her. She obeyed him; she always did as she was told.

When the family found a young man in the next village to be her husband, she stood tractably beside the best rooster, his proxy, and promised
before they met that she would be his forever. She was lucky that he was
her age and she would be the first wife, an advantage secure now. The
night she first saw him, he had sex with her. Then he left for America. She
had almost forgotten what he looked like. When she tried to envision
him, she only saw the black and white face in the group photograph the
men had had taken before leaving.

The other man was not, after all, much different from her husband.
They both gave orders: she followed. "If you tell your family, I'll beat you.
I'll kill you. Be here again next week." No one talked sex, ever. And she
might have separated the rapes from the rest of living if only she did not
have to buy her oil from him or gather wood in the same forest. I want
her fear to have lasted just as long as rape lasted so that the fear could
have been contained. No drawn-out fear. But women at sex hazarded
birth and hence lifetimes. The fear did not stop but permeated everywhere. She told the man, "I think I'm pregnant." He organized the raid
against her.

On nights when my mother and father talked about their life back
home, sometimes they mentioned an "outcast table" whose business they
still seemed to be settling, their voices tight. In a commensal tradition,
where food is precious, the powerful older people made wrongdoers eat
alone. Instead of letting them start separate new lives like the Japanese,
who could become samurais and geishas, the Chinese family, faces averted
but eyes glowering sideways, hung on to the offenders and fed them left-
overs. My aunt must have lived in the same house as my parents and
eaten at an outcast table. My mother spoke about the raid as if she had
seen it, when she and my aunt, a daughter-in-law to a different household, should not have been living together at all. Daughters-in-law lived
with their husbands' parents, not their own; a synonym for marriage in
Chinese is "taking a daughter-in-law." Her husband's parents could have
sold her, mortgaged her, stoned her. But they had sent her back to her
own mother and father, a mysterious act hinting at disgraces not told me.
Perhaps they had thrown her out to deflect the avengers.

She was the only daughter; her four brothers went with her father,
husband, and uncles "out on the road" and for some years became western men. When the goods were divided among the family, three of the
brothers took land, and the youngest, my father, chose an education.
After my grandparents gave their daughter away to her husband's family,
they had dispensed all the adventure and all the property. They expected

her alone to keep the traditional ways, which her brothers, now among the barbarians, could fumble without detection. The heavy, deep-rooted women were to maintain the past against the flood, safe for returning. But the rare urge west had fixed upon our family, and so my aunt crossed boundaries not delineated in space.

The work of preservation demands that the feelings playing about in one's guts not be turned into action. Just watch their passing like cherry blossoms. But perhaps my aunt, my forerunner, caught in a slow life, let dreams grow and fade and after some months or years went toward what persisted. Fear at the enormities of the forbidden kept her desires delicate, wire and bone. She looked at a man because she liked the way the hair was tucked behind his ears, or she liked the question-mark line of a long torso curving at the shoulder and straight at the hip. For warm eyes or a soft voice or a slow walk—that's all— a few hairs, a line, a brightness, a sound, a pace, she gave up family. She offered us up for a charm that vanished with tiredness, a pigtail that didn't toss when the wind died. Why, the wrong lighting could erase the dearest thing about him.

It could very well have been, however, that my aunt did not take subtle enjoyment of her friend, but, a wild woman, kept rollicking company. Imagining her free with sex doesn't fit, though. I don't know any women like that, or men either. Unless I see her life branching into mine, she gives me no ancestral help.

To sustain her being in love, she often worked at herself in the mirror, guessing at the colors and shapes that would interest him, changing them frequently in order to hit on the right combination. She wanted to look back.

On a farm near the sea, a woman who tended her appearance reaped a reputation for eccentricity. All the married women blunt-cut their hair in flaps about their ears or pulled it back in tight buns. No nonsense. Neither style blew easily into heart-catching tangles. And at their weddings they displayed themselves in their long hair for the last time. "It brushed the backs of my knees," my mother tells me. "It was braided, and even so, it brushed the backs of my knees."

At the mirror my aunt combed individuality into her bob. A bun could have been contrived to escape into black streamers blowing in the wind or in quiet wisps about her face, but only the older women in our picture album wear buns. She brushed her hair back from her forehead, tucking the flaps behind her ears. She looped a piece of thread, knotted into a circle between her index fingers and thumbs, and ran the double strand across her forehead. When she closed her fingers as if she were making a pair of shadow geese bite, the string twisted together catching the little hairs. Then she pulled the thread away from her skin, ripping the hairs out neatly, her eyes watering from the needles of pain. Opening her fingers, she cleaned the thread, then rolled it along her hairline and the tops of the eyebrows. My mother did the same to me and my sisters and herself. I used to believe that the expression "caught by the short hairs" meant a captive held with a depilatory string. It especially hurt at the temples, but my mother said we were lucky we didn't have to have our feet bound when we were seven. Sisters used to sit on their beds and cry together, she said, as their mothers or their slave removed the bandages for a few minutes each night and let the blood gush back into their veins. I hope that the man my aunt loved appreciated a smooth brow, that he wasn't just a tits-and-ass man.

Once my aunt found a freckle on her chin, at a spot that the almanac said predestined her for unhappiness. She dug it out with a hot needle and washed the wound with peroxide.

More attention to her looks than these pullings of hairs and pickings at spots would have caused gossip among the villagers. They owned work clothes and good clothes, and they wore good clothes for feasting the new seasons. But since a woman combing her hair hexes beginnings, my aunt rarely found an occasion to look her best. Women looked like great sea snails—the corded wood, babies, and laundry they carried were the whorls on their backs. The Chinese did not admire a bent back; goddesses and warriors stood straight. Still there must have been a marvelous freeing of beauty when a worker laid down her burden and stretched and arched.

Such commonplace loveliness, however, was not enough for my aunt. She dreamed of a lover for the fifteen days of New Year's, the time for families to exchange visits, money, and food. She plied her secret comb. And sure enough she cursed the year, the family, the village, and herself.

Even as her hair lured her imminent lover, many other men looked at her. Uncles, cousins, nephews, brothers would have looked, too, had they been home between journeys. Perhaps they had already been restraining their curiosity, and they left, fearful that their glances, like a field of nesting birds, might be startled and caught. Poverty hurt, and that was their first reason for leaving. But another, final reason for leaving the crowded house was the never-said.

She may have been unusually beloved, the precious only daughter, spoiled and mirror-gazing because of the affection the family lavished on her. When her husband left, they welcomed the chance to take her back from the in-laws; she could live like the little daughter for just a while longer. There are stories that my grandfather was different from other people, "crazy ever since the little Jap bayoneted him in the head." He used to put his naked penis on the dinner table, laughing. And one day he brought home a baby girl, wrapped up inside his brown western-style greatcoat. He had traded one of his sons, probably my father, the youngest, for her. My grandmother made him trade back. When he finally got a daughter of his own, he doted on her. They must have all loved her, except perhaps my father, the only brother who never went back to China, having once been traded for a girl.

Brothers and sisters, newly men and women, had to efface their sexual color and present plain miens. Disturbing hair and eyes, a smile like no other, threatened the ideal of five generations living under one roof. To focus blurs, people shouted face to face and yelled from room to room. The immigrants I know have loud voices, unmodulated to American tones even after years away from the village where they called their friendships out across the fields. I have not been able to stop my mother's screams in public libraries or over telephones. Walking erect (knees straight, toes pointed forward, not pigeon-toed, which is Chinese-feminine) and speaking in an inaudible voice, I have tried to turn myself American-feminine. Chinese communication was loud, public. Only sick people had to whisper. But at the dinner table, where the family members came nearest one another, no one could talk, not the outcasts nor any eaters. Every word that falls from the mouth is a coin lost. Silently they gave and accepted food with both hands. A preoccupied child who took his bowl with one hand got a sideways glare. A complete moment of total attention is due everyone alike. Children and lovers have no singularity here, but my aunt used a secret voice, a separate attentiveness.

She kept the man's name to herself throughout her labor and dying; she did not accuse him that he be punished with her. To save her inseminator's name she gave silent birth.

He may have been somebody in her own household, but intercourse with a man outside the family would have been no less abhorrent. All the village were kinsmen, and the titles shouted in loud country voices never let kinship be forgotten. Any man within visiting distance would have been neutralized as a lover—"brother," "younger brother," "older brother"—115 relationship titles. Parents researched birth charts probably not so much to assure good fortune as to circumvent incest in a population that has but one hundred surnames. Everybody has eight million relatives. How useless then sexual mannerisms, how dangerous.

As if it came from an atavism deeper than fear, I used to add "brother" silently to boys' names. It hexed the boys, who would or would not ask me to dance, and made them less scary and as familiar and deserving of benevolence as girls.

But, of course, I hexed myself also—no dates. I should have stood up, both arms waving, and shouted out across libraries, "Hey, you! Love me back." I had no idea, though, how to make attraction selective, how to control its direction and magnitude. If I made myself American-pretty so that the five or six Chinese boys in the class fell in love with me, everyone else—the Caucasian, Negro, and Japanese boys—would too. Sisterliness, dignified and honorable, made much more sense.

Attraction eludes control so stubbornly that whole societies designed to organize relationships among people cannot keep order, not even when they bind people to one another from childhood and raise them together. Among the very poor and the wealthy, brothers married their adopted sisters, like doves. Our family allowed some romance, paying adult brides' prices and providing dowries so that their sons and daughters could marry strangers. Marriage promises to turn strangers into friendly relatives—a nation of siblings.

In the village structure, spirits shimmered among the live creatures, balanced and held in equilibrium by time and land. But one human being flaring up into violence could open up a black hole, a maelstrom that pulled in the sky. The frightened villagers, who depended on one another to maintain the real, went to my aunt to show her a personal, physical representation of the break she made in the "roundness." Misallying couples snapped off the future, which was to be embodied in true offspring. The villagers punished her for acting as if she could have a private life, secret and apart from them.

If my aunt had betrayed the family at a time of large grain yields and peace, when many boys were born, and wings were being built on many houses, perhaps she might have escaped such severe punishment. But the men—hungry, greedy, tired of planting in dry soil, cuckolded—had been forced to leave the village in order to send food-money home. There were ghost plagues, bandit plagues, wars with the Japanese, floods. My Chinese brother and sister had died of an unknown sickness. Adultery, perhaps only a mistake during good times, became a crime when the village needed food.

The round moon cakes and round doorways, the round tables of graduated size that fit one roundness inside another, round windows and rice bowls—these talismans had lost their power to warn this family of the law: A family must be whole, faithfully keeping the descent line by having sons to feed the old and the dead who in turn look after the family. The villagers came to show my aunt and lover-in-hiding a broken house. The villagers were speeding up the circling of events because she was too shortsighted to see that her infidelity had already harmed the village, that waves of consequences would return unpredictably, sometimes in disguise, as now, to hurt her. This roundness had to be made coin-sized so that she would see its circumference: Punish her at the birth of her baby. Awaken her to the inexorable. People who refused fatalism because they could invent small resources insisted on culpability. Deny accidents and wrest fault from the stars.

After the villagers left, their lanterns now scattering in various directions toward home, the family broke their silence and cursed her. "Aiaa, we're going to die. Death is coming. Death is coming. Look what you've done. You've killed us. Ghost! Dead Ghost! Ghost! You've never been born." She ran out into the fields, far enough from the house so that she could no longer hear their voices, and pressed herself against the earth, her own land no more. When she felt the birth coming, she thought that she had been hurt. Her body seized together. "They've hurt me too much," she thought. "This is gall, and it will kill me." With forehead and knees against the earth, her body convulsed and then relaxed. She turned on her back, lay on the ground. The black well of sky and stars went out and out forever; her body and her complexity seemed to disappear. She was one of the stars, a bright dot in blackness, without home, without a companion, in eternal cold and silence. An agoraphobia rose in her, speeding higher and higher, bigger and bigger; she would not be able to contain it; there would be no end to fear.

Flayed, unprotected against space, she felt pain return, focusing her body. This pain chilled her—a cold, steady kind of surface pain. Inside, spasmodically, the other pain, the pain of the child, heated her. For hours she lay on the ground, alternately body and space. Sometimes a vision of normal comfort obliterated reality: She saw the family in the evening gambling at the dinner table, the young people massaging their elders' backs. She saw them congratulating one another, high joy on the mornings the rice shoots came up. When these pictures burst, the stars drew yet further apart. Black space opened.

She got to her feet to fight better and remembered that old-fashioned women gave birth in their pigsties to fool the jealous, pain-dealing gods, who do not snatch piglets. Before the next spasms could stop her, she ran to the pigsty, each step a rushing out into emptiness. She climbed over the fence and knelt in the dirt. It was good to have a fence enclosing her, a tribal person alone.

Laboring, this woman who had carried her child as a foreign growth that sickened her every day, expelled it at last. She reached down to touch the hot, wet, moving mass, surely smaller than anything human, and could feel that it was human after all—fingers, toes, nails, nose. She pulled it up on to her belly, and it lay curled there, butt in the air, feet precisely tucked one under the other. She opened her loose shirt and buttoned the child inside. After resting, it squirmed and thrashed and she pushed it up to her breast. It turned its head this way and that until it found her nipple. There, it made little snuffling noises. She clenched her teeth at its preciousness, lovely as a young calf, a piglet, a little dog.

She may have gone to the pigsty as a last act of responsibility: She would protect this child as she had protected its father. It would look after her soul, leaving supplies on her grave. But how would this tiny child without family find her grave when there would be no marker for her anywhere, neither in the earth nor the family hall? No one would give her a family hall name. She had taken the child with her into the wastes. At its birth the two of them had felt the same raw pain of separation, a wound that only the family pressing tight could close. A child with no descent line would not soften her life but only trail after her, ghostlike, begging her to give it purpose. At dawn the villagers on their way to the fields would stand around the fence and look.

Full of milk, the little ghost slept. When it awoke, she hardened her breasts against the milk that crying loosens. Toward morning she picked up the baby and walked to the well.

Carrying the baby to the well shows loving. Otherwise abandon it. Turn its face into the mud. Mothers who love their children take them along. It was probably a girl; there is some hope of forgiveness for boys.

"Don't tell anyone you had an aunt. Your father does not want to hear her name. She has never been born." I have believed that sex was unspeakable and words so strong and fathers so frail that "aunt" would do my father mysterious harm. I have thought that my family, having settled among immigrants who had also been their neighbors in the ancestral land, needed to clean their name, and a wrong word would incite the kinspeople even here. But there is more to this silence: They want me to participate in her punishment. And I have.

In the twenty years since I heard this story I have not asked for details nor said my aunt's name; I do not know it. People who comfort the dead can also chase after them to hurt them further—a reverse ancestor worship. The real punishment was not the raid swiftly inflicted by the villagers, but the family's deliberately forgetting her. Her betrayal so maddened them, they saw to it that she would suffer forever, even after death. Always hungry, always needing, she would have to beg food from other ghosts, snatch and steal it from those whose living descendants give them gifts. She would have to fight the ghosts massed at crossroads for the buns a few thoughtful citizens leave to decoy her away from village and home so that the ancestral spirits could feast unharassed. At peace, they could act like gods, not ghosts, their descent lines providing them with paper suits and dresses, spirit money, paper houses, paper automobiles, chicken, meat, and rice into eternity—essences delivered up in smoke and flames, steam and incense rising from each rice bowl. In an attempt to make the Chinese care for people outside the family, Chairman Mao encourages us now to give our paper replicas to the spirits of outstanding soldiers and workers, no matter whose ancestors they may be. My aunt remains forever hungry. Goods are not distributed evenly among the dead.

My aunt haunts me—her ghost drawn to me because now, after fifty years of neglect, I alone devote pages of paper to her, though not origamied into houses and clothes. I do not think she always means me well. I am telling on her, and she was a spite suicide, drowning herself in the drinking water. The Chinese are always very frightened of the drowned one, whose weeping ghost, wet hair hanging and skin bloated, waits silently by the water to pull down a substitute.

CONSIDERATIONS

Thinking

What ideas about cultural origins appear in "No Name Woman"? Which cultural attitudes does Kingston feature most prominently? Why?

What significance does Kingston give to the Chinese family "circle" and the "roundness" of family life? In what ways are secrecy and silence determining factors in the cultural experience Kingston describes?

Connecting

Consider ways in which your own family uses family stories as vehicles of instruction, as forms of entertainment, or as bonds of social solidarity.

Compare the way Kingston blends fact and fiction in "No Name Woman" with the way Loren Eiseley seems to combine fact and fiction in "The Dance of the Frogs."

Writing

Tell a story that has been part of your family lore. Be sure to account for the story's significance—for what it reveals (or conceals) about family values and attitudes.

Tell a series of family stories that reveal significant ideals of the race, culture, or ethnicity to which your family belongs.

Discuss the ways Kingston's essay and Amy Tan's "Mother Tongue" reflect and resolve differences between Chinese and American cultural practices.

Silence

When I went to kindergarten and had to speak English for the first time, I became silent. A dumbness—a shame—still cracks my voice in two, even when I want to say "hello" casually, or ask an easy question in front of the check-out counter, or ask directions of a bus driver. I stand frozen, or I hold up the line with the complete, grammatical sentence that comes squeaking out at impossible length. "What did you say?" says the cab driver, or "Speak up," so I have to perform again, only weaker the second time. A telephone call makes my throat bleed and takes up that day's courage. It spoils my day with self-disgust when I hear my broken voice come skittering out into the open. It makes people wince to hear it. I'm getting better, though. Recently I asked the postman for special-issue stamps; I've waited since childhood for postmen to give me some of their own accord. I am making progress, a little every day.

My silence was thickest—total—during the three years that I covered my school paintings with black paint. I painted layers of black over houses and flowers and suns, and when I drew on the blackboard, I put a layer of chalk on top. I was making a stage curtain, and it was the moment before the curtain parted or rose. The teachers called my parents to school, and I saw they had been saving my pictures, curling and cracking, all alike and black. The teachers pointed to the pictures and looked serious, talked seriously too, but my parents did not understand English. ("The parents and teachers of criminals were executed," said my father.) My parents took the pictures home. I spread them out (so black and full of possibilities) and pretended the curtains were swinging open, flying up, one after another, sunlight underneath, mighty operas.

During the first silent year I spoke to no one at school, did not ask before going to the lavatory, and flunked kindergarten. My sister also said nothing for three years, silent in the playground and silent at lunch. There were other quiet Chinese girls not of our family, but most of them got over it sooner than we did. I enjoyed the silence. At first it did not occur to me I was supposed to talk or to pass kindergarten. I talked at home and to one or two of the Chinese kids in class. I made motions and even made some jokes. I drank out of a toy saucer when the water spilled out of the cup, and everybody laughed, pointing at me, so I did it some more. I didn't know that Americans don't drink out of saucers.

I liked the Negro students (Black Ghosts) best because they laughed the loudest and talked to me as if I were a daring talker too. One of the Negro girls had her mother coil braids over her ears Shanghai-style like mine; we were Shanghai twins except that she was covered with black like my paintings. Two Negro kids enrolled in Chinese school, and the teachers gave them Chinese names. Some Negro kids walked me to school and home, protecting me from the Japanese kids, who hit me and chased me and stuck gum in my ears. The Japanese kids were noisy and tough. They appeared one day in kindergarten, released from concentration camp, which was a tic-tac-toe mark, like barbed wire, on the map.

It was when I found out I had to talk that school become a misery, that the silence became a misery. I did not speak and felt bad each time that I did not speak. I read aloud in first grade, though, and heard the barest whisper with little squeaks come out of my throat. "Louder," said the teacher, who scared the voice away again. The other Chinese girls did not talk either, so I knew the silence had to do with being a Chinese girl.

Reading out loud was easier than speaking because we did not have to make up what to say, but I stopped often, and the teacher would think I'd gone quiet again. I could not understand "I." The Chinese "I" has seven strokes, intricacies. How could the American "I," assuredly wearing a hat like the Chinese, have only three strokes, the middle so straight? Was it out of politeness that this writer left off the strokes the way a Chinese has to write her own name small and crooked? No, it was not politeness; "I" is a capital and "you" is lower-case. I stared at that middle line and waited so long for its black center to resolve into tight strokes and dots that I forgot to pronounce it. The other troublesome word was "here," no strong consonant to hang on to, and so flat, when "here" is two mountainous ideographs. The teacher, who had already told me every day how to read "I" and "here," put me in the low corner under the stairs again, where the noisy boys usually sat.

When my second grade class did a play, the whole class went to the auditorium except the Chinese girls. The teacher, lovely and Hawaiian, should have understood about us, but instead left us behind in the classroom. Our voices were too soft or nonexistent, and our parents never signed the permission slips anyway. They never signed anything unnecessary. We opened the door a crack and peeked out, but closed it again quickly. One of us (not me) won every spelling bee, though.

I remember telling the Hawaiian teacher, "We Chinese can't sing 'land where our fathers died.'" She argued with me about politics, while I meant because of curses. But how can I have that memory when I couldn't talk? My mother says that we, like the ghosts, have no memories.

After American school, we picked up our cigar boxes, in which we had arranged books, brushes, and an inkbox neatly, and went to Chinese school, from 5:00 to 7:30 P.M. There we chanted together, voices rising and falling, loud and soft, some boys shouting, everybody reading together, reciting together and not alone with one voice. When we had a memorization test, the teacher let each of us come to his desk and say the lesson to him privately, while the rest of the class practiced copying or tracing. Most of the teachers were men. The boys who were so well behaved in the American school played tricks on them and talked back to them. The girls were not mute. They screamed and yelled during recess, when there were no rules; they had fistfights. Nobody was afraid of children hurting themselves or of children hurting school property. The glass doors to the red and green balconies with the gold joy symbols were left wide open so that we could run out and climb the fire escapes. We played capture-the-flag in the auditorium, where Sun Yat-sen and Chiang Kai-shek's pictures hung at the back of the stage, the Chinese flag on their left and the American flag on their right. We climbed the teak ceremonial chairs and made flying leaps off the stage. One flag headquarters was behind the glass door and the other on stage right. Our feet drummed on the hollow stage. During recess the teachers locked themselves up in their office with the shelves of books, copybooks, inks from China. They drank tea and warmed their hands at a stove. There was no play supervision. At recess we had the school to ourselves, and also we could roam as far as we could go—downtown, Chinatown stores, home—as long as we returned before the bell rang.

At exactly 7:30 the teacher again picked up the brass bell that sat on his desk and swung it over our heads, while we charged down the stairs, our cheering magnified in the stairwell. Nobody had to line up.

Not all of the children who were silent at American school found voice at Chinese school. One new teacher said each of us had to get up and recite in front of the class, who was to listen. My sister and I had memorized the lesson perfectly. We said it to each other at home, one chanting, one listening. The teacher called on my sister to recite first. It was the first time a teacher had called on the second-born to go first. My sister was scared. She glanced at me and looked away; I looked down at my desk. I hoped that she could do it because if she could, then I would have to. She opened her mouth and a voice came out that wasn't a whisper, but it wasn't a proper voice either. I hoped that she would not cry, fear breaking up her voice like twigs underfoot. She sounded as if she were trying to sing through weeping and strangling. She did not pause or stop to end the embarrassment. She kept going until she said the last word, and then she sat down. When it was my turn, the same voice came out, a crippled animal running on broken legs. You could hear splinters in my voice, bones rubbing jagged against one another. I was loud, though. I was glad I didn't whisper.

How strange that the emigrant villagers are shouters, hollering face to face. My father asks, "Why is it I can hear Chinese from blocks away? Is it that I understand the language? Or is it they talk loud?" They turn the radio up full blast to hear the operas, which do not seem to hurt their ears. And they yell over the singers that wail over the drums, everybody talking at once, big arm gestures, spit flying. You can see the disgust on American faces looking at women like that. It isn't just the loudness. It is the way Chinese sounds, ching-chong ugly, to American ears, not beautiful like Japanese sayonara words with the consonants and vowels as regular as Italian. We make guttural peasant noise and have Ton Duc Thang names you can't remember. And the Chinese can't hear Americans at all; the language is too soft and western music unhearable. I've watched a Chinese audience laugh, visit, talk-story, and holler during a piano recital, as if the musician could not hear them. A Chinese-American, somebody's son, was playing Chopin, which has no punctuation, no cymbals, no gongs. Chinese piano music is five black keys. Normal Chinese women's voices are strong and bossy. We American-Chinese girls had to whisper to make ourselves American-feminine. Apparently we whispered even more softly than the Americans. Once a year the teachers referred my sister and me to speech therapy, but our voices would straighten out, unpredictably normal, for the therapists. Some of us gave up, shook our heads, and said nothing, not one word. Some of us could not even shake our heads. At times shaking my head no is more self-assertion than I can manage. Most of us eventually found some voice, however faltering. We invented an American-feminine speaking personality.

CONSIDERATIONS

Thinking

Kingston suggests that her silence was not peculiar to her, that instead, "the silence had to do with being a Chinese girl." Do you think her gender or her race and ethnicity were more important? Why?

What do you think about the "American-feminine speaking personality" she and her friends invented?

Connecting

Have there been times in your own life when you preferred silence to speech? On what occasions might you have wished to avoid speaking? Why?

Consider to what extent silence is encouraged or valued in different social situations and cultural contexts.

Writing

Discuss how attitudes toward language and ways of using it differ among racial, cultural, and ethnic groups. Focus on two or perhaps three groups.

Or explain the major differences Kingston identifies between Chinese and American ways of speaking.

On Discovery

Once upon a time, a man, named Tang Ao, looking for the Gold Mountain, crossed an ocean, and came upon the Land of Women. The women immediately captured him, not on guard against ladies. When they asked Tang Ao to come along, he followed; if he had had male companions, he would've winked over his shoulder.

"We have to prepare you to meet the queen," the women said. They locked him in a canopied apartment equipped with pots of makeup, mirrors, and a woman's clothes. "Let us help you off with your armor and boots," said the women. They slipped his coat off his shoulders, pulled it down his arms, and shackled his wrists behind him. The women who kneeled to take off his shoes chained his ankles together.

A door opened, and he expected to meet his match, but it was only two old women with sewing boxes in their hands. "The less you struggle, the less it'll hurt," one said, squinting a bright eye as she threaded her needle. Two captors sat on him while another held his head. He felt an old woman's dry fingers trace his ear; the long nail on her little finger scraped his neck. "What are you doing?" he asked. "Sewing your lips together," she joked, blackening needles in a candle flame. The ones who sat on him bounced with laughter. But the old woman did not sew his lips together. They pulled his earlobes taut and jabbed a needle through each of them. They had to poke and probe before puncturing the layers of skin correctly, the hole in the front of the lobe in line with the one in back, the layers of skin sliding about so. They worked the needle through—a last jerk for the needle's wide eye ("needle's nose" in Chinese). They strung his raw flesh with silk threads; he could feel the fibers.

The women who sat on him turned to direct their attention to his feet. They bent his toes so far backward that his arched foot cracked. The old ladies squeezed each foot and broke many tiny bones along the sides. They gathered his toes, toes over and under one another like a knot of ginger root. Tang Ao wept with pain. As they wound the bandages tight and tighter around his feet, the women sang footbinding songs to distract him: "Use aloe for binding feet and not for scholars."

During the months of a season, they fed him on women's food: the tea was thick with white chrysanthemums and stirred the cool female winds inside his body; chicken wings made his hair shine; vinegar soup improved his womb. They drew the loops of thread through the scabs that grew daily over the holes in his earlobes. One day they inserted gold hoops. Every night they unbound his feet, but his veins had shrunk, and the blood pumping through them hurt so much, he begged to have his feet rewrapped tight. They forced him to wash his used bandages, which were embroidered with flowers and smelled of rot and cheese. He hung the bandages up to dry, streamers that drooped and draped wall to wall. He felt embarrassed; the wrappings were like underwear, and they were his.

One day his attendants changed his gold hoops to jade studs and strapped his feet to shoes that curved like bridges. They plucked out each hair on his face, powdered him white, painted his eyebrows like a moth's wings, painted his cheeks and lips red. He served a meal at the queen's court. His hips swayed and his shoulders swiveled because of his shaped feet. "She's pretty, don't you agree?" the diners said, smacking their lips at his dainty feet as he bent to put dishes before them.

In the Women's Land there are no taxes and no wars. Some scholars say that that country was discovered during the reign of Empress Wu (A.D. 694–705), and some say earlier than that, A.D. 441, and it was in North America.

E.B. White
(1899–1985)

E. B. White is generally recognized as one of America's finest writers. Long associated with *The New Yorker,* for which he wrote stories, sketches, essays, and editorials, White also contributed to another prominent magazine, *Harper's,* writing a monthly column, "One Man's Meat," from 1938 to 1943. These columns were collected and published with a few additional pieces from *The New Yorker* as *One Man's Meat* (1944). This book was followed by two other collections of miscellany, *The Second Tree from the Corner* (1954) and *The Points of My Compass* (1962). Besides these collections, White published, over a slightly longer span of years, three children's books: *Stuart Little* (1945), *Charlotte's Web* (1952), and *The Trumpet of the Swan* (1970). In 1976, White published a selection of his best essays, those, as he says, which had "an odor of durability clinging to them." *The Essays of E. B. White* was followed a year later by a selection of White's letters, titled simply enough, *Letters of E. B. White. Poems and Sketches of E. B. White* appeared in 1981.

Although not a complete bibliography of White's published work, this list does suggest something of White's range and versatility, as well as something about the way writing has been for him steady work over a long stretch of time. And the steadiest of White's work, in both senses of the word, has been his essays. In fact, it is as an essayist that White is best known and most highly acclaimed. And it is as an essayist that he identifies himself, defining an essayist as "a self-liberated man sustained by the childish belief that everything he thinks about, everything that happens to him, is of general interest." And again, as one who is "content with living a free life and enjoying the satisfactions of a somewhat undisciplined existence."

Edward Hoagland has recently noted that White's name has become almost synonymous with *essay*. And for good reason, we might add, since it is the form most congenial to his temperament, a form that allows him the latitude he needs to roam freely in thought, a form that he has been able to stamp with his own imprint. This imprint is reflected in the following elements: a scrupulous respect for his readers; an uncanny accuracy in the use of language; and an uncommon delight in common, everyday things. White sees the extraordinary in the ordinary, noticing and valuing what most of us either overlook or take for granted. And from his repeated and respectful acts of attention flow reminiscences, speculations, explorations, and questions about our common humanity, about our relationships with one another, with the past, with the worlds of technology and nature.

White is a writer whose insights derive directly from his literal observations, from what he sees. Thoreau, one of White's favorite writers—and one with whom White has much in common—once remarked that "you can't say more than you can see." White's writing bears this out. The relationship between sight and insight, between observation and speculation, is evident in essays such as "The Ring of Time," which begins with a description of a circus act and ends with speculations about time and change, and "Once More to the Lake," in which White reminisces about his boyhood summer holidays in Maine, both describing the place with startling vividness and offering unsettling speculations about the meaning of his memories. In these and in other essays, White's writing is rooted in the crucial act of vision, a vision which sees into and beyond the surface of his subjects.

White's best writing, however, is more than a record of what he has seen and thought. It is also art, literature. His best work is crafted, shaped, formed with the same attention to details of structure, texture, image, and tone that poets or painters, sculptors or novelists give their work. In "The Ring of Time," "Once More to the Lake," and "The Geese," matters of fact, details of time, place, and circumstance give way to larger concerns. The circus is more than a circus ring: it becomes an emblem of time and change; the lake is more than a summer vacation place: it becomes an image of serenity and a reminder of time, change, even death; the old gander's plight becomes White's. The images of light and water, the symbolism of circus ring and lake, along with a concern for understanding the present in relation to the past and the future, the emblematic nature of the geese—these emphases lift their respective essays beyond the merely personal and reminiscent, beyond the ordinary and the everyday into the extraordinary universality of art.

About writing itself, White has said a good deal, and said it well. In the chapter he contributed to the now famous *Elements of Style,* White notes that when we speak of a writer's style we mean "the sound his words make on paper." The voice that we hear is what distinguishes one writer from another; and it is one good reason why, to get a good sense of a writer's style, we should read his or her work aloud. Beyond this concern for hearing what language can do, White notes that a writer's style "reveals something of his spirit, his habits, his capacities, his bias . . . it is the Self escaping into the open." And, as White suggests, this Self cannot be hidden, for a writer's style "reveals his identity as surely as would his fingerprints."

Recognizing that writing is hard work requiring endurance, thought, and revision ("revising is part of writing"), White advises that beginning writers let their ears be their guide, that they avoid all tricks and mannerisms, that they see writing as "one way to go about thinking," and, finally, that they achieve style both by affecting none and by believing "in the truth and worth of the scrawl."

Throughout his years as a writer, White has often been asked for advice about writing. To one seeker he wrote: "Remember that writing is translation, and the opus to be translated is yourself." On another occasion he responded to a seventeen-year-old girl this way:

> You asked me about writing—how I did it. There is no trick to it. If you like to write and want to write, you write, no matter where you are or what else you are doing or whether anyone pays any heed. . . . If you want to write about feelings, about the end of summer, about growing, write about it. A great deal of writing is not "plotted"—most of my essays have no plot structure, they are a ramble in the woods, or a ramble in the basement of my mind.

There is a naturalness, an ease about White's writing, both in these offhand remarks from his letters and in his more elaborately plotted essays. It is an ease that derives in part from a refusal to be either pompous or pedantic; it is an ease that derives also from a consistent attempt to be honest, to achieve the candor he admires in Montaigne;

and it is a naturalness that is reflected in his style, a style that mingles the high subject and the low, the big word and the small, without flamboyance or ostentation. White's style, in short, is a badge of his character—intelligent, honest, witty, exact, and fundamentally endearing.

Once More to the Lake

One summer, along about 1904, my father rented a camp on a lake in Maine and took us all there for the month of August. We all got ringworm from some kittens and had to rub Pond's Extract on our arms and legs night and morning, and my father rolled over in a canoe with all his clothes on; but outside of that the vacation was a success and from then on none of us ever thought there was any place in the world like that lake in Maine. We returned summer after summer—always on August 1st for one month. I have since become a salt-water man, but sometimes in summer there are days when the restlessness of the tides and the fearful cold of the sea water and the incessant wind that blows across the afternoon and into the evening make me wish for the placidity of a lake in the woods. A few weeks ago this feeling got so strong I bought myself a couple of bass hooks and a spinner and returned to the lake where we used to go, for a week's fishing and to revisit old haunts.

I took along my son, who had never had any fresh water up his nose and who had seen lily pads only from train windows. On the journey over to the lake I began to wonder what it would be like. I wondered how time would have marred this unique, this holy spot—the coves and streams, the hills that the sun set behind, the camps and the paths behind the camps. I was sure that the tarred road would have found it out and I wondered in what other ways it would be desolated. It is strange how much you can remember about places like that once you allow your mind to return into the grooves that lead back. You remember one thing, and that suddenly reminds you of another thing. I guess I remembered clearest of all the early mornings, when the lake was cool and motionless, remembered how the bedroom smelled of the lumber it was made of and the wet woods whose scent entered through the screen. The partitions in the camp were thin and did not extend clear to the top of the rooms, and as I was always the first up I would dress softly so as not to wake the others, and sneak out into the sweet outdoors and start out in the canoe, keeping close along the shore in the long shadows of the pines. I remembered being very careful never to rub my paddle against the gunwale for fear of disturbing the stillness of the cathedral.

The lake had never been what you would call a wild lake. There were cottages sprinkled about the shores, and it was in farming country although the shores of the lake were quite heavily wooded. Some of the cottages were owned by nearby farmers, and you would live at the shore and eat your meals at the farmhouse. That's what our family did. But although it wasn't wild, it was a fairly large and undisturbed lake and there were places in it which, to a child at least, seemed infinitely remote and primeval.

I was right about the tar: It led to within half a mile of the shore. But when I got back there, with my boy, and we settled into a camp near a farmhouse and into the kind of summertime I had known, I could tell that it was going to be pretty much the same as it had been before—I knew it, lying in bed the first morning, smelling the bedroom, and hearing the boy sneak quietly out and go off along the shore in a boat. I began to sustain the illusion that he was I, and therefore, by simple transposition, that I was my father. This sensation persisted, kept cropping up all the time we were there. It was not an entirely new feeling, but in this setting it grew much stronger. I seemed to be living a dual existence. I would be in the middle of some simple act, I would be picking up a bait box or laying down a table fork, or I would be saying something, and suddenly it would be not I but my father who was saying the words or making the gesture. It gave me a creepy sensation.

We went fishing the first morning. I felt the same damp moss covering the worms in the bait can, and saw the dragonfly alight on the tip of my rod as it hovered a few inches from the surface of the water. It was the arrival of this fly that convinced me beyond any doubt that everything was as it always had been, that the years were a mirage and there had been no years. The small waves were the same, chucking the rowboat under the chin as we fished at anchor, and the boat was the same boat, the same color green and the ribs broken in the same places, and under the floor-boards the same fresh-water leavings and debris—the dead hellgrammite, the wisps of moss, the rusty discarded fishhook, the dried blood from yesterday's catch. We stared silently at the tips of our rods, at the dragonflies that came and went. I lowered the tip of mine into the water, tentatively, pensively dislodging the fly, which darted two feet away, poised, darted two feet back, and came to rest again a little farther up the rod. There had been no years between the ducking of this dragonfly and the other one—the one that was part of memory. I looked at the boy, who was silently watching his fly, and it was my hands that held his rod, my eyes watching. I felt dizzy and didn't know which rod I was at the end of.

We caught two bass, hauling them in briskly as though they were mackerel, pulling them over the side of the boat in a businesslike manner without any landing net, and stunning them with a blow on the back of the head. When we got back for a swim before lunch, the lake was exactly where we had left it, the same number of inches from the dock, and there was only the merest suggestion of a breeze. This seemed an utterly enchanted sea, this lake you could leave to its own devices for a few hours and come back to, and find that it had not stirred, this constant and trustworthy body of water. In the shallows, the dark, watersoaked sticks and twigs, smooth and old, were undulating in clusters on the bottom against the clean ribbed sand, and the track of the mussel was plain. A school of minnows swam by, each minnow with its small individual shadow, doubling the attendance, so clear and sharp in the sunlight. Some of the other campers were in swimming, along the shore, one of them with a cake of soap, and the water felt thin and clear and unsubstantial. Over the years there had been this person with the cake of soap, this cultist, and here he was. There had been no years.

Up to the farmhouse to dinner through the teeming, dusty field, the road under our sneakers was only a two-track road. The middle track was missing, the one with the marks of the hooves and splotches of dried, flaky manure. There had always been three tracks to choose from in choosing which track to walk in; now the choice was narrowed down to two. For a moment I missed terribly the middle alternative. But the way led past the tennis court, and something about the way it lay there in the sun reassured me; the tape had loosened along the backline, the alleys were green with plantains and other weeds, and the net (installed in June and removed in September) sagged in the dry noon, and the whole place steamed with midday heat and hunger and emptiness. There was a choice of pie for dessert, and one was blueberry and one was apple, and the waitresses were the same country girls, there having been no passage of time, only the illusion of it as in a dropped curtain—the waitresses were still fifteen; their hair had been washed, that was the only difference— they had been to the movies and seen the pretty girls with the clean hair.

Summertime, oh summertime, pattern of life indelible, the fade-proof lake, the woods unshatterable, the pasture with the sweetfern and the juniper forever and ever, summer without end; this was the background, and the life along the shore was the design, the cottages with their innocent and tranquil design, their tiny docks with the flagpole and the American flag floating against the white clouds in the blue sky, the little paths over the roots of the trees leading from camp to camp and the paths leading back to the outhouses and the can of lime for sprinkling, and at the souvenir counters at the store the miniature birch-bark canoes and the post cards that showed things looking a little better than they looked. This was the American family at play, escaping the city heat, wondering whether the newcomers in the camp at the head of the cove were "common" or "nice," wondering whether it was true that the people who drove up for Sunday dinner at the farmhouse were turned away because there wasn't enough chicken.

It seemed to me, as I kept remembering all this, that those times and those summers had been infinitely precious and worth saving. There had been jollity and peace and goodness. The arriving (at the beginning of August) had been so big a business in itself, at the railway station the farm wagon drawn up, the first smell of the pine-laden air, the first glimpse of the smiling farmer, and the great importance of the trunks and your father's enormous authority in such matters, and the feel of the wagon under you for the long ten-mile haul, and at the top of the last long hill catching the first view of the lake after eleven months of not seeing this cherished body of water. The shouts and cries of the other campers when they saw you, and the trunks to be unpacked, to give up their rich burden. (Arriving was less exciting nowadays, when you sneaked up in your car and parked it under a tree near the camp and took out the bags and in five minutes it was all over, no fuss, no loud wonderful fuss about trunks).

Peace and goodness and jollity. The only thing that was wrong now, really, was the sound of the place, an unfamiliar nervous sound of the outboard motors. This was the note that jarred, the one thing that would sometimes break the illusion and set the years moving. In those other summertimes all motors were inboard; and when they were at a little distance, the noise they made was a sedative, an ingredient of summer sleep. They were one-cylinder and two-cylinder engines, and some were make-and-break and some were jump-spark, but they all made a sleepy sound across the lake. The one-lungers throbbed and fluttered, and the twin-cylinder ones purred and purred, and that was a quiet sound too. But now the campers all had outboards. In the daytime, in the hot mornings, these motors made a petulant, irritable sound; at night, in the still evening when the afterglow lit the water, they whined about one's ears like mosquitoes. My boy loved our rented outboard, and his great desire was to achieve singlehanded mastery over it, and authority, and he soon learned the trick of choking it a little (but not too much), and the adjustment of the needle valve. Watching him I would remember the things you could do with the old one-cylinder engines with the heavy flywheel, how you could have it eating out of your hand if you got really close to it spiritually. Motor boats in those days didn't have clutches, and you would make a landing by shutting off the motor at the proper time and coasting in with a dead rudder. But there was a way of reversing them, if you learned the trick, by cutting the switch and putting it on again exactly on the final dying revolution of the flywheel, so that it would kick back against compression and begin reversing. Approaching a dock in a strong following breeze, it was difficult to slow up sufficiently by the ordinary coasting method, and if a boy felt he had complete mastery over his motor, he was tempted to keep it running beyond its time and then reverse it a few feet from the dock. It took a cool nerve, because if you threw the switch a twentieth of a second too soon you could catch the flywheel when it still had speed enough to go up past center, and the boat would leap ahead, charging bull-fashion at the dock.

We had a good week at the camp. The bass were biting well and the sun shone endlessly, day after day. We would be tired at night and lie down in the accumulated heat of the little bedrooms after the long hot day and the breeze would stir almost imperceptibly outside and the smell of the swamp drift in through the rusty screens. Sleep would come easily and in the morning the red squirrel would be on the roof, tapping out his gay routine. I kept remembering everything, lying in bed in the mornings—the small steamboat that had a long rounded stern like the lip of a Ubangi, and how quietly she ran on the moonlight sails, when the older boys played their mandolins and the girls sang and we ate doughnuts dipped in sugar, and how sweet the music was on the water in the shining night, and what it had felt like to think about girls then. After breakfast we would go up to the store and the things were in the same place—the minnows in a bottle, the plugs and spinners disarranged and pawed over by the youngsters from the boys' camp, the Fig Newtons and the Beeman's gum. Outside, the road was tarred and cars stood in front of the store. Inside, all was just as it had always been, except there was more Coca-Cola and not so much Moxie and root beer and birch beer and sarsaparilla. We would walk out with a bottle of pop apiece and sometimes the pop would backfire up our noses and hurt. We explored the streams, quietly, where the turtles slid off the sunny logs and dug their way into the soft bottom; and we lay on the town wharf and fed worms to the tame bass. Everywhere we went I had trouble making out which was I, the one walking at my side, the one walking in my pants.

One afternoon while we were there at that lake a thunderstorm came up. It was like the revival of an old melodrama that I had seen long ago with childish awe. The second-act climax of the drama of the electrical disturbance over a lake in America had not changed in any important respect. This was the big scene, still the big scene. The whole thing was so familiar, the first feeling of oppression and heat and a general air around camp of not wanting to go very far away. In midafternoon (it was all the same) a curious darkening of the sky, and a lull in everything that had made life tick; and then the way the boats suddenly swung the other way at their moorings with the coming of a breeze out of the new quarter, and the premonitory rumble. Then the kettle drum, then the snare, then the bass drum and cymbals, then crackling light against the dark, and the gods grinning and licking their chops in the hills. Afterward the calm, the rain steadily rustling in the calm lake, the return of light and hope and spirits, and the campers running out in joy and relief to go swimming in the rain, their bright cries perpetuating the deathless joke about how they were getting simply drenched, and the children screaming with delight at the new sensation of bathing in the rain, and the joke about getting drenched linking the generations in a strong indestructible chain. And the comedian who waded in carrying an umbrella.

When the others went swimming my son said he was going in too. He pulled his dripping trunks from the line where they had hung all through the shower, and wrung them out. Languidly, and with no thought of going in, I watched him, his hard little body, skinny and bare, saw him wince slightly as he pulled up around his vitals the small, soggy, icy garment. As he buckled the swollen belt suddenly my groin felt the chill of death.

CONSIDERATIONS

Thinking

White's essay is, in part, a meditation on time. What ideas about time do you find White exploring? What do you think he means by saying that he "seemed to be living a dual existence"? Why is this statement important?

In what sense is White's essay about a trip to a place—a trip into his past, a projection into his future?

Connecting

To what extent can you share in the experience White describes? Why? Identify another work you have read (or viewed) that can be linked with the experience White describes or the ideas he explores.

Or consider how and why the world White describes is alien to you, how it makes assumptions or expresses values at odds with or perhaps different from your own.

Writing

Develop your own essay about time and change, perhaps using White's as a jumping-off point. You may wish to ground your essay in your experience, or you may wish to draw upon your reading of other works to develop your thinking, or you may wish to do both.

Or analyze how White's choices of language, image, and organization convey his meaning.

Or discuss the implications of the images White uses to convey a sense of what the world was like for him in the period of time spanned by the essay.

The Ring of Time

Fiddler Bayou, March 22, 1956

After the lions had returned to their cages, creeping angrily through the chutes, a little bunch of us drifted away and into an open doorway nearby, where we stood for a while in semidarkness, watching a big brown circus horse go harumphing around the practice ring. His trainer was a woman of about forty, and the two of them, horse and woman, seemed caught up in one of those desultory treadmills of afternoon from which there is no apparent escape. The day was hot, and we kibitzers were grateful to be briefly out of the sun's glare. The long rein, or tape, by which the woman guided her charge counterclockwise in his dull career formed the radius of their private circle, of which she was the revolving center; and she, too, stepped a tiny circumference of her own, in order to accommodate the horse and allow him his maximum scope. She had on a short-skirted costume and a conical straw hat. Her legs were bare and she wore high heels, which probed deep into the loose tanbark and kept her ankles in a state of constant turmoil. The great size and meekness of the horse, the repetitious exercise, the heat of the afternoon, all exerted a hypnotic charm that invited boredom; we spectators were experiencing a languor—we neither expected relief nor felt entitled to any. We had paid a dollar to get into the grounds, to be sure, but we had got our dollar's worth a few minutes before, when the lion trainer's whiplash had got caught around a toe of one of the lions. What more did we want for a dollar?

Behind me I heard someone say, "Excuse me, please," in a low voice. She was halfway into the building when I turned and saw her—a girl of sixteen or seventeen, politely threading her way through us onlookers who blocked the entrance. As she emerged in front of us, I saw that she was barefoot, her dirty little feet fighting the uneven ground. In most respects she was like any of two or three dozen showgirls you encounter if you wander about the winter quarters of Mr. John Ringling North's circus, in Sarasota—cleverly proportioned, deeply browned by the sun, dusty, eager, and almost naked. But her grave face and the naturalness of her manner gave her a sort of quick distinction and brought a new note

729

into the gloomy octagonal building where we had all cast our lot for a few moments. As soon as she had squeezed through the crowd, she spoke a word or two to the older woman, whom I took to be her mother, stepped to the ring, and waited while the horse coasted to a stop in front of her. She gave the animal a couple of affectionate swipes on his enormous neck and then swung herself aboard. The horse immediately resumed his rocking canter, the woman goading him on, chanting something that sounded like "Hop! Hop!"

In attempting to recapture this mild spectacle, I am merely acting as recording secretary for one of the oldest of societies—the society of those who, at one time or another, have surrendered, without even a show of resistance, to the bedazzlement of a circus rider. As a writing man, or secretary, I have always felt charged with the safekeeping of all unexpected items of worldly or unworldly enchantment, as though I might be held personally responsible if even a small one were to be lost. But it is not easy to communicate anything of this nature. The circus comes as close to being the world in microcosm as anything I know; in a way, it puts all the rest of show business in the shade. Its magic is universal and complex. Out of its wild disorder comes order; from its rank smell rises the good aroma of courage and daring; out of its preliminary shabbiness comes the final splendor. And buried in the familiar boasts of its advance agents lies the modesty of most of its people. For me the circus is at its best before it has been put together. It is at its best at certain moments when it comes to a point, as through a burning glass, in the activity and destiny of a single performer out of so many. One ring is always bigger than three. One rider, one aerialist, is always greater than six. In short, a man has to catch the circus unawares to experience its full impact and share its gaudy dream.

The ten-minute ride the girl took achieved—as far as I was concerned, who wasn't looking for it, and quite unbeknownst to her, who wasn't even striving for it—the thing that is sought by performers everywhere, on whatever stage, whether struggling in the tidal currents of Shakespeare or bucking the difficult motion of a horse. I somehow got the idea she was just cadging a ride, improving a shining ten minutes in the diligent way all serious artists seize free moments to hone the blade of their talent and keep themselves in trim. Her brief tour included only elementary postures and tricks, perhaps because they were all she was capable of, perhaps because her warmup at this hour was unscheduled and the ring was not rigged for a real practice session. She swung herself off and on the horse several times, gripping his mane. She did a few knee-stands—or whatever they are called—dropping to her knees and quickly bouncing back up on her feet again. Most of the time she simply rode in a standing position, well aft on the beast, her hands hanging easily at her sides, her head erect, her straw-colored ponytail lightly brushing her shoulders, the blood of exertion showing faintly through the tan of her skin. Twice she managed a one-foot stance—a sort of ballet pose, with arms outstretched. At one point the neck strap of her bathing suit broke and she went twice around the ring in the classic attitude of a woman making minor repairs to a garment. The fact that she was standing on the back of a moving horse while doing this invested the matter with a clown-ish significance that perfectly fitted the spirit of the circus—jocund, yet charming. She just rolled the strap into a neat ball and stowed it inside her bodice while the horse rocked and rolled beneath her in dutiful inno-cence. The bathing suit proved as self-reliant as its owner and stood up well enough without benefit of strap.

The richness of the scene was in its plainness, its natural condition—of horse, of ring, of girl, even to the girl's bare feet that gripped the bare back of her proud and ridiculous mount. The enchantment grew not out of anything that happened or was performed but out of something that seemed to go round and around and around with the girl, attending her, a steady gleam in the shape of a circle—a ring of ambition, of happiness, of youth. (And the positive pleasures of equilibrium under difficulties.) In a week or two, all would be changed, all (or almost all) lost: the girl would wear makeup, the horse would wear gold, the ring would be painted, the bark would be clean for the feet of the horse, the girl's feet would be clean for the slippers that she'd wear. All, all would be lost.

As I watched with the others, our jaws adroop, our eyes alight, I became painfully conscious of the element of time. Everything in the hideous old building seemed to take the shape of a circle, conforming to the course of the horse. The rider's gaze, as she peered straight ahead, seemed to be circular, as though bent by force of circumstance; then time itself began running in circles, and so the beginning was where the end was, and the two were the same, and one thing ran into the next and time went round and around and got nowhere. The girl wasn't so young that she did not know the delicious satisfaction of having a perfectly behaved body and the fun of using it to do a trick most people can't do, but she was too young to know that time does not really move in a circle at all. I thought: "She will never be as beautiful as this again"—a thought that made me acutely unhappy—and in a flash my mind (which is too much of a busybody to suit me) had projected her twenty-five years ahead, and she was now in the center of the ring, on foot, wearing a conical hat and high-heeled shoes, the image of the older woman, holding the long rein, caught in the treadmill of an afternoon long in the future. "She is at that enviable moment in life [I thought] when she believes she can go once around the ring, make one complete circuit, and at the end be exactly the same age as at the start." Everything in her movements, her expression, told you that for her the ring of time was perfectly formed, changeless, predictable, without beginning or end, like the ring in which she was traveling at this moment with the horse that wallowed under her. And then I slipped back into my trance, and time was circular again—time, pausing quietly with the rest of us, so as not to disturb the balance of a performer.

Her ride ended as casually as it had begun. The older woman stopped the horse, and the girl slid to the ground. As she walked toward us to leave, there was a quick, small burst of applause. She smiled broadly, in surprise and pleasure; then her face suddenly regained its gravity and she disappeared through the door.

It has been ambitious and plucky of me to attempt to describe what is indescribable, and I have failed, as I knew I would. But I have dis-charged my duty to my society; and besides, a writer, like an acrobat, must occasionally try a stunt that is too much for him. At any rate, it is worth reporting that long before the circus comes to town, its most notable performances have already been given. Under the bright lights of the finished show, a performer need only reflect the electric candle power that is directed upon him; but in the dark and dirty old training rings and in the makeshift cages, whatever light is generated, whatever excitement, whatever beauty, must come from original sources—from internal fires of professional hunger and delight, from the exuberance and gravity of youth. It is the difference between planetary light and the combustion of stars.

The South is the land of the sustained sibilant. Everywhere, for the appreciative visitor, the letter "s" insinuates itself in the scene: in the sound of sea and sand, in the singing shell, in the heat of sun and sky, in the sultriness of the gentle hours, in the siesta, in the stir of birds and insects. In contrast to the softness of its music, the South is also cruel and hard and prickly. A little striped lizard, flattened along the sharp green bayonet of a yucca, wears in its tiny face and watchful eye the pure look of death and violence. And all over the place, hidden at the bottom of their small sandy craters, the ant lions lie in wait for the ant that will stumble into their trap. (There are three kinds of lions in this region: the lions of the circus, the ant lions, and the Lions of the Tampa Lions Club, who roared their approval of segregation at a meeting the other day—all except one, a Lion named Monty Gurwit, who declined to roar and thereby got his picture in the paper.)

The day starts on a note of despair: the sorrowing dove, alone on its telephone wire, mourns the loss of night, weeps at the bright perils of the unfolding day. But soon the mockingbird wakes and begins an early rehearsal, setting the dove down by force of character, running through a few slick imitations, and trying a couple of original numbers into the bargain. The redbird takes it from there. Despair gives way to good humor. The Southern dawn is a pale affair, usually, quite different from our northern daybreak. It is a triumph of gradualism; night turns to day imperceptibly, softly, with no theatrics. It is subtle and undisturbing. As the first light seeps in through the blinds I lie in bed half awake, despairing with the dove, sounding the A for the brothers Alsop. All seems lost, all seems sorrowful. Then a mullet jumps in the bayou outside the bedroom window. It falls back into the water with a smart smack. I have asked several people why the mullet incessantly jump and I have received a variety of answers. Some say the mullet jump to shake off a parasite that annoys them. Some say they jump for the love of jumping—as the girl on the horse seemed to ride for the love of riding (although she, too, like all artists, may have been shaking off some parasite that fastens itself to the creative spirit and can be got rid of only by fifty turns around a ring while standing on a horse).

In Florida at this time of year, the sun does not take command of the day until a couple of hours after it has appeared in the east. It seems to carry no authority at first. The sun and the lizard keep the same schedule; they bide their time until the morning has advanced a good long way before they come fully forth and strike. The cold lizard waits astride his warming leaf for the perfect moment; the cold sun waits in his nest of clouds for the crucial time.

On many days, the dampness of the air pervades all life, all living. Matches refuse to strike. The towel, hung to dry, grows wetter by the hour. The newspaper, with its headlines about integration, wilts in your hand and falls limply into the coffee and the egg. Envelopes seal themselves. Postage stamps mate with one another as shamelessly as grasshoppers. But most of the time the days are models of beauty and wonder and comfort, with the kind sea stroking the back of the warm sand. At evening there are great flights of birds over the sea, where the light lingers; the gulls, the pelicans, the terns, the herons stay aloft for half an hour after land birds have gone to roost. They hold their ancient formations, wheel and fish over the Pass, enjoying the last of day like children playing outdoors after suppertime.

To a beachcomber from the North, which is my present status, the race problem has no pertinence, no immediacy. Here in Florida I am a guest in two houses—the house of the sun, the house of the State of Florida. As a guest, I mind my manners and do not criticize the customs of my hosts. It gives me a queer feeling, though, to be at the center of the greatest social crisis of my time and see hardly a sign of it. Yet the very absence of signs seems to increase one's awareness. Colored people do not come to the public beach to bathe, because they would not be made welcome there; and they don't fritter away their time visiting the circus, because they have other things to do. A few of them turn up at the ballpark, where they occupy a separate but equal section of the left-field bleachers and watch Negro players on the visiting Braves team using the same bases as the white players, instead of separate (but equal) bases. I have had only two small encounters with "color." A colored woman named Viola, who had been a friend of my wife's sister years ago, showed up one day with some laundry of ours that she had consented to do for us, and with the bundle she brought a bunch of nasturtiums, as a sort of natural accompaniment to the delivery of clean clothes. The flowers seemed a very acceptable thing and I was touched by them. We asked Viola about her daughter, and she said she was at Kentucky State College, studying voice.

The other encounter was when I was explaining to our cook, who is from Finland, the mysteries of bus travel in the American Southland. I showed her the bus stop, armed her with a timetable, and then, as a matter of duty, mentioned the customs of the Romans. "When you get on the bus," I said, "I think you'd better sit in one of the front seats—the seats in back are for colored people." A look of great weariness came into her face, as it does when we use too many dishes, and she replied, "Oh, I know— isn't it silly!"

Her remark, coming as it did all the way from Finland and landing on this sandbar with a plunk, impressed me. The Supreme Court said nothing about silliness, but I suspect it may play more of a role than one might suppose. People are, if anything, more touchy about being thought silly than they are about being thought unjust. I note that one of the arguments in the recent manifesto of Southern Congressmen in support of the doctrine of "separate but equal" was that it had been founded on "common sense." The sense that is common to one generation is uncommon to the next. Probably the first slave ship, with Negroes lying in chains on its decks, seemed commonsensical to the owners who operated it and to the planters who patronized it. But such a vessel would not be in the realm of common sense today. The only sense that is common, in the long run, is the sense of change—and we all instinctively avoid it, and object to the passage of time, and would rather have none of it.

The Supreme Court decision is like the Southern sun, laggard in its early stages, biding its time. It has been the law in Florida for two years now, and the years have been like the hours of the morning before the sun has gathered its strength. I think the decision is as incontrovertible and warming as the sun, and, like the sun, will eventually take charge.

But there is certainly a great temptation in Florida to duck the passage of time. Lying in warm comfort by the sea, you receive gratefully the gift of the sun, the gift of the South. This is true seduction. The day is a circle—morning, afternoon, and night. After a few days I was clearly enjoying the same delusion as the girl on the horse—that I could ride clear around the ring of day, guarded by wind and sun and sea and sand, and be not a moment older.

P.S. (April, 1962).   When I first laid eyes on Fiddler Bayou, it was wild land, populated chiefly by the little crabs that gave it its name, visited by wading birds and by an occasional fisherman. Today, houses ring the bayou, and part of the mangrove shore has been bulkheaded with a concrete wall. Green lawns stretch from patio to water's edge, and sprinklers make rainbows in the light. But despite man's encroachment, Nature manages to hold her own and assert her authority: high tides and high winds in the gulf sometimes send the sea crashing across the sand barrier, depositing its wrack on lawns and ringing everyone's front door bell. The birds and the crabs accommodate themselves quite readily to the changes that have taken place; every day brings herons to hunt around among the roots of the mangroves, and I have discovered that I can approach to within about eight feet of a Little Blue Heron simply by entering the water and swimming slowly toward him. Apparently he has decided that when I'm in the water, I am without guile—possibly even desirable, like a fish.

The Ringling circus has quit Sarasota and gone elsewhere for its hibernation. A few circus families still own homes in the town, and every spring the students at the high school put on a circus, to let off steam, work off physical requirements, and provide a promotional spectacle for Sarasota. At the drugstore you can buy a postcard showing the bed John Ringling slept in. Time has not stood still for anybody but the dead, and even the dead must be able to hear the acceleration of little sports cars and know that things have changed.

From the all-wise *New York Times,* which has the animal kingdom ever in mind, I have learned that one of the creatures most acutely aware of the passing of time is the fiddler crab himself. Tiny spots on his body enlarge during daytime hours, giving him the same color as the mudbank he explores and thus protecting him from his enemies. At night the spots shrink, his color fades, and he is almost invisible in the light of the moon. These changes are synchronized with the tides, so that each day they occur at a different hour. A scientist who experimented with the crabs to learn more about the phenomenon discovered that even when they are removed from their natural environment and held in confinement, the rhythm of their bodily change continues uninterrupted, and they mark the passage of time in their laboratory prison, faithful to the tides in their fashion.

CONSIDERATIONS

Thinking

What ideas about time emerge in this essay? Why does White visualize time as running both in a straight line and in circles?

What do the two parts of White's essay have in common? What does the second part contribute to your understanding of the first part? How does it alter or otherwise modify your understanding of the first part? Why?

Connecting

Relate what White describes in either part of "The Ring of Time" to your own experience. Explain how your experience links up (or doesn't link up) with something White mentions in his essay.

Relate the ideas that emerge in your reading of "The Ring of Time" to ideas that animate White's "Once More to the Lake" or "The Geese," or both essays.

Consider Martin Luther King, Jr.'s "Letter from Birmingham Jail" in conjunction with the second part of "The Ring of Time."

Writing

Write your own essay about a ring of time of which you are a part. Consider how your own family exemplifies (or doesn't exemplify) the ideas White conveys in "The Ring of Time." You may wish to focus on one of your parents or perhaps one of your grandparents in developing your essay.

Or compare White's treatment of the subject of time and change in "The Ring of Time" with his handling of that subject in "The Geese" or "Once More to the Lake."

The Geese

Allen Cove, July 9, 1971

To give a clear account of what took place in the barnyard early in the morning on that last Sunday in June, I will have to go back more than a year in time, but a year is nothing to me these days. Besides, I intend to be quick about it, and not dawdle.

I have had a pair of elderly gray geese—a goose and a gander—living on this place for a number of years, and they have been my friends. "Companions" would be a better word; geese are friends with no one, they badmouth everybody and everything. But they are companionable once you get used to their ingratitude and their false accusations. Early in the spring, a year ago, as soon as the ice went out of the pond, my goose started to lay. She laid three eggs in about a week's time and then died. I found her halfway down the lane that connects the barnyard with the pasture. There were no marks on her—she lay with wings partly outspread, and with her neck forward in the grass, pointing downhill. Geese are rarely sick, and I think this goose's time had come and she had simply died of old age. I had noticed that her step had slowed on her trips back from the pond to the barn where her nest was. I had never known her age, and so had nothing else to go on. We buried her in our private graveyard, and I felt sad at losing an acquaintance of such long standing—long standing and loud shouting.

Her legacy, of course, was the three eggs. I knew they were good eggs and did not like to pitch them out. It seemed to me that the least I could do for my departed companion was to see that the eggs she had left in my care were hatched. I checked my hen pen to find out whether we had a broody, but there was none. During the next few days, I scoured the neighborhood for a broody hen, with no success. Years ago, if you needed a broody hen, almost any barn or henhouse would yield one. But today broodiness is considered unacceptable in a hen; the modern hen is an egg-laying machine, and her natural tendency to sit on eggs in springtime has been bred out of her. Besides, not many people keep hens anymore—when they want a dozen eggs, they don't go to the barn, they go to the First National.

Days went by. My gander, the widower, lived a solitary life—nobody to swap gossip with, nobody to protect. He seemed dazed. The three eggs were not getting any younger, and I myself felt dazed—restless and unfulfilled. I had stored the eggs down cellar in the arch where it is cool, and every time I went down there for something they seemed silently to reproach me. My plight had become known around town, and one day a friend phoned and said he would lend me an incubator designed for hatching the eggs of waterfowl. I brought the thing home, cleaned it up, plugged it in, and sat down to read the directions. After studying them, I realized that if I were to tend eggs in that incubator, I would have to withdraw from the world for thirty days—give up everything, just as a broody goose does. Obsessed though I was with the notion of bringing life into three eggs, I wasn't quite prepared to pay the price.

Instead, I abandoned the idea of incubation and decided to settle the matter by acquiring three ready-made goslings, as a memorial to the goose and a gift for the lonely gander. I drove up the road about five miles and dropped in on Irving Closson. I knew Irving had geese; he has everything—even a sawmill. I found him shoeing a very old horse in the doorway of his barn, and I stood and watched for while. Hens and geese wandered about the yard, and a turkey tom circled me, wings adroop, strutting. The horse, with one forefoot between the man's knees, seemed to have difficulty balancing himself on three legs but was quiet and sober, almost asleep. When I asked Irving if he planned to put shoes on the horse's hind feet, too, he said, "No, it's hard work for me, and he doesn't use those hind legs much anyway." Then I brought up the question of goslings, and he took me into the barn and showed me a sitting goose. He said he thought she was covering more than twenty eggs and should bring off her goslings in a couple of weeks and I could buy a few if I wanted. I said I would like three.

I took to calling at Irving's every few days—it is about the pleasantest place to visit anywhere around. At last, I was rewarded: I pulled into the driveway one morning and saw a goose surrounded by green goslings. She had been staked out like a cow. Irving had simply tied a piece of string to one leg and fastened the other end to a peg in the ground. She was a pretty goose—not as large as my old one had been, and with a more slender neck. She appeared to be a cross-bred bird, two-toned gray, with white markings—a sort of particolored goose. The goslings had the cheerful, bright, innocent look that all baby geese have. We scooped up three and tossed them into a box, and I paid Irving and carried them home.

My next concern was how to introduce these small creatures to their foster father, my old gander. I thought about this all the way home. I've had just enough experience with domesticated animals and birds to know that they are a bundle of eccentricities and crotchets, and I was not at all sure what sort of reception three strange youngsters would get from a gander who was full of sorrows and suspicions. (I once saw a gander, taken by surprise, seize a newly hatched gosling and hurl it the length of the barn floor.) I had an uneasy feeling that my three little charges might be dead within the hour, victims of a grief-crazed old fool. I decided to go slow. I fixed a makeshift pen for the goslings in the barn, arranged so that they would be separated from the gander but visible to him, and he would be visible to them. The old fellow, when he heard youthful voices, hustled right in to find out what was going on. He studied the scene in silence and with the greatest attention. I could not tell whether the look in his eye was one of malice or affection—a goose's eye is a small round enigma. After observing this introductory scene for a while, I left and went into the house.

Half an hour later, I heard a commotion in the barnyard: the gander was in full cry. I hustled out. The goslings, impatient with life indoors, had escaped from their hastily constructed enclosure in the barn and had joined their foster father in the barnyard. The cries I had heard were his screams of welcome—the old bird was delighted with the turn that events had taken. His period of mourning was over, he now had interesting and useful work to do, and he threw himself into the role of father with immense satisfaction and zeal, hissing at me with renewed malevolece, shepherding the three children here and there, and running interference against real and imaginary enemies. My fears were laid to rest. In the rush of emotion that seized him at finding himself the head of a family, his thoughts turned immediately to the pond, and I watched admiringly as he guided the goslings down the long, tortuous course through the weedy land and on down across the rough pasture between blueberry knolls and granite boulders. It was a sight to see him hold the heifers at bay so the procession could pass safely. Summer was upon us, the pond was alive again. I brought the three eggs up from the cellar and dispatched them to the town dump.

At first, I did not know the sex of my three goslings. But nothing on two legs grows any faster than a young goose, and by early fall it was obvious that I had drawn one male and two females. You tell the sex of a goose by its demeanor and its stance—the way it holds itself, its general approach to life. A gander carries his head high and affects a threatening attitude. Females go about with necks in a graceful arch and are less aggressive. My two young females looked like their mother, particolored. The young male was quite different. He feathered out white all over except for his wings, which were a very light, pearly gray. Afloat on the pond, he looked almost like a swan, with his tall, thin white neck and his cocked-up white tail—a real dandy, full of pompous thoughts and surly gestures.

Winter is a time of waiting, for man and goose. Last winter was a long wait, the pasture deep in drifts, the lane barricaded, the pond inaccessible and frozen. Life centered in the barn and the barnyard. When the time for mating came, conditions were unfavorable, and this was upsetting to the old gander. Geese like a body of water for their coupling; it doesn't have to be a large body of water—just any wet place in which a goose can become partly submerged. My old gander, studying the calendar, inflamed by passion, unable to get to the pond, showed signs of desperation. On several occasions, he tried to manage with a ten-quart pail of water that stood in the barnyard. He would chivvy one of his young foster daughters over to the pail, seize her by the nape, and hold her head under water while he made his attempt. It was never a success and usually ended up looking more like a comedy tumbling act than like coitus. One got the feeling during the water-pail routine that the gander had been consulting one of the modern sex manuals describing peculiar positions. Anyway, I noticed two things: the old fellow confined his attentions to one of the two young geese and let the other alone, and he never allowed his foster son to approach either of the girls—he was very strict about that, and the handsome young male lived all spring in a state of ostracism.

Eventually, the pond opened up, the happy band wended its way down across the melting snows, and the breeding season was officially opened. My pond is visible from the house, but it is at quite a distance. I am not a voyeur and do not spend my time watching the sex antics of geese or anything else. But I try to keep reasonably well posted on all the creatures around the place, and it was apparent that the young gander was not allowed by his foster father to enjoy the privileges of the pond and that the old gander's attentions continued to be directed to just one of the young geese. I shall call her Liz to make this tale easier to tell.

Both geese were soon laying. Liz made her nest in the barn cellar; her sister, Apathy, made hers in the tie-ups on the main floor of the barn. It was the end of April or the beginning of May. Still awfully cold—a reluctant spring.

Apathy laid three eggs, then quit. I marked them with a pencil and left them for the time being in the nest she had constructed. I made a mental note that they were infertile. Liz, unlike her sister, went right on laying, and became a laying fool. She dallied each morning at the pond with her foster father, and she laid and laid and laid, like a commercial hen. I dutifully marked the eggs as they arrived—1, 2, 3, and so on. When she had accumulated a clutch of fifteen, I decided she had all she could cover. From then on, I took to removing the oldest egg from the nest each time a new egg was deposited. I also removed Apathy's three eggs from *her* nest, discarded them, and began substituting the purloined eggs from the barn cellar—the ones that rightfully belonged to Liz. Thus I gradually contrived to assemble a nest of fertile eggs for each bird, all of them laid by the fanatical Liz.

During the last week in May, Apathy, having produced only three eggs of her own but having acquired ten through the kind offices of her sister and me, became broody and began to sit. Liz, with a tally of twenty-five eggs, ten of them stolen, showed not the slightest desire to sit. Laying was her thing. She laid and laid, while the other goose sat and sat. The old gander, marveling at what he had wrought, showed a great deal of interest in both nests. The young gander was impressed but subdued. I continued to remove the early eggs from Liz's nest, holding her to a clutch of fifteen and discarding the extras. In late June, having produced forty-one eggs, ten of which were under Apathy, she at last sat down.

I had marked Apathy's hatching date on my desk calendar. On the night before the goslings were due to arrive, when I made my rounds before going to bed, I looked in on her. She hissed, as usual, and ran her neck out. When I shone my light at her, two tiny green heads were visible, thrusting their way through her feathers. The goslings were here—a few hours ahead of schedule. My heart leapt up. Outside, in the barnyard, both ganders stood vigil. They knew very well what was up: ganders take an enormous interest in family affairs and are deeply impressed by the miracle of the egg-that-becomes-goose. I shut the door against them and went to bed.

Next morning, Sunday, I rose early and went straight to the barn to see what the night had brought. Apathy was sitting quietly while five goslings teetered about on the slopes of the nest. One of them, as I watched, strayed from the others, and, not being able to find his way back, began sending out cries for help. They were the kind of distress signal any anxious father would instantly respond to. Suddenly, I heard sounds of a rumble outside in the barnyard where the ganders were—loud sounds of scuffling. I ran out. A fierce fight was in progress—it was no mere skirmish, it was the real thing. The young gander had grabbed the old one by the stern, his white head buried in feathers right where it would hurt the most, and was running him around the yard, punishing him at every turn—thrusting him on ahead and beating him unmercifully with his wings. It was an awesome sight, these two great male birds locked in combat, slugging it out—not for the favors of a female but for the dubious privilege of assuming the responsibilities of parenthood. The young male had suffered all spring the indignities of a restricted life at the pond; now he had turned, at last, against the old one, as though to get even. Round and round, over rocks and through weeds, they raced, struggling and tripping, the old one in full retreat and in apparent pain. It was a beautiful late-June morning, with fair-weather clouds and a light wind going, the grasses long in the orchard—the kind of morning that always carries for me overtones of summer sadness, I don't know why. Overhead, three swallows circled at low altitude, pursuing one white feather, the coveted trophy of nesting time. They were like three tiny fighter planes giving air support to the battle that raged below. For a moment, I thought of climbing the fence and trying to separate the combatants, but instead I just watched. The engagement was soon over. Plunging desperately down the lane, the old gander sank to the ground. The young one let go, turned, and walked back, screaming in triumph, to the door behind which his newly won family were waiting: a strange family indeed—the sister who was not even the mother of the babies, and the babies who were not even his own get.

When I was sure the fight was over, I climbed the fence and closed the barnyard gate, effectively separating victor from vanquished. The old gander had risen to his feet. He was in almost the same spot in the lane where his first wife had died mysteriously more than a year ago. I watched as he threaded his way slowly down the narrow path between clumps of thistles and daisies. His head was barely visible above the grasses, but his broken spirit was plain to any eye. When he reached the pasture bars, he hesitated, then painfully squatted and eased himself under the bottom bar and into the pasture, where he sat down on the cropped sward in the bright sun. I felt very deeply his sorrow and his defeat. As things go in the animal kingdom, he is about my age, and when he lowered himself to creep under the bar, I could feel in my own bones his pain at bending down so far. Two hours later, he was still sitting there, the sun by this time quite hot. I had seen his likes often enough on the benches of the treeless main street of a Florida city—spent old males, motionless in the glare of the day.

Toward the end of the morning, he walked back up the lane as far as the gate, and there he stood all afternoon, his head and orange bill looking like the head of a great snake. The goose and her goslings had emerged into the barnyard. Through the space between the boards of the gate, the old fellow watched the enchanting scene: the goslings taking their frequent drinks of water, climbing in and out of the shallow pan for their first swim, closely guarded by the handsome young gander, shepherded by the pretty young goose.

After supper, I went into the tie-ups and pulled the five remaining, unhatched eggs from the nest and thought about the five lifeless chicks inside the eggs—the unlucky ones, the ones that lacked what it takes to break out of an egg into the light of a fine June morning. I put the eggs in a basket and set the basket with some other miscellany consigned to the dump. I don't know anything sadder than a summer's day.

CONSIDERATIONS

Thinking

One way to think of White's essay is in terms of a fable whose animal characters reveal human characteristics and qualities. What is the moral of White's essay, as revealed by the fable?

What feelings does White express in the course of telling his story? What does the expression of his sympathies reveal about him?

Connecting

Relate the situation of "The Geese" to another work you have read (or viewed). How are the two works similar? How are they different? What might we observe by considering them together?

Compare White's presentation and portrayal of the geese with Annie Dillard's presentation of the weasel in "Living Like Weasels" or with Edward Hoagland's presentation of the turtle in "The Courage of Turtles."

Writing

Write your own animal fable; that is, tell a story with animals as characters. Be sure that your animals can be interpreted in human terms—that their actions can be explained in terms of human motivation.

Analyze the way White writes about animals in "The Geese" with the way he or another writer does so in another work.

Student Essays
Based on Maxine Hong
Kingston's "On Discovery"

Maxine Hong Kingston's "On Discovery" comes from her book *China Men*, which, along with *The Woman Warrior*, explores Kingston's view of the cultural roles of men and women in China. Although brief, "On Discovery" is thought-provoking, as the three student essays presented in this section demonstrate.

Each of the three essays about "On Discovery" offers a different analysis and interpretation of Kingston's essay. Each of the student essays offers a valid and interesting way to interpret and understand Kingston's piece, even though the students' views, focuses, and analyses differ. The student writers cite some of the same details. Occasionally, one writer overlaps an idea or perspective suggested by one or both of the others. Overall, the three student pieces reveal how a variety of analytical essays can be written about a single text without agreeing on every point, and indeed, by offering quite different ways of interpreting the text.

M ichelle Bowman

Gender Switching

S ociety has often used the Asian woman as an example of sexual mystery but also of docility and subservience, which are often considered "second nature" to her. Ironically, Kingston's "Land of Women" in "On Discovery" is inhabited by Asian women. Much like the matriarchal society in the Amazon, women also rule on the "Gold Mountain." By accident, Tang Ao is unfortunate to find himself among them. Kingston shows us in "On Discovery" that in any society, there is a hierarchy of authority. Kingston uses the classic tale of pre-wedding preparations as a symbolic reference to domination and subservience.

Through a series of steps, we see Tang Ao emasculated by the same steps that a traditional Asian woman might take to become feminized, beautiful. Without these steps she would be considered an anomaly in her culture. For the sake of beauty, Tang Ao's feet are broken and bound tightly: "they bent his toes so far backward that his arched foot cracked." His ears are pierced daily with hot needles: "they strung his raw flesh with silk threads; he could feel the fibers." These pains, which the older women must inflict on Tang Ao, are not intentionally malicious; rather, they are part of womanly traditions handed down for generations of women, who also comfort him in traditional ways: "the women sang foot-binding songs to distract him."

Kingston's demonstration of these careful preparations before Tang Ao's first meeting with the queen suggests something grander, perhaps a wedding. Delicate foods are given to Tang Ao, such as vinegar soup, which "improved his womb" or tea "thick with white chrysanthemums," which "stirred the cool female winds inside his body." There are several other foods given to him to smooth his skin or gloss his hair, but I would like to focus on the vinegar soup and chrysanthemum tea. The desired effects from either of these two foods would suggest that Tang Ao could produce a child or is being made ready to bear children. This beautification process alludes to the pre-wedding rituals. The older knowledgeable women constantly surround him, poking and probing at him. As in all cultures, these women already know what will befall the bride on her wedding night. They may joke with him, nurture him, or even torture him, only to postpone his inevitable encounter or to alleviate his fright. The jokes and sly nudges of the women before the bride meets her groom exclude her because she doesn't know yet that her life will be as theirs, the other married women. Tang Ao is the bride awaiting her wedding night.

Tang Ao accepts their behavior with only one question, "What are you doing?" And this is spoken before his features have been altered. Why does Tang Ao allow the women to mummify him? At the introduction Tang Ao is discovered searching for the Gold Mountain, Kingston's allusion to North America or the United States. Tang Ao has "crossed an ocean" and landed here. Before his crossing, perhaps he thought the Gold Mountain to be an oasis of opportunity. Possibly he is married in his land and seeking fortune to send to his wife. Perhaps his journeys have tired him and he would gladly go with the women who capture him. Or perhaps his interest has been piqued when the women tell him, "we have to prepare you to meet the queen." Regardless of his reasons, Tang Ao seals his fate by accompanying the women.

However, Kingston writes, "if he had had male companions, he would've winked over his shoulder." This makes Tang Ao's capture impure. His thoughts are lewd and lecherous; already his inner feelings for women are of debasement. Suddenly, he has found something better than the Gold Mountain, and it looks good. His next impression of the castle is of "a canopied apartment equipped with pots of makeup, mirrors, and a woman's clothes." With the removal of his clothes, he experiences more sexual feelings. Kingston sets up the first part of this essay with subtle sexual nuances. First, a man alone searching for fortune suddenly encounters a band of women who capture him. The women do not use any violent measures to apprehend him; he comes along gladly. Next, he is in a feminine boudoir and his clothes are being taken from him. With an abrupt twist, his wrists are "shackled" and his ankles "chained." Expecting a fight, instead he is met by "two old women with sewing boxes in their hands."

The stripping of Tang Ao's identity is a slow process of emasculation. Tang Ao loses a little bit of himself each day with the alterations being made to his body. There are people who, when lost in the wilderness, exist like the animals in their own environment. They revert to a prehuman state: hunting and eating from the land, their voices becoming thick with disuse, their memories of human life fading. As identity becomes stifled, Tang Ao's voice is muted, and he reverts to sounds and gestures: he cries, weeps, and begs. His role in society becomes increasingly dehumanized. Adding to his physical changes is the degrading shame to his dignity: "They forced him to wash his used bandages, which were embroidered with flowers and smelled of rot and cheese." He suffers with embarrassment because he has to hang the bandages out to dry, "streamers that drooped and draped wall to wall." Although this daily shame promotes cleanliness and serves a general purpose that his feet will not become infected and gangrenous, to perform this task is to admit to the world his body is producing something rank and foul that he cannot control. Tang Ao no longer has any power over his own bodily functions.

"On Discovery" is a disturbing account of gender role reversal. Both male and female audiences might agree that Tang Ao's physical transformation is both painful and revolting. However, the binding of Tang Ao's feet and consequent breaking of bones is perhaps the most vivid illustration of a vanity which goes too far: "The old ladies squeezed each foot and broke many tiny bones along the sides." The fact that he must wash out his dirty bandages nightly is also a distasteful image. Initially, it may seem that Kingston is merely relating this image to vanity. Perhaps we can also dismiss it as such until the next to last paragraph, where we read that "his hips swayed and his shoulders swiveled because of his shaped feet." This image of weakness created through self-mutilation could hardly be considered beautiful.

Or could it? One of the most attractive images of being feminine is weakness. Ironically, Tang Ao is in the Land of Women ruled by women, but made appealing because of his physical weaknesses created by their feminine standards of self-mutilation. Kingston plays with this image of culturized feminine weakness throughout "On Discovery." The binding can also be compared with other symbols of feminine vanity, such as the tight elastic of a brassiere, the metal wire inside corsets, or even hot sticky nylon pantyhose, which bring women no pleasure. These objects were designed to alter a woman's appearance and disguise her physical flaws to make her more sexually alluring.

Kingston's essay opens with sexual innuendo and moves to the nurturing of the virgin bride awaiting her wedding night. Sometimes the bride is apprehensive, and other times she is quite excited. Lastly we see Tang Ao as female servant to the queen, as Kingston returns once again to the bride metaphor. In most cultures when a woman marries she becomes the property of her husband and his family. Most often in translation, she becomes a domestic slave with few of the privileges granted to men. The married wife becomes a second-rate person, her worth no better than the family cow. She is not allowed to dine with the family; she must clean the house and work the fields. Whereas men in other countries may dress in western attire with shirt, tie, and pants, women are still confined to traditional garb in many cultures. Kingston grapples with one feminine image throughout "On Discovery," that of the slave. The woman is slave to fashion, to culture, and to her dominator. The anticipatory bridal image ironically contrasts with the dominating husband symbol represented by the queen.

"Smacking their lips at his dainty feet," the queen's court comment on Tang Ao's physical attributes. This demonstration of the beautification process for women in preparation for final inspection or the symbolic marriage and its subsequent slavery plays on the culturized lowly feminine status of women, which has taken place for centuries. Kingston breaks it down from the beginning much like the women break down Tang Ao's individuality. The women are seen as charming or inviting to Tang Ao, and he enters their world readily. Although the beautification process seems barbarous, consider the results: smooth skin, glossy hair, and shapely dainty feet. But then, Kingston delivers her punch line: all this preparation is only for Tang Ao to become a weak slave.

While Kingston's essay may be seen as an allegorical diatribe on the evils of men against women, it is not enough for Kingston to merely suggest that women are subjugated into slavery everyday. She suggests that it is inevitable for any group of people. In any society, there will always be a dominating group that sets the standards for everyone else. Perhaps the discovery in "On Discovery" suggests that when there is a dominating group, there too must be a servant underclass. Moreover, just because the Land of Women is a matriarchal society does not exclude class and gender prejudices among the women.

Kingston ends her essay by noting that "in the Women's Land there are no taxes and no wars . . . and it was in North America." She makes the reader believe she is narrating historical facts. There are several ways to look at this final paragraph: It is true that Asian people did populate North America in the early eighth century. It is also true that there have been several matriarchal societies. However, with this final observation, Kingston reminds the reader that oppression exists between both genders and races, and it has so for ages. Because of her ethnic background, she has an innate sense of ethnocentrism and because of her gender, she has an innate sense of feminism. However, she neither places blame nor allies herself with either group.

H an N. Pham

In Essence

When I was little, meaning too little to argue, too little to know better, I would always hear my mother telling me certain things with a stern face, old and worried even then, staring into mine: You can't go there. You're a girl. You can't ride the bus alone. You're a girl. The list ran on through my childhood, never seeming to stop, even when my mother told me I could do anything, be anything. But she forgot to tell me what girls could do, when rattling off that list of what we couldn't. The world seemed a place where little boys could run wild and free, the door to the world's secret pleasures flung wide open, while their female counterparts could only sit at home and stare out the window. So when I was little, too little to argue, too little to know better, I was taught that the world was a man's world, seemingly, with no place for me.

Maxine Hong Kingston turns these notions upside down with a rebellious and (for some) disturbing twist in her piece "On Discovery," a brief parable from *China Men*.

"On Discovery" describes the wayward fortunes of one man, Tang Ao, who carelessly wanders into the women's land to be caught and brought to a "canopied apartment equipped with pots of makeup, mirrors, and a woman's clothes," where he would stay while the servants of the queen, old women who bounced with laughter as they sat on him, broke his feet, pierced his ears, and stripped away every ounce of his masculinity, which they peeled off and discarded like the dirty bandages wrapped about his feet, bandages which smelled of "rot and cheese."

Perhaps this was one of the most stirring images of the story, one of feet "squeezed" in order to break "many tiny bones along the sides" and toes gathered "over and under one another like a knot of ginger root." I have seen people cringe while reading the description; Kingston's words, while innocent, take on a macabre aspect. Readers know that with each crack of bone, every tear of pain, the man that is—was—Tang Ao is dying, to be replaced by the woman within, who begged to have his feet rebound when the bandages were taken off for cleaning, because the pain that coursed through shrunken veins was too much for him to bear. I have watched faces soften with sympathy as they read the passage where Tang Ao is forced to wash his own bandages, "streamers that drooped and draped wall to wall." Like Tang Ao, they too are embarrassed, feeling, perhaps as Tang Ao did, that the "wrappings were like underwear, and they were his."

I did not soften with sympathy.

I read the passage over, rereading and finding new insights, new images that whispered and teased my mind. When I felt that I understood, when all traces of understanding of what Tang Ao had to experience left me, hardened, I read the passage out loud to a male friend, laughing at the look on his face.

Kingston does not tell this story because it is the "classic fairy tale of the modern feminist," as my male friend declared; rather she tells it to show the gender roles that men and women played in China, and still play today. She describes the foot binding realistically, knowing that generations of young Chinese girls had to go through the same ordeal, male counterparts looking on with dispassion. Indeed, the girls' feet were bound and their cries of pain and tears went unheard for the pleasures of men. Where small waists and big bosoms and backsides are the Western ideal for women, small feet made male Chinese hearts patter with desire. Moreover, broken feet lent another attractive aspect to women, in the eyes of men—with feet so small, so broken, women could not walk without aid. Their fidelity was ensured; they could not run off to meet their lovers. So men received a double pleasure—small feet that warmed their hearts and loins and an assurance that their wives were forever their own, at their mercy, like caged birds with clipped wings.

So I did not cringe at the thought of feet being bound, of a man's ability to walk taken away. It has happened before, I tell myself, and it will happen again. One more promise of fidelity. One more pair of feet for diners to smack their lips at.

Yet, as much as I may sound like a rampant feminist, demanding justice for generations of young girls crippled in their youth, I understand that the point of Kingston's essay lies deeper than a cruel story wrought for the simple pleasure of a literary revenge. "On Discovery" is an artful illustration of Chinese talk-story, one in which Kingston, with a simple and direct language so characteristic of her style, allows for no musings about her characters, their actions, their motives. Instead, she tells the story as an onlooker might, recalling the experience. "Tang Ao wept with pain," she says, speaking of his footbinding. Not "he wailed in anger and frustration and humiliation as they bound his feet, breaking his male spirit, taking away from him his freedom." Simply, "[he] wept with pain," those few words giving the reader a glimpse of a man, once so confident, weeping softly, powerlessly, accepting, his male spirit, as it were, draining away with every tear. Kingston does not try to humiliate Tang Ao by revealing his distress; she does not use him as an object upon which to vent her anger and frustration at the roles Chinese women have been forced into through the centuries. Instead, she plays the facts as they are, the roles remaining the same, only taking on a more drastic coloration because a man has now slipped into a woman's dress, her bridge-like shoes.

Grasping this idea firmly, of a switch of roles, of power, Kingston weaves it through her story. She is not obvious, elaborate, overwhelmingly dramatic in what she has to say. Rather, she tells the story, perhaps as it was handed down to her, and allows the reader to make the connections, to find the ideas that emerge, some hitting with a blinding force, others with a subtle coyness: "What are you doing?" Tang Ao asks of the woman who scratches his ear thoughtfully, a needle in her hand, searching for a place to pierce and loop the string that will become gold hoops then, finally, jade studs, signaling the final transformation of Tang Ao from man into woman. "Sewing your lips together," she jokes, throwing her companions into cackling laughter. The irony and symbolism of this statement are lost on the reader until later, when Tang Ao is seen with broken feet, swaying gently as he bends to serve the Queen's court. His masculine lips have been metaphorically sewn together; his masculinity is bound and held captive by the bandages about his feet, the earrings in his ears.

Kingston throws us another curve, almost whizzing by us in its seeming innocence, the allure with which it passes us by before we recognize it, and pull it gently back to analyze it.

She says that there is a woman in every man.

"During the months of a season," she says, "they fed [Tang Ao] . . . tea [that] was thick with white chrysanthemums [that] stirred the cool female winds inside his body." With this small statement, Kingston lays the foundation for the theory that crowns the story of Tang Ao with a stunning blow to the senses, something that may have sent, more than all the images of broken feet and humiliating acts, past readers of this essay cringing with the impact of its significance: that men, within, are inherently women, and, consistently, that women, within, could be men. "On Discovery," along this line of thought, is no longer a cruel story of a man degraded to the status of a woman, but rather a story of role "reversal" and fate realized. Kingston tells the story "objectively," with acceptance, as one might have if this were just another story of a woman forced into a subservient social role, not to maintain her omniscient narrator status, but rather to show that Tang Ao's fate was no more poignant, no more significant, simply because he was a man. Silently, she tells us, there is man and woman. We are the same. What separates us is the fact that there are essentially two roles, one of which will fall to each of us. The fact that men, historically, have had the "more powerful" and "superior" role is irrelevant. Chance, she whispers, fate, a luck of the draw. Tang Ao's fate was one of the two roles that, unfortunately, he drew. It has happened before, and it will happen again, regardless of whether the "victim" is a man or a woman.

In a final gesture Kingston teases us into thought with her statement that "In the Women's Land there are . . . no wars," and ends by stating the various dates and places that scholars say the land was discovered. The fact remains that there is no such land, that never in the known history of the world has there been evidence that any such Women's Land ever existed. Why, then, does Kingston tack it onto the story in such an awkward yet prominent fashion? She does it to remind us, as my mother tried to remind me, that women *can* do anything, even turn the world upside down to show that a *man* can be anything—even a woman.

D ennis Son

Men at the Mercy of Women

Many say that finding a significant other is one of the greatest things that can happen to a man. A man needs someone to care about, someone to listen to, someone to love. But everything comes at a price, and, oftentimes, the price is exorbitantly high. Things happen to a man when he finds a woman, but he is unfortunately unaware of these changes most of the time. Indeed, a female can alter a man from the inside out, affecting every aspect of his essence and soul.

In her essay "On Discovery," Maxine Hong Kingston writes about a man named Tang Ao who, searching for his dream of "the Gold Mountain," came upon a "Land of Women." Because they were women, he did not have his guard up when he encountered them. It was possibly the greatest mistake of his life. They captured him and told him he was going to see their queen. What he saw instead were two old women who began the painful process of turning him into a woman. Eventually, after months of their treatment, they finished with him, and no one could tell that under all of the makeup and clothing there were the remnants of what had once been a man.

The parallels between Tang Ao's situation and a man's situation with a woman are painfully evident. Like many young men, Tang is looking for a Gold Mountain, the greatness that a man seeks to achieve throughout his life, before he is distracted. He is ambitious and courageous, willing to do almost anything to bring his goals to fruition. But his search is cut off while he is still far short of his objective. He stumbles upon a Land of Women whose inhabitants represent a girlfriend and her friends and what they can do to a man. He is distracted by these females, and before any-one knows what is going on, he has been "captured," unable to continue on his quest. Men, of course, are not literally captured, but they are in a sense enslaved by their masters, the women with whom they fall in love.

Tang also notices that this new land he has stumbled upon has no male inhabitants, only females. Such is the fate of someone who has been "whipped" by his master. Undoubtedly, he will spend most of his free time with his special friend, occasionally seeing her friends when they visit, leaving little time to acknowledge the existence of his other male friends. In essence, he is being confined to a world of females.

Tang's hell began when he was shackled and told he was going to be taken to see the queen. He was, understandably, excited. "A door opened, and he expected to meet his match, but it was only two old women with sewing boxes in their hands." But they added insult to injury. Two women sat on him and another held his head in place while the two old women jabbed needles through his earlobes to pierce them. At the same time, the women sitting on him broke several bones in his feet and wrapped them tight with bandages. He wept in pain, while the women sang songs to distract him.

The choice of details at this point in the story reflects the author's desire to reveal how painful Tang's ordeal is. Kingston describes graphically the manner in which they put holes in his ears and then break his toes: "They worked the needle through—a last jerk for the needle's wide eye. . . . They strung his raw flesh with silk threads. . . . They bent his toes so far backward that his arched foot cracked. . . . [They] broke many tiny bones along the sides. They gathered his toes . . . like a knot of ginger root." She describes his misery as accurately as possible to illustrate vividly what women can figuratively do to a man.

A man's hell begins in a very similar fashion. A man is socially shackled by his new woman. The shackles represent what men like to refer to as the "ball and chain" or being whipped. Just as the women all cooperated like a well-oiled machine to work on Tang in the story, a hapless man's woman and her friends will make sure that he does not do anything that he should not. Soon, after all the pretenses have been dropped, the doors of truth open. But he does not see a lovely queen before him. He sees someone wrought with imperfections, just like any other person. Women might as well be "old women with sewing boxes" saying, "The less you struggle, the less it'll hurt." Nothing makes her any more special than anyone else. But soon this woman begins to change her new slave, making him give up anything that takes him away for any amount of time.

The two women sitting on top of Tang Ao are symbolic of the burden a man soon begins to feel. And it is not only the burden of his woman, but also of her friends. They gang up on him until the point that he is powerless even to stand up on his own two feet. Their watchful eyes are everywhere, ready to report back to his master about any wrongdoing.

The process of a man losing his freedom, which his parents have tried to instill in him since birth, is as painful as Tang's being tortured by the women working on him.

As time progressed, Tang came closer and closer to becoming a woman. The women inserted gold hoops in the holes they had made in his ears and "fed him on women's food: the tea was thick with white chrysanthemums and stirred the cool female winds inside his body; chicken wings made his hair shine; vinegar soup improved his womb." This was a key sentence in the essay. He is now being referred to as a woman. Kingston still employs the use of the pronoun "he," but he has now been given distinctly female characteristics, including a womb.

The clincher is the wrappings around his feet. His feet had been wound so tightly for so long that the veins in his feet had shrunk, and it was agonizing to have the wrappings off. They "hurt so much, he begged to have his feet rewrapped tight." So now he asked, begged even, to have them back. He took care of them and washed them every night. Now things had changed and a crucial turning point had been reached. This is another important moment. What once had to be forced upon him, what once put him through excruciating pain, what once was something that he never would have dreamed would be a part of his life, he now actively sought. He had passed the point of no return. They had succeeded. He now asked, of his own volition, for the things that they gave and did to him.

All that the women had to do now was implement the final touches. They replaced the gold hoops in his ears with jade studs and gave him shoes that curved like bridges. "They plucked out each hair on his face, powdered him white, painted his eyebrows like a moth's wings, painted his cheeks and lips red." He was now ready to be their servant as a woman. He served food at the queen's court and "his hips swayed and his shoulders swiveled" as he walked. So perfect was Tang Ao's transformation that the people he served commented on her beauty.

Such is the fate of any man who falls in love with a woman. Tang Ao's plight is symbolic of a female's impact on an unwary man. Before much time has passed, a man will grow so accustomed to having his woman around and having her love and attention that he will find it difficult to adjust to life alone. The changes she imposes on him will be sought after, even begged for, just as Tang wanted the bandages. And a life without the love and attention he is receiving becomes an unbearable possibility.

Kingston's choice of verbs is reflected in Tang Ao's position. After his capture by the women, he is always having things done to him. Whether the women are shackling him, singing to him, or feeding him, his passive position is evident. Rarely does he do anything. He just has those things done to him that the women decide to do.

Throughout the piece, Kingston's tone of cool acceptance induces a feeling of acceptance in the reader as well. Even the dialogue contributes to this feeling. Whenever anything is said, it is something that might be said if what was happening was nothing special, and merely another occurrence in the daily course of events. When Tang Ao is taken to the old women with sewing kits, they calmly joke with him. There are no specific points in the story that the reader would find particularly shocking or offensive. In this way Kingston delivers her message all the more effectively.

Kingston can also be ironic. "On Discovery" concentrates on Tang Ao's capture and transformation into a woman by women. Is it not ironic that a brave explorer, one who has reached the pinnacle of machismo, is completely conquered both physically and mentally by females? The strong is now helpless against the weak. He ends up serving women their food as some kind of waitress in the queen's court. And worse yet, he does not even make an attempt to struggle, losing his manliness altogether.

There is also irony in the fact that the things that the women do to him are the things that women do to themselves in real life to make themselves more attractive to men, so that they may have the power to control them. What Tang Ao undoubtedly liked to see females do to themselves was now being done to him. It goes to the point that the women now look at him in ways men look at women in the real world. Men are apt to make comments about women's appearances and are very blunt about it many times. But the tables have been turned. The diners at the end of the story smacked "their lips at his dainty feet as he bent" over and commented, "She's pretty, don't you agree?" They said this right in front of him and without hesitation.

In addition to being changed, Tang loses his will. Tang was put through many things that most would consider torture, but he never resists. He accepts anything that the women do to him. Not once does he attempt to free himself or bother asking them to stop, even when what they do causes him to weep in pain. The one time that he does speak up, he only asks a question, which demonstrates his passivity. His silence represents a man's willingness to submit to a woman's wishes and desires, despite any amount of pain it may cause him. If a man cannot make up his own mind, what good is he? The individuality that makes a person and defines his character is no more. He is nothing more than an automaton with a woman at the controls. Just as Tang Ao becomes a woman, the man has essentially become one as well, allowing her to run his life and define who he is. Kingston's choice of turning him into a woman instead of something else reflects this fact.

Kingston also makes a forceful statement about power in her essay. Men are put into a superior position by society. In almost every professional field men dominate. Men on average make more money. Even in social settings, it is customary that a man approaches a woman and asks her out on a date. So, by that token, men possess greater power. But who really controls this power and makes the decisions? If a woman can get a stranglehold on a man and control him, then she possesses the power. Not directly of course, but she has the ability to get what she wants nonetheless.

Kingston's final paragraph suggests some differences that would exist if women controlled the world. "In the Women's Land," Kingston writes, "there are no taxes and no wars." In their world, things that we see as necessarily evils do not exist. Maybe women are kinder and should rule the world. But in our world these are two very grim realities, implying that women are not in control. Kingston realizes that not all women control their men, and this is the reason that we are taxed and kill our fellow human beings. It is also a statement, though, of the fact that the men who are in power have not been oppressed by their women. The powerful politicians and leaders who have reached considerable heights would not be making these decisions if they were at the mercy of their women. Kingston may be trying to say that these men who climb to greatness have not been affected to nearly as great a degree as other men who may be wallowing in their mediocrity, making the unpleasant but possibly true implication that women make men complacent and lazy. These people have not been distracted from their search for the Gold Mountain.

The last sentence also makes an interesting suggestion about the uncertainty of the whole topic. The entire thing is so subjective that there are no absolutes. There are no applicable equations. Nothing is certain, and there are as many variables in individual relationships as there are quirks of peoples' personalities. In like manner, Kingston makes no definitive statements about the location and time this land was discovered. "Some scholars say that that country was discovered during the reign of Empress Wu . . . and some say earlier than that . . . and it was in North America," but no one is sure, and it will remain that way.

To an outside observer, a man in love is a sick puppy. He is a manifestation from the deepest reaches of his soul of what every man fears that he may one day become. He accepts what was previously unacceptable. But to the man who is being affected, nothing else matters.

Student Research Essays Based on the Work of E. B. White

The students whose essays appear in this section were asked to write about the work of a single author but not to restrict their discussion to a single piece by that author. Christian D'Andrea's "The Human Atlas: Locating E. B. White" identifies time as an important topic in White's work.

Christian looks at White's ideas about time as they are explored in nearly a dozen of White's essays. He develops his idea about White's concern with time by looking at its appearance in White's essays, taking them up one after another.

Radhika Jones does something a bit different. She too refers to a dozen or so of White's essays and other prose pieces. But instead of discussing each in turn, Radhika weaves back and forth between White's works, referring to some of them in half a dozen places in her essay.

Both Christian D'Andrea and Radhika Jones use passages from White's work to illustrate and clarify their own ideas. Both student writers reveal White's accomplishments as a writer, and both offer thoughtful analyses and interpretations that integrate and connect different pieces of White's work that span many years, including letters and children's fiction as well as essays.

As you read these students' research essays, notice how they cite White's texts, documenting their references carefully. Notice, too, how Radhika Jones cites secondary sources, references to books and articles written by others about White's work.

C hristian D'Andrea

The Human Atlas: Locating E. B. White

E.B. White lived in all but the last sixteen years of this century, and those years of experience are still alive in his sparkling, compact essays. But to capture life he shows his subjects—a pig or a goose, a man or a car—deteriorating under a pressure they cannot escape: time. White is just as hungry to relive the decay of beauty as he is to preserve it. Things are falling apart, losing their worth. In light of this, White discovers himself. Married to words and pitted against time, he turns his work into a study of himself and his opponent, of the power of corrosive time and its agents, and of his own power.

At face value, White is a humble chronicler of a charming America that no longer exists. No shroud of modern angst, yearning, or sadness surrounds his writing. And indeed, at times, the raw celebration of a memory takes over. He can be jubilant and nothing else, as he is when writing about the era of the Model T in "Farewell, My Lovely!" Out of the fusion of parts powering the car, on the basis of nothing more than a "dull rapport" between them, comes a strange, idiosyncratic harmony (*Second Tree* 33). All the efforts of a man—his placebos, his showering the car with trinkets and gizmos—not only kept the metaphysical functions in order, they also turned him into the king of all this magic, a man on par with the mystery. White knows the glory of the Model T. Not only was a man bound to his car—each stage of deterioration now a glorious dilemma for "both man and machine" (37)—man was also bound to other men. Being a "Ford owner" gave you friends across the country. A man had allies, kindred spirits, everywhere. But White was more than a part-time mechanic and comrade. While most men only swapped stories, White could recognize a Ford owner by the "hunger in (a man's) eyes that set him off from other men" (39). Rather than just acknowledging that there is a camaraderie of memory, he looks into it. He sees that the awkward charm and simple brotherhood spawned by a Model T are as obsolete in 1936 as its parts are absent from the pages of a Sears Roebuck catalogue. Value has decayed.

Although a response to the perfidious decay of the mystical will take White many years to formulate, he identifies the problem, as a thirty-year-old. The decaying metal of the Ford was endearing; the decay of America's vitality is a horror. So he exposes this horror's symptoms in hints and allegories. As he lies in bed in "A Weekend with the Angels," recovering from a nose operation during World War II, White imagines the hot-water bottle as having "to be exhumed from its cold grave at the foot of the bed" (*Second Tree* 7). The bottle is dead, without power, without the heat that gives it its purpose, and so is life dead in the modern era. Cars zoom today, they do not sputter and buck you like the Model T, and that is the tragedy. Even words are eulogized in White's short piece on grammar, "English Usage." "People are afraid of words" these days White claims (151). They are blinded and cannot see that the usage of words is sometimes "sheer luck, like getting across a street." Just as the language, White's true love, has been corralled and bereft of its spirit by the worshippers of so-called "taste" and "education," so has life itself slowly been enervated by the much more neutral but ubiquitous, powerful force of time.

But time and its partner change are not themselves horrors. After all, White declares, the sense of time is the only sense "that is common" to man ("Ring" 155). Time alone is too huge and invisible to be a foe, but it seems to bring with it states of mind that can erase the universal charm of a Model T and breed a hunger for perfection. World War II and the Industrial Revolution brought a hunger for mechanical perfection, encouraged America to let its wily spark die. Those consorts of time are the evils against which White writes.

The problem of how to fight them is the crux of White's personal search; it shapes all his scenarios and gives employment to all his characters. In "The Departure of Eustace Tilley," a genteel old man, presumably a thinker of some kind, is about to leave his anonymous town. White is the fictitious reporter for the local gab rag, ludicrous in his prying and ignorance, employing the editorial "we" that he hates so much in reality. When prodded by the reporter, Tilley reveals his poisonous predicament. "We live in a new world," he says, one from which he must escape (*Second Tree* 152). Ancient trees that "shelter the graves and throw their umbrage upon the imponderable dead" are now alive with loudspeakers.

Tilley will think on "the faces of motorists drawn up for the red light," because "in their look of discontent is the answer to the industrial revolution" (153). And in this concern is Tilley's identity with White. The unwanted interview yields an admission: "I have certain macabre pilgrimages to make" (153). Indeed, this is White's calling. As Tilley pulls away from the hubbub, a single vision remains. The ground on which Tilley stood while he put his yearning into words is now nothing but a pool of tears.

But the tormented Tilley only helped clarify White's subject and quest; he only named the decay that White himself must engage in the world of his essays. White does indeed leave town and embark on strange pilgrimages, and he converts his journeys into lasting weapons against time. But White is not cocky; he even seems to question whether writing is the right mode of action. But it is his only hope, his talent, and he turns it against those consorts in the oddest ways. "The Decline of Sport" paints a not-so-farfetched picture of sports worship and statistics hoarding run amok. Out of the comedy White creates there emerges a tragic hero. Mr. Parkinson, overcome by the bad news of defeat from four simultaneous contests, draws a gun and shoots the wide receiver, the disinterested symbol of this chaos, on the field. Panic ensues; 20,003 are killed. Yet the effects are salutary. "Sport waned" and motorists "rediscovered the charms of old twisty roads . . . and barnyards" (*Second Tree* 45). White vanquishes sport, the farcical brother of Industry and War. But can he fight foe after foe with only words as his weapon, without the brute force of a gun? Yes, he seems to think, words are enough, but the search over time for the right words is exhausting.

Must a fighter against War and Industry fight alone? White looks for help in "A Weekend with the Angels," the story of his wartime convalescence. Back home in the United States, recovering, he gets a double dosage of second-hand war: a vicarious taste of combat and the grim sobriety of the hospital staffers. Overreacting to his window's "sticky transom," White enjoys the "nonsensical sensation of being in contact with the enemy" (*Second Tree* 6). But he is really not at war. Nor is he allied with the people around him. He reads the mysteriously anonymous early morning visits of a nurse as the "beauty and lunacy of which life is so subtly blended" (9). He speaks, calls her "Cousin," tries to cement their bond, and gets this reply: "There's a war on, Bud . . . so just for the heck of it I start with you." White is to have no partner in the mysteries of life's madness and beauty, no human partner in the non-fiction stories of his prose. He must fight his fictive war alone.

But even in childhood White was a loner. "Afternoon of an American Boy" is the story of his monumental first date. Having witnessed the spectacle of tea-dancing at the New York Plaza Hotel with his sister, he decides to return with a girl of special interest. Proposing to Eileen Parnell required the defeat of his "bashfulness and backwardness" (*Second Tree* 18). It looked to be an "expedition of unparalleled worldliness" (20). But in this hope for some unparalleled and yet tethered world we see White's problem. No one can match the meteoric quality of his wishes, the dazzling goals of his mind. He is looking for accompaniment, even in this date, that he will never find. Time blurs all things, and in the face of loss, even imagined loss, White's feelings go internal. Afterward, this "journey into ineptitude" with the girl leaves him stunned but inwardly "happy" (23). Later in life, as he writes, his senses yearn back to his teens, when the drumbeat of the dance melded with cinnamon on his tongue and gave the wild spirit of such moments a taste and sound, much like later moments in his life. In journeying back to his youth, White is rediscovering life's nuggets of worth, but he still is not beating down oppressive War and Industry. The recoveries are always temporary. Nothing lasts, and White laments.

Ultimately for White the wisdom, the potent attitude or aphorism from experience, that can refute the War-and-machine state of mind and hold it at bay, must lurk outside the city, where Tilley wanted to go. White makes the farm his home and attempts to ally himself with the animals. Despite the awe he feels for the mysteries of birth and creation on a farm, decay seems as evident in rural America as it is in the city. Mixed in with the seasonal progressions and their accompanying decay is the blessing of solitude; White can struggle with both practical problems and metaphysical quandaries on his own with the animals. Or so he thinks.

In "The Geese," White tends to a burgeoning family of geese, a family built up from a single widowed gander. In searching for foster children, White realizes that the dead mother goose's eggs will go without a broody hen, because "today broodiness is considered unacceptable" (*Prose Pieces* 145). This convention, a touch of the modern allegiance to efficiency, infiltrates his secluded barnyard, but White hardly notices it. With the widowed gander's acceptance of the foster goslings, White's previously sporadic understanding of the birds is sealed as he throws his lot in with the goose family. "Summer was upon us, the pond was alive again" (147), and White is riding the crest of this experience—one of those natural spontaneous combinations that constitute life's rich moments.

But War and Industry are not to be beaten by some rural commune. Everything quickly comes to a head—geese, White, and philosophy ride the course of nature and are dropped at the truth. The intensity of the farm scene peaks with the sudden fight between father and son for "the dubious privilege of . . . parenthood" (148). Bubbling within White is his lifelong respect for the miracle of incubation, the "strange calm of broodiness," and birth itself (Second Tree 239). Yet while the birds fought for supremacy, White "just watched" (149). In this, a deed as nondescript as the half sentence that houses it, White understands his place on the farm and his place in the world. His only soul brother is the beaten gander; the gander's sorrow, defeat, and "broken spirit" are White's own. The goose is cast off by his own family, and the man is not a part of his society. Both are "spent old males" (149). White has trouble going it alone, or with humans or animals; he watches, reports, broods on the human condition.

In "The Ring of Time" White again leaps back to a happier day. As if he is a boy enraptured by the barefoot circles of a practicing horseback acrobat, White's sense for genuine beauty and charm strikes gold in the girl's expression and concentration—wherein is seen the ambition, happiness, and youth that turn with the acrobat in suspended loops of time that began just where they had ended. Even as a young boy, White could tell she would "never be as beautiful as this again" (Prose Pieces 152). The circus is best raw, "before it has been put together," when rank smells and original sources exude real courage and sincerity. But as an adult writing the essay, White harps on the passive nature of his role. He declares he is "merely acting as recording secretary for one of the oldest of societies— the society of those who . . . have surrendered . . . to the bedazzlement of a circus rider" (151). He knows the raw stuff of life when he sees it throughout his life, but he is rarely active in making it. When young, he could surrender himself to the moment, enter a trance. Older, he implies, he must be rational and systematic and astute; as a middle-aged man his time is already up.

White tries to ward off the retreat of his youth—that time of the elemental America before it has been put together and bastardized—but he still faces the modern day and age. The geese told an allegorical story of alienation and profound anachronism, of beings out of time, but the death of a pig, in an essay of that name that seems strictly elegiac on the surface, is restorative on a deeper level. But it too leaves White wispy.

White quips that he was lucky it was the pig who died and not himself, otherwise there would be "none left to do the accounting" (Second

Tree 243)—a distinct role that has become White's own. In dealing with
the pig's frightening lack of hunger, White gets to know the animal intimately. He realizes that just as he had felt healthy in feeding a healthy pig,
the "pig's imbalance becomes the man's, vicariously" (247). The pig's earlier struggle between the satisfaction of being scratched and the indignity
of the enema parallel White's predicament: his recollections of happiness
jar with his attempts to deal with the modern dilemma. With their lots
"inextricably bound" (248), White reacts strongly to the veterinarian's
diagnosis. "Deep hemorrhagic infarcts" are a vague concept. He does not
know the name, but he knows the sickness. But this deeper world of con-
founded pig and man bubbles up into the narrative. At the pig's passing,
White weeps "deep hemorrhagic intears" (251). What was once a horrifying, unknown specter becomes the palpable tears of a man who knows
"what could be true of my pig could be true of the rest of my tidy world"
(249). The injustice is that White is responsible for both himself and the
pig, and possibly more. Whether his particular brand of salve is the
proper one becomes an important question. White, a man who, in his
own words, felt a sense of "personal deterioration" (243) in his recurring
uncertainty of dates, at the end concludes he is "a man who failed to raise
his pig" (253). But, in the deeper sense, White has not failed. Burial is the
deserved right of things past; their memory is best preserved when their
flesh is safe. The grave takes care of the flesh; White takes care of the
spirit. The pig's life deteriorated, but White's work as a writer does not.
Thirty years later after the events, at age eighty, he understands.

In the introduction to *The Second Tree from the Corner,* a collection of
pieces that includes "Death of a Pig," White remarks that for all the
farewells he bade the world in these essays written during the fifties, he
has "failed to disappear" (xi). He is very much alive and has reached a
state of modest control over his adversaries. The "flagless memorial days
of our own choosing" ("Pig" 253) that commemorate the pig not only
keep him alive but they also apply to the men and women of the war—
remembered, yet allowed to lie in their graves in peace. Time has illuminated for White the best weapon against itself.

White recognizes the power of words that can satisfy the humdrum
while tickling the cosmic. For this he celebrates Don Marquis, whose
book, "the lives and times of archy and mehitabel," conveys his thoughts
through the fictional cockroach Archy, a literary bug eager in all things
but unable to use the shift key on his typewriter. Just as there was much
more to White's relationship with the pig than the "slapstick" *(Second Tree
244)* of their shared medical exploits, the stories of Archy are much more

than simply gaudy and irreverent. In Marquis, White sees a genuine ally. Both Marquis and White have the skill of deep vision born of awareness of deaths. Archy's falling to the floor exhausted and his creeping "feebly into a nest of . . . poems" after one draining session with his column is actually Marquis' "own obituary notice" (*Second Tree* 182).

Archy's prose has the "unmistakable whiff of the tavern" (186), the humid stickiness of originality—much like the musky air of the circus tent. This feel is a product of Marquis' unique perspective. He saw the world from its underside, as did White. Using the voice of a cockroach, Marquis could shun the constrictions of editing as well as open himself up to the loose power of free verse and get away with both. Marquis' discussions of the Almost Perfect State in his daily columns reverberate in White's mind because White knew that era. It was a time when purchasing the daily paper was "quietly exciting" (189), a nearly perfect act itself. Those days are gone. But although the savvy writer and the joy of purchasing papers have both faded, something vital is still alive, still selling copies thirty-four years after its first publication. The magic is in the book; Marquis left his energy and his song masquerading forever as the works of a wily cockroach—masked, they still live. White and his book still live, too, without the preservative quirk of a cockroach ghostwriter.

White's essays are not the armor of an embittered man. His works stand as quietly defiant acts, as bursts of value in the face of technological progress. As we survey the modes of writing and thought in White's essays, we see that as he thinks, searches, and celebrates in his prose, he looks slant at the specters of World War II and the Industrial Revolution. Nostalgic, he nevertheless confronts chaos and decay. Natural decay is sad, but it is not to be struggled against. Artificial decay—the oppressive, mechanized deterioration induced by War and Industry—is too big finally to be vanquished, but can be held at bay, kept at a safer distance from life. The secret is to trust the folly of grammar, a date, the Model T, and the geese.

Works Cited

White, E. B. *The Second Tree from the Corner.* New York: Harper and Row, 1984.
——. "The Geese" and "The Ring of Time." *Prose Pieces.* Ed. Pat C. Hoy II and Robert DiYanni. New York: Random House, 1988.

Radhika A. Jones

Essentially Egg-Shaped: E. B. White's Image of Life

I don't know of anything in the entire world more wonderful to look at than a nest with eggs in it. An egg, because it contains life, is the most perfect thing there is. It is beautiful and mysterious. An egg is a far finer thing than a tennis ball or a cake of soap. A tennis ball will always be just a tennis ball. A cake of soap will always be just a cake of soap—until it gets so small nobody wants it and they throw it away. But an egg will someday be a living creature.

E. B. WHITE
The Trumpet of the Swan

The reverent admiration that Sam Beaver, young hero of *The Trumpet of the Swan,* has for eggs can only be rivaled by that of his creator. E. B. White's work, from his essays to his children's literature, is replete with eggs—as objects of natural beauty and as sources of life. A relatively small and simple object with an infinite number of thematic associations, the egg as subject matter perfectly reflects White's ability to transform concrete observations into clear, universal conclusions. White's eggs are rich with meaning; they are links in a never-ending cycle of life; they are sources of continuity in a world fragmented by passing time. And even in those essays that do not figure literal eggs, the sanctity, the beauty, and the fragility of life that they represent pervades White's work.

Perhaps only a writer so attuned to simplicity and detail could write an essay that is just about brown and white eggs, as is White's "Riposte." In this essay he takes issue with an Englishman who believes that Americans prefer white eggs to brown because white eggs seem more hygienic and brown eggs more countrified. "My goodness" is White's comment (*Essays* 60); "there is no such thing as an *un*natural egg" (*Essays* 61). Mr. Priestley (the Englishman) has missed the point altogether—an egg is an egg; its color is irrelevant to its identity. That White would devote an entire essay to discussing this topic is a testimonial to his interest in the egg. He would not have it misjudged.

In and of themselves eggs—oval shells of calcium carbonate—are not terribly exciting, but as sources of new life they hold magical and exhilarating properties. In the spectrum of White's work, eggs hatch right and left, and White revels in each birth. One pictures White as his own character Sam Beaver, sitting awed and motionless as he witnesses the miracle of the cygnets' birth (*Trumpet* 29–30). Or as Charlotte the spider, offering her "sincere congratulations" on the occasion of the newly hatched barnyard goslings (*Web* 44). In "The Geese" White appoints himself caretaker of three goslings and meticulously looks after their eggs as a tribute to a goose acquaintance who had died of old age (*Prose* 145–49). "Spring" finds him caring for "254 little innocents"—chicks for whom he and his stove act as mother-hen (*Meat* 234–37). In short, White hails eggs as producers of life; in his writing and in his life they are objects to be revered and tended appropriately.

It would not be enough, however, simply to say that White is a writer with a healthy respect for the wonder of an egg; to do so would be to take the egg out of context. White's eggs remain very much in context; they are part of the natural cycle of life, of development. The hatching of eggs is not a once-in-a-lifetime occurrence. It happens every spring, and every spring it brings the renewal of youth and hope. "Each spring," writes White in *Charlotte's Web*, "there were new little spiders hatching out to take the place of the old" (183). Likewise, the three new goslings and their offspring in "The Geese" continue the tradition of the original pair of geese with whom White had "an acquaintance of such long standing— long standing and loud shouting" (*Prose* 145). Eggs come as dependably as the seasons; they are at once sources of stability and continuity; they are links in a natural chain.

Indeed, if White can be said to have a central preoccupation, then it is certainly the mystery of time's cyclic nature, and the precarious yet precious relationships that ensue. His literal tales of hatching eggs are only a few of his many essays and stories that address the topic of passing time and chronicle the natural cycles of life. Such is clearly the case in *Charlotte's Web*, which begins with the birth of Wilbur the pig and follows him into old age, while also telling the story of his spider friend Charlotte and her descendants. Wilbur is saved from an untimely, unnatural death by the resourceful and clever Charlotte; he lives out his life as Nature intended, as does she (White, *Web*). But *Charlotte's Web* is more than a story of animal progeny; it is a tale of how the love between two friends enriched both of their lives. White has taken us beyond the simple hatching of eggs to life outside' the eggshell, where we can see his joy for life reflected in the relationships he creates among living things.

"Once More to the Lake" and "The Ring of Time" move to the realm of human relationships and life cycles, away from literal eggs. "Once More to the Lake" involves the time lapse between being a son and then becoming a father of one's own son, and depicts the change in temperament that naturally accompanies those passing years. White so vividly remembers the summers when he was a boy that he is lulled into thinking "there had been no years," but as he gradually notices subtle changes in the lake and in himself—the cacophonous sounds of the new outboard motors, his reluctance to swim in the rain as he would have done long ago—he realizes that life may be cyclic but it spirals ever forward: he has aged and there have undeniably been years (*Essays* 191–202).

"The Ring of Time" addresses the illusion of the young that time has no ramifications. "She is at that enviable moment in life," White writes of a young circus performer who is riding her horse around the ring, "when she believes she can go once around the ring, make one complete circuit, and at the end be exactly the same age as at the start" (*Essays* 145). Later in the essay he refers to this feeling as "true seduction" and a "delusion," for "time has not stood still for anybody but the dead, and even the dead must be able to hear the acceleration of little sports cars and know that things have changed" (*Essays* 148–49).

Eggs may come every spring, in other words, but they are not the same eggs; Charlotte's children and grandchildren cannot really replace Charlotte in Wilbur's eyes. White recognizes the new eggs each spring for what they are worth—sources of continuity yet also subtle change. Life is not merely seasonal repetition, even though this spring may be reminiscent of the last.

The egg is a tiny microcosm of life, and as such it is a perfect example of White's tendency to look to the smaller things in order to facilitate a better understanding of the larger issues of his day. "Who has the longer view of things, anyway, a prime minister in a closet or a man on a barn roof?" he asks in "Clear Days" (*Meat* 20), written slightly before the outbreak of World War II. Later, in 1941, he writes, "I sometimes think I am crazy—everybody else fighting and dying or working for a cause or writing to his senator, and me looking after some Barred Rock chickens" (*Meat* 236). White is clearly concerned with the topic of war, but he continues to write about it in the context of his experiences on his farm.

In his review of *One Man's Meat,* Benjamin DeMott dismisses White's subjects because they are so ordinary: he lists them as "Maine, progress as disaster, frustrations of urban life, and so on" (63) as if it bores him to include them at all. But I am more inclined to agree with the reviewer who wrote, "It is the gift of the poetic imagination to shape commonplace things into conclusions of considerable weight" (DeVane 164). To the attentive artist no place does not lend itself to observation, no topic is too mundane. White commits himself to reporting what he sees and thinking about what meaning he can derive from his observations, not to merely musing on grandiose abstractions. Likewise, he commits himself to preserving and protecting what life there is around him, instead of lamenting the lives he cannot save in Europe.

> I soon knew that the remaining warmth in this stubborn stove was all I had to pit against the Nazi idea of *Frühling.* . . . Countries are ransacked, valleys drenched with blood. Though it seems untimely I still publish my belief in the egg, the contents of the egg, the warm coal, and the necessity for pursuing whatever fire delights and sustains you. (*Meat* 237)

White invests in the egg the ultimate sanctity of human life, and he will go to great lengths to uphold it. He works within his sphere of influence to comment on more universal themes; his sight and his actions lead to insight and speculation (Hoy and DiYanni, *Prose* 144).

> "Look," he [Templeton] began in his sharp voice, "you say you have seven goslings. There were eight eggs. What happened to the other egg? Why didn't it hatch?"
> "It's a dud, I guess," said the goose. (White, *Web* 45)

E. B. White does not write fairy tales; not all of his eggs hatch. White's world has a dual nature, where happiness and sorrow co-exist peacefully, naturally. Perhaps this co-existence is the reason children recognize him as a wonderful writer, for he does not hide from them what well-meaning adults would. White has the ability to gently exploit the contradictions in life; his essays and stories probe the reality of not-so-happy endings.

When I was eight I cried for Charlotte, who died alone at the Fair Grounds (White, *Web* 171). I felt that it was grossly unfair that she who had worked so hard should perish so soon after her triumph—felt that she should at least be able to return home with Wilbur. Now I realize that White has too much respect for Nature to have permitted me that miracle. Charlotte was a spider with a spider's life span; such things cannot be altered, and certainly not by a writer as familiar with and respectful of life cycles as E. B. White.

However much White might want to promote life among his fellow creatures, he is not idealistic enough to suppose that he can always be successful. In "The Geese" he expresses a desire to hatch the old goose's three eggs as a tribute to her, but he finds himself not obsessed enough to devote himself to an incubator for the necessary thirty days. Instead, he purchases three newborn goslings from a neighbor (*Prose* 145–46). Where there is life, there is also, so to speak, non-life, and White presents this contrast directly: "Summer was upon us, the pond was alive again. I brought the three eggs up from the cellar and dispatched them to the town dump" (*Prose* 147). We are not told what to make of this incongruence, we are merely given it, and we know by the startling juxtaposition of those two sentences that White is thinking about it himself. His closing sentence is along similar lines: "I don't know anything sadder than a summer's day" (*Prose* 149). Summer days in "Once More to the Lake" are tinged with sadness as well, as the son prepares to bathe in the rain, the father feels "the chill of death" (*Essays* 202). But on the other hand, those same summer days are also replete with the joy of new life—the three goslings nurtured by White, the son who feels no chill of death. White's world is by no means pessimistic, nor is it idealistically optimistic. It is a depiction of reality as seen through the eyes of a man who acknowledges the unfortunate, yet is always willing to "publish his belief in the egg" (White, *Meat* 237). . . .

> The world White loves is more than a collection of things, natural and man-made, or a fascinating organization of reassuring cyclical, ongoing processes: it is a world in which the motive for creating, nurturing, teaching, encouraging, singing, and celebrating is love. (Elledge 303)

This love pervades White's works: it is implicit in all of his essays, all of his children's stories. It motivates him to take his son to visit his old haunt in "Once More to the Lake"; it motivates him to keep a vigil by the stove that warms the chicks in "Spring"; it motivates him to raise three goslings in memory of the old goose in "The Geese." In short, it motivates him to cherish life, and to cherish the eggs, symbolic and literal, that bring life into the world. In White's world, life is nothing short of a miracle, and "to him a miracle was essentially egg-shaped" (qtd. in Elledge 25).

Works Cited

DeMott, Benjamin. "Books: Pick of the List." Rev. of *Essays of E. B. White,* by E. B. White. *Saturday Review* 20 Aug. 1977: 63.

DeVane, William C. "A Celebration of Life." Rev. of *One Man's Meat,* by E. B. White. *The Yale Review* 1942: 163–165.

Elledge, Scott. *E. B. White: A Biography.* New York: W. W. Norton & Company, 1984.

Hoy, Pat C. II and Robert DiYanni. Headnote: "E. B. White." *Prose Pieces: Essays and Stories, Sixteen Modern Writers.* New York: Random House, 1988. 143–145.

White, E. B. *Charlotte's Web.* New York: Harper & Brothers, 1952.

———. *Essays of E. B. White.* New York: Harper & Row, 1977.

———. "The Geese." *Prose Pieces: Essays and Stories, Sixteen Modern Writers.* Ed. Pat C. Hoy II and Robert DiYanni. New York: Random House, 1988. 145–149.

———. *One Man's Meat.* 2nd ed. New York: Harper & Row, 1944.

———. *The Trumpet of the Swan.* New York: Harper & Row, 1970.

Acknowledgments

Student essays are reprinted by permission of the authors.

Abbott, Lee K., "The True of Why I Do What I Do." Copyright © 1987 by Lee K. Abbott. Lee K. Abbott is the author of five collections of stories. He directs the MFA Program in Creative Writing at The Ohio State University in Columbus.

Anzaldúa, Gloria, "How to Tame a Wild Tongue," from *Borderlands/La Frontera: The New Mestiza* © 1987 by Gloria Anzaldúa. Reprinted with permission from Aunt Lute Books.

Baldwin, James, "Stranger in the Village" from *Notes of a Native Son* by James Baldwin. Copyright © 1955, renewed 1983, by James Baldwin. Reprinted by permission of Beacon Press.

Berger, John, "Ways of Seeing: Men Looking at Women," chapter 3, from *Ways of Seeing* by John Berger. Copyright © 1972 by Penguin Books, Ltd. Used by permission of Viking Penguin, a division of Penguin Books USA.

Cofer, Judith Ortiz, "Silent Dancing" from *Silent Dancing: A Partial Remembrance of a Puerto Rican Childhood,* by Judith Ortiz Cofer. by Arte Publico Press. Reprinted with permission from the publisher.

Danto, Arthur C., "Gettysburg." Copyright © 1988 by Arthur C. Danto. Reprinted by permission of Georges Bourchardt, Inc. for the author. This essay originally appeared in *Grand Street.*

Davenport, Guy, "The Geography of the Imagination" by Guy Davenport. Reprinted by permission of Guy Davenport.

Didion, Joan, "Georgia O'Keeffe" from *The White Album* by Joan Didion. Copyright © 1979 by Joan Didion. Reprinted by permission of Farrar, Straus and Giroux.

Dillard, Annie, "Living Like Weasels" from *Teaching a Stone to Talk* by Annie Dillard. Copyright © 1982 by Annie Dillard. Reprinted by permission of HarperCollins Publishers, Inc.

Dorris, Michael, "Fetal Alcohol Syndrome: A Parent's Perspective" from *Paper Trail* by Michael Dorris. Copyright © 1994 by Michael Dorris. Reprinted by permission of HarperCollins Publishers, Inc.

Ehrlich, Gretel, "Looking for a Lost Dog," by Gretel Ehrlich. Copyright © Gretel Ehrlich. Reprinted by permission of the author.

Eiseley, Loren D., "The Dance of the Frogs" From *The Star Thrower* by Loren D. Eiseley. Copyright © 1978 by the Estate of Loren D. Eiseley, Mabel L. Eise-

773

ley, Executrix. Reprinted by permission of Times Books, a division of Random House, Inc.

Forster, E.M., "What I Believe" from *Two Cheers for Democracy.* Copyright © 1939 and renewed 1967 by E.M. Forster. Reprinted by permission of Harcourt Brace & Company, and King's College, Cambridge, and The Society of Authors as the literary representatives of the E.M. Forster Estate.

Fussell, Paul, "Indy" from *Thank God for the Atom Bomb and Other Essays* by Paul Fussell. Summit Books.

Geller, Anne Ellen, "The Truth, Teased Out, and Told," Reprinted by permission of Anne Ellen Geller.

George, Diane Hume, "Wounded Chevy at Wounded Knee." Copyright Diane Hume George. Originally appeared in *The Missouri Review.* Reprinted in *The Lonely Other: A Woman Watching America (Essays),* Diane Hume George, University of Illinois Press, 1996.

Gordimer, Nadine, "Where do Whites Fit In?" from *The Essential Gesture* by Nadine Gordimer and Stephen Clingham. Copyright © 1988 by Felix BVIO. Reprinted by permission of Alfred A. Knopf, Inc.

Gordon, Mary, "Mary Cassatt" from *Good Boys and Dead Girls* by Mary Gordon. Copyright © 1991 by Mary Gordon. Used by permission of Viking Penguin, a division of Penguin Books, USA.

Gould, Stephen Jay, "Women's Brains." Reprinted from *The Panda's Thumb: More Reflections in Natural History* by Stephen Jay Gould, with the permission of W.W. Norton & Company, Inc. Copyright © 1980 by Stephen Jay Gould.

Hoagland, Edward, "The Courage of Turtles." Copyright © 1968 by Edward Hoagland. From *The Courage of Turtles* published by Lyons & Burford. Reprinted by permission of Lescher & Lescher, Ltd.

Hoy, Pat C. II, "Immortality" from *Instinct for Survival,* pp 140-152. Reprinted by permission of The University of Georgia Press.

Hughes, Langston, "Salvation" from *The Big Sea: An Autobiography* by Langston Hughes. Copyright © 1940 by Langston Hughes. Copyright renewed © 1968 by Arna Bontemps and George Houston Bass. Reprinted by permission of Hill and Wang, a division of Farrar, Straus & Giroux.

Hurston, Zora Neale, "How it Feels to be Colored Me." Reprinted by permission of Edgar Hurston. Originally appeared in The World Tomorrow in 1928.

Jordan, June, from "Many Rivers to Cross," *On Call.* Reprinted by permission of South End Press.

Kincaid, Jamaica, "On Seeing England for the First Time." Originally published in *Transition, 1991.* Reprinted by permission of Oxford University Press.

King, Martin Luther, Jr., "Letter from Birmingham Jail." Reprinted by arrangement with The Heirs to the Estate of Martin Luther King, Jr., c/o Joan Daves as agent for the proprietor. Copyright © 1963, 1964 by Martin Luther King, Jr., copyright renewed 1991, 1992 by Coretta Scott King.

Kingston, Maxine Hong, "No Name Woman" from *The Woman Warrior* by Maxine Hong Kingston. Copyright © 1976 by Maxine Hong Kingston. Reprinted by permission of Alfred A. Knopf, Inc.

Kingston, Maxine Hong, "Silence" from *The Woman Warrior* by Maxine Hong Kingston. Copyright © 1976 by Maxine Hong Kingston. Reprinted by permission of Alfred A. Knopf, Inc.

Kingston, Maxine Hong, "On Discovery" from *China Men* by Maxine Hong Kingston. Copyright © 1980 by Maxine Hong Kingston. Reprinted by permission of Alfred A. Knopf, Inc.

Kriegel, Leonard, "Falling into Life" from *Falling into Life* by Leonard Kriegel, 1991 North Point Press. Reprinted by permission of Leonard Kriegel. Copyright © 1988. This essay was originally published in *The American Scholar.*

Lawrence, D.H., "Cocksure Women and Hensure Men." Copyright © 1928 by Forum Publishing Co., renewed 1956 by Freida Lawrence Ravagli, from *Phoenix II: Uncollected Papers of D.H. Lawrence,* edited by Roberts and Moore. Used by permission of Viking Penguin, a division of Penguin Books USA Inc.

Lopez, Barry, "The Stone Horse" from *Crossing Open Ground* by Barry Lopez.

Lowell, Robert, "Returning Turtle" from *Selected Poems* by Robert Lowell. Copyright © 1977 by Robert Lowell. Reprinted by permission of Farrar, Straus & Giroux.

Mairs, Nancy, "On Being a Cripple" from Nancy Mairs, "On Being a Cripple," in *Plaintext.* Reprinted by permission of The University of Arizona Press.

Momaday, N. Scott, "A First American Views His Land" by N. Scott Momaday. This essay originally appeared in *National Geographic.*

Morrison, Toni, "The Site of Memory" by Toni Morrison from *Inventing the Truth: The Art and Craft of Memoir,* edited by Zinsser. Copyright © 1994 by Toni Morrison. Permission granted by International Creative Management.

Oates, Joyce Carol, "On Boxing" from *On Boxing.* Copyright © 1985 by *The Ontario Review, Inc.* Reprinted by permission of John Hawkins & Associates, Inc.

O'Brien, Tim, "How to Tell a True War Story" from *The Things They Carried.* Copyright © 1990 by Tim O'Brien. Reprinted by permission of Houghton Mifflin Co./Seymour Lawrence. All rights reserved.

Orwell, George, "Marrakech" from *Such, Such Were the Joys* by George Orwell. Copyright 1953 by Sonia Brownell Orwell and renewed 1982 by Mrs. George K. Perutz, Mrs. Miriam Gross, and Dr. Michael Dickson, Executors of the Estate of Sonia Brownell Orwell. Reprinted by permission of Harcourt Brace & Company. This material is also Copyright © The estate of the late Sonia Brownell Orwell and Martin Secker and Warburg Ltd.

Ozick, Cynthia, "The Seam of the Snail" from *Metaphor and Memory* by Cynthia Ozick. Copyright © 1989 by Cynthia Ozick. Reprinted by permission of Alfred A. Knopf, Inc.

Pickering, Sam, "Trespassing" from *Trespassing* © 1994 by Sam Pickering. Reprinted by permission of University Press of New England.

Porter, Katherine Anne, "The Necessary Enemy" by Katherine Anne Porter from *The Collected Essays and Occasional Writings.* Reprinted by permission of Barbara Thompson Davis, trustee for the literary estate of Katherine Anne Porter.

Reed, Roy, "Spring Comes to Hogeye" from *Looking for Hogeye.* Copyright 1986 University of Arkansas Press. Reprinted by permission.

Rodriguez, Richard, "The Achievement of Desire" from *Hunger of Memory* by Richard Rodriguez. Reprinted by permission of David R. Godine Publisher, Inc. Copyright © 1982 by Richard Rodriguez.

Rose, Phyllis, "Tools of Torture: An Essay on Beauty and Pain." Copyright © 1984, 1985, 1986, 1987, 1988, 1989, 1990 by Phyllis Rose. Reprinted by permission of Georges Borchardt, Inc.

Russell, Sharman Apt, "Homebirth" from *Songs of the Flute Player: Seasons of Life in the Southwest,* © 1991 Sharman Apt Russell. Reprinted by permission of Addison-Wesley Publishing Company, Inc.

Sanders, Scott Russell, "Wayland" from *Secrets of the Universe* by Scott Russell Sanders. Copyright © 1993 by Scott Russell Sanders. Reprinted by permission of Beacon Press.

Selzer, Richard, "A Mask on the Face of Death." Copyright © 1987 by Richard Selzer. Reprinted by permission of Georges Borchardt, Inc. for the author.

Shilts, Randy, "Talking AIDS to Death." This essay originally appeared in *Esquire.*

Silko, Leslie Marmon, "Landscape, History, and the Pueblo Imagination." Copyright © 1987 by Leslie Marmon Silko. Reprinted by permission of Wylie, Aitken & Stone, Inc.

Sontag, Susan, "AIDS and its Metaphors." Excerpts from *Aids and Its Metaphors* by Susan Sontag. Copyright © 1988, 1989 by Susan Sontag. Reprinted by permission of Farrar, Straus, and Giroux.

Staples, Brent, "Just Walk On By: A Black Man Ponders His Power to Alter Public Space." Reprinted by permission. Brent Staples writes editorials for The New York Times and is author of the memoir *Parallel Time: Growing Up in Black and White.*

Strand, Mark, "Crossing the Tracks to Hopper's World" from *Antaeus.* Copyright 1990.

Tan, Amy, "Mother Tongue" Copyright © 1990 by Amy Tan. First appeared in *The Threepenny Review.* Reprinted by permission of Amy Tan and The Sandra Dijstra Literary Agency.

Thomas, Lewis, "The Corner of the Eye" from *Late Night Thoughts on Listening to Mahler's Ninth* by Lewis Thomas. Copyright © 1981. Used by permission of Viking Penguin, a division of Penguin Books, USA Inc.

Tuchman, Barbara, "History by the Ounce" from *Practicing History* by Barbara Tuchman. Copyright © 1981 by Barbara Tuchman. Reprinted by permission of Alfred A. Knopf, Inc.

Walker, Alice, "Beauty: When the Other Dancer is the Self" from *In Search of Our Mothers' Gardens: Womanist Prose.* Copyright © 1983 by Alice Walker. Reprinted by permission of Harcourt Brace & Company.